THE ENGLISH CHURCH
1000–1066

FRANK BARLOW

The English Church
1000–1066

*A history of the later
Anglo-Saxon church*

Longman
London and New York

Longman Group Limited London

*Associated companies, branches and representatives
throughout the world*

*Published in the United States of America
by Longman Inc., New York*

*First published 1963
Second impression 1966
Second edition and first appearance in paperback 1979*

ISBN 0 582 49049 9

British Library Cataloguing in Publication Data

Barlow, Frank
The English Church, 1000–1066 – 2nd ed.
1. Great Britain – Church history – Anglo-
Saxon period, 4449–1066
274.2   BR749   78–40984

ISBN 0–582–49049–9

Printed in Great Britain by
Richard Clay (The Chaucer Press) Ltd,
Bungay, Suffolk

Contents

Maps and Diagrams

Preface

This book, a view of the English church on the eve of the 'Hildebrandine' or 'Gregorian' reform, is self-contained. But I hope to continue the constitutional history of the *ecclesia anglicana* in other volumes.

Some aspects of my attitude and treatment need explanation. The sub-title – A Constitutional History – defines fairly well the purpose and scope of the work, although, of necessity, there is more description and analysis than historical development. Some fields of ecclesiastical history I have deliberately excluded – for example, religious thought, which is beyond my powers, and art and archaeology, because they lie outside my main interests. Nor in this study have I examined the monastic houses individually or monasticism as a separate entity. Professor David Knowles and others have paid great attention to the monastic order, and it is possible that through their devoted efforts the general picture is in danger of distortion. Although I would be the first to affirm the importance of the monastic contribution to the English church, in my view of Old-English conditions monasticism is something which pervades the structure, and I prefer to see it within and throughout the whole. As for treatment, in order to give as much life as possible to a study which inevitably inclines to generalization and abstraction, I have included all the concrete illustrations that I could find. Some – perhaps many – of these may not be historically true. But I hope I have avoided anachronism, and would justify them as typical, and so both instructive and recreational. And if I find myself here in the goodly company of the hagiographers, I still am not dismayed. Finally I must apologize for quoting continental chronicles and writers usually from Migne's *Patrologia*. I am aware that there are often better editions, and I remember the precepts of my teachers. But Migne is generally available, and easily accessible references are sometimes the most useful.

I wish to thank Professor C. N. L. Brooke and Mr G. W. Greenaway for their valuable criticism of my draft and Mrs Valerie A. Hawgood for her help in reading the proofs. And it would be ungrateful not to mention Professor R. R. Darlington's inspiring article, 'Ecclesiastical Reform in the late Old English period', *English Historical Review*, vol. li (1936). It is on Darlington's foundations that I have tried to build.

University of Exeter   FRANK BARLOW
25 *July* 1962

Preface to Second Edition

This volume was intended to be the first of a series; and to complement the belated appearance of *The English Church, 1066–1154* it has been reprinted. I am grateful to Messrs Longman for their sustained interest in my works. I have taken the opportunity to correct misprints and errors and, very occasionally, an interpretation, and to modernize some of the references. Although with the passing of the years my view of the pre-Conquest period has altered here and there, I have had no real change of heart and am not much out of sympathy with what I wrote almost two decades ago. I have therefore preferred not to tinker unnecessarily with the original text. One feature of the first edition, however – the omission of a separate chapter on the monasteries – I have since regretted, and have now tried to remedy. It would have been difficult for several reasons to insert a new chapter in the body of the work, so the supplement appears as an appendix, where the inevitable repetitions and overlaps will, I hope, cause less offence; and if I am guilty of incoherence, this also is characteristic of the late Old English church.

Anglo-Saxon studies flourish exceedingly and great advances in our knowledge have occurred in the fields of archaeology, numismatics, place names, palaeography, language, and literature, but less perhaps in political and ecclesiastical history. I have been able to take advantage of some of the new discoveries; and I have used the unpublished Exeter PhD thesis (1976) of my pupil, Guy Lanoë, 'Anglo-Saxon Bishops, 899–1066: a List', to correct some of the regnal dates. To all who have helped me in various ways I offer my grateful thanks.

Middle Court Hall, Kenton, Exeter   FRANK BARLOW
5 September 1978

ABBREVIATED REFERENCES

Ælfric, *Catholic Homilies* .. .. ed. B. Thorpe, Aelfric Soc. (1843–6)

— *Lives of Saints* .. .. .. ed. W. W. Skeat, EETS, 76, 82, 94, 114 (1881–1900)

Anglia Sacra .. .. ed. H. Wharton (1691)

ASC .. .. *Anglo-Saxon Chronicle* (conveniently translated and arranged in *EHD*; and revised and issued separately, ed. Dorothy Whitelock, 1961)

BJRL .. .. *Bulletin of the John Rylands Library* (Manchester)

Bouquet, *Recueil* .. .. .. *Recueil des historiens des Gaules et de la France*, ed. M. Bouquet and the Congregation of St Maur (Paris 1738 ff.)

Camb HJ .. .. *Cambridge Historical Journal*: after 1957 *The Historical Journal*

Chron. Abingdon.. .. .. .. *Chronicon monasterii de Abingdon*, ed. J. Stevenson, RS (1858)

Chron. Evesham .. .. *Chronicon abbatiae de Evesham*, ed. W. D. Macray, RS (1863)

Chron. Peterborough .. .. .. *The Chronicle of Hugh Candidus, a monk of Peterborough*, ed. W. T. Mellows (1949)

Chron. Ramsey .. .. *Chronicon abbatiae Rameseiensis*, ed. W. D. Macray, RS (1886)

DB .. .. *Domesday-Book seu Liber Censualis Willelmi Primi* (1783–1816)

Eadmer, *Historia Novorum* .. .. .. *in Anglia*, ed. M. Rule, RS (1884)

Ecclesiastical Documents .. .. viz. I. *A brief History of the Bishoprick of Somerset*, ed. J. Hunter, Camden Soc. (1840)

EETS .. .. Early English Text Society (London)

EHD .. .. *English Historical Documents*, ed. D. C. Douglas: (1955), ed. Dorothy Whitelock; ii (1953), ed. Douglas and G. W. Greenaway

EHR .. .. *English Historical Review*

Enc. Emmae .. .. *Encomium Emmae Reginae*, ed. Alistair Campbell, Royal Hist. Soc. Camden 3rd ser. lxxii (1949)

Florence .. .. Florence of Worcester, *Chronicon ex chronicis*, ed. B. Thorpe (Eng. Hist. Soc. 1848–9)

Fournier and Le Bras .. .. Paul Fournier and Gabriel le Bras, *Histoire des Collections canoniques en Occident*, i (1931)

Freeman, *NC* .. .. E. A. Freeman, *The History of the Norman Conquest of England* (i–ii, 2nd edn. 1870; iii–v, 1st edn. 1869–75)

ix

Gesta abbatum monasterii S. Albani .. .. ed. H. T. Riley, RS, i (1867)

Gilbert Crispin, *Vita Herluini*   in J. Armitage Robinson, *Gilbert Crispin abbot of Westminster* (1911)

Goscelin, *Liber Confortatorius*   C. H. Talbot, 'The Liber confortatorius of Goscelin of Saint Bertin', *Studia Anselmiana*, fasc. xxxviii = *Analecta Monastica*, 3rd ser. (Rome 1955), 1–117

— *Vita S. Edithe* .. .. .. A. Wilmart, 'La légende de Ste Édith en prose et vers par le moine Goscelin', *Analecta Bollandiana*, lvi (1938), 5–101, 265–307

— *Vita Wlsini* .. .. C. H. Talbot, 'The Life of Saint Wulsin of Sherborne by Goscelin', *Revue Bénédictine*, lxix (1959), 68–85

Grierson, *England and Flanders*   Philip Grierson, 'Relations between England and Flanders before the Norman Conquest', *Trans. R. Hist. Soc.* 4th ser. xxiii (1941), pp. 71–112.

Haddan and Stubbs, *Councils* ..   *Councils and Ecclesiastical Documents relating to Great Britain and Ireland*, ed. A. W. Haddan and W. Stubbs, iii (1871)

Harmer, *Writs* .. .. F. E. Harmer, *Anglo-Saxon Writs* (1952)

Hauck, *Kirchengeschichte Deutschlands* .. .. A. Hauck, . . . , iii (Leipzig 1920)

HBS .. .. Henry Bradshaw Society

HCY .. .. *The Historians of the Church of York and its Archbishops*, ed. J. Raine, RS (1879–94)

Hemingi Chartularium .. .. *Hemingi Chartularium ecclesiae Wigorniensis*, ed. Tho. Hearne (Oxford 1723)

HLF .. .. *Histoire Littéraire de la France*, by the Congregation of St Maur (Paris 1733 ff.)

Hugh the Chantor, *HCY* .. .. *Hugh the Chantor: The History of the Church of York, 1066–1127*, ed. Charles Johnson, Nelson's Medieval Texts (1961)

JTS .. .. *Journal of Theological Studies* (London and Oxford)

K. .. .. J. M. Kemble, *Codex diplomaticus Aevi Saxonici* (1839–1848)

Leechdoms .. .. *Leechdoms, Wortcunning, and Starcraft of Early England*, ed. O. Cockayne, RS, iii (1866)

Liber Eliensis .. .. ed. E.O. Blake, Royal Hist. Soc. Camden 3rd ser. xcii (1962)

Liebermann, *Gesetze* .. .. .. F. Liebermann, *Die Gesetze der Angelsachsen* (Halle 1903)

Lingard, *Antiquities* .. .. .. J. Lingard, *The History and Antiquities of the Anglo-Saxon Church* (1845)

Lloyd, *A History of Wales* .. J. E. Lloyd, . . . , 3rd edn. (1939)

Makower .. .. Felix Makower, *The Constitutional History and Constitution of the Church of England* (1895)

Malmesbury, *De antiqu.*
  Glaston. ecclesiae .. .. .. in *Adami de Domerham historia*, ed. Tho. Hearne (Oxford 1727)

— *GP.* .. .. *De gestis pontificum Anglorum*, ed. N. E. S. A. Hamilton, RS (1870)

— *GR.* .. .. *De gestis regum Anglorum*, ed. W. Stubbs, RS (1887–9)

Memorials of St Dunstan .. .. ed. W. Stubbs, RS (1874)

Monasticon. .. .. *Monasticon Anglicanum*, ed. W. Dugdale, rev. by Caley, Ellis, and Bandinel (1817–30)

MPL .. .. *Patrologia Latina*, ed. J. P. Migne

Napier, *Wulfstan Sammlung* .. *Wulfstan: Sammlung der ihm zugeschiebenen Homilien*, ed. A. Napier (Berlin 1883)

Plummer .. .. C. Plummer and J. Earle, *Two of the Saxon Chronicles parallel*, vol. ii, Plummer's introduction, notes, and index (1899)

Regularis Concordia .. .. .. ed. T. Symons, Nelson's Medieval Classics (1953)

Robertson, *Charters.* .. .. A. J. Robertson, *Anglo-Saxon Charters* (1939)

— *Laws* .. .. *Laws of the Kings of England from Edmund to Henry I* (1925)

RS .. .. Chronicles and Memorials of Great Britain and Ireland during the Middle Ages, publ. under the direction of the Master of the Rolls

Schramm, *Herrschaftszeichen*
  und Staatssymbolik .. .. P. E. Schramm, . . . , Schriften der Monumenta Germaniae historica (1954–6)

SSC .. .. W. Stubbs and H. W. C. Davis, *Select Charters . . . of English Constitutional History*, 9th edn. (1921)

Symeon, *HDE* .. .. *Historia ecclesiae Dunhelmensis*, in *Opera Omnia*, ed. T. Arnold, RS (1882–5)

The Bosworth Psalter. .. .. F. A. Gasquet and Edmund Bishop, *The Bosworth Psalter* (1908)

Thorpe, *Ancient Laws* .. .. B. Thorpe, *Ancient Laws and Institutes of England* [&c], 2 v. (1840)

— *Diplomatarium* .. .. .. *Diplomatarium Anglicum Ævi Saxonici* (1865)

VCH .. .. *Victoria County History*

INTRODUCTION

1. THE WESTERN CHURCH

The vitality of the Christian religion during turbulent and materialistic times made it one of the great formative influences of the Middle Ages, for in its institutions, laws, art, and ceremonial was a picture of the Roman antique. The vitality can be variously explained. The Old Testament history of the Jews, with its stories of warfare, bravery and treachery, famine and enslavement, made an immediate appeal to men living under similar stresses; and the God of Hosts, the Righteous Avenger, was easily assimilated to, and also influenced, their idea of a perfect lord.[1] The Gospel, too, although it enshrined themes without meaning for a brutal society, had some compelling aspects. Its pastoral imagery was familiar and its simple messages could at least be understood. Moreover, Christianity was without peer as a miraculous cult. It had conquered rivals in a period of high civilization and could not be challenged by more primitive and rustic competitors in the early Middle Ages. Its ancient ritual served as a perfect focus for communal devotion; and its myths, so primeval in structure, could be adorned with the garlands of any age. The disharmonies also were important. Christianity offered antidotes to men sickened by the world. Excesses of violence and greed engendered pacifism and renunciation. Men sated with activity turned away from their world and found the church offering another world, an antithesis. And for those not ready to take the radical cure, there were restoratives for the wounded: absolution of sin through confession and penitence and the mystical communion with God in the sacrament of the Eucharist.

Christian thought had from the beginning been heterogeneous, and, although some formulations fell by the wayside or were condemned as heretical, the bequest of the primitive church to the Middle Ages was a body of writing in which many different attitudes of mind could be found. Especially were there two dissimilar views of the world in which the faithful were forced

---

[1] At the end of the tenth century Ælfric translated parts of the historical books of the O.T. into English for the benefit of the nobility; and of his translation of 'Judith' he wrote that it was done 'for your example, that you may also defend your country by force of arms against the invasion of a foreign army': *The Old English Version of the Heptateuch, Ælfric's Treatise on the Old and New Testament, and his Preface to Genesis*, ed. S. J. Crawford, EETS, 160 (1922), p. 48.

to live. The one advocated withdrawal and the performance of Christian virtues in solitude or in select communities. The other envisaged the active participation of Christians in affairs, the building of an organized church, and a
zealous ministry to the sinful and heathen. These two complementary attitudes, which found their formal expression in monasticism and the clerical
hierarchy, could usually live peacefully together in Christendom, all the more
because in practice the two spheres were never self-contained. Monks were
seldom entirely cloistered: they often undertook a limited ministry,[1] some
monks became bishops, and the great monastic leaders lived almost as much
in the world as the secular clergy; while these, although merging too often
into secular society, had their time for prayer and meditation and frequently
lived in regular communities. In the eleventh century the cleavage was not
at its sharpest.[2] Yet, however worldly the church might become, however
much engaged in constructing a system of government and reforming the
world by precept and even compulsion, the dominant impression remained
that the holiest life could be achieved only out of the world. Just as the laity
acknowledged that celibacy was a higher state than Christian marriage, so it
regarded the piety of the monk as superior to the mode of life of the secular
clerk. It made practical use of both. From the secular priests it accepted the
sacraments of the church and formal instruction in good living. But the
influence of the monks may often have been greater. If they lived up to their

---

[1] For example, Ælfric, 'monk and masspriest', probably preached while at the monastery of
Cerne, before he became abbot of Eynsham, those sermons which he collected into two volumes:
Kenneth Sisam, *Studies in the history of Old English Literature* (1955), pp. 174-5. A generation
later Wulfstan, the future bishop and saint, preached, heard confessions, and baptized when he
was prior of Worcester (*Vita Wulfstani*, pp. 11-15). St Peter Damiani wrote a tract, *Apologeticus
monachorum adversus canonicos*, against canons who denied that monks had the right to administer
the sacraments (*MPL*, cxlv, coll. 511 ff.).

[2] Edmund Bishop attacked such a view as misconceived – the attitude of an outsider. He wrote,
the monk is constituted by his "profession" or vow, and by that alone. Degrees of strictness are
no doubt fit subjects for moral reflexions, but in the tenth century, as indeed before or subsequently,
men became monks by taking the vows of religion and not by "assuming the name and dress"':
The Bosworth Psalter, p. 128. Bishop is, of course, right. But in fact an age which believed that the
exteriora should reveal the *interiora* wrote much of the dress and behaviour and little of the vow.
The eleventh-century observer naturally recognized a monk by these signs. Cf. Symeon of Durham
on Bishop Aldhun, a monk among canons, 'Erat . . . habitu, sicut omnes praedecessores ejus, et
actu probabilis monachus', *HDE*, p. 78, and Ralf abbot of Séez to the dying Gundulf of Rochester
(1108), both monks of Bec, 'sum enim habitu monachus etsi non vita': *Vita Gundulfi*, *Anglia Sacra*,
ii. 290. And he had good authority for his view; cf. *Institutio Canonicorum* of the Council of Aachen,
817, c. li, 'Habitus namque singulorum ordinum idcirco in ecclesia ab invicem discreti sunt, ut
his visis cuius propositi sit gestans, vel in qua professione domino militet, liquide cognoscatur': *Enlarged Rule of Chrodegang*, ed. A. S. Napier, EETS, 150 (1916), p. 63. Cf. also *Vita Wulfstani*, pp. 7-8.

ideals they showed the perfect pattern of life and offered grace and comfort to the sinful beholder. And when they were organized in communities for prayer and intercession, they worked for the salvation of all souls, the quick and the dead.

Just as the antisocial tendencies in the Christian religion had usually been kept under control, so had its anti-governmental inclinations. Christianity had arisen under a great system of secular government and had eventually enjoyed its patronage. The powers of the world had soon adopted a Christian colouring, so that princes, once divine or at least descended from the gods, had become the servants of God, divinely called to rule. The church assumed the vestments, symbols, and claims of the secular kingdom, and temporal rulers enriched their state by borrowing from the church.[1] A process of mutual imitation began, complicated, and often strange, in its detailed history, which by the tenth century had gone so far that a bishop was installed in his office with all the trappings of a secular ruler except for the crown and sceptre, and a king was enthroned just as a bishop except for the laying on of hands. On the Bayeux Tapestry Kings Edward and Harold, in their tunic, robe, and mantle, and Archbishop Stigand, in his alb, stole, and chasuble, had the basic garments in common. There was differentiation in detail, especially in colour; but the ceremonial costume of both kings and bishops was derived from the same Roman secular models, and had developed together.

This complementary process, the *imitatio regni/imperii* and the *imitatio sacerdotii*, was inspired up to the eleventh century less by hostile rivalry than by the natural interplay of influences between the two most active political forces in Christendom. The interpenetration was the result of a basic harmony and a common agreement on ideals. There was no real rivalry between the secular and ecclesiastical organizations. The renunciation of the monks put them apart and led them to passive acceptance of sinful government. Their hope was for pious rulers who would establish the peace in which their quiet lives could be lived.[2] The secular church, although through its governmental claims more liable to come into conflict with the *regnum*, was not yet aggressive in temper. Each was engaged in a battle against the same or similar enemies, and each needed the help of the other. In the conversion of Europe

---

[1] See P. E. Schramm, 'Sacerdotium und Regnum im Austausch ihrer Vorrechte', *Studi Gregoriani*, ii. 403 ff.; *Herrschaftszeichen und Staatssymbolik*.

[2] Cf. the attitude of St Odilo, abbot of Cluny, as stated by his biographer, the monk Jotsalus, 'Principibus et potestatibus Christianis secundum apostolicam sententiam (Mat. 5: 39) in nullo restitit, sed ita amicabilem et officiosum se reddidit, ut tanquam alter Joseph ab omnibus amaretur et celebriter veneraretur.' *Vita S. Odilonis*, I, c. vii, *MPL*, cxlii, col. 902.

to Christianity the secular sword had been decisive. The blood of martyrs had sanctified the cause in all heathen lands, but it had usually been through conquest or political influence that tribal or national conversions had been made. At the same time Christian kings had seen in the church a means of pacifying and subordinating frontier territories. Bishops had been encouraged to missionary work and archbishops had been helped to establish their power over foreign bishops. So it was, too, within the Christian kingdoms. The church needed lay help against the rivalry of magical cults and heretical beliefs, for the maintenance of its internal discipline, and for the raising of revenue.[1] The temporal rulers welcomed the moral support of the church for their undertakings, and found in the non-hereditary bishops a body of servants, literate and often skilled in Roman and canon law, who were more reliable and less dangerous than the nobles.

The more important the kingdom, the more ambitious the ruler, the more influential the church in the early Middle Ages. In Germany, the most powerful kingdom in Western Christendom, the Saxon dynasty – the three Ottos (936–1002) – and the second Salian, Henry III (1039–56), had built new Christian empires through military strength and control of the church. The physical power at the disposal of these men made their achievements possible; but they reformed and cultivated the church in order to give their government moral sanction and to facilitate administration. Even those who reacted against this policy, such as Conrad II, the father of Henry III, were obliged to have their children educated by the clergy and so prepare for a reversal of their outlook.

The influence exerted by the church on the kings and their government was matched by the influence which secular society had exerted on the church. In northern Christendom the church had been 'Germanized'.[2] The whole organization of the 'national' churches owed more to Old-German custom than to Roman law. In England the two ecclesiastical provinces illustrated the sometime political cleavage at the Humber, the dioceses corresponded to once independent Germanic kingdoms or folks, and the lesser churches followed a completely secular pattern. Although kings recognized that the church was subject to 'Christ's law', this law, from the penitential codes to the laws of property, bore an unmistakable Germanic stamp. Moreover, all ecclesiastical relationships were affected, often transformed, by ideas current in lay society; and in kingdoms which had become feudalized the church too

---

[1] Cf. Burchard, *Decretum*, XV, xliii.
[2] See Hans Erich Feine, *Kirchliche Rechtsgeschichte*, i. 129 ff.

had been feudalized. In England, just as the king referred to his earls and thegns, so he addressed his archbishops, bishops, and abbots.[1] The prelates were his men, his servants; their churches and estates were in his gift and under his protection and control. He could even grant the rank of bishop without the office or benefice.[2] It was he who decided under what rule his monasteries should live,[3] what saints should be recognized, what festivals observed.[4] The earls and thegns likewise had a proprietary attitude towards their churches,[5] but they were without the religious authority of the king.

The church never completely accepted this Germanization of its law and institutions, although it was rarely able before the eleventh century to influence actual conditions by its theories. Its characteristic attitude towards secular domination consisted in allowing the office of advocate to the laity, an office so inspired by disinterestedness, a quality rarely to be found in political life, that in practice it was always out of equilibrium. The papacy, whenever it felt threatened by the emperor, stressed the old Roman idea that the *advocatus* was merely an agent without initiative (the *brachium*, or strong arm), who owed the duty to protect, but only when summoned to perform it. No secular ruler, however, was constrained by this interpretation. As a divinely appointed agent to govern he had an independent responsibility for the state of the church, and, even as advocate, he must use his judgment as to the moment to intervene and the nature of the remedy. Nor had the secular ruler need to justify his attitude. In every other sphere of society those who sought protection accepted also dependence – *protectio trahet subjectionem;* and so defenceless an institution as the church found it hard to escape the implication of its necessity and to resist its protectors.[6] It had to content itself with complaints that the *advocatus*, instead of being *patronus et defensor*, behaved like a *dominus*. Especially did the church dislike the domination of women. Here natural prejudice was reinforced by historical examples. The

---

[1] Cf. the address in the writ-charters.   [2] Harmer, *Writs*, no. 44.

[3] e.g. *Regularis Concordia*.

[4] Cf. V Æthelred, 14–19. The Old-English 'Poetical Menology' of the tenth century, printed G. Hickes, *Thesaurus*, i (1703), 207, professes to give a list of the feasts prescribed by the king of England for general observance. Bishop, *The Boswell Psalter*, p. 24, does not take kindly to the observations of Lingard, *Antiquities*, i. 314, *n.* 2. For the recognition of St Wulfsige as a saint by King Æthelred, Archbishop Ælfheah, and the witan, see *Vita Wlsini*, p. 80; for the establishment of St Edward King and Martyr's feast day, see V Æthelred, 16.

[5] Cf. 'We enjoin that God's servants . . . be also to their temporal lords faithful and true [according to God's law, *added by one MS.*]': Wulfstan, 'Canons enacted under King Edgar' (written between 1004–8), c. i, in Thorpe, *Ancient Laws*, ii. 245.

[6] See Walter Ullmann, ' The origins of the *Ottonianum*', *Camb. HJ*, xi. 114–29.

rule of the 'Pornocracy' at Rome in the tenth century had been calamitous; and the control of the Empress Agnes after the death of Henry III and during the minority of Henry IV was resented by reformers.[1] Yet the influence of pious queens on ecclesiastical policy was always considerable and cannot as a rule have been harmful.

In England the lively apprehension of the monk-reformers actually increased royal power, for to escape from the interference of local founders and benefactors the abbots and abesses were anxious to be under the direct patronage of the crown. This policy was enshrined in the *Regularis Concordia*,[2] where Edgar was given responsibility for the abbeys and his queen, Ælfthrith, for the nunneries; and it was proclaimed by Archbishop Wulfstan a generation later.[3] Ælfric, writing in 991, denounced the malpractices of advocates, and allowed them merely the duty of helping the servants of God in their worldly concerns.[4] But he avoids mention of the king; and, indeed, without royal help local servitude was inescapable. At the end of the tenth century Glastonbury Abbey had obtained a papal letter against an oppressive earl;[5] but a papal letter was unlikely to be effective without the *brachium* of the king.

Thus the laity were dominant everywhere in the early eleventh century. At Rome the papacy was either under the control of the local aristocracy or subject to the German king. In the kingdoms and duchies the secular rulers kept their hands on the church. But the theme of the later reformers, that the laity had enslaved the church,[6] was more a general moral observation than an historical judgment on secular lords. The times had been bad; and even had the laity feared to place sacrilegious hands on church property and treat

---

[1] Cf. Cardinal Humbert of Silva Candida, *Contra simoniacos libri tres*, III, c. xii, *MPL*, cxliii, col. 1158.

[2] See also the historical fragment, probably by Æthelwold of Winchester, in *Leechdoms*, iii. 441; and cf. Eric John, 'The Kings and the Monks in the tenth-century Reformation', *BJRL*, vol. xlii (1959).

[3] Cf. V Æthelred, 10. 1 and VI Æthelred, 13 (1008): 'And all churches shall be under the special protection of God and of the king and of all Christian people.'

[4] *Catholic Homilies*, II, 'On the dedication of a church' (ii. 592–3; *EHD*, i. 852). In the preamble to vol. I, Ælfric is careful to say that he 'was sent in the reign of King Æthelred by Bishop Ælfheah ... to a monastery which is called Cerne, at the request of the thegn Æthelmaer', who was its founder (i. 2–3; *EHD*, i. 850).

[5] *Memorials of St Dunstan*, p. 396; Malmesbury, *GR*, i. 172. It is not certain which Pope John it was. Stubbs decided for XV against XIII (*ibid.* p. 396 *n.*). D. J. V. Fisher, 'The anti-monastic reaction in the reign of Edward the Martyr', *Camb. HJ*, x (1950–2), 257, favours XIV.

[6] e.g. Cardinal Humbert's *Adversus simoniacos libri tres*, written in 1057, *MPL*, cxliii, where, it is true, there are historical judgments on the German and French kings.

what had been granted to God as a private estate and the ministers of the church as personal servants, it is unlikely that the clergy could have risen much higher than the general standards of the age. Indeed, secular control of the church did not always have a depressive effect. There were always land-owners who abused their position, but only the most brutal and uncultured were uninterested in the condition of the clergy in their churches. Owing to a dominant thread in Christian theology the state of the secular clergy was of least concern, for the church, despite temptation, clung resolutely to the thesis that the worthiness of the priest did not affect the efficacy of the sacraments.[1] There was no wish to give cause for scandal to 'the contentious and foolish multitude'.[2] Even so, it was a widespread, and natural, popular heresy to doubt the efficacy of the ministration of an evil priest,[3] and the superstitious belief in the magical properties of virginity and all self-denial exerted some influence on the behaviour of the clergy. Of more immediate concern to the great men, however, was the condition of the monks in their abbeys. No one doubted that the more pious the monks the more valuable their prayers; and the landowner who inherited or founded a colony of monks, whose tasks included intercession for the souls of his family, was usually anxious that its behaviour should at least be seemly. Hence many of the reform movements of the period were due to the initiative or patronage of pious laymen and were mainly to be found in connexion with monasteries.

The eleventh-century church followed the general political pattern in its fragmentation into local groupings, and these did not always make much ecclesiastical sense. The *ecclesia anglicana*, however, was, after the national church in Germany, the largest coherent unit in Western Christendom. It was a backwater, but in a church without a main stream. Springs of reform

---

[1] This was a burning question in the mid-eleventh century because simony and unchastity (*Nicolaita haeresis*) were recognized as heresies. Cardinals Humbert and Hildebrand threatened the orthodox line to which Peter Damiani clung. Cf. Peter, 'sed donum dei, quod per illum [*sc.* simoniacum etc.] transit, nullius labe polluitur, nullius contagione foedatur. Purum namque est quod per illum fluit . . . Ponamus ergo ut mali sacerdotes quodammodo lapidei sint canales . . .', *Liber qui dicitur gratissimus*, c. xii, *MPL*, cxlv, col. 115; and see his *De sacramentis per improbos administratis, ibid.* col. 523.

[2] 'scandalum contentiosae et ineptae multitudinis devitantes', Humbert, *Adversus simoniacos libri tres*, I, c. ii, *MPL*, cxliii, col. 1013. Humbert is at pains to distinguish between the *mercenarii*, the unworthy shepherds, who must be obeyed until deposed, and the *fures et latrones*, the heretics (here simoniacs), whose authority is null.

[3] The heretics tried by the Council of Arras, 1035, gave as one of their objections to baptism, 'quia vita reproba ministrorum baptizandis nullum potest praebere salutis remedium', *Acta synodi Atrebat., MPL*, cxlii, col. 1272.

erupted here and there, and eddies could sometimes travel far, though un-predictably. Some of the most fervent upsurges in the early eleventh century, like the eremitical movement in Italy, spread hardly at all. The violent tracts of St Peter Damiani were directed to a small audience, and, even though this included the church leaders, had no measurable effect. Rule over wide areas was impossible more because of lack of information – and so a reason for government – than because of the absence of governmental machinery. There were men who advanced great claims for the papacy; but neither the popes nor their champions knew anything of conditions in those churches outside their personal acquaintance. Italy was as provincial as England. The Continental churches knew little about the English except what they learned from Bede.

It was a situation which awaited its exploiters. The religious beliefs of the people endowed the church with great latent power. Not all men were true believers, most true believers were sinful, but none doubted divine providence and the interpenetration of the natural and the supernatural. There was indeed a living God for the eleventh-century man, and there were angels and devils who lived, plucking at his shoulder as he went his way. The truths of the Christian faith were more certain than the laws of nature, and men often preferred to explain phenomena in terms of the miraculous rather than of physical causality.[1] At its best this frame of mind produced a noble serenity, secure from the buffetings of this world. At its worst it pandered to ignorance, stupidity, and childishness. Even St Peter Damiani could write, c. 1067, a tract for Pope Alexander II on the shortness of the life of popes (although really it was the shortness of their pontificates which was note-worthy), in which he explained that their lives were cut untimely short by God so as to instil the fear of death into the human race. To meet a possible difficulty, he added that kings were not subject to the same fate because the lesson would be only local in effect.[2]

When God ruled, the church, which alone could explain His laws and actions, possessed powers which could hardly be opposed on a theoretical level. And yet there was passive resistance among men, a sinful pride which the church could never entirely overcome. There were other social habits and

---

[1] Vacandus, monk of Moyenmoutier (Vosges), opened his *Vita S. Deodati* with, 'Catholica fides et Christiana pietas quanto vivacius aciem mentis in invisibilibus defigit, tanto segnius visibilia attendit, quia eorum vanitate se posse caecari animadvertit', *MPL*, cli, col. 611. This Life was read to a papal synod in Rome, 1049.

[2] *De brevitate vitae pontificum Romanorum et divina providentia*, *MPL*, cxlv, col. 471.

other loyalties. There was often in everyday life a worldly indifference which was the closest an eleventh-century man came to scepticism. There was often a feeling that the church expected too much and interfered too much. This is why the tremendous claims which the church advanced from the middle of the eleventh century were never realized in full. Given the premises, they seem irresistible; given the faith, invincible. But secular societies were always stronger than the theory allowed, and ecclesiastical statesmen themselves were not always completely free from the attitudes which they denounced. Few prelates were as logical and reckless in deed as they were in their literary works.

Christianity is an historical religion and the church was both consciously and unconsciously historical. It wrote its history eschatologically if not apocalyptically and was also wrapped in its traditions. Especially did it remember its dead, because they were not dead but living, and particularly the saints, for they lived with God. The church calendars, with the companion book of saints, taught the general and local ecclesiastical history to the faithful. The English calendars of the eleventh century are, indeed, revealing. Bishops formed the largest class of English saints and the seventh century produced the most. Holy virgins from the late seventh and early eighth centuries were almost as numerous. Abbots were few, largely because many abbots had become bishops; anchorites were fewer. The lower clergy was almost unrepresented except by the great name of Bede. From the saints' lives a history of the English church could be read, from Albanus, by way of the Celtic saints, the Roman missionaries and their worthy successors, and the reformers of the tenth century, to Ælfheah, the latest English martyr. The tenth century had improved on the ninth and eighth. But, as with all churches, the greatest piety was in the past.[1] All reforms were an attempt to recover a past formulated in the terms of the present.

The intelligentsia of the early twelfth century were often scornful of conditions in the eleventh. They remembered too well the paucity of teachers, how men hungry for learning or holiness sought in vain for instruction, when

[1] And the best miracles also were in the past. Cf. Coleman – Malmesbury, *Vita Wulfstani*, pp. 42–3, 'Veniam ad illud miraculum quod, quia nostris temporibus est factum, pene sibi fidem abrogat. . . . Nec diffitendum est nostro tempore potuisse fieri quod aliquotiens per antiquos sanctos deus fecerit.', and Malmesbury, *GP*, p. 289, on Bishop Wulfstan, 'Et profecto, si facilitas antiquorum hominum adjuvaret, jamdudum elatus in altum sanctus praedicaretur. Sed nostrorum incredulitas, quae se cautelae umbraculo exornat, non vult miraculis adhibere fidem etiamsi conspicetur oculo, etiamsi palpet digito.'

even good masters of grammar were rare.[1] They considered its logicians and theologians elementary or stupid.[2] They condemned its ignorant credulity.[3] It was the age of the simoniac and the married priest, of unreformed monasticism. In England a foreign conquest intensified this attitude.[4] The contempt is a measure of the advance which had been made. But the advance, of course, was simply a widening and development of movements started in the previous century. What had been sporadic and revolutionary had become accepted and general. And with acceptance had come a change in tone. The eleventh-century critics and reformers were bitter, violent, and sometimes almost hysterical. Twelfth-century writers, when looking back, were ironical, malicious, often complacent. But on the whole they preferred to forget the stridency of the earlier critics and the fumbling work of the older masters. This confidence gave to their age a warm liveliness which has been hailed as a renaissance. But in truth it was early summer, when men put out of mind the harsh contrasts, the brave starts in cold ground and inclement weather, the painful spring of the eleventh century.

2. ENGLAND'S CULTURAL RELATIONS

The two most powerful cultural forces in England were consciousness of Germanic race[5] and gratitude to Christian Rome. The English, turning their backs upon the Celtic fringe,[6] always maintained easy relations with the

---

[1] Cf. Gilbert Crispin, *Vita Herluini*, especially pp. 89–92, Guibert of Nogent, *De vita sua libri tres*, I, cc. iv–vi, *MPL*, clvi, coll. 844–8. Guibert, born at Beauvais a few years before 1066, writes, col. 844, 'Erat paulo ante id temporis et adhuc partim sub meo tempore tanta grammaticorum charitas, ut in oppidis pene nullus, in urbibus vix aliquis reperiri potuisset, et quos inveniri contigerat, eorum scientia tenuis erat, nec etiam moderni temporis clericulis vagantibus comparari poterat.'

[2] R. W. Southern, 'Lanfranc of Bec and Berengar of Tours', *Studies in Medieval History presented to F. M. Powicke* (1948), pp. 27–8.

[3] Guibert of Nogent, *De pignoribus sanctorum*, *MPL*, clvi, coll. 607 ff. Among other things he attacks inept saints' lives, coll. 613–14, the unnecessary exhumation of bodies (the treatment of St Edmund by Abbot Leofstan *c*. 1065 is quoted, col. 628; cf. *De vita sua*, coll. 958–9; Malmesbury, *GP*, pp. 155–6), and fraudulent exploiters of relics (he mentions Lanfranc's and Anselm's misgivings over Ælfheah, coll. 614–15).   [4] Exemplified by William of Malmesbury.

[5] The popularity of Bede kept everyone in mind of the Angles, Saxons, and Jutes. Abbo abbot of Fleury began his *Vita S. Eadmundi* with an account of them, *MPL*, cxxxix, coll. 508–9.

[6] The English chronicles give little information about Irish, Welsh, or Scottish affairs. There was, of course, some traffic between the western ports and the Ostmen towns – St Wulfstan of Worcester was honoured by Irish kings (*Vita Wulfstani*, p. 59) and his monk Patrick, the second bishop of Dublin (1074–84), sent to Worcester the poems and tracts he composed in Ireland (Aubrey Gwynn, *The Writings of Bishop Patrick*, Scriptores Latini Hiberniae, vol. i, 1955) – and there was

northern peoples of Europe and were ever attracted towards the mother church of St Peter's and the Christian Orient. But there were times when Frankish civilization rose so much above the English level that the restraining barriers were breached. In this period trade played only a small part in

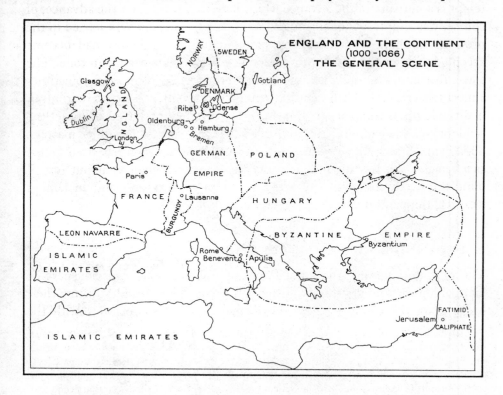

cultural exchange.[1] Far more important were diplomatic missions, the movement of soldiers and churchmen on business, and educational and devotional journeys. All these caused the transfer of objects of high – and often artistic –

frequent military and diplomatic contact with Wales and Scotland; but there is no sign that the Celtic parts exerted any cultural influence on England in this period. Ireland, in fact, seems to have by-passed England. It was in 1056 that Marianus Scotus travelled to join the Scottish community at Cologne (*Chronicon Mariani Scotti, MPL*, cxlvii, col. 786), and it is in his chronicle that we learn of the interesting school in Ireland, which possibly he had attended, conducted by the famous and wonderfully religious Aed, or Æderic, for both sexes, in which the women were tonsured instead of veiled, and which was dispersed on the master's expulsion from Ireland in 1053 (*ibid*. coll. 785–6).

[1] Cf. the views of Philip Grierson, 'Commerce in the Dark Ages: a critique of the evidence', *Trans. R. Hist. Soc.*, 5th ser., ix (1959), 123–40. It has been suggested that the Middle Ages were a deflationary depression.

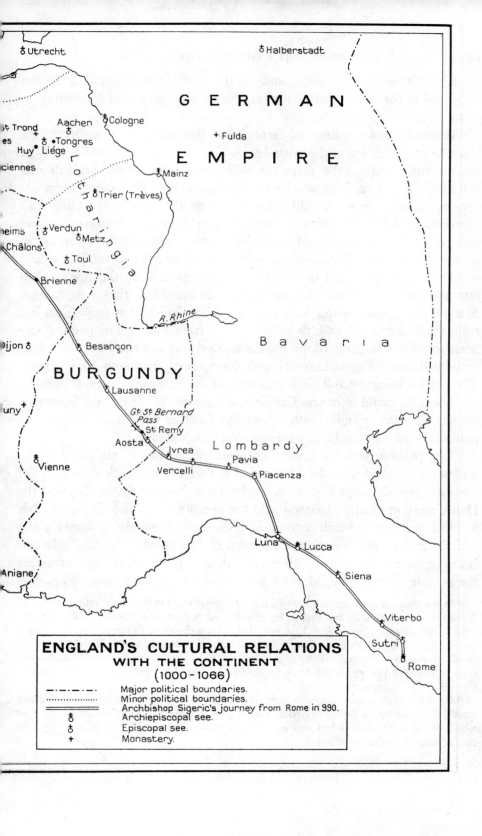

ठ Utrecht

ठ Halberstadt

G E R M A N

Aachen
ठ Cologne

St Trond
Huy ठ•Tongres
Liége

ciennes

+ Fulda

E M P I R E

ठ Mainz

Lotharingia

ठ Trier (Trèves)

heims   ठ Verdun
ठ Metz
Châlons

ठ Toul

Brienne

R. Rhine

B a v a r i a

Dijon ठ   ठ Besançon

B U R G U N D Y

uny +

ठ Lausanne

Gt St Bernard
Pass
ठ St Remy

Aosta
ठ Ivrea   L o m b a r d y
Pavia
Vercelli   ठ Piacenza

ठ Vienne

Aniane

Luna • Lucca

ठ Siena

ठ Viterbo

Sutri

Rome

ENGLAND'S CULTURAL RELATIONS
WITH THE CONTINENT
(1000 - 1066)

—·—·—	Major political boundaries.
·············	Minor political boundaries.
═══════	Archbishop Sigeric's journey from Rome in 990.
ठ	Archiepiscopal see.
ठ	Episcopal see.
+	Monastery.

value,[1] information, and ideas, and, as the traffic was generally from the backward to the more advanced areas, the wide geographical dissemination of art styles and ways of thought.

Although southern England faces the north coast of France, the easiest Channel crossings are to the ports between the Somme and the Scheldt. In the eleventh century the main trans-Channel port for the English was Wissant in Flanders, from which easy connexion could be made to the road-system radiating from the old Roman port of Boulogne, long silted up.[2] Hence there have been prolonged periods when intercourse between England and France has been small, when English traffic has mostly flowed round it, northwards through Flanders and the Rhineland or towards the Baltic, and southwards to Spain and the Mediterranean. Historically the English had few ties with the Franks. The islanders remembered that they were Angles, Saxons, and Jutes and that they had been christianized not from Gaul but from the Celtic north and, more effectively, from Rome. The political importance of the kingdom of the Franks between the sixth and the ninth centuries had drawn England into its orbit, but without creating much intimacy. The great missionary and civilizing work of the Anglo-Saxons was done on the northern marches of the Carolingian Empire, in Frisia and Germany, among Teutonic peoples with whom the English felt akin. Cultural and political relations with Gaul were always a little uneasy.

This position was not greatly changed by the Viking raids and settlements on both sides of the Channel in the ninth and tenth centuries, for hostility soon developed between England and Normandy. In England the Danes were gradually absorbed into the kingdom, and the kings, whether English or, in the eleventh century, Danish, feared intervention from the less orderly and almost autonomous county of Normandy. Political relations between the two states were often strained, and the Normans, by controlling the mouth of the Seine, blocked the easiest entry into France. The main

---

[1] In the early eleventh century Earnwi, the schoolmaster at Peterborough Abbey, wrote and illuminated a Sacramentary and Psalter. He gave the one to Cnut and the other to Emma in the hope of ecclesiastical advancement. Cnut sent them to the church of Cologne to get its prayers. In 1054 the archbishop presented them to Bishop Ealdred who was there on a diplomatic mission, and Ealdred passed them on to the prior of Worcester, St Wulfstan, who, he considered, deserved them. This closed a circle, because Wulfstan, when a pupil at Peterborough, had had the books in his care: *Vita Wulfstani*, pp. 5, 15-16.

[2] Grierson, *England and Flanders*, pp. 72-81. But Abbo of Fleury, when he went to Ramsey, crossed from *Morini*, 'a quibus brevissimus ad Anglos transitus est', after waiting for almost a month on the shore owing to bad weather: *Vita S. Abbonis abbatis*, *MPL*, cxxxix, col. 391. See also William of Poitiers, p. 6 and *n*.

cultural effect on England of this Viking expansion was to bring England into direct contact with Scandinavia, to increase her connexion with Germany, and to expand her horizon in several directions. Byzantium, for example, could be reached by more routes than before.[1]

It was Cnut, a Scandinavian emperor with a two-faced seal, signifying perhaps that he ruled two kingdoms,[2] who again obtained for England an important place in Christendom and who created the complicated dynastic web in which his successors were caught. The formal connexion with Denmark ended with Harthacnut's death; but Anglo-Scandinavian relations still remained important when Edward's half-cousin (and his wife's full cousin), Svein Estrithson, was king of Denmark.[3] Although Scandinavian influence on England was considerable, the far North had little to offer England in the form of Christian culture. The Scandinavian church looked to England.[4]

[1] It has been shown that Harold Hardrada's return to Norway from Constantinople in 1046 with a great treasure (Adam of Bremen, *Gesta Hammaburgensis ecclesiae pontificum*, III, c. 51, Schol. 84; *MPL*, cxlvi, col. 597) caused Svein Estrithson of Denmark to change the design of his coinage from the English to the Byzantine pattern. See Philip Grierson, 'Commerce in the Dark Ages', *ut supra*, p. 136.

[2] Harmer, *Writs*, pp. 97–101; see also below p. 127.

[3] Adam of Bremen, who knew Svein and questioned him about Scandinavian and English affairs (*Gesta Hammaburgensis ecclesiae pontificum*, III, c. 22, col. 477, c. 53, col. 599, IV, c. 21, col. 637, c. 25, col. 642), considers him to have been a standing claimant to the English throne. He asserts that Edward nominated him as his heir (II, c. 74, col. 554, III, c. 11, col. 566) and that this policy was opposed by the Godwin family (III, c. 13, col. 567). Adam names Ribe as a port for English traffic (IV, c. 1, col. 621); cf. *Gesta abbatum monasterii S. Albani*, i. 16. For trade, see Grierson, *England and Flanders*, p. 105.

[4] See below p. 233. The East-Anglian monasteries, because of the Scandinavian nobility in the area, were closely connected with the North. Before 1006 Bishop Siward and the Ramsey monk Wulfred, who had been missionaries, presumably in Scandinavia, returned to Ramsey: Goscelin, *Miracula S. Yvonis, Chron. Ramsey*, pp. lix–lx. Sigefred, 'bishop of Norway', a Glastonbury monk, sent four copes, two adorned with lions, two saffron, to his old house: Malmesbury, *De Antiqu. Glaston. ecclesie*, i. 94. Two northern bishops retired to England in Edward's reign. Rothulf, Edward's kinsman, was appointed abbot of Abingdon in 1051 (*ASC C* 1050, *E* 1048; Florence, i. 204; Plummer, p. 234; *Chron. Abingdon*, i. 463–4, ii. 281). According to Adam of Bremen (*op. cit.* II, cc. 55, 98, *MPL*, cxlvi, coll. 540–1, 545) Rothulf had been taken by Olaf of Norway from England and had been among those sent to evangelize Sweden and Gotland. Bishop Osmund of Sweden who, after spending some time at Edward's court, entered Ely Abbey as a domestic bishop (*Liber Eliensis*, II, c. 99, pp. 168–9), is given a very bad name by Adam (*op. cit.* III, c. 14, col. 568). Sent to the school at Bremen by a Norwegian bishop, he went ungratefully to Rome for ordination, but, repulsed there, wandered around until he was ordained by some Polish archbishop. He then entered Sweden, claiming that the pope had consecrated him archbishop of that country, and actually obtained the office from King Edmund (1056–60), to Hamburg – Bremen's indignation. Later, however, Archbishop Adalbert seems to have accepted him (*ibid.* III, c. 44, col. 617). This *acephalus gyrovagus* no doubt suited Ely well.

England's ties with Germany were tightened by Cnut. There was a trading connexion with the Rhineland[1] and Oldenburgh.[2] The presence of German artificers in England was noticed by William of Poitiers.[3] Edward's seal and some of his coins were based on German imperial models.[4] And with Cnut there began frequent diplomatic contact between the royal courts. Cnut settled the Eider boundary dispute with Conrad II, visited Rome for his coronation, and betrothed his daughter to the Emperor's son. Edward at the beginning of his reign was in military alliance with his brother-in-law, Henry III. The German kingdom was at the height of its power; and the influence of the German and Lotharingian churches must have spread in England through the many contacts.[5] But Germany itself took little account of England. Adam of Bremen, because he was concerned with both the past and the present evangelization of the North, included lively if inaccurate scraps of English history in his writings. In central Germany, however, the Hersfeld monk, Lambert, referred to England only in connexion with Halley's Comet – 'At which time a savage and lamentable battle took place in the northern world, in which a king of the Anglo-Saxons completely destroyed three kings with their enormous army',[6] – a quite inadequate account of the Norman Conquest.

England's interests reached also to Germany's neighbours. Cnut's mother was a Pole. Æthelred's grandson, Edward 'the Exile', had fled to Hungary; and other Englishmen travelled through Hungary to Jerusalem. For the coronation of King Solomon of Hungary in 1059 use was made of an English *Ordo;* and Anglo-Saxon rites passed from Hungary to Poland, possibly as a result of the marriage of Solomon's widow to King Wladislaw.[7] The main route to Rome was through the Middle Kingdom and Burgundy.

---

[1] IV Æthelred, 2. 8.

[2] According to the miracles of St Bernard, bishop of Hildesheim (*ob.* 1022), some merchants bound for England out of Bremen were saved from shipwreck by that saint, *MPL*, cxl, col. 438.

[3] p. 258. These were probably mostly goldsmiths and moneyers. For Theodoric *aurifaber*, see below p. 123, *n.* 4.

[4] J. P. C. Kent, 'From Roman Britain to Saxon England', *Anglo-Saxon Coins*, ed. R. H. M. Dolley (1961), p. 14; Dolley and F. Elmore Jones, 'A new suggestion . . .', *ibid.* pp. 220 ff.

[5] In 1046 there were three or four bishops with German/Lotharingian connexions in English sees. Also Bishop Brihtheah of Worcester accompanied Cnut's daughter to her wedding in Germany (*Hemingi Chartularium*, i. 267; *Monasticon*, i. 596a) and Bishop Ealdred spent a year at Cologne (below p. 87). It is perhaps significant that St Bruno of Toul, who was born in Alsace, composed responsories in honour of 'the venerable doctor Gregory, the apostle of the English' (Wibert = Cardinal Humbert, *Vita S. Leonis*, I, c. xiii, *MPL*, cxlviii, col. 481).

[6] *MPL*, cxlvi, col. 1089.

[7] Schramm, *Herrschaftszeichen und Staatssymbolik*, pp. 744 and *n.*, 944.

In 1027 Cnut made a treaty with the king of Burgundy in favour of English pilgrims.[1] The church of Utrecht was conscious of its debt to the English,[2] and traders from Nivelles and from Huy and Liége on the Meuse were familiar in London.[3] Liége at this time had a famous school, to which many foreigners went.[4]

England's relations with Flanders were intimate, although, politically, often unfriendly. Economic ties were close and each country depended to some extent on the other;[5] but the Flemish counts were attracted more to France and often pursued a policy which aimed at making the most of both worlds. The counts of Boulogne, although Flemish vassals and on the marches of France, were better disposed politically towards England, probably in order to safeguard their independence. Edward's sister, Godgifu, married Eustace II of Boulogne after the death of her first husband, Drogo, count of the Vexin. Flemish monasteries, especially St Peter at Ghent and St Bertin at St Omer, had important connexions with the English church and were centres for cultural exchange.[6] On 15 May 1060 Bishop William of London was at Bergues St Winnoc on the Flemish coast, in company with the count and countess of Flanders, Drogo bishop of Thérouanne, and a large body of Flemish nobles, when the relics of St Ursmar were exhibited in that monastery.[7] The purpose of the visit is, however, unknown and can hardly be guessed.

Naturally there was some traffic with Gaul. A great cultural stream had flowed from Fleury on the Loire into England in the tenth century,[8] carrying

[1] Cnut's proclamation of 1027, cc. 6, 8 (Liebermann, *Gesetze*, pp. 276–7).

[2] In the early eleventh century Adelbold bishop of Utrecht wrote a life of St Waldburg, the sister of Willibald and Wynbald, *MPL*, cxl, col. 1091.

[3] IV Æthelred, 2. 7.

[4] *Vita Vasonis Leodiensis episcopi*, *MPL*, cxlii, coll. 725–7. Wazo's successor as schoolmaster, Adelman, a pupil of Fulbert of Chartres, in an alphabetical poem in praise of great scholars, commemorates among three 'citizens' of Liége, Alestanus, possibly an Æthelstan: 'Tres mihi, Camena, cives memora de pluribus, / Illum, procul quem extinctum Transalpinis febribus / Lugent artes, lugent urbes cum suis primatibus. / Vix amissum queremur, Odulfo superstite, / Alestantum, quantus erat veteris scientiae, / Sicut hi quos erudivit, satis pollent hodie.', *MPL*, cxliii, col. 1297. See also Fournier and Le Bras, i. 385–7.

[5] Grierson, *England and Flanders*, pp. 104–6. Cf. IV Æthelred, 2. 6.

[6] Grierson, *op. cit.* pp. 89 ff.

[7] 'Miracula S. Ursmari', ed. O. Holder-Egger, *Monumenta Germaniae historica*, SS, xv (2), 839–40. I owe this reference to the kindness of Mr Philip Grierson. There was a cult of St Oswald at Bergues: see below, p. 176.

[8] Cf. Eric John, 'The King and the Monks in the tenth-century reformation', *BJRL*, xlii (1959), pp. 75–6.

in its depths the theological and liturgical heritage of the Carolingian renaissance and, on its surface, such fashions as the Carolingian minuscule and a wave of devotion to the Blessed Virgin, manifest in church dedications, the increased importance of the Feast of the Annunciation, and the reckoning of the start of the year from Lady Day.[1] The close tie between Fleury and the Fenland abbey of Ramsey remained.[2] There had also been the impact of Breton Christianity, when refugees from the Vikings had fled to Athelstan's court, bringing their cults and customs with them.[3] But in the eleventh century England was less receptive and the Frankish church had little more to give. There were, of course, some contacts. 'Pictish' clerks, possibly Bretons, travelling with the shrine of St Iwi, called at Wilton.[4] Englishmen visited the monastery at Fécamp and one retired to St Bénigne at Dijon.[5] Cnut exchanged embassies with the duke of Aquitaine and aroused some interest in English affairs at Limoges and Angoulême.[6] He sent a gift to

---

[1] R. L. Poole, *Studies in Chronology and History* (1934), pp. 13–18.

[2] See above, pp. 10, *n*. 5, 14, *n*. 2. *Chron. Ramsey*, pp. 42–3, 73, 159–60. Cf. *Regularis Concordia*, prolog. c. 5.

[3] Influence was strong at Winchester, *The Bosworth Psalter*, pp. 53–7. There was some opposition to Breton linguistic and liturgical customs. Ælfric refers in the preface to his *Grammar*, p. 2, to the Welsh manner (*Brittonice*) of pronouncing Latin short vowels in open syllables, e.g. *păter*, *mălus*. The school of Winchester obviously pronounced them long. There was also resistance to the Breton method of observing Ember days; see Kenneth Sisam, *Studies in the History of Old English Literature* (1953), pp. 55–6, 281.   [4] *Vita Edithe*, pp. 273–4.

[5] *Vita S. Guillelmi abbatis S. Benigni Divion.*, *MPL*, cxli, col. 864.

[6] The connexion was occasioned, or fostered, by the interest of the church of Limoges in establishing the claims of St Martial, the patron saint of Aquitaine, to be an apostle, for the case of St Augustine, the apostle to the English, was considered apposite. The campaign on behalf of St Martial seems to be associated with the rebuilding of the basilica of St Sauveur at Limoges, of which the apse was dedicated in 1028. As Cnut was at Rome at Easter 1027, it is possible that he visited Limoges on the outward or return journey and so became involved in the business. Cnut had sent *c*. 1024 to Duke William of Aquitaine an illustrated Book of Saints, written in gold, which was held to support the case, and two monks of Limoges were sent to England before 1031 to study English evidence (they visited St Augustine's, Canterbury) and probably to collect money for the rebuilding. For the frequent exchange of legations and gifts between the two courts and the English evidence produced to support St Martial's claims, see Ademar of Chabannes, *Historiarum libri tres*, *MPL*, cxli, coll. 56, 66; *Commemoratio abbatum Lemovicensium*, *ibid*. col. 84; *Epistola de apostolatu S. Martialis*, *ibid*. col. 99; *Sermo III*, *ibid*. col. 122; *Acta Concilii Lemovicensis II*, *MPL*, cxlii, coll. 1368–9. Six English manuscripts, possibly from the second quarter of the eleventh century, contain litanies which include St Martial among the apostles; and the attribution of five of them to Winchester, Winchcombe, Christ Church Canterbury, Bury St Edmunds, and St Germans Cornwall, shows how widely and quickly the new cult was disseminated. See Francis Wormald, 'The English saints in the Litany in Arundel MS. 60', *Analecta Bollandiana*, lxiv (1946), Appendix, pp. 84–6.

Chartres.[1] There were trading connexions. The men of Rouen had their own harbour in London,[2] and the men from Ponthieu and the Isle de France were also expected there.[3] Æthelred was anxious for an alliance with Normandy against the Vikings, and it is said that he sent gifts to, and sought help from, Robert I of France.[4] Towards Cnut, Normandy followed a policy of neutrality. Count Richard II allowed the supplanter to marry his sister, Æthelred's widow, but carefully protected the sons of her first marriage. It was the accession of the half-Norman, French-educated, Edward to the English throne and the re-emergence of Normandy as an important power under William the Bastard which substantially affected England's traditional diplomatic and cultural relations. There were contacts between the English and French courts [5] and there was established that political understanding between Edward and William which was to have such dire results. Edward brought some Normans into the English church and a few French, Normans, and Bretons into the lay nobility. French fashions found a place at court. But the effect was to increase the number of cultural forces in England rather than to disrupt the old pattern. Some circles reacted against, many were unaffected by, the new French influence. Only by taking a back trail and searching diligently for clues can a case be made for the theory that the Norman Conquest began in Edward's reign.

The English church calendars and litanies [6] also give a guide to English cultural relations. Most of the important cults of the Low Countries are honoured – Valery, Medard, Richarius, and Wulfmaer (Picardy), Bertin and Omer (St Omer), Fursey (Péronne – his head was at Canterbury), Vedast (Arras), Salvius (Valenciennes), Bavo and Armand (Ghent), Trudo (St

---

[1] Fulbert of Chartres, *Epistolae*, no. lxix, *MPL*, cxli, col. 236, where dated 1021, presumably because the gift was probably intended for the rebuilding of the church burnt down in 1020. It should be noticed that Fulbert, who addresses Cnut simply as king of Denmark, clearly knew little about him. Yet it has been suggested (Bouquet, *Recueil*, x. 466, *n*.) that Archbishop Æthelnoth, on his way to Rome for the pallium, took Cnut's gifts to Chartres, in which case the date would be 1022 (*ASC*). Larson, *Canute the Great*, p. 227, associates the gift with Cnut's visit to Rome in 1027.   [2] IV Æthelred, 2. 5.   [3] *Ibid.* 2. 6.

[4] R. Glaber, *Historiarum libri quinque*, III, c. ii, *MPL*, cxlii, col. 649, mentions Æthelred, Rudolf III of Burgundy, and Sanchio III of Navarre as clients of King Robert. He clearly exaggerates Robert's importance.

[5] Edward kept in touch with Henry I, king of the French (1031–60) through Helinand, a native of Pontoise, a chaplain sent to Edward by his nephew, Walter III of Mantes, and who became, as a result of these embassies, bishop of Laon in 1052, and later archbishop of Rheims. See Guibert of Nogent, *De vita sua libri tres*, *MPL*, clvi, col. 99.

[6] Francis Wormald, *English Kalendars before A.D. 1100*, HBS, lxxii (1934); 'The English saints in the Litany in Arundel MS. 60', *ut supra*.

Trond), and Landbert (Liége), together with Wandrille (Normandy) and Winnoc and Judoc (Brittany), whose cults had been transferred to Flanders.[1] No other regional group of the post-Roman period can compare.

Besides this natural intercourse between England and the maritime countries of northern Europe and its ties with Germany, there were the roads to Rome, Byzantium, and Jerusalem. The English had always been travellers and Christianity had given wanderers new goals, without, however, cleansing all worldliness from their proceedings. There were English harlots in Italian cities in the mid-eighth century,[2] an English colony in Rome by the ninth,[3] and probably English soldiers among the Scandinavians in the Varangian Regiment of the Imperial Guard at Byzantium in the eleventh century.[4] The road to Rome was a familiar one. It was trodden by prelates on business, by pilgrims of all classes, by the sick [5] and the penitent, and by merchants. Ælfric, when re-telling Bede's story of how St Gregory became interested in converting the English, wrote, 'It happened then at this time, as it yet often does, that English chapmen brought their wares to Rome, and Gregory went along the street to the Englishmen, viewing their things.'[6] Ælfric was aiming at striking a familiar note. Much trash came out of Italy but also some beautiful things. St Albans had a collection of cameos fashioned from sardonyx.[7] One of these, as large as the palm of the hand, carved with the figure of Asclepius, accompanied, perhaps, by the boy Telesphorus, was the gift of King Æthelred. Characteristic of the time, it was valued more for its virtue to alleviate the pangs of women in difficult labour than for its beauty.[8] Some monks of Bury St Edmunds believed that the wonderful

---

[1] Cf. '1030 comes Balduinus, qui dictus est Barbatus, congregatis marchisiae suae sanctorum corporibus, Bavonis, Wandregisili, Amandi, Vedasti, Bertini, Winnoci, cum aliis innumerabilibus sanctorum reliquiis ... pacem ab omni populo conjuratam firmari fecit', Afflighem additions (*Auctarium Affligemense*) to Sigebert of Gembloux's *Chronica*, MPL, clx, col. 281.

[2] Boniface, *Epistolae* (Wilkins, *Concilia*, i. 93a).   [3] See below, pp. 290-1.

[4] A. A. Vasiliev, 'The opening stage of the Anglo-Saxon immigration to Byzantium in the eleventh century', *Annales de l'Institut Kondakov (Seminarium Kondakovianum)*, ix (Prague, 1937), 39-70.

[5] A dumb man from Canterbury in Edward's reign spent three years in Rome for a cure, 'Mirac. S. Egwini', *Chron. Evesham*, p. 47.   [6] Ælfric, *Catholic Homilies*, ii. 120-1.

[7] 'quos sardios oniclios appellamus, et vulgariter cadmeos nuncupamus', *Gesta abbatum monasterii S. Albani*, i. 83-4. The word 'cameo' has, according to lexicographers, an unknown derivation. But it seems that for this author *cadmeus* (a calamine stone (i.e. hemimorphite), means 'cameo', and such a derivation makes sense.

[8] 'insculpitur autem in eodem imago pannosa, tenens in una manu hastam, per quam repens ascendensque serpens apparet, et in alia manu puerum, clypeum bajulantem. Et praeterea ante pedes imaginis aquila insculpitur, alas expandens elevatas', *ibid*. i. 84.

rood-cross over the altar of St Peter was exactly modelled on the Volto Santo that Abbot Leofstan (1044–65) had seen and admired at Lucca when visiting Rome.[1]

Then in Edward's reign England was affected by the increase in the power and range of papal government, inaugurated by Leo IX.[2] The volume of ecclesiastical business increased. Summonses to papal councils introduced English bishops to the authority of a new monarchy in Christendom. And Italy was probably the main centre of cultural exchange within that community. The feasts of the Conception of the Blessed Virgin Mary and of her Oblation in the Temple are thought to have been introduced into England in the early eleventh century through contact with Greeks in southern Italy, or possibly in Rome itself.[3] And a Greek monk named Constantine, who carried an archbishop's pall in his scrip, could even find a home until his death in Malmesbury abbey, apparently in Æthelred's reign. He planted a vineyard and was long remembered as a holy if somewhat mysterious guest.[4]

If many could visit Rome some could go even further afield. Byzantium was probably more often a stage on the journey to Jerusalem than an end in itself. There were two main routes from Western Europe to the Holy Land in the eleventh century, overland by way of Bavaria, Hungary, and Byzantium, and by sea from some Italian port. The latter was the more rewarding as it included Rome both old and new, but was probably the more dangerous. Even men as far south as Angoulême seem to have preferred the northern journey by land, which, indeed, only took from four to five months.[5] English pilgrims were to be found on both routes.[6]

---

[1] 'Sancta uero crux, que ibidem erecta est, sancta est et antiqua, et antecessoribus nostris in magne sanctitatis ueneracione uenerata, et multa miracula ante ipsam perhibebant celebrata. Nam quidam ante monachos introductos in ecclesiam sancti Edmundi longum tempus ibidem hanc fuisse putant; alii quando Leofstanus abbas iuit Romam crucem sacram que ueneratur in ciuitate Lucana in itinere contemplasse, quam expressius habere formam et magnitudinem dominici corporis, prebeat et mensuram eius sumptam domum reuersus hanc ad modum eius et secundum ipsam fieri fecisse.' Registrum Album monasterii S. Edmundi, Brit. Mus. Add. MS. 14,847, fo. 21ʳ.

[2] Cf. G. Tellenbach, 'Die Bedeutung des Reformpapsttums für die Einigung des Abendlandes', Studi Gregoriani, ii. 125 ff.

[3] The Bosworth Psalter, pp. 43–52.   [4] Malmesbury, GP, pp. 415–16.

[5] Pilgrimages from Aquitaine to Jerusalem were very popular in the early eleventh century. In 1026 the count of Angoulême and a party left on 1 October, and travelling by way of Bavaria, Hungary, Byzantium, and Asia Minor were at the Holy Places by the first week in March, and were back by the third week in June. Ademar of Chabannes, Historiarum libri tres, MPL, cxli, coll. 75–6.

[6] For English travellers to Jerusalem, see Vita Ædwardi, p. 69 n. Others thought of going: cf. Aldwin monk of Worcester and prior of Great Malvern, Malmesbury, GP, p. 286; Vita Wulfstani,

Rome, Byzantium, Bethlehem, and Jerusalem, and many towns and cities associated with the Christian faith, were familiar to Christians through the Bible lessons, the homilies, and the lives of the saints. But ecclesiastical geography can hardly have prepared the traveller for all the marvels that lay on his path, the corrupt glories of Rome and the more living classical features of its eastern rival. These journeys cannot have been without some effect both on the pilgrims [1] and on their society at home. Oriental and Roman traits in English artistic and political life hardly need elaborate explanation.

The coinage provides the best index to England's cultural relations.[2] The silver pennies were vernacular in name as in basic style. After Cnut there was the persistent influence of the German empire. But every now and then the designer copied some Roman imperial coin.[3] Byzantine traits are only to be found in detail and were probably taken at secondhand. King Harold's issue in 1066 exemplifies the assimilation of the dominant themes. On the reverse is the word PAX, as with Edward's first issue. It is the promise of peaceful continuity. The portrait is based on a Roman first-century bust. The crown and sceptre are of the contemporary English-German type; but the diadem-tails are of fourth-century Rome. There are, perhaps, indistinct Byzantine pendants below the ears, as had been clearly shown on Edward's last issue and were to be prominent on William's second. The inscription on the obverse is HAROLD REX ANGLORUM.

England was 'on the outer edge of the earth's extent',[4] set in an angle.[5] But it was neither isolated nor barbarous. Men were as restless then as now,

p. 26. St Wulfstan of Worcester carried as a talisman a golden bezant which, he believed, had been perforated by the head of the lance which had pierced Christ's side, *ibid.* p. 33. Bishop Ealdred travelled by way of Hungary in 1058 (Florence, i. 217). In 1055 Æthelwine monk of Canterbury returned by way of Byzantium, Apulia, Rome, and Lombardy (Eadmer, 'Mirac. S. Dunstani', *Memorials of St Dunstan*, pp. 245-6). There were many variations on the sea route. A man from Toulouse sailed from *urbs Lunae* (Sarzana, nr. La Spezia, Italy): Bernard scholasticus of Angers, *Miracula S. Fidis*, *MPL*, cxli, col. 148.

[1] Gundulf, the future bishop of Rochester (1077-1108) and William Bona Anima, archdeacon, and future archbishop, of Rouen went to Jerusalem before 1057, 'ut agnitis locis incarnationis, passionis, et ascensionis dominicae, dulciori haec omnia memoria postmodum teneant': *Vita Gundulfi*, *Anglia Sacra*, ii. 274.

[2] Cf. J. P. C. Kent, P. D. Whitting, R. H. M. Dolley, and F. Elmore Jones, *Anglo-Saxon Coins*, ed. Dolley (1961), pp. 14, 35, 215 ff.

[3] Æthelred 'Helmet', 1003-9 (Brooke 4); Edward 'Radiate Small Cross', 1044-6 (Brooke 2); 'Sovereign/Eagles', 1056-9 (Brooke 7); Harold 'Pax', 1066.

[4] Ælfric, *Lives of the Saints*, i. 290-1.

[5] The two puns, that the English were angelic and lived in an angle, were very popular. For the latter cf. Widukind of Corvey, *Res gestae saxonicae sive annalium libri tres*, I, c. 8, and Thietmar bishop of Merseburg, *Chronicon*, VII, c. 26, *MPL*, cxxxix, col. 1381.

and, as now, it was not primarily trade which caused men to travel, but the simple curiosity to see other places. Ralf Glaber wrote of a native of Gaul who wandered in Africa that 'he was one of those globe-trotters who are never sated by their experiences or by the novelties they find'.[1] There were many like him in eleventh-century Europe. And England itself could attract the traveller. It was extremely rich. It had paid countless pounds of silver to the Viking despoilers and after half a century of peace could again yield great treasure to the Norman conquerers. Men visited the royal court in the hope of gifts, and English kings were generous.[2] Magnanimity and liberality were lay virtues which the church encouraged. With such inward and outward traffic, there was a considerable exchange of information, although in popular dress. Men found it easier to tell marvellous stories than to convey ideas. News of monastic revivals springing from Burgundian Cluny, Lorraine, and Flanders in the tenth century, of the great changes in the secular church made by the Saxon and Salian emperors, of the regeneration of the papacy under Leo IX and his successors, reached England without delay, but in a form which robbed it of meaning except for the most perceptive hearers. English society was generally conservative. Most thegns and some bishops never went abroad. And even those who were not ignorant of the transformations which were taking place in the more progressive regions of Christendom were under no pressure to introduce novelties. In the main England stood firmly on its past.

3. THE INTERPRETATION OF ENGLISH CONDITIONS

In English history the period 1000–66 is roughly the life-span of some of its important characters, such as King Edward and Archbishops Stigand and Ealdred. A few men baptized by St Dunstan, St Æthelwold, or St Oswald could have lived to see Stigand deposed. It is a short period and also has a unity. It witnessed the establishment, attenuation, and extinction of the Danish and Anglo-Danish monarchy. There was no major disturbance in the church. But it is, partly because of the growing peacefulness of the kingdom, an obscure period and exceptionally difficult to interpret. We have little information about the reign of Cnut. Almost nothing is known about the major

---

[1] *Historiarum libri quinque*, V, c. i, *MPL*, cxlii, col. 692.

[2] Freeman, *NC*, ii. 535; *Vita Ædwardi*, pp. 40–1. Between 1020 and 1035 the bishop of Benevento came to England with the arm of St Bartholomew to raise funds for his Apulian city suffering from famine. Queen Emma bought the arm. He was also given by Canterbury a splendid cope, which Eadmer recognized at the Council of Bari, 1098. Eadmer, *Historia Novorum*, pp. 107–10.

part of Edward's life, the period before he ascended the throne, and there is an embarrassing conflict or cleavage between contemporary writers on the few events which were considered important at the time or in retrospect, such as the 'revolutions' of 1051–2 and Anglo-Norman and Anglo-Papal relations. Moreover, this poorly and fitfully illuminated scene is then obscured by two great shadows, the one cast by the Norman Conquest and the other by Edward's cult and canonization.

William of Malmesbury's *Gesta pontificum Anglorum*, the first ecclesiastical history of the English people to be written since Bede, exemplifies these points. For the period 1000–66 William only provides one set-piece and a few scraps. Goscelin of St Bertin, who lived into the twelfth century, had known about 1060 at Sherborne a monk who remembered St Wulfsige.[1] Osbern, the Canterbury historian, overlapped Dean Godric, who had been St Ælfheah's pupil and who in 1023 had opened Ælfheah's tomb at St Paul's together with his fellow monk Ælfweard the Long, a man who had served under St Dunstan.[2] But between the Norman Conquest and 1118–25, when William wrote his histories, English bishops and abbots had been replaced by Normans; there had disappeared from the cloisters and chapters those who remembered even the day on which King Edward was alive and dead; and the removal of several episcopal sees had broken continuity and tradition. The revival of interest in English history, in the kingdom's Anglo-Saxon past, came too late to recover much of the story of the church in the period which the Normans had chosen to condemn. William of Malmesbury could write at some length about a few of the tenth-century prelates, for their deeds had been recorded and remembered. Goscelin, Eadmer, and Osbern had even produced some ' modern ' lives of the saints. But no one had recorded the life of any English bishop who had died after Oswald and before St Wulfstan.

William wrote in the prologue to his book:[3]

What task could be more agreeable than to tell of the favours conferred on us by our ancestors, so that you may get to know the deeds of those from whom you have received both the rudiments of your faith and the encouragement to right living. I thought it was very slack and shameful not to know at least the names of the leaders of our province, when in other respects our knowledge extends to the lands of India and whatever lies beyond hidden by the boundless ocean. And so, for these reasons, I have dragged my pen, both here and elsewhere, through the obscurest histories, although the sources

[1] *Vita Wlsini*, prologue.   [2] Osbern, *Translatio S. Elphegi*, c. 6, *MPL*, cxlix, col. 390.
[3] *GP*, p. 4.

for this work are not as plentiful as for the *Gesta Regum*. For there, when I had made an abstract of the chronicles which I had in front of me, I was advised, just as by a torch shining from a high watch-tower, in what direction I could freely bend my steps. But here, deprived of almost all comfort, I grope within the thick dark clouds of ignorance, making my own path, with no lantern of history to lead the way.

Unfortunately, the path that William blazed is not one which can be confidently followed by his successors. Some fundamental prejudices, which he shared with his sources, can lead us badly astray. For his sources the story was the swift ebb of that great tide of reform which was associated in all men's minds with Edgar's reign. William accepted this interpretation all the more readily because he was aware that a new tide had flowed in with the Normans. Then there is the associated monastic prejudice. Histories and Lives were written in the monasteries, and no bishop received a good notice unless he was a monk or favoured monasticism. William gives only one eleventh-century English bishop – St Wulfstan – extensive treatment, and for the simple reasons that Wulfstan lived almost to the end of the century and that his Life had been written. But to the modern observer Wulfstan's contemporaries Stigand and Ealdred appear more interesting and important. William pays no attention at all to the continuous reform drive in the diocese of York, for it concerned secular minsters. Non-monastic reformers get short shrift. Giso of Wells is but mentioned,[1] Leofric of Exeter is disparaged,[2] and for Walter of Hereford there is an unseemly story.[3] Even more unbalanced is the short notice which he gives to the first Wulfstan, the lawgiver and homilist, who, in view of the literary works now attributed to him, can be regarded as the giant of the period. Because there was no Life, and presumably because Peterborough Abbey disliked him for abandoning his intention to be buried there, William merely compares him unfavourably with his predecessor, Ealdwulf, a former abbot of Peterborough whom the monks revered: 'Ealdwulf can be pardoned for holding the two sees [of Worcester and York] contrary to canon law because of his sanctity, and because he did it not through ambition but by necessity. But not Wulfstan, who differed from him both in sanctity and habit.'[4] This judgment is not only ludicrously inadequate and unfair. It is also based on a falsehood. Wulfstan, like Ealdwulf, was a monk. The suppression of this fact by Peterborough was an effective revenge.

[1] *GP*. pp. 194, 251.　　　　　　　[2] *Ibid*. p. 201.　　　　　　　[3] *Ibid*. p. 300.
[4] *Ibid*. p. 250. But, as Karl Jost, *Wulfstanstudien* (1950), p. 51, has pointed out, Wulfstan was very familiar with the Rule of St Benedict.

In addition, William had little true historical sense and was not completely free from Norman prejudice or its effects. When he was faced with discordant English and Norman traditions, he usually at least recorded the conflict of views.[1] But when, as so often, he unearthed a simple version, he merely accepted it and made no allowance for the bias of the source. Although he himself tried to avoid racial prejudice, it had some effect on his writings. He relates that Thorney Abbey possessed the bodies of many saints.

> But I must decline to give their names, for they strike us as barbarous. Not that I would doubt or deny that they were saints. What authority have I to dispute what holy antiquity has consecrated? But because, as I have said, their names have an uncouth ring and a rough flavour, I have no wish to expose saints to the derision of foolish men, who are produced in such plenty by our age. Also, since not even the community [*inhabitatores*] reads their lives, it seems silly to preach the merits of men whose miracles cannot be found.[2]

The names he suppressed were Athulf, Firmin, Herefrith, Botulf, Cissa, Huna, Tancred, Torthred, and Tova.[3] He had not discovered Folcard's Life of St Botulf.[4] And we notice the deep prejudice against the 'uncouth' English vernacular. William could himself read and translate Old-English. But he set no value on, indeed almost completely ignored,[5] the literary achievements of the English.

Medieval man was obsessed with the idea of deterioration. He was a sturdy pessimist when regarding the Church Militant and its obvious backsliding, an optimist only in selecting a few men and women whose outstandingly different way of life or whose spectacular death seemed to qualify them for eternal life outside this world. Few would deny that he had cause for dismay. Laws and standards, so often proclaimed, were as rarely observed. The pessimism of the monastic writers of the early eleventh century is readily understandable. They lived in communities which owed their re-establishment, their Rule, and their ideals to the great figures of the tenth-century reformation. The abbeys were the fruit of that reform and were not

---

[1] e.g. on Robert of Jumièges, *ibid.* p. 35.

[2] *Ibid.* pp. 327–8. Similarly, when translating Coleman, he suppressed the names of almost all the witnesses to Wulfstan's miracles, 'ne vocabulorum barbaries delicati lectoris sauciaret aures', *Vita Wulfstani*, p. 23.

[3] *Chron. Peterborough*, p. 63.

[4] *Acta Sanctorum* (Paris and Rome 1868), June, iv. 327; prologue in T. D. Hardy, *Descriptive catalogue of materials relating to the history of Great Britain and Ireland*, I, i. 373.

[5] He badly confused various Ælfrics, *GP*, pp. 404–7. His composite figure 'reliquit aliquantos codices, non exigua ingenii monimenta:... libros multos ex Latino in patrium sermonem versos.'

inclined to undervalue it. They were blind to its limitations and completely uncritical of its aims. A kingdom filled with reformed monasteries was their ideal. The severe check to the movement which developed in Æthelred's reign with the death of the monastic leaders, the fighting in England, and the exorbitant taxation and tributes which fell especially heavily on the monasteries, was therefore to be lamented. And nothing, they considered, occurred between then and 1066 which entirely restored the position.

The general truth of this view – that the period was in fact the slack water between two tides of reform – can be accepted. Such ebbs and flows are characteristic of ecclesiastical history. But whereas the water had gone far out in the ninth century and came in majestically and with gathering momentum in the tenth, so that it crashed almost all barriers, the retreat and advance was much less in the eleventh. The unrelieved gloom of the monastic writers is far too black. Even on the monastic side, although with two of the four monastic sees held by a secular priest and the other two arousing the cupidity of the ambitious, by the eve of the Conquest an important policy of the reformers seemed to have failed, some houses like Sherborne and the East-Anglian abbeys remained at least respectable, and at Worcester there was a revival which renewed the glories of the past. Furthermore, monastic eyes were blind to new movements and ideals. The monastic archbishops of York were obviously regarded as traitors to the movement because they fostered non-monastic institutions. The rash and violent Earl Tostig, who was occasionally generous to monasteries, was viewed with sympathy, while the steadier Harold, who founded a college at Waltham, was judged no friend to the church. In any case there seems no good reason why the modern historian should necessarily identify himself with the aims of reformers and treat with their severity periods which fell short of their ideals. The Church Militant is a society of sinners, and a truer historical tone is achieved if the observer finds himself more at home with the weaker brethren than in the company of those who demanded the impossible. As Goscelin of St Bertin wrote,[1] at Domesday there will be two columns of the elect. The first will consist of those saints who have abandoned everything for Christ. The second, however, and the larger, will consist of those less perfect,

such as good and faithful married folk who have refrained from unlawful acts and have bestowed their earthly possessions in alms and hospitality, who will be saved through the

[1] *Liber confortatorius*, pp. 110–11; cf. St Gregory, *Moralia in Job*, XXVI, 50–1, *MPL*, lxxvi, coll. 378–80.

fire of their labours here and through the fire of purgatory there; or such as the largest part of our Order – men who, although despising the common life, are unable to ascend with the Lord on to the heights, and do not rise to the greatest virtue.

The real task of the historian after William of Malmesbury is to withstand monastic prejudice in detail, to revalue persons and movements according to their own aims, and to create a new pattern which is not illuminated from a single source of light and distorted by shadows cast by events to come. His task is not to rehabilitate but to reconstruct an age which has been neglected because of its shortcomings, aware that in the long run quiescence is more characteristic – more normal – than revolution in the history of institutions, and that to give all attention to periods of reform and ignore the usual scene is to falsify the past. To compare moral tones, to estimate just how deep the trough was, to decide whether a native reform movement had already begun before the Norman Conquest are difficult tasks and can lead to unprofitable controversy. The Normans when rewriting the lives of the tenth-century English saints were occasionally disturbed by customs and actions quite irregular by their own standards. St Wulfstan's behaviour was often most unconventional, and we read with surprise of the Worcester monks loaning land to individual nuns until they should have need of it.[1] Each age has its own moral and disciplinary susceptibilities and its characteristic blind spots. The monks in the Old-English church after Edgar's death believed that they lived in a degenerate period, that Edward was no Edgar (although it was the grandson who was canonized),[2] that there was never again an earl like Æthelwin, and that the government in church and state lacked moral purpose. The Normans after the Conquest disapproved of much that they found. The limited view of the monastic writers has already been discussed. The scornful attitude of the Normans was not devoid of self-interest and prejudice. About 1080 Goscelin of St Bertin, who had lived for twenty years in Wiltshire under the protection of Bishop Herman, and who had personal reason at that time to lament the Norman Conquest, wrote from Peterborough, where he was taking temporary refuge,

---

[1] 'Hec hida T.R.E. reddebat in praedicto manerio sacam et socam et omne regis servitium et est de dominico victu monachorum, sed praestita fuit cuidam Edgidae moniali ut haberet et deserviret quamdiu fratres voluissent et carere possent. Crescente vero congregatione T.R.W. reddidit et ipsa adhuc vivens inde est testis', DB, i. 173 b ii. Another nun also held a hide: 'Elfgivae [sic] monialis tenuit sicut deprecari poterat', DB, i. 173 b i.

[2] There was a cult of Edgar at Glastonbury, where he was buried. For his rather unseemly translation in 1052 by Abbot Ælfweard, and miracles at his tomb, see Malmesbury, De Antiqu. Glaston. ecclesie, i. 90–1, GR, p. 180.

to an old pupil and friend now at Angers, some bitter words about the new masters of the English church.[1]

First he expresses sorrow for the victims of the Conquest:

How many thousands of the human race have fallen on evil days! The sons of kings and dukes and nobles and the proud ones of the land are fettered with manacles and irons, are in prison and in gaol. How many have lost their limbs by the sword or disease, have been deprived of their eyes, so that when released from prison the common light of the world is a prison for them! They are the living dead for whom the sun – mankind's greatest pleasure – now has set. Blessed are those who are consoled by eternal hope; and afflicted are the unbelieving, for, deprived of all their goods and also cut off from heaven, their punishment has now begun.

He then turns to a change he has found in the church:

Those who through fear of pride forbid learning are mistaken, seeing that the more learned a man the humbler he is. . . . It would be just as crazy to condemn chastity, abstinence, prayers, and all other virtues which are a source of exaltation. They would do far better to learn through education how to preserve humility, which is the guardian of all virtues, and to stamp out the barbarous pride and bragging of the undisciplined. We shall soon see the unlearned deriding and despising the learned and counting illiteracy secular wisdom or holiness of life. No wonder that they neglect what they do not know and prefer what they do know, that the blind despise those who can see and ignorant men take pride in the cult of humility.

For Goscelin the Norman Conquest brought in the rule of the ignorant, proud, and prejudiced barbarian, men who could not appreciate English scholarship and civilization. Later he became reconciled to the new way of life and may even have thought it an improvement. But at first he could not contain his indignation.

[1] *Liber confortatorius*, pp. 77, 82.

CHAPTER I

The Persons

I. THE MONARCHY

The kingdom of England had only a monarchical unity. Its kings had become landlords, and the kingdom was in many ways a private estate. Alfred had divided the territory with Guthrum, Edmund Ironside with Cnut. Lothian was sometimes granted to the king of Scots, sometimes withheld. But the vigour of the monarchical principle in these Germanic lands is remarkable. By the eleventh century English kingship was like a great tree with roots pushed into every pocket of soil that could nourish it. The unbroken descent from Woden, the Germanic cult of the leader, the transformation through unction at the crowning, the piety of the priest-king, the belligerency of the gods both old and new, the ceremonial splendour of Rome, administrative techniques, all fed the growth. Several kings had been great and none completely worthless since Alfred's day, and the monarchy suffered no irreparable harm from the irresponsibility of Æthelred or the rapid changes in dynasty. Kingship had become a powerful office, which supported the incumbent. It could maintain a man like Edward the Confessor who had no taste for pomp. The queen saw to it that he was dressed properly on ceremonial occasions,[1] and the bureaucratic government did not need close supervision. Indeed, England had a structure which can be termed 'neo-Carolingian'. The kingdom was governed by royal officials.[2]

The active principle of monarchy, working within a rather inert society and a somewhat motiveless administration, explains some of the startling contrasts to be found in the last years of the Anglo-Danish kingdom. The kings since Æthelred were foreigners: Cnut was a mixture of Dane and Pole; Harold Harefoot added Anglo-Scandinavian and Harthacnut Norman blood; Edward was Anglo-Norman, and Harold Anglo-Danish. The official aristocracy – earls and thegns – was no less heterogeneous. The half-West-Saxon,

---

[1] *Vita Ædwardi*, p. 41.

[2] As Ælfric wrote in the preface to his third book of homilies, 'our nation is subject to one king. . . . An earthly king has many servants [thegns] and divers stewards; he cannot be an honoured king unless he has the state which befits him and serving men to offer him their obedience.' *Lives of Saints*, pp. 4, 7.

half-Danish, Tostig, married to a Flemish countess, ruled the Northumbrians; Ralf from the French Vexin ruled on the Welsh march. Similarly in the church. A Lotharingian had the bishopric of Wiltshire, a Saxon Somerset, a Norman London. Yet the offices held by these men of Germanic descent were expressed in the ecclesiastical documents in Romano-Greek terms – *basileus, dux, minister, episcopus.*

With so many foreigners at the English court, and with so much diplomacy on a European scale, there must have been linguistic difficulties, for Latin cannot have been an entirely satisfactory *lingua franca* even among clerks. Those who spoke one of the branches of the Germanic tongue – the Scandinavians, Saxons, Lotharingians, and English – could, no doubt, make adjustments. Many of the English nobility must have been familiar with both Danish and English. The real barrier was between the Germanic and the Romance tongues. Doubtless King Edward could speak both Norman and English. It is possible that some men were tri-lingual. Earl Harold, we know, was carefully educated for his duties [1] and had travelled abroad. His brother, Earl Tostig, was several times in his wife's country, Flanders. Educated men were aware of these language difficulties [2] and may have taken steps to overcome them. At a time when little was read and much important business was transacted orally and carefully remembered, learning to speak a new language may have been relatively easy. The problem of communication is not mentioned by any contemporary observer; and we must conclude, therefore, that it was satisfactorily solved.

Basically English kingship was still Germanic in character, and the Danish conquest intensified this aspect. In skaldic verse the kennings convey only military virtues. The prince is the son of princes, the 'bold son of Svein'. He is 'protector of the land' and of his men. He is a terror to his foes: in 'the storm of the corpse-fire' he feeds the raven and the wolf. He is rich and generous – a 'gold-giver', a 'distributor of rings', a 'scatterer of the ice of the hand'. Here was the call to the deepest loyalties. But there was also the Christian side.

English kings had been protectors of the church since the conversion. There was no history of persecution, and the only famous ecclesiastical martyr had suffered at the hands of the heathen Danish invaders. Many of

[1] *Vita Ædwardi*, pp. 6, 33.
[2] Goscelin of St Bertin, a Flemish monk serving a Lotharingian bishop of Wiltshire in the last years of Edward's reign, refers several times to the different languages spoken in western Europe. Cf. his *Liber confortatorius*, pp. 41, 86–7, 107, 113, 115.

the great saints had been associated with holy kings. From Æthelberht, by way of Oswiu, Alfred, and Æthelstan, to Edgar the story was one of Christian grandeur. Five kings – Oswald, Æthelberht of East Anglia, Kenelm, Edmund, and Edward – were generally regarded as saints and martyrs. One English queen, Ælfgifu of Wessex, and the Frankish Bathild of English origin, were among the confessors. Most of the holy virgins were of royal birth. In Edgar, despite the stories of his cruelty and lust,[1] the English church had found its greatest advocate. 'With due rites the faithful monks, and above all the shepherds of the people, pray for him, for he was not only their lord but also their father. O Benedict our king, help him, the defender of thy servants, with thy bounteous prayers, and make him to sit on the right hand in majesty, who was ever thy revered friend', wrote a Ramsey monk a quarter of a century after his death.[2] The royal family had produced many saints, and so great was the respect for the dynasty that any unfortunate royal death could be interpreted as a martyrdom. The shrine of St Edward at Shaftesbury [3] was as popular as that of St Ælfheah at Canterbury.[4] English kings did not have to assert themselves against the church. They could be sure of unquestioning obedience.

It has been suggested that the office of emperor, when revived by the Carolingian and then the Saxon kings, was more an ecclesiastical than a

[1] These stories were current in the eleventh century. Goscelin of St Bertin gives a graphic description of Edgar's pursuit of nuns at Wilton in his *Vita S. Uulfhilde*, ed. Mario Esposito, *Analecta Bollandiana*, xxxii (1913), pp. 10–26. See also Osbern, 'Vita S. Dunstani', in *Memorials of St Dunstan*, pp. 111–12, Malmesbury, *GR*, i. 178–80; C. E. Wright, *The Cultivation of Saga in Anglo-Saxon England*, pp. 146–55. They were used, rightly or wrongly, to explain Edgar's 'delayed' coronation. Since Osbern believed that Edward the Martyr was Edgar's child by a nun (an assertion which was hotly denied by some of the writer's contemporaries: cf. Nicholas monk of Worcester, *Memorials of St Dunstan*, pp. 422–4, Stubbs, *ibid*. pp. lxvii, lxix) it is possible that these stories originated in the circles opposed to Edgar's patronage of monasticism and were used to discredit him and his murdered son during Æthelred's reign. Geographically they are associated with Winchester and may represent an answer to Æthelwold and Edgar's reforms there.

[2] *Vita Oswaldi, HCY*, i. 443. Note the deliberate echo of the Rule of St Benedict, c. 2, where 'abbas . . . dirum magistri pium patris ostendat affectum'.

[3] Edgar's elder son, murdered at Corfe in 979 by the adherents of his half-brother and supplanter, Æthelred. Archbishop Sigeric had suggested that Æthelred should commemorate Edward at Shaftesbury (Goscelin, *Vita S. Yvonis, MPL*, clv, coll. 87–8). For the popularity of his shrine, see Malmesbury, *GP*, pp. 187–8. A proper mass is in the Missal of Robert of Jumièges (printed *The Leofric Missal*, ed. F. E. Warren, pp. 282–3).

[4] Monk of Deerhurst, hermit at Bath, succeeded Æthelwold at Winchester and then Dunstan at Canterbury, murdered by the Danes in 1012, and translated from London to Canterbury in 1023. See Osbern's *Vita et Translatio (MPL*, cxlix, coll. 371 ff.), *ASC DE* 1023. A proper mass is in Corpus Christi College, Cambridge MS. 270 (printed *The Leofric Missal*, p. 302).

secular institution – that it gave the holder ecclesiastical privileges and duties rather than additional temporal power.[1] A similar view can be held of the anointing of a king at his coronation. The great reformer, St Peter Damiani (ob. 1072), wrote in his Sermon on the Dedication of a Church:[2]

The fifth sacrament is the unction of a king. Exalted is this anointing because it creates exalted power. For when the noblest blood, either on account of descent or as the result of election, is to be consecrated king, the church and the whole nobility of the kingdom are called together. On the one side stands the glorious company of the primates, metropolitans, and bishops, and, on the other, the not despicable nobility of the dukes, counts, and castellans; and through the middle goes the man who is to rule over men, thronged by his own personal servants. He is led to the altar of the High Prince, to obtain there the principality of the kingdom from Him by whom kings reign (Prov. 8: 15). But before he is clothed in imperial raiment, the will of the clergy and people is sought, and with his own hand he swears to preserve the liberties of the churches. He is then divested, and asperged with the oil of sanctification, so that, drenched with allegorical dew, he may glory in the fullness of the heavenly unguent. Next he is dressed in purple, which is the token of royal majesty, and bears in his hands the sceptre of the kingdom for ruling God's holy people. A crown of gold, stamped with the symbol of holiness, the ornament of honour, and the strength of valour (Ecclus. 45: 12), is put on his head. A sword is carried before his eyes, so that he shall know that he is the avenger of God's wrath, set up for that very purpose. When he has been initiated by these and such mysteries, he is carried back to his palace, from that day forward a man to be feared as well as loved. Blessed is he if he shall join the sword of the kingdom to the sword of the priesthood, so that the sword of the priesthood shall soften the sword of the king, and the sword of the king sharpen the sword of the priesthood. These are the two swords of which we read in the Lord's passion: 'Behold, here are two swords. And he said unto them, It is enough' (Luke 22: 38). For the kingdom is exalted, the priesthood enhanced, and both are honoured, when those things which the Lord has predetermined are joined in blessed alliance.

Thus unction gave to the king Christian duties, which are expressed in the *ordo* for his coronation. Certainly English kingship assumed a strong ecclesiastical colour; and just as the English church takes on sharper form when seen in relation to the monarchy, so kingship appears in its greatest amplitude when regarded from an ecclesiastical standpoint. The Christian view of kingship is firmly stated by Wulfstan of York in his 'Institutes of Polity', cc. ii–iv.[3] Moreover, imperial ideas were current in the English church in the eleventh century.[4] Whether these were drawn from memory of the

---

[1] Cf. W. Holtzmann, 'Imperium u. Nationen' in *Relazioni, X congresso internazionale di Scienze storiche Roma 4–11 Settembre 1955*, iii. 279–81; discussion in *Atti*, pp. 330 ff.

[2] *Sermo* lxix, *MPL*, cxliv, coll. 899–900.   [3] *Polity*, pp. 40–58.

[4] See R. Drögereit, 'Kaisertitel u. Kaiseridee bei den Angelsachsen' in *Zeitschrift d. Savigny-Stiftung für Rechtsgesch.* (Germ. Abt. 69) (1952), pp. 24–73; cf. R. S. Lopez, 'Le problème des relations Anglo-Byzantines du viime au xme siècle', *Byzantion*, xviii (1948), pp. 139–62; A. Vasiliev,

old *bretwaldaship*, taken directly from Byzantium, or imitated from Germany, the urge must have been to exalt the king in his religious character, strengthen his position as *Christus dei*, and justify the effigy of the king as it appeared on his seal – crowned in majesty.

English unity was a product of the tenth century. And just as the successors of Alfred expanded their boundaries to take in the other kingdoms and also made arrangements for the government of the whole, so they extended their ecclesiastical patronage and created an *ecclesia anglicana*. Their control over the newly acquired bishoprics does not seem to have been seriously disputed, although it was not before the reign of Cnut that Durham came under royal influence. An attempt was also made to inspire the priests with loyalty towards king and bishop.[1] Royal control over monasticism was the achievement of St Æthelwold and King Edgar in the latter half of the tenth century, the effect of their work being the establishment of new reformed monasteries, detached as far as possible from local influence and depending directly on the king and queen. These new royal *Eigenklöster* served the king as royalist centres in the provinces and supplied abbots who were useful not only in the royal councils but in the local moots as well.[2] The political gain to the crown was considerable.

The English kings governed the church and made use of its administrative techniques. The prologues to the 'royal' charters, composed by churchmen, are mostly concerned with the uselessness of worldly goods and the transitoriness of earthly life, but occasionally they express a clerical view of royal power. The sentiments attributed to Cnut never outstep simple piety: 'Peace and victory of the apostolic faith to its worshippers for ever! We desire that the everlasting and indefatigable authority of the catholic church should endure.'[3] Edward's prologues, however, occasionally strike a more active note: 'It behoves us, whom God has set up as ruler over his people in this world, to do justice to all, and especially to the church, the mother of our salvation, through whom all Christians may come to the eternal mercy of the

'The opening stages of the Anglo-Saxon immigration to Byzantium in the eleventh century', *Annales de l'Institut Kondakov (Seminarium Kondakovianum)* ix (Prague, 1937), 39–70; Eric John, 'An alleged Worcester charter of the reign of Egar', *BJRL*, xli (1958), 59–63.

[1] 'And we enjoin that every priest be able to declare when he fetches chrism [from the cathedral] what he has done in prayers for the king and bishop': Wulfstan, 'Canons enacted under King Edgar', c. 67, Thorpe, *Ancient Laws*, ii. 259.

[2] Cf. Eric John, 'The King and the Monks in the Tenth-century Reformation', *BJRL*, xlii (1959), 82 ff.

[3] K. 746, charter to Abingdon Abbey, 1032.

Lord, who will judge the kings of the earth and render to each according to his works.' [1]

Even more revealing is the proem to the charter which records Edward's transfer of the see of the bishopric of Devon from Crediton to Exeter:

As all things have been founded well by God in his wisdom, heaven and earth, and all things that are therein (Acts xiv: 15), it is clear that, although the incapacity of suffering mankind confuses the acts of men with many mishaps, it will be right and proper for us [Edward], who are said to have been appointed by God as ruler over men, prudently to endeavour, by the inspiration of divine mercy and after the measure of our judgment, to seek for the justice of political science, and, especially, to take in hand, and in kindly measure investigate, the affairs of the church, putting to right those things which in our eyes do not appear to be just, and, when we have established them correctly, directing them to the advancement of innocence and the strengthening of both this and the other life. [2]

These clerical draftsmen regarded the king as the servant of the church. But at the same time he was God's deputy, *rex dei gratia*,[3] entrusted with a temporal magistracy. He was the guardian of justice, responsible for restoring to the best of his ability God's plan for His creation. Accordingly the affairs of the church were under his care; and a servant who is a protector is also a kind of master. It was, indeed, the successful joining of the secular and ecclesiastical structures which gave to the English monarchy its remarkable strength and prestige; [4] and the unity of the church under the king produced a pattern for a state and a nation. The provinces lay restless or supine, wrapped in their traditions, conscious of their own history. Earls could rebel, secede, or usurp. But the bishops and abbots looked only to the English king, their advocate and protector.

---

[1] K. 808, a judicial sentence in favour of Peterborough Abbey, 1060.

[2] K. 791 (1050). Exeter Dean and Chapter MS. 2072, the 'original' foundation charter, gives a better, although not perfect, text. Both manuscripts have a common error in this passage—ęcclesiasticę for ęcclesiasticas or ęcclesię; and I have preferred to amend *corroborando* to *corroborationem*.

[3] This style, or variations on it, was used in most charters of Kings Æthelred, Cnut, Harthacnut, and Edward, except in those granting land to thegns. *Dei gratia* – Æthelred (K. 1289, 1300, 1309), Cnut (730, 753), Edward (771, 776, 791, 793); *divina favente gratia* – Cnut (737), Edward (781, 786, 787, 810); *dei nutu* – Æthelred (1305, 1307), Cnut (1316), Edward (778); *dei dono* – Edward (813); *christo annuente/conferente* – Æthelred (1278, 1306), Cnut (751), Harthacnut (762), Edward (792, 796, 800). Numerous other, usually more elaborate, variations were used.

[4] W. Holtzmann has suggested that one of the great differences between Germany and France as they developed out of the Carolingian empire was that in Germany the church was incorporated into the state in the Ottonian period whereas in France the crown lost control over it ('Imperium u. Nationen', *ut supra*, iii. 277).

2. THE KINGS

Despite the frequent political revolutions which took place during the last phase of the Anglo-Saxon kingdom there was no break in the traditions of government. The renewed Viking incursions into England, already half-Scandinavian, at the end of the tenth century, far from provoking English nationalism, had led to even more assimilation. The West-Saxon Æthelred married the able and ambitious Norman princess, Emma, enrolled Scandinavian auxiliaries, and fought against the Danish Svein on equal terms; [1] and when their sons, Edmund Ironside and Cnut, disputed the crown, the conflict must have appeared to contemporaries more as a contest of rivals than as a struggle between nations. The successful, but hardly victorious, Cnut married Æthelred's widow, thereby facilitating a continuity which he had no interest in destroying,[2] and the reigns of his two sons, Harold Harefoot and Harthacnut, and of his stepson, Edward, which followed in turn, were little more than attenuated projections of the pattern which their father had made.

After the savage and often purposeless violence of Æthelred's reign a deep peace fell on England. Cnut's reign is devoid of great incident; Harold Harefoot and Harthacnut disturbed only by their entry; and if in Edward's reign there were undercurrents that sometimes whipped up the surface, it was again because the succession to the crown was uncertain. The cost of the wars had been great; the political revolution had left a legacy of military government which was expensive; and we can discern in the country a revulsion from savagery and a distaste for violence. The dynastic confusion caused insecurity and internal faction. But from 1035 to 1066 all disputes were compromised. None of the kings was a great warrior. Cleverness and eloquence were highly esteemed. Throughout political life there was a reaction from the heroic. The country was recovering its wealth.

All but one of the kings after Æthelred were under-educated for the task of ruling England. Cnut, the younger son of a Danish king, adroit by nature and impressionable, was schooled by events and in time achieved a stature commensurate with his position. Harold Harefoot was unprepared for his

---

[1] Wulfstan, in his *Sermo Lupi ad Anglos* (1014), not only stresses the treachery of the period, but also states that many Englishmen became Vikings (*EHD*, i. 855-8).

[2] Emma's view that the marriage reconciled the English and the Danes (*Enc. Emmae*, p. 32) has been ridiculed (A. Campbell, *ibid.* pp. xxi, xlv); but one can understand what she meant. She had been married to Æthelred for some fourteen years, at an impressionable age, and no doubt was able to teach her second husband much about the ways of English royalty. The marriage gave continuity to the court and improved Cnut's title.

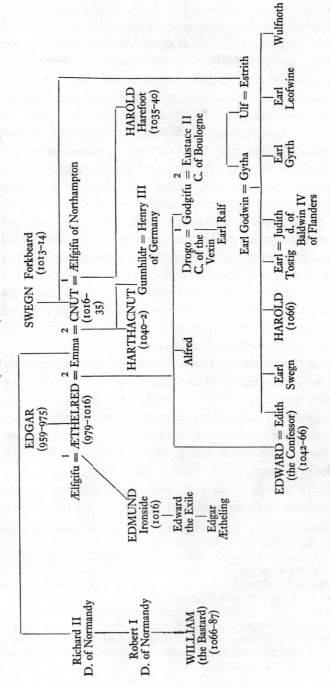

KINGS OF ENGLAND
(1000 – 1066)

fortuitous elevation; Harthacnut knew more of Denmark than of England; and neither survived long enough to impress. And Edward during his long exile abroad had not been trained to rule and had shown no great inclination to seek out his inheritance. Edward, however, lived long and acquired passively with the accumulation of the years a semblance of royalty. Only Harold Godwinesson, the weakest in title, had had a political education suitable for the office.

The lack of breeding and the foreign extraction of these kings made them very dependent on the servants of the court. Bishops were especially influential, for they represented a sphere in which the kings were conscious of inferiority, and at the same time offered no affront to royal dignity or power. Menial in attitude, yet informed with divine authority, learned and wise in the ways of the world and the secrets of government but incapable of dynastic or the grosser forms of temporal ambition, anxious to strengthen the monarchy, the rule of law, and the reign of peace, they had every attraction for semi-barbarian rulers. The church was, therefore, in a most advantageous position, but one which held subtle dangers. Such kings could not put high ideals before their clerical servants or do other than encourage their more useful accomplishments. And when rewards were lavish there were temptations to the spirit which few could resist.

There is no evidence that any of these kings had a personal ecclesiastical policy. But the reformers had captured the government under Edgar (959-75) and, despite the reaction after his death,[1] a clerical party remained entrenched in the organs of government. His successors, therefore, were expected to display the proper pietistic attitude at the appropriate times, and, as long as the church itself had a policy, to carry that out. This they did, for the church had offerings which none of these kings could afford to disregard. To Æthelred it averred that the political disasters were due to sin;[2] and Æthelred in his last years clutched at any helping hand. To Cnut it offered

[1] *Vita Oswaldi, HCY,* i. 444 ff.; D. J. V. Fisher, 'The anti-monastic reaction in the reign of Edward the Martyr', *Camb. HJ,* x (1950–2), 254–70.

[2] Cf. a prayer and a hymn to Dunstan (*Memorials of St Dunstan,* pp. 440–1); Wulfstan's *Sermo Lupi ad Anglos,* where the author, basing himself on a letter from Alcuin to Archbishop Æthelhard, compares himself to Gildas (*EHD,* i. 859; D. Bethurum, 'Archbishop Wulfstan's Commonplace Book', *PMLA,* lvii (1942), 920–1); *Vita Ædwardi,* p. lxii. A simple theology of heaven and hell was proclaimed to all: cf. I Cnut, 25, 'And likewise we earnestly enjoin all men to have the fear of God constantly in their hearts, and day and night to be in terror of sin, dreading the Day of Judgment and shuddering at the thought of Hell, and ever expecting the last day to be close at hand.' Contempt of God's commands, especially in the withholding of tithe, was, of course, one of the reasons for God's wrath. Cf. IV Edgar.

the paraphernalia of civilized Christian kingship; and Cnut accepted this eagerly. To Edward it gave a sphere of influence which was invaluable to him in his straitened circumstances. So, up to Cnut's death the royal government had a reforming aspect. Wulfstan I of Worcester and archbishop of York (*Lupus*) rewrote almost all the laws in Christian terms. But this was the watershed. During the times of peace and renewed prosperity religion lost some of its power, and in Edward's reign a sophisticated worldliness appeared. The reform movement had lost its momentum and so the royal government was left without an ecclesiastical policy.

When Svein Forkbeard died full of sins at Gainsborough, he exhorted his younger son and companion, Cnut, to pay attention to the Christian religion.[1] This precept was faithfully obeyed. Cnut was not a great warrior and had no reputation for strength or bravery.[2] He exposed that other side of the Viking character, a sharp wit, a delight in the law, and the ability to organize. Soon after his acquisition of England and the crimes necessary to safeguard his position, he and his dispersed followers became subject to English pressure,[3] and he showed much skill in cloaking his despotism and cultivating the church. He was greatly influenced by the skills, the pomps, and the outward displays of religion.[4] He was ostentatious in all the observances fashionable at the time: he built a minster to expiate the battle of *Assandun*;[5] he collected relics;[6] he was lavish with gifts to English and foreign monasteries,[7] to the poor, and to the orphan;[8] he had his name entered in the necrologies of many churches;[9] he always stopped at a

[1] *Enc. Emmae*, p. 14. Svein was a Christian, and his body was taken from England for reburial at Roskilde. See also C. E. Wright, *The Cultivation of Saga in Anglo-Saxon England*, pp. 172–4.

[2] A. Campbell, *Enc. Emmae*, pp. lx–lxi; but cf. the poems on Cnut, *EHD*, i. 308–12.

[3] For stories of Danes in the neighbourhood of Ramsey giving up through fear of the English the lands that Cnut had granted them, see *Chron. Ramsey*, pp. 140–1, 143–4; cf. pp. 135 ff. In this way the monastery was able to get land cheaply. The ecclesiastical charges brought against Earl Thorkell and Countess Edith, *c.* 1020, were regarded as an attack by the English on a Dane: *ibid.* p. 132; for the case, see below, pp. 273–4.

[4] His personal interest in the translation of Archbishop Ælfheah comes out clearly in Osbern's account of it (*MPL*, cxlix, coll. 387 ff.). For his reverence for St Edith at Wilton, see Goscelin, *Vita S. Edithe*, pp. 278–80, and a rather different version in Malmesbury, *GP*, p. 190.

[5] *ASC* 1020. Cnut gave a pall adorned with peacock feathers to Glastonbury for Edmund's tomb, Malmesbury, *De Antiqu. Glaston. Ecclesiae*, i. 88.

[6] Cf. *Vita S. Wistani*, *Chron. Evesham*, pp. 325–6.

[7] See Plummer, p. 203.   [8] *Enc. Emmae*, pp. 34–8.

[9] At Bremen under his baptismal name of Lambert, 'Lambrecht rex Danorum et Imma regina et Knut filius eorum devote se commendaverunt orationibus fratrum Bremensium': Schol. 38 on Adam of Bremen, *Gesta pontificum Hammaburgensis ecclesiae*. Cf. also *Enc. Emmae*, pp. 36–8.

shrine [1] and visited Rome at least once; [2] and he had his son Harthacnut baptized in infancy.[3] He relied much on his bishops and executed the policy which they suggested to him. The letters he sent to England from abroad are concerned almost exclusively with church affairs. The missive of 1020, instigated by a message which Archbishop Lyfing had brought from the pope, was intended to secure a reform of morals,[4] and the letter of 1027, written while Cnut travelled from Rome to Denmark, ordered the payment of all church dues.[5] Cnut had a saintly archbishop of Canterbury, a reforming archbishop of York, was in close touch with Rome, and seems to have done all that was required of him. But that was not enough. In his period the church still required a lead from the enlightened laity, and Cnut could not give that inspiration or stimulus. He was a pupil not the master. Hence the English church was maintained at the best average standard of the time, but did not rise high above it.

It is, perhaps, significant that, except for the praise in the *Encomium Emmae*,[6] the writers of the time were reserved and showed no inclination to compare him with Edgar. Political prejudice and a suspicion of unauthenticity may account for this. He was a usurper of heathen race, and, although he played chess at night like a civilized Viking [7] and is known to have had a bath,[8] he kept two wives and provided for two families. Christian influence had penetrated deeply without completely transforming the man. In his religion he protested a little too much.

Cnut's legitimate wife, Emma/Ælfgifu of Normandy, was moved by the same type of religious zeal. She had left England in 1013 in company with an abbot,[9] and she was extravagantly pious in all the conventional 'monastic' ways. About the year 1023 she was described as governing the monastery of

---

[1] Cf. Cnut's letter of 1027 describing his visits: Liebermann, *Gesetze*, i. 276. He is supposed to have walked barefoot the six miles from Garmondsway Moor to Durham because of his reverence for St Cuthbert, Symeon, *HDE*, p. 90.

[2] See below, p. 291.   [3] *Enc. Emmae*, p. 34.

[4] Liebermann, *Gesetze*, i. 273-5.   [5] *Ibid.* i. 276-7.

[6] As a result of his marriage to Emma, 'Amicus vero et familiaris factus est viris ecclesiasticis, adeo ut episcopis videretur coepiscopus pro exibitione totius religionis, monachis quoque non secularis sed caenobialis pro continentia humillimae devotionis', etc.: *Enc. Emmae*, pp. 34-6. At the end of the century, Goscelin of St Bertin, at St Augustine's Canterbury, had a high opinion of him. For references, see *Vita Ædwardi*, p. 5 *n.*   [7] *Chron. Ramsey*, p. 137.

[8] There is a graphic passage in Osbern, *Translatio S. Elphegi*, c. 4 (*MPL*, cxlix, col. 389), describing how Cnut dashed from his bath to help Archbishop Æthelnoth disinter Ælfheah at St Paul's.

[9] *ASC* 1013; Florence, i. 167; *Chron. Peterborough*, pp. 48-9. Ælfsi of Peterborough was also a great collector of relics.

Evesham,[1] and she avidly collected relics of the most expensive sort.[2] Emma probably inspired even more suspicion than Cnut, for her vain, ambitious character, her determination always to be near the centre of power,[3] must have led to an interference in ecclesiastical affairs without the justification of high ideals or obvious purpose. Religious women had a special and honoured place in the church, but it was a place of retirement.

That there was no reaction during the eight troubled years after Cnut's death, such as had occurred in rather similar circumstances after the death of Edgar, is proof that Cnut and Emma had not forced the pace in ecclesiastical affairs.[4] Their extravagances had been private and had not disturbed vested interests. Harold Harefoot, the son of Cnut and Ælfgifu of Northampton, who obtained the crown in 1037 owing to Harthacnut's delay in returning from Denmark, seems to have been weak but in no way anticlerical,[5] and there is no evidence for hostility to the church in the provinces. Harthacnut, who secured his inheritance belatedly in 1040, was under the influence of his mother and under the shadow of death. He was highly regarded for his religion in at least one monastery.[6] These two half-brothers ruled too briefly to develop an ecclesiastical policy, and the irregularities which are reported seem due simply to inexperience.[7] The accession of the third half-brother, Edward, in 1042, at first merely confirmed the somewhat provisional character which the English monarchy had acquired. But Edward reigned long and became, if not a force, at least a new symbol of kingship. The reputation for sanctity, which was already forming in some circles before his death,[8] was a strange epilogue to a career which had aroused little contemporary enthusiasm. The annalists were cool before they entered

[1] Robertson, *Charters*, no. 81. For Emma and Wilton, see *Vita Edithe*, pp. 281–2.

[2] Plummer, p. 223. She was especially interested in heads.

[3] A. Campbell, *Enc. Emmae*, p. xxiii.

[4] There was possibly a decline after Archbishop Wulfstan's death in 1023. The visit to Rome and the letter of 1027 show that the high tone was still being maintained; but it cannot be without significance that Cnut's first Code was also his last.

[5] Freeman, *NC*, i. 504–5. For a story of his being deceived by an abbot who suborned his steward, and his lying ill at Oxford in company with a bishop and a monk, see Robertson, *Charters*, no. 91.

[6] *Chron. Ramsey*, pp. 151–2; 'vir praedicandae indolis et eximiae in miseros pietatis', *ibid.* p. 154. He gave a shrine to Glastonbury: Malmesbury, *De Antiqu. Glaston. ecclesiae*, i. 89. Norman writers were, naturally, hostile to Harold Harefoot and partial to Harthacnut: cf. William of Poitiers, I, cc. 2–5.

[7] It is reported that Harold sold the bishopric of Selsey to Grimketel (Malmesbury, *GP*, p. 205) and Harthacnut Durham to one of the clerks of St Cuthbert (Symeon, *HDE*, p. 91).

[8] *Vita Ædwardi*, pp. lxix ff.

an obituary poem.[1] His mother's encomiast seems to have thought him un-enterprising.[2] And the queen's panegyrist was not entirely uncritical.[3] The enormous political difficulties which he overcame could earn him no praise because all ended in ruin: sanctity was the only possible reward.

Edward was born to Æthelred and Emma of Normandy, at Islip in Oxfordshire,[4] after the end of 1002, and, according to the *Vita Ædwardi*,[5] had been proclaimed heir to the throne while still in his mother's womb. The story is told in order to show that Edward, chosen as king before his birth, was divinely called to rule, and that God's purpose was fulfilled when he succeeded in 1042. If historical fact underlies this 'prodigy', Emma probably married Æthelred, as later Cnut,[6] on condition that the descent of the crown should be limited to the issue of her marriage and all children of the half-blood disinherited. Yet, according to an oral tradition embedded in the twelfth-century Ely chronicle,[7] but uncontaminated by the hagiographical legend, Edward was given by his parents to the abbey as an oblate, the child being offered on the altar swathed in a fine pall which was still on show in the monastery. Moreover there had been seniors in the house who remembered him learning psalms and hymns with the other boys being educated in the cloister. The Ely story is used to introduce a forged charter attributed to Edward and to explain his benefaction. But the prologue to the charter has no connexion with the story, and the obvious falsity of the one does not necessarily involve the credit of the other.

Although Edward was born during a period of deep penetration by Viking armies into England it is hard to believe that Emma was capable of sacrificing her firstborn in this way in order to avert God's wrath. Nor is it likely that Edward would have been placed at so early an age in a monastery

---

[1] *ASC CD*. Even the poem is not extravagant: Edward had had a prosperous reign, his power had been extensive and his kingdom peaceful. He was virtuous, chaste and mild, blithe and guiltless. There is no hint of sanctity. His *obit* was established at Bury St Edmunds by his doctor, Abbot Baldwin (1065–97/8), when he is called 'the good king' (Robertson, *Charters*, pp. 197, 199), the usual epithet before canonization.

[2] *Enc. Emmae*, p. 48.   [3] *Vita Ædwardi*, pp. 17 ff.

[4] Harmer, *Writs*, no. 104. See also pp. 334 ff. See further F. Barlow, *Edward the Confessor* (1970, 1979).   [5] pp. 7–8, 60.

[6] Emma always behaved as though legitimate claims to England were vested in her. Cf. *Enc. Emmae*, p. 32.

[7] 'Illuc enim delatus in cunabulis a patre rege et matre regina super sanctum altare oblatus fuerat, palla involutus orbiculata brevibus circulis non plene viridi coloris; adhuc ibi ostenditur, et sicut seniores ecclesiae, qui videre et interfuere, nararre consueverant, cum pueris in claustro illic diu alitus est, psalmos et ymnos dominicos cum illis didicit': *Liber Eliensis*, II, c. 91, p. 160.

for his education. Indeed, if there is any truth in the story,[1] the likeliest interpretation is that the court merely disembarrassed itself of the child at a moment of great danger by putting him in a famous refuge,[2] from which, in the last resort, he could be carried by water to Normandy. Edward need not have remained long at Ely. In 1013 Emma left England for Normandy with the abbot of Peterborough, while Edward and his brother Alfred travelled under the care of the bishop of London. But it may have been the first of a series of absences from a court which had become a military headquarters. And such a separation would help to explain how Emma could so easily abandon interest in her first brood after Æthelred's death and how Edward could at first behave so coldly towards her when events drew them together again. Ely has no part in Edward's ecclesiastical legend. But if he did spend some time in that abbey at an impressionable age, with an abbot acting as a substitute father, he may well have acquired there his taste for the company and advice of ecclesiastical persons which could have facilitated the formation of his legend.

However that may be, Edward did not become a monk. After Svein's death on 3 February 1014, Edward was back in England with his father's messengers to prepare for Æthelred's return; and from then, until the position was finally clarified by his mother's marriage to Cnut in 1017, he may have crossed the Channel several times.[3] From 1017 until 1041 he was an exile on the Continent, and had ceased to be of political account, for the English throne seemed assured to the issue of his mother's second marriage. The situation was not transformed before the deaths of Duke Robert of Normandy and Cnut in 1035 and the usurpation of the English throne by Harold Harefoot. But Edward was without a really influential backer until Earl Godwin of Wessex took him up. Banished *aethelings* were usually on the move, taking hospitality where they could. Edward's sister was married to Drogo, count of the Vexin, until his death in 1035, and later to Eustace II, count of Boulogne. Edward is known to have visited Flanders

---

[1] Ely certainly regarded Æthelred as a benefactor; cf. *Liber Eliensis*, II, cc. 58, 76–9. But none of Æthelred's sales or gifts to Ely is explicitly connected with Edward, and Ely, so far as we know, never claimed Islip, which was Emma's birthday gift to Edward and would surely have been granted with him if he had been an oblate.

[2] St Albans, in fear of a Danish invasion early in Edward's reign, sent relics to Ely for safety, 'Erat enim eorum insula intransmeabilibus circumdata paludibus et arundinetis, unde hostium incursus nequaquam timuerunt': *Gesta abbatum monasterii S. Albani*, i. 34.

[3] The movements of Emma's children are discussed by A. Campbell, *Enc. Emmae*, pp. xliv–xlv. Edward was probably at Ghent at Christmas 1016 (*ibid.* p. lxiv, *n.* 3).

twice. He seems also to have had friends in Brittany.[1] In his first Life it is said that many French nobles sent representatives to his coronation and did him fealty, and that Edward rewarded them with great gifts.[2] Although the tradition may be wildly inflated, it is likely that there were many debts of gratitude owed in Neustria which in his new fortune Edward was called upon to repay. Norman historians maintained that it was due to William's counsel and aid that Edward obtained the crown, and that the obligation was acquitted when he adopted the duke as heir. This also contains an exaggeration, but may also have an aspect of truth.[3]

Later an attempt was made to associate Edward with religion even in this period of his life. His first biographer was told that Edward had performed miracles in the duchy.[4] Certainly Edward made a friend of Robert Champart, prior of St Ouen, who became abbot of Jumièges in 1037; and on his deathbed, it seems, his thoughts turned to two monks who had been friends of his youth in Normandy.[5] But it can hardly be credited that Edward and Alfred were educated in St Ouen at Rouen or in Jumièges close by, for the chronicler William of Jumièges, who was unlikely to conceal their connexion with his own house or any other, states explicitly that they were brought up in the ducal hall and were adopted almost as brothers by Duke Robert.[6] Moreover, to judge by Edward's later interests, he must have passed his life like any other nobleman, in hunting and fighting. In northern saga he was remembered as a warrior who, standing by his half-brother, Edmund Ironside, almost killed Cnut in the battle for London in 1016.[7] According to the Norman historians he made an exploratory invasion of England, probably from Normandy, after Harold Harefoot had usurped the crown, and fought a successful, although unexploitable, battle at Southampton.[8] But after his

[1] He granted lands to Bretons after he became king: see F. M. Stenton, *Anglo-Saxon England*, pp. 419–20.   [2] *Vita Ædwardi*, pp. 10–11.

[3] William of Jumièges, VII, c. xxi, and William of Poitiers, I, cc. 2, 14. But on the latter's own showing (I, c. 6) the young duke only began to make himself felt after 1042. Edward and Alfred (*Hetwardus* and *Helwredus*) witness a charter of Duke Robert's, *c.* 1030, and Edward (*Hatuardus rex*) witnesses one of Duke William's, *c.* 1041. In both cases the *aethelings* are surprisingly low in the order of precedence. Léopold Delisle, *Histoire du château et des sires de Saint-Sauveur-le-Vicomte* (Paris and Caen 1867), pièces justificatives, nos. 10, 17.

[4] *Vita Ædwardi*, p. 62.   [5] *Ibid.* p. 75.

[6] William of Jumièges, VI, c. ix, p. 109; cf. William of Poitiers, I, c. i. See also above, *n.* 3.

[7] *Flateyjarbók*, c. 20; cf. *Longer Saga of Olaf Tryggvason*, cc. 285–6.

[8] Between Cnut's death (12 Nov. 1035) and before Emma's banishment (1037). William of Jumièges, VII, c. v, pp. 120–1, and William of Poitiers, I. c. 2. No English writer mentions this invasion, but probably for obvious reasons. In any case, it had not the same dramatic interest as Alfred's.

brother Alfred had lost his life in a similar expedition from Flanders,[1] Edward seems to have become discouraged, in 1038 refusing his mother's request to try again and disclaiming immediate interest in English affairs.[2] Edward may have become reconciled to exile. But there is no good evidence for his having adopted a quasi-monastic life.

Although few of the events of Edward's career before 1041 can be established with certainty, an examination of this obscure period does help to explain his character and behaviour as king. We cannot think him inexperienced in the way of the world. Indeed, he was probably well versed in the shifts of feudal politics and skilled in using others. He cannot have wanted to begin his travels again. He was bound to be conciliatory. His best years had been spent in idle pursuits. He had not married, possibly for the simple reason that he had lacked a landed estate, and even the hope of one; but he was probably a confirmed bachelor. He must have been cosmopolitan by education. To identify him too closely with Norman culture would be mistaken, and to associate him with the monastic life would be unwarranted. The known companions of his return were a count of the Vexin, two priests (one born, the other educated, in Lotharingia), and a Norman abbot.[3] As far as we can see this group is a typical embodiment of his preferences. He retained a taste for foreigners, and at no time was his favour given only to Normans. His interest in monasticism seems to have grown with advancing age, but he never gave it his exclusive attention.

This view of Edward's character, although at variance with his legend, seems to be supported by the events of his reign. In the first seven years resolute military preparations, skilful foreign diplomacy, and a great deal of luck enabled him to keep his throne despite the ambition of Scandinavian

---

[1] Within the same period as Edward's. This expedition is discussed by A. Campbell, *Enc. Emmae*, pp. lxiv ff.

[2] According to *Enc. Emmae*, p. 48, Emma summoned him to Bruges, but Edward, after listening to his mother's woes, 'se matris fortunas edocet miserari, sed nullo modo posse auxiliari, cum Anglici optimates nullum ei fecerint iusiurandum'. He advised her to turn to Harthacnut, and returned to Normandy. We can accept that Edward refused to invade, but we do not have to believe anything more.

[3] Earl Ralf (*Chron. Ramsey*, p. 171); but he signs no charter in any capacity before 1050. The priests Herman and Leofric (K. 762, 767; *Ordnance Survey Facsimiles*, ii, Exeter charters, no. 12), and the abbot Robert of Jumièges (*Vita Ædwardi*, p. 17). According to William of Poitiers, I, c. 14, Edward returned with a small escort of Norman knights, the most that the English would allow. The number of foreigners endowed by Edward is probably usually exaggerated. Few can be traced in England, and it is by no means certain that all these had come to England at the same time. A king's court was the mecca of every adventurer.

claimants. And the external danger gave him power at home. Although his private resources were slender, and he had to manage proud and powerful earls, royal government was traditional and highly respected in England. Each earl had his own interests and ambitions; but they had learned to work together under Cnut, and in the last resort they always acted to preserve the unity of the kingdom.[1] If we can rely on the witness lists to charters,[2] Edward often gathered all the earls at court. He may not always have been able to get his own way, but since the earls were sometimes divided in counsel he had opportunities for taking the lead. It is possible to regard Edward's rule as a passive acceptance of forces too great for his control, interrupted by bouts of wilfulness.[3] Such in the main was the contemporary view, and it harmonizes with what we know of his father's character. Yet it is easy to overlook the achievements of a manager.

Edward soon established his power over the royal ecclesiastical patronage. In the first years there were rumours of simony,[4] and between 1043 and 1047 twice as many priests as monks were promoted bishop. The influence of the 'chapel'[5] which Edward inherited from his predecessors cannot be disregarded. It contained priests of long experience, such as Stigand, Cynsige, and Eadweald,[6] and Edward introduced Herman and Leofric,[7] and later others of the same type – men born or educated in Lotharingia, interested in the canonical but not necessarily monastic life, progressive and able, ready to use their administrative skill and royal favour to restore dilapidated cathedral churches. Among the familiar monks promoted was Robert Champart, abbot of Jumièges, whom Edward rewarded at the first opportunity, and whose translation from London to Canterbury had disastrous results.

---

[1] Cf. *Vita Ædwardi*, p. 53, in connexion with Tostig's deposition, 'quia in eadem gente horrebat quasi bellum civile'.

[2] Tryggvi J. Oleson, *The Witenagemot in the Reign of Edward the Confessor* (1955), uses the witness lists to illustrate the composition of the king's council. There is, indeed, no other evidence. But if the diploma was more of a private ecclesiastical document than an official royal charter (see below, p. 126), the lists could easily be ideal. To take an extreme example, a diploma granting land to St Michael's Mount (K. 914) is attested by King Edward, Robert archbishop of Rouen, Herbert bishop of Lisieux, Robert bishop of Coutances, and five men with Norman names. Presumably this is a charter drawn up on the authority of Edward's writ; cf. his writ to St Denis Paris, authorizing the creation of such a charter (Harmer, *Writs*, no. 55). It is a surprising feature of the schedules that all or most of the earls are usually included. It may be, of course, that land was only granted on special occasions.

[3] According to the *Vita Ædwardi* he was liable to bouts of passionate anger (pp. 12, 28, 53), but without the use of oaths (p. 12).

[4] See below, p. 109.   [5] See below, pp. 130 ff., 156 ff.
[6] See below, pp. 132 ff.   [7] See above, p. 45, n. 3.

The house of Godwin regarded Robert as the king's evil genius,[1] and when he broke loose he nearly ruined the kingdom. At a time when Edward was moving towards ecclesiastical reform, and entrusting other agents with his negotiations with the pope,[2] Robert used the new weapon in his vendetta against Godwin and badly blunted it.

In 1051 Edward ruined Earl Godwin and his whole family. The causes of this revolution are complex. The stability of the kingdom had depended in part on the fact that the power of Godwin, which included the earldoms of his sons Swegn and Harold and of his nephew Beorn, and the influence of his daughter, the queen,[3] had been balanced by the power of earls Leofric of Mercia and Siward of Northumbria. On some important occasions Godwin had been overruled by the king; but he was patient and experienced and could take hard knocks.[4] In 1050–1, however, he was not only constrained but also subjected to venomous attacks. It was the emergence of William the Bastard, duke of Normandy, as a European power after 1048 which disturbed the settled alliances in north-western Europe and caused trouble in England. A party at court led by Robert of Jumièges favoured closer relations with the duke, a policy to which Edward was probably sympathetically inclined, and which Godwin probably opposed, presumably because it was advocated by men he disliked.

With the king's councillors divided on this issue, ecclesiastical promotions became of exceptional importance.[5] Edward, no doubt to increase his personal power, had been appointing his own clerks and foreigners to bishoprics at the expense of English monks.[6] Although Godwin was not a champion of monks as such, the monks and abbots deprived of promotion were members of the nobility, often related to the earls. Hence Edward's policy struck against vested interests.[7] Godwin objected to the appointment of the Norman Ulf, one of Edward's priests, to Dorchester in 1049, and he attempted to get a kinsman into Canterbury in the winter of 1050–1. The Canterbury election was a real trial of strength. A royal council held at London in mid-Lent 1051 was uncompromising: Robert was translated from London to the arch-see, as the king willed;[8] his place was filled by Spearhavoc, abbot of Abingdon,

---

[1] *Vita Ædwardi*, pp. 17 ff.   [2] See below, pp. 301–2.
[3] 'erat enim in omnibus regalibus consiliis, ut ita dicamus, moderatrix et quoddam principium totius honestatis', *Vita Ædwardi*, p. 23.   [4] *Ibid.* pp. 6, 19.
[5] *Ibid.* p. 18.   [6] See below, pp. 76–7.
[7] Cf. 'cum obeuntibus possessoribus suis evacuatas dignitatum sedes hii optarent suis, illi distraherent alienis', *Vita Ædwardi*, p. 18.
[8] ' regio favore ', ' regis munere ', *ibid.* pp. 17, 19.

the king's goldsmith; [1] and to Abingdon was sent a Scandinavian bishop, a kinsman of the king. There was little if anything in this for Godwin. It is possible that the vacancy at York also was filled at this council, and again Godwin may have been snubbed. Instead of the usual promotion of the bishop of Worcester – in this case, Ealdred, who was friendly towards Godwin's family – a royal priest, an Englishman, Cynsige, was preferred. Moreover, if we can believe Norman tradition, it was at this council that the *witan* decided that William should be Edward's heir to the throne.[2] Once more Godwin was in the minority, for he was compelled to give a son and grandson as hostages to William.[3] The council also dismissed the last of the standing fleet and abolished *heregeld*, the tax imposed for the support of the royal forces, a measure which may have made a reform of the coinage possible. These may have been acts to buy the support of the earls for Edward's policy. It is clear that Godwin was not getting his own way, but equally clear that he was not being wantonly provoked. His power was as great as ever, for in the previous year Edward had forgiven, at Bishop Ealdred's instigation, his eldest son, the outlawed Swegn.[4]

It was the new archbishop of Canterbury who rashly provoked Godwin beyond endurance. On his way to Rome for the pallium he visited Normandy to confirm that Edward recognized William as his heir, and at the papal curia intrigued again to Godwin's discomfiture. Leo IX cannot have been happy about English affairs. In 1049 after the council of Rheims he had announced that he was sending a legate to inquire into the state of the English sees,[5] and at Vercelli in 1050 he had almost quashed the election of Bishop Ulf, probably as a result of complaints. He would, therefore, have been predisposed to accept Robert's information that Spearhavoc was an

---

[1] *Chron. Abingdon*, i. 462–3; Plummer, p. 228. For Goscelin's story of how Spearhavoc lost a precious ring of Queen Edith and found it again after praying to St Letard at St Augustine's, Canterbury, in Abbot Ælfstan's time (*ante* 1046), see *Historia translat. S. Augustini episcopi*, *MPL*, clv, col. 46. Spearhavoc has sometimes been considered Godwin's candidate, on the grounds that Robert of Jumièges disapproved of him. But it should be noticed that Abingdon, as represented by the 'C' version of the Chronicle, was hostile to the earl. It may be that Edward was choosing someone agreeable to Godwin, but clearly Spearhavoc was Edward's man.

[2] Since, according to William of Poitiers, I, c. 14, and William of Jumièges, VII, c. 13, p. 132, Archbishop Robert was the ambassador, the only possible date for the mission is the pallium journey of 1051, immediately after this council. The former states that the decision was taken with the assent of the English nobles.

[3] For a discussion of this see Barlow, *Edward the Confessor*, Appendix B.

[4] Florence, i. 203.

[5] Letter printed *The Leofric Missal*, ed. F. E. Warren, p. 2.

unsuitable candidate for London. Robert seems to have been transported by
these diplomatic triumphs. On his return to England he refused to consecrate
Spearhavoc [1] – suggesting, apparently, his replacement by another Norman,
one of the king's clerks named William – accused Godwin of the usurpation
of Canterbury estates,[2] and finally alleged that just as the earl had murdered
the king's brother Alfred, so he was planning to kill the king.[3] A visit to the
royal court of Edward's brother-in-law, Eustace II of Boulogne, touched off
the explosion. This man was a Flemish vassal, but probably a friend of Duke
William's. Doubtless he came on an important diplomatic mission,[4] and one
unwelcome to Godwin, who was at this very time celebrating the marriage
of his son Tostig to Judith of Flanders, the sister of the count and a kins-
woman of Edward; [5] and when Eustace attacked Godwin's port of Dover,
and Edward ordered Godwin to punish the burgesses for their part in the
affray,[6] the earl and his sons, Swegn and Harold, raised the forces of their
earldoms and threatened the king and his guest as he held court at Gloucester.[7]

Edward handled the crisis adroitly. He firmly contained Godwin's half-
hearted rebellion, gave it time to collapse, and then, in the autumn of 1051,
banished the whole family, except Queen Edith whom he sent to a convent.
He had, however, more difficulty in restraining the more extreme of his
friends. He did not follow Archbishop Robert's advice to divorce Godwin's
daughter.[8] But, after Godwin's expulsion, he allowed the priest William to

[1] *ASC E* 1048.   [2] With justice, according to *Vita Ædwardi*, p. 19.

[3] *Ibid.* pp. 20–1.

[4] Eustace had a strategic geographical position and also interesting connexions. Moreover, his
stepson, Edward's nephew, Walter III, count of the Vexin, was a man of political importance,
for he not only had the chance of succeeding to England but also to Maine. Walter's brother-in-law,
Hugh IV of Maine, had died in 1051 leaving young children; and it is significant that eventually
Walter and his wife were imprisoned, and perhaps poisoned, by Duke William of Normandy.

[5] *Vita Ædwardi*, pp. 24–5. Judith was, like William of Normandy, Edward's cousin once
removed.

[6] For a discussion of these events, see Freeman, *NC*, ii. 125–62, 575–81; Plummer, pp. 234–6;
Bertie Wilkinson, 'Freeman and the Crisis of 1051', *BJRL*, xxii (1938), 368–87; D. C. Douglas,
'Edward the Confessor, Duke William of Normandy, and the English succession', *EHR*, lxiii (1953),
526–45; R. W. Southern, 'The First Life of Edward the Confessor', *EHR*, lviii (1943), 392–5;
T. J. Oleson, 'Edward the Confessor's promise of the throne to Duke William of Normandy',
EHR, lxxii (1957), 221–8. See also Barlow, *op. cit.*, Appendix C.

[7] It should be noticed that in *Vita Ædwardi*, pp. 21 ff., all the troubles are reduced to a lawsuit: Godwin requests permission to purge himself of the charges brought by Robert and is forced
into exile by the king's refusal to do justice. No doubt there was this defensive side to Godwin's
stand, and his passive behaviour when in arms proves that he could have been placated. It is
possible that his children, especially Swegn, were wilder than he.   [8] *Vita Ædwardi*, p. 23.

replace Spearhavoc in the see of London.[1] Spearhavoc, who had been engaged in making a new 'imperial' crown for Edward, left England secretly
with the booty.[2] Although Edward had manipulated the forces well, his
moves were opportunist and his measures inconclusive. There is a provisional air about all the arrangements. And it is hard to believe that the more
realistic courtiers thought that Godwin's family could be permanently
exiled from the country. Indeed, when Godwin and his sons invaded in the
following year, clearly prepared to fight,[3] Edward had to make what terms he
could. The exiles were restored to their former positions. Archbishop
Robert, Bishops William and Ulf, and some others who feared Godwin's
vengeance, fled the country as soon as it was decided to treat with the
invaders. But although after the counter-revolution the outlawry was proclaimed of all those Frenchmen who had perverted the law and given bad
counsel, this measure was probably aimed principally, if not exclusively, at
the fugitive bishops – Robert who had brought vindictive lawsuits against
Godwin, and Ulf who did nothing worthy of a bishop.[4] The king was
suffered to keep such Frenchmen as were true also to the people, his nephew
Ralf stayed as earl in Herefordshire, for Swegn had died on pilgrimage, the
Norman soldiers remained on the Welsh march, and the Norman William
was allowed to return and hold the see of London, 'for he was a good man'.[5]

It is possible that Godwin's successful return affected English foreign
policy. But there is little to show. Relations with Flanders improved.[6] But the
count of Flanders was Duke William's father-in-law, and Godwin's hostages were still in Normandy. Indeed, it was not until after Godwin's death
that search was started for an alternative heir to the throne. One clear result
of the revolution, although possibly accidental, was a misunderstanding with
the papacy. Archbishop Robert and Bishop Ulf had abandoned their sees
and were replaced, the one by Stigand, bishop of Winchester, and the other
by Wulfwig, a royal clerk. Godwin may have exerted an influence, but it was
Edward's doing; and such old-fashioned behaviour was unwise in view of

---

[1] *ASC E* 1048.

[2] *Chron. Abingdon*, i. 463. Spearhavoc's later movements are unknown.

[3] Although, according to *Vita Ædwardi*, p. 27, Godwin expressly stated that he would not use
force against the king.

[4] This outlawry of Frenchmen has sometimes been understood in a wide sense. But since the
texts are specially concerned with courtiers – and only some of these – and we know that the Frenchmen in Herefordshire were not banished, presumably because Swegn was not there to demand it,
the list can probably be restricted to those few who fled abroad. Cf. Freeman, *NC*, ii, 336–7.

[5] Florence, i. 210.   [6] Grierson, *England and Flanders*, pp. 100–2.

England's close relations with the reformed papacy. Bishoprics could no longer safely be treated simply as earldoms. The irregularities produced by these promotions not only harmed the English church as an institution but also confirmed the suspicion which had been forming in the papal curia that there was something rotten in England.[1]

Edward's mother, Emma of Normandy, died in March 1052 and Earl Godwin, Edward's father-in-law, followed a year later. These deaths mark the real turning-point in the reign. When the excitement of the political crises had subsided, Edward found himself not only free from long-standing restraints but also able to work with new and younger men. Much of the frustration and tension had disappeared from the government. For the first time Edward could lean without repugnance on the Wessex family. With the trustworthy Harold ruling Wessex, the favourite Tostig Northumbria, and their sister Edith the court, the monarchy recovered its strength. Wales was mastered and Scotland brought to heel. First Harold and then Tostig went on pilgrimages to Rome. A great kingdom was once more consolidating its position. The only weakness was the want of a natural heir.

In the last decade of his reign Edward began to take an interest in his approaching end. He was generous with alms and rebuilt Westminster Abbey as his mausoleum.[2] But he remained physically vigorous. In 1065 he would have gone hunting in the Welsh marches with Harold had not the Welsh destroyed the hunting lodge prepared at Portskewet, and when the Northumbrian rebellion broke out while he was hunting with Tostig near Wilton, only Harold's desertion prevented him from marching against the rebels. Mass followed by hunting seems to have been his usual day.

In this same period the queen, restored again to the court, became more influential. According to the *Vita Ædwardi*, she was Edward's prop in ecclesiastical and secular affairs. More generous than he, she gave in such a way that the honour always fell to him; more serious in her piety, she was content to work through her husband. The bias is unmistakable, but it may not distort too drastically. Edith had been educated in the nunnery at Wilton.

---

[1] See below, pp. 302 ff.

[2] If Jumièges was the model for Westminster, the latter was most likely started before 1052, when Robert of Jumièges was banished. Edward certainly made gifts to monasteries, mainly in northern Francia; but whether he was exceptionally generous is uncertain. It is striking that he made no grant to the new cathedral church of Exeter in 1050, but perhaps he regarded earlier gifts to Leofric as serving this purpose. On the whole royal grants were made to individuals rather than to corporate bodies. According to *Vita Ædwardi*, pp. 41–2, Queen Edith was more generous than her husband.

Her passion for relics is well attested; she rebuilt the church at Wilton; and her influence on ecclesiastical matters is occasionally mentioned. In several senses she can be considered one of the makers of the saint. An Abingdon story,[1] which if true is to be dated 1045-8, shortly after her marriage, supports the legend. On a visit to the abbey with the king and his mother, while the party was on a tour of inspection, Edith noticed in the refectory that the children, as was usual and correct, were taking lunch before the mealtime of the monks. And when on closer investigation she saw that they had nothing but bread, she asked, being a woman of fashion (*utpote urbana*), why they were lunching so early and also so frugally. On being told that now they rarely had anything other than bread to eat, she was moved to pity and pressed the king to grant the abbey some revenue to commemorate their visit to this 'banquet'. Edward laughingly replied that he would be glad to give them something if he had anything at hand to give. Whereupon Edith said that, if it pleased him, she would willingly grant the village of Lewknor which she had just acquired. And so it was done.

It detracts a little however from Edith's generosity that she had obtained the village in somewhat doubtful circumstances.[2] And it must be allowed that her behaviour could be viewed less charitably by others. She could even be accused of political assassination.[3] It can be suspected that she was an ambitious intriguer, hard on occasion and always tenacious, well able to look after herself. Her favourite brother, and very like in character, was Tostig, who was often at court. Harold, the head of the family, although serious and responsible in his actions, was not religiously inclined and seems to have stood a little apart. Yet, despite the suggestion of a high moral tone in the household, the ecclesiastical policy was rather worldly. With Stigand at Canterbury, and influential at court, the leadership was uninspiring; Ealdred of Worcester and then of York typifies the splendid and artistic tastes of the period; and, although some reforming clerks and a few good monks were promoted, one appointment was scandalous. The court was probably to some extent the victim of circumstances. The monastic revival was almost spent, foreign monks were politically unacceptable, and use had to be made of inferior material.

Edward's legend emasculates a passionate, active, and resourceful man. Most of his panegyrists stress his goodness and attribute errors and defects

---

[1] *Chron. Abingdon*, i. 459-61.
[2] This was not the only time that an alleged legacy to Edith was disputed: cf. K. 808.
[3] Florence, i. 223. Cf. *Vita Ædwardi*, pp. lxvi-lxvii.

to his simplicity and the unwise advice of others.[1] Coleman, as translated by
William of Malmesbury, paid unqualified tribute to Edward's integrity.[2]
One of the earliest interpretations of Edward's reign is in the *Vita Ædwardi*,
a work probably commissioned by the queen from a Flemish monk resident
in England, and completed just after Edward's death. The author's task, to
glorify most members of Queen Edith's family, was, because of their quarrels,
by no means easy. He was therefore compelled to push as hard as he dared
the natural inclination of an encomiast to typify his characters. Anything too
lifelike would have hurt. And in this setting Edward had to suffer the most,
for by devitalization he could be drained of evil intent. In any case, the stock
figure of a good old king, a little simple in the ways of the world, was to
hand and sure to please. Accordingly Edward was like Solomon.[3] And, as
Ælfric tells us,[4] 'in English Solomon is interpreted *gesibsum* [the peaceable]:
he is the type of our Saviour Christ, who brought us peace and is the prince
of peace'. Earl Godwin was like David,[5] who was 'strong of hand'.[6] And
Godwin's children were like the four waters out of one well spring which ran
out of Paradise, that is to say the four gospels,[7] sent to irrigate all parts of the
realm.[8]

This writer and some of his successors were creating a legend, and we
may think that the tradition of a good man, occasionally misled through his
ignorance of the world of politics, is both a hagiographical simplification and
also a judgment based on Edward's last years. It is the author of the *Vita
Ædwardi*, a late-comer to England who learned little of the past, who has
transmitted the only surviving, and so almost inescapable, literary portrait of

---

[1] Cf. the later Ramsey view, interesting because, although Abbot Ælfwine was greatly trusted
by the king, the succession of Ramsey monks to Dorchester was stopped in 1049. 'Erat autem vir
simplex et rectus, in dei rebus strenuus, vir qui propter mansuetudinem innatam vix etiam injuriis
impetitus nosset irasci, unde, quia sine severitate causali nullum congrue regi potest imperium,
pluribus propter indulgentiam ejus et simplicitatem parum idoneum eum ad tractanda regni negotia
arbitrantibus, deus tamen, opera ejus dirigens, et imperium timeri et majestatem ejus ab omnibus
fecit adorari': *Chron. Ramsey*, p. 155.

[2] 'in cuius pectore nichil unquam nundinator ecclesiarum, nichil unquam deprehendit avarus,
quod suis conduceret artibus': *Vita Wulfstani*, p. 18. On the other hand it was believed that Edward
would accept gifts in connexion with lawsuits. See *Chron. Ramsey*, p. 170; *Hemingi Chartularium*,
i. 268-9 (St Wulfstan himself giving a valuable gold cup); Whitelock, *Wills*, no. 11; Harmer,
Writs, no. 62 (unauthentic).

[3] *Vita Ædwardi*, pp. 3, 12, 74, 120. See also Barlow, *op. cit.*, Appendix A.

[4] *Treatise on the Old and New Testament*, ed. S. J. Crawford, EETS, 160 (1922), 37; 'On the
dedication of a church', *Catholic Homilies*, ii. 579.

[5] *Vita Ædwardi*, pp. 28-30. [6] Ælfric, *Treatise*, p. 35.

[7] *Ibid.* p. 53. [8] *Vita Ædwardi*, pp. 4, 15-16, 56-7.

the king: [1] royal yet saintly in appearance – snowy locks and beard, pink complexion, emaciated white hands, and long translucent fingers – the good simple king, who, freed from the cares of state by the labours of his brothers-in-law, divided his time between hunting and the company of religious men, mostly foreign abbots and monks attracted by his piety and generosity; devout and humble in the presence of his monkish guests, with the pomp of monarchy maintained only by the sedulous care of the queen; attentive to mass, generous to the poor, able to work miracles through his holiness, the builder of Westminster Abbey. And this picture seems to be the work of a few foreign clerks at court. Although English kingship had developed a strong odour of sanctity, it was in France that the church was almost consciously engaged in endowing the weak Capetian monarchy with religious attributes, in order to strengthen it as the protector of the church and the guardian of justice and order; [2] and Frenchmen at Edward's court seem to have encouraged the belief that Edward had been divinely called to rule, had been crowned by St Peter, had preserved the virtue of his coronation and unction by a life of chastity, and possessed the power of miraculous healing.

To liken the king's coronation to the ordination of a priest [3] and to make of the king a kind of ecclesiastical person was, of course, a commonplace idea.[4] But it depended on confusions which were about to be dispelled. The church was beginning to extricate itself again from lay society, to observe the rule of celibacy, and to emphasize and develop its own Order. And this daring attempt to apply the new sacramental theology to the king – to suggest that, just as a priest after ordination, so the king must remain chaste because of his coronation – was naturally without a future. Indeed, it reveals the absurdity of much of the muddled thinking on this subject. Only for a moment, with an ageing and childless king, who had become pious in his habits and whose interrupted marriage to a younger woman had taken on a

---

[1] *Vita Ædwardi,* pp. xli ff. Both Goscelin and Folcard, who have been suggested as possible authors, came to England only shortly before Edward's death.

[2] Cf. Jean-François Lemarignier, *Autour de la royauté française du ixe au xiiie siècle,* Bibl. de l'École des chartes, cxiii (1955), 9–13.

[3] The great festival of Easter Day was probably deliberately chosen by the bishops for Edward's belated coronation in 1043. Although it has been suggested that Edgar's coronation was delayed until 973, some fourteen years after his accession, to allow him to attain the canonical age for a bishop (30), H. G. Richardson and G. O. Sayles, *The Governance of Mediaeval England* (1963), pp. 399 ff., argue that Edgar had been anointed at least once and crowned probably several times before the ceremony of 973.

[4] Cf. Fritz Kern, trans. S. B. Chrimes, *Kingship and Law in the Middle Ages* (1948), pp. 27 ff.

father-daughter appearance, could the idea be other than ridiculous. However, it helped to establish a cult which in the end justified Edward's canonization.

The theme of Edward's sanctity, although interesting in itself and revealing one aspect of the religious life at court, has little relevance to Edward's true character or the ecclesiastical policy of his government. It is doubtful indeed whether Edward had a policy. Impressed and formed by his long exile, simple in his habits, rustic in his pleasures,[1] kind and, up to a point, loyal to his friends, martial in temper, terrible in his anger, easily vindictive, rash and passionate when his interest was aroused or his interests involved, sometimes capable of manipulating forces, sometimes if not patient at least long-suffering, mindful of his father's fate, without great aims or noble intentions, without real ambition, often incurious and neglectful of his duties, inclined to rely on others and to give them a free hand, careless as to ways and means, Edward's actions make little sense outside their immediate context. What can appear systematic, such as the promotion of monks and royal priests in equal numbers to bishoprics, was only the chance effect created by the interplay of the various interests within an ancient and strong tradition. The English church was ruled by the king but to little purpose and to no true ecclesiastical end.[2]

3. THE NOBILITY

King Edgar's enthusiasm for monasticism had not been shared by the aristocracy as a whole, although some ealdormen, notably his foster-brother, Æthelwine of East Anglia, had been fired by his example.[3] But there does not seem to have been an active opposition, for the attack on some monasteries which followed his death was part of a political struggle, intended to hurt rivals.[4] Monasteries were, indeed, valuable private property, and were treated as such. Normally they were ruled by men of noble birth, and, although genealogical details are scarce, it is likely that the abbot was often a relative

---

[1] For grants by Edward to his forest officials, see DB, i. 61 b i (Kintbury, Berks), i. 167 b i (Forest of Dene, Glos.), and i. 254 a i (Montgomery, Salop.).

[2] Edward's treatment of Peterborough Abbey towards the close of the reign should be noticed: Chron. Peterborough, pp. 66–7. Queen Edith was disliked there because she 'stole' the rich bequests to the house which Archbishop Cynsige of York made with his body (1060), ibid. p. 73.

[3] Chron. Ramsey, p. 72; Vita Oswaldi, HCY, i. 428–9, 445.

[4] D. J. V. Fisher, 'The anti-monastic reaction in the reign of Edward the Martyr', Camb. HJ, x (1950–2), 254–70.

of the founder.[1] In these circumstances secular interference in church endowments was inevitable. Reformers would reorganize arbitrarily or even confiscate superfluous wealth in order to reduce the monks to a proper state To rob one church in order to enrich another was common practice.[2] And to the lay mind it was less than robbery to demand loans of land from ecclesiastical estates. An attitude to the church which alternated between indulgence and exploitation was probably usual among landowners: indulgent, even craven, when spiritual benefits were required, harsh when temporal benefices were wanted.[3]

The earls,[4] no less than the kings, were subject to ecclesiastical influence, for they normally kept domestic chaplains [5] and were associated with the shire bishops in several official capacities; but their representative character was less pronounced than the king's, and some earls were not closely connected with the earldoms they ruled. Their religious activities were tied more to their private estates than to their office. Two of the earldoms, however, Mercia and Wessex, became hereditary, and these can be regarded as organic units.

Leofric, son of Leofwine who was ealdorman of the Hwicce and of Mercia under Æthelred, was promoted earl soon after Cnut's accession and later ruled over the whole of Mercia.[6] He was succeeded in 1057 by his son, Ælfgar,[7] and, about 1062, by his young grandson, Edwin.[8] His wife, Godgifu or Godiva,[9] was closely associated with his religious activities. Leofric earned an ambivalent reputation. On the one hand he was praised as the founder and builder of Coventry Abbey, where he was buried, and the munificent patron of the monasteries at Leominster, Wenlock, Chester (St John's and St Werburg's), Stow St Mary (a secular minster), Worcester, and Evesham.[10]

[1] To judge by their names.

[2] 'Spoliant ecclesias et rapinis ipsis alias ditant', William of Poitiers, II, c. 42, p. 258 – like William the Conqueror, although his encomiast carefully distinguishes him from such.

[3] Cf. Æsgar the Staller and Ely (Liber Eliensis, II, c. 96). For a discussion of some invasions of church lands, see Freeman, NC, ii, Appendix E.

[4] For the Christian duties of earls, see Wulfstan, Polity, pp. 78–80. Earls kept a great state. Cf. 'eadem quoque tempestate quidam consul [= comes] regis nimium dilectus, in caducis praepotens rebus, cum ingenti comitatu, sicut mos est Anglosaxonibus, properanter equitabat ad quemdam vicum, in quo grandis apparatus ad necessarios convivandi usus erat illi opipare constructus': Miracula S. Swithuni, MPL, clv, col. 79.

[5] The name of Earl Godwin's chaplain, Brand, has been preserved in legend: Walter Map, De Nugis Curialium, Dist. V, cap. 4, ed. M. R. James, p. 217.

[6] For Leofwine, see Robertson, Charters, p. 396; for Leofric, see Harmer, Writs, pp. 565–6.

[7] See Harmer, Writs, pp. 546–7.   [8] See ibid. p. 560.   [9] See ibid. p. 561.

[10] Florence, i. 216; ASC E 1066; Robertson, Charters, nos. 113, 115.

And, on the other, he and his family were accused of despoiling Worcester of land, in one instance transferring an estate to Coventry.[1] Leofric seems to have been a religious man, but in no way a reformer. He had his nephew and namesake appointed abbot of Burton, Coventry, Crowland, Thorney, and Peterborough – pluralism of an excessive kind.[2] As Peterborough considered Abbot Leofric its greatest patron – 'in his day there was every happiness and every good . . . and he was beloved by everyone'[3] – he cannot have been austere. Earl Leofric is praised for his religion not only in the D version of the Chronicle[4] but also in the *Vita Ædwardi*.[5] But we can see that it was devotion of a fashionable type; and neither his son, Ælfgar,[6] nor his grandson, Edwin,[7] showed similar inclinations.

Earl Leofric was in the tradition of his master, Cnut. Godwin, however, a thegn whom Cnut showered with favours, made no pretence of an interest in religion.[8] Earl of Wessex (1018–53), the brother-in-law of his patron, the uncle of Svein of Denmark, the father-in-law of Edward, and the father of five earls, one of them a future king of England, Godwin had useful political qualities – industry, patience, affability, eloquence, and guile. He was careful of his children's education. And yet he felt no need to display even conventional piety. His rule coincided almost exactly with the great depression in the religious life of the kingdom. The *Vita Ædwardi*, which is really a eulogy of his family, is significantly silent about his religion, and the only gifts he is known to have made to the church were those in preparation for his burial in the Old Minster at Winchester.[9] Hostile writers accused him of robbing

---

[1] R. R. Darlington, *Vita Wulfstani*, pp. xxii, *n.* 2, xxiv; *Hemingi Chartularium*, i. 261–2; Malmesbury *GP*, p. 311. See also below, pp. 173, 175. There is a slightly more favourable account of the family in *Hemingi Chartularium*, ii. 406.

[2] Plummer, p. 241; Harmer, *Writs*, p. 565.

[3] *ASC E* 1066; *Chron. Peterborough*, pp. 65–7.

[4] 'who was very wise in divine and temporal matters. That was a benefit to all this realm', *s.a.* 1057.

[5] 'vir scilicet eximius, ut plurimum deo devotus', p. 21.

[6] Ælfgar took part in the sack of Hereford and its cathedral in 1055 (*ASC CE*). Coleman paid him the cool compliment of pairing him disadvantageously with Earl Harold: 'par insigne fortitudinis non ita religionis' (*Vita Wulfstani*, p. 18).

[7] According to Hemming (*Hemingi Chartularium*, i. 262), Edwin and his brother Morcar frustrated Leofric's intention to make restitution to Worcester. Marianus Scotus, however, believed that a hundred priests as well as a thousand laymen were killed when the brothers were defeated by Harold Hardrada and Tostig at Gate Fulford in 1066: *Chronicon Mariani Scotti, MPL*, cxlvii, coll. 788–9.

[8] See especially C. E. Wright, *The Cultivation of Saga in Anglo-Saxon England*, pp. 213–29, 233–6.   [9] *Vita Ædwardi*, p. 30.

churches ¹ – charges which are illustrated by Domesday Book.² If Godwin forced churches to enfeof him and his friends with land, and repaid with protection, it was not remembered with gratitude. Whenever he interfered in ecclesiastical business the result was unhappy, and the bishops with whom he is occasionally found in collaboration were of the more worldly type. His Danish wife, Gytha, obtained later a reputation for religion which does not seem to depend only on her seemly ending.³ She refounded Hartland in Devonshire as a college ⁴ and is known to have disapproved of her husband's treatment of Berkeley Abbey.⁵ It is, therefore, curious that she is almost completely ignored in the Life of her son-in-law the king, dedicated to her daughter.⁶

Their eldest son, Earl Swegn, banished from England in 1046, 1049, and 1051, and dying shortly afterwards on a pilgrimage to Jerusalem (doubtless a penance imposed on him for his sins), seems to have had no apologist except his indulgent father. The church of Worcester remembered the neighbouring earl with dislike and contempt. Hemming wrote ⁷ that Swegn was so addicted to vainglory and pride that he claimed that Cnut not Godwin was his true father. He was of the Danish royal line. His indignant mother had to call the noble matrons of Wessex to witness to his parentage. He was so depraved that (in 1046) he abducted the abbess of Leominster and kept her as his wife for almost a year.⁸ Only the threats of Archbishop Eadsige and Bishop Lyfing brought him at length to his senses; but in revenge he despoiled Worcester of lands in Shropshire. Hemming does not add that in 1049 Swegn murdered his cousin, Earl Beorn, and was pronounced *nithing* by the army. This lawless man is possibly the 'gulping monster' of the poem on Godwin's children.⁹

The second son, Harold, king in 1066, cannot be dismissed so shortly. The author of Edward's Life had a high opinion of him as man and as earl,

---

¹ *Vita Ædwardi*, p. lxiv. The 'C' version of the Chronicle, referring to his restoration in 1052, says, 'but he did all too little reparation about the property of God which he had from many holy places'.   ² Freeman, *NC*, ii. 543.

³ For Gytha's adventures after the Conquest, see *ibid.* iv. 158–60, 756.

⁴ No authority beyond the unsupported statement of antiquarians can now be found. Gytha certainly held the manor in Edward's reign, *DB*, i. 100 b ii.

⁵ *DB*, i. 164 a ii: 'Gueda mater comitis Heraldi tenuit Vdecestre. Goduinus comes emit ab Azor et dedit suae uxori ut inde viveret donec ad Berchelai maneret. Nolebat enim de ipso manerio aliquid comedere pro destructione abbatiae.'

⁶ *Vita Ædwardi*, p. lxv.   ⁷ *Hemingi Chartularium*, i. 275–6.

⁸ Cf. the account in *ASC C* 1046; according to Florence, i. 201–2, Swegn wished to marry her. She had the popular noble name of Eadgifu.

⁹ *Vita Ædwardi*, p. 16.

a view shared in several other quarters.[1] He had great physical and mental endurance; he was patient, kindly, and loyal, a strong ruler but relaxed and open in private; he took counsel and combined steadfastness of purpose with caution, shrewdness, and enjoyment of life. He passed through the dangers of the world with watchful mockery. He had been educated by his father to rule and had studied diplomacy and statesmanship through observing the Frankish principalities. He was a second Judas Maccabeus. Happy the king with such a second-in-command![2] But the writer says nothing about Harold's generosity or religion, and he sadly admits that he was too free with his oaths.[3] It is, indeed, clear that Harold was secular in outlook and pagan in morals; and it may be that the Danish side of his character was dominant, for he lived with a mistress until his promotion to the throne,[4] had an unbaptized son buried near the altar at Christ Church, Canterbury,[5] and displayed characteristic Viking virtues. Like his father he made use of church estates,[6] and his priest Leofgar, who was appointed bishop of Hereford presumably through his influence, was as unconventional and martial as his master.[7] Nevertheless, there was no inclination in England to regard Harold as evil or worthless. He refounded the collegiate church at Waltham,[8] possibly as a thanksgiving for his recovery from an illness after the Welsh campaign,[9] and it was believed at Waltham that his endowment in lands, ornaments, and relics was princely and that the schoolmaster he appointed, Ailred the physician, was distinguished.[10] He visited Rome and made great gifts.[11] Although, perhaps deliberately, he did not found a monastery, he had monkish friends. Coleman reports that he valued St Wulfstan highly, would deviate thirty miles from his route to converse with him and make his confession, and would do anything that Wulfstan asked. In return

[1] See Freeman, *NC*, ii, Appendix D, and above, p. 53.

[2] *Vita Ædwardi*, pp. 30–3.

[3] 'ad sacramenta nimis, proh dolor, prodigus': *ibid*. p. 53.

[4] Freeman discusses Harold's concubines, *NC*, iii, Appendix NN.

[5] Osbern, *Miracula S. Dunstani, Memorials of St Dunstan*, pp. 141–2. For Harold's daughter, Gunnhild, who became a nun at Wilton, see *Vita Wulfstani*, p. 34, A. Wilmart, 'La destinaire de la lettre de St Anselme sur l'état et les voeux de religion', *Revue Bénédictine*, xxxviii (1926), 331–4, and 'Une lettre inédite de S. Anselme à une moniale inconstante', *ibid*. xl (1928), 319–32.

[6] Cf. his frustration of the will of Bishop Duduc of Wells (*Ecclesiastical Documents*, p. 16) and his 'unjustly' despoiling St Peter's, Exeter, of an estate (Robertson, *Charters*, p. 227). *DB* contains many charges against him: see Freeman, *NC*, ii, Appendix E.   [7] See below, p. 81.

[8] K. 813.   [9] *Vita Haroldi*, c. 2.   [10] *Ibid*. cc. 2–3, 7.

[11] *Vita Ædwardi*, p. 33; *Vita Haroldi*, c. 7, where the story of Harold's search at Rome for relics is weakened by obvious confusion with Tostig's adventures.

he had Wulfstan's prayers.[1] Ælfwine, abbot of Ramsey, intercepted him on his march to Stamfordbridge to cheer him with the news that King Edward had appeared to him in a vision and intimated that God would cure Harold's leg and give him victory in the battle.[2] There was also a belief in Harold's justice and a conviction that as king he would assume a different character.[3] Even if he allowed Stigand of Canterbury to crown him,[4] it was Bishop Wulfstan whom he took with him on a tour of Northumbria.[5] Leofric, the magnificent abbot of Peterborough, was with the army at Hastings.[6] Harold's character is fairly clear. He was not devout, but he was reasonable and just.

The third son of Earl Godwin, Tostig, earl of Northumbria and North-ampton (1055-65),[7] was regarded by the author of Edward's Life as in no way inferior to Harold. They were both chips off the old block, but were unlike in temperament. Tostig was more secretive and vindictive, harder, swifter, more imaginative, perhaps more brilliant.[8] He seems to have been closer in sympathy to his sister and his brother-in-law the king, and shared some of their religious interests, for he and his wife, Judith of Flanders,[9] were

---

[1] Vita Wulfstani, p. 13. Wulfstan cured Harold's daughter of an eye complaint, 'memorie paterne non nichil deferendum arbitratus' (ibid. p. 34).

[2] Osbert of Clare, Vita beati ac gloriosi regis Anglorum Eadwardi, Marc Bloch, 'La vie de S. Édouard le Confesseur par Osbert de Clare', Analecta Bollandiana, xli (1923), p. 114; Vita Haroldi, c. 10.

[3] 'Florence of Worcester', i. 224-5, wrote that on becoming king Harold 'leges iniquas destruere, aequas coepit condere, ecclesiarum ac monasteriorum patronus fieri, episcopos, abbates, monachos, clericos colere simul ac venerari, pium, humilem, affabilemque se bonis omnibus exhibere, male-factores exosos habere, nam ducibus, satrapis, vicecomitibus, et suis in commune praecepit ministris fures, raptores, regni disturbatores comprehendere, et pro patriae defensione ipsemet terra marique desudare'. This passage may possibly be based on a letter Harold sent to the shires announcing his coronation and the intentions of his government – an embryonic coronation charter – or may simply be an elaboration of his coronation promises. Harold promised to restore his 'thefts' from Wells (Ecclesiastical Documents, p. 18; Monasticon, ii. 287).

[4] Freeman, NC, iii, app. D (with some hesitation) and F. M. Stenton, The Bayeux Tapestry (Phaidon, 1957), pp. 17-18, decide, relying on Florence, i. 224, and rejecting William of Poitiers, II, c. 1 (p. 146), and the implication of the Bayeux Tapestry, pl. 33, that Ealdred not Stigand crowned and consecrated Harold. But Florence, when unsupported by ASC, is only a twelfth-century authority, and a late Worcester-York tradition – especially when primatial rights are involved – inspires little confidence. The failure of the English annalists to name the consecrator seems definitely to tip the balance in favour of Stigand.   [5] Vita Wulfstani, pp. 22-3.

[6] ASC E 1066. Harold had given estates to Peterborough, Chron. Peterborough, p. 70.

[7] For biographical summary, see Harmer, Writs, p. 575.

[8] Vita Ædwardi, pp. 31-2. Cf. 'Inceptum suum uterque satis constanter urguere, sed hic [Tostig] fortiter, ille [Harold] sapienter; hic in actu suo consummationem, ille intendebat pariter et felicitatem.' Cf. 'nec fortitudine degenerer, si ardens ingenium tranquillis studiis applicare maluis-set': Vita Wulfstani, p. 22.   [9] See Plummer, p. 249, Vita Ædwardi, p. 32.

benefactors of Durham and generous to good causes.[1] But Tostig spoke very sharply to the pope after the humiliations that he and his party suffered in 1061.[2] He was praised for the purity of his life [3] and blamed for his tyranny and wilfulness. The panegyrist of these two brothers regarded their quarrel in 1065 as the great tragedy of the reign. As it was, the careers of both were cut short; but it seems unlikely that either would have contributed much to the church.

The one earl of this period who earned golden opinions in ecclesiastical circles was Odda of Deerhurst, also known as Æthelwine, who died in 1056. But his renown, which was local, was due to his private virtues and to his taking the cowl on his deathbed.[4] He was a good man, and did good things, such as building a church [5] and founding a monastery,[6] and his death was characteristic of his life.

Even less is known about the attitude to the church of the other earls of this time; but the scanty evidence reinforces the impression of general indifference combined with concern for individual or family salvation. The earls in Northumbria at the beginning of the century had treated the bishop of Durham as a nobleman with an estate, out of which he could provide a dowry for his daughter.[7] Siward, earl of Northumbria (*ante* 1033–55) was remembered for replacing the monk-bishop Æthelric who had been expelled by the clerks of Durham,[8] and for building a church in York dedicated to St Olaf.[9] Earl Ralf of Hereford and Oxfordshire (*c.* 1053–7) was a benefactor of Peterborough Abbey, where he was buried,[10] but demanded and received an estate for life from Ramsey Abbey.[11]

The piety of the royal court did not set a pattern for the higher nobility, and the lack of a royal ecclesiastical policy was not supplied by a drive in any of the earldoms. There were religious earls and careless earls, and, especially, there were good women. The devout pampered, the profane hindered the fashionable expressions of religion; but all accepted the conditions. Nor is

[1] Symeon, *HDE*, p. 94.
[2] *Vita Ædwardi*, pp. 36–7; *Vita Wulfstani*, p. 16; Malmesbury, *GP*, p. 252; and below, p. 297. [3] According to *Vita Ædwardi*, p. 32, he was faithful to his wife.
[4] *ASC D* 1053, *CD* 1056; Florence, i. 215; *HCY*, ii. 345. For biographical details, see Robertson, *Charters*, pp. 456–8.
[5] At Deerhurst in memory of his brother Ælfric (Plummer, p. 238).
[6] At Great Malvern (R. R. Darlington, *Vita Wulfstani*, p. xli).
[7] See below, pp. 172–3. [8] Symeon, *HDE*, p. 91; see below, p. 85.
[9] At Bootham Bar, in which he was buried, *Vita Ædwardi*, p. 31, *ASC CD* 1055; Florence, i. 212.
[10] *ASC D* 1057; *Chron. Peterborough*, p. 69. [11] *Chron. Ramsey*, pp. 171–2.

there evidence of a popular movement in the church. Thegns seem to have
taken their religious duties seriously, and the building of churches went on
apace; but no thegn is known to have renounced the world in a spectacular
fashion.[1] Nor are there stories of men abandoning their farms for the
wilderness, living in passionate austerity as a reproach to the complacent.
Even the hermits seem to have been respectable.[2]

4. THE BISHOPS

The three great tenth-century monastic reformers died in quick succession –
Æthelwold in 984, Dunstan in 988, and Oswald in 992. They were all monks
and bishops, all saints, and with them closed an epoch. But their memory was
kept green for at least a generation. Ælfric, archbishop of Canterbury 995–
1005, commissioned the writing of the first Life of Dunstan,[3] and his successor, Ælfheah the Martyr, the second.[4] Oswald's Life was written around
the turn of the century in his monastery of Ramsey;[5] and two biographies
of Æthelwold were composed about the same time, one in his see of Winchester[6] and the other by a pupil, Ælfric, abbot of Eynsham.[7] Their lives
and works, so far as we know, were not written of again until after the Norman
Conquest.

[1] About 980, however, when St Ælfheah left Deerhurst to become a hermit at Bath, some nobles
joined him and formed a monastic community. But this quickly became dissolute. Osbern, *Vita S.
Elphegi*, cc. 1–2, *MPL*, cxlix, coll. 377–8.

[2] Cf. the will of Mantat the Anchorite, a man patronized by Cnut and Emma (Whitelock,
Wills, no. 23). For Wulfsi, who is supposed to have persuaded St Wulfstan to accept Worcester
(below, p. 106, *n*. 5), see Sir Ivor Atkins, 'The Church of Worcester from the eighth to the
twelfth century', *The Antiquaries Journal*, xx (1940), 37–8. A good picture of the eremitical life in
North Italy at this time is to be found in St Peter Damiani's *Vita S. Romualdi*, *MPL*, cxliv. The
terrible austerity, stark principles, and complete independence of St Romuald, who died in 1027,
made him a revolutionary.

[3] By B., a Saxon, a clerk who had been under the patronage of the bishop of Liége, *Memorials
of St Dunstan*, pp. x–xxvi. See also *EHD*, i. 826–31.

[4] By Adelard, monk of St Peter's, Ghent, written between 1006 and 1011, Grierson, *England
and Flanders*, pp. 106–7.

[5] Possibly by Byrhtferth of Ramsey, the author of the famous *Manual*, and revised and
interpolated in a Mercian monastery. See S. J. Crawford, 'Byrhtferth and the anonymous Life of
St Oswald', *Speculum Religionis, Essays . . . presented to C. G. Montefiori* (1929); J. Armitage
Robinson, 'Byrhtferth and the Life of St Oswald', *JTS*, vol. xxx (1929); D. J. V. Fisher, 'The
anti-monastic reaction in the reign of Edward the Martyr', *Camb. HJ*, x (1950–2), 254–70; *EHD*,
i. 839–46.

[6] By Wulfstan, precentor of Winchester. See D. J. V. Fisher, 'The early biographers of St
Ethelwold', *EHR*, lxvii (1952), 381–91; *EHD*, i. 831–2.

[7] Ælfric the Homilist. See *EHD*, i. 831–9.

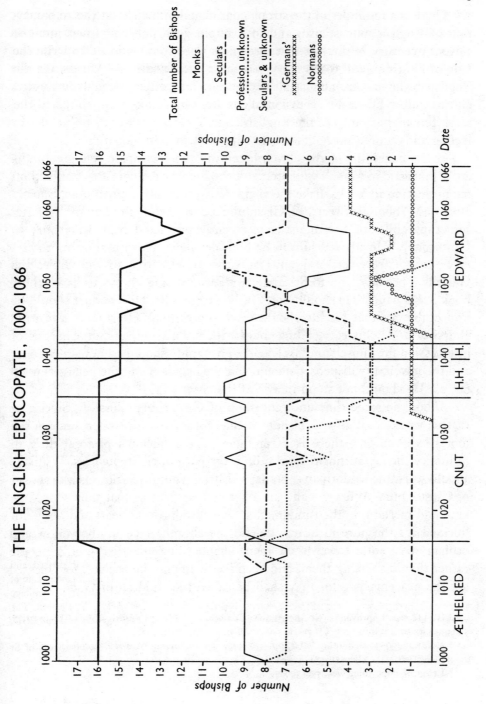

THE ENGLISH EPISCOPATE, 1000–1066

Total number of Bishops
Monks
Seculars
Profession unknown
Seculars & unknown
'Germans' xxxxxxxxxxxxx
Normans ooooooooooooooo

There is a reminder of the strong continental influence on the refoundation of English monasticism and of a pupillage which continued into the
eleventh century in the fact that foreigners were commissioned to write the
Life of Dunstan, and that Fleury was most interested in it.[1] Until 1042 the
English bishops were almost all native-born but often affected by foreign
culture; after Edward's accession aliens were more often appointed to the
sees. The higher ranks of the English church were not, therefore, insular in
feeling and showed no reluctance to support a foreign monarchy.

At the beginning of the eleventh century the episcopate was predominantly monastic in tone. Two letters, on the model of Alcuin's to Eanbald on
his promotion to York, strike the characteristically Carolingian note. Shortly
after 990 Abbot Ælfweard of Glastonbury wrote to his old pupil, Sigeric,
sometime abbot of St Augustine's, recently promoted from Ramsbury to
Canterbury.[2] He advised him to be humble, generous with alms, more of a
giver than a receiver, assiduous at services, attentive to the Bible, the
Gospels especially, and to St Gregory's Pastoral, and always to have a holy
book in his hands. He should not sell the sacraments. His conduct should be
impeccable 'so that his life should teach the people'. He should adorn the
churches under his care, filling them with psalms, prayers, and masses of
intercession for himself and his friends. His family should eschew splendour;
and the hospitality dispensed should suit the occasion and the persons enter-
tained. He should not stand in awe of the lay power.

About the same time an archbishop of Canterbury, possibly Sigeric or
Ælfric, wrote to Wulfsige, bishop of Sherborne.[3] In this letter, besides the
moral exhortations, there is a reminder of the bishop's pastoral duty to
influence the lay authorities to walk in the path of righteousness. Wulfsige
should warn the ealdorman – perhaps Ælfric, whom we know as a despoiler
of Glastonbury Abbey [4] – and all other secular princes that they should be
kind and merciful in their judgments, love cleanliness of heart and body, for
'blessed are the pure in heart', defend the church, succour the widow and
orphan, be gentle towards all men, shepherding together God's people
rather than dispersing them, and keep peace among themselves, for 'blessed
are the peacemakers, for they shall be called the children of God'.

[1] B's life was 'improved' at St Augustine's, Canterbury, and then sent to Abbo of Fleury with
a request to turn it into verse (*Memorials of St Dunstan*, pp. xxvii, 409).
[2] *Ibid.* pp. 400–3; cf. another letter, pp. 399–400. See Alcuin, ep. lvi, *MPL* c, coll. 221 ff.
[3] *Memorials of St Dunstan*, pp. 406–8.
[4] Letter of Pope John, *ibid.* pp. 396–7.

These letters, written by monks to monks, present the monastic view of a bishop's vocation. Similar conventions rule the few biographies. St Wulfsige was remembered at Sherborne only for his holy life.[1] His efforts to reform his diocese [2] had been forgotten by 1080. Wulfstan of York's chapters on the episcopal office in his *Institutes of Polity* [3] are inspired by the same feeling. The bishop must be a good man and must also practise some handicraft.[4] He should pray and intercede with God, instruct his flock, and protect it from the wolves. But there is also a significant development. The bishop is the upholder of righteousness and justice. He must have wisdom and prudence and promulgate divine law in the moots. Especially is he responsible for weights and measures. He is a judge and, together with temporal judges, must make just judgments. This is the nearest we get to a view of the bishop as an administrator and governor, and it is clear that the monastic convention has falsified the picture transmitted to us of these times. Bishops who diverged too far from the ideal found no biographer and those remembered were ideally portrayed.

The monastic character of the English church was by 1066 threatened both by the decay in the monastic order itself and by the impact of other more active influences. Had there been no Conquest it might easily have disappeared. But it had not been lost and was capable of partial revival. Since the beginning of the century more than thirty monks associated with at least sixteen English monasteries had been promoted bishop, and, although about half the promotions were made from Christ Church, Canterbury, Winchester, Ramsey, and Glastonbury, there was clearly no favourite house or anything like a school for bishops. The king and his advisers were able to review the whole field whenever a vacancy occurred.

This dominant monastic tone was an aberration from the general pattern in western Christendom. Under weak monarchies a monk was unlikely to get a bishopric, and in strong monarchies the king usually preferred to promote clerks from his household chapel, men educated in his ways whom he had learned to trust. Bishoprics were a reward for royal service and the bishops were the king's agents in the provinces. In Germany, for example, there was a prejudice against monastic and locally-educated bishops. When Wazo was

---

[1] Goscelin, *Vita Wlsini*.   [2] See below, p. 282.

[3] *Polity*, pp. 59–61, 67–77; Liebermann, *Gesetze*, i. 477–9.

[4] Presumably some ecclesiastical craft, such as goldsmithery, bookbinding, or music, although St Paul, the tentmaker, may be the model. Cf. Wulfstan's 'Canons enacted under King Edgar', c. 11 (Thorpe, *Ancient Laws*, ii. 247).

elected to the church of Liége in 1042 and went to Henry III for his consent, the courtiers were outraged at an election made without the king's permission, and they urged that Henry should appoint a royal chaplain, one who had sweated in the royal court to earn such an honour, instead of admitting someone who had been brought up under monastic discipline to be a good man rather than a ruler.[1] In England, once the monastic revival had begun to lose its impetus, royal clerks again began to receive bishoprics. But English conditions remained individual. The more important abbeys were royal foundations and the abbots were often at court. There could be no objection to the promotion of these on the ground of unworldliness. Hence Edward at least seems to have chosen with more regard to the person than to a policy, and monks were appointed to rule over secular chapters and clerks over monasteries. Nor by the middle of the eleventh century did the profession indelibly stamp the prelate. It would be difficult to tell from the behaviour of some of Edward's bishops which was the monk, which the canon, and which the royal clerk.

The bishops whom Cnut inherited from Æthelred seem to have been more than respectable.[2] At Canterbury was Lyfing-Ælfstan, formerly abbot of Chertsey and bishop of Wells, 'a sagacious man, both before God and before the world',[3] whom Cnut entrusted with an important mission at Rome.[4] At York was the great Wulfstan. Ælfgar of Elmham provided a direct link with Dunstan. He had been the archbishop's private chaplain and had had a vision of the saint being received into glory.[5] In an age lavish with alms he earned the name of the 'almsgiver'.[6] The bishops of Dorchester,[7] Ramsbury,[8] Wells,[9] Worcester,[10] and Durham[11] were monks, and Æthelstan of

---

[1] *Vita Vasonis Leodiensis episcopi, MPL*, cxlii, col. 740.

[2] For episcopal *curricula vitae* with revised dates, see Guy Lanoë, 'Anglo-Saxon Bishops, 899–1066', unpubl. Exeter DPhil. Thesis, 1976).

[3] *ASC D* 1019; Harmer, *Writs*, p. 567.   [4] Liebermann, *Gesetze*, i. 273.

[5] Adelard in *Memorials of St Dunstan*, p. 64.   [6] *ASC* 1021.

[7] Æthelric from Ramsey, where he was buried (Florence, i. 189). He had a fine reputation in his own monastery (*Chron. Ramsey*, pp. 120 ff.).

[8] Brihtwold, monk and abbot of Glastonbury, promoted bishop in 995 or 1005 (Robertson, *Charters*, p. 405; R. R. Darlington, *VCH Wilts*, ii. 29). He died on 22 April 1045 and was buried at Glastonbury, of which he was so great a patron (Malmesbury, *GP*, p. 182) that he was accused of despoiling his diocese for the abbey (*Idem, De antiqu. Glaston. ecclesiae*, i. 94–6). It was he who had the famous vision of King Edward the Confessor being crowned by St Peter and granted a life of celibacy (*Vita Ædwardi*, pp. 8–9). See also Lanoë, p. 123.

[9] Æthelwine, abbot of Evesham. See J. Armitage Robinson, *The Saxon Bishops of Wells*, Brit. Acad. supplemental papers, iv (1918), 50, 68–9.

[10] Leofsige, abbot of Thorney, who was buried at Worcester. Bishop 1017–33, 'magnae religionis et modestiae vir . . . ad coelica regna migravit, ut credi fas est': Florence, i. 180, 189.

[11] Aldhun presumably took monastic vows on his election as bishop. See below, p. 230.

THE BISHOPRICS

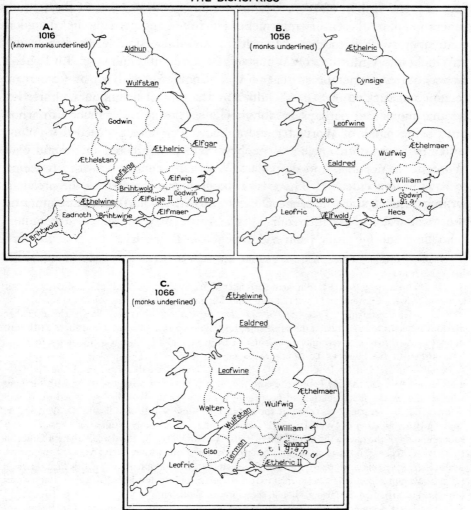

Hereford obtained a reputation for sanctity before he ended his long life.[1] Of the other eight bishops little is known save their names.

Wulfstan, *Lupus episcopus*, bishop of London 996, archbishop of York 1002–23, and bishop of Worcester in plurality 1002–16,[2] was of the second generation of tenth-century reformers.[3] His friend and perhaps slightly older contemporary, Ælfric abbot of Eynsham, was educated under St Æthelwold at Winchester. Unfortunately Wulfstan's background is unknown. Ely, where he was buried, remembered that he was of noble stock, born by Caesarean section and suckled on a cow's udder by the care of neighbours.[4] Later he became monk and perhaps an abbot. His sister's son was Brihtheah, who, after being monk of Worcester and abbot of Pershore, succeeded to Worcester in 1033. Both uncle and nephew were remembered ungratefully at Worcester as nepotists and despoilers. Wulfstan's connexion with Ely seems to have been accidental.[5] There is no biographical material in the prelate's writings. But in spirit he seems closer to St Æthelwold than to any other of the great leaders, his intercourse with Ælfric may be due to a common schooling, and his sister's son had kinsmen in Berkshire.[6]

[1] Bishop 1012–56. Buried in the church he had built at Hereford. 'magnae vir sanctitatis': Florence, i. 214.

[2] It has been suggested that Wulfstan surrendered Worcester as a result of the division of the kingdom between Edmund and Cnut (A. Hamilton Thompson, 'The jurisdiction of the archbishops of York in Gloucestershire', *Trans. Bristol and Glos. Arch. Soc.*, xliii (1921), 86 *n*.). However that may be, he seems to have treated the substitute, Leofsige, as a *chorepiscopus*. Goscelin of St Bertin, in his *Vita S. Wlsini*, c. x, recounts a miraculous cure at St Wulfsige's tomb at Sherborne obtained by a bishop of the Hwicce, the saint's colleague and namesake. This prelate, 'chosen for the salvation of many' but for long racked by illness, was carried paralysed to the shrine and rode away on a horse. On the day before the cure the other priests had been discussing with the king whether the bishop should be retired because of his illness; and 'Wulfsige' surprised them, still deliberating, by returning to court fit for duty. The story is full of difficulties. 'Wulfsige' is apparently a conflation of 'Wulfstan' and 'Leofsige' and may possibly recall a joke based on the subordination of the one to the other. There is also a contradiction in the date. Although Goscelin twice writes (cc. vii, ix) that no miracle occurred at the tomb within twelve years of the saint's death, i.e. *c*. 1013, this cure apparently took place before the translation of St Wulfsige in Æthelred's reign by Bishop Æthelric of Sherborne (1001/2–1009/12) and Archbishop Ælfheah of Canterbury (1005–12) (c. xii). The sick bishop should, therefore, be Wulfstan.

[3] The latest account of Wulfstan and his works is in Dorothy Bethurum, *The Homilies of Wulfstan* (1957), where the important work of Dorothy Whitelock and Karl Jost is used. There is a full bibliography. See also D. Whitelock's edition of *Sermo Lupi ad Anglos* (1939) and 'Archbishop Wulfstan, Homilist and Statesman', *Trans. R. Hist. Soc.*, 4th ser., xxiv (1942), pp. 25–45; K. Jost, *Wulfstanstudien* (Berne, 1950); and below, pp. 283 ff.

[4] *Liber Eliensis*, II, c. 87.   [5] *Ibid.*; *Chron. Peterborough*, p. 73.

[6] *Hemingi Chartularium*, i. 266. Ælfric mentions with respect Wulfstan, *cantor* of Winchester, in connexion with a miracle performed at Æthelwold's tomb, *Vita S. Æthelwoldi*, *Chron. Abingdon*, ii. 266.

Ælfric and Wulfstan regarded Edgar's reign as the Golden Age [1] and Wulfstan especially viewed the Viking invasions as God's punishment for the sins of the English people. Under different conditions, which affected Wulfstan more than Ælfric, both widened the influence of the tenth-century reform movement. Dunstan, Æthelwold, and Oswald, although not exclusively concerned with monks, of necessity followed the usual pattern of reforming the monasteries first. And, also typically, they restored monasticism before they troubled about perfecting the Rule. There is no evidence that any of them made a serious study of canonical literature, and, apart from the *Regularis Concordia*, they bequeathed no substantial body of writings to their followers.[2] With Ælfric and Wulfstan there is a significant change. Both paid attention to the systematic presentation of Christian moral teaching and to programmes of reform. They were concerned with the education and ministry of the priesthood and the morals of the laity. Both were good Latinists who were familiar with the theological literature of the Carolingian renaissance and with the Fathers popular at that time,[3] but both wrote much in the English language in order to achieve a wider circulation. In character and purpose, however, they were most unlike. Ælfric in his southern cloister was more speculative, more interested in pure theology, deeply attached to the saints of the monastic calendar. He was the great vulgarizer of Christian history and traditional Christian morality. His stories of the saints and his model sermons, although adorned by concrete illustration and contemporary colouring, have the serenity of an untroubled man. With the detachment of a monk, yet with his feet fixed firmly on English soil and his eyes on the public at which he aimed his message, he wrote for all times. Wulfstan, on the other hand, a prelate who was both important in the king's council and also responsible for the wild and partly heathen province of York, was much concerned with the present state and practical reform. His problem was the

[1] Characteristically in Ælfric's *Grammar*, pp. 8, 11, *Edgarus, Athelwoldus*, and *Dunstanus* are given as examples of proper nouns. Cf. Wulfstan, *Polity*, p. 81. Strangely enough, in the panegyric on Edgar in *ASC D* 959, written under the influence of Wulfstan, occurs the mysterious reservation, 'Yet he did one ill-deed too greatly: he loved evil foreign customs and brought too firmly heathen manners within this land, and attracted hither foreigners and enticed harmful people to this country.'

[2] H. W. Keim, 'Aethelwold und die Mönchreform in England', *Anglia*, xli (1917), 405–43, ascribes to Æthelwold the *Regularis Concordia*, a translation of the Rule of St Benedict, the historical tract in English on the reforms, and, with hesitation – but mistakenly – the *Canons enacted under King Edgar*.

[3] It is possible that Wulfstan took his nom-de-plume of *Lupus* in imitation of Carolingian practice.

Scandinavian wars and settlements and the Danish conquest with their disruption of the ecclesiastical organization and their threat to Christianity itself. He put monks into St Peter's, Gloucester;[1] but he was no monastic leader. His task was the elementary education of his flock in Christian practices and the reorganization of his clergy. His emphasis was on duty – the duties of the various ranks which made up society. More direct than Ælfric, more practical, simpler, he dispensed with all amenities of composition except rhetorical colour. There are no *exempla* in his sermons, no topical allusions. He disregarded the saints and their popular cults. He seems to have had no interest in the arts or literature as such, although the 'D' version of the Chronicle prospered under his care.[2] His eye was always on the essentials and he showed a puritanical dislike of the popular approach, the disguised medicine and the padded message. Only in his *Sermon to the English* does he turn from the eternal verities to a passionate consideration of present ills in the terms of the present. He had no time for scholarly speculation: it was alien to his purpose. But Wulfstan wrought well within his limitations. His homilies, like Ælfric's, were still in use in the twelfth century.

Ælfric composed lawbooks (his pastoral letters) for St Wulfsige, abbot of Westminster and bishop of Sherborne 992–1001/2, and for Wulfstan, which are in the form of a bishop's charge to his clergy, explaining their duties and correcting the common abuses.[3] 'The monks have the Rule of St Benedict. You too have a rule; and if you will read it you will see what is ordained for you.'[4] Wulfstan compiled canonist manuscripts at Worcester, where he found a useful library, consulted and used the knowledge of Ælfric, and then, as the great legal expert, rewrote almost the whole body of English enacted law. He drafted, or inspired, the royal codes from V Æthelred (1008) until the great codification under Cnut (1018–23).[5] At London he made a formulary of penitential letters.[6] For his northern province he issued

---

[1] *Historia mon. S. Petri Gloucestriae*, ed. W. H. Hart (RS, 1863), i. 8, *sub anno* 1022, which raises difficulties.

[2] K. Jost, 'Wulfstan und die angelsächsische Chronik', *Anglia*, xlvii (1923), 105–23.

[3] Bernhard Fehr, *Die Hirtenbriefe Ælfrics* (Hamburg, 1914).

[4] Latin version of Ep. I, cap. 34, *MPL*, cxxxix, col. 1476.

[5] D. Whitelock, 'Wulfstan and the Laws of Cnut', *EHR*, lxiii (1948), 433–52, 'Wulfstan's authorship of Cnut's Laws', *EHR*, lxx (1955), 72–85. But K. Jost, *Wulfstanstudien* (1950), p. 183, holds that, although some of Wulfstan's language is used in these laws, the archbishop had no part in drafting them.

[6] Printed D. Bethurum, *op. cit.* Appendix II.

a special edition of the royal laws,[1] ecclesiastical canons for his clergy,[2] and pastoral letters for his flock.[3] He probably composed or prompted the code known as the *Law of the Northumbrian priests*. Attributed to him are several tracts on legal and administrative subjects, including the *Rectitudines Singularum Personarum* and the *Gerefa*, and the interesting essay on the duties of various ranks – the *Institutes of Polity*.[4] He systematically collected and recorded Worcester's charters and leases.[5] For his minsters he translated a chapter of Amalarius's *De regula canonicorum*, and he probably had a translation of Theodulf's *Capitula* to hand.[6] These and his other legal writings reveal a bishop using every resource of church and state to achieve a Christian way of life. Wulfstan was a moral crusader. He was the friend of kings, and by asserting his influence over the young Cnut assured the continuity of the English ecclesiastical tradition. Just as his elders had imposed the Rule of St Benedict on the English monasteries, so he composed the rule for the secular clergy and laity, and tried to enforce it.

In his general purpose Wulfstan can be compared with Burchard bishop of Worms, the greatest canonist of his day, the representative of Imperial reform.[7] But Wulfstan's writings are less systematic, narrower in scope, less scholarly, stamped with the English characteristic of emphasis on duties rather than on rights. He was in no way original and his various works are repetitive. He had a limited number of points to make and he hammered them home. But he and Ælfric had made an important contribution to the study of canon law in England. And if Wulfstan marks the end of a period, if the reform movement which began with Dunstan in some ways ends with him, it is because what had been started had been completed. The law, both ecclesiastical and lay, had been codified. From a practical point of view what was required after Wulfstan was not more research but more enforcement of the law which had been declared.

---

[1] 'Edward and Guthrum' (Robertson, *Laws*, pp. 102–9); VI Æthelred and the Latin version: see D. Whitelock, 'Wulfstan and the so-called Laws of Edward and Guthrum', *EHR*, lvi (1941), 1–21, and her other articles cited; Kenneth Sisam, 'The relationship of Æthelred's Codes V and VI', *Studies in the History of Old English Literature* (1953), pp. 278 ff.

[2] 'Canons of Edgar', Thorpe, *Ancient Laws*, ii. 245 ff. See K. Jost, 'Einige Wulfstantexte und ihre Quellen', *Anglia*, lvi (1932), 288 ff. Ælfric's Epp. II and III, ed. B. Fehr, *op. cit.*

[3] E.g. Homily xiii (ed. D. Bethurum).

[4] Cf. D. Bethurum, *op. cit.* pp. 45–6. Possibly the whole collection of legal essays printed Liebermann, *Gesetze*, i. 442–79 are Wulfstan's.

[5] N. R. Ker, 'Hemming's Cartulary', *Studies in Medieval History presented to F. M. Powicke* (1948), pp. 68–72.

[6] See K. Jost, 'Wulfstantexte', pp. 267–8.   [7] Fournier and Le Bras, i. 455.

Within a decade of Cnut's accession twelve bishops had died and had been replaced almost exclusively by monks. There seems to have been some irregularity at first while the newcomer secured the loyalty of Wessex. Cnut expelled Brihtwine from Sherborne and replaced him for a time by Ælfmaer, abbot of St Augustine's, Canterbury.[1] He also apparently wished to intrude the prior of St Augustine's, Ælfstan, into Winchester. But Ælfstan preferred to succeed Ælfmaer as abbot.[2] Other appointments were more regular. Æthelnoth 'the good' succeeded Lyfing at Canterbury in 1020. The son of a thegn, probably a pupil of Ælfric, and dean of Christ Church, Canterbury, he was greatly loved and respected as archbishop.[3] William of Malmesbury had heard that Æthelnoth had rebuked Cnut for his doubt and profanity at Wilton,[4] and Queen Emma praised his wisdom.[5] Ælfwine, oblate and monk of Ely, whose wealthy parents greatly enriched the monastery, ruled Elmham after Ælfgar resigned in 1016. He helped to refound Bury St Edmunds and granted estates to his old home, to which he also retired. Naturally Ely regarded him as a man of saintly life.[6] The abbot of Glastonbury, Brihtwig Merewit, succeeded to Wells in 1023/4.[7]

Wulfstan of York survived Lyfing of Canterbury by three years, and was followed by Ælfric Puttoc, provost of Winchester, and as loyal as

[1] Goscelin of St Bertin wrote two versions of this affair, one for Sherborne and therefore hostile to Ælfmaer (*Vita S. Wlsini*, p. 82), and one for St Augustine's and naturally favourable to its abbot (*Historia translat. S. Augustini, MPL*, clv, coll. 29–30). The basic facts – Brihtwine's expulsion, Ælfmaer's intrusion, blindness, and return to St Augustine's and Brihtwine's restoration – are not in doubt. The date, however, remains uncertain. According to *Chronologia Augustiniensis* in *Historia Mon. S. Augustini Cantuariensis*, ed. Ch. Hardwick (RS, 1858), p. 24, Ælfmaer's 'election' took place in 1022. This date is followed by Wm. Thorne, *De rebus gestis Abbatum S. Augustini*, in Twysden, *Anglic. Hist. Script. X*, col. 1782. But when Thorne, a little later (col. 1783), turns to the story of how Ælfstan was offered Winchester (see below, *n.* 2) he gives the date as 1017. Ælfmaer witnesses as abbot in 1022 (K. 734) and 1023 (Robertson, *Charters*, no. 82), but he may have been a pluralist for a time.

[2] 'nulla ratione acquiesceret episcopatum suscipere, fraternis pulsus precibus et regiis coactus hortamentis': Wm. Thorne, *op. cit.* col. 1783; see above, *n.* 1. Ælfsige II was bishop of Winchester 1012/4–32.

[3] *ASC* 1020, 1038; Florence, i. 183, 192–3; K. 1314; *GP*, p. 311. He was the son of Æthelmaer, the founder of the monastery of Cerne Abbas, and had probably been Ælfric's pupil there. He went to Rome for his pallium in 1022 and may have taken Cnut's gifts to Chartres (*HLF*, x. 466 *n.*). About 1036 he bought an estate to give to the refectory at Christ Church (Robertson, *Charters*, no. 89). Æthelric bishop of Selsey did not want to live any longer than his beloved father in God, Æthelnoth, and died seven nights after him (Florence, i. 192). [4] *GP*, p. 190.

[5] 'vir omni virtute et sapientia praeditus': *Enc. Emmae*, p. 40. No doubt his coolness to the intruder, Harold Harefoot, earned him Emma's praise.

[6] *Liber Eliensis*, II, cc. 75, 86. Lanoë, p. 258.   [7] *Ecclesiastical Documents*, p. 15.

Æthelnoth to the memory of Cnut. Although his violent and revengeful championship of Harthacnut earned him the censure of William of Malmesbury,[1] the midland chronicler, who must have seen Ælfric as bishop of Worcester, considered him 'very venerable and wise'.[2] Wulfstan had provided a rule for his canons. Ælfric began the rehabilitation of the archiepiscopal minsters, a work completed by his two immediate successors. In 1037 he translated the eighth-century archbishop of York, St John of Beverley, to a magnificent shrine in Beverley, thus encouraging a popular cult, and by re-endowing the church and starting new buildings, laid plans for the regular canonical life of the clergy.[3] Ælfric bequeathed with his body to Peterborough splendid vestments – an alb, copes, a dalmatic, a chasuble, and two palls – his altar with two great silver candlesticks, and his pastoral staff.[4]

In 1027 Lyfing, abbot of Tavistock, was raised to the episcopal bench. Lyfing's career illustrates the dangers which faced political bishops once Cnut's firm hand was removed.[5] Monk of Glastonbury or Winchester [6] and then abbot of Tavistock, Lyfing found favour with Cnut, accompanying him to Rome in 1027. It was he who brought back the king's admonitory letter to the English church, and he discharged his commission so well that he was appointed to succeed Bishop Eadnoth of Crediton who had died on the journey. At about the same time, on the death of his uncle Brihtwold, he added the bishopric of Cornwall.[7] Lyfing may have been a reformer of a kind,[8] but clearly he was an avidly political bishop, who could even work with the irreligious Godwin, earl of Wessex. Like Godwin he adhered to Harold Harefoot after Cnut's death, receiving as reward the bishopric of Worcester on Brihtheah's death in 1038; and, like Godwin, he was punished when

---

[1] GP, pp. 250–1; Florence, i. 184, 194–6.

[2] ASC D 1052. He went to Rome for his pallium: 'Chron. of the archbps. of York', HCY, ii. 342–3.   [3] Ibid. ii. 343, 353.

[4] Chron. Peterborough, pp. 72, 85, 87. He also gave some vestments to Ramsey: Chron. Ramsey, p. 199.

[5] For Lyfing see ASC D 1047; Florence, i. 185, 194, 196–7, 238; Malmesbury, GP, pp. 200–1; Plummer, pp. 225–6. He is found with Harold Harefoot at Oxford (Robertson, Charters, no. 91). Worcester charters of his are K. 760, 764–5, 777, and Robertson, no. 94.

[6] Monk of Winchester, Malmesbury, GP, p. 200. Idem, De Antiqu. Glaston. Eccles. i. 94, lists a bishop Lyfing, whose obit. was celebrated on 19 March, as a Glastonbury monk, who was buried there, i. 43. There is confusion here, for Lyfing of Crediton was buried at Tavistock and Lyfing of Canterbury is believed to have died on 12 June 1020.

[7] But Florence (i. 238) places the event in Edward's reign.

[8] Much depends on the meaning of Malmesbury's words (GP, p. 200): 'Ambitiosus et protervus, ecclesiasticarum legum tirannus, ut fertur, invictus, qui nichil pensi haberet quominus omni voluntati suae assisteret.'

Harthacnut gained the throne in 1040, losing Worcester for a time to Ælfric Puttoc of York who accused him of having been involved with Godwin in the murder of Alfred the Ætheling. But both bishop and earl made their peace with the king, and on his death in 1042 they backed the claim of Edward. So Lyfing was still in possession of the three sees when he died in 1046. This 'eloquent bishop' was buried at Tavistock, where the monks half-a-century later still remembered him as a great benefactor. Perhaps like some other monastic bishops of this time he had cared more for his monastery than for his episcopal churches. The story went that an earthquake had accompanied his death. Political insecurity had given him too free a rein.

In the last four years of Cnut's reign there were deaths which removed almost the last of Æthelred's bishops. Again monks were favoured: Æthelric I at Selsey (1032), Brihtheah at Worcester (1033), Eadnoth II at Dorchester (1034), and Ælfweard at London (1035). The bishop of Selsey came probably from Christ Church, Canterbury.[1] The bishop of Worcester was the nephew of Wulfstan I of Worcester and York and had been monk of Worcester and abbot of Pershore, a house reformed by St Oswald.[2] He was the patron of another and even more famous Wulfstan, but he also left a bad name at Worcester for nepotism.[3] Typically, while Brihtheah ruled from St Mary's, St Oswald's new cathedral, his brother Æthelric held St Peter's, the old minster.[4] The bishops of Dorchester and London were both Ramsey monks, and both benefactors of their old home.[5] Ælfweard of London, a kinsman of Cnut, had been promoted to the abbacy of Evesham in 1014 and retained this office after his consecration as bishop. He collected books as well as relics for Evesham; but when he had to retire in 1044, owing to

---

[1] See above, p. 72, *n*. 3. One of Eadmer's sources for his Life of St Dunstan was Æthelred, subprior and precentor at Canterbury and then prior at Worcester under St Wulfstan, who had learned much about Dunstan from the saint's 'near contemporary', Æthelric 'bishop of Chichester'. Stubbs identified this bishop as Ælfric II, deposed in 1070. But he is surely Æthelric I. Eadmer describes him as 'homo magnarum rerum peritia praeditus' (*Memorials of St Dunstan*, p. 164).

[2] Florence, i. 189. Abbot possibly *c*. 1020 when the monastery was rebuilt. Sir Ivor Atkins, 'The Church of Worcester from the Eighth to the Twelfth Century', *The Antiquaries Journal*, xx (1940), 17. For his possible witness as a monk in company with his uncle, see Robertson, *Charters*, no. 76, Atkins, *op. cit.* pp. 16-17.

[3] *Vita Wulfstani*, p. xxiv. His brother, Æthelric, and his brother-in-law were beneficiaries according to Hemming (*Hemingi Chartularium*, i. 266) as were Brihtwine (*ibid.* i. 267) and Atsur, his kinsman and chamberlain (*ibid.* i. 267; cf. Robertson, *Charters*, pp. 458-9). See below, p. 174.   [4] *Hemingi Chartularium*, ii. 342-3.

[5] *Chron. Ramsey*, pp. 148, 159. Eadnoth, who was buried at Ramsey, was remembered as 'the good bishop of Oxfordshire' (*ASC C* 1049).

leprosy, the cowardly monks refused to admit him, and he took all his acquisitions to Ramsey.[1]

The monastic chroniclers took pride in noticing the promotion of a monk, and it is possible that most bishops for whom we have no biographical details were secular priests, some of whom may have risen through service in the royal household. But it is not until the end of the reign that we have clear evidence of this policy.[2] In 1032 one of Cnut's priests was appointed to Winchester, a monastic foundation. It seems to have been an unfortunate break with precedent, and Ælfwine acquired a scandalous reputation.[3] In the next year Duduc, a Saxon or Lotharingian,[4] was appointed to Wells. Although Duduc left his church in poor shape, aggravated by King Edward's refusal to allow him to bequeath to Wells the estates which he had received from Cnut before his promotion, he seems to have been a cultured man. Among his ineffectual bequests were vestments, relics, altar vases, and many books; and his successor, an active reformer, had nothing to say against him.[5]

Cnut's promotions seem to have been respectable, but unadventurous. Monks from some of the better English houses were rewarded; but the ruler of three kingdoms, who was in close contact with Germany and Rome, and whose generosity to the church was famous, attracted few distinguished foreign clerks to his court. The view that Cnut was a traditionalist seems right. In ecclesiastical affairs he must have been dominated by insular advisers.

[1] Chron. Evesham, p. 83; 'Translat. et mirac. S. Odulphi', ibid. pp. 313–14; Chron. Ramsey, pp. 148–51, 157–8; ASC D 1044; Florence, i. 198–9.
[2] It is to be noticed that in 1028–32, 1033, and 1035 royal priests witness charters (K. 1318, 1322, 1324).   [3] ASC E 1032; Anglia Sacra, i. 233–9.
[4] 'de Lotharingia' (Florence, i. 218); 'genere Saxonicus' (ibid. i. 237 ; Ecclesiastical Documents, p. 15), which is to be preferred. He signs a charter of 1033 as presbyter (K. 1318).
[5] Ecclesiastical Documents, pp. 15–16; cf. Freeman, NC, ii, Appendix FF. In Giso's account of his predecessor's pontificate there is listed among the estates which Cnut had given Duduc the monastery of St Peter's, Gloucester, and we are told that when Earl Harold and Archbishop Stigand invalidated Duduc's will (in 1061), the latter persuaded King Edward to grant the monastery to him. This story, however, cannot be reconciled with Ealdred's known connexion with the house (below, p. 88, n. 5). But the difficulty is solved by a later passage in Giso's history (Ecclesiastical Documents, p. 18), where we learn that King William restored one of the estates to Wells and also promised to restore the monasterium Oswaldi. As Stigand is shown in DB (i. 164 b i) as having held some of St Oswald's estates, it is quite clear that the reference to St Peter's is a mistake and that we are concerned throughout with the secular minster of St Oswald's. In the event, King William disregarded his promise to Giso and, after Stigand's deposition, granted most of St Oswald's to Thomas, archbishop of York. This reconstruction of the story clarifies A. Hamilton Thompson's account of St Oswald's minster in 'The jurisdiction of the archbishops of York in Gloucestershire', Trans. Bristol and Glos. arch. soc., xliii (1921), 87 ff. See also GP, pp. 263 n., 293.

The short reign of Harold Harefoot introduced disorder rather than a change of policy. Five vacancies occurred in 1038–9. Æthelnoth 'the good', archbishop of Canterbury, was replaced by his suffragan bishop of St Martin's, Eadsige, one of Cnut's priests who had become a monk at Christ Church, Canterbury, a man whose effectiveness was limited by bad health.[1] Two appointments were scandalous. Lyfing of Devon and Cornwall was given Worcester as well, solely as a reward for his political support,[2] and Grimketel, otherwise unknown, is said to have bought Selsey from the king.[3] For Ælfric III of Elmham 'the small'[4] and Wulfsige of Lichfield, biographical details are lacking. In the even shorter reign of Harthacnut politics again disturbed the position.[5]

Edward inherited only two of his father's bishops, Æthelstan of Hereford,[6] and Brihtwold of Ramsbury, and about nine of Cnut's; but all these had gone by 1051, except Æthelstan and Duduc of Wells. Changes occurred frequently and regularly, and the vacancies were filled with monks and priests from the royal household in almost equal numbers. Monks were appointed to Durham in 1042 and 1056 (Æthelric and Æthelwine from Peterborough), London in 1044 (Robert, abbot of Jumièges), Sherborne in 1046 (Ælfwold II from Winchester, the brother of his predecessor), Worcester in 1046 (Ealdred, abbot of Tavistock) and 1062 (Wulfstan, prior of Worcester), Canterbury in 1051 (Robert of Jumièges), Lichfield in 1053 (Leofwine, abbot of Coventry), Selsey in 1057 (Ælric II from Christ Church), Rochester in 1058 (Siward, abbot of Chertsey), and York in 1060 (Ealdred), so that all dioceses, except Winchester, Wells, and Elmham, were ruled by a monk for part of the reign. Royal priests were appointed to Elmham in 1043 (Stigand), Ramsbury in 1045 (Herman, a Lotharingian), Devon and Cornwall in 1046 (Leofric), Selsey (Heca) and Winchester (Stigand) in 1047, Dorchester in 1049 (Ulf, a Norman) and 1053 (Wulfwig), York (Cynsige) and London (William, a Norman) in 1051, Canterbury in 1052 (Stigand), and Wells (Giso, a Lotharingian) and Hereford (Walter, a Lotharingian)

---

[1] *ASC CE* 1038, 1044, 1048; Florence, i. 193; Robertson, *Charters*, 85, 86, 108; see Plummer, pp. 217, 223–4; Harmer, *Writs*, p. 559.   [2] See above, p. 73.

[3] Florence, i. 193; Malmesbury, *GP*, pp. 150, 205. He was buried at Christ Church, Canterbury, *ASC C* 1047.   [4] See Robertson, *Charters*, p. 425; Harmer, *Writs*, p. 549.

[5] E.g. the punishment of Lyfing of Worcester.

[6] He was blind for the last thirteen years of his life (Florence, i. 214). He died in 1056. Nevertheless, he attests charters until 1050. Tremerig, 'the Welsh bishop', was Æthelstan's vicar during his infirmity until his death in 1055 (*ASC CD* 1055).

in 1060, while Stigand's brother, Æthelmaer, succeeded him at Elmham in 1052 and Earl Harold's priest, Leofgar, obtained Hereford in 1056.

The tendency to reduce the number of monastic bishops and to increase the foreign element, which is a feature of Edward's reign, was much more marked in the first half, and reached its climax during the period of Edward's greatest independence. It is, indeed, difficult to avoid the conclusion that it represented the king's own inclinations. The new pattern is seen at its most extreme in 1051–2, when, of the fifteen bishops, only four were monks (including one Norman) and ten were seculars (five English, three 'German', and two Norman).[1] By 1057 the number of bishops had dropped to twelve, of whom four were monks and eight seculars (five English, two 'German', and one Norman). By the end of the reign the situation had become more normal. Of the fourteen bishops, holding seventeen dioceses, half were monks and half seculars. But monks held the less important sees. Their eight dioceses – York, Durham, Worcester, Lichfield, Rochester, Selsey, and Ramsbury and Sherborne – were no match for the nine, including Canterbury, Winchester, and London, held by the seculars. And there were still five foreigners. The Lotharingians were grouped in the West, in relatively unimportant sees – Ramsbury and Sherborne, Wells, Devon and Cornwall, and Hereford. But the one Norman bishop held London.

The character of the episcopate thus changed considerably under Edward. On the whole, it may be thought, the quality of the bishops improved. The tragedy of the reign was undoubtedly Stigand's unsatisfactory position at Canterbury which cast a quite undeserved shadow over the English church.

Stigand spans the whole period. A priest of Cnut, he was deposed by William I. He is a link between one great reformer, Wulfstan I, who in 1020 dedicated the church at Ashingdon which seems to have been Stigand's first benefice,[2] and another, Lanfranc, who succeeded him at Canterbury. By 1070 he was a lonely survivor, exemplifying in his ecclesiastical position many of the basic weaknesses of the Old-English church and in his career its slow deterioration while a new and revolutionary reform movement had been gaining ground outside.[3] Stigand, probably from East Anglia and of Anglo-

---

[1] See diagram, p. 63.

[2] *ASC F* 1020; 'Chron. of the archbps. of York', *HCY*, ii. 342. He signs as priest K. 1318, 1322, 1324.

[3] It is characteristic of Stigand that, unlike most of his colleagues, he seems never to have travelled abroad.

Scandinavian descent,[1] was a careerist who, by always supporting the party in power and rarely misreading the situation, rose rapidly under Edward, becoming bishop of Elmham in 1043, bishop of Winchester in 1047, and archbishop of Canterbury in plurality after Robert of Jumièges had been expelled in 1052. He also controlled various monasteries or their estates.[2] His position was therefore irregular. He was a pluralist; he had invaded Canterbury in the lifetime of his predecessor; and the pallium he obtained from Benedict X in 1058 was useless, even harmful, because the donor was an intruder. Such irregularities were common in Christendom and pluralism had become characteristic of the English church. But Stigand was more careless of proper form than most of his colleagues.

Moreover, he was outstandingly worldly. By birth and career he represented the Anglo-Scandinavian interest in the kingdom, an interest which, while conservative in regard to some of Edward's policies, was insecurely fixed in England's past, and so more than usually opportunist and historically aimless. It seems therefore in character that Stigand should have been the intermediary between the royalists and Earl Godwin in 1051–2, one of the half-hearted backers of Edgar Ætheling after the battle of Hastings, and then a firm supporter of the Conqueror. The anonymous author of the *Vita Ædwardi* was connected with the court circle and involved, although only as an historian, in the same conflicting loyalties as Stigand. His references to the archbishop are acute and rather unkind. He makes it clear that in 1051 Stigand did his best for Earl Godwin and was deeply affected by the earl's disgrace, but never considered abandoning his implacable royal master.[3] And he portrays him at Edward's death-bed as a worldly prelate unmoved by religious manifestations and indecently ready to disregard the dying man and ingratiate himself with the next king.[4] The writer's reports are perhaps accurate, but his moral judgments too severe.

[1] His name is Old-Norse. His sister lived in Norwich (*DB*, ii. 116) and his brother Æthelmaer married a woman who brought him the manor of Blofield near Norwich (*DB*, ii. 195). Æthelmaer held the church of St Simon and Jude in Norwich, 'non de episcopatu sed de patrimonio' (*DB*, ii. 117b). If they came from Norse trading stock their business acumen is understandable.

[2] The diocese of Rochester (to which Stigand consecrated in 1058 the abbot of Chertsey) was traditionally under Canterbury's control. And when, likewise in 1058, Stigand consecrated a Christ Church monk as bishop of Selsey, he probably rounded off his south-eastern ecclesiastical 'empire'. According to *Liber Eliensis*, II, c. 98 (but cf. Freeman, *NC*, iii. 636–9), Stigand prolonged vacancies in monasteries, including Winchester, Glastonbury, St Albans, St Augustine's, and Ely, in order to enjoy their revenues, but also was most generous to them. Cf. Malmesbury, *GR*, p. 36, 'praeterea multas abbatias solus ipse possidebat'. See also Eadmer, *Hist. Novorum*, p. 37.

[3] p. 22.   [4] pp. 76–7.

Stigand was active in the royal government,[1] and used his position to make himself rich.[2] To combine the two wealthiest dioceses – Winchester and Canterbury – was indefensible when most other English bishoprics were poorly endowed, and for a secular clerk to hold two of the four monastic sees was unseemly. His attitude towards ecclesiastical institutions was that of an administrator rather than a pastor,[3] and he also accumulated a large private estate, so making himself one of the greatest magnates in the kingdom. At the same time he was a man of cultured tastes,[4] a patron of the arts who was generous to the monasteries which he held. To Ely he gave gold and silver vessels for the altar, and he manufactured, apparently in the abbey itself, a great cross covered with silver bearing a life-size image of Christ, which, together with statues of St Mary and St John the Evangelist, were cast from bronze. He also had made an alb and a cope for the precentor and a chasuble of priceless workmanship and value, thought to be the most precious in the kingdom.[5] At Winchester he used gifts of Queen Emma to provide a great cross bearing the images of St Mary and St John, richly adorned with gold and silver.[6] In fact Stigand represents the bankruptcy of

[1] According to the Ely chronicler, Stigand controlled the ecclesiastical patronage of Kings Edward and Harold (*Liber Eliensis*, II, c. 98). Malmesbury's version is that he sold bishoprics and abbeys (*GP*, pp. 35–6, but see below, pp. 112 ff.). It should be noticed that Stigand administered at various times those monasteries whose abbots were supposed to share the 'chancellorship' (see below, p. 125). Winchester, of course, was the seat of the treasury.

[2] Besides the ecclesiastical endowments of Canterbury and Winchester and a number of manors in Wessex (especially in Gloucestershire), Stigand had handsome estates in East Anglia, consisting mostly in rights over scattered freemen and sokemen. As the foci of the four principal complexes were North Elmham, Norwich, Hoxne, and South Elmham (two see-towns and two boroughs), it looks as though this great territorial interest was created out of Stigand's tenure of the East Anglian see, reinforced by his brother's succession. Stigand also had rights in Cambridgeshire, Bedfordshire, and Hertfordshire. See Olaf Feilitzen, *The pre-Conquest personal names of Domesday Book* (1937). He extracted estates from Ely (*Liber Eliensis*, II, c. 98), he forced loans of land from Abingdon (*Chron. Abingdon*, i. 462), St Edmund's (*DB*, ii. 288b; Harmer, *Writs*, p. 436), and Bath (Robertson, *Charters*, no. 117). In 1061 he frustrated Bishop Duduc's bequest of a secular minster to Wells and persuaded the king to grant it to him (above, p. 75, *n*. 5). He benefited from wills (Whitelock, *Wills*, nos. 29, 31). It was popularly thought that Stigand was immensely rich (Malmesbury, *GP*, pp. 35–7).

[3] Cf. Malmesbury, *GP*, p. 36: 'errore . . . rem ecclesiasticorum negotiorum sicuti publicorum actitari existimans.'

[4] About 1055 (for he met an imperial army in Lombardy) a monk of Christ Church, Æthelwine, visited Jerusalem and returned by way of Constantinople, where he bought a splendid pall for St Dunstan: Eadmer in *Memorials of St Dunstan*, pp. 245–6. It should also be noticed that there was an artistic revival in the English coinage while Stigand was Edward's first minister.

[5] *Liber Eliensis*, II, c. 98.

[6] The untrustworthy *Annales de Wintonia* in *Annales Monastici* (ed. H. R. Luard), ii. 25.

the tenth-century reformation. His pluralism, concern with royal government, and interest in the arts all had respectable antecedents in that movement. But the moral purpose which had justified them had disappeared.

Clearly Stigand was neither a good bishop nor a satisfactory metropolitan. He was not recognized in England as an archbishop except in 1058 and after the Conquest; and the papacy may have taken an even severer view.[1] His faults were notorious and were proclaimed by his detractors – by some monks who were outraged by the rule of a secular clerk over the monastic churches of Winchester and Canterbury and by the Normans who thus justified his deposition. But irregularity and worldliness seem to be the only true charges which can be brought against him. No attack was ever made on his private life; and it is only in the twelfth century that we hear of his simony and illiteracy, amid general abuse which served both to exaggerate the achievements of the Norman successors and to provide a scapegoat for reproaches which might otherwise have been directed at Edward.[2] In truth Edward was guilty of making use of Stigand's administrative talents without exercising sufficient control or directing him to his spiritual duties, so that the prelate was able to exploit his commanding position within a disorganized church. And Stigand was guilty of giving no heed to the tide of reform which was to overtake him. In 1043 he was a respectable bishop by the standards of that age. By 1066 he had become a scandal even in England. And after the Conquest he epitomized the vices of a church which the Normans had condemned. He cannot have been worthless.[3] He was clearly an intimate of Edward and Edith [4] and he even captured the Conqueror himself for a

[1] See below, pp. 302 ff.

[2] Malmesbury, *GP*, pp. 35–6.

[3] In England he was strongly disliked at Canterbury and Winchester. See Osbert and Eadmer, *Memorials of St Dunstan*, pp. 141–2, 229, 237–8, 245. Yet, according to E. Bishop, he appears, together with Harold, Cnut, and Emma, in a thirteenth-century Christ Church calendar, Cant. MS. E. 19. Winchester pointedly omitted his name from the mortuary roll of Abbot Vitalis in 1122–3: *Rouleau Mortuaire du B. Vital, abbé de Savigni* (ed. Léopold Delisle), p. xliii, tit. 182. Abingdon cared little for him (*Chron. Abingdon*, i. 462–3). On the other hand two monasteries associated with him regarded him favourably – Ely (*Liber Eliensis*, II, c. 98) and St Augustine's Canterbury (obituary, Brit. Mus. Vitell. C xii, fo. 120: 8 Kal. March, 'Stigandus archiepiscopus'). He was allowed his full style on the Bayeux Tapestry and in *DB*. Even Malmesbury permitted a few grudging words of praise: 'Alias sane nec imprudens nec inefficax' (*GR*, p. 35).

[4] The author of the *Vita Ædwardi* tries to separate Stigand and Edward – for obvious reasons. But Stigand's career is only explicable in terms of royal favour. The prelate was in regular attendance at court and witnesses all the 'royal' diplomas. According to Malmesbury, *GP*, p. 252, Queen Edith was one of the friends of Stigand who, after his deposition and imprisonment at Winchester visited him and begged him to take more care of his health.

time.[1] Nor was he singular. Bishops of his type were usually to be found in royal courts. But it was this very curial position which made him so vulnerable in 1070. He had no secure standing in the church and he had outlived his usefulness to his new royal master.

Most of the other secular clerks appointed by Edward to bishoprics were foreigners. Among the exceptions were Cynsige of York (1051–60), one of Edward's priests,[2] and Leofgar, Earl Harold's priest. Cynsige, another thought to have been delivered by Caesarean section, continued his predecessor's work at Beverley. He built the tower, in which he placed two bells, adorned the church with books and ornaments, and gave bells to Southwell and Stow. He must have enjoyed some reputation in the North, for he consecrated two bishops to Glasgow and one to 'Llandaff'.[3] Peterborough, where he was buried, regarded him as a monk and saint. He lived most abstemiously while his household feasted, and, especially in Lent, he travelled on foot, sometimes barefooted, preaching and distributing alms. He may have taken the cowl while archbishop. He bequeathed to Peterborough with his body a richly adorned text of the Gospels, an estate, and ornaments worth £300, all of which Queen Edith took away.[4] Leofgar's actions were less edifying. He wore moustaches until appointed bishop of Hereford in 1056 and lost his life fighting against the Welsh in the same year.[5]

Of the foreign royal clerks who obtained bishoprics, two were Normans and four 'Lotharingians'. The Normans were involved in the events which led to the revolutionary episode of 1051–2. Ulf's appointment to Dorchester in 1049 was regarded as scandalous, no doubt partly because his three predecessors in the see had all been Ramsey monks; but the charges are without detail.[6] William's appointment to succeed Robert at London in 1051 caused,

---

[1] In 1067 Stigand consecrated Remigius to Dorchester. He was treated with great honour in Normandy (Malmesbury, *GP*, pp. 36–7; William of Poitiers, II, cc. 28, 35, 40). On the charter granted by William to St Denis, Paris, 13 April 1069, a year before Stigand's deposition, there appears at the head of the witness list after the royal family, 'Ego Stigandus ecclesie Cantuariensis archiepiscopus confirmavi' (T. A. M. Bishop and P. Chaplais, *Fascimiles of English Royal Writs to A.D. 1100*, pl. xxviii, text). His despair was so great when he fell (Malmesbury, *GP*, p. 252) that he could not have expected disgrace. [2] Florence, i. 204.

[3] 'Chron. of the archbps. of York', *HCY*, ii. 343–4, 353; below, pp. 232–3. He witnesses as priest K. 743, 796, 800. [4] *Chron. Peterborough*, pp. 70, 73; cf. Florence, i. 218; *ASC D* 1060. [5] *ASC CD* 1056; Florence, i. 214.

[6] 'A bad appointment', *ASC C* 1049; 'but he was expelled from it afterwards because he did nothing like a bishop in it, so much that we are ashamed to say anything more about it', *ASC D* 1050; cf. *ASC E* 1047, Florence, i. 203: he was almost broken by the council of Vercelli in 1050 for unsuitability.

apparently, no more than transitory resentment, for he was allowed to keep the see after Earl Godwin's triumphant return.[1]

The Lotharingians were mostly satisfactory bishops. Herman,[2] who accompanied Edward to England and was appointed to Wiltshire (Ramsbury) in 1045, appalled by the poverty of his see, tried to move it into Malmesbury Abbey. But he was successfully opposed by the monks and by the house of Godwin and in 1053 retired to the monastery of St Bertin at St Omer, where he became a monk. The death of Godwin and a vacancy at Sherborne induced him to return three years later, when he was satisfied with the government of the re-united dioceses. Towards the end of his life he planned the removal of his see to (Old) Salisbury. Herman was certainly in Edward's confidence. In 1050 he was sent with Bishop Ealdred to Leo IX's Easter synod at Rome. And he seems to have been especially close to Queen Edith.[3] This 'famous and well-educated bishop'[4] is perhaps to be regarded as an obstructed or ineffective reformer. His greatest contribution to English culture was to bring over the hagiographer Goscelin from St Bertin's c. 1060. But Goscelin's works from this period have been lost,[5] and it was not until after his patron's death that he produced his Lives of St Wulfsige of Sherborne and St Edith of Wilton with apologies for his remissness. It is noticeable that Goscelin treats Herman with no great warmth in his writings,[6] and it may be that he, too, found conditions in the diocese frustrating.

Giso, who was born near the abbey of St Trond (Liége),[7] which was reformed by Bishop Dietrich of Metz (1030–47),[8] was similarly distressed by

[1] ASC D 1052, E 1048.

[2] For Herman and Goscelin, see Vita Ædwardi, pp. xlv ff., 91 ff.

[3] Edith had been educated at Wilton Abbey, which she rebuilt in stone, Herman officiating at the dedication ceremony. It was the queen who had made Herman's return in 1058 possible.

[4] Vita Ædwardi, p. 47. Part of a Salisbury pontifical, based on a 'Romano-Germanic' pontifical originating from Mainz in the mid-tenth century, written in two German hands probably mid-eleventh century, can be associated with Herman: N. R. Ker, 'Three Old English Texts in a Salisbury Pontifical', The Anglo-Saxons, ed. Peter Clemoes (1959), p. 263.

[5] Unless, of course, the Vita Ædwardi is his.   [6] He is especially cold in his Vita Wlsini.

[7] At Hasbengau, 'Hasbaniensis incola', Ecclesiastical documents, p. 17. It is interesting to note the personal foreign elements in a Wells calendar (Francis Wormald, English Kalendars before A.D. 1100, HBS, 1934, no. 8), which is probably his (The Bosworth Psalter, pp. 163–4): Ansbert of Rouen, Romanus abbot of Mont-Jura, Servatus of Tongres, Desiderius of Vienne, Gaugericus of Cambrai, Philibert of Jumièges, Remaclus of Stavelot, Mansuetus of Toul, Benedicta of Laon region, Gangolfus of Varennes in Burgundy, Lupus bishop (of Angers), the Eleven Thousand Virgins of Cologne, Severinus of Cologne, Hubert of the Ardennes, Nicasius of Rheims, Servulus (a poor man of Rome mentioned by St Gregory). This 'uninteresting miscellaneous list' (Bishop) has some geographical significance.

[8] 1005/34. A. Hauck, Kirkengesch., iii, 503. K. Hallinger, Gorze-Cluny, ii. 830–1.

the conditions at Wells to which he was appointed in 1060. He applied himself strenuously to the restoration of the dilapidated property, enlisted the help of the royal family, and wrote a history of the church to safeguard his acquisitions.[1] The author of the *Vita Ædwardi* considered him a fit and learned bishop.[2] Walter, a chaplain of the queen, appointed to Hereford in the same year, and earning a similar eulogy from Edward's biographer, was less fortunate in his memorials.[3]

Perhaps the most distinguished of these foreign clerks is Leofric, bishop of Devon and Cornwall in 1046. His origin is not clear. Although his name is English, he is described as *Brytonicus* – presumably, a Cornishman – by Florence of Worcester.[4] However that may be, he was reared and educated in Lotharingia,[5] probably in a reformed house of canons.[6] He may have met Edward at Bruges in 1039, and he accompanied the *aetheling* to England two years later.[7] At Edward's court he was employed as a scribe,[8] and his literary interests are proved not only by his fine collection of manuscripts [9] but also by the liturgical pieces he added to a Gregorian sacramentary,

[1] *Ecclesiastical documents*, pp. 16–17; *ASC D* 1060; Florence, i. 218; Malmesbury, *GP*, p. 194. For his writs, see Harmer, *Writs*, nos. 64–72. Giso also, but probably after the Conquest, increased the number of canons (*clerici, fratres*), built for them a cloister, refectory, and dormitory, and imposed on them a more canonical rule (*Ecclesiastical documents*, p. 19).

[2] *Vita Ædwardi*, p. 35.

[3] *Ibid.* where he is styled 'presbiter regis'. Florence, i. 218, calls him 'reginae capellanus'. See Plummer, p. 249. Malmesbury, *GP*, p. 300, reports that he was killed with scissors when attempting to rape a seamstress, but that King William had the affair hushed up.

[4] Florence, i. 199. F. Barlow, K. M. Dexter, A. M. Erskine, L. J. Lloyd, *Leofric of Exeter* (1972).

[5] Malmesbury, *GP*, p. 201.

[6] Lotharingia proper was roughly equivalent to the ecclesiastical province of Trèves, including the dioceses of Metz, Toul, and Verdun, together with, perhaps, the region of Liége. Leofric reveals a connexion with Trèves and with Mainz to the East and with Bruno of Toul, Pope Leo IX (below, p. 84, *n.* 4). His reverence for St Leo may be due merely to the pope's favour in 1050 and his special interest in canons, but they may have met at Toul, where Bruno was a canon of St Stephen's, 1017–24, and bishop after 1027. Leofric's collectar is based on the *Liber capitularis* of Stephen, bishop of Liége, or Tongres: *The Leofric Collectar*, ed. E. S. Dewick and W. H. Frere (HBS, 1913, 1918), ii, pp. xii, xxii, xxiv–xxv. It is unfortunate that the two bishops whom Leofric held in special esteem (below, p. 84, *n.* 4) cannot be securely identified. The first could be the eighth-century Madalveus of Verdun and the other possibly the seventh-eighth-century Omotarius or his successor Madalgarius of Laon. If there was a mistake in the description, Madalbert, saint and virgin, whose relics were at Liége, would be an obvious candidate for the first.

[7] K. 762, 767; *Ordnance Survey Facsimiles*, ii, Exeter charters, no. 12.

[8] 'regis cancellarius', Florence, i. 199.

[9] Robertson, *Charters*, pp. 477–80; Max Förster, 'The Donations of Leofric to Exeter', *The Exeter Book of O.E. poetry* (1933); N. R. Ker, *Medieval Libraries of Great Britain* (R. Hist. Soc. Guides and Handbooks, no. 3, 1941).

written at St Vaast's (Arras) in Flanders *c.* 900,[1] and an Anglo-Saxon calendar, written probably at Glastonbury *c.* 970, to make his 'full Mass book'.[2] These additions show the foreigner adapting himself to the place and the times. He supplemented the Sacramentary with masses for festivals popular in England [3] and for special occasions. A benediction for the king, a mass for the king and queen, a benediction and a mass for the king in synod, masses for peace, for enemies, for a tribulation, for a friend afflicted by his adversaries, a benediction and a mass for those undertaking a journey, a blessing for a bell, and – a strange provision for a south-western church – a mass for rain, reveal the interests of this conscientious and cultured bishop.

He remained nevertheless much of a foreigner. There was at least one Lotharingian priest in his household,[4] and he had no patience with the conditions he found in his diocese. Within a short time he had by papal authorization and royal help moved his see from Crediton to Exeter, reorganized his chapter according to the Rule of St Chrodegang, and begun to use his own talents and his interest at court to restore the dilapidated estates of the church. By the time of his death he had re-founded, physically and spiritually, his episcopal church. He inherited a rich, if miscellaneous, reliquary, and he bequeathed a valuable library.[5] He left only the task of building a great church to his successors. According to his obituary notice he was a good man, an active visitor and preacher, an instructor of the clergy, and a builder of churches.[6] He exemplifies the foreign prelate at his best: detached from, but not insensitive to, local tradition; free from dynastic and tenurial ties, so that, instead of ecclesiastical property being used to endow dependants, private fortune could be put to the use of the church; an able administrator and a progressive force. Yet there is no evidence that he was much loved or even, in the widest sense, important.

[1] Grierson, *England and Flanders*, p. 92.

[2] *The Leofric Missal*, ed. F. E. Warren (Oxford, 1883).

[3] *Ibid.* pp. lv–lviii.

[4] His ambassador to Pope Leo IX in 1049 was his priest, Landbert (named after the patron saint of Liége), *ibid.* p. 2a. His list of those to be prayed for includes, among the living, Utbert, his maidservant Bernoz, and Becco, and, among the dead, bishops Madalbert and Odolgarius, the priests Peter, Leotfrid, Eleneus, and Odolbramnus, and Gontran, Centulf, Aldo, Rotbert, Elena, Utberga, Ermengardis, and Ildeardis, *ibid.* p. 6b. In a litany, Brit. Mus., Harl. MS. 863, which is probably Leofric's (*The Bosworth Psalter*, pp. 162–3), the three last invocations of confessors are St Leo IX, St Bardo (bishop of Mainz, 1031–51), and St Simon (? the hermit of the Black Gate at Trèves).

[5] Malmesbury, *GP*, p. 201; Robertson, *Charters*, Appendix I, no. 1.

[6] 'vita moribusque modestus', *The Leofric Missal*, p. 2a.

Although the secular bishops of Edward's reign seem to lack brilliance, it must be remembered that their obscurity is partly due to their appointment to churches with no tradition of historical writing and to the monastic interest of the chroniclers. Several impress as energetic administrators, some were learned, and only a few incurred a censure which seems deserved.

Much more is known about the monks promoted by Edward; and they prove to be at least as heterogeneous as the seculars. The monks of Peterborough who became bishops of Durham, the brothers Æthelric (1042) and Æthelwine (1056), were hated in their secular chapter.[1] Although their unpopularity is to some extent a testimonial,[2] they do not seem to have been entirely satisfactory bishops. A greater admirer of St Cuthbert was Ælfwold II of Sherborne (1045/6–58), a monk of Winchester, the brother of his predecessor, the unfortunate Brihtwine. Ælfwold rebuilt the monastery at Sherborne and gained a great reputation for asceticism. He also had the courage to withstand Earl Godwin.[3] Leofwine of Lichfield (1053) had been the first abbot of Earl Leofric's house at Coventry;[4] but he married and in 1070 he resigned in order to avoid his deposition.[5] Æthelric of Selsey (1058), a monk of Christ Church, Canterbury,[6] was deposed in 1070, but possibly unjustly.[7] Siward of Rochester (1058), abbot of Chertsey,[8] survived the purge. No less disparate were the three outstanding monk-bishops of the reign, Robert, Ealdred, and Wulfstan.

Robert Champart was one of the principal actors in the dramatic events of 1051–2 and has been vilified by English historians, contemporary and modern. Prior of St Ouen at Rouen and in 1037 abbot of Jumièges, a Norman house which had been reformed by William of Dijon at the beginning of the century, he accompanied Edward to England, and was appointed bishop of London in 1044 and archbishop of Canterbury in 1051. He was regarded by

---

[1] Symeon, *HDE*, i. 87, 89, 91–2, 94; *ASC D* 1041, 1073; Harmer, *Writs*, p. 556.

[2] Æthelric retired to Peterborough and was imprisoned by the Conqueror at Westminster. He was regarded as a saintly monk at both houses, *Chron. Peterborough*, pp. 74–6, Malmesbury, *GP*, p. 271. Æthelwine was expelled from Durham and put into Abingdon.

[3] *Vita Wlsini*, pp. 82–3; Malmesbury, *GP*, pp. 179–80; Harmer, *Writs*, p. 552.

[4] *ASC C* 1053; Florence, i. 211; *FNC*, ii. 361; Harmer, *Writs*, p. 567.

[5] See below, p. 218.   [6] *ASC E* 1058; Florence, i. 216–7; Plummer, p. 248.

[7] See below, p. 114. The Conqueror had him brought out of his enforced retirement and taken in a carriage to the trial on Penenden Heath, ?1072, to testify to Canterbury's rights. In the report of the trial Æthelric is described as 'episcopus de Cicestra, vir antiquissimus et legum terre sapientissimus', *Anglia Sacra*, i. 335; J. H. Le Patourel, 'The reports on the trial on Penenden Heath', *Studies in Medieval History presented to F. M. Powicke*, p. 23.

[8] *ASC E* 1058; Florence, i. 217; Plummer, p. 248.

the party of Earl Godwin as the king's evil genius and his policy of opposition to the earl as raving madness.[1] There can be no doubt that he influenced Edward to follow a political course which was unpopular in the kingdom as a whole and that he recklessly provoked a fight with the earl of Wessex. It is, therefore, important to establish whether he was an ecclesiastical reformer.

Robert was a great builder at Jumièges,[2] and, when bishop of London, he gave to his monastery a fine Missal, written at Winchester c. 1008–25,[3] and probably a Pontifical.[4] We can infer that he had cultured tastes. To assume more would be dangerous. Gilbert Crispin's view of the Norman church in the decade before the foundation of Bec (1040) could not be gloomier.[5] And if St Ouen or Jumièges were among the houses that Herluin visited from Brionne when he was thinking of becoming a monk,[6] they must have been below the standard even of English monasteries at that time. The ideals which were to put English monasticism to shame after 1066 were those of Herluin's new monastery of Bec.

It is probable, therefore, that Robert's background was fairly worldly. And so his vendetta against Earl Godwin can be viewed as more political than ecclesiastical and one more of persons and nations than of principle. If Robert could have retained Canterbury the English church would certainly have been more lively and interesting, but his political sense was so poor, his rancour so marked, and his behaviour so unrestrained, that the activity might have been dearly bought.

In contrast to the embittered expatriate Robert, the English Ealdred impresses as a cultured man of the world. What we know of him only makes us wish to know more, for he was the closest to a 'prince-bishop' that England could produce. But although he dazzled contemporaries and also later generations at York he could not have been a saint.[7] He inspired no biographer, and the twelfth-century York historians had to rely on the

[1] 'dementia et insania', *Vita Ædwardi*, pp. 17 ff. His ejection and spoliation 'was God's will, in that he had obtained the dignity when it was not God's will', *ASC E* 1052.

[2] Malmesbury, *GR*, i. 244; Georges Lanfry, *L'abbaye de Jumièges, plans et documents* (Rouen, 1954).   [3] *The Missal of Robert of Jumièges*, ed. H. A. Wilson, HBS, 1896.

[4] Usually called 'the Abp. Robert Benedictional': ed. *idem*, HBS, 1903.

[5] *Vita Herluini*, p. 89. Naturally, he exaggerates. Cf. J. Leclercq, and J.-P. Bonnes, 'Un maître de la vie spirituelle au XIᵉ siècle: Jean de Fécamp', *Études de théologie et d'histoire de la spiritualité*, ix (Paris, 1946).   [6] *Vita Herluini*, pp. 91–2.

[7] William of Poitiers pays the warmest tribute, presumably because Ealdred crowned, and then supported, the Conqueror. He is described as, 'aequitatem valde amans, aevo maturus, sapiens, bonus, eloquens, . . . aeque sancta vita carus et inviolata fama' (p. 220), and another eulogy (p. 270) has been lost owing to the truncation of the manuscript.

midland and northern versions of the Anglo-Saxon chronicle for material. Ealdred has been called 'the central person in Anglo-Saxon chronicle D', [1] and he is also prominent in 'Florence of Worcester'. For Ealdred, therefore, we have little more than a record of his public acts, and, although these show the quality and importance of the man, they help little to an understanding of his character and views.

Ealdred's early life followed the familiar pattern of the monastic careerist: monk of Winchester and abbot of Tavistock in Cnut's reign,[2] and bishop of Worcester in 1046.[3] At this time he was probably associated with Godwin, earl of Wessex,[4] and it is, perhaps, significant that he was not promoted to York in 1051 when Ælfric Puttoc died. However that may be, he had not compromised himself, and in the years after 1052 he was in the entire confidence of the court and allowed to display talents not usually associated with monks. In 1050 he and Herman, bishop of Wiltshire, attended the Easter synod of Rome 'on the king's business', [5] and in 1054 he led the legation to Germany to negotiate for the return of Edward 'the Exile' as a possible successor to the throne.[6] The war with Wales then occupied his energies. He had already, in 1049, fought against the Welsh.[7] In 1056, after Bishop Leofgar of Hereford's death in the battle of Glasbury-on-Wye, he administered that diocese for four years and helped Earls Leofric and Harold in the work of pacification.[8] Since he also controlled the bishopric of Wiltshire during Herman's withdrawal (c. 1055–8), he ruled a sort of ecclesiastical palatinate on the March which was politically convenient. When Herman returned to Ramsbury and added Sherborne, Ealdred left the country and travelled to Jerusalem by way of Hungary.[9] Edward 'the

[1] *EHD*, ii. 108. [2] Florence, i. 199; Malmesbury, *GP*, p. 251.

[3] *ASC D* 1046. Miss Robertson has suggested that he may have held some other office between his abbacy and bishopric, *Charters*, p. 448: he possibly acted as Lyfing's *chorepiscopus* in the diocese of Worcester, H. P. R. Finberg, *Tavistock Abbey* (1951), p. 4.

[4] He persuaded King Edward to remit the outlawry incurred by Godwin's eldest son, Swegn, for killing his cousin Beorn (Florence, i. 203), and, although he was sent by the king to intercep Harold in 1051, 'they could not or would not' (*ASC D* 1052).

[5] *ASC C* 1049, 1050, *D* 1050, *E* 1047; Florence, i. 204; *MPL*, cxliii, col. 617; Goscelin, *Hist. translat. S. Augustini episcopi*, *MPL*, clv, col. 32.

[6] *ASC CD* 1054; Florence, i. 212; *Vita Wulfstani*, pp. 15–16. He was accompanied possibly by Abbot Ælfwine of Ramsey (cf. *DB*, i. 208 a i: 'sed [E.] rex dedit terram . . . S. Benedicto de Ramesy propter unum servitium quod abbas Alwinus fecit ei in Saxonia') and may have left Æthelwig (abbot of Evesham 1058) as his deputy (*Chron. Evesham*, p. 87).

[7] *ASC D* 1050; Florence, i. 203, who makes him the leader; Lloyd, *A History of Wales*, ii. 362.

[8] *ASC C* 1056; Florence, i. 205; Lloyd, *op. cit.* ii. 367–8.

[9] *ASC D* 1058; Florence, i. 217.

Exile' had returned from Hungary to his unexpected death in England in the previous year, and it is possible that Ealdred was again seeking news of English princes, and took the opportunity of following his old friend, Earl Swegn, to the Holy Land.[1] The death of Cynsige of York occurred shortly after his return, and this time Ealdred obtained the traditional promotion, surrendering Hereford to Walter the Lotharingian.[2] But his visit to Rome in 1061 with Earls Tostig and Gyrth and the countess of Northumbria to get the pallium and do the king's business ended in disaster,[3] and the pope's decision that he must surrender Worcester must have been a bitter pill to swallow. Between 1055 and 1058 Ealdred had been the ruler of three dioceses and the abbey of Winchcombe.[4] He was left with little more than a great honour. However, he salvaged what he could,[5] and gave his attention to York, where he gained a great reputation. He lived to crown King William,[6] and although he had not unnaturally favoured the crowning of Edward the Exile's son, Edgar the Ætheling, after the battle of Hastings,[7] he gave William loyal service and helped to establish respect for the conquered.

The incapacity of the archbishop of Canterbury had given Ealdred an opportunity which he had used to the full. He was at the centre of affairs for over a decade. Contemporaries praised his skill in administration rather than his holiness.[8] William of Malmesbury drew attention to the boldness of his

---

[1] This was probably the occasion on which he was in danger of shipwreck in the Adriatic and saved by the intercession of St Edith, a characteristic invocation for a curial bishop. Goscelin, *Vita S. Edithe*, pp. 279–80.   [2] *ASC DE* 1060; Florence, i. 218.

[3] *ASC D* 1061; Florence, i. 218; *Vita Ædwardi*, pp. 34–7; *Vita Wulfstani*, pp. 16–17; Malmesbury, *GP*, pp. 251–2; 'Chron. of the archbps. of York', *HCY*, ii. 346.

[4] *ASC D* 1053; Florence, i. 211.

[5] He retained paramount control over Worcester, kept twelve of its estates, and also held on to some manors which he had acquired from St Peter's, Gloucester. See R. R. Darlington, *Vita Wulfstani*, pp. xxvi ff.; A. Hamilton Thompson, 'The jurisdiction of the archbishops of York in Gloucestershire', *Trans. Bristol and Glos. Arch. Soc.*, xliii (1921), 91 ff. Ealdred, if not as greedy as Stigand, behaved in a similar way. Gloucester Abbey preserved several versions of how it was treated by Ealdred. It seems that the estates were given him, perhaps for life, to recompense him for his rebuilding the abbey in 1058, although later the monks complained that he took them 'causa magis hospitii quam operis sui' (*Historia monasterii S. Petri Gloucestriae*, ed. W. H. Hart, i. 9). And it was also said in this connexion that Ealdred actually held the whole monastery, during a vacancy and when deprived of his see, 'ad sui sustentationem' (*ibid.* ii. 112), and that the Worcester monk Wilstan, whom Ealdred appointed abbot of Gloucester in 1058, was the bishop's kinsman (*ibid.* ii. 115). Moreover, Ealdred always retained two manors of Tavistock Abbey, Finberg, *Tavistock Abbey*, p. 4. See also above, p. 75, *n.* 5, and *GP*, p. 292.

[6] *ASC D* 1066; 'Chron. of the archbps. of York', *HCY*, ii. 349; Hugh the Chantor, *HCY*, p. l.

[7] *ASC D* 1066; Florence, i. 228.

[8] 'Vir multum in secularibus astutus nec parum religiosus', *Vita Wulfstani*, p. 13. Coleman also writes of the 'arrogantis animi cupiditas', *ibid.* p. 20.

spirit.[1] He was undoubtedly a courageous man. The story of his rebuke to the sheriff Urse rings true,[2] even if we can hardly believe that he had King William grovelling at his feet.[3] The words that the chronicler gives him, however, show at least the remembered stature of the man – 'Leave him, good sirs, leave him lying there. For he does not lie at the feet of Ealdred but at the feet of St Peter. It is right that he should feel the power of St Peter since he has not feared to harm his vicar.'

Ealdred must often have been away from his dioceses. Apart from the year at Cologne, the journey to Jerusalem, and the two visits to Rome, the king's business limited his pastoral work. But he does not seem to have been remiss. In 1058, before his visit to Jerusalem, he dedicated to St Peter the monastic church he had built at Gloucester.[4] In old age, with his diocese confined to York, he put the finishing touches to the work of Wulfstan, Ælfric, and Cynsige.[5] At the first opportunity after his election he sent his *chorepiscopus*, Bishop Wulfstan of Worcester, to visit the diocese;[6] and by retaining estates from Worcester he was able to complete the building programme. He bought lands for the great minsters, endowed prebends at York, Beverley, Ripon, and Southwell, finished the refectory at Beverley, and added there a presbytery dedicated to St John the Evangelist. Like Stigand he was a patron of the arts. At our Lord's tomb in Jerusalem Ealdred offered a golden chalice of very wonderful workmanship.[7] At Beverley he provided furnishings of great splendour. He covered the whole of the church from his presbytery to Cynsige's tower with a painted and gilded ceiling, and he installed above the entrance to the choir a bronze pulpit or *ambo* adorned with gold and silver, flanked with arches, and bearing, on an arch above, a rood made out of the same metals. Shortly before 1066 he commissioned Folcard, a monk of St Bertin, who like Goscelin accepted literary commissions in England, to write

[1] 'libertas animi ejus', *GP*, p. 253; cf. 'vir magnanimus', 'Chron. of the archbps. of York' *HCY*, ii. 351.
[2] ' "Hattest thu Urs, have thu Godes kurs" . . . et quod Anglice non apposui, "meam et omnium consecratorum capitum, nisi castellum hinc amoveris. Et scias profecto quod progenies tua non diu de terra S. Mariae haereditabitur" ': Malmesbury, *GP*, p. 253. For the language, see Robertson, *Charters*, p. 210, lines 26–8.
[3] 'Chron. of the archbps. of York', *HCY*, ii. 351. Malmesbury writes that Ealdred, after rebuking the king for his extortionate danegeld, cursed him, *GP*, pp. 252–3.
[4] *ASC D* 1058; Florence, i. 217.
[5] 'Chron. of the archbps. of York', *HCY*, ii. 344–54; *Memorials of Ripon*, ed. J. T. Fowler, Surtees Soc., lxxviii (1886), ii. 182.
[6] *Vita Wulfstani*, p. 19.
[7] *ASC D* 1058.

responsories in honour of St John of Beverley and then a life of the saint, a work which is prefaced by a very flattering notice of the patron.[1]

The pulpit at Beverley was of cast bronze – *opus Theutonicum* – like those he had seen at Cologne.[2] And also from Germany he had derived the impulse to reform his secular chapters.[3] Like Leofric at Exeter and Giso at Wells, Ealdred, by establishing common refectories and dormitories, made provision for a more regular canonical life. He improved the customs at Beverley[4] and he issued for the clergy of his diocese synodical constitutions concerning their dress, almsgiving, the washing of the feet of the poor, and masses for the dead.[5]

York was flattered by Ealdred's appointment. According to Folcard, under Ealdred's rule York 'had cast off its old provincialism'. He was 'a lantern shining in a dark place'. Ealdred outgrew the cloister in which he had been reared and used his talents in a larger world. He obtained papal privileges and royal charters.[6] He became a great man. If it was he who ensured that William the Conqueror took the traditional coronation oath before receiving the crown at his hands, that was his finest hour. Amid the storm of rebellion and invasion he was buried at York [7] – a more fitting resting place than Peterborough or Ely where his recent predecessors had been entombed.

It had been usual in the Anglo-Saxon church for the Life of a saintly or eminent prelate to be written shortly after his death. But after that great trinity – Dunstan, Oswald, and Æthelwold – had been commemorated, the tradition languished, and it was not until the end of the eleventh century that a revival took place. Among the biographies then produced was Coleman's

---

[1] 'ecclesia tui praesulatus tempore priscam rusticitatem exuerit, et in dei laudibus, rudi novitate, tuis doctrinis commonita, decenter adoleverit': *Vita S. Johannis, HCY*, i. 239–42. For the date, see *Vita Ædwardi*, pp. liii ff. It is in any case more likely that Ealdred would have occupied himself with such patronage and reform in the peaceful years 1062–6 than in 1066–9.

[2] The cities of the Rhine were famous for their metalwork. Willigis, archbishop of Mainz, introduced bronze foundries there, A. Hauck, *Kirchengeschichte Deutschlands*, iii. 416. Cf. also the pulpit put in the abbey of Verdun by Abbot Richard (*post* 1004): 'Pulpitum autem aere crebris tunsionibus in laminas tabulasque producto, et deaurato factum esse constat satis accurate et eleganter, et per 12 tabulas 12 prophetarum imagines 12 apostolorum formas subvehentium, sculptorio et polimito opere exaratae sunt' etc. etc.: Hugh abbot of Flavigny, *Chronicon*, II, c. 8, *MPL*, cliv, col. 208.

[3] At Cologne, 'multa quae ad honestatem ecclesiasticae observantiae, multa quae ad rigorem ecclesiasticae disciplinae pertinent audivit, vidit, et memoriae commendavit, quae postea in ecclesiis Anglorum observari fecit': ' Chron. of the archbps. of York ', *HCY*, ii. 345.

[4] 'consuetudinibus ammelioravit', *ibid*. ii. 353.

[5] *Vita S. Johannis, HCY*, i. 241; 'Chron. of the archbps. of York', *HCY*, ii. 354.

[6] *Ibid* ii. 347.   [7] *Ibid*. ii. 350.

Life of Wulfstan, bishop of Worcester 1062–95, written in English, and as old-fashioned as the man it honoured, which survives only in a translation made by William of Malmesbury in the second quarter of the twelfth century. Coleman had been Wulfstan's chaplain in his later years, and his *Vita* is very much a chaplain's story, with the emphasis on the sanctity of the bishop and his pastoral work. Wulfstan appears as a monolithic survival, with all the rugged virtues of the golden age of English piety. There is no subtlety in the portrait, and it seems that we have the picture of an old man, simplified into a type.

Wulfstan, the son of a vassal of the bishop of Worcester, was carefully groomed for a distinguished ecclesiastical career. After elementary education at Evesham abbey he was sent for more advanced instruction to Peterborough abbey, probably through the influence of his bishop, Leofsige (1017–33), who had been abbot of Thorney. He entered the household of the next bishop, Brihtheah (1033–8), and after receiving the priesthood was given one of the country churches on the episcopal estates.[1] At this time he had a religious experience, gave up the eating of meat, refused the bishop's offer of a rich suburban church, and decided to become a monk.[2] This was a true renunciation, for he had found the bishop's favour, and Brihtheah, nephew of an archbishop of York, and himself not averse to nepotism, was a useful patron. Wulfstan rose steadily in the small monastery through the offices of schoolmaster, precentor, and sacristan to the priorate. Extraordinary piety, relentless discipline, and, we may think – although Coleman ignores this side – good education and administrative ability[3] were the qualities which brought him to the

[1] *Vita Wulfstani*, pp. 4–8. Although he lived *in seculo* (p. 7), he was of course a clerk.

[2] *Ibid.* pp. 8, 47. The later reference to Wulfstan as priest at Hawkesbury helps us to understand the progress of his renunciation, which was not as abrupt as appears in the earlier passage.

[3] Coleman, perhaps, takes Wulfstan's scholarship for granted. The bishop's love of religious books is illustrated (*ibid.* pp. 5, 16); and he is often portrayed with a book. But it is always devotional study. Wulfstan's administrative ability seems to have been deliberately depreciated by Coleman, who contrasts Wulfstan's 'simplex religio in deo' with Æthelwig's 'perspicax industria in seculo' (p. 18), and we are given the impression that Wulfstan's only concern was to get enough money to give to the poor. But we know that he was careful about the episcopal estates, which had suffered from Brihtheah's nepotism and Ealdred's usurpations (*ibid.* pp. xxiii–xxiv, 19–20, 24–5), that he employed the sub-prior, Hemming, to reform the church's cartulary (*Hemingi Chartularium*, i. 282 ff.), and that he greatly increased the number of monks at Worcester (*Vita Wulfstani*, p. xxv). It seems improbable, indeed, that so great a disciplinarian would have allowed the secular side of his rule to go untended. Hemming says of him (*Chartularium*, i. 284), 'Erat namque idem reverentissimus pater noster, licet secularium rerum minime cupidus, hujus monasterii plurimum studens semper utilitatibus, et ne sua, ut quorundam predecessorum suorum, negligentia, comissa sibi ecclesia damnum aliquod posteris temporibus pateretur, pro posse suo precavebat providus.'

top; but his appointment to the bishopric in 1062 was due to unusual factors, and the rival candidate, Æthelwig, abbot of Evesham, would probably have been preferred under more ordinary conditions.[1] Wulfstan resisted the appointment with undoubted sincerity; but once he had been persuaded to accept he threw his enormous energy into the task. When the Gospels were opened at his consecration, Archbishop Ealdred read, 'Behold an Israelite indeed in whom is no guile!',[2] a *prognosticon* which was considered truly prophetic.

Coleman believed with justification that Wulfstan harmonized the monk and the prelate, the tenth-century ideal. He was, indeed, a perfect example of a monk-bishop – monk in way of life, bishop in office – performing his duties so simply and ruthlessly that he made no concessions to current fashions. He was imbued with a sense of discipline and duty. Ealdred, until his death, was his superior, first as bishop and then as archbishop; and Wulfstan accepted the unusual burdens which Ealdred put on him sometimes reluctantly but always without resistance. He had learned to obey. But in his own sphere he knew how to rule. Coleman, who informs us fully about the monks' criticism of his external ministry – his 'acting as bishop' – when he was prior,[3] hides from us the tension caused in the monastery by his acting as abbot when bishop,[4] although he makes the reasons for the unrest – Wulfstan's appointment of his brother as nominal prior and his strong, direct, and almost tyrannical government – abundantly clear. Both as monk and bishop Wulfstan's first concern was the cure of souls. Within his small diocese he could display the rustic episcopal virtues of a missionary age. He travelled incessantly, conferring sacraments, dedicating churches, and preaching to the people.[5] He was a true ordinary, supplying the wants left by

---

[1] *Vita Wulfstani*, p. 18. Both Coleman and Hemming (*Hemingi Chartularium*, i. 270-1) contrast Æthelwig's skill in worldly affairs with Wulfstan's unworldliness. Both of course were prejudiced, for Worcester claimed that it had been despoiled by Evesham, and Wulfstan brought a suit against Æthelwig in the Conqueror's reign. Wulfstan's dislike of his adversary is revealed by one of Hemming's stories. Æthelwig died of gout before the end of the case, and Wulfstan, moved by compassion, prayed for him, but was himself immediately attacked by gout. And he told Hemming that it was revealed to him by Heaven that this was a punishment for the prayers he was saying for Æthelwig. So he stopped the prayers and was cured (*ibid.* i. 272-3).

[2] John i: 47; *Vita Wulfstani*, p. 19; cf. Lingard, *Antiquities*, ii. 26, *n.* 2.

[3] *Vita Wulfstani*, pp. 11-15. Bishop Ealdred was probably often absent.

[4] He had, no doubt, the example of St Oswald before him: see *Vita S. Oswaldi*, *HCY*, i. 420-1.

[5] *Vita Wulfstani*, pp. 21, 36-9, 51; Malmesbury, *GP*, p. 281. Wulfstan's compendious breviary for use when travelling, written in 1065-6, has survived: *The Portiforium of Saint Wulstan*, ed. Dom Anselm Hughes, HBS, lxxxix, xc (1956, 1960).

a remiss and scanty priesthood. People flocked to meet him, to confess their sins, to present their children for baptism, to hear him preach. His themes were simple and compelling. Christian peace was his mission and Christ was the model he put before his hearers.

He was tempted by lust and gluttony in his youth; [1] and we can see from his prayers how strong his passions were.[2] He was not meek or gentle. He had to struggle to be good. He confessed to a weakness for idle stories and the vainglories of the world; but the delights of the classical authors,[3] the seduction of eloquence, and the fascination of the arts seem not to have existed for him. Plain rather than extravagantly ascetic in his mode of life,[4] he was a true up-country bishop, rude in health, direct in speech, single-minded in purpose. Only once is there a hint of mortal weakness in his biography. He esteemed beauty in the young men being educated in his household. Coleman says that he embraced in them the grace of divine harmony and from the beauty of their features he deduced the existence of good, saying 'How fair is the Creator who makes creatures so fair.' [5] But he detested the effeminate locks which had come into fashion.[6]

Wulfstan was in the tradition of St Oswald, an earlier bishop of Worcester, whose chasuble he may sometimes have worn,[7] and whose miracles he used to quote.[8] He lived into the reign of William Rufus, a native bishop who exemplified the foreigner's conception of English virtues.[9]

---

[1] Vita Wulfstani, pp. 6–7, 47; Malesmbury, GP, pp. 278–9. Wulfstan esteemed larks above all other food.   [2] The Portiforium of Saint Wulstan, ii. 1 ff.

[3] 'Quamquam non ita hebes in litteris, ut putabatur, fuerit, qui cetera necessaria sciret, praeter fabulas poetarum et tortiles sillogismos dialecticorum, quae nec nosset nec nosse dignaretur': Malmesbury, GP, pp. 280–1.

[4] His rival in this field, the priest Eilmer, was more severe and disapproved of Wulfstan's lighter discourse (Vita Wulfstani, p. 31). Cf. also Malmesbury, GP, pp. 278–9, 281.

[5] Vita Wulfstani, p. 50. Such behaviour was expressly condemned by the Regularis Concordia, c. 11. It was, however, a natural weakness. Cf. the biographer of St Odilo of Cluny (ob. 1049), 'Amabat enim pueros, non lasciviam sectans, sed aetatis innocentiam pie in illis amplexans': Jotsaldus, Vita S. Odilonis, II, c. ii, MPL, cxlii, col. 917.

[6] Any luxuriant head which bowed before him was in danger of mutilation from Wulfstan's pocket-knife (Vita Wulfstani, p. 23).

[7] It was recovered at the translation of the saint in 1004 and preserved and occasionally used at Worcester (Eadmer, Mirac. S. Oswaldi, HCY, ii. 50).

[8] Ibid. ii. 53. When defending in the royal council Worcester's independence of York, Wulfstan had the lives of St Dunstan and St Oswald in his hands and had a vision of them (Vita Wulfstani, p. 25). In the Worcester calendar which has been thought to be his personal possession (English Kalendars before A.D. 1100, HBS, 1934, no. 17) there is a high grading for the feasts of St Oswald.

[9] Cf. the joking exchanges between Geoffrey bishop of Coutances and Wulfstan, Vita Wulfstani, p. 46.

Goscelin of St Bertin, writing *c.* 1100 at St Augustine's Canterbury, re-membered a great speech that his first patron, Herman, bishop of Wiltshire, had made before the pope at the Easter council at Rome in 1050. Herman had spoken of English hospitality offered to all races, of England herself, full of churches, and every day adding new ones to the old, of the innumerable ornaments and bells (*signa*) to be found in these oratories, and of the great benefactions given to Christ by the kings and rich men. England, he went on to say, had a venerable hierarchy of great nobility; and he claimed for her representatives their proper places in the assembly.[1] Some thirty-five years earlier, however, Goscelin, or some other monk of St Bertin, in the book written to honour Queen Edith, had expressed a poor opinion of the late Edwardian church. He reported that Edward on his death-bed had a vision in which he was warned by two holy Norman monks that all the clergy in England were servants of the devil.[2] If Edward indeed had such thoughts he was slipping back to the days when Robert was poisoning his mind. His biographer, however, remarks that the queen and others of the court had been disturbed because the pope had often denounced English laxity through legates and letters, and that although the king and queen had publicized the admonitions, the warnings fell on deaf ears, because the English priests were so attracted by riches and earthly glory that they neglected the true rule.

There is, of course, an exaggerated antithesis here between a saintly court and a corrupt clergy, and a too conventional and sweeping attribution of all the ills to riches and greed.[3] No doubt Stigand was seduced by wealth and Ealdred, perhaps, by worldly glory. Too many bishops had accepted too readily the unsatisfactory arrangements and atmosphere in which they found themselves. There was complacency and, possibly, hedonism, and, despite the example of practical reform given by some of the seculars and the demon-stration in holy living given by some of the monks, there was a general mediocrity.

But material prosperity was really only an aggravating factor. The bishops seem in the main to have been recruited from the middle ranks of the nobility.[4] The kings produced few lawful sons and fewer bastards. Earls

---

[1] *Hist. translat. S. Augustini episcopi, MPL*, clv, col. 32.   [2] *Vita Ædwardi*, p. 75.

[3] St Wulfstan of Worcester was another who bewailed the effeminacy and immorality of these soft days, *Vita Wulfstani*, p. 23.

[4] This seems to have been equally true of the monasteries. At the end of the tenth century Abbot Leofric (perhaps *recte* his brother Ælfric, the future archbishop of Canterbury) of St Albans, the son of an earl of Kent, 'nullum nisi genere clarum vel saltem legitimum in monachatum admittit, asserens ignobiles et illegitimos, ignotos maxime et instabiles, ad enormia fore proniores': *Gesta*

did not commonly put their younger sons into the church.[1] No custom could be better designed to avoid resounding scandal and likewise fame, greatness, or splendour. In England there were no Odos of Bayeux or Poppos of Trèves. The English thegn-bishops, especially if they had been bred as monks, needed a leader; and the basic weakness in the church was the lack of direction both from the throne and from the see of Canterbury. Monks had too often displayed only monastic virtues in their higher office and had counted it a virtue to rob the diocese for the monastery, while the reforms of the seculars had been unco-ordinated. Since Dunstan the best men had been sent to York. And if, in 1066, Ealdred had held Canterbury and Stigand York, the flaws in the church would at least have been gilded over. All the same, a sense of proportion must be kept. It would be hard to find in 1066 a national or ducal church in Christendom where the bishops were distinctly superior as a whole to the English and easy to name several in which the standards were much lower. By the measure of perfection the English episcopate is found wanting. But nowhere was the ideal to be seen.

abbatum monasterii S. Albani, i. 31. Abbot Leofsige of Ely (*ante* 1044) is said to have laid down the policy, 'ut neminem in congregatione monachum susciperent, nisi electos in scientia et praeclaros genere, quorum largitione ecclesia sublimius ditaretur, et fratres solito deinceps victum et vestitum abundantius haberent': *Liber Eliensis*, II, c. 84.

[1] Abbots were, of course, often kinsmen of earls and frequently related to the royal house. But the relationship was seldom very close.

CHAPTER II

The Church and the Kingdom

I. THE BISHOPS AND THE KINGDOM

All ecclesiastical persons held a spiritual office, but most of them had other characters too. The fortunate had lands attached to their office. Many had private estates [1] or family interests. There were few who were not in some sense the servant of a layman. In England in the eleventh century these different capacities seem to have caused little strain, either in *foro conscientiae* or in the public view, and, although the emphasis varied with each individual, it is the unquestioned acceptance of an ambiguous role which is characteristic of the church at this time.[2] Only simple monks could live divorced from all worldly interests. Even St Wulfstan could not forget that his bishopric had estates and that a bishop was by tradition a royal servant. Under these conditions the behaviour of the clergy was not far removed from that of the laity of equivalent social standing, and when they were landholders their interests were similar to those of other landholders. They had a special and accepted function as priests, abbots, or bishops, but in that respect were not different from other men. Society was divided into legal ranks. Since Æthelberht's code, the clergy had had their appropriate position, and while there were, no doubt, problems special to each rank, there is no more evidence of a deliberate and formulated policy common to bishops, abbots, or priests than there is of a concerted movement by earls, thegns, or ceorls. At a time when travelling was restricted and means of publicity and organization did not exist, men were concerned exclusively with the maintenance of their individual rights under the law, and in that way preserved the privileges of their rank.

In royal documents bishops had precedence over earls. This was a relic of the old days when the bishop in his diocese was at least as politically important as the ealdorman of the shire. With the rise of the great earldoms

---

[1] E.g. Cynsige of York gave an estate to Peterborough, where he chose to be buried, 'de patrimonio suo': *Chron. Peterborough*, p. 70.

[2] Cardinal Humbert, *Adversus Simoniacos libri tres*, III, c. ii, *MPL*, cxliii, coll. 1141–2, stresses the inseparability of the office, the diocese, and the estates as a defence against those simoniacs who claimed that they had merely purchased the estates and not the sacred office.

under Cnut the bishop fell behind.[1] Archbishop Wulfstan in his *Institutes of Polity* refers to the bishop as 'Christ's sheriff'.[2] Yet despite this sudden change in the situation it is not difficult to see affinities between the office of bishop and earl. Both were appointed by the king with the advice of his *witan*. Both held an office for life, although the earls, unhampered by any canonical rule, were rapidly transforming the office into an hereditary property. Both assumed the administration of estates and revenue attached to their office and neither found it easy to differentiate between official and private interests. Both owed such independent power as they possessed to the same circumstances – their possession of land and their ability to attract a clientèle, for the bishop had no clerical hierarchy beneath him and could draw little prestige from his spiritual authority over the lowly parish priests, and the power of the earl did not rest principally on the royal reeves who were under his control. There were, no doubt, occasions when the bishop in his vestments surrounded by his robed assistants stood as the representative of the heavenly kingdom, wielding supernatural powers against which the rough swords and spears of the military could be of no avail; but, in general, the bishop, riding with his cnihts and thegns, appeared similar to any other magnate. What is more, there are signs that the bishoprics were developing in the same way as the earldoms. The pluralism for which the Edwardian church is so often blamed was certainly in part due to the dominance of the idea of private property over that of office. Bishops would not surrender one diocese when translated to another. But it may also reflect, under the guise of administrative expediency, an unconscious striving on the part of the bishops, abetted by the king, to recover their old parity with the earls.

Through the endowment of their bishoprics, the archbishop of Canterbury and the bishop of Winchester were among the greatest nobles of the kingdom, and all the bishops had what can be called a magnate's estate. Although all the benefactions had been made to their church, often personified in its patron saint, and the responsibility for the whole was the bishop's, in an economic context there was an inclination to separate the bishop's holding from the rest. Probably in all dioceses there existed in the eleventh century a division between the estates assigned to the episcopal *mensa* and

---

[1] According to II Cnut, 58.1, and other legal tracts of the period, an archbishop was equivalent to an aetheling and a bishop to an ealdorman, and the precedence of the clergy over the laity was always observed in official documents. We can see, however, from Cnut's letter of 1020, c. 11 (Liebermann, *Gesetze*, i. 274), that from an administrative point of view the diocesan bishop had fallen to the level of the shire-reeve. [2] *Polity*, pp. 144-5.

those assigned to the chapter's, and the tendency noticeable in Domesday Book to describe lands held by the chapters as belonging to the church, minster, or patron saint reveals that in ordinary thought the episcopal estate was less integrally within the church than the chapter's. This attitude, although incapable of much development, did allow the bishop some freedom in the arrangement of his lands and give him much of the appearance of a lay nobleman. The main endowment of the bishoprics was book-land, that is to say land held in permanent tenure and free from the king's *feorm*; but most of the land was assessed in hides, carucates, or sulungs, even if beneficially, and therefore subject to the common burdens placed on all land. In the eleventh century this meant that the bishoprics were assessed to the maintenance of bridges and fortifications and to military service,[1] and so to geld and tribute, the one probably a commutation of or supplement to *fyrd*-service, the other an arbitrary application of the idea. Some bishops were even responsible for raising and commanding the contingent of troops that they owed to the king's army;[2] the defence of the episcopal city was at least partly in their charge[3] and their military importance had increased with the acquisition of hundreds, a military unit. They did not however come anywhere near the earls, the king's principal military officers, and their franchises at their best kept out only the officials of the hundred and the sheriff.

All the same, the bishops and some of the abbots had become great landowners, important royal officials, and powerful lords of men, with an influential position in local affairs and a large stake in the kingdom's fortunes. There must have been some provision for the government of the 'honour' after the death of a prelate. Orderic Vitalis, writing in the 1130s, claimed that before the Conquest vacant abbeys were in the hands of the diocesan bishop, and vacant bishoprics in the custody of the archbishop who applied the revenues to good causes.[4] Although evidence is lacking, it is difficult to believe that the king took no interest in the temporalities.

The changing position in England invites comparison with what had happened in other European countries. There had been no uniform develop-

---

[1] Nicholas Brooks, 'The Development of military obligations in eighth and ninth-century England', *England before the Conquest* (Whitelock Festschrift, 1971) 69.

[2] No doubt they were intended, and usually preferred, to provide a suitable deputy commander. But in Edward's reign Bishops Ealdred of Worcester and Leofgar of Hereford commanded armies on the Welsh march.

[3] The bishop of Worcester had, with the king and the earl, the third penny from the city of Worcester: *DB*, i. 173 b i.

[4] *The Ecclesiastical History of Orderic Vitalis*, ed. and trans. M. Chibnall (Oxford Med. Texts) iv (1973) 174.

ment since Carolingian times. In Italy and France, where the royal power had been weak, royal officials had become independent and the bishops had fallen under the control of the usurping powers. At Rome the papacy had become the spoil of the local aristocracy. In Normandy it was the count who appointed to bishoprics. In Germany, on the other hand, the rise of the great tribal, or 'stem', duchies in the ninth century had led to a natural alliance between the episcopate and the relatively strong monarchy and to the deliberate strengthening of the bishops by the king as a counterpoise to the dukes. Otto I (936–73) had changed the bishops into princes under his immediate control, had prevented them from falling under the control of the dukes, and had exploited them as crown agents within duchies which might otherwise have become autonomous units. Until the accession of Edward the Confessor English cultural and political relations with Germany had been close. Cnut especially had been influenced by the traditions of the other great northern power. But no exact parallel can be found. Strains which could arise within the great area of Germany were bound to be less dangerous within the smaller and more coherent English kingdom. And, moreover, owing to the Norman Conquest, these early eleventh-century developments were never fully worked out. The great provincial earldoms disappeared before they had given proof of independent vitality and the bishoprics were filled with men trained under different traditions. Even so, it is German rather than French or Italian history which serves best as a commentary on English affairs.

2. APPOINTMENT TO BISHOPRICS

The collections of canon law did not give clear guidance on the procedure to be followed in choosing a bishop. Election by the clergy and people of the episcopal city had been the primitive practice, and was well supported by the texts; but the need to allow the participation of other interested parties – the fellow bishops, the metropolitan, and the prince – had introduced the factor of consent. Hence the generally accepted canonical form was popular election followed by the appropriate confirmations, a framework which could tolerate most political stresses. Since, however, in the stronger kingdoms royal *consensus* had become nomination and the popular *electio* had been reduced to an acceptance, the roles had been reversed and the intention perverted. In 1057 the reforming Cardinal Humbert, in his *Adversus simoniacos libri tres*, insisted on three stages: election by the clergy, request by the people, and consecration by the bishops of the province on the authority of the metropolitan. Even so, he admitted that only consecration was essential and that the omission of the other requirements could be excusable.[1] He knew enough history to be aware that there had been much variety of procedure in the past, and he was sufficiently adroit to avoid the demand for an impossible uniformity in the present and future.[2] But his formulation, by omitting royal consent from the necessary stages,[3] had true revolutionary purpose; and his argument that the consent of the lay power should be the last stage in the process, and never the first,[4] was a direct attack on current practice.[5] The papal election decree of 1059, inspired by such reasoning, is of interest as an early and timid attempt to establish a new and more acceptable procedure. It gave the first voice to the cardinal-bishops, then allowed for the presence of the other cardinals, and reduced the participation of the general body of clergy and people to a ratifying consent. Although the decree was studiously vague about the powers of the emperor, as was proper in a statement of ecclesiastical law, in the historical context it was aimed much more against the local nobles and their mobs than against him; and so is typical of the period.[6]

The papacy was determined to free itself eventually from lay control, whether it was popular election, aristocratic pressure, or imperial superintendence. But only extremists aimed at the complete freedom of bishops from the secular rulers, and extremists rarely dominated papal counsels. Pope Alexander II did not hesitate to confirm William I's translation of Bishop John of Avranches to Rouen and did not avoid writing of his election by the king.[7] The essential demand of most reformers was for the observance of the

---

[1] III, cc. 5–6, *MPL*, cxliii, coll. 1017–20.

[2] St Peter Damiani claimed that Pope Stephen IX had forced him uncanonically into a cardinal-bishopric – 'non canonice traditum sed violenter injectum': *De abdicatione episcopatus*, *MPL*, cxlv, col. 423.

[3] St Peter Damiani, who was not hostile to royal power, composed an interesting debate on 'utrum sine regis assensu Romani pontificis fieri possit electio' in connexion with Alexander II's election in 1061 without imperial consent: *Disceptatio Synodalis*, *ibid*. coll. 67 ff.

[4] *Adversus simoniacos libri tres*, III, cc. 5–6, *MPL*, cxliii, coll. 1148–9.

[5] Goscelin of St Bertin, writing *c*. 1078 about the appointment of St Wulfsige to Sherborne *c*. 980, uses a more realistic formula – 'Ita dei disposicione et regio favore clerique ac populi acclamacione intronizatur pontificali ipsius ecclesie cathedre': *Vita Wlsini*, p. 76. Cf. the expression used at the beginning of the eleventh century, 'rex . . . iniit post haec consilium cum suis, et elegit eum ad gubernandum episcopatum' (*Vita S. Oswaldi*, *HCY*, i. 406), to which Eadmer adds, 'Primo tamen requiritur voluntas cleri et populi super re ipsa, et cum ingenti exultatione et vociferatione fit vox omnium una': *ibid*. ii. 16.

[6] Cf. H. L. Mikoletzky, 'Bemerkungen zu einer Vorgeschichte des Investiturstreites', *Studi Gregoriani*, iii (1948), 275–80.

[7] Alexander to John, 'comperimus . . . te ex electione principis tui . . . Guillelmi . . . ad majorem sedem promovendum si ex auctoritate sedis apostolicae fuerit assensus': *Ep*. lvi, *MPL*, cxlvi, col. 1339.

law when a bishop was appointed.[1] And the law was gradually declared. The result was to make royal participation less offensive but hardly less effective. In the eleventh century, however, nomination and election worked in harmony as component parts of the procedure to secure the appointment of a bishop.[2] Indeed, it was essential that they should, for the one represented political reality and the other the law. Chroniclers tended to regard them as two aspects of the same event, writing of the election of a bishop or of the king's grant of the office according to the context. *Electio* always had a predominantly passive sense. It was a procedure for giving legal validity to a decision which had usually already been taken. It was only when the demand arose for *libera electio*, and by new bodies of electors, that an active force was created capable of opposing the will of the king.

The law was uncertain because the general conditions had changed enormously since the early days of the church and because local conditions were various. England had one peculiarity – the monastic cathedral – for which the canons offered no special guidance. It had been the aim of the English tenth-century reformers to enforce the Rule of St Benedict, and, according to the Rule, the election of an abbot was to be made unanimously by the whole community of monks or by its *sanior pars*; but should an unworthy abbot be elected, the diocesan bishop, or other abbots, or even Christian neighbours, should intervene and appoint a worthy custodian.[3] As the reformers wished to make the bishop of a monastic see the real abbot of the community, they enacted in the synod of Winchester, held about 970 shortly after the re-establishment of a bishopric of this type, that the election of such a bishop should be conducted in the same way as that of an abbot, that is to say, with the consent and advice of the king and according to the teaching of the Rule of St Benedict. If, however, no monk in the cathedral community was suitable – owing to ignorance or sinfulness – a monk should be chosen from another distinguished monastery with the consent of the king

---

[1] Canon 1 of the synod of Rheims (Leo IX), 1049, insisted on the observance of the traditional form, 'Ne quis sine electione cleri et populi ad regimen ecclesiasticum proveheretur', but made no other demands.

[2] Cf. Hauck, *Kirchengeschichte Deutschlands*, iii. 590, *n.* 4, 'Ernennung und Wahl bilden keinen Gegensatz.' Some historians have caused themselves unnecessary trouble by disregarding the limited significance of the word *electio*. It is best understood as a procedure. This observation applies also to the treatment of the 'election' of kings.

[3] c. 64. A convenient edition, with an English translation, is Abbot Justin McCann, *The rule of St Benedict* (1952). A Latin text with an Anglo-Saxon gloss, apparently of the early eleventh century, is printed EETS, vol. 90, ed. H. Lodgeman (1888).

and the counsel of the brethren of the cathedral church. This rule was to be followed as long as the see remained monastic.[1]

The English law then was clear. There was to be an election whenever possible out of the community, under the guidance of the king. The purpose too was clear. A good king like Edgar was to help the monks to choose the most suitable candidate and to prevent unwise actions and the intervention of the local nobility.[2] The desire was to secure the accession of a good monk – who was to live with the monks as an abbot and not with the pride of a secular bishop.[3] And to achieve this end, since the reformers were not afraid of royal power, the law was weighted in favour of the monarchy. There was, of course, a fundamental ambiguity and the theoretical possibility of a clash. But the law was framed to suit English conditions and seems, for a time at least, to have worked well.

The monastic chapters, familiar with the Rule of St Benedict and the English law,[4] were by no means passive recipients of royal nominees. Now and then they tried to play an effective part in the selection of their bishop. But they were well aware that if they proceeded in too independent a way they ran the risk not only of the king refusing his consent but of his anger as well. A glance at the history of some of the better-documented monastic sees will show the interplay of the forces.

Sherborne certainly resented Cnut's expulsion of Bishop Brihtwine and his intrusion of Ælfmaer, abbot of St Augustine's Canterbury. When the intruder had to retire owing to blindness, Brihtwine was restored and, on his death in 1045, was succeeded by his brother Ælfwold, a Winchester monk.[5] But Herman, appointed in 1058, was Queen Edith's choice.[6]

Between 1006 and 1049 three successive bishops of Dorchester were

---

[1] *Regularis Concordia*, c. 9. These electoral rules were written into the (?) spurious charter of Edgar to Ramsey Abbey, dated December 974: *Chron. Ramsey*, pp. 187–8.

[2] Earl Æthelwin, the lay patron of Ramsey abbey, when it seemed that he and Archbishop Oswald, the abbot, were nearing the end of their lives (992), humbly begged the monks, should they have to elect an abbot, to choose Germanus, a disciple of Oswald and the expelled abbot of Winchcombe, 'cum concordia pacis, sicuti moniti decernunt S. Benedicti': *Vita Oswaldi*, HCY, i. 468. Actually they elected Eadnoth, a monk who had been in charge of *exteriora*, and King Æthelred appointed Germanus abbot of Cholsey: *Chron. Ramsey*, p. 110.   [3] *Regularis Concordia*, c. 9.

[4] W. H. Stevenson was suspicious of clauses in charters granting the right of free election to abbeys: *Cartularies of Muchelney and Athelney*, Somerset Rec. Soc. xiv (1899), 41, *n*. But Eric John, 'Some Latin Charters of the Tenth Century Reformation in England', *Revue Bénédictine*, lxx (1960), 339, is more trusting. Cf. *Vita Ædwardi*, p. 18: 'huncque [Ælric] et affectu communi et petitione eligunt preesse regulari.' The monks petition the king to accept him, 'utpote in eadem ecclesia nutritum et secundum canonica instituta electum'.

[5] See above, p. 72.   [6] *Ibid.*, p. 82.

taken from the abbey of Ramsey, and, although the see was not moved into the monastery, the connexion was most intimate. Ramsey was in close contact with Fleury and the Continent, and nowhere in England was the cult of St Benedict stronger. Archbishop Oswald had obtained a papal privilege for his favourite abbey giving the community the right of free election, and between 992 and 1043, on the strength of this, the monastery seems to have been successful, except in one case, in electing its abbot freely.[1] It must also have had a say in the selection of the two bishops who followed Eadnoth I [2] – Æthelric in 1016 [3] and Eadnoth II in 1034. Indeed, the notice of the 1034 election states the proceedings in the strictest canonical form.[4] In 1049, however, King Edward broke with tradition and appointed a clerk from his household.

Canterbury, although not always truly monastic, also tried occasionally to make a free election. In 994 Sigeric archbishop of Canterbury died, and the intention of translating Ælfric, sometime monk of Abingdon and abbot of St Albans, from Ramsbury seems to have alarmed the chapter, for the monks of Christ Church had degenerated into secular clerks and Ælfric was to prove himself a stronger reformer than Sigeric. Two of the clerks raced Ælfric to Rome and tried to buy the pallium for one of themselves. But the pope required the royal letter, and the scheme failed.[5] In 1051, according to the *Vita Ædwardi*, which is sympathetic to Earl Godwin and his family, the people

---

[1] In 992 (*Chron. Ramsey*, p. 110), 1006 (p. 116), 1020 (p. 124), and 1043 (p. 156). But the monastery was in trouble at the beginning of Cnut's reign, for in 1016 Bishop Eadnoth I of Dorchester, a former Ramsey monk, and Abbot Wulfsi were killed in the defeat of Edmund Ironside's army at Ashingdon. Cnut allowed another Ramsey monk, Æthelric, to go to Dorchester, but he appointed a fierce German, Wythman, to the abbey. Wythman failed to control the monks, naturally received no support from his bishop, and left to go on a pilgrimage to Jerusalem (pp. 118–24). Doubtless connected with these events is the Peterborough story that Cnut, because of the crimes of some Ramsey monks, ordered the abbey to be destroyed and the monks 'exterminated'. Abbot Ælfsi of Peterborough, with the aid of the queen and the advantage of finding Cnut merry from his cups, got the king to mitigate the sentence – on condition that Ælfsi assumed responsibility for Ramsey and appointed a Peterborough monk as its abbot. 'Set ille amiciciam quam inceperat vicinis suis servans, . . . abbatem illis ex propria congregacione constituit, libertatemque imperpetuum donavit' (*Chron. Peterborough*, p. 50). Ramsey, however, claimed to have elected Æthelstan as abbot in 1020 after Wythman's departure (*Chron. Ramsey*, p. 124). A later proposal of Cnut, to establish a sister nunnery at Ramsey, although opposed, was not necessarily a sign of his displeasure (*ibid*. p. 126).

[2] 'conclamante in ejus electionem tam clero quam populo': *ibid*. p. 115.

[3] 'rege tam cleri quam populi votis consentiente': *ibid*. p. 120.

[4] 'vota et voces tam cleri quam populi in Ædnothum coalumnum ipsius [Æthelric] conveniunt, et, rege Cnutone assentiente, post eum in episcopum consecratur': *ibid*. p. 148.

[5] *ASC F* 995, in a later insertion which contains some spurious matter; but this story may be true.

and monks of the church elected Ælric, one of the monks and a kinsman of Godwin, as archbishop, and asked the earl to use his influence with the king to get his assent. But Edward refused the petition and appointed his own candidate, the bishop of London.[1]

Where there was a true community of monks, or even of degenerate monks, there was a domestic policy and a voice which could make itself heard. But clearly it was often ignored; and by the end of Cnut's reign the distinction between monastic and other sees was becoming blurred. Just as monks were appointed to secular churches, so monastic cathedrals were given to clerks. Only at Worcester and Sherborne was no violence done to the *Regularis Concordia*. King's priests were appointed to Winchester in 1032 (Ælfwine) and 1047 (Stigand), and to Canterbury in 1052 (Stigand). The Ramsey-Dorchester connexion was broken in 1049. The resentment this caused in monastic circles helps to explain the evil reputations which Ælfwine, Ulf, and Stigand enjoy.

In the case of abbeys the king seems sometimes to have allowed, or promised to allow, free election.[2] The monastic sees were treated with less indulgence. Had they been unimportant they might have escaped this close control; but the archbishop of Canterbury and the bishop of Winchester were key officials in the kingdom, and the wishes of the monks were unlikely to suit the policy of the court. The disregard of free election caused some bad feeling, but no real clash on principle. The whole church cried out against the rejection of Ælric and the appointment of Robert to Canterbury in 1051, according to the *Vita Ædwardi*.[3] And in the same way most chroniclers condemned Edward's grant of Dorchester to his priest Ulf in 1049.[4] But in each case it was the unwisdom of the choice rather than unconstitutional behaviour which was blamed.

[1] pp. 18–19.

[2] At Ramsey (above, p. 102, n. 1). King Eadwig, according to a diploma of 959 (Thorpe, *Diplomatarium*, p. 193), gave permission for the monks of Abingdon to elect their next abbot, 'secundum regularia beati Benedicti instituta', and Edward on nominating Rothulf as abbot in 1051, promised free election next time (*Chron. Abingdon*, i. 463). The *Chron. Peterborough* uses perhaps significantly different language for the various Peterborough elections: Ælfsi (1006) 'quem sibi omnis concors congregatio abbatem elegerat et postulaverat' (p. 48); Earnwi (*c.* 1055) 'electus est ab omni congregacione' (p. 65); Leofric (*c.* 1057) 'electus est cum consensu regis et ipsius . . . a tota congregatione' (p. 65) . . . 'a rege Edwardo et regina Edgit in tantum dilectus est ut pro amore eius dederunt S. Petro et ipsi alias abbacias' (p. 66).

[3] 'totius ecclesie filiis hanc iniuriam pro nisu suo reclamantibus', p. 19.

[4] *ASC* C 1049, D 1050. The indignation was probably largely due to Edward's failure to appoint a Ramsey monk.

If there was little free election to monastic sees, even less is to be expected in the case of the secular bishoprics.[1] On the Continent at this time chapters of canons occasionally tried to elect freely. But in England, where the non-monastic sees were generally poor, the clerks or canons few, and the sense of community weak, there seems to have been little spirit in these churches. Durham was the most independent, and its history in this period illustrates what may have been a general trend.

As a result of the Viking conquests, which almost completely disorganized religious life in Northumbria, the succession of bishops was a purely domestic affair in the tenth century: the survivors of the Lindisfarne church, the clerks of St Cuthbert, and their descendants had elected bishops out of their own community during their stay at Chester-le-Street.[2] But in the relatively quieter conditions which prevailed after Bishop Aldhun moved the see to Durham (995) the bishops began to play a part in the political life of the province;[3] and when Cnut re-established the English monarchy, the Durham church sought his patronage. Edmund was freely elected by the clerks in 1020, after a vacancy of almost three years due simply to domestic difficulties, but he was taken to the king for his approval, a step, so far as we know, without precedent. Cnut gave a cheerful consent and issued the order for Edmund's consecration.[4] Edmund died when with King Harthacnut at Gloucester, and the dean of the clerks hurried to the king to buy the succession. But the simoniac king and bishop died soon after; and during the reign of Edward the brothers Æthelric and Æthelwine, Peterborough monks, the former a man whom Edmund had chosen to instruct him in the monastic life, ruled in turn.[5] Both these appointments were against the desire of the clerks of St Cuthbert; and it is clear that the influence of the earls of Northumbria, probably supporting the policy of Edward, had become decisive. In this story can be seen a distant church gradually brought under the control of the resurgent monarchy and the appointment of monks secured by lay authority.

But elsewhere there was no tradition of independence. Most cathedral minsters seem to have been served by a very small and undistinguished body of clerks or canons – apparently from five to seven on the eve of the Conquest[6]

---

[1] Lingard, *Antiquities*, i. 92–6.   [2] Symeon, *HDE*, i. 56–78.

[3] Cf. *De obsessione Dunelmi, ibid.* i. 215–20. Aldhun witnessed a royal charter in 1009 (unpublished document in the William Salt Collection, Stafford, quoted *EHD*, i. 96).

[4] Symeon, *HDE*, i. 85–6.

[5] *Ibid.* i. 91–2.   [6] See below, p. 241.

– and these obscure communities cannot have exerted much influence on the king and *witan*. That they did not freely elect their bishop is proved by the rarity of promotions *e gremio*.[1]

The Anglo-Saxon chronicles often notice the succession of bishops, but in laconic words. The usual form is that X died and Y succeeded him. The Abingdon version (*C*), however, sometimes states that the king gave the office. This seems nothing more than individuality of style, and, when the different notices are read together, the impression is strong that it was so generally understood that the king appointed that it was hardly worth mentioning.[2] No evidence can be brought against this hypothesis, and, whenever greater detail is given, either in the chronicles or elsewhere, it is supported. Yet the will of the king is often a fiction, and Edward the Confessor is usually regarded as a weak ruler. Obviously behind each appointment lies a story; but as few of these histories have come down to us, the interplay of the various interests can rarely be analysed.

The appointment recorded in most detail is that of Wulfstan to Worcester in 1062. When Ealdred of Worcester was promoted to York in 1060, the pope granted the pallium only on condition that he should surrender the other see and substitute the best man he could find in his diocese. Legates returned with the archbishop from Rome to see that it was carried out.[3] According to the most trustworthy authority, Coleman, Wulfstan's chaplain, whose life of the bishop has survived in its translation by William of Malmesbury,[4] Ealdred hesitated between Æthelwig abbot of Evesham and Wulfstan prior of Worcester; but he left the legates with the latter while they waited during Lent for the royal court to meet. When, at Easter, the matter of the election came before the court, possibly at Winchester, the legates advocated Wulfstan's appointment; the king was sympathetic; the archbishops of Canterbury and York and then the earls of Wessex and Mercia supported the proposal, each in his own way; and finally the thegns (*milites*) acclaimed the decision. Wulfstan was sent for and ordered to assume the office. He refused, and was only brought to acceptance by the legates' reminder of the obedience he owed the pope.[5] Coleman clearly regarded Ealdred as the prime mover in the

---

[1] The only bishops known to have been promoted from the chapter are the monks Æthelnoth to Canterbury in 1020 and Wulfstan to Worcester in 1062.

[2] The argument that *C* was royalist, *E* pro-Godwin, and *D* remote from court, cannot be pressed.

[3] *Vita Wulfstani*, pp. 16–17; *Vita Ædwardi*, pp. 34–7; Florence, i. 218.

[4] *Vita Wulfstani*, p. 18.

[5] According to Florence, i. 220, it was the hermit Wulfsi who convinced Wulfstan.

business, manipulating others to achieve his ends. This accords with what we know of Ealdred, and certainly he arranged the surrender of Worcester in a way which suited himself.[1]

The chronicle of 'Florence of Worcester', which is not completely independent of Coleman's Life,[2] gives the story a different twist, due doubtless to the fact that the author was adapting and not translating. In this version the king allowed free election and the legates incited the clergy and people to elect Wulfstan.[3] The emphases here seem false.

The papal ultimatum and the presence of the legates in England and at the king's council give the appointment unusual features. But some general points can be made. The nomination is the concern of the king and *witan*. The witenagemot is a fluid institution which can easily accommodate papal legates. The king presides and controls, and on this occasion seems to do no more than preside. Among the *witan* the interested parties have their say, first the archbishops, then the earls, Harold, the senior earl, taking precedence over Ælfgar in whose earldom Worcester was. The thegns concur, and faintly in the background can be heard the voices of the clergy and people.

It is, indeed, likely that the feeling that the king should not act without counsel, and that important acts should receive the widest publicity and be performed in the most solemn manner, applied to the appointment of bishops.[4] But references to the participation of the *witan* are few [5] and allow the construction of no elaborate conciliar machinery.[6] Although on some

---

[1] Malmesbury, *GP*, p. 280, makes Ealdred propose Wulfstan because of his incapability, simplicity, and holiness, under cover of which the archbishop's depredations would be safe. Hemming wrote, 'Cernens autem venerandus archiepiscopus Aldredus hunc servum dei bonis operibus insudare, . . . in episcopatum . . . decrevit eum sullevare' (*Hemingi Chartularium*, ii. 406).

[2] R. R. Darlington, *Vita Wulfstani*, pp. xi–xvi.   [3] Florence, i. 218–21.

[4] The author of the first *Vita Oswaldi*, an early-eleventh-century monk of Ramsey, possibly Byrhtferth, always describes the king as taking council in appointing to bishoprics (*HCY*, i. 406, 420).

[5] The author of the first *Vita Dunstani*, the Saxon priest writing *c.* 1000, describes Dunstan as being elected bishop in a council, by the wish of the king, then states that the king appointed him to Worcester and London, and finally has King Edgar translate him to Canterbury 'ex divino respectu et sapientium consilio' (*Memorials of St Dunstan*, pp. 36–8). In 995 Ælfric was translated from Ramsbury to Canterbury 'by King Æthelred and all the witan' (*ASC F*). The Abingdon chronicle states that in 1051 King Edward held a council at London in mid-Lent and appointed Robert as archbishop of Canterbury and Spearhavoc as bishop of London, and gave Rothulf his kinsman the abbey of Abingdon. The D and E versions simply say that the king appointed these men (*ASC C* 1050, *D* 1051, *E* 1048). See also below p. 109, n. 1.

[6] See Tryggvi J. Oleson, *The Witenagemot in the Reign of Edward the Confessor* (1955).

occasions no doubt the king received a delegation from the vacant church or sent for representatives,[1] and although the king may often have granted bishoprics at the larger courts which assembled at the great church festivals, there is no evidence to support the view that the king had to summon a formal meeting of interested members to transact this type of business. It is possible that some of the allusions in eleventh-century writers to the king's independent action may have had a reproachful colouring; [2] but the grievance was probably wilful and unwise decisions rather than neglect of lawful procedure.

The earls seem to have been frequently at court. But there is little evidence that either as a class or even as individuals they were specially interested in the appointments to bishoprics. Most episcopal estates were modest and their regalities insignificant. The office was not coveted for the younger sons of leading noble families. Bishops were traditionally royal creations, and the earls had no motive to dispute the arrangement. Pluralist bishops held sees in several earldoms, and the connexion between Worcester and York had no political significance. Godwin was earl of Wessex for over thirty years and in four reigns. He was a strong and cunning man with a craving for power. But he never acquired control over the nomination to bishoprics within his earldom; indeed, he seems to have had little influence over appointments. It cannot be claimed that he raised Lyfing, abbot of Tavistock, to Crediton in 1027,[3] even though they were often in association later; Grimketel bought Selsey from King Harold Harefoot in 1039,[4] and king's priests were appointed to Winchester in 1032 (Ælfwine), Ramsbury in 1045 (Herman), Devon and Cornwall in 1046 (Leofric), and Selsey in 1047 (Heca). Nor can Stigand's rise from king's priest to archbishop of Canterbury, by way of the bishoprics of Elmham (1043) and Winchester (1047), be regarded as the work of Godwin. Both seem to have been opportunists whose interests occasionally coincided.

The powerlessness of Godwin, especially in 1045-6, when he is thought to have dominated the king, is all the more remarkable since he is believed to have taken a rather sinister interest in church matters. It is known that he interfered in Canterbury affairs. In 1044 Archbishop Eadsige of Canterbury

---

[1] Cf. *Vita Wlsini*, p. 79, where the priests (? of Worcester) discussed with King Æthelred a replacement for the sick Bishop 'Wulfsige' of Worcester: 'Pridie autem quam ascenderat sanus, reliqui sacerdotes coram rege consultabant de dando eidem Wlsino successore'.

[2] Cf. the statement that Robert of Jumièges was appointed to London *regio favore* (*Vita Ædwardi*, p. 17) and then made archbishop *regis munere* (*ibid*. p. 19).

[3] See Florence, i. 185.   [4] Malmesbury, *GP*, p. 205.

wished to retire – temporarily, it seems – owing to bad health. 'By the permission and on the advice of the king and Earl Godwin' he consecrated
Siward, abbot of Abingdon, as suffragan. This he did secretly because he
feared that if his intention were more widely known someone else would ask
for the post or someone less suitable would buy it.[1] Clearly Edward was
still not master in his house and a faction dared not work in the open. By the
time that Eadsige died in 1050 Edward had become independent, and he
rejected the earl's petition for his kinsman.[2] Nor is there evidence that any
other of the great earls of this period had an exclusive influence over the
giving of bishoprics in their earldoms.[3]

There seems no reason to doubt, therefore, that as a rule these kings gave
greatest weight to the advice of their ecclesiastical counsellors when making
church appointments; and even if the queens, Emma and Edith,[4] were at
times influential, their interventions were probably inspired by their own
clerical advisers. Æthelred and Cnut were swayed by a church in which the
monastic reform of Edgar's reign was still a vital force, and there were some
powerful bishops among their domestic counsellors.[5] Edward's behaviour has
been variously explained,[6] but it seems capable of bearing the same simple
interpretation.

In England as in Germany the king nominated the bishops. But were the
canonical forms observed? Was there a regular *electio*? English practice is
not clear. Certainly the monastic writers describe the proper procedure,[7]

---

[1] *ASC* C 1044, E 1043; Malmesbury, *GP*, p. 34. But Florence, i. 199, writes that Siward was
appointed by the consent of the king and the magnates of the kingdom.

[2] *Vita Ædwardi*, p. 19.

[3] The only clear example of comital influence is the appointment of Harold's clerk, Leofgar,
to Hereford in 1056. But Leofwine was probably promoted from Coventry to Lichfield in 1053
through the influence of Earl Leofric's family.

[4] Edith's interest is well attested. Cf. *Vita Ædwardi*, pp. 41–2. She helped Bishop Giso of Wells
(*Ecclesiastical Documents*, p. 17), and is said to have promised Bishop Herman that he should have
Sherborne as well as Ramsbury (Malmesbury, *GP*, p. 183). Walter bishop of Hereford is described
as having been her chaplain (Florence, i. 218).

[5] We learn that Archbishop Dunstan persuaded King Æthelred to appoint Ælfheah to Winchester
n 984, Adelard in *Memorials of St Dunstan*, pp. 61–2.

[6] Freeman's view that Edward advanced Normans while the house of Godwin favoured
Lotharingians is an improbable simplification. Why should Godwin have desired the promotion
of royal clerks?

[7] See above, pp. 102, n. 4; 103, nn. 2–4; 104, n. 2. In Osbern's Life of St Dunstan, written at the
end of the eleventh century, there may be anachronisms. He describes Dunstan, seeking consecration to Worcester, presenting the archbishop of Canterbury with the petition of the clergy and
people (*Memorials of St Dunstan*, p. 103), and Dunstan's promotion to London in the words,

and, although it may be that they were simply using the appropriate form of words, it is likely that a bishop appointed to a monastic see would normally be sent to the chapter to get its formal approbation and be welcomed by the clergy and laity of the cathedral city. For the secular sees there is no direct evidence, and it is possible that a preliminary visit to a distant church served by a few priests might sometimes be shirked. Bishops were presumably appointed at a ceremony as solemn as the resources of the court permitted.[1] On occasion, as at Worcester in 1062, the court was not far distant. It may be that at other times representatives of the chapter who announced the death, or who arrived after hearing of it, were retained at court. But we may well believe that the acclamation which a new bishop received often represented his election by the clergy and people of his cathedral city in a very attenuated form.

We are also ill-informed about the investiture ceremony. In the empire of Charlemagne it had been usual for a royal precept to be issued ordering the consecration of the bishop whom the king had appointed. The metropolitan acted on the mandate and conferred the office by giving the bishop his ring and pastoral staff. Such a procedure is envisaged in a form for an investiture ceremony, entitled 'a prayer on the occasion of a bishop's election', included by Bishop Leofric of Exeter among the liturgical pieces he collected. The brethren pray that they and their elect may be illuminated by the grace of the Holy Ghost. The bishop is admonished before making his profession. He is then given the ring, 'the symbol of discretion, honour, and faith', and the staff, 'the symbol of sacred government'.[2] The occasion would seem to be the visit of the metropolitan to the church of the bishop-elect. In the ninth century, however, the custom arose of the king investing the bishop with the symbols, and it became normal practice in the tenth century. Soon the ceremony was affected by feudal ideas. The German king granted the church – *accipe ecclesiam* – just as he granted a lay honour or fief, and the oath which the bishop then took was assimilated to an oath of fealty. English habit in the eleventh century is uncertain. Usually the bishop-elect was issued with at least two writs: one informing the appropriate shire court or courts of the

'rogatu regis ac principum . . . annuentibus quoque omnibus ejusdem urbis habitatoribus et importunis vocibus illius nomen acclamantibus': *ibid.* p. 105.

[1] For the credulous, the tenth day of the moon would have been auspicious. See *Leechdoms*, iii. 178–9.

[2] *The Leofric Missal*, ed. F. E. Warren, pp. 215–17. Cf. the forms for the consecration of a bishop in *The Benedictional of Archbishop Robert*, ed. H. A. Wilson, HBS, xxiv (1903), 128–9, and in *The Lanalet Pontifical*, ed. G. H. Doble, HBS, lxxiv (1937), 58–9.

appointment,[1] and another requiring the metropolitan to consecrate.[2] In the first the king states baldly that he has granted the bishopric,[3] and Edward the Confessor had been brought up in Normandy where the church was feudalized. Nevertheless, the similarity to Carolingian procedure makes it possible that the old custom still prevailed in England,[4] and we should note that the English monk Eadmer believed that there were many ecclesiastical innovations after 1066.[5]

The church always laid emphasis on correct procedure because this preserved a principle through the shifts of social and political forces. Yet the form could be without significance at the time. Even if canonical procedure was observed in the English kingdom it cannot be inferred that there was a greater refinement of attitude than in the other kingdoms of the West. The king gave the bishopric, the whole episcopal dignity, the spiritual office and the worldly goods, all the rights and possessions of the see. The English, Norman, and German priests and monks who accepted the royal gift were not likely to question this assumption, for it was general in Europe.

These perverted, but ubiquitous, practices were sharply criticized by Cardinal Humbert. Undue secular interference in ecclesiastical affairs was bad, and lay investiture of bishops was wrong. Humbert wrote forcefully, and he harshly censured the German and French monarchies for their behaviour. His views here were radical and revolutionary and were to cause an upheaval in western Christendom. But his main attack was against simony – the buying and selling of spiritual offices – and an important distinction in his attitude must be noticed. Irregularities in procedure, even serious irregularities,

---

[1] Cf. Harmer, *Writs*, nos. 50, 64, 115; for an abbot, see *ibid.* no. 23; for supplementary or confirmatory writs, see *ibid.* nos. 65, 110. In 1051 Spearhavoc on his appointment to London must have presented this type of writ first, for he remained in possession of the bishopric through the summer and autumn despite his failure to get consecration (*ASC E* 1048). In Cnut's reign, however, the writ to put the bishop in possession of the bishopric seems to have been issued, on one occasion at least, after the archbishop had certified that he had consecrated (K. 1314).

[2] In 1051 Spearhavoc approached Archbishop Robert of Canterbury with the king's writ and seal to the effect that he should consecrate him as bishop of London (*ASC E* 1048). A similar letter must have been sent to the pope when he was asked to consecrate. In 995, according to doubtful evidence, the pope refused to consecrate a clerk as archbishop of Canterbury because he could not show a royal letter (see above, p. 103).

[3] 'ich habbe geunnan . . . thes bissopriche' (Harmer, *Writs*, no. 64, 1060/1, no. 115, 1062); 'ich habbe unnen . . . the abbotriche' (no. 23, 1065/6); 'ego concessi . . . istum episcopatum' (no. 50, Latin translation of a writ of 1061).

[4] One of the fullest literary accounts of the making of a bishop – Edmund of Durham in 1020 (Symeon, *HDE*, i. 85–6) – gives that impression that Cnut's part was confined to assent.

[5] *Historia Novorum*, pp. 9–10.

and likewise reprehensible conduct, did not necessarily invalidate the authority of a properly consecrated bishop. He was a true bishop until he was canonically deposed. But when a bishopric was purchased, then the act was null and void. The simoniac, as a heretic, was a *pseudo-episcopus*, a thief and a robber in the Lord's sheepfold, his ministrations were ineffective, and his deposition was merely the publication of the nullity.[1] Humbert's attitude towards simoniacs was too extreme for many other ardent reformers,[2] and his views on lay investiture were at the time simply idealistic. Most men were aware that the canonical procedures for the making of a bishop were obsolete as well as unenforceable and that all kinds of irregularity had to be tolerated. But there was little sympathy anywhere for the simoniac; and those bishops who had purchased their office were usually ashamed of their action, and normally confessed and resigned their bishopric when taxed with this heretical crime. All the same, moralists pushed their definition of simony farther than customary behaviour would allow. The custom that every gift should be met with a counter-gift was deep-rooted in Germanic society and fundamental to the law of property.[3] To break this rule in connexion with the sacraments was the aim of the reformers. But when all the clergy felt that it was, to say the least, impolite to receive a bishopric or an abbey without making a present in return, few could have resisted what good breeding required. Hence simony could cover anything from the naked purchase of a church to the customary token in return, and probably no community was ever guiltless of its more innocent forms.

In England there is no evidence that Kings Edgar, Æthelred,[4] or Cnut sold bishoprics, and it is not likely that they did. Simony is mentioned a few times in the disturbed period 1038–44; but the orders of the English bishops seem to have passed the test at the council of Rheims in 1049; and it was not until after the Norman Conquest that serious charges were brought against the English episcopate. In 1070 three bishops were removed; and in the twelfth century William of Malmesbury expressed the Norman view that

---

[1] Humbert's general attitude is epitomised by 'in tantum haeretici differunt a catholicis, ut quantumlibet criminosus catholicus acceptior sit deo et tolerabilior hominibus, quam quantumlibet justus, si dici potest, haereticus': *Adversus simoniacos libri tres*, III, c. xxxii, *MPL*, cxliii, col. 1193.

[2] St Peter Damiani, for instance, in his *Liber qui dicitur gratissimus* (*MPL*, cxlv, coll. 99 ff.) argued that 'donum dei nulla ministrorum contagione polluitur', and, on the analogy of baptism by heretics, that simoniacs should not be re-ordained. He himself followed this course when he reconciled the simoniacs of Milan, *Actus Mediolani, ibid.* coll. 94 ff.

[3] Cf. H. D. Hazeltine in Whitelock, *Wills*, p. xxv.

[4] Æthelred, however, certainly sold the abbey of Abingdon (K. 684).

Archbishop Stigand (also deposed in 1070) had made a public market of bishoprics and abbeys,[1] a way of saying that the simple Edward had been the victim of an unscrupulous man.[2] Cardinal Humbert charged metropolitans with simony and quoted the proverb that the hawk cannot rob without feathers.[3] And when we consider the worldly atmosphere of Edward's court, Malmesbury's charges are not completely incredible. It is, however, difficult to get at the truth, especially since the line between permissible and unlawful gifts was, in the absence of an investigation and verdict, a matter for the consciences of the persons involved. What does seem clear is that no legal charge of simony was brought by the Normans against Edward's prelates and that few, if any, of these were guilty of it in a gross or open form.

Stigand himself was not accused of simony in 1070.[4] This silence seems by itself to be almost conclusive. Then if the bishops promoted after 1052 are examined, it seems most unlikely that many of them were parties to a simple mercenary bargain. Between 1052 and 1066 all the English sees fell vacant except for Canterbury-Winchester (Stigand), Elmham (Æthelmaer, Stigand's brother), London (William), Ramsbury-Sherborne (Herman), and Exeter (Leofric). Six monks and four clerks were promoted bishop, of whom Stigand consecrated certainly two and possibly three.[5] The orders of the others were faultless. Of the ten, one monk-archbishop (Ealdred) and two secular bishops, none defamed of simony, died before 1070. In that year twelve of Edward's bishops, seven promoted in Stigand's time, came under review. Of the older five, Stigand and his brother Æthelmaer were deposed. Of the junior seven, three monks lost their sees. Leofwine of Lichfield, a married man, resigned,[6] Æthelwine of Durham, a political rebel, was driven out; and Æthelric of Selsey was deposed at the second (Whitsun) council for unknown reasons.[7] Spared were the monks, Siward of Rochester (consecrated

---

[1] 'publicas nundinas ex episcopatibus et abbatiis faciens', *GP*, pp. 35–6.

[2] Coleman, as translated by Malmesbury, wrote of Edward, 'in cuius pectore nichil umquam nundinator ecclesiarum, nichil unquam deprehendit avarus, quod suis conduceret artibus': *Vita Wulfstani*, p. 18.

[3] 'accipiter, licet conetur, sine pennis et plumis non praedatur', *op. cit.* III, c. xvi, col. 1165.

[4] See below, pp. 302 ff.

[5] The consecrator of Leofgar of Hereford (1056) is unknown; but Leofgar may well have been killed before consecration.

[6] Wulfstan of Worcester was put in charge of the see as a temporary measure: *Vita Wulfstani*, p. 26.

[7] If he were deposed because Stigand had consecrated him, the decision was unjust. It is possible that King William wanted a safe and younger man in his strategic see. Æthelric, described as a

by Stigand) and St Wulfstan of Worcester, and the Lotharingian clerks, Giso of Wells and Walter of Hereford. Clearly no one principle or common charge justified the several removals, and Pope Alexander II was troubled by the action taken. In one letter to Lanfranc he complained that the case against Æthelric was defective. It had been heard by delegates of the legates (*suppositi*) and appeared not to have been fully investigated (*non ad plenum tractata*). Æthelric was to be reinstated and then canonically tried by Lanfranc as papal delegate.[1] In a second letter, defending the monastic constitution of Winchester against its opponents, he inquired anxiously about the fate of an imprisoned bishop whose liberation he had ordered.[2] The pope had little doubt that, in some cases at least, ecclesiastical justice had been perverted by reasons of state.

The charge that Stigand sold abbeys as well as bishoprics cannot be investigated owing to the lack of evidence. But no abbot, so far as is known, was deposed after the Conquest because he had bought his abbey. The formal verdict is clear. Seven English bishops, four promoted in Stigand's time, including one consecrated by him, survived the scrutiny of 1070, and those removed do not seem to have been accused of simony. And no other verdict could be expected. William I can hardly have wished to inculpate his predecessor, the man who had bequeathed him the throne. Nor was it necessary for his purpose. Yet the impression remains that Edward's court was to some extent shielded. Edward and Edith readily accepted gifts.[3] And curious transactions are to be found. Bishop Herman, who had been Edith's priest, through her good offices added Sherborne to Ramsbury on Ælfwold's death in 1058. The statement in Domesday Book that the manor of Sherborne had been held before Bishop Osmund by Queen Edith, and before her by Bishop Ælfwold,[4] suggests that the queen's generosity had a price. Giso, another royal priest, who obtained Wells in 1060, likewise lost the manor of

---

very old man, was, after his deposition, taken in a carriage on the king's orders to the Trial on Penenden Heath to give expert advice on English law (*Anglia Sacra*, i. 335). According to Florence, ii. 6, he was imprisoned at Marlborough.

[1] *Ep*. lxxxiii, *MPL*, cxlvi, coll. 1365–6.

[2] 'Praeterea de liberatione capti episcopi quod experientiae tuae commisimus, valde miramur an hoc tua praetermiserit negligentia, an regis poenam adjiciens contempserit inobedientia. Per praesentiam etiam latorem dilectionem tuam interpellare curavimus, ut quae apud te impetrare desiderat, dummodo concedenda sint, tua sibi benignitas pro nostra charitate concedat.' (*Ep*. cxliii, *loc. cit.* col. 1416.) Although the context is Winchester, Æthelwine of Durham is probably the bishop in question.

[3] See above, p. 53, *n*. 2.   [4] *DB*, i. 77 a i.

Milverton to Edith.[1] And Edith was Stigand's friend.[2] Spearhavoc's promotion from abbot of Abingdon to bishop of London in 1051 cost the abbey the loan of an estate to Stigand.[3] Also one case is known of the buying and selling of a church by Edward's household servants.[4] There is just enough evidence of irregularity to cause uneasiness. But it is probably fair to hold that by the standards of the time the English church was irregular rather than criminal. It had become worldly, but not to the point of heresy. Cardinal Humbert's reluctant mercy towards the irregularities of the day would surely have spared it had there not been a Norman Conquest and a purge dictated in part by political motives.[5]

3. THE CHURCH AND THE ROYAL COURT

The king was always accompanied by his *witan*, his wise men, and, apart from Æthelred 'Unraed' (no-counsel), he took advice from them.[6] The king's council was formless. It was essentially a private meeting of the king's household and guests, its membership varied according to the place and the season, and it probably always kept some of the festive character of a sitting at the mead-bench, which it had had in the heroic age. The local nobility and the more important local churchmen came into court and then took their leave as the king travelled about; and at the great church festivals a larger concourse of guests than usual assembled round the king.[7] But even the biggest assemblies were primarily domestic, and the kings never had to take counsel which was not familiar counsel.[8] An established king, even on the most

[1] *DB*, i. 87 a i, 89 b ii. But after 1066 she granted Mark to him: *Ecclesiastical Documents*, p. 17, *Monasticon*, ii. 287. [2] See above, p. 80.

[3] *Chron. Abingdon*, i. 462–3. The suggestion seems to be that the loan was Stigand's fee for his advocacy (*uti callidus perorator*). King Edward is said to have approved of the transaction (p. 463). The estate, *Cyrne* in Glos., is identified as Cernel (Dorset) in the index. But it was North or South Cerney, near Cirencester, worth £16. According to *DB*, i. 169 a i, 'Hoc manerium calumniatum est ad aecclesiam S. Mariae de Abendone; sed omnis comitatus testificatus est Stigandus archiepiscopus x annis tenuisse vivente E. rege'. Stigand held other estates in this area, 164 b i. [4] See below, pp. 192–3.

[5] Cf. Florence, ii. 5: Bishop Æthelmaer and some abbots were deposed, 'ob confirmationem scilicet sui quod noviter adquisierat regni. Hic et nonnullos, tam episcopos quam abbates, quos nulla evidenti causa nec concilia nec leges seculi damnabant, suis honoribus privavit.' Bishop Æthelric 'non canonice degradatur . . . sine culpa': *ibid*. ii. 6.

[6] Cf. 'and gelome with witan wisdom smeagan, gyf he Gode wile rihtlice hyran': Wulfstan, *Polity*, p. 48. For the King's government in general, see F. Barlow, *Edward the Confessor*, pp. 158 ff.

[7] Cf. *Vita Ædwardi*, pp. 71–3; and cf. below, p. 136.

[8] Tryggvi J. Oleson, *The Witenagemot in the Reign of Edward the Confessor* (1955). Cf. J. E. A. Jolliffe, 'Familiar Counsel', *Angevin Kingship* (1955), ch. viii.

ceremonial occasions, was surrounded by his creatures, by his family and household, his priests and clerks, his housecarles and thegns, and by the bishops, abbots, and earls whom he had appointed. He was their master; he knew them all; and they gave advice as a servant advises his master, with circumspection, if not with obsequiousness.

Among the *witan* the ecclesiastical servants always had a background importance, but their influence on policy varied according to the nature of the business and the strength of character and the inclinations of the persons involved.[1] A prelate such as Dunstan occasionally ruled the court. A Cnut would listen to his English bishops when the affairs of the church were discussed, but would hardly ask their advice when he planned some Scandinavian adventure. Edward in the early years of his reign clearly relied much on his earls.[2] A foreign monk, Robert of Jumièges, bishop of London in 1044, is said to have had great influence before 1052.[3] And later the queen is believed to have been powerful in the royal councils.[4] But we do not know enough about the intimacies of the court to write its history in detail. All that can be said is that in the late Old-English period the bishops and abbots were in a position to advise the king and that on many topics their advice would have been heard with respect.[5]

We can take as an example Edward's court in the summer of 1050, a period when the king had to decide some matters of the highest importance: the reduction of the mercenary fleet, the reform of the coinage and of taxation, the imminent death of the archbishop of Canterbury, the dissatisfaction of his father-in-law, Earl Godwin, the pardoning of his brother-in-law, Earl Swegn, an alliance, involving the succession to the throne, with the count of Normandy, and church reform and relations with the papacy. Here was weighty business indeed; and decisions made at this time, or shortly after, led to the revolt and outlawry of Earl Godwin, an estrangement with the papacy, and the Norman Conquest.

In mid-Lent (22–23 March) the king held a large court in London, at which it was decided to pay off nine of the fourteen ships' crews,[6] and then travelled to Exeter, where on 29 June he installed Leofric in his new cathedral. On the outward or return journey he visited Abingdon. The composition

---

[1] For an ecclesiastical view of the *witan*, see Wulfstan, *Polity*, pp. 62 ff.

[2] E.g. Edward's action against his mother in 1043, *ASC CDE*; Florence, i. 197.

[3] *Vita Ædwardi*, pp. 17–18.   [4] *Ibid.* pp. 15, 23, 31, 42, 54.

[5] Karl Jost, *Wulfstanstudien*, pp. 104–9, suggests that Wulfstan's Homily LI was the archbishop's address to the *witan* on the subject of legislation.   [6] *ASC CE*.

of the court is illustrated by five charters, four granted to Abingdon and the other (in two versions) to Exeter.[1] Besides the king (and the queen, who does not sign, although we know that she was at Exeter), five classes of persons are shown in the witness lists: bishops, earls, together with a few familiar nobles, abbots, priests, and thegns. There are usually nine to eleven bishops, five earls, two to five nobles, three abbots, up to six priests, and up to a dozen thegns. The thegns, who appear at the foot of the list, are the local nobility and form the most variable component.

According to these witness lists all the actors in the political drama which was unfolding were gathered at court. On the lay side were all the great earls: Godwin of Wessex, Leofric of Mercia, Siward of Northumbria, Harold of East Anglia, and Ralf, the king's nephew, of the west-midlands. As witness to one of the Exeter charters appears also Godwin's eldest son, Earl Swegn, the murderer of his cousin Beorn, the outlaw whom Bishop Ealdred had just brought back from Flanders and reconciled to the king.[2] Two other sons of Godwin, not yet earls, were there, Tostig and Leofwine, together with Odda of Deerhurst, Edward's kinsman, who was to benefit by Godwin's disgrace, and Ralf the Staller, who was to get an earldom after the Conquest. On the ecclesiastical side, Eadsige of Canterbury, now close to death, witnesses all these charters, but Ælfric Puttoc of York, who was to last a little longer, signs only at Exeter. Stigand of Winchester follows the archbishops, and lower on the lists is Robert of London, both future archbishops of Canterbury. Duduc of Wells, who had been to Leo IX's council at Rheims in the previous autumn, and Herman of Wiltshire and Ealdred of Worcester, both just back from the pope's Easter council at Rome, were present; and Ulf, the new bishop of Dorchester, about to set off for an uncomfortable interview with the pope at Vercelli, was at Abingdon. The curial bishop, Heca, recently appointed to Selsey, and Ælfwold, the ascetic bishop of Sherborne, were in attendance at Abingdon. Leofric of Exeter was naturally at court. Absent were the bishops of the more distant parts, Rochester, Elmham (Stigand's brother), Hereford, Lichfield, and Durham. The abbots of Abingdon,[3] Ely, Ramsey, and Glastonbury were, as usual, with the king – Spearhavoc of Abingdon soon to be promoted ineffectually to London. Ælfwine of Ramsey had been with Wulfric of St Augustine's and Duduc to Rheims in the previous year. Wulfweard, possibly abbot of Exeter, was with the court; and at Exeter the neighbouring abbot, Sihtric of Tavistock, added his witness.

---

[1] See below, Appendix A, p. 154.   [2] Florence, i. 203; cf. *ASC CE*.
[3] Spearhavoc (K. 793); Ordric, a later abbot (K. 792, 796, 800).

Among the group of priests were Regenbald, who was granted a bishop's
rank without the duties,[1] Cynsige and William, shortly to be appointed to
York and London respectively, Peter and Robert, possibly the men who obtained the sees of Lichfield and Hereford in William's reign,[2] and Godman,
whose son, Godric, was later to be made abbot of Winchcombe.[3] Future
abbots of Evesham and Malmesbury may also have been at Abingdon.[4]

When the court is thus viewed in the middle of Edward's reign, it gives
the impression of organic growth and continuity. The two archbishops and
the three greatest earls had been created by Cnut, and there were present
seven who were to be bishops and one to be earl under the Conqueror.
Among the earls were Edward's father-in-law, a brother-in-law, and a
nephew; but it is likely that the prelates were more manageable than the
laity. Apart from the archbishops there was hardly a bishop, abbot, or priest
who did not owe everything to the king.

The clergy had a share in the formulation of royal policy and also a share
in carrying it out. Again there is the broad division between secular and
ecclesiastical business, with the earls and sheriffs the royal agents in the one
and the bishops and abbots in the other. But, so characteristic of the period,
the clergy intruded as much into secular affairs as the laity into ecclesiastical. Earls as well as bishops and abbots [5] served as royal ambassadors; and
a bishop could be put in charge of the defences against Wales [6] and an archbishop could formulate, and a bishop pronounce, judgment on an earl.[7] The

[1] Harmer, *Writs*, no. 44.

[2] The identity of the two Peters, a relatively uncommon name, is likely. The future bishop of
Lichfield was put in control of the diocese of Dorchester by the Conqueror in 1067 on the death
of Wulfwig: *Chron. Abingdon*, i. 492. Robert, however, was a common name. The bishop of Hereford
(1079–95), a great friend of St Wulfstan of Worcester, was probably related to Herbert bishop of
Thetford/Norwich (1091–1119), for both were described as *de Losinga* or *de Lotharingia*.

[3] Symeon, *HR*, ii. 171.

[4] Æthelwig (abbot of Evesham, 1058–77), K. 796, and Beorhtric (of Malmesbury, 1062–70),
K. 793, 800; cf. K. 817 and Malmesbury, *GP*, p. 420. But these must be considered most doubtful
identifications. The latter was prior before becoming abbot of Malmesbury.

[5] King Edward, for example, used Earls Harold and Tostig. Obviously bishops and, especially,
abbots were used more frequently. Ælfwine, abbot of Ramsey, was sent to the Council of Rheims
in 1049 (*Chron. Ramsey*, p. 170), to Rome in 1062–5 (*ibid.* pp. 176–7), and at an unknown date in,
Edward's reign (possibly in 1054 with Ealdred) to 'Saxony' (*DB*, i. 208 a i). It is not surprising
that Ælfwine's health broke down just before the end of the reign (*Chron. Ramsey*, p. 177). Also he, or
his temporary replacement, Æthelsige of St Augustine's (for the confusion see *FNC*, iv. 135–7 and
Appendix P) was in Denmark, but possibly after the Conquest (*DB*, i. 208 a i).

[6] Ealdred of Worcester: see above, p. 87.

[7] Robert of Canterbury and Stigand of Winchester in 1051 against Earl Godwin, *Vita Ædwardi*
p. 22.

tradition of literacy among the English nobility [1] and the tradition of royal service among the higher clergy reduced the cleavage between the two orders and made for an integrated society. Nevertheless, the basic direction of the government remained secular. We can hardly believe that even a pious king lived in a predominantly ecclesiastical environment. And the English monarchy cannot be regarded as a slave to the church, even in its governmental techniques.

We know nothing about the ceremonial of the king's court, little about its staff, and not much about its work. Its organization, therefore, is a teasing problem.[2] Only one contemporary writer, the anonymous author of the *Vita Ædwardi*, attempts to describe the court; but he is disappointingly vague, and, moreover, as a foreigner, must be read with caution. For him the *regalis curia* was a *palatium*, with an *aula*, *thalamum* and *oratorium*,[3] inhabited by *palatini*, and possibly to some extent controlled by a *regalis palatii stabilator*, who, in 1065, was a secular kinsman of the king.[4] It may be that the writer was familiar only with the royal palace at Westminster. The important men at court are *a secretis*,[5] and they can be *ordinarii secretorum consilii regis et rectores rerum regalis palatii*.[6] Robert bishop of London could intrude himself more than was necessary *in disponenda regalium consiliorum et actuum serie*,[7] and Tostig earl of Northumbria could be detained at court *in disponendis regalis palatii negotiis*.[8] With this class it is doubtful whether we go much below bishops and earls. In a lost passage he probably mentioned the king's *cubicularii*.[9] Apart from describing Giso and Walter as royal priests when promoted to bishoprics,[10] no attention is given to the lower clergy at court. But we learn that Edward attended mass daily and maintained the poor and sick at his court. Similarly the hunt-servants are ignored, although we are told about the hounds and birds.[11] Only once does he mention – and in an obscure sentence – duties and functions, and these probably go beyond the

---

[1] The most outstanding example is the ealdorman Æthelweard, the patron of Ælfric the Homilist and the author of a Latin version of the Chronicle. See L. Whitbread, 'Æthelweard and the Anglo-Saxon Chronicle', *EHR*, lxxiv (1959), 577 ff. Cf. also C. P. Wormald, 'The uses of literacy in Anglo-Saxon England and its Neighbours', *TR Hist. Soc.*, 5th ser. xxvii (1977), 95–114.

[2] L. M. Larson, in his doctoral thesis, *The King's Household in England before the Norman Conquest* (Madison, Wisconsin, 1904), was more successful on the lay than the ecclesiastical side.

[3] *Vita Ædwardi*, pp. 7, 29; 14, 28, 29; 63. Cf. R. Elze, 'Das "Sacrum Palatium Lateranense" im 10. und 11. Jahrhundert', *Studi Gregoriani*, iv (1952), pp. 27–54.

[4] *Vita Ædwardi*, p. 76. Robert fitzWimarch, a Norman, or possibly a Breton.

[5] *Ibid.* pp. 6, 17, 62.   [6] *Ibid.* p. 17.   [7] *Ibid.* p. 18.   [8] *Ibid.* p. 50.

[9] *Ibid.* p. 65.   [10] *Ibid.* p. 35.   [11] *Ibid.* p. 40.

palatini. Edward entrusted the cause of God to his bishops and to men skilled in canon law, warning them to act according to the case, and he ordered his secular judges, princes, and palace lawyers (*palatii sui causidici*) to distinguish equitably.[1]

To this observer, probably a monk, the important men at court were, after the king and queen, earls, bishops, and laymen. The only abbots he mentions are foreign visitors. We know from other evidence that this is an incomplete picture, but it is a salutary warning not to go to the other extreme and lay all emphasis on an obscure clerical element.

As Edward was brought up in *Francia*, and both he and Cnut were subject to foreign influences, and as the English church was deeply affected by Carolingian and neo-Carolingian reform, it is natural to expect that the Old-English court would have borne some resemblance to the royal courts in the Carolingian successor kingdoms.[2] And it is easily presumed that there must have been a court treasury in the chamber and a chapel based on the royal oratory, with some sort of writing office within the chapel, and that each department had its appropriate officials and clerical staff. It is also tempting, when officials such as *thesaurarius* (treasurer), *cancellarius* (chancellor), and *capellani* (chaplains) are not found under those names, to ascribe the absence to vernacular terminology and translate Anglo-Saxon terms into Latin, or, going further, attribute titles to men on the grounds that these describe the function which they performed.[3] This substitution and attribution was attempted first by the compilers of Domesday Book in 1086 and then by twelfth-century chroniclers of the Old-English scene and fabricators or revisers of land-books. The witness list to Edward's charter of 1062 granting Waltham to Earl Harold for the foundation of a minster [4] identifies Esgar as

[1] *Vita Ædwardi*, pp. 12–13.

[2] Josef Fleckenstein, *Die Hofkapelle der deutschen Könige*, vol. i: *Die karolingische Hofkapelle* (Schriften der Monumenta Germaniae historica, 16, 1959), where the derivation and various meanings of the words *capella* and *capellani* are discussed.

[3] J. H. Round, in a rather casual Note, 'The Officers of Edward the Confessor', *EHR*, xix (1904), 90–2, identifies a marshal (Alfred), a constable (Bondi), a steward (Eadnoth), the king's butler (Wigod), the queen's butler (Harding), a chamberlain (Hugo) – and 'the name of the chamberlain's office suggests that of the *treasurer*, as to which we read . . . that "Henricus thesaurarius" had a house in the city [of Winchester] "in King Edward's time".' – and a chancellor (Regenbald), and concludes, 'A comparison of the offices I have enumerated with those named in the "Constitutio Domus Regis" certainly seems to suggest that in the names of his chief officers, as in sundry other respects, Edward had Normanised his court'. G. H. White, however, 'The Household of the Norman Kings', *Trans. R. Hist. Soc.* 4th ser., xxx (1948), 127, traced back the post-Conquest steward, butler, chamberlain, constable, and chancellor – he regarded the treasurer as a later introduction – first to the Norman ducal and then to French royal court.   [4] K. 813.

regiae procurator aulae, Rodbert and Osbern as kinsmen of the king, Ralf as *regis aulicus*, Bondi as *regis palatinus*, Regenbald as *regis cancellarius*, and Peter and Baldwin as *regis capellani*. There are also *pincernae* and *dapiferi*. Similarly a Westminster forgery, dated 28 November 1065, claiming to record Edward's benefactions to that house,[1] lists Regenbald, the king's chancellor, and Osbern, Peter, and Rodbert his chaplains.

But all these later observers may have been looking for officials who were not in fact there, and, by asking the wrong questions, and accepting approximations, produced a wrong answer. There is no great harm in substituting *capellani* for *presbyteri regis*,[2] provided that it is not consequently assumed that they were members of a *capella* in the Carolingian sense. It is, however, more dangerous to select a seemingly important priest and assign to him the title of chancellor. And it is completely wrong to take a named official like the *bur-thegn* (*cubicularius*) and rename him *thesaurarius*, or treasurer. It is more prudent to start with the presumption that the English court was relatively formless and ask if there is any good evidence for the existence of a rudimentary departmental system and a settled routine, and to assume, unless there is evidence to the contrary, that although the king needed at all times some basic servants – chamberlains for his bed-chamber, priests to say mass and hear confessions, and the various servants of the hall and courtyard – other requirements from such men need not have been specialized. The tasks of the court were not constant. Law suits could have been heard only occasionally. The military duties of the court may have declined under Edward. If in 1051 he abolished *here-geld* he would also have removed some financial work. But about the same time the court seems to have taken a greater interest in the coinage. We should not exaggerate the amount of business transacted by the court. And it is obvious that, when duties were sporadic, changeable, and miscellaneous, a group of useful men rather than units of experts would be more serviceable.

We can start our inquiry from two entries in the Chronicle of Ramsey Abbey. Describing arrangements made when a loan of land was granted to Edward's nephew, Earl Ralf, it states that a chirograph was drawn up, and

---

[1] K. 825.

[2] Some documents for which the Lotharingian-educated Leofric bishop of Exeter was probably responsible do so: Edward, 1044, to *meo idoneo capellano Leofrico* (*Ordnance Survey Facsimiles of A.S. MSS*, ii, Exeter xii), Edward, 1050, for Leofric, *presentibus . . . capellanis* (*ibid*. Exeter xiii; K. 791). The vernacular for a household chaplain was *hirdprest* (cf. Whitelock, *Wills*, no. 29), which was often translated later as *capellanus* (cf. K. 968).

that by the king's command one part was placed for safe custody in his chapel with his collection of saints' relics.[1] And in connexion with the custody of the decrees of the Council of Rheims (1049) it states that Edward ordered that one copy should be placed in his treasury (*gazophilacium*), where all his most precious treasures were kept, under the diligent care of his chamberlain Hugelin.[2] Here we have references to two places which are often mentioned, the king's sanctuary (*haligdom*)[3] and his chamber treasury. The entries raise two important questions: first were the *haligdom* and the treasury identical,[4] and, second, was there a chancery distinct from the one or both? Ælfric in his Vocabulary tried to identify rooms in a Roman house. He translates *thesaurus* (treasure chamber) as *goldhord* and *gazophilacium* as *madmhus*.[5] A supplement is more ambitious: it adds *scriptorium = pisleferhus* and *oratorium vel oraculum = gebedhus*.[6] These equivalents as spacial terms inspire no confidence. And when we read that *ypodromum* (treasury or latrine) means *goldhordhus*[7] we see how low the treasury could sink. Even if we turn from rooms to furniture or servants we remain on treacherous ground. *Scrinium* originally meant a box for writings, and so an archive, but also for money, and so a treasury, or for relics[8] (hence shrine). The ambiguity prepares us for difficulties. But when the supplement to Ælfric informs us that *cancellarius vel scriniarius* means *burthen*,[9] the confusion is at least revealing. The *bur-thegn* we know. He is the servant in the chamber or bedroom, and so *camerarius* or *cubicularius*. And it is obvious that the *cancellarius* and *scriniarius* are phantoms. Our inquiry, therefore, must be conducted on a more primitive level, and we must ask whether there were in the court one, two,

[1] *Chron. Ramsey*, p. 172.

[2] *Ibid.* pp. 170–1. As Hugolin, *cubicularius regis* at the palace of Westminster, he appears in one of Edward's miracles related by Osbert of Clare: Marc Bloch, 'La Vie de S. Édouard le Confesseur par Osbert de Clare', *Analecta Bollandiana*, xli (1923), 82–3; and see below, p. 123.

[3] Whitelock, *Wills*, pp. 46, 151; *Liber Eliensis*, pp. 146–7; cf. V. H. Galbraith, *Studies in the Public Records* (1948), pp. 40–1. At the court of the Emperor Henry III even a precious dish of Alexandrine glass, which was produced at banquets, was under the care of junior clerks, of whom two became bishops later. See *Vita S. Odilonis Cluniacensis abbatis*, II. c. xii, *MPL*, cxlii, coll. 925–6.

[4] Larson, *The King's Household*, pp. 129–33, in his discussion of the treasury, treats them as identical.

[5] *Anglo-Saxon and Old English Vocabularies*, ed. T. Wright and R. P. Wülckur (1884), i. 164.

[6] *Ibid.* i. 186. For *thesaurarium* he gives *goldhold*.

[7] *Ibid.* i. 184.

[8] Cf. 'benedictio scrinii vel arcae', *The Lanalet Pontifical*, ed. G. H. Doble, HBS, lxxiv (1937), 128.

[9] Wright and Wülckur, i. 190. The next entry is *sacri scriniarius = cyrcweard*. For the *scriniarius* in the 'Lateran palace', see Elze, *op. cit.*, pp. 37–40.

or three boxes, one for relics and sacred treasures kept in the oratory, another for money kept in the chamber, and a third for documents located elsewhere, each with its proper servants.

As the cult of St Edward the Confessor was in its earliest days associated with the king's chamber – a fact significant in itself – we have some traditional lore about Edward's court-treasury. The fullest description is in a popular story related by Ailred of Rievaulx in 1163,[1] and so of doubtful accuracy. According to the anecdote, Edward, while resting on a couch (*lectulus*) and unable to sleep, watched first a clerical servant (*aedituus = ? capellanus*) go to the chest (*theca, arca*) in which the king's money was kept and, after putting something in or taking it out, forget to shut it up, and then a poor table-servant, who had noticed the omission, enter three times to steal money from it. On the third occasion, the king, divining the approach of the keeper of his treasures – who turns out to be Hugelin, his *cubicularius* or *camerarius* – warns the boy of his danger. The story has no obviously twelfth-century colouring and can be accepted in the main as a picture of the conditions a century earlier. The tradition that Hugelin was Edward's chamberlain [2] and had custody of his treasure is strong, and we can believe in the existence of a treasury box. But of an office or department there is no sign.[3] We know that Spearhavoc, abbot of Abingdon, whom Edward tried to make bishop of London, was the king's goldsmith.[4] But no one mentions a treasurer (*hordere*, in charge of the gold-hoard) at court. All the same, kings who collected a tax, the geld, from most of the kingdom, rents from the demesne, and a variety of royal customs, who could vary the assessment to the geld, who often required payments adjusted to a fixed standard of monetary fineness, and who distributed their treasures among several treasuries, needed

---

[1] *Vita S. Edwardi regis, MPL*, cxcv, col. 746.

[2] Hugo or Hugelin held one hide in Berks worth £8, eight hides in Oxon worth £8, and one hide three virgates in Warwicks worth £1: *DB*, i. 63 a i, 157 a ii, 239 a ii. Edward, of course, had other chamberlains, e.g. Wynsige who had estates in Bucks and Beds: *DB*, i. 151 a ii, 209 a ii.

[3] Galbraith, *Studies*, pp. 41–6, is one of the strongest supporters of a treasury organization. But it should be noticed that his evidence, like Round's, refers to local treasuries and has little bearing on the organization of the court for financial matters. Richardson and Sayles, *The Governance of Med. Eng.*, p. 223, suggest that Hugelin was 'the chamberlain who was in direct charge of the treasury'.

[4] See above, pp. 47–8. Other goldsmiths held of Abingdon or in the neighbourhood. Leofwine *aurifaber* and the priest Alweard held in Berks of the abbot of Abingdon: *DB*, i. 58 b i. In 1086 Alweard *aurifaber* was holding an estate in Berks which his father had held of Queen Edith: *DB* i. 63 b i. Theodoric *aurifaber* held an estate of the king in Survey: *DB*, i 36 b ii, and possibly married an Englishwoman, for in 1086 he held also two estates which she had held of King Edward in Oxon: *DB*, i. 160 b ii. King William gave him lands in Berks: *DB*, 63 a ii.

some clerks familiar with finance, even if accountancy was done by tallies or some other primitive method. Also a land tax presupposes a cadastral survey; and it could have been the loss, or insufficiency, of such a one which led to the Domesday Inquest.[1] Yet, if financial records were kept, they have all disappeared; and we look in vain for anything which could suggest an elaborate or specialized organization.

The evidence for a department based on the king's oratory with its own box for relics and ecclesiastical treasures is less circumstantial. There were certainly priests and clerks in the household whose duty it was to minister to the spiritual needs of the court, and clearly it was believed in the abbeys that these had charge of a *haligdom*. As one chest would hardly carry all the court treasures, it is tempting to suppose that there was some specialization of contents and custodianship, and that there was a *haligdom* in a spacial sense – a box in the oratory. Yet Ailred's story of the *aedituus* using a money box in the chamber makes it possible that all the treasure chests were kept in that room. In the proem to one of Cnut's charters it is written, based on the Gospels,[2] 'ad sacra autem sanctuaria in domini gazophilacio diversa iubentur iactari ac offerri munuscula'.[3] Those who read the Bible knew of the *gazophylacium sanctuarii*,[4] and also were accustomed to the association of *scribae* with the *gazophylacium in domo regis*.[5] There can have been no reluctance to put holy things in the chamber. As we have seen, one eleventh-century scholar regarded the *bur-thegn* as a *cancellarius* or *scriniarius*. And for several observers of Edward's court Hugelin the chamberlain was the most important servant about the king. We find him concerned with royal priests in ecclesiastical business: he bought the church of Huntingdon from two of the king's priests named Vitalis and Bernard and then sold it again.[6] But we hear nothing of a priest in charge of the oratory. The evidence, such as it is, points to the superiority of the chamber over the oratory in Edward's later years, although this may not have been the usual arrangement.

The problem of the physical independence of the chancery is in some ways simpler. It is agreed that in this period chanceries as independent departments did not exist in western Christendom. Some kings had officials styled chancellors and scribes called notaries, but the production of documents was one of the duties of the chapel. There was only a 'notional'

---

[1] D. Clementi, 'Notes on Norman Sicilian surveys', in V. H. Galbraith, *The Making of Domesday Book* (1961), p. 58.   [2] Cf. Luc 21: 1, Marc 12: 41-4.
[3] K. 746.   [4] Ezech. 44: 19; 46: 19.
[5] 4 Kings 12: 10 (vulg.); Jerem. 36: 12.   [6] *DB*, i. 208 a i.

chancery.[1] But in England, just as there was no *capella*, so there was no *cancellarius* and no *notarii*. Later references to royal chancellors of this period carry little weight. Sometimes royal priests who were promoted bishop are said by post-Conquest writers to have been the king's chancellor.[2] 'Chancellors' of Kings Edgar and Æthelred became prelates.[3] We hear, again later, of Cnut's *secretarii*;[4] but these are men who, presumably, were *a secretis*, the king's confidential *witan*.[5] The most elaborate attempt to credit Æthelred and his successors with a chancellor is a statement in the Ely chronicle that King Æthelred had given to the abbots of Ely, St Augustine's, and Glastonbury the office of chancellor, with the duty of caring for the sanctuaries and their ornaments. Each abbot, or his deputy, was to serve at court for four months, the abbot of Ely commencing duty on 2 February. The chronicler also maintains that this system lasted until the Conquest.[6] If we look again at Edward's court in 1050, there is some slight support for the statement. Both the abbots of Ely and Glastonbury were at Abingdon, the former witnessing one and the latter three other charters, but only Glastonbury signs at Exeter on 29 June. It may be, therefore, that Glastonbury took over from Ely in June. But it must be confessed that in general no neat rotation of the three abbots can be established. This result is a little disappointing, for, if the story were watered down a little, it would not be incredible. To appoint abbots, on a characteristic English rotation, to supervise the notarial work done in or out of court, and at a time when the writ-charter may have been introduced, would suit the general situation. Yet, in the absence of an organized chapel, it is unlikely that there was an organized chancery.

English kings had, of course, scribes, and the names of a few of them have been preserved.[7] It can hardly be doubted that some royal letters and official documents were written in court. But if we look at the problem from the

---

[1] Josef Fleckenstein, *Die Hofkapelle der deutschen Könige*, i. 74 ff. Larson, *The King's Household*, p. 144, however, decided that it cannot be doubted that a chancery existed in England just before the Conquest.

[2] See H. W. C. Davis, *Regesta Willelmi Conquestoris et Willelmi Rufi* (1913), pp. xi–xv; Galbraith, *Studies*, pp. 36–41; Harmer, *Writs*, pp. 57–61; T. A. M. Bishop and P. Chaplais, *Facsimiles of English Writs to A.D. 1100* (1957), pp. xii, xvii.

[3] Ealdwulf, a married man who accidentally suffocated his son, and who became abbot of Peterborough, bishop of Worcester, and archbishop of York: *Chron. Peterborough*, pp. 29–31. Ælfric, the son of an earl of Kent, abbot of St Albans, bishop of Ramsbury, and archbishop of Canterbury: *Gesta abbatum monasterii S. Albani*, i. 32.

[4] *Chron. Ramsey*, p. 135.

[5] See above, p. 119.

[6] *Liber Eliensis*, II, c. 78; cf. c. 85.

[7] See references above, *n*. 2.

diplomatic angle,[1] we find little to support the existence of even a 'notional' chancery. Leaving aside the chirograph as probably an essentially private document – although the third part was sometimes put in the king's hands – our concern is with three types of document which may have been produced in court: 'codes' of law, diplomas, and writs. There is little evidence about the way in which legislation was promulgated. But, as Archbishop Wulfstan was directly or indirectly responsible for the codes issued in this period,[2] it is quite possible that his own scribe produced at least the master copy and that the archbishop himself authenticated it. The diploma, charter, or land-book had been introduced into England by the church, and it remained an essentially ecclesiastical document. It bore no seal, but was attested by crosses and 'signatures' and dated by the year, indiction, epact, and con-current.[3] Its first line was often written in majuscules, and it is not unlike a papal privilege. A religious proem and an anathema clause, composed in special hieratic Latin, give it a sacred character particularly suited to a land title. These diplomas were issued in the name of the king, and may at times have been written in the royal court.[4] But frequently they were drawn up with the king's permission by the interested party or a suitable helper;[5] and it is not impossible that Æthelred's alleged grant of the chancellorship to three geographically discrete monasteries should be understood in the sense that Ely, St Augustine's, and Glastonbury were appointed official centres for the issue of diplomas. These documents were not without quasi-dispositive features.[6] The land-book was transferred with the land, and

[1] Much remains to be done in Anglo-Saxon diplomatics, especially on the charters; but see the new editions published by the British Academy.   [2] See below, pp. 137–9.

[3] This was simply the hocus-pocus of men fascinated by ecclesiastical arithmetic and the intricacy of calendars. See Heinrich Henel, *Studien zum altenglischen Computus* (Leipzig, 1934). It contributed nothing to precision; indeed, it could confuse, for the calculations were often wrong.

[4] R. Drögereit, 'Gab es eine angelsächsische Königskanzlei?', *Archiv für Urkundenforschung*, xiii (1935), 335–436; Harmer, *Writs*, p. 39.

[5] Harmer, *Writs*, pp. 38–41; cf. V. H. Galbraith, *Studies in the Public Records*, pp. 31–5; Eric John, 'Some Latin Charters of the Tenth Century Reformation in England', *Revue Bénédictine*, lxx (1960), 334–5, 340 n., 357. The Exeter charter of 1050 (below, p. 154) raises the baffling question of how it is that a charter can exist in two versions with different, albeit reasonable, witness lists. Is one a copy of the draft and the other of a revision? And why is a grammatical error (above, p. 35, n. 2) left in both? Exeter A is usually regarded as the 'original' and 'authentic' 'royal' charter.

[6] The old controversy over whether the diploma was evidentiary or dispositive has been re-opened by Eric John, *Land Tenure in Early England*, Appendix II, where he argues that they were 'doing' instruments and dispositive. It may possibly be that at times, especially when they were

possession of the document was believed to give a claim to the land granted by it. But essentially they represented the authority of God and the church invoked to protect and perpetuate the memory of the deed, and basically against its revocation by the king.[1] They were better testimony than the fallible witness of the king's *witan* or the shire court, and they contained a safeguard which was not in the writ. There was an element of magic in them.[2]

In contrast, the royal writ was secular in tone.[3] It was in letter form, and letters are as old as writing; but those which have survived are notifications of royal grants of lands or rights, or confirmations of previous grants. They were used to give the recipient livery of seisin and to publicize the transaction, and therefore could serve as title deeds and were preserved by the beneficiary. This type of writ, the only type to survive from Anglo-Saxon days, can properly be called a 'writ-charter'. It was written briefly in English, so that when read in the shire court all would understand. It was essentially technical: its formulas were regular and it employed the alliterative jingles and other mnemonic devices of the popular law and public courts. Since its authenticity must be obvious it bore the king's seal, and, as it was to be kept and exhibited on later occasions, it was sealed open.

The diploma and the writ were alternative, and complementary,[4] types of title deed. The one invoked an impressive list of witnesses and the authority of God and the church. The other relied simply on the king's will, symbolized by his effigy on his seal. The different nature of these documents is well shown by their representation of the royal style. The inscription on

'in chancery', they had this character. But John does not, in this context, consider such a case as when permission was given by the king in a writ to draw up a book – such a diploma was obviously *post factum* – or a diploma like the Exeter 'foundation charter' which clearly describes an event which had already taken place.

[1] All the same, the king occasionally revoked them arbitrarily, and in the interest of the church: *ibid*. pp. 135 ff.

[2] These remarks have an important bearing on the vexed question of authenticity. In fact the problem does not arise. No diploma is authentic in the technical sense. Some may be genuine originals, others true copies of such, and others copies spurious in part or in whole; but diplomatic tests are hardly possible. The important question is whether a diploma is a true record. It should be regarded as a literary source and criticized as such.

[3] For the writ, see Galbraith, *op. cit.* pp. 35–6; Harmer, *Writs;* G. Barraclough, 'The Anglo-Saxon Writ', *History* (n.s.), xxxix, no. 137, pp. 193–215; Bishop and Chaplais, *Facsimiles of English Royal Writs to A.D. 1100.*

[4] Complementary also in content, for the land-book gave the grant in more detail and listed the estate boundaries, written, significantly, in English. This was a part which had to be intelligible to be of use.

Edward's seal is 'Sigillum Eadwardi Anglorum basilei',[1] and in the writs he is described simply as 'Eadward cing'. The diplomas, however, show a deliberate search for elegant variation, characteristic of literary rather than legal documents. At least twenty-five different forms of graces can be found in the diplomas of this period [2] and every resource of synonym and permutation is employed on the king's title. The simplicity of 'Ego Eadwardus dei gratia Anglorum rex' [3] – a precursor of the official style of Edward's successors – is less characteristic than such forms as 'Ego Eadweardus diuina adridenti gratia Angol-Saxonum et aeque totius Albionis rex' [4] and 'Ego Eadwardus desiderio regni coelestis exardens fauente superno numine basileus industrius Anglorum cunctarumque gentium in circuitu persistentium'.[5] To the Normans they sounded *pompatice*.[6]

The 'writ-charter' may have been developed in the reign of Æthelred or Cnut to replace the mission of the king's representative, bearing some symbol of royal authority, to put the recipient in seisin of the lands granted. It may have been formed out of a less specialized 'writ-mandate', a simple administrative order, which, being of ephemeral importance, was not preserved. However that may be, it seems to be a creation of the early eleventh century, and its devising is probably to be connected with the equally important invention of the two-sided seal, attributed to Cnut,[7] for it was probably as much the need to seal such documents open as the desire to show two aspects of royal power which led to this more expensive method of authentification.

The writ, but not the diploma, appears to be a typical 'chancery' production. It was drawn up according to formulae, and it needed the impression of the king's seal, which was presumably kept in the court. But it does not seem that even the writs were always written by royal household clerks. A monastic beneficiary could supply its own scribe.[8] And this lack of jealousy does much to persuade us that no proper writing-office existed in the royal court. It seems, indeed, that within a formless 'chapel' there was an equally formless secretariat. Some royal clerks were probably better scribes than others and

---

[1] Harmer, *Writs*, pl. 2. Only the 'second' seal of Edward is genuine: Bishop and Chaplais, *Facsimiles*, p. xxii.   [2] See above, p. 35, *n*. 3.

[3] K. 791.   [4] K. 787.   [5] K. 783.

[6] 'Denique Graeci involute, Romani splendide, Angli pompatice dictare solent. Id in omnibus antiquis cartis est animadvertere, quantum quibusdam verbis abstrusis, et ex Graeco petitis, delectentur': Malmesbury, *GP*, p. 344. For the fashion of using Greek words, see Stubbs, *Memorials of St Dunstan*, p. cxxii, and for some examples, see below, p. 234, *n*. 6.

[7] Harmer, *Writs*, pp. 92 ff.; Bishop and Chaplais, *Facsimiles*, pp. xix ff.

[8] Bishop and Chaplais, *Fascimiles*, pp. xii–xiii.

were given notarial work to do as a more or less regular task. Such a one in Edward's reign was Regenbald,[1] whom we have noticed at court in 1050, and who remained to serve King William as chancellor. One of William's first actions was to reward him, no doubt for his transfer of allegiance.[2] At a time when a foreign king was taking over his conquest and enfeoffing his new barons with their lands, a scribe experienced in the ways of the English court was for a time indispensable. But Regenbald cannot have been Edward's chancellor. He is given no title and no prominence in the witness-lists to contemporary charters. No one thought of him as chancellor. And the reward he got from Edward, although substantial, was less than that given to Osbern, a noble clerk at court.

The royal court was also occasionally a court of law. It may be presumed that cases which came for the king's judgment were considered, like any other problem, by the king and his *witan* in sessions which, although formal in the contemporary sense, were somewhat informal by ours, and that there was no sharp distinction between legal hearings and the determination of other matters.[3] The author of the *Vita Ædwardi* refers to legal experts at court. But perhaps too much should not be made of this. Doubtless there were among the king's counsellors and clerks some men more skilled in the law than others, and it should be noticed that on one occasion (although the pre-Conquest date is not certain) Bishop Wulfstan, Abbot Æthelwig of Evesham, and 'the chancellor' Regenbald were sent out of court to hear a case.[4] The hearing of lawsuits can only have been an occasional function of the court and could not have justified a special organization.

Although we can find little evidence for the existence of specialized departments, there was certainly a group of priests and clerks at court, whom we can think generally useful and often specially employed according to individual skills. It is difficult to get a clear view of this society.[5] The characteristically uncertain terminology does not help. The collective term for the lower clergy in royal service was *clerici regis*, the king's clerks, in which were lumped together men in priest's, deacon's, and minor orders. And although sometimes *presbyteri regis*, the king's priests, are distinguished, and it may be that these were often men in priest's orders, as opposed to *clerici*

---

[1] J. H. Round, art. in *D.N.B.*, and 'Regenbald, priest and chancellor', *Feudal England*, pp. 421 ff; H. W. C. Davis, *Regesta*, i, p. xv. [2] Round, *Feudal England*, pp. 422–5.
[3] Cf. the account of the trials of Earl Godwin in 1051, *Vita Ædwardi*, pp. 21–2, and in 1052, pp. 27–8. [4] Davis, *Regesta*, no. 213.
[5] For a list of *clerici regis*, see below, Appendix B, p. 156.

construed in a stricter way,[1] we have insufficient information to enable us to discuss usefully how many priests there were among the clerks at court, or their relative proportions, whether there was internal promotion from grade to grade, and whether these servants had functions appropriate to their orders – priestly duties for the priests and clerical duties for the clerks. The lack of statistics hinders the formulation of a general thesis about the responsibilities of the clerical staff. If priests were in the minority, there would be evidence for an administrative secretariat, if the reverse, evidence for more strictly religious duties.

Some information about the men described as *presbyteri regis* can be gained from the charters. None witnesses a charter of Æthelred. Eleven priests, usually in twos or threes, but once five, witness seven charters of Cnut which are well spaced over the last twelve years of the reign.[2] One charter of Harthacnut has six priest witnesses.[3] About sixteen priests appear on Edward's charters. But the spacing and reliability of these lists is unsatisfactory. Three priests witness a charter of 1043,[4] eleven or twelve the group of charters from 1050 which have already been discussed,[5] three a doubtful charter of 1062,[6] and four two forgeries dated 1065.[7] The reason for the occasional inclusion of royal priests among the witness-lists is not obvious. But it may simply be the whim of the beneficiary or of the monastic house which drew up the book for him. Although the appearance of Abingdon and Westminster in this company makes for suspicion there is no cause to think that all charters containing priest witnesses are late fabrications. The witness lists must be taken for what they are worth – contemporary or later views on the composition of the court, often arbitrarily shaped to a pattern or the space available on the parchment.[8]

These lists can be supplemented from other sources. Sometimes we are informed in the chronicles that a bishop had been a royal priest. In Domesday Book landholders are usually listed within the shire in exactly the same order

---

[1] Yet there is usually some doubt. In Old English *preost* means clerk, and the clerk in priest's orders is distinguished only by the suffix *maesse-*. Hence contemporary Latin equivalents (e.g. *presbyter* in Anglo-Saxon charters) as well as some modern translations (e.g. *ASC D* 1060: 'Gisa preost' = 'the priest Gisa') may be misleading.

[2] K. 741 (1024), 743 (1026), 1324 (1027–32), 746 (1032), 751 (1033), 1318 (1033), 1322 (1035).
[3] K. 762.   [4] K. 767.   [5] Above, pp. 117–8.
[6] K. 813.   [7] K. 815, 825; Regenbald 'the chancellor' also on K. 824.

[8] Drafters showed a preference for neat groups. Exeter 1050 (*Ordnance Survey Fascimiles*, ii, Exeter xiii), lists the king and 2 archbishops + 3 bishops, 3 abbots + 3 priests, 6 earls, 6 nobles, and 6 thegns.

of dignity as witnesses to charters – the king, archbishops, bishops, abbots, *clerici regis*, earls, barons, *taini regis*, and other *ministri*. And again royal priests and clerks do not always appear, and there is some uncertainty about their status.[1] More than thirty priests and clerks are named in twelve shires under headings such as 'Quod clerici regis tenent'. Not all these men, of course, were in royal service before 1066. Ranulf Flambard, for example, holds in Oxfordshire, and William's doctor, Nigel, has been enfeoffed partly out of lands held by Edward's priest Spirites. Beorhtweard and Earnwig are the sons of Edward's men. But it does not seem that a revolution has occurred between 1066 and 1086 or that the number of men has changed much. Although some of the charter witnesses can be found either as tenants or as *antecessores*, it is not necessary to think that all these *clerici regis* had places at court. Some of them may have had local duties in connexion with the king's churches, houses, and estates. There are also some significant groups in Domesday Book. In 1066 there were twenty canons of St Martin's, Dover, then holding the prebends in common.[2] Four of them are charter-witnesses: Archbishop Stigand, Leofwine, Smelt, and Spirites. And Wulfwig, who was succeeded by his son Wulfstan, Alwine, and Godric, bear the names of the bishop of Dorchester and two of his brothers. Bosham, with which Edward's priest and kinsman Osbern was endowed, supported also the priests Radulf and Godwin.[3]

About a dozen 'priests' attest the charters of 1050. If we add as many *clerici*, the number required by the king in attendance at court at any one time would seem already to be exceeded. It is possible that there was a system of rotation at least among those who had been endowed with churches and estates. It may be that there was a household nucleus and that local royal priests and clerks came into court as the king travelled about. All the same, there was, if not a department, at least a society. The continuity in this body, despite the changes of king, is most striking. It cannot be proved that Cnut took over Æthelred's priests; but we can assume that he did. And no break

---

[1] After royal demesne: Wilts, no heading (fo. 65 b i). At the end of the ecclesiastical tenants-in-chief: Dorset – 'xxiiii. Terra elemosinariorum regis' (fo. 79 a i); Somerset – index, 'Clerici tenentes de rege' (fo. 86 a i), text, 'xvi. Quod clerici regis [tenent]' (fo. 91 a ii); Devon – (not indexed or numbered) 'Quod tenent clerici de rege' (fo. 104 a ii); Oxon – index, 'Canonici de Oxeneford et alii clerici' (fo. 154 a ii); Northants – 'xvii. Terra elemosinariorum regis' (fo. 222 b ii); Leics – index, 'Godvinus presbiter et alii elemosinarii', text, 'viii. Elemosinae regis' (fo. 231 a ii). Occasionally priests are included in a miscellaneous group at the end of the shire folios, e.g. Beds – 'Terra prepositorum regis et elemosinariorum' (fo. 218 b i), and Lincs – 'lxxviii. Terra Sortebrand et aliorum tainorum' (fo. 371 a i).

[2] *DB*, i. 1 b i–ii.   [3] *DB*, i. 17 b i, 27 a i–ii, 43 a i.

can be seen thereafter. Stigand was at court, as priest, bishop, or archbishop, from, possibly early in, Cnut's reign until 1070. Edward retained at least three of Cnut's priests. Spirites, a favourite of Harold Harefoot and Hartha-cnut,[1] was with Edward until exiled, probably in 1065. Edward on his death-bed urged Harold to take over his men.[2] And William kept several of Edward's priests. At the same time each king introduced his own creatures and doubtless retired some of the old. A charter of Harthacnut,[3] dated 1042, witnessed also by his half-brother and successor Edward, illustrates in its attestations this process of growth. At least three of the bishops – Eadsige of Canterbury, Ælfwine of Winchester, and Duduc of Wells – had been Cnut's priests. The serving priests are headed by Eadweald and Stigand, old ser-vants of Cnut. Ælfwine, otherwise unknown unless he be the same as Alwine, and Spirites follow. Edward's men, Herman and Leofric, bring up the rear. In all likelihood these priests are listed in strict order of seniority, and, two by two, they represent three periods. Moreover, the two junior will be bishops at William's court.

The basis of the continuity was, of course, long service. Herman and Leofric, possibly because they had been in Edward's household overseas, were quickly promoted bishop. But their case seems to have been excep-tional. Eadsige served at least six years, Ælfwine eight, Cynsige fifteen, Stigand twenty, Peter as much, and Osbern ten before they obtained bishop-rics. And if it was Edward's priest Rodbert who was given Hereford in 1079, he had been thirty years at court. Eadweald served from before 1024 until after 1043, Smelt from before 1035 until after 1066, Spirites from before 1040 until about 1065, and Regenbald from before 1050 until after the Conquest, all without promotion to the episcopal bench. Besides these im-portant priests were others of whom we hear only once or twice and those who do not appear in any of the extant witness lists. Some of these, too, since they were rewarded by the king, may have had long, if obscure, service. Others may have been failures.

Since household clerks can have had no security of tenure, long service is evidence for a menial position. It may be thought that they were not exposed to the risk of giving counsel. Spirites fell in a spectacular way. But 1065 was a dangerous year. The terms *presbyter regis* and *clericus regis*, and the verna-cular renderings, suggest that these men were commended to the king and

---

[1] *Hemingi Chartularium*, i. 254.   [2] *Vita Ædwardi*, pp. 79–80.

[3] K. 762. Although in favour of Abingdon, this charter, because of its unusual collection of witnesses, merits respect.

under his jurisdiction. Edward, when dying, invited Harold to take oaths of fealty from those of his men whom he wished to retain.[1] The priests are the ecclesiastical counterpart to the *taini regis*, the king's thegns. According to Domesday Book the priest Earnwig held one hide of land in Bedfordshire which his father, a vassal (*homo*) of King Edward, had held. He had succeeded without authority.[2] But as Earnwig is listed, with some other priests, among the thegns in Lincolnshire,[3] we are possibly concerned here with a thegnly family. Yet the very confusion is interesting. And the king treats his priests much as he treats his thegns, and for each the coveted reward is a benefice. At Edward's court, just as there were foreign secular servants, so there were aliens among the priests. Edward's weakness for aliens no doubt played its part, but, as his priests were recruited widely from northern Christendom, he may well have been looking for skills in short supply in England. The presence of these strangers, completely dependent on their patron, must have strengthened the king's hand. The king's priests were very definitely his men.

Unfortunately we know nothing about the origin, education, or affinities of the English royal priests of this period. There were certainly clerical families in the shires. Among the canons of St Martin's, Dover, in 1066 were Dyring, his father Sired, and Sired's father, and Sigar and his father.[4] But none of the priests who witnessed charters is known to have been related to another, although it is just possible that Wulfwig and his two brothers all served the king. Little, however, should be made of this negative evidence. The approach to the king must have been through kinsmen and friends.

Despite cohesion and continuity, the clerical component in the royal court did not form a chapel in the Carolingian and post-Carolingian sense because the typical officials were missing and because the specialization was rudimentary. The lack of form is due probably more to the intimacy of English conditions than to backwardness. Bishops and abbots were often at court, and were present in large numbers at the principal feasts when much business was done. Also at court, certainly in the tenth century, but less noticeably in the eleventh,[5] were noble clerks, like Dunstan and Æthelwold, merely waiting for a suitable abbey or bishopric. The presence of these

---

[1] *Vita Ædwardi*, pp. 79–80.   [2] *DB*, i. 211 a i.   [3] *DB*, i. 371 a i–ii.

[4] *DB*, i. 1 b i–ii. Sigar also held an estate in Kent worth £40 from Queen Edith. He was the *antecessor* of Albert *capellanus*, *DB*. i. 14 b i.

[5] Rodbert and Osbern, however, are each described as *regis consanguineus* on the Waltham charter (K. 813).

clerical courtiers and prelates made unnecessary the organization of a chapel to carry out the king's ecclesiastical policy and negotiate with synods and the local bishops and abbots. As all the prelates were in a sense the king's chaplains (and several had been in fact his priests) the establishment of a formal chapel was hindered. The proximity of the abbey, in which Edward was much interested, to the palace of Westminster may also have had a cramping effect on the spacial development of a court chapel. We can only speculate on how the clerical duties were allocated and supervised in the absence of departments. It is not unlikely that the king himself was often in direct command. The court was probably small enough. The senior priest may have had some responsibility without a title. Or it is possible that the king delegated the duty to one of the prelates in attendance. The archbishop of Canterbury always claimed to be the king's chief counsellor and clearly he was often with the king. Stigand especially appears to have been a domestic archbishop. And from what we know of him it would be easy to believe that he was in charge of the clerical servants of the household. Such a position would explain his reputed control of the king's ecclesiastical patronage, his influence over lawsuits, his ability to enrich himself, and his undoubted background importance.[1]

Service at court was attractive to clerks because they could influence royal patronage. But the king was not undiscriminating. Bishoprics were only for the few. And although there were in 1050 and 1066 seven bishops who had been the king's priests, that is to say about half the total number, the royal household cannot be regarded as a school for bishops. At the other extreme there were clerks who perhaps never obtained more than their livery in the court and others who, on Domesday evidence, received only small estates. Churches seem to have been granted generally to the more important men. For a few with special claims on the king's gratitude there were rich benefices. The Norman Osbern, a kinsman of Edward, held part of the princely estate attached to the church of Bosham [2] while he waited for a bishopric. The other part, rated at sixty-five hides, and worth £65 a year, was held by the priest Godwin, sixteen hides from the king and forty-nine originally from Earl Godwin. Regenbald 'of Cirencester' who could not take a bishopric, presumably because of his marriage or unchastity, did not suffer unduly. He eventually assembled an honour of scattered estates, rated at

[1] See above, pp. 77-80.
[2] For the partition of the church of Bosham and the value of Osbern's share, see below, pp. 190-1.

some ninety hides, which stretched from Boveney (Bucks.) in the east, to Wellington (Som.) in the west, and to Elmstone Hardwick (Glos.) and Rothwell and Brigstock (Northants.) in the north. Some of this, especially the complex round Cirencester, was acquired after the Conquest,[1] when he received grants out of the forfeited estates of Earl Harold and of several thegns. Regenbald's family, too, was established in that area. In 1086 his brother was holding eleven hides in Ampney St Peter on the fief of the abbey of Gloucester [2] and his son, Edward (a significant name), two hides at Aldsworth (Glos.).[3] Although Regenbald held some 'secular' estates before 1066, such as the ten hides at Pulham (Dorset), the five hides at Eldersfield (Worcs.), and the fifteen hides at Hagbourne (Berks.), the foundations of his honour were the churches he possessed – possibly most of those which he held in 1086 – Wellington, Milborne Port, and Frome (Som.), Cheltenham (Glos.), Avebury and Pewsey (Wilts.), Shrivenham, Cookham, and Bray (Berks.), and Passenham (Northants.). The value of his estate in 1066 is difficult to establish. But it was probably worth at least £40 a year. And Edward even granted him the legal status of a diocesan bishop.[4] In contrast, Spirites, who was in 1065 perhaps even more richly endowed than Regenbald, had an estate more secular in appearance. Apart from canonries in St Martin's, Dover, and St Mary's, Bromfield, there is nothing remarkable about his lands. His largest holding was in Wiltshire, and he had modest estates in Shropshire and Herefordshire and something smaller in Somerset and Hampshire. In all his benefice was rated at 77 hides and was worth about £60. But these large complexes were exceptional. Smelt had an estate in Kent worth £20 and a prebend in St Martin's, Dover. Peter held in Berkshire two-thirds of a church with four hides worth £3 and in Somerset two churches worth 30s. and 20s. and an estate let at 20s. p.a.

What the king could give he could also take away. When Edward banished Spirites, apparently in 1065, he kept all the escheated estates in his own hands except for the prebend in St Mary's, Bromfield, rated at ten hides, which he gave to his kinsman and staller Robert fitzWimarch, a layman, to hold *ut canonicus*. Robert then transferred it to his son-in-law, and the canons complained. Edward decided that the prebend should be returned

---

[1] The development of Regenbald's honour can be studied by comparing Henry I's grant of it to St Mary's, Cirencester, *Monasticon*, vi. 177, with *DB*.   [2] *DB*, i. 165 b i.

[3] 'Elward f. Reinbald', listed under royal thegns: *DB*, i. 170 a ii.

[4] 'and that his *wite* be equivalent to that of a diocesan bishop in all things': Harmer, *Writs*, no. 44.

immediately to the church, but gave respite until the approaching Christmas court when he would order Robert to make a substitute grant to the son-in-law. However, the king died at that time and the church lost its land.[1] The story is interesting in several ways. Again we meet Edward's careless attitude towards ecclesiastical benefices and traffic in them at court. And we notice that the king disposes of them freely. It is unlikely that benefices and estates granted to priests and clerks were normally given in full inheritance, as by a book. Osbern and Peter kept their endowments on promotion, the one to Exeter the other to Lichfield in 1072. But Peter's, after his death in 1085, returned to the king, because 'non erant de episcopatu'.[2] In 1086 the jurors stated that the priest Rodbert, who had held one carucate of land of the king *in elemosina*, had become a monk of St Mary's, Stow, and had taken the land with him – 'but it is not lawful to pass the land to anyone without the king's consent'.[3] On the death of a clerk the king seems to have expected the grant to revert. Cases of hereditary succession are noted in Domesday Book, but in one instance the jurors stated significantly that they had not seen livery given on the king's writ.[4] No doubt a bishop always had to obtain permission to bequeath estates granted to him by the king; and on two occasions Edward and Edith invalidated a will. Duduc of Wells was not allowed to leave to his cathedral church lands which Cnut had given him,[5] and Cynsige of York's bequests to Peterborough were defeated.[6] Both these men had been royal priests and had profited from royal generosity. And on their death the court decided what should happen to their wealth. Although ecclesiastical heriots had been abolished, the king seems to have claimed a limited *ius spolii*, and to have treated at least his own priests and clerks as dominical vassals with no right in the benefices created from royal demesne and with no full right even in their chattels.

A sacramental king, responsible for the welfare of the church, needed ecclesiastical advice and clerical servants. In England the idea was carried so far that in the eleventh century the whole church was at his disposal. Most of the bishops and many of the abbots were among his familiar counsellors. And he had priests and clerks to carry out more menial administrative work. There were limitations on the power of the king over the laity. In 1065

---

[1] *DB*, i. 252 b ii. Robert was with the king at his death: *Vita Ædwardi*, p. 76. For Bromfield, see F. E. Harmer, 'A Bromfield and a Coventry Writ of King Edward the Confessor', *The Anglo-Saxons*, ed. Peter Clemoes (1959), pp. 90–8. [2] *DB*, i. 57 a i, 91 b i, 98 b ii.
[3] *DB*, i. 345 a i. [4] Earnwig, *DB*, i. 211 a i.
[5] See above, p. 75 *n*. 5. [6] See above, p. 81.

Edward had to accept a revolution in Northumbria. But the only check on royal power over the church was the novel intractability of the popes after 1049, and the matters which concerned the pope were few. There seems to have been no hindrance to the king's will in the English church itself. No archbishop could have been more useful than Ealdred, more docile than Stigand. The abbot of Ramsey wore himself out in Edward's service. Priests with their eye on a bishopric or other benefice are unlikely to have been difficult. The king was more than the patron of the English church: he was its lord and master. But like all masters he was often the servant of his servants.

4. ROYAL LEGISLATION AND ECCLESIASTICAL JURISDICTION

The importance of the bishops and abbots among the *witan*, already seen in their influence over the king's ecclesiastical patronage, is further illustrated by their success in using royal government for urging the observance of Christian standards in political behaviour, for the reformation of morals, and for the maintenance of the church's discipline. They exploited the traditional power of the king to legislate on any subject, and put to work in their service the machinery which existed to enforce royal decrees.

Most of the ecclesiastical legislation of the Anglo-Saxon period has been transmitted in the form of royal laws, written in the vernacular,[1] and it seems that a 'national' assembly of the higher clergy and nobles, under the presidency of the king, was considered a proper enacting authority. Such a body could be called a synod.[2] The king's leadership was an accepted European

---

[1] The ecclesiastical codes are I Edmund (942, 944–6), II Edgar (959–63), VIII Æthelred (1014), and I Cnut (1018, 1020–3). Mixed codes are IV Edgar (962–3), V Æthelred (1008), VI Æthelred (? 1008), and VII Æthelred (1009). II Cnut, 'The secular ordinance', also contains some ecclesiastical matter. Non-royal codes and treatises, for which Archbishop Wulfstan is probably responsible, are 'Edward and Guthrum', 'Canons enacted under King Edgar', *Northhymbra preosta lagu* (Law of the Northumbrian priests) = *Law NP*, *Ordal*, *Becwaeth*, *Gethynctho*, *Northleoda laga*, *Ath and Hadbot*, *Grith*, *Northhymbra cyricfrith*, *Iudex*, and *Episcopus*. The best edition is Liebermann, *Gesetze*. But the laws can be read conveniently, text and translation, in Robertson, *Laws*; and selections of the laws and treatises are translated in *EHD*, i. For important studies on Wulfstan and the laws, see Miss Whitelock, 'Wulfstan and the so-called laws of Edward and Guthrum', 'Wulfstan and the laws of Cnut', and 'Wulfstan's authorship of Cnut's laws', *EHR*, vols. lvi, lxiii, lxx; Karl Jost, *Wulfstanstudien* (Swiss Studies in English, 23, Bern 1950), pp. 13–44, 94–103.

[2] Cf. 'Haec itaque legalia statuta vel decreta (VI Æthelred) in nostro conventu sinodali a rege N (*sc.* Æthelred) magnopere edicta, cuncti tunc temporis optimates se observaturos fideliter spondebant; idcircoque ego N (*sc.* Wulfstan), gratia domini disponente Eboracensium archiepiscopus, eadem ad sequentium memoriam, necnon et ad praesentium vel futurorum salutem,

custom,[1] and when Æthelred declared, 'For a Christian king is Christ's deputy in a Christian people, and he must avenge very zealously offences against Christ',[2] he was asserting a duty which no contemporary would have denied.

From Æthelberht to Athelstan royal codes, although they had contained a sprinkling of ecclesiastical enactments, had been essentially secular. With the tenth-century reformation of the English church, however, a change occurred which led rapidly to a reversal of the old position. From the reign of Edmund distinct ecclesiastical codes were issued alongside laws of the old type. The duality, however, was unstable, and from 1008 to 1023, confusion reigned again, but in a new form – secular legislation was assimilated to the ecclesiastical, and all royal enactments had a homiletic colouring. After 1023 no more laws were issued. The progression is significant and illustrates the phases of the reform movement.

The influence of the church on legislation had always been considerable, for not only the mechanical processes of drafting and writing but also the very idea of reforming and promulgating laws was peculiar to the church. Hence the periods of royal legislative activity were usually those in which the church was particularly influential and unusually solicitous for the welfare of the kingdom. The first purely ecclesiastical code issued by an English king, so far as is known, is I Edmund (942, or 944–6), promulgated on the advice of the two archbishops and many of the other bishops.[3] Archbishop Dunstan is credited with influencing Edgar to issue laws in reform of morals.[4] Edgar's first code (II and III Edgar, 959–63) was divided into an ecclesiastical and a secular section,[5] and there is internal evidence that Dunstan inspired IV Edgar (962–3),[6] mixed legislation with a penitential flavour, intended to

litteris infixi, Domini videlicet proximique dilectione conpunctus', VI Æthelred, 40.2, cf. Robertson, *Laws*, pp. 334–5. A meeting of the *witan* at Cirencester, at which Ælfric Cild was convicted of treason against the king, and banished, is called a synodal council in Æthelred's charter of ? 999 (K. 1312). In Ælfric's *Grammar*, p. 30, 'haec sinodus = this witenagemôt'.

[1] Cf. the action of King Conrad of Germany after his coronation (1024) travelling to Aachen where he was enthroned, 'Quo sedens excellentissime rempublicam ordinavit, ibique publice placito et generali concilio habito, divina et humana jura utiliter distribuebat': Wipo, *Vita Conradi Salici, MPL*, cxlii, col. 1230. There is a mass 'pro rege dicenda tempore sinodi' in the Gregorian Sacramentary, and Bishop Leofric of Exeter included in his miscellany another mass and a benediction for the king on such an occasion: *The Leofric Missal*, ed. F. E. Warren, pp. 9 a, 19.

[2] VIII Æthelred, 2.1. A phrase of Archbishop Wulfstan, used with modification in II Cnut, 40.2, and *Polity*, pp. 42–3.   [3] I Edmund, preamble.

[4] Osbern, *Memorials of St Dunstan*, p. 110.

[5] III Edgar is described as a secular (*worldcunde*) ordinance; but II Edgar has no special description. A similar method of distinction is used for I and II Cnut.   [6] IV Edgar, 1.4.

ward off the plague which had been ravaging England. In 1008 Archbishop Wulfstan of York began to write or draft the enactments,[1] and he imposed his homiletic style on the secular as well as the religious laws.

Although there was always some confusion between what was properly an ecclesiastical and what a secular decree,[2] the distinction between church law and secular law was well understood. The two are frequently contrasted;[3] ecclesiastical ordinances are usually grouped together in the mixed codes; and some attempt was made to distinguish the promulgating authority. Almost all codes which retain a preamble are described as having been issued by the king with the advice of his *witan*. Sometimes the description 'both ecclesiastical and lay' is added.[4] There is no significant variation between the form of the religious and secular enactments, and clearly the ultimate authority in both cases was the king and the whole body of his councillors. Yet there was a feeling that, although lay laws were the concern of both estates, purely ecclesiastical rules were a matter for the church alone, and phrases such as 'these are the injunctions of the bishops'[5] and 'I and the archbishop enjoin'[6] point to subject divisions and, perhaps also, to separate deliberation.

The purpose of issuing ecclesiastical canons in the form of royal laws was twofold. In the first place it was the most convenient method. It saved the church the trouble of constructing a separate and redundant administrative machinery. These laws, decreed by the *witan*, could be published in the shire courts by the bishops, and, of course, elsewhere according to their pleasure.[7] Secondly, the church was inviting the king to impose secular

---

[1] K. Jost, *Wulfstanstudien*, pp. 104 ff., thinks that Wulfstan's Homily LI was the archbishop's address to the *witan* on the subject of legislation. But Jost does not believe that Wulfstan wrote I and II Cnut – they merely contain excerpts from his legal writings: *ibid*. p. 183.

[2] Cf. II Cnut, 'the secular ordinance', which contains some ecclesiastical decrees and also a homiletic section.

[3] The commonest antithesis is 'for Gode & for worolde'; cf. V Æthelred, 1.1, 4, 9.2; VI Æthelred, 2, 8.2, 39, 40.1, 53; II Cnut, 2, 11.1, 38.1. For this phrase of Wulfstan's, see D. Bethurum, *The Homilies of Wulfstan*, pp. 72 ff. Other antitheses are 'godcunde lara & woroldlaga' (X Æthelred, 1), 'Godes riht & woroldriht' (III Edgar, 5.2, VI Æthelred, 30; II Cnut, 18.1), and 'Godes riht & manna riht' (VI Æthelred, 50). Similarly there is the antithesis between sins (synna) and misdeeds (misdaeda), cf. VI Æthelred, 52.

[4] Cf. I Edmund, preamble; V Æthelred, preamble.

[5] VI Æthelred, 1.   [6] IV Edgar, 1.4.

[7] Kenneth Sisam, 'The Relationship of Æthelred's Codes V and VI', *Studies in the History of Old English Literature* (1953), p. 287, has suggested that royal laws were sent to the bishops for distribution among the parish priests. But it hardly seems likely that a bishop's household could prepare copies on this scale.

penalties, in addition to the ecclesiastical punishments, for ecclesiastical offences.[1]

This royal ecclesiastical legislation recalls the capitularies which the Frankish kings had issued and which some eleventh-century German kings imitated. It presupposes two conditions: the dominance of the secular government and anxiety to introduce reform. But the second factor could take various guises, and each of the three examples cited has special characteristics. In all of them the king regarded himself as the representative of God on earth (*vicarius Dei*) and hence no less responsible for the welfare of the church than for that of the state. Both the secular and ecclesiastical hierarchies reached their apex in him.[2] But the motives could be very different. Charlemagne had an untroubled concept of his mission, and he was, with all his insufficiencies, the master of the plan. The German kings of the eleventh century were generally more secular in tone and their patronage of the church was more calculated, more exploitive. In England the stimulus to reform came essentially from the church, and it was the moral influence of the bishops and abbots among the *witan* which sustained its impetus. The kings co-operated for different reasons. Edgar was a sincere reformer. Æthelred accepted the view that the misfortunes of his kingdom were due to sin, and anxiously wooed the cementing authority of the church.[3] Cnut needed ecclesiastical help and was not unaffected by some aspects of Christianity. These kings, therefore, put their physical force behind the moral drive of the church. This they could do without fear because the English church had none of that independent political and territorial power which the German had acquired. In England to strengthen the influence and discipline of the church was to reinforce royal authority. The bishops were the shire bishops. They were servants of the king.

[1] The imposition of secular penalties begins perhaps more truly with Edgar than with Edmund. I Edmund mentions only ecclesiastical penalties, except, possibly, in c. 1, where unchaste clergy are to forfeit their worldly possessions in addition to other canonical penalties.

[2] Cf. VI Æthelred, 40, 'And constant thought shall be taken in every way how best to determine what is advisable for the public good, and how best to promote true Christianity, and to suppress with all diligence every injustice. For it is only by the suppression of injustice and the love of righteousness in matters both religious and secular that any improvement shall be obtained in the condition of the country.' X Æthelred, 1, 'Frequently and often it has come into my mind that sacred precepts and wise secular decrees promote Christianity, strengthen royal authority, further public interests, are the source of honour, bring about peace and reconciliation, put an end to strife, and improve the whole character of the nation.'

[3] In 1009, 'when the great army came to the country', a national fast was declared (VII Æthelred), and all Æthelred's codes lay emphasis on loyalty to God and the king.

From a strict canonist standpoint the promulgation of ecclesiastical decrees under royal authority was unnecessary and ineffective. Even when an eleventh-century German king issued the decisions of a church synod as royal precepts, it was not the form which gave them validity.[1] There was a gain only in weight and prestige. But the English church was requiring from the king more than his prestige. It required secular penalties. According to V Æthelred, c. 31, 'If anyone is guilty of offering obstruction (*forsteal*) or open opposition anywhere to the law of Christ or of the king, he shall pay either *wergeld*, or *wite*, or *lahslit* according to the nature of the offence'.[2] In other words, all ecclesiastical offences were made also secular offences, liable to secular penalties. And there is evidence that this sweeping principle was observed, for in the *Law of the Northumbrian Priests* secular penalties are mentioned which are not listed in the extant royal codes.[3] Hence in England a true theocratic government was created, yet one, despite the common charge of confusion against the Anglo-Saxon church, remarkably free of confusion in theory. The duality of the two spheres was emphatically proclaimed. There were God's rights and the king's rights, Christ's laws and the laws of the world. There was an independent ecclesiastical jurisdiction under the control of the bishop, but there was also the helping hand of the secular power which the church had invoked and which it could use at its discretion.

The ecclesiastical codes are concerned with five main subjects: the protection of churches, the morals of the clergy, the morals of the laity, church dues, and festivals and fasts. I Edmund legislates on all these subjects, except the last, which is introduced for the first time in II Edgar,[4] and the legislation develops more by elaboration than by the introduction of new topics. From 1008, when Archbishop Wulfstan of York began to write the codes, until II Cnut, when they ended, the law was declared in ever greater detail. A few new subjects were introduced. In V Æthelred there is a section of religious and moral precepts for the laity,[5] in VI Æthelred (a version for the province of York) sorcery attracts more attention,[6] in VIII Æthelred there are enactments about criminous clerks,[7] and in Cnut's reign is noticed a growing concern with heathen practices.[8] A few matters were dropped –

---

[1] Hauck, *Kirchengeschichte Deutschlands*, iii. 586.
[2] Cf. also VI Æthelred, 38, II Cnut, 83, 'Edward and Guthrum', 2.2.
[3] Oppression and sale of churches (cc. 20–2) and heathenism and witchcraft (cc. 48–54).
[4] c. 5. There is the rather weak precedent of Wihtred, 9.   [5] cc. 22–6.
[6] c. 7.   [7] cc. 19–27.   [8] II, c. 5.

Edmund's enactment about the restoration of church buildings,[1] and Æthelred's decrees concerning simony and lay ownership,[2] vagrant monks,[3] and the communal life of canons.[4] But, in general, the legislation was remarkably consistent in substance.

Protection of the persons of the clergy and of their churches was the earliest responsibility of the state. For calculating the value of the clergy, so that the proper *wer* or *bot* could be enforced, archbishops were equated with princes, bishops with earls, and celibate priests with thegns.[5] The *wer* was paid to the kinsmen, the *had-bot* (*ordinis emendatio*) to the church, to be divided one part to the bishop, one to the altar, and the third to the brotherhood,[6] presumably either the monastic or canonical community or the gild. Special penalties were imposed for attacks on clerks, nuns, and religious women.[7] Each church had its own peace (churchgrith), which was protected by a tariff according to its status,[8] and also limited powers of sanctuary.[9] Æthelred legislated against the oppression of churches, their sale.(simony), and the expulsion of a priest without the bishop's consent,[10] without naming penalties; but in the *Law of the Northumbrian Priests* the penalty for all these offences is given as *lahslit*.[11]

The tenth-century reformers had realized that the morals of the clergy could be corrected only with the help of the king. Bishops Æthelwold and Oswald had used the royal power to free their minsters from the grasp of secular canons. And, according to Dunstan's biographers, Edgar, at the archbishop's instigation, attacked various classes of sinner and decreed penalties for ministers of the church who indulged in hunting, secular business, or lechery.[12] Accordingly there was much royal legislation about clerical celibacy[13] and the obligation of priests, monks, nuns, and canons to

---

[1] I Edmund, 5.   [2] V Æthelred, 10.2, VI Æthelred, 15.

[3] V Æthelred, 5-6, VI Æthelred, 3-4.   [4] V Æthelred, 7, VI Æthelred, 4.

[5] II Cnut, 58.1 for archbishops and bishops; V Æthelred, 8-9, VI, 5, VIII, 28, for celibate priests; cf. also *Northleoda laga*, 2, 3, 5, *Ath and Hadbot*, 'Canons enacted under King Edgar', 60.

[6] *Ath and Hadbot.*

[7] VIII Æthelred, 33-4, II Cnut, 39, 42; cf. *Gethynctho*, 8, *Law NP*, 23-4. In all cases amends were to be made both to church and state.

[8] VIII Æthelred, 1-5, I Cnut, 3-3a; *Grith, Northhymbra Cyricfrith;* Wulfstan, 'Be cyrican', *Polity*, pp. 138 ff.

[9] Cf. II Edmund, 2, VI Æthelred, 14, VIII Æthelred, 1.1, 'Edward and Guthrum', 2.1.

[10] V Æthelred, 10.2, VI Æthelred, 15.   [11] *Law NP*, 20-2.

[12] Osbern, in *Memorials of St Dunstan*, p. 110; cf. also p. 106; Auct. B., *ibid.* p. 49; Eadmer, *ibid.* pp. 200-2. See also 'Canons enacted under King Edgar', 14, 64.

[13] I Edmund, 1, IV Edgar, 1.7-8, V Æthelred, 8-9, VI Æthelred, 5, 41, VIII Æthelred, 28-30, I Cnut, 6a. 1-2a. See also Makower, para. 22, pp. 212-16.

observe their rules.[1] Professional irregularities, such as misdirecting the people about a festival or fast, failing to collect chrism, or withholding baptism, could also, apparently, be punished by secular penalties.[2] Edmund threatened unchaste clerks with the loss of their possessions,[3] Edgar offered the power of the secular arm,[4] and Cnut threatened apostate monks and priests with banishment.[5] But the church probably used this help with circumspection. Forfeiture of estates could lead to the church losing endowments.[6] In any case it is clear that the delinquent could always make his peace with the church,[7] and that the bishop had no need, except when faced with a rebel, to use the secular procedure.

The position of clerks accused of breaches of the secular law was also a matter for royal legislation. There seems to have been no type of case or charge which could not be brought against them in the public courts,[8] and they had to clear themselves in the usual way, by oaths calculated according to a tariff, or, if they could not produce compurgators, by the ordeal of consecrated bread.[9] If they failed in the proof they were liable to the ordinary compensatory payments (*bot* or *wer*) and to the fines (*wite*) and forfeitures. In these 'civil' cases they were treated according to the ideas of the time, that is to say, according to their status and rank. For those offences which were beginning to be regarded as crimes, special penalties were decreed by the laws. Priests guilty of false witness or perjury, theft or being the accessory or accomplice of thieves, were to be degraded from their office, unless they made full amends to God and men, as the bishop should direct, and find

[1] V Æthelred, 4–7, VI Æthelred, 2–4, VIII Æthelred, 31, I Cnut, 6a.

[2] 'Edward and Guthrum', 3. 1–2.

[3] I Edmund, 1, in addition to canonical penalties, including burial in unconsecrated ground.

[4] IV Edgar, 1.8, 'I and my thegns shall enforce upon our priests the duties prescribed for us by the guardians of our souls, namely the bishops, whom we ought never to disobey in any of those matters which they, as representatives of God, prescribe for us, so that we, through the obedience which we show them as representatives of God, may inherit the eternal life to which they draw us by their teaching and by the example of good works.'

[5] II Cnut, 4a. 1.

[6] Bishop Æthelwold warned secular lords not to take advantage of an abbess being convicted of a crime against church or state and confiscate estates which had been given to God: *EHD*, i. 849. Cf. also Eric John, 'The King and the Monks in the Tenth-Century Reformation', *BJRL*, xlii (1959), 80–1.

[7] Unchaste priests shall incur that which is ordained in the canon (I Edmund, 1); cf. also V Æthelred, 6, VI Æthelred, 3.1, II Cnut, 4a. 1.

[8] Monks, however, were free from the vendetta, VIII Æthelred, 25, I Cnut, 5.2d: 'he leaves the law of his kindred behind when he accepts the monastic rule'.

[9] VIII Æthelred, 19–27, I Cnut, 5–5.4, II Cnut, 41, 43.

sureties for their good behaviour in the future.[1] Priests guilty of great crimes, including homicide, were to suffer degradation and banishment, and were to accept penance from the pope.[2] And priests guilty of the greatest, capital, crimes – probably murder, treason, arson, attacks on houses, and open theft [3] – were to be arrested and their case reserved to the bishop, who was to give judgment according to the nature of the deed.[4] We can hardly believe that the bishop would pronounce a sentence of mutilation or death on a clerk in Holy Orders. The binding and whipping of priests is expressly forbidden by the law.[5] It may appear paradoxical that the more serious the offence the more ecclesiastical the penalty. But it was the church itself which had been influential in stigmatizing certain offences as crimes, and it had acquired a special competence in such cases.

Thus benefit of clergy consisted in the right to use an appropriate method of defence and in immunity from the physical penalties of the law. Degradation and banishment (with the duty of seeking absolution from the pope) was probably the penalty for hardened clerical criminals. The procedure would hardly have satisfied the twelfth-century canonists, but nevertheless the clergy were treated as a privileged class and, in criminal matters, were made subject to their own judges. They enjoyed all the benefits that the age could contrive.

The immoral conduct of the laity was also made liable to secular penalties. King Edgar is said at Dunstan's request to have attacked the unlawfully married, false coiners, servants of diabolical evil, thieves, the sacrilegious, breakers of faith, sorcerers (*veneficii compositores*), whoremongers, traitors, slayers of kinsmen, 'women who killed their husbands by adulterous deceit', and those whose life was hateful to God.[6] In the laws secular penalties are specified principally for sexual offences – adultery, incest,[7] and the unseemly remarriage of widows [8] – for heathen practices and witchcraft,[9]

---

[1] VIII Æthelred, 27, I Cnut, 5.3.   [2] VIII Æthelred, 26, II Cnut, 41.

[3] See II Cnut, 64.

[4] II Cnut, 43; Wulfstan, *Polity*, pp. 144-5. We can see from *Law NP*, 2, that it was assumed that a priest guilty of a capital crime would lose his church.

[5] II Cnut, 42.   [6] See above, p. 142, *n*. 12.

[7] Penalties for adultery, II Cnut, 53-5, 'Edward and Guthrum', 3; for incest, II Cnut, 51, 'Edward and Guthrum', 4.1; for fornication with or marriage to a nun, I Edmund, 4, Cnut, 1020, 16-17, *Law NP*, 63-4. It is clear, however, that the main responsibility rests with the church, cf. II Cnut, 53.

[8] Cf. V Æthelred, 21.1, VI Æthelred, 26, II Cnut, 73a. See *DB*, ii. 199a, Plumstead in Norfolk, where Bishop Æthelmaer had confiscated a widow's land, 'pro forisfactura quia mulier quae tenuit nupsit intra annum post mortem viri'.

[9] II Cnut, 5.1; *Law NP*, 48-54, penalties to be divided between the church and the king.

and for crimes which the church regarded as heinous sins, murder,[1] perjury,[2] and the violation of oaths and pledges.[3] The church used excommunication to enforce its discipline, and in the laws it was regarded as the ecclesiastical counterpart to outlawry.[4] Hence the king was willing to supplement the one with the other, and to decree penalties for harbouring excommunicates.[5]

The enforcement of ecclesiastical taxation came increasingly under secular control. The four main items – tithe, church-scot, Peter's Pence, and plough–alms – were to be paid under ecclesiastical threats in Edmund's reign.[6] But Edgar took tithe [7] and Peter's Pence [8] under his aegis, and Æthelred the rest.[9] According to VIII Æthelred, cc. 14–15, if anyone refused to pay God's dues he should be brought to justice with a secular penalty, which was to be divided between Christ and the king, according to former custom. Cnut [10] put the penalty at the full *wite* (probably 60s.) [11] or *lahslit* in the Danelaw, and in his proclamation of 1027, cc. 16–17, ordered royal officials to exact the dues in case of non-payment. The render of soul-scot and light-dues was ordered by the secular laws, but without mention of a secular penalty.[12]

The attitude of the state towards festivals and fasts developed in a similar way. By VIII Æthelred festivals and fasts were to be observed and Sunday markets abolished under penalty of a secular *wite*,[13] and Cnut protected the Sunday holiday and fasts with *wite* or *lahslit*.[14]

It seems therefore that any sin or offence which was liable to punishment under ecclesiastical law was also, through royal legislation, awarded a secular penalty. No real threat to ecclesiastical jurisdiction, however, can be seen in this procedure. The church was invoking the aid of the secular *brachium*

---

[1] II Cnut, 56: the bishop to pronounce judgment.

[2] II Cnut, 36: wergild to be divided between the king and bishop; cf. II Cnut, 6, 'Edward and Guthrum', 2.3.

[3] Cnut, 1020, 14: 'For all the bishops declare that very severe amends must be made to God for the violation of oaths and pledges.'

[4] Cf. II Cnut, 4a. 1. Excommunication formulae are in Liebermann, *Gesetze*, i. 432 ff.

[5] VIII Æthelred, 42, II Cnut, 66: life and property to the deputies of Christ, possibly the secular powers (cf. VIII Æthelred, 2.1), but more probably the bishops.   [6] I Edmund, 2.

[7] II Edgar, 3.1; repeated IV Edgar, 1.4, VIII Æthelred, 7, I Cnut, 8; cf. also *Law NP*, 60.

[8] II Edgar, 4; cf. VII Æthelred, 7, VIII Æthelred, 10.1, I Cnut, 9; cf. also *Law NP*, 57.1–59.

[9] VIII Æthelred, 11, I Cnut, 10.1; VIII Æthelred, 12.

[10] II Cnut, 48; cf. Ine, 4.   [11] Cf. Ine, 43, II Edgar, 3.

[12] II Edgar, 5.2, V Æthelred, 12, VI Æthelred, 20, VIII Æthelred, 13, I Cnut, 13; V Æthelred, 11.1, VI Æthelred, 19, 42; VIII Æthelred, 12.1, I Cnut, 12; but cf. 'Edward and Guthrum', 6.

[13] VIII Æthelred, 16–17; cf. also *Law NP*, 55–6.

[14] II Cnut, 45–6; cf. also *Law NP*, 57, 'Edward and Guthrum', 7–8.

to enforce its own discipline, but was not thereby necessarily surrendering its jurisdiction to the state. We find, in fact, the basic medieval attitude displayed: that the church had a primary responsibility in the sphere of morals and that it was the duty of the Christian state to come to its aid when required. Emphasis varied according to the relative strengths and needs of the two authorities. In Germany in 1063, when some of the monks rebelled against the abbot of Fulda, the king ordered the abbot to put down the revolt by force; and the abbot, once order had been restored, discussed with his advisers whether to punish the rebels according to ecclesiastical or secular law. He decided to use the latter, presumably because it was the more severe.[1] Here we have a choice between two systems. In Normandy the duke intervened uninvited to supplement inadequate ecclesiastical penalties and to punish lenient ecclesiastical judges.[2] In England, on the other hand, the church was the petitioner, and it made use of the state in a way which the thirteenth-century canonists would have considered dangerous, if not reckless. But although the royal laws exaggerate the active side of secular patronage, they nevertheless proclaim the duality of authority. God's rights and the rights of men, and God's law and the world's law, are the themes of the legislation, and if there was a striving to bring them into harmony, that was one of the dominant ideals of the Middle Ages.

So far we have been considering laws and penalties rather than courts. The only courts mentioned in the laws are the public courts – the meetings of the shires, boroughs, and hundreds.[3] This does not mean that other courts did not exist. But these others were not the direct concern of the king, and references to them are disguised under phrases expressing rights of jurisdiction.[4] The secular content of the legislation was, of course, intended for the instruction of the public courts, especially the shire moots. And it cannot be doubted that the imposition of secular penalties for ecclesiastical crimes was also a matter for the public courts.

According to II Cnut, c. 18, the shire court was to meet at least twice a year. Its presidents were the bishop and ealdorman,[5] with the sheriff gradually replacing the ealdorman or earl.[6] The suitors to the court were mostly

---

[1] Lambert of Hersfeld, *Annales, MPL*, cxlvi, col. 1077.

[2] William of Poitiers, I, c. 51, *ad fin.*   [3] Cf. III Edgar, 5, II Cnut, 17–20.

[4] Inevitably, because the only *gemote* were the shire, borough, and hundred assemblies. The compound *ciriscgemot* is unrecorded, because purely ecclesiastical tribunals could hardly be considered *gemote*. It should be noted that in Latin documents the expression *placita* is earlier and more common than *curia*.

[5] III Edgar, 5.2, II Cnut, 18.1.   [6] Cf. Cnut, 1020, 11.

laymen, principally the thegns of the shire, and, according to Germanic procedure, the judges declared the law and the suitors pronounced the judgments. We have an account of the sessions of the Herefordshire court, sitting at Aylton near Ledbury, in Cnut's reign at which a plea concerning land was heard and determined.[1] There were present Bishop Athelstan, Earl Ranig, the local nobility, the sheriff Bryning, and all the thegns of the shire. The president was clearly the bishop, and the court's judgment was recorded in the gospel book of the cathedral church. According to Canterbury tradition secular cases from the whole kingdom which could not be determined in the hundreds, shires, or the king's court were decided in the south porch of Christ Church.[2] However that may be, the modes of proof used in the secular courts – the oaths and ordeals – all supposed divine intervention, and were administered by the church.[3] Indeed, so ritualistic were the processes of law that the church naturally took command, a position which it retained at least until the thirteenth century. Bishops were typically royal justiciars, and were given special duties by the laws.[4]

The tenth-century reformers seem to have thrown themselves into judicial work without scruple. St Dunstan is reported to have refused to say mass one Whitsunday until some false coiners had been executed [5] – overriding the law against Sunday and feast-day executions because of his detestation of the crime. And St Ælfheah sentenced a thief to be flogged and

---

[1] Robertson, *Charters*, no. 78.

[2] 'Quarum una (turris), quae in austro erat, sub honore B. Gregorii papae altare in medio sui dedicatum habebat, et in latere principale ostium ecclesiæ quod antiquitus ab Anglis et nuncusque Suthdure dicitur. Quod ostium in antiquorum legibus regum suo nomine saepe exprimitur, in quibus etiam omnes querelas totius regni quae in hundredis vel comitatibus, uno vel pluribus, vel certe in curia regis non possent legaliter definiri, finem inibi, sicut in curia Regis Summi, sortiri debere decernitur': Eadmer, *De reliquiis S. Audoeni et quorundam aliorum sanctorum quae Cantuariae in ecclesia domini Salvatoris habentur*, HCY, i, p. xlvi.

[3] *Law NP*, 39, ecclesiastical penalty for a priest who conducts the ordeal wrongly. For liturgies for the ordeals (cold water, hot iron and hot water, and bread and cheese), see Liebermann, *Gesetze*, i. 386 ff, *The portiforium of Saint Wulstan*, ed. Dom Anselm Hughes, HBS, lxxxix (1956), 166 ff., *The Lanalet Pontifical*, ed. G. H. Doble, HBS, lxxiv (1937), 108–9, 116–25. The sins/crimes used as examples in the formulae are theft, homicide, adultery, and sorcery (*maleficium*).

[4] Cf. *Iudex*. Archbishop Ælfric, on Æthelred's orders, heard a case against thegns: Robertson, *Charters*, no. 68. Bishop Wulfstan of Worcester, Abbot (Æthelwig) of Evesham, and Regenbald 'the chancellor' determined a suit for the king either late in Edward's reign or early in William's: Davis, *Regesta*, no. 213. Bishops are expressly required to exact the *bot* for false judgment, III Edgar, 3, to watch over the judgments and penalties of the [? shire] – reeves, Cnut, 1020, 11, to sentence adulterers, II Cnut, 53.1, and to pronounce capital sentences on murderers, II Cnut, 56.1. According to Wulfstan, *Episcopus*, they were to safeguard weights and measures.

[5] Eadmer in *Memorials of St Dunstan*, pp. 202–3; cf. Osbern, *ibid.* p. 106.

imprisoned.[1] But among those better acquainted with canon law there developed some reluctance to act as criminal justiciars. Archbishop Wulfstan showed mercy in the royal laws for which he was responsible. Ælfric, in his pastoral letter for the archbishop, protested against the judging of thieves by ecclesiastical persons.[2] Abbot Manni of Evesham (1044–59), when rendered £15 by one of his reeves, took £5, *quia de recto lucro erat*, and rejected £10 *de placitis et diversis culpis acquisitis*.[3] And Bishop Æthelwine of Durham refused in 1070 to sentence robbers delivered to him by the royal power, although these in the previous year had stripped the jewels from a crucifix given to the cathedral by Earl Tostig.[4] A saint is reported even to have shown disinterest in all the secular business done in the shire court. William of Malmesbury wrote of St Wulfstan, 'taking his seat, he applied his mind intently if a religious affair was under discussion; but if, as was more usual, it was a secular matter, he disdainfully fell asleep'.[5]

A bishop we notice was not only the president of the shire court with a general competence, he was also there as an ecclesiastical judge.[6] Bishop and earl were considered the two pillars of justice. By III Edgar, c. 5. 2, the bishop of the diocese and the ealdorman were to be present at the shire court to expound, respectively, the ecclesiastical and secular law.[7] The author of the first life of Edward the Confessor writes that the king 'entrusted the cause of God to his bishops and men skilled in that branch of the law, and instructed them to act in accordance with God's law; and he ordered his secular judges, earls (*principes*), and curial lawyers to judge justly, so that good men should have the protection and evil men the reprobation of the king'.[8]

[1] Ælfric, *Vita S. Æthelwoldi, Chron. Abingdon*, ii. 266.
[2] *Die Hirtenbriefe Ælfrics*, ed. B. Fehr, p. 227; cf. Ælfric, *Lives of Saints*, ii. 330 f.
[3] *Trans. et Mirac. S. Odulphi, Chron. Evesham*, pp. 321–2.
[4] Symeon, *HDE*, p. 101.   [5] *GP*, p. 282.
[6] In the following pages I diverge from the attitude taken by T. P. Oakley, *English Penitential Discipline and Anglo-Saxon Law in their Joint Influence* (New York, 1923), 'Secular requirement of ecclesiastical penalties', pp. 141 ff. As I understand him, he regards royal ecclesiastical legislation as essentially a reinforcement of the confessional, and does not envisage the bishop administering canon law in the shire court. Cf. p. 143, 'The terms of these laws make certain that they directly referred to ecclesiastical penance, rather than to money compensation to the church, although this is sometimes mentioned in addition and is found in other sections.' I would take a contrary position: although these laws, by drawing attention to sin, ordering confession, etc., were obviously in support of ecclesiastical penance, their main purpose was to supplement that discipline.
[7] Cf. also II Cnut, 18.1; Wulfstan, *Episcopus, Polity*, pp. 75–6. I take a contrary view to Makower, para. 59, pp. 386–8, who argued that the ealdorman and bishop had the joint duty of expounding both laws and that the shire court could in no sense be regarded as an ecclesiastical tribunal.
[8] *Vita Ædwardi*, pp. 12–13.

The official attitude was that the ecclesiastical and secular judges were complementary, and the theory is not in doubt. The laws contain instructions to both ecclesiastical and lay judges [1] and impose on the bishop the statutory duty of expounding canon law.[2] It is certain therefore that, besides the secular law, canon law also ran in the shire court and that some, if not all, ecclesiastical cases were tried according to it. Indeed, when we consider all the circumstances and take into account the belief in the application of that law which is appropriate to the person and to the case, we cannot fail to presume that in most cases concerning ecclesiastical persons and in most cases concerning sin or ecclesiastical crime, it was the bishop who held the plea, expounded the law, and pronounced the sentence. Theoretically therefore the shire court was both a secular and an ecclesiastical tribunal. It must be remembered that place is no guide to jurisdiction. As late as the end of the twelfth century Hubert Walter held successive courts in York minster in his various capacities as royal justiciar and papal legate,[3] and the confusion of courts is often bewildering throughout the Middle Ages. The only true guide to jurisdiction is the law under which a case is heard and the guilty punished. A secular penalty enforced by the state at the request of the church is theoretically irrelevant to the matter of jurisdiction. And by the test of law the shire court splits into two.

In practice, however, we must probably allow for some confusion. For example, Bishop Giso, after his accession to Wells in 1061, took action against a man, Ælfsige, who had received a loan of land from one of Giso's predecessors and was not performing services for it. According to Giso's own account,[4] he first gave Ælfsige frequent canonical warnings, then secured a judgment of the shire court ejecting the tenant and replacing the bishop in possession of the land, and finally, when Ælfsige resisted the judgment by arms, excommunicated him. Here the bishop seems to have used a mixture of canonical and secular procedures in a land case.

The introduction of secular penalties for ecclesiastical crimes also was a confusing factor. These penalties were presumably enforced by the lay power – and hence the usual division of the fines between the church and the king.

[1] Cf. VI Æthelred, 52–3, II Cnut, 38.2, 68–9.

[2] Cf. VI Æthelred, 50, 52, II Cnut, 38.1–2, 68.1, 1c. II Cnut, 38.2, declares, 'And ecclesiastical amends (*bote*) shall always be diligently exacted in accordance with the directions contained in the canon law, or in the penitentials (*be boctale*), and secular amends in accordance with secular law.'

[3] *Chronica magistri Rogeri de Hovedene*, ed. W. Stubbs, RS, iii (1870), 293 ff.

[4] 'quem crebro canonice ammonitum, et post judicium provincialium, quo ille excludi et ego debebam introduci, armis repugnantem, non timui anathematizare': *Ecclesiastical documents*, p. 17.

'Edward and Guthrum', c. 2,[1] states that as some men were unwilling to submit to ecclesiastical jurisdiction and pay the penalties required by the church and determined by the bishops, the kings had fixed secular penalties which were divided between Christ and the king. This was a sensible working arrangement. But for a short time in Æthelred's reign the church secured exclusive right to the secular penalty. VI Æthelred (1008), cc. 50-1, reveals the change. After enacting that violators of the laws of God shall make appropriate amends to the ecclesiastical authority and violators of the laws of men shall pay the penalty demanded by the secular law – and giving advice to the ecclesiastical and secular judges on the selection of the appropriate penalties (cc. 52-3) – the law adds, 'payment for the needs of religion shall take the place of payments to the secular authorities, whether they are *wites*, wergilds, *healsfang*, or *lahslit*, whether they affect land or chattels, whether they be large or small' (c. 51). And earlier it is decreed (*ibid.*) that these monetary penalties, imposed by secular law and taken by the church, are to be applied solely to religious purposes at the discretion of the bishop. This change destroyed the interest of the secular authorities, and the church soon found it desirable to return to the original scheme. VIII Æthelred (1014), cc. 55-9, informs us that in the good old days the secular councillors of the king had enacted secular laws for the maintenance of religious rights, and the penalties had been divided between Christ and the king, but, since Edgar's reign, partly because the secular penalties which had been common to Christ and the king had been separated, the laws both ecclesiastical and secular had fallen into disrepute. And in caps. 14-15 it is ordered that church dues are to be paid under pain of a secular penalty which is to be divided between Christ and the king, as it used to be. The same system is revealed by the *Law of the Northumbrian Priests*, also composed by Archbishop Wulfstan, in which the penalties, both ecclesiastical and lay, are set out in more detail. According to this source, secular penalties were usually shared half and half with the king or the owner of private jurisdiction.[2] A variation of the scheme was that in cases of incest the king had possession of the man and the bishop of the woman,[3] a division which outlasted the Norman Conquest.[4]

---

[1] For the date, see D. Whitelock, 'Wulfstan and the so-called laws of Edward and Guthrum', *EHR*, lvi (1941), 1-21.   [2] *Law NP*, 10.1, 48-54, 58-9.

[3] 'Edward and Guthrum', 4; cf. Robertson, *Charters*, no. 54, p. 113, Archbishop Oscytel of York (956-71) had obtained Helperby (N. Riding, Yorks) because there were two brothers who had one wife.

[4] *DB*, i. 1 a ii, for the Kentish custom that in a case of adultery the king should have the man and the archbishop the woman. Cf. *The Domesday Monachorum of Christ Church, Canterbury*, ed. D. C. Douglas (1944), p. 98.

Our concern so far has been with the shire court. King William's famous writ of *c.* 1072 refers to ecclesiastical cases which were heard in the hundred court, and forbids bishops and archdeacons to hear cases there in the future. The hundred or wapentake was basically a police and military organization, responsible with its subordinate tithings for local peace and order, for schemes devised for the prevention of theft, especially of cattle,[1] and for providing a contingent of troops for the royal army.[2] Its court met once a month,[3] and in it, as in the other *gemote*, ran the public law (*folcriht*).[4] Appeals lay from it possibly to the shire court, and, in default of justice, to the king.[5] Many hundred courts, or fragments of them, were in private hands. The competence of the court is nowhere stated, but it is likely that the distinction between the *gemote* lay less in jurisdiction than in their suitors. The hundred court was, in the main, for the humbler people, and its president, a reeve, was less distinguished than the presidents of the shire court.

Although no Anglo-Saxon law concerning the hundred court mentions ecclesiastical pleas, it is possible that church cases punishable by secular penalties could go before it and the borough court. What is more, since the hundreds and tithings were part of the police organization, it is likely that those inquisitions into heinous sins which were ordered periodically were the responsibility of the hundred courts. VIII Æthelred, c. 40, ordered, so as to purify the land, that inquiry and search should be diligently made for the dwelling-places of the wicked who would not abstain from evil or make amends in the sight of God, and that wherever they were found they should be brought to justice willy-nilly, or be banished from the land unless they would submit and amend their ways. II Cnut, c. 4, ordered a similar purification of the land, and, amplifying V Æthelred, cc. 23–6, VI Æthelred, c. 7, another purification decree, and 'Edward and Guthrum', c. 11, gives a list of sinners which probably reveals those who were to be rounded up – witches, sorcerers, murderers, whores, apostates, thieves and robbers, heathens, perjurers, injurers of the clergy (and, less emphatically, hypocrites and liars, robbers and plunderers).[6] These sweeps seem to be

---

[1] III Edmund, I Edgar, III Edgar, 5, IV Edgar, 3–11.

[2] Eric John, *Land tenure in Early England* (1960), pp. 115 ff.

[3] I Edgar, 1.   [4] I Edgar, 7.   [5] III Edgar, 2, II Cnut, 17.

[6] Cf. Wulfstan, *Sermo Lupi ad Anglos*, *EHD*, i. 858–9, 'Here there are manslayers and slayers of their kinsmen, and slayers of priests and persecutors of monasteries, and traitors and open apostates, and here there are perjurers and murderers, and here there are injurers of men.' Cnut, 1020, 15, 'the bishops teach that we should avoid every form of unrighteousness, such as the deeds of parricides, murderers, perjurers, witches, sorceresses, adulterers, and the incestuous'.

precedents for, or at least similar to, the Assizes of Clarendon and Northampton in Henry II's reign.

The hundred courts were admirably suited to this type of inquiry, for among their suitors were the priest and reeve and representative men from each village and the heads of the tithings. These men could present delinquents. We find, for example, that the national fast ordered by VII Æthelred was to be enforced by the priest and reeve of every village and the heads of the tithings, who were to be sworn on holy relics, and that fines imposed for breaches of the fast were to be divided among the poor.[1] Here we have the hundred court administering an ecclesiastical expedient, decreed and enforced by the state.

We have suggested that the shire court splits theoretically into ecclesiastical and secular components. It would be pressing theory too hard to force such a division on the hundred court. Priests attended and could act as doomsmen in ecclesiastical cases; but there is no convincing evidence for clerical presidents. The shire bishop could not have attended hundred courts, or their franchisal fragments, as a rule, for they were too many and met too often. Nor, as far as we know, had the bishop spiritual representatives who could have taken his place. It is unlikely that any bishop had more than one archdeacon.[2] The implication of William I's writ, that bishops and archdeacons had been hearing cases in the hundred courts, is only intelligible in a very limited sense. Bishops who owned hundreds, or parts of them, may have been using their courts for ecclesiastical purposes. But we have no other evidence for this custom.

In the Old-English kingdom the alliance between church and state was probably more intimate than anywhere else in Europe. As a result there was a certain conflation of royal and ecclesiastical institutions, but, according to the ideas of the time, no real confusion and little behaviour that was truly uncanonical. At all times the church required the state to help it in its work, and usually it asked the lay power to add secular penalties for some sins, especially for the supreme sin of heresy. Moreover, the participation of the king was supplementary. He did not deny, or encroach upon, a bishop's ecclesiastical jurisdiction.[3] And it may be that the main function of royal

---

[1] VII Æthelred, 2.4–5 (Latin), 3–4 (Old English).

[2] See below, pp. 247–9. Makower, para. 59, p. 385, took the contrary view: 'Similarly the hundred-moot seems to have been held by the bishop or his archdeacon in conjunction with the temporal official', relying on William's writ and III Edgar, 5, and II Cnut, 18, laws which have to be badly strained to bear this interpretation.

[3] For purer ecclesiastical jurisdiction, see below, chapter V.

ecclesiastical legislation always was to give publicity to that part of the canon law which the bishops desired to make known throughout the kingdom. How much the church availed itself of secular help and penalties in the maintenance of its discipline will always remain unknown owing to the absence of court records.

APPENDIX A

Edward's Charters from 1050

Five charters, none impeccable, and only persuasive because of the agreement between two separate traditions, deserve attention: three Abingdon charters, K. 792 (dated 1050), 796 (dated 1052), and 800 (dated 1054), and one in which Abingdon had an interest, 793 (dated 1050), and the Exeter 'foundation charter' (dated 1050), which exists in two versions, A (*Ordnance Survey facsimiles*, Exeter xiii) and B (K. 791). Abingdon charters have not a very high reputation. K. 792 and 796 have the same preamble. K. 792 and 793 give Earl Siward's name as 'Sihroth'. K. 793 and 800 refer apparently to the same piece of land, and, if so, can hardly have been granted on the same occasion. Two of the charters, K. 796 and 800, have wrong dates, and these, together with K. 792, include among the witnesses Abbot Ordric (*c.* 1052–66), who could not have signed with the others. The Exeter charter is no less puzzling, for, although the two versions of the text are substantially the same, the witness lists have important differences. Despite these serious difficulties, all the witness lists have no obvious fault (except for Ordric's signature on some of the Abingdon charters); and the substantial agreement between the Exeter and Abingdon schedules, which are of independent origin, is a strong argument in favour of their being a fairly accurate list of the *witan* at the time of the grants. The *terminus ad quem* for all these witness lists is 29 October 1050, when Archbishop Eadsige died. The Abingdon lists cannot be so late, for Bishop Ulf witnesses. He was at Toul on 21–22 October and Vercelli on 1 September, and therefore cannot have been in England after 1 August. The *terminus a quo* for all is 1049, for Pope Leo IX is mentioned in the Exeter charter and Bishop Ulf was appointed no earlier than that year; and, as three of the charters are dated 1050 and the others later, 1050 can be accepted. Bishop Herman, who signs all, and Bishop Ealdred, all but 796, were at the Easter council at Rome. Hence a date before 15 March or after 15 May is indicated; but, as Earl Swegn witnesses Exeter A, the later period is preferable. The most suitable day for the ceremony at Exeter was St Peter's day, 29 June. There is no difficulty in accepting this date. The Abingdon charters would seem to be dated 15 May–1 August.

Since it is now believed that the land-books of this period were not products of the royal writing office, but were usually drawn up by the interested party, their witness lists cannot be regarded as official records of attendance. We must allow for partiality and wishful thinking. Nevertheless, since the charter was written to commemorate an act of gift, the more reputable memorials are unlikely to be completely irresponsible in the naming of participants in the ceremony. The principal witnesses to these charters (omitting some nobles and most thegns) are as follows: *archbishops:* Eadsige (all), Ælfric (Exeter A, B); *bishops:* Stigand (all), Herman (all), Ulf (all Abingdon), Heca (K. 792–3), Duduc (K. 792–3, 800, Exeter B), Leofric (all Abingdon), Ælfwold II (K. 792–3), Ealdred (all except K. 796), Robert (K. 792–3, 800, Exeter B); *abbots:* Æthelweard (of Glastonbury) (all except K. 800), Ordric (of Abingdon) (K. 792, 796, 800), Spearhavoc (of Abingdon) (K. 793), Wulfweard (K. 792–3, 800),Ælfwine (of Ramsey) (K. 796, 800, Exeter A, B), Leofsige (of Ely) (K. 800), Sihtric (of Tavistock) (Exeter A); *priests:* Regenbald (all except K. 791), Rodbriht (all Abingdon), Godwine (all except K. 796), Lifing (K. 792–3), William (K. 792–3, 800), Kinsige (Unsige and Winsige, K. 792 ; Kinsige min., K. 793; 796, 800), Brihtric (K. 793, 800), Æthelwig (K. 796), Godman (Exeter A, B), Peter (Exeter B); *earls :* Godwin, Leofric, Harold, Siward, Ralf (all), Swegn (Exeter A); *nobles:* Tostig (all; *minister*, Abingdon; *nobilis*, Exeter), Odda (Exeter only); *thegns:* Ralf (Exeter only), Leofwine (K. 800).

APPENDIX B

Royal Priests and Clerks, 1024-66

Listed in order of occurrence

(OD, OG, ON, OSW = Old-Danish, -German, -Norse, -Swedish)

Eadsige 1024, 1032 (K. 741; 745); bp. of St Martins *ante* 1038, archbp. of Canterbury 1038-50.

Eadweald 1024, 1032, 1033, 1035, 1042, 1043 (K. 741; 745-6; 751, 1318; 1322; 762; 767).

Ælfwine 1024, 1032 (K. 741; 745-6); bp. of Winchester 1032-47.

Kinsige (Cynsige) 1026 (K. 743)/1050 (K. 796, 800); archbp. of York 1051-60.

Leofstan 1026 (K. 743).

Wynsige 1026 (K. 743)/?1050 (K. 792)/1066, *camerarius regis* E., *DB*, i. 151 a ii, 209 a ii.

Stigand (ON) 1027-32, 1033, 1035, 1042 (K. 1324; 751, 1318; 1322; 762); bp. of Elmham 1043-7, Winchester 1047-70, archbp. of Canterbury 1052-70.

Duduc (OG; Saxon/Lotharingian) 1033 (K. 1318); Congresbury and Banwell minsters; bp. of Wells 1033-60.

Godwine [1] 1033 (K. 1318)/1050 (K. 791-3, 800)/*ante* 1053-?1066 holding part of the church of Bosham, *DB*, i. 17 b i, 27 a i-ii, 43 a i.

Wulfnoth 1033 (K. 1318).

Smelt 1035 (K. 1322); 1066 *capellanus regis* E., canon of St Martin, Dover, *DB*, i. 1 b i, landholder in Dorset, *ibid*. i. 24 b ii.

Ælfwine 1042 (K. 762): possibly identical with Alwine (below).

Spirites 1042 (K. 762); brother of Earnwig, a secular reeve of St Mary, Worcester, *Hemingi Chartularium*, i. 254; exiled by Edward *c*. 1065, *ibid*., *DB*, i. 252 b ii; canon of St Martin, Dover, *DB*, i. 1 b ii, of St Mary, Bromfield, i. 252 b ii; landholder in Shropshire, Herefords, Somerset, Wilts, and Hants, i. 258 a ii, 260 b ii; 183 a i; 91 a ii; 73 a i, ii; 49 a ii; *antecessor* of Nigel *medicus*.

Herman (OG; Lotharingian) 1042, 1043 (K. 762; 767); bp. of Ramsbury 1045-78, of Sherborne 1058-78.

Leofric 1042, 1043 (K. 762; 767); estate in Devon *ante* 1046; bp. of Devon and Cornwall 1046-72.

Heca bp. of Selsey 1047-57.

[1] Although a common name, the landholder was associated with Earl Godwin, and we are probably here concerned with one man.

Ulf (ON; Norman) bp. of Dorchester 1049–52.

Regenbald (Reinbald OG; ?German) 1050, 1062, 1065 (K. 791–3, 796, 800; 813; 815, 825); for his lands and churches, see above, pp. 134–5.

Godman 1050 (K. 791); father of Godric abt. of Winchcombe; ?landholder in Devon, *DB*, i. 106 b i, 107 b, 108 b.

Peter (Norman) 1050, 1062, 1065 (K. 791; 813; 815, 825); 1066 held land and churches in Berks and Somerset, *DB*, 57 a i, 91 b i, 98 b ii; custodian of Dorchester 1067; bp. of Lichfield 1072–85.

Rodbert (OG; ?Norman) 1050, 1062, 1065 (K. 792–3, 796, 800; 813; 825); ?bp. of Hereford 1079–95; ?monk of St Mary, Stow, *ante* 1086, *DB*, i. 345 a i.

Lyfing 1050 (K. 792–3).

William (OG; Norman) 1050 (K. 792–3, 800); bp. of London 1051–75.

Beohrtric 1050 (K. 793, 800).

Leofwine 1050 (K. 792–3); ?canon of St Martin, Dover, *DB*, i. 1 b i; ?landholder in Northants 1066, 1086, *DB*, i. 222 b ii.

Æthelwig 1050 (K. 796).

Wulfwig bp. of Dorchester 1053–67.

Walter (OG; Lotharingian) bp. of Hereford 1060–79; 1066 landholder in Hants., *DB*, i. 43 a i.

Giso (OG; Lotharingian) bp. of Wells 1060–88.

Baldwin (?Fleming) 1062 (K. 813).

Osbern (ON; Norman) 1062, 1065 (K. 813; 815, 825); churches in Hants. and Wilts. 1066, 1086, *DB*, i. 17 a i, b i; 65 b i; bp. of Exeter 1072–1103.

Vitalis (?Norman) *ante* 1066, *DB*, i. 208 a i; church in Wilts., *DB*, i. 65 b i.

Bernard (OG; ?German) *ante* 1066, *DB*, i. 208 a i; 1068.[1]

Albert the Lotharingian [2] (OG; Lotharingian) *ante* 1066; estates in Middlesex, Beds, and Rutland, churches of Oakham, Hambledon, and St Peter's, Stamford 1066, *DB*, i, 129 a i, 216 b ii, 294, 336 b ii; prebendary of Maplebury, St Paul's, London.

Ingelric[3] (OG) *ante* 1066; estates in Oxon, Herts, and Essex 1066, *DB*, i. 137 a ii, 142 a i, 159 b i, ii. 26 b, 27 b, 29, 32 b; he and his brother Æirad (? OD Elaf) founded the canonry of St Martin-le-Grand, London, for the souls of Kings Edward and William and their own, *ante* 1067.

[1] W. H. Stevenson, 'An Old-English charter of William the Conqueror in favour of St Martin's-le-Grand, London', *EHR*, xi (1896), 744.

[2] J. H. Round, 'Ingelric the Priest and Albert of Lotharingia', *The Commune of London* (1899), pp. 36–8; C. N. L. Brooke, 'The composition of the Chapter of St Paul's 1086–1163', *Camb. HJ*, x (1951), 122.

[3] *FNC*, iv. 726; W. H. Stevenson, *op. cit.* and *EHR*, xii (1897), 108 *n.*; Round, *op. cit.* pp. 28–30, 36; D. C. Douglas, *Feudal Documents from the Abbey of Bury St Edmunds* (Br. Acad.: Records of Social and Ec. Hist. vii. 1932), p. xcix *n.* Ingelric's nationality is uncertain; but he was probably a foreigner.

Leofa 1066 estate in Somerset, *DB*, i. 91 b i.

Beohrtfrith 1066 estate in Devon, *DB*, i. 104 a ii.

Brun 1066–86 landholder in Oxon., *DB*, i. 157 a i.

Leofgeat 1066 estate in Beds., *DB*, i. 211 a i.

Alwine 1066 canon of St Martin, Dover, *DB*, i. 1 b i, landholder in Kent and Hunts., *DB*, i. 13 b ii, 208 a i; ?brother of Wulfwig (above), holding in Bucks. and Beds., *DB*, i. 151 b ii, 211 b i, 218 b ii.

Godric 1066 canon of St Martin, Dover, *DB*, i. 1 b i; ?brother of Wulfwig (above), holding in Bucks., *DB*, i. 144 a i; several priests and clerks of this name are in *DB*.

Radulf 1066–86 church in Wilts., *DB*, i. 65 b i.

Alweard (ON) 1066–86 church in Wilts., *ibid*.

Beorhtweard 1066–86 churches in Dorset, *DB*, i. 79 a i, 1086 his father's church in Wilts., 65 b i.

Bolla 1066–86 churches in Dorset, *DB*, i. 79 a i, 1086, 78 b i, 84 a i, Somerset, 92 a ii; Bolla's wife held of Peter (see above), 98 b ii.

Ælfgeat 1066–86 land in Somerset, *DB*, i. 91 b i.

Thorsteinn (OD) 1086 his father's land in Somerset, *ibid*.

Ælfgar 1086 land in Devon, *DB*, i. 104 a ii.

Edward 1086 landholder in Oxon, Dorset, and Devon, *DB*, i. 157 a i; 77 b i; 113 b i, 117 b ii.

Earnwig 1086 his father's lands in Lincs., *DB*, i. 211 a i, 371 a i, ii. The name occurs elsewhere in Lincs. and Northants.

Ælfric 1066 canon of St Martin, Dover, *DB*, i. 1 b i; 1086 lands in Leics. and Rutland, *DB*, i. 231 a ii, 294 a i.

Wulmaer 1066 land in Bucks., *antecessor* of William the chamberlain, *DB*, i. 151 a ii.

CHAPTER III

The Geographical Organization and Economy of the English Church

I. TEMPORALITIES AND SPIRITUALITIES

Ecclesia has many meanings, ranging from the building which housed the altar to the whole body of Christian people, dead and alive. Among the narrower senses is the concept of an individual physical church together with all its lands, rights and privileges, and its jurisdictional area. It was primarily the home of one or more saints, who were sometimes very much alive. St Yves appeared to a Ramsey monk who had failed to bow before his shrine, and exclaimed, 'You listless idle brother! Why do you neglect the salvation of your soul? Why do you not pay me proper reverence?' And, pointing to his tomb, he went on, 'Who do you think is resting there? Not some paltry fellow, I suppose?' [1] An Ely monk, who claimed not to have heard of St Yves, was given no uncertain proof of his existence. Waylaying him with the words, 'Do you not know me? This is my house', the saint gave him a belt which squeezed him almost to death.[2] Yet it was also such a church that an owner or patron gave to a priest as a benefice. Both the donor and the bishop (or, with a bishopric, the metropolitan and fellow bishops) played a part in the investiture. And it is theoretically possible, and was sometimes attempted, to draw a distinction between a church's temporalities and spiritualities, to segregate the purely ecclesiastical functions from the administration of lands, secular jurisdictions, and regalities. But it is doubtful whether this distinction was clearly apprehended in the early eleventh century or whether under English conditions it had any practical significance.

The basic endowment of a church was the land it stood on and the usually necessary curtilage. There were private oratories within secular buildings and itinerant chapels which travelled on carts. More substantial churches were occasionally transported to a new site. But in general a church was founded on the rock of its own hallowed ground. It usually needed a graveyard, and, if it was served by a resident priest or a community, it also

[1] Goscelin, *Miracula S. Yvonis, Chron. Ramsey*, p. lxvi.   [2] *Ibid.* p. lxxi.

required agricultural land, or the 'superiority' over such land, for the support of its ministers. These basic needs were often, of course, supplemented by the bequests of the faithful. Every type of temporal right could be granted to a church, from the administration of hundreds, the ownership of a mint,[1] or the privilege of holding a market, to the right to keep a bull on the common, or pasture swine without payment [2] – and it would be profitless to attempt an enumeration. A church as a landholder was like other landholders except that its right to alienate its property was restricted. And like other land-holders it had a lord or patron whose domination was always real and, at some levels, could be oppressive.

There were also some financial rights peculiar to the church, principally the five customs which, in the tenth and eleventh centuries, were sanctioned by the royal laws: tithe, church-scot, plough-alms, light-dues, and soul-scot.[3] A sixth customary payment, Romescot, similarly enforced, went to the church of Rome.[4] These taxes were not originally of the same nature. Whereas light-dues were essentially a local payment to an individual church, tithe had had a wider purpose and a less particular application. But, on the whole, by the eleventh century they had all been divided out and had become customs pertaining to a church. That is to say, individual churches had definite claims to all or some of them from defined areas or persons. Of these customs tithe was the most important. All men who bred animals or raised crops were bound to pay a tenth of the yield to the church, to be divided into three parts, one for the maintenance of the fabric, one for the ministers of the church, and one for the poor.[5] The tithe of young stock was to be paid by Pentecost and the tithe of all fruits of the earth by the Equinox or All Saints' Day (1 November).[6] In the eleventh century, it seems, the tenth acre, instead of a tenth of the crop, was often allocated to the church.[7] The tax was rather different from church-scot, or first-fruits, which was paid on the feast of St Martin (11 November) [8] in the form of a load of grain per

---

[1] The bishop of Hereford's moneyer in the city is noted *DB*, i. 179 a, 181 a ii, and the bishop of Thetford's right to one in Norwich, ii. 117 b.

[2] The priests of Lambourne (Berks) had free pasture for 40 pigs: Robertson, *Charters*, Appendix i, no. 5.   [3] See above, p. 145.   [4] See below, pp. 295-7.

[5] Cf. *Institutio Canonicorum* of the Council of Aachen, 817, c. lxxiii, *Enlarged Rule of Chrodegang*, ed. A. S. Napier, EETS, 150 (1916), 81; VIII Æthelred, 6; Lingard, *Antiquities*, i. 181-90.

[6] V Æthelred, 11.1; I Cnut, 8.1; Napier, *Wulfstan Sammlung*, nos. XXIII, LXI. For tithe-collectors after the Conquest, see R. Lennard, 'Peasant Tithe-collectors in Norman England', *EHR*, lxix (1954), 580-96.   [7] *Chron. Abingdon*, ii. 25; cf. VIII Æthelred, 7, I Cnut, 8.2.

[8] Cnut 1027, 16, Liebermann, *Gesetze*, i. 277; Napier, *ibid*. According to Homily XXIII it was due from the 'English law'.

THE DIOCESES
AND MAIN CHURCHES
1000 - 1066

- - · - Diocesan Boundaries
· · · · · · · Shire Boundaries (when
        different from Diocesan)
● Monastic Church
○ Secular College
‡ Archbishop's See
+ Bishop's See

DURHAM

Ripon
YORK
Beverley

Chester

Stow
Lincoln
Southwell
Grantham

Burton
Wenlock   LICHFIELD   Crowland
Bromfield   Peterborough   Thorney   ELMHAM
Leominster   Ramsey Ely Soham   Norwich
            Coventry   Huntingdono   Hoxne
      Pershore Evesham   St Ives
WORCESTER   St Neots   Bury
HEREFORD Deerhurst   St Edmunds
ST DAVIDS   Winchcombe
      Gloucester Eynsham Buckingham
            Berkeley   Aylesbury St Albans
LLANDAFF   Abingdon DORCHESTER   Waltham
      Hawkesbury Cholsey Bensington Ashingdon
      Bath Malmsb'y   LONDON
            RAMSBURY Sonning Westminster ROCHESTER CANTERBURY
WELLS   Bedwyn   Chertsey   St Augustines
      Amesbury   WINCHESTER   Dover
Glastonbury   Wherwell
Athelney   Wilton o(Old) Salisbury
Hartland Taunton Shaftesbury Mottisfont
CREDITON Muchelney SHERBORNE Romsey Bosham
      Cerne Abbas   SELSEY
BODMIN Tavistock EXETER
ST GERMANS   Abbotsbury

taxation hide, although this too could sometimes mean an acre of corn or
4d.[1] Plough-alms were a penny for each plough or ploughland, paid fifteen
days after Easter.[2] Light-dues were paid three times a year.[3] And soul-scot
(mortuary) was required when a Christian was buried.[4]

Attached to each church was an area of jurisdiction, its parish, a spirituality, although determined almost always by secular boundaries. The parish
did not necessarily coincide with the district under tribute to a church, nor
did all churches have equal rights over their parishioners. The subdivision of
the bishop's parish – his diocese – into lesser parishes had led to a partition of all jurisdictional and financial rights between the various churches.
But the parish did serve to direct to the local church the customary payments
and also the voluntary gifts in connexion with the sacraments and other
spiritual services performed by the priest or community. Although there
were always inequalities and irregularities, there was a natural tendency for
parish and tributary area to coincide.

For any church, then, it can be asked what was its parish, what rights it
possessed over its parishioners, what customs it enjoyed, and what were its
temporal possessions. These questions, however, cannot always be answered
for the eleventh century.

2. THE DIOCESES

The arrangement of the English church owed more to secular history than to
Roman geography or an ecclesiastical plan. The two provinces perpetuated

---

[1] Robertson, *Charters*, nos. 35, 109; Lingard, *Antiquities*, i. 190-1; N. Neilson, *Customary
Rents* (Oxford Studies in Social and Legal History, ii, 1910), pp. 192-6. It was often reserved when
land was leased by a church: cf. Robertson, nos. 34, 81, 112. According to *DB*, i. 174 a i (*Hemingi
Chartularium*, i. 49-50), the bishop of Worcester should have one *summa* of corn from each hide,
whether free or villein land, which belonged to his church. The tenant's liability is occasionally
mentioned in *DB*. Four freemen held in Fladbury from the bishop, rendering all sake and soke,
church-scot, soul-scot, *expeditiones et navigia*, and pleas to Oswaldslow (i. 173 a i); from ⅓ hide at
Lippard were rendered annually 8d. for church-scot and *recognitio terrae* (i. 174 a i). Pershore had a
similar render from each freeman holding a hide or more within Oswaldslow, *DB*, i. 175 b i.
Aylesbury (Bucks) had one *summa* of corn, apparently commuted into one acre of corn or 4d, from
every sokeman who held one hide or more in the eight hundreds pertaining to that *tun*, *DB*, i.
143 b ii.   [2] V Æthelred, 11.1; Napier, *ibid.*; Lingard, *Antiquities*, i. 191-2.

[3] V Æthelred, 11.1; Napier, *ibid.*: a halfpenny's worth of wax at Candlemas, Easter, and All
Saints (XXIII); Christmas, Candlemas, and Easter, or oftener (LXI); Lingard, *Antiquities*, i. 192;
Neilson, *Customary Rents*, p. 192.

[4] V Æthelred, 12; Napier, *ibid.*; Lingard, *Antiquities*, i. 192. Payment had to be made at the
open grave. A nobleman's payment was heavy and his burial well worth having: see Whitelock,
Wills, nos. 15, 18-21, 24, 29.

the political frontier on the Humber. Most of the dioceses represented submerged peoples or kingdoms, or a combination of such ancient units. South of the Thames ecclesiastical institutions had developed naturally within the political framework of kingdom and shire.[1] Kent had kept two dioceses for east and west, with sees at Canterbury and Rochester; and sometimes there was a suffragan bishop with his see in St Martin's, Canterbury.[2] Selsey was the see for the bishop of the South Saxons. In Wessex there were six bishops for eight shires – Hampshire and Surrey (Winchester), Wiltshire and Berkshire (Ramsbury), Dorset (Sherborne), Somerset (Wells), Devon (Crediton), and Cornwall (St Germans). In western Mercia, however, owing to the recent and artificial introduction of shires, there was no coincidence. The diocese for the Magonsaetan, with its see at Hereford, overstepped the shire boundary into Shropshire, and the diocese for the Hwicce, by which name it was still sometimes called,[3] with its see at Worcester, comprised Worcestershire, Gloucestershire, and the southern half of Warwickshire. To the east and north, where several dioceses had disappeared during the period of the Viking invasions, the survivors were large. The diocese of Lichfield included northern Warwickshire, Staffordshire, north-east Shropshire, Chester, the land between Mersey and Ribble, and Derbyshire. On Dorchester depended part of Nottinghamshire, Lincolnshire, Leicestershire, Rutland, Northamptonshire, Huntingdonshire, Cambridgeshire, Oxfordshire, Buckinghamshire, and Bedfordshire. Elmham sufficed for East Anglia. Only London (Middlesex, Essex, and Hertfordshire) kept its old boundaries. In Northumbria, where Whithorn and Hexham had been abandoned, there was no more than the large diocese of York and, north of the Tees, the newly founded see of Durham.

The Scandinavian invasions had destroyed what little had remained of Pope Gregory I's plan for the English church, and if King Edward and his bishops had had their way, and managed to combine even more dioceses,[4] a real transformation would have occurred. But amalgamations had probably

---

[1] Archbishop Wulfstan, 'Be cyrican', *Polity*, pp. 144–5, refers to the bishop as 'Cristes scirgerefa'. Cf. Napier, *Wulfstan Sammlung*, p. 118 *n.*, 'on his b. scire'.

[2] E.g. Bishop Godwin who died in 1061 (*ASC DE* 1061). See also Plummer on Siward, pp.223–4.

[3] *Vita Wlsini*, p. 79. Cf. also F. M. Stenton, *The Early History of the Abbey of Abingdon* (University College, Reading, Studies in Local History, Oxford, 1913), pp. 20–1.

[4] Devon and Cornwall had been united since 1027. Stigand in 1052 joined Winchester and Canterbury, adjacent except for dependent Rochester. Herman in 1058 reunited Wiltshire and Sherborne. Ealdred held various combinations of dioceses and in 1060 tried to attach Worcester to York again.

gone as far as was desirable. The existing arrangements corresponded roughly to the density of population, except for the immoderately large diocese, with ill-sited see, of Dorchester-on-Thames. So that after this bishopric had been divided, and a diocese created for Carlisle,[1] no great change in the boundaries took place before the sixteenth century.

Although great emphasis was placed on the maintenance of a fixed territorial organization, the concept of a neat governmental area within a ringfence ran counter to ordinary habits. In a kingdom where one lord could have a man's commendation and another his soke, and some men were free to change their lord and even take their land with them, temporary personal relationships often governed territorial arrangements. The bishoprics were not as unstable as the earldoms in this period, but they were by no means unalterable. Hence the bishop's most important possession was the symbol of his authority, his throne, *cathedra*, his see. Among words expressing a bishop's parish, *bisceop* is more generally and frequently compounded with *setle*, *sethel* (settle), *seld* (seat), or *stol* (stool) than with words referring to jurisdiction, *dom* (judgment), or to area, *scir*. It was from his high seat that the bishop ruled, and it was on his stool that he died.[2] A folding chair would be carried on his progresses; and when he changed decisively his governmental centre, then, it seems, he would uproot his stone *cathedra* and erect it in his new church. In this way the present throne in Norwich cathedral probably came there from Dunwich by way of Elmham and Thetford.[3]

The siting of the sees within the dioceses was in the eleventh century rather unsatisfactory. The relative importance of places had changed, and by 1000 the position of some sees could be defended only on the grounds of sacred tradition or recent necessity. William of Malmesbury considered that half the Anglo-Saxon sees were unsuitable. London was a noble city, York a fine metropolis with evidence of Roman elegance, Hereford showed signs of former greatness, Exeter was a fine city, Durham had a spectacular site, and Canterbury was of moderate size [4] (he does not describe Winchester and Worcester, which were, presumably, satisfactory, or Selsey, which was probably not); but Rochester was constricted, Elmham rather small, Crediton a

---

[1] Carlisle and Ely were established by King Henry I.

[2] Bishop Wulfsige of Sherborne died at the episcopal manor of Beaminster (*Bega monasterium*), Dorset, *c.* 1001, 'Regente ergo extrema hora in sella episcopali, uti mos erat, eger collocatus, et . . . misterio sancte unctionis insignatus': *Vita Wlsini*, p. 78. Cf. *Vita Wulfstani*, p. 61.

[3] Report of its restoration in *The Times*, 11 January 1960.

[4] *GP*, pp. 140; 208; 298; 201; 270-1; 3.

village, Dorchester tiny and remote, and Ramsbury poor.[1] Of Sherborne he wrote that it was a little place without activity or beauty, and that it was a matter for wonder, almost for shame, that a bishop's see had been there for so many centuries; [2] and of Lichfield that it was small and off the map, that its church was cramped and revealed the poverty of olden times, and that it was a place of which contemporary bishops would be ashamed.[3]

Although William was justifying the removal of sees by the Normans, his observations seem fair, and reveal a remarkable situation. England had few ancient and enduring cities. Some bishops' towns had not prospered. In general, wealth had come to the monasteries founded or refounded since the tenth century,[4] and only four sees – Canterbury, Winchester, Worcester, and Sherborne – had benefited from this movement. Some of the secular minsters had fallen by the wayside. Served by only a handful of canons or priests, they were without obvious attraction. Durham, with St Cuthbert, was the exception, and it prospered exceedingly. On the other hand, monastic reform was creating places of new importance. For example, the East-Anglian monasteries of Ely, Peterborough, Bury St Edmunds, and Ramsey were dynamic institutions with attractive shrines, centres of art and industry and active in estate management. The result was that some abbots and monks when appointed to an unfashionable see, never changed their allegiance, and so added to the existing disorder.

About half the bishops' sees were sited within boroughs over which they did not have exclusive control. Boroughs were essentially royal institutions, created for the defence of the shire, and under the special care of the earl. But the bishop, too, seems to have had some responsibility for the defence of the borough,[5] and, in the absence of the earl, it would be to him, rather than to the port-reeve or sheriff, that the burgesses would turn. In most, if not all, cases the bishop's church and men formed a privileged enclave within the borough. The position at York is described in Domesday Book: [6]

In the city of York in the time of King Edward there were six shires besides the archbishop's shire. From one of these [six] shires the archbishop still has a third part. . . . From his own shire, however, the archbishop used to have the full dues [consuetudo]. In the

[1] GP, pp. 133; 148; 200; 311; 182.   [2] Ibid. p. 175.   [3] Ibid. p. 307.

[4] In 1052 Pope Leo IX issued a Bull to Italy denouncing abbots and monks who persuaded laymen to give all their possessions to monasteries and cut out the churches which had given them baptism, penance, and eucharist, and ordering that in future at least half must be given to the donor's parish church (MPL, cxliii, coll. 685–6).

[5] The bishop of Worcester had the third penny of the borough: DB. i. 173 b i.

[6] DB, i. 298 a i–ii.

archbishop's shire there were 189 dwelling houses. . . . In this shire the archbishop has as much as the king has in his shires. . . . In the same way in all the land of St Peter of York [and of four other churches] neither the king nor the earl nor anyone else has any dues.

In Lincoln in 1086 Bishop Remigius held one little manor (*maneriolum*) of one carucate, with the right of sake and soke and toll and team, which also extended over two churches and some eighty houses. Only one of these houses was free from all customs. The others paid the king's geld with the burgesses.[1] This sort of arrangement seems to have been acceptable to all concerned and to have caused no trouble. Leofric deliberately moved his see from rural Crediton into the protection of the walls of Exeter. And if Herman removed from the borough of Wilton into Sherborne Abbey it was probably more because he was a monk than that he had quarrelled with royal reeves.

The Normans found the cathedral churches, as well as their sites, unsatisfactory, and rebuilt all of them in a different style. The Norman aim was to improve on unfashionable, small, and probably decayed buildings. We are not well informed about the history of the fabric of the Old-English cathedrals. But, except for the revolutionary period of the tenth-century reforms, when there was a special need for reconstruction and a conscious desire to break with the past, renovation, usually after some natural or military disaster, seems to have been the rule.[2] The most radical rebuilding was at Worcester, and some anecdotes concerning it were recorded.[3] A man Wiferd and his wife Alta gave land to St Peter's, Worcester (where their parents lay buried); and after their death a stone monument bearing a cross was erected over their tomb,[4] situated, apparently, outside the east-end of the cathedral. It was by this stone, because of the flatness of the ground, that St Oswald used to preach to the people. The minster was in fact too small to accommodate the multitude of worshippers, and later Oswald built a new cathedral church, dedicated to St Mary, on a new site. The old minster was given by

---

[1] *DB*, i. 336 a i.

[2] In 962 St Paul's, London, was burnt and, according to *ASC A* 962, rebuilt in the same year. North Elmham seems to have been rebuilt in the late tenth or early eleventh century, probably after Viking destruction. Hereford, possibly because of damage by the Welsh, was rebuilt by Bishop Æthelstan (1012–56). Sherborne was restored owing to its dilapidated state by Bishop Ælfwold (1045/6–58).   [3] *Hemingi Chartularium*, ii. 341–3.

[4] 'lapidum structura more antiquorum super sepulchrum eorum opere artificioso cum cruce dominica ob monumentum largitatis et monimentum animarum ipsorum composita est': *ibid*. ii. 342. It is also called 'lapidum congeries' and was a mile from a similar stone called 'candidus lapis', outside the city to the north, which was pulled down in William I's reign when the monks' lavatory was built on the site: *ibid*. ii. 343. For the pyramids in the churchyard at Glastonbury, see Malmesbury, *De Antiqu. Glaston. Ecclesiae*, i. 43–5.

Bishop Brihtheah, a great nepotist, to his brother Æthelric; and this man, in Edward's reign, extended the presbytery of his church and destroyed the monument to Wiferd and Alta. Generally, however, once the revolution had subsided, the old feeling that it was vandalism to destroy ancient churches was intensified, for there developed a natural reluctance to throw down a fabric associated with saintly predecessors. Prelates living under the influence of the tenth-century reformation had no wish to uproot their heritage. St Wulfstan often prayed in the old minster [1] and wept unconsolably during the next rebuilding of St Mary's, Worcester,[2] and several who planned a reconstruction were dissuaded by visions of those whom they proposed to disturb.[3] It needed a measure of detachment and a certain disrespect for the past – such as the Normans possessed – to take this drastic step. Goscelin of St Bertin, a foreigner in England, could write,[4]

He destroys well who builds something better. Although I am myself a useless little man, an inhabitant only of the earth, I greatly dislike little buildings, and, although poor in goods, design great things. And so, if given the means, I would not allow buildings although much esteemed to stand, unless they were, according to my idea, glorious, magnificent, most lofty, most spacious, filled with light, and most beautiful.

He had seen his bishop, likewise a foreigner, plan a new cathedral church at Salisbury.

A bishop took possession with his diocese of a collection of rights and claims to property and financial customs. His basic source of revenue was his church's estates, situated for the most part within his diocese; and, as a landlord, he drew profit from markets, jurisdiction, and other 'regalities' possessed by his church. This property was very unstable. The heart of the endowment was book-land, land held under charter in perpetual inheritance, a tenure as absolute as Anglo-Saxon wit could contrive. But the church sometimes wrongfully alienated this land by charter, and sometimes a king would

[1] *Vita Wulfstani*, pp. 9–10.
[2] *Ibid*. p. 52: 'Nos inquit miseri sanctorum destruimus opera, pompatice putantes nos facere meliora. Quanto prestantior nobis sanctus Oswaldus, qui hanc fecit ecclesiam! Quot sancti viri religiosi in ea deo servierunt !'
[3] Siward of Abingdon planned to rebuild St Æthelwold's church *c*. 1034, but instead gave away the money to the poor: *Chron. Abingdon*, i. 444. Wulfric of St Augustine's, Canterbury, after getting Leo IX's permission at the Council of Rheims, 1049, to restore the abbey, changed his mind: Goscelin, *Historia translat. S. Augustini*, *MPL*, clv, coll. 32–3. Herluin, the founder of Bec, strongly resisted Lanfranc's scheme to rebuild: Gilbert Crispin, *Vita Herluini*, pp. 98–9. Guibert of Nogent was opposed to the indiscriminate exhumation of the bodies of saints: *De pignoribus sanctorum*, I, c. iv. *MPL*, clvi. coll. 626–7, *De Vita sua*, III, c. xx, coll. 958–9.
[4] *Liber confortatorius*, p. 93.

impiously grant it away. Probably more serious, however, were the losses due
to enfeofments. Nobles demanded loans; benefactions were often burdened
with life-interests;[1] lawsuits were usually compromised by allowing some
interest to the loser; and the bishop had both the need to grant leases to
servants and the temptation to reward his kinsmen and friends. A few estates
were usually kept relatively unencumbered. These were the slave and serf
estates under the direct control of the bishop's servants, although even these
were often 'farmed' by bailiffs. And beyond this 'inland' was an 'outland' of
indeterminate area – a collection of reversionary claims with an entitlement
to rents, services, and customs in the meanwhile.[2]

A few episcopal sees were forcibly re-endowed in the tenth century. In
964 King Edgar and the bishops decided to recover all alienations and usurpations in some bishoprics.[3] At Winchester and Worcester all grants that had
been made to nobles in hereditary tenure out of church lands were abrogated
and the charters voided. At Worcester, it seems, Bishop Oswald was em-
powered to convert these book-lands [4] into loan-land for two or three lives,[5]

[1] Ramsey Abbey often put a kinsman of the benefactor in possession for life, *vice firmarii*,
paying *census* and the agreed *feorm; cf. Chron. Ramsey*, pp. 144–5, 153–4, 175. In the first two cases
the tenant was a Ramsey monk.

[2] As Worcester enfeofments are usually quoted (thanks to Hemming), here are three typical
bargains from St Albans: Abbot Ælfric or Leofric, probably in Cnut's reign, granted land to
Leofsige and his *socii* in pledge for £10 – the land was redeemable at the will of the abbot, otherwise
it reverted on the death of the creditors: *Gesta abbatum monasterii S. Albani*, p. 33; Abbot Leofstan
in Edward's reign granted a vill to the widow Tova at farm for three marks of gold as *gersum* and
one measure of honey *p.a.: ibid.* p. 39, and a manor to Turnoth and two other 'knights' for 5 oz.
of gold, a palfrey, and a hound and for the service of protecting the monastery from the wild beasts
and robbers of the Chilterns and the danger of general war in the kingdom: *ibid.* p. 40. Glastonbury's
lease of Uffculme in Edward's reign is discussed by H. P. R. Finberg in W. G. Hoskins and Finberg,
Devonshire Studies (1952), pp. 59 ff.

[3] Eric John, 'The King and the Monks in the Tenth-century Reformation', *BJRL*, xlii (1959),
70 ff.; 'Some Latin charters of the Tenth-century Reformation in England', *Revue Bénédictine*,
lxx (1960), 338, 340; *Land Tenure in Early England*, ch. VII.

[4] John, *Land Tenure*, has reconsidered the nature of book-land. Among its characteristics were
hereditary tenure, *ius perpetuum*, freedom from contribution to the royal *feorm*, and, although
Mr John would not express it in these words, a *dominium* over the estate granted as full as was
possible at the time. Cf. 'quidam predives ... eam [villam] hereditate parentorum suorum possidebat
liberaliter, habens videlicet potestatem donandi sive vendendi eam cuicumque vellet, utpote
paternam hereditatem, nulli inde aliquid servitium nisi regi faciens': *Hemingi Chartularium*, i. 263.

[5] 'beatus Oswaldus archiepiscopus, cum adjutorio regis Ædgari, terras, injuste a viris potentibus
aliquanto tempore possessas, ditioni ecclesie attitulavit; easque regali auctoritate et senatorum
consensu et principum patrie testimonio, data unicuique cirographi cautione, post duorum vel
trium heredum tempora juri ecclesie absque contradictione reddendas, ... suis scriptis successoribus
manifestavit', *ibid.* i. 285; cf. i. 292 ff.

thus creating more 'feudal' tenancies. Also some book-lands created from royal demesne were handed over to the churches and similarly treated. At Winchester a number of thegns, to their great displeasure, were mediatized under the bishop. At the same time the canons serving the cathedral churches who owned prebends, thus holding church property *quasi propria*, were violently uprooted and replaced by monks holding the property in common. This tenurial revolution had wide repercussions in the shires and brought the reformed churches into conflict with the local landed families. Only the most ruthless of the reformers – Æthelwold and Oswald – were able to carry it through. Dunstan was clearly less extreme at Canterbury.

The attack was on radical alienations, not on enfeofments. And the effect was to put the reformed churches in an extremely vulnerable position. Only the most consistent royal support could protect them from a counter-revolution or from a steady erosion of their rights. The despoiled noble families could recover much of their losses by withholding the services due to the church from their loan-lands and by refusing to surrender the leases at their termination.[1] Any temporary weakness in the monarchy led to some loss by the church, and it is no wonder that the monasteries were among the staunchest supporters of the crown.

Edgar and his successors, possibly to make the changes more secure, also granted, or restored, wide powers of local government to the reformed monasteries. The concessions were normally either in the form of grants of whole hundreds – such as the triple hundred of Oswaldslow to Worcester,[2] and the even larger groups made over to the East-Anglian monasteries [3] – or in the form of exemption for the church's estates from hundredal jurisdiction, such as Canterbury apparently possessed.[4] It was in any case a natural step to take. The monasteries were usually reformed minsters situated in royal vills on royal estates now granted to them; and it was convenient to transfer to the monastery the hundredal rights and jurisdiction which had been centred in

---

[1] In 995 Æthelred restored to Muchelney Abbey an estate in Ilminster which it had *inepte* loaned for three lives, and for which the holders had wrongfully obtained an hereditary charter. When the fraud was discovered the book was annulled. *Cartulary of Muchelney and Athelney*, Somerset Rec. Soc. xiv (1899), 44.

[2] *Hemingi Chartularium*, i. 287–8. For the association between churches and hundreds, see W. Page, 'Some remarks on the Churches of the Domesday Survey', *Archaeologia*, lxix (1915), 61 ff.

[3] Helen M. Cam, 'Early Groups of Hundreds', *Liberties and Communities in Medieval England* (1944), pp. 100 ff.; cf. also pp. 184 ff.

[4] *De placito apud Pinendenam inter Lanfrancum archiepiscopum et Odonem Baiocensem episcopum*: *Anglia Sacra*, i. 334 ff.

that royal *tun*,[1] and make the abbot or bishop provide the reeves. Thus the parochial rights of the old minsters and the king's hundredal jurisdiction were brought together in the same hands. And even greater jurisdictional franchises were accorded to some favoured houses.[2] With responsibility for local peace and justice went also military duties. Although it is probable that most of the reformed monasteries had at least their 'inland' freed again from the common burdens which lay on land,[3] the grant of hundreds to churches made bishops and abbots personally responsible for the military duties of this unit.[4] For example, the triple hundred of Oswaldslow created for Worcester was a *scipsocn*, and Oswald became responsible for the provision and command of 60 warriors, the complement of a warship. It seems that Oswald, in order to perform this duty, granted land to thegns on loan for three lives,[5] and would naturally rate each holding at five hides. But the church had probably to enfeof more thegns than it required, just as with knights after the Conquest. We learn that Earl Leofric compelled Prior Æthelwine (*c.* 1040– *c.* 55) to grant a parcel of the monastic inland to one of the earl's thegns (*miles*), a Dane named Simund, in return for military service (*expeditio terra marique*) to be performed for the church. And this military service, we are told, was being demanded frequently at that time.[6] Nor was it obsolete after the Conquest, for Bishop Wulfstan brought a claim that the abbot of Evesham held as a vassal of the bishop in Oswaldslow, and expressly demanded the abbot's contribution to *expeditiones in terra et mari* due from that franchise.[7] And one of the bishop's witnesses in the case was Eadric, who in King Edward's time had been the captain (*stermannus*) of the bishop's ship and leader of the bishop's army in the royal service.[8] Eadric had held an estate rated at five hides.[9] Hence it is probably no accident that several abbots

---

[1] Helen M. Cam, 'Manerium cum Hundredo', *Liberties and Communities*, pp. 64 ff.

[2] Naomi D. Hurnard, 'The Anglo-Norman Franchises', *EHR*, lxiv (1949), 314 ff., 446 ff.

[3] John, *Some Latin Charters*, pp. 337–8.

[4] Helen M. Cam, 'Early Groups of Hundreds', pp. 93–4; John, *Land Tenure*, chs. VI, VIII.

[5] Some of the details of the tenure are given in *DB*. Four freemen held in Fladbury from the bishop. They owed to the hundred sake and soke, church-scot, *sepultura, expeditiones et navigia*, and pleas: *DB*, i. 173 a i. Sirof held five hides at Croome from the bishop, and on his death after the Conquest the bishop gave his daughter in marriage to one of his knights who could look after the mother and perform the service: *DB*. i. 173 a ii. See also C. Warren Hollister, *Anglo-Saxon Military Institutions* (1962), especially pp. 98–102.

[6] *Hemingi Chartularium*, i. 264–5: Crohlea.

[7] *Ibid.* i. 80.   [8] *Ibid.* i. 81.

[9] *DB*, i. 173 b i: 'Edricus stirman tenuit et deserviebat cum aliis servitiis ad regem et episcopum pertinentibus.'

were at the battle of Hastings. They had conducted their quotas of thegns in person.[1]

As a result of these changes in the tenth century the abbots became important men in the kingdom and appear as witnesses to the diplomas. But the bishops only got the full benefit from this policy when they had monastic sees. It may well be that bishops with unreformed sees who had manors which once had been royal *tuns* possessed also the hundreds attached to them. For example, Ramsbury's manors of Potterne and Canning were hundredal.[2] But in general these bishops were less bountifully endowed.

King Louis VII of France, according to Walter Map,[3] said that the Emperor of the Germans had many soldiers but no riches or splendour, for Charlemagne had given everything except the castles to the archbishops and bishops. As part of an aphorism it will pass. The problem of the accumulation of wealth by the church through benefactions could, of course, be serious. Sometimes uncontrolled despoilers, whether internal or external, solved the problem for a kingdom. Sometimes the church itself scattered what it had received. Sometimes the king had to confiscate superfluous ecclesiastical wealth by the favourite medieval method of placing burdens on the land, such as military service, food rents, or taxation. The English church had been robbed from every quarter in the eighth and ninth centuries. The generosity of the tenth had not created serious disequilibrium in the kingdom as a whole. Certainly there were areas – such as East Anglia – where clerical ambition was creating problems. But there were other areas where the church was, on balance, probably losing land.

It is not surprising, therefore, that histories of churches at this time should consist largely of the story of their estates and moveable property.[4] There were some amazing stories to tell. Bishop Aldhun (990–1018) has an honoured place in Durham tradition.[5] It was he who brought the body of St Cuthbert to its last resting place, built the first cathedral at Durham, and re-established the bishopric. According to the Durham chronicler he was a man of great religion and humility, friendly to all good men.[6] 'This bishop', he

---

[1] Aluric, a man of the abbey of Ramsey, to whom the abbot had granted two estates for life, was killed in the battle: *DB*, i. 208 a i.   [2] Helen M. Cam, p. 81.

[3] *De nugis Curialium*, dist. V, cap. v, ed. T. Wright (Camden Soc. 1850), pp. 215–16; ed. M. R. James (Anecdota Oxoniensia, med. and mod. ser. pt. xiv, 1914), p. 225.

[4] E.g. Wells (*Ecclesiastical Documents*), *Chron. Abingdon*, *Chron. Ramsey*, *Liber Eliensis*.

[5] At the end of the Durham ritual (fo. 73) are the words, 'Dominus salvet, honoret, amet Aldhunum antistitem', words borrowed from Alcuin's dedication of his treatise on the Trinity to Charlemagne: *MPL*, ci, col. 14.   [6] Symeon, *HDE*, p. 83.

writes, 'was noble by birth and even nobler in his behaviour, which was pleasing to God. He was, like all his predecessors, a professed [*probabilis*] monk in habit and deed. His countrymen keep fresh the memory of his righteousness, which they praise before that of almost all other men, just as though he was still alive today.' [1] He obtained rich gifts of land for Durham *in aeterno jure*, but leased [*ad tempus praestitit*] much of it to the earls of Northumbria, and these estates could seldom be recovered from their successors.[2] He had also to provide for his daughter. A Durham tract, composed towards the end of the century, is concerned with the fate of six vills which Aldhun gave from the episcopal estates with his daughter Egfrith when he married her to the son of the earl of Northumbria.[3] To explain the descent of these vills the author produces a genealogy running to six generations and complicated through the looseness of the marriage tie in Scandinavian Northumbria.[4] Egfrith had two husbands and was repudiated by both. Her first

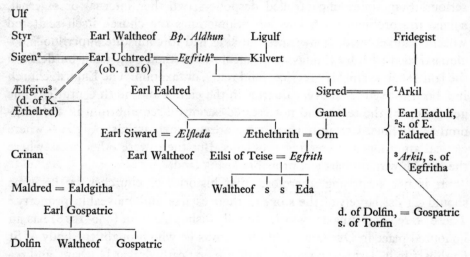

husband made two subsequent marriages. Her daughter by her second husband had three successive lords. By the end of the century some of the vills had been returned to Durham but at least two were in the hands of Egfrith, Aldhun's great-great-granddaughter. Yet Aldhun was not considered a dilapidator of the church by the Durham chronicler, presumably

[1] Symeon, *HDE*, p. 78.   [2] *Ibid.* pp. 83–4.
[3] *Symeonis monachi opera omnia*, i. 215–20.
[4] Here is a reconstruction of part of the genealogy. See also *De Northymbrorum comitibus* in *Symeonis Dunelmensis opera et collectanea*, ed. Hodgson Hinde, Surtees Soc., li (1868), 212–3. Persons known to have held vills are in italic.

because the estates should have returned at the daughter's repudiation or death.

Owing to the care of St Wulfstan and the industry of Hemming we are well informed about the ways in which the church of Worcester lost some of its lands.[1] Hemming regarded the Danes as the first great despoilers. Earl Hacon and his men seized various estates, and all that Worcester recovered was an image of the B.V.M. given by the Countess Gunnhild.[2] Earl Ranig and his men were equally acquisitive in Herefordshire.[3] The depredations of other Danes are mentioned.[4] Many of these 'invasions' seem to have been connected with tributes and taxes imposed by the Danish kings.[5] It was a rule that if the tax was not paid by the appointed day, anyone who acquitted the liability could have the estate. Hence the poverty or carelessness of Worcester tenants, especially in remote areas, could cause the church serious loss. But Hemming also alleges that despoilers made a pact with the sheriff and acquired estates by paying the tax although the church or the tenant was willing to pay.[6]

The English earls of Mercia also robbed Worcester. Two of the estates unjustly held by Leofwine were returned by his son Leofric, but he retained the rest for life. On his death his widow Godgifu gave Worcester rich gifts and had the leases transferred to her. But again there was no reversion, and her sons, Edwin and Morcar, kept the estates in their hands.[7] Leofric's brother, Edwin, likewise detained Worcester property.[8]

---

[1] See N. P. Ker, 'Hemming's Cartulary', *Studies in Medieval History presented to F. M. Powicke* (1948), pp. 49–75. Hemming is only concerned with estates which should pertain *ad victum monachorum* (p. 63), and the trustworthiness of his detail is doubtful (pp. 64–5).

[2] *Hemingi Chartularium*, i. 251: Clifton and Eastham.

[3] *Ibid*. i. 274–5.

[4] *Ibid*. i. 255–6: Æstlege, i. 256: Ribetforde, i. 280 (Oxfords).

[5] Cf. *ASC* C 1018: 'In this year tribute was paid over all England, namely 72,000 pounds in all apart from what the citizens of London paid, namely 10½ thousand pounds.' Other churches also lost in this way. For Malmesbury, see Malmesbury, *GP*, p. 411; for Peterborough, *Chron. Peterborough*, pp. 64–5; for Gloucester, see *Historia Mon. S. Petri Gloucestriae*, ed. W. H. Hart, i. 8–9. In this last case Abbot Eadric in 1022 granted three estates to a man for life, 'et hoc feci pro ejusdem placita pecunia mihi pro xv. libris, quibus redemi omnia alia praedia monasterii ab illa magna heregeldi exactione, quae per totam Angliam fuit'; for Glastonbury, see Malmesbury, *De Antiqu. Glaston. Ecclesiae*, i. 95–6.

[6] 'Constituerunt enim ut siquid vectigalis ad terminum constituti diei deesset, quisquis prius peccuniam pro ea solveret, ejus possessioni subjaceret. Hac calliditate inventa, quisquis aliquam terram de monasterio concupierat, peccunia data vicecomiti, vectigali refutato, etiamsi satis tempestivo, quod male concupierat, pro libitu injuste rapiebat': *Hemingi Chartularium*, i. 278.

[7] *Ibid*. i. 261–2: Ceadeslaeh and Broctune.   [8] *Ibid*. i. 278–9.

The church's loan-lands were subject to many hazards.[1] Bishop Briht-heah (1033–8) granted leases to his kinsmen from Berkshire,[2] and these proved troublesome. With the permission of the monks he granted two vills to his brother-in-law. But on the death of the sister and her husband one vill was invaded by Richard fitz Scrob (one of the Norman knights settled on the Welsh march before 1051), who bequeathed it to his son (probably Osbern fitz Richard),[3] and the other was appropriated by Brihtheah's brother, Æthelric, who then gave it to his son, Godric.[4] After the Conquest Æthelric and Godric seem to have lost all their estates to Normans. Another vill, which Brihtheah gave to a servant, was recovered through litigation by his successor, Bishop Lyfing (1038–46); but Lyfing then leased it to one of his own thegns for life. This man after the Conquest lost the land to a Norman.[5] There were also enfeofments made by the church for fear or favour.[6]

The kinsmen of the dead tenant could be obstructive. Sometimes Worcester with obviously bad grace had to renew the lease to an heir.[7] Bishop Oswald (961–92) granted a vill to a priest for the service of writing books for the church; but on the priest's death his kinsmen kept it until the French came and took it.[8] Prior Godwin (? c. 1016) granted a hide of land to a clerk for the rent of 5s. a year; but on the clerk's death his kinsmen seized it and also refused to perform the service.[9] Other claimants could come forward. Abbot Æthelwig of Evesham once prevented the reversion of a thegnland to Worcester.[10]

A tenant could forfeit his land as a judicial penalty, although such losses were always regarded as illegal by the church.[11] A rich secular reeve of Goodrich, Earnwi, gave this land to his brother Spirites, a royal clerk, so that Spirites could take hospitality there when he came to visit his brother.

[1] 'Ac primo videndum que terre trium heredum temporibus accomodate sint, post quorum decessum juri monasterii redderentur, que-ve postea juxta hanc conventionem reddite, que-ve injuste sunt retente, sivè ipsorum, qui eas exigere deberent, negligentia, sive denegati sint iniquorum hominum potentia': ibid. i. 259. Cf. also Chron. Abingdon, i. 481.

[2] Ibid. i. 266–7, 269.   [3] For this family, see J. H. Round, Feudal England, pp. 320 ff.

[4] Hemingi Chartularium, i. 255: Ælfintun and Sapian.   [5] Ibid. i. 267–8: Elmlaege.

[6] See above p. 170; Eadric the Wild (see Florence, ii. 1, 7; FNC, iv, Appendix I) persuaded Bishop Ealdred and Prior Wulfstan to lease a vill to his priest: Hemingi Chartularium, i. 256: Witlaege.

[7] Cf. ibid. i. 252–3: Lawerna.   [8] Ibid. i. 265–6: Bradicote.

[9] Ibid. i. 264: Odduncgalea.   [10] Ibid. i. 250–1: Actune.

[11] Cf. Abbot Eadric of Gloucester's grant of estates to a man for one life, 'Quare si forisfecerit ille qui terram tenet, de se et de suo emendet: terra autem sit libera et iterum monasterio reddatur post mortem ejus': Historia Mon. S. Petri Gloucestriae, i. 9.

But Spirites was banished by King Edward, probably in 1065, and Richard fitz Scrob 'invaded' the estate.[1]

Such losses the church of Worcester attempted to recover whenever the opportunity arose. When Prior Wulfstan and Wilstan (later abbot of Gloucester) were called to perform the last rites for Godwin, the brother of Earl Leofric, they claimed and recovered some land from him, and imposed penance for its unjust detention. But then Godwin's son, Æthelwine, who had had his hands cut off when a hostage of the Danes, with the support of his uncle Leofric, repudiated his father's will.[2] When Earngeat, the son of Grim, wanted his son to become a monk of Worcester, Bishop Wulfstan demanded that an estate which he claimed for his church should be given with the boy. But Earngeat, supported by Earl Leofric, would only offer the reversion of the estate after the death of all his sons. So Wulfstan would not take the boy.[3] According to Hemming many of Worcester's despoilers were punished by God. There seem, however, to have been few cases of true repentance.

It is axiomatic in the chronicles and other memorials produced by the clergy that no church held an estate illegally or was deprived of it with justice. But the laity, as we can see from their actions, viewed ecclesiastical behaviour differently. The church, it was clearly thought, was greedy and took undue advantage of its position. It persuaded the godly, or the repentant sinner, to defraud heirs of their expectations. It tried to turn other persons' hereditary possessions into leases and its own usufructs into inheritance. And the church, no doubt, always had an advantage in the courts, to which the only answer was force. Hence for ecclesiastical writers old men and women were benefactors and their children robbers of the church. We are presented with a completely one-sided picture which cannot possibly be true. But it was a necessary exaggeration at a time when the church found it difficult to retain its estates.

No more secure than landed property were church ornaments and relics. Churches had to surrender their furnishings to meet catastrophes and taxation. Worcester, as a result of the tribute levied by Æthelred to pay Svein, the taxation of Cnut, and the ravages of Harthacnut, was stripped of much of its gold and silver: the altar tables were despoiled, books had their covers torn off, chalices were broken up, and crosses melted down.[4] The devastation and instability of the once flourishing and pious kingdom of Northumbria

---

[1] *Hemingi Chartularium*, i. 254: Coddarycge.   [2] *Ibid*. i. 259–60: Salewarpe.
[3] *Ibid*. i. 260–1: Heamtune. Cf. i. 249–50: Peonedoc, where Wulfstan temporarily recovered an estate with an oblate.   [4] *Ibid*. i. 248–9.

attracted relic hunters in the eleventh century. In 1038 a certain Balger pro-
cured some relics of St Oswald of Northumbria and St Edburga (of Winchester) for the abbey of St Winnoc at Bergues.[1] During Edward's reign the
chaplain of a rich Danish housecarl obtained a relic of St Wilfrid in Yorkshire, 'where owing to the devastations hardly a church was to be found'.
This he bequeathed to Abingdon.[2] The Durham canon Alfred collected
assiduously for his church, and visited Jarrow every year until he succeeded
in stealing the body of Bede, which he secretly placed in the shrine of St
Cuthbert.[3] But Durham lost as well as gained. The two brothers from
Peterborough Abbey, Æthelric and Æthelwin, who became bishop in turn,
took what they could from the cathedral to send to their old home.[4]

In the south of England 'body-snatching' had to be organized as a military expedition. After 1020 Abbot Æthelstan of Ramsey, at the instigation of
Bishop Æthelric of Dorchester, and with Cnut's consent, sent raiders along
the waterways to Soham in order to seize the body of St Felix, and they only
escaped from a naval battle with the monks of Ely through the appearance of
a miraculous mist.[5] In 1023 Archbishop Æthelnoth, a holy man, with Cnut's
connivance, removed the body of St Ælfheah from St. Paul's, London,
while housecarles stood on guard at various strategic points against the
hostile citizens. After two Canterbury monks had broken the sarcophagus
open, using as crowbar an iron candlestick which stood near, the corpse was
put on a plank removed from the tomb and concealed partly by a cloth taken
from the high altar. It was then swiftly carried across the river in the royal
barge, and at Plumstead, near Woolwich, the escort took up battle positions
to cover the retreat to Canterbury.[6] In 1035, again with Cnut's permission,
Abbot Ælfstan of St Augustine's invaded Thanet to snatch the body of St
Mildred.[7] The possession of a relic which caught the popular imagination

---

[1] Grierson, *England and Flanders*, p. 101.   [2] *Chron. Abingdon*, ii. 47.
[3] Symeon, *HDE*, i. 88-9.
[4] *Ibid.* pp. 87, 91-2, 94. For other Peterborough schemes, see *Chron. Peterborough*, pp. 50-1.
[5] *Chron. Ramsey*, pp. 127-8.
[6] Osbern, *Translatio S. Elphegi*, *MPL*, cxlix, coll. 387 ff. Osbern's graphic and highly-coloured
account, which includes such details as Cnut hurrying half-clad from his bath to take part in the
raid and later taking the tiller of the boat, is professedly based on the recollections of Godric,
one of the participant monks, who later became dean of Christ Church, Canterbury (col. 390).
Ælfheah himself is said to have taken the head of St Swithun with him from Winchester to Canterbury:
Eadmer, *De reliquiis S. Audoeni et quorundam aliorum sanctorum quae Cantuariae in ecclesia domini
salvatoris habentur*, *HCY*, i, p. xlvi.
[7] See F. Barlow, 'Two Notes: Cnut's Second Pilgrimage and Queen Emma's Disgrace in 1043',
EHR, lxxiii (1958), 650-1.

could make the fortune of a place. At the beginning of the century the body of St Neot was removed from Cornwall to the recently founded monastery of Eynesbury in Huntingdonshire,[1] and proved so valuable an acquisition that the place assumed the saint's name. Slepe became St Ives after the discovery there of the body of that Persian saint.

The authenticity of some of the relics was, of course, doubtful.[2] Glastonbury claimed to have raided Canterbury after its sack by the Danes and the martyrdom of Ælfheah in 1012, removed the body of St Dunstan from the deserted cathedral, and translated it to a tomb in the abbey whose secret was passed down through a small number of senior monks.[3] In the twelfth century Odense in Denmark, Ely, and St Albans all claimed to have the bones, except for the left scapula which was supposed to be in Spain, of England's 'protomartyr'. There was every reason for the uncertainty. According to the legend created by the monastery of St Albans, the house was located on the site, the 'Calvary' of Verulamium, formerly called Holmhurste, where King Offa, informed by a vision, had discovered the relics.[4] Towards the end of the ninth century Danish invaders stole the shrine and took it to Odense. But the sacristan went in secret pursuit, rose to be sacristan of Odense, and managed to steal it away again.[5] The story of the subsequent loss of the shoulder is no less remarkable. King Cnut, sailing to Rome in 1027, took refuge from a storm on the coast of Spain, formed a friendship with the local duke, a convert from paganism, helped him against his rebel Saracen subjects, and on the return journey picked up his son to give him an English education. The boy was placed in St Alban's for the sake of his health, and, on succeeding to his father's duchy, begged for a relic of the saint to take home with him. Hence the presence of the scapula in the

---

[1] 'Et in Enolfesbiri sanctus Neotus presbyter': *Chron. Peterborough*, p. 63. For a discussion of the translation, see W. H. Stevenson, *Asser's Life of King Alfred*, pp. 296-9.

[2] Naturally scepticism was reserved for the relics possessed by other churches. Cf. 'Tunc temporis [*c*. 1027] contigit innoti ossa hominis de loco abjectissimo a quodam mangone collecta et feretro imposita, in monasterio S. Mariae apud Seusiam [Soissons] sub nomine Justi martyris a Mainfredo marchione fuisse reposita. Sed licet religiosis id vanissimum et stultissimum fuisse multis et probatis documentis demonstratum sit, vulgus tamen injustum pro Justo venerans in suo permansit errore': Hugh, abbot of Flavigny, *Chronicon*, II, c. 17, *MPL*, cliv, coll. 241-2. Cf. also Ralf Glaber, *Historiarum libri quinque*, IV, c. iii, *MPL*, cxlii, col. 673.

[3] Malmesbury, *De Antiq. Glaston. Ecclesiae*, i. 31 ff. Eadmer wrote a refutation *c*. 1120, *Epistola ad Glastonienses, Memorials of St Dunstan*, pp. 412 ff.

[4] *Gesta abbatum monasterii S. Albani*, p. 18.

[5] *Ibid.* pp. 12-19, 84-5. Matthew Paris seems to have got this episode from Danish sources (p. 19).

cathedral church of *Naumucia*, built specially to house it.[1] With the Ely episode we reach sophisticated fraud. Early in Edward's reign, when there was the threat of a new invasion by the Danes, the abbot decided to take precautions. Secretly he hid the feretory of St Alban under the altar of St Nicholas, but publicly he sent to ask the abbey of Ely if it would take safe custody. This was a trick to deceive both the expected invaders and the monks of Ely, and pseudo relics were sent with the church's ornaments to the Fens. A year later, when the panic had subsided, Ely, after first refusing to return the supposed relics, eventually sent back another fraudulent substitute, which the abbot of St. Albans, in order to avoid scandal, received with due reverence.[2]

Such fluctuations, if accompanied by less fraud, were common to all estates. The church was receiving and giving all the time. On one hand were the grants of the faithful and on the other the enfeofments made by the church. And as well there were the 'invasions' and usurpations, the many illegalities of a society whose respect for the law was matched only by its disregard of it. No balances between profit and loss were struck at the time, and today it is impossible to analyse the position in detail. It is clear, however, that the churches were on a slippery slope, and that with lax control the situation could easily get out of hand. The benefactions were usually purchased, or encumbered with conditions, and to raise the money other lands had to be leased. But a prudent administrator, who checked the outgoings, could accumulate much wealth. The estates in which a church had an interest had become extensive – often too extensive for proper control.

In comparison we hear little about the church's more truly spiritual

---

[1] *Gesta abbatum monasterii S. Albani*, pp. 87–91. We are, of course, in the realm of fantasy. The loss of the scapula was discovered at the translation in 1129, and was then inexplicable. A later visit (1129–46) from two regular canons from the cathedral church of *Naumucia* allowed the mystery to be solved. But where is this Spanish church? There is no such bishopric in Spain. Cnut was troubled by a south-westerly gale. The west, or the north, coast is indicated. Namancos of Milton's *Lycidas* comes to mind. But Namancos, reputedly in Gallicia, near Cape Finisterre, does not appear on modern maps. The only famous church on the western and northern seaboards with a name something like *Naumucia* is Naranco (S. Maria, ninth-century, associated with King Ramiro I of Asturia), on the slope of the Sierra de Naranco, one-and-a-quarter miles and a fatiguing ascent (Baedeker) from Orviedo. It is just possible that canons from Orviedo, who said that there was a relic of St Alban at Naranco, visited St Albans in the thirteenth century. But it is hard to say whether there is even a grain of truth in this story.

[2] *Gesta abbatum*, pp. 34–6. In the thirteenth century even a St Albans monk had doubts over the exact location of the relics: *ibid.* p. 37.

rights. Less lucrative, they may sometimes have been less esteemed. But it is also possible that they were not so unstable. Certainly we can assume from the relative neglect of this subject that they were not usually subject to secular 'invasion'.

The bishop's parish, his diocese, had been divided and subdivided into smaller parishes. There was primarily the network of old minsters, and secondarily the 'manorial' parishes within this.[1] Perhaps from the beginning the bishop's minster had been financially on an equal footing with the other minsters in the diocese, drawing tribute only from its own smaller parish. Certainly in the tenth and eleventh centuries there seem to have been few financial levies on a diocesan basis. Hence the royal ecclesiastical laws, which were inspired by the bishops, tried to safeguard the rights of the old minsters as a class against the encroachments of manorial churches.[2] And it seems that all the old minsters, including the bishop's minster, had the same kind of claim to the five ecclesiastical customs – tithe, church-scot, plough-alms, light-dues, and soul-scot. They each collected them from their own parish and made their own terms with the smaller churches.

This circumscription could not, however, seriously affect the bishop's ordinary powers within his diocese and the revenues associated with their exercise. He had to share jurisdiction with the priests, especially the hearing of confessions.[3] But it is likely that the more substantial penances, producing the larger *bots*, were awarded by him; and penal slaves were always plentiful on episcopal estates.[4] He also received the royal penalties on sinners which the king shared with the church.[5] Some functions he could not lose, and, although to sell the sacraments was simony, all gifts tended to attract a counter gift. The bishop consecrated on Maundy Thursday the oil used for baptism, chrism; and all the parish priests in his diocese had to obtain it, in return for a few pence, directly or indirectly from the cathedral church.[6] The Whitsuntide processions to the mother church were expected to bring

---

[1] See below, pp. 184 ff.   [2] See below, pp. 194–6.   [3] See below, pp. 262 ff.

[4] On the evidence of *DB* there were few episcopal estates in 1086 without them. For an episcopal manumission, see Whitelock, *Wills*, no. 18.   [5] See above, pp. 149–50.

[6] In the diocese of Canterbury 7*d*. (see below). In the diocese of Rochester 9*d*. for churches and 6*d*. for chapels: 'De numero ecclesiarum Rofensis episcopatus et de reddittibus quos singulae reddunt quando accipiunt sanctum crisma a matre ecclesia episcopatus', *Textus Roffensis*, ed. T. Hearne (1720), pp. 228–31. In 1121 Archbishop Thurstan of York remitted the ancient custom by which churches paid 6*d*. and chapels 4*d*. for chrism: Hugh the Chantor, *HCY*, p. 101. See also H. Böhmer, 'Das Eigenkirchentum in England', *Texte und Forschungen zur englischen Kulturgeschichte, Festgabe für Felix Liebermann* (Halle 1921), p. 333.

gifts.[1] The bishop could take hospitality when a church was dedicated.[2] And freewill offerings for spiritual services were not always declined.

For the diocese of Canterbury we have several lists of churches, all connected with 'spiritual' customs payable to the archbishop. There are two lists of customs due at Easter from priests and churches, one the *institutio antiqua* and the other Lanfranc's reform of it.[3] The older schedule contains thirteen churches, and these head the much longer list of Lanfranc's revision, in which payments in kind have been commuted (except for St Augustine's), the items consolidated, and the liability has been spread more widely. Under the ancient arrangement there was a render of honey or mead, sheep, and loaves (30 or 60), and payments usually in units of 6*d.* for wine and 7*d.* for chrism. A few churches, Milton Regis and St Augustine's (possibly a transfer of the same obligation), Dover, and Folkestone, also paid a sum of 600*d.* For example, St Augustine's paid 7*d.*, 30 farthing-loaves, 2 best-quality sheep, 2 ambers of mead and one of ale, and 600*d.*, all due on Maundy Thursday. Milton paid 2 sesters of honey, 2 sheep, 7 lambs, 60 loaves, 12*d.*, and at Pentecost 600*d.* Maidstone, Charing, Wye, Teynham, and Eastry paid each one sester of honey, 7 ewes, 60 loaves, 12*d.* for wine, and 14*d.* for oil. At the bottom of the list the two Boughtons and Ruckinge paid each 3 lambs, 30 loaves, and 13*d.* (= 6*d.* + 7*d.*).

At least four separate customs are to be distinguished here. There are the payments in money for communion wine and chrism. Then there are the food renders, which are probably a contribution to the archbishop's Maundy gifts to the poor. We know how lavish St Wulfstan was on that day and how his face was sometimes saved only by last-minute gifts.[4] Lastly, there are the three or four units of 600*d.*, which may be hearth-pennies.[5] As ten of these thirteen churches are in another list of twelve mother churches with their dependants,[6] we cannot doubt that normally the old minsters collected chrism and wine from the archbishop for distribution among their daughter

---

[1] Cf. F. Barlow, *Durham Jurisdictional Peculiars*, pp. 70-2.

[2] Cf. *Vita Wulfstani*, p. 55.

[3] 'Haec est institutio antiqua ante adventum domini Lanfranci archiepiscopi . . . Sed beatae memoriae Lanfrancus ut in antea scriptum est ordinavit et instituit'; 'Haec sunt consuetudines archiepiscopi in pascha de presbiteris et aecclesiis'; 'Haec sunt quae debentur de S. Augustino singulis annis aecclesiae Christi': *The Domesday Monachorum of Christ Church Canterbury*, ed. D. C. Douglas (1944), pp. 77-9; cf. 5 ff. See also W. Urry, *Canterbury under the Angevin kings* (1967), pp. 76-9.   [4] *Vita Wulfstani*, pp. 57-9.

[5] For Maundy hearth-pennies, and the confusion with Rome-pennies, see below, p. 295, *n.* 7; cf. also, p. 197.

[6] *The Domesday Monachorum*, pp. 78-9; cf. 8-13.

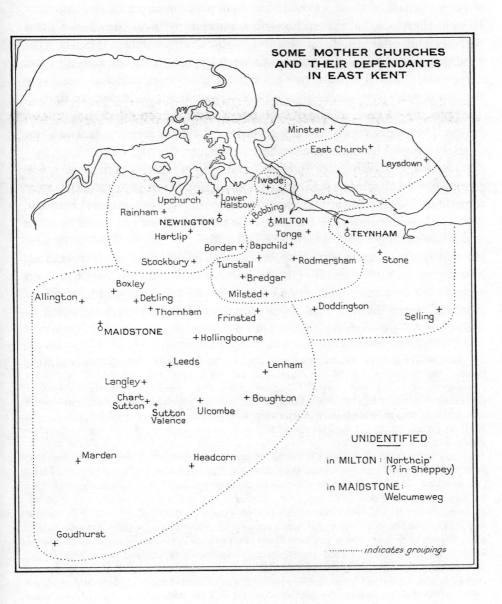

SOME MOTHER CHURCHES
AND THEIR DEPENDANTS
IN EAST KENT

Minster +

East Church +

Leysdown +

Iwade +

Upchurch + + Lower Halstow

Rainham +

NEWINGTON ⚲

Bobbing

MILTON ⚲

Hartlip +

Tonge +

TEYNHAM ⚲

Borden + Bapchild +

Stockbury + Tunstall + + Rodmersham Stone +

Boxley + Bredgar

Allington + + Detling Milsted +

+ Thornham Frinsted + + Doddington Selling +

MAIDSTONE ⚲ + Hollingbourne

+ Leeds Lenham +

Langley +

Chart Sutton + + Boughton + Ulcombe

Sutton Valence

Marden + Headcorn +

UNIDENTIFIED

in MILTON : Northcip'
(? in Sheppey)

in MAIDSTONE :
Welcumeweg

Goudhurst +

·········· indicates groupings

churches, and that, although they seem to have made payments to Canterbury on behalf of these,[1] the arrangement was lucrative to the minsters. It was, therefore, in the archbishop's interest to break down the great parishes and establish direct relations with more churches. This is what Lanfranc did. And as the various Canterbury schedules are rarely in full agreement, and it is difficult to work out the old system in detail, it is likely that his predecessors too had varied the arrangements from time to time.

Thus the diocese, although hierarchical and decentralized, was still an entity. The rights which an English bishop exercised were at least as great as those enjoyed by bishops elsewhere in western Christendom.

The English bishoprics differed greatly in wealth. There were a few plums, but many which by Edward's reign seemed jejune. Royal clerks were sometimes dismayed on appointment. Giso found Wells mediocre.[2] Herman, appointed to Ramsbury, by no means the poorest of the sees, tried to move into Malmesbury Abbey and in the end added Sherborne. His views after his appointment, as reported by William of Malmesbury,[3] are revealing: Ramsbury, he said, was all right for his predecessors, for they had been natives; but he was a foreigner and forced to make do without the wealth of kinsmen. Some bishops with private means did leave their possessions to their church,[4] although their intention was sometimes frustrated.[5] Some rich

---

[1] Gordon Ward, 'The lists of Saxon churches in the Domesday Monachorum, and White Book of St. Augustine', *Archaeologia Cantiana*, vol. xlv (1933), and Douglas, *The Domesday Monachorum*, p. 14, seem to imply that the four items of 600d. were chrism money in respect of dependent churches. It can be accepted that the old minsters collected chrism from Christ Church and then sold it to their chapels. St Augustine's, for example, collected the 7d. fee from its own churches (Ward, pp. 84 ff.). And it is possible that the payments of the old minsters to the archbishop include a lump sum for this privilege. But it is difficult to explain the units of 600d. as such. According to the *institutio antiqua*, Maidstone (17 dependant churches), Eastry (10), Lyminge (10) Wye (8), etc., all paid 14d. for chrism. Why should Milton Regis (10), Folkstone (10), and Dover (19) pay 600d.? With the church on the great royal manor and half-leet of Milton the inquiry can be conducted in more detail. In one Christ Church list it is credited with 10 daughter churches. In Stigand's day it paid food-renders, 12d. (? *recte* 13 or 14), and 600d. In Lanfranc's revision Milton, like Maidstone, Charing, Wye, and Eastry, is debited with 116d. William I granted it with all its chapels to St Augustine's, and according to that abbey's list it paid 32d. and its chapels 7d. each. If we can believe that 116d. represents the consolidation of 32d. and twelve units of 7d., we shall think that the 32d. is the commutation of the food-rent and the 84d. the lump sum for chrism. It is possible that Milton's liability for 600d. was transferred immediately to St Augustine's and that later the abbey gained the right to collect for itself the other customs. Indeed, everything points to the dissociation of the units of 600d. from chrism.

[2] *Ecclesiastical Documents*, pp. 16–17.   [3] *GP*, p. 182.

[4] E.g Leofric of Exeter, Robertson, *Charters*, Appendix I, no. 1.

[5] Cf. Duduc's bequest to Wells, *Ecclesiastical Documents*, p. 16.

bishops were no more than stepfathers to their sees: some monk-bishops were little more than robbers. It is no wonder that the Normans, in order to re-endow the sees, moved several into monasteries – a kind of pluralism which the church was prepared to tolerate.

3. PARISH CHURCHES AND THEIR PARISHES

In the Germanic lands north of the Alps the Roman ecclesiastical organization of a bishop's church in the city ruling over baptismal churches in the countryside was soon engulfed by a rising tide of private churches, founded and owned by the local landowners, and serving their estates. During the same period the new conception strongly influenced the old arrangements, so that baptismal churches began to be regarded as the private possessions of the bishops. By the eleventh century the ancient baptismal churches often enjoyed a title of honour (the mother church), vestiges of once paramount parochial rights, and generally a collegiate establishment, but had retained little or nothing of the public character which they had possessed under Roman law.[1]

England was Christianized relatively late; the Roman missions operated within a largely Germanized society; and Celtic Christianity gave no support to Roman organization. Moreover, England was converted partly by monks. Hence it is doubtful whether the sixth-century Roman system of baptismal churches was ever properly introduced into the outpost province. It seems rather that a network of mission churches, in part monastic,[2] was established during the conversion period, an organization consisting basically in one church, a bishop's church, for each Germanic kingdom, and that offshoots were planted when a more intensive ministry was attempted or new ground taken in.[3] But in England it is likely that private churches are almost as old as the mission centres of the bishops.[4] The private church was a pagan custom which the Germans introduced into Christian organization. Its origin lay in the family assembly for religious services and the cult of the ancestral graves.[5] In 601 Pope Gregory reversed his earlier instructions to

---

[1] Cf. Hans Erich Feine, *Kirchliche Rechtsgeschichte*, vol. i, *Die katholische Kirche* (Weimar 1950), pp. 129–78.

[2] But monastic, of course, only in the contemporary sense. For the background and literature, see J. C. Dickinson, *The Origins of the Austin Canons and their Introduction into England* (1950), p. 15.

[3] William Page, 'Some remarks on the Churches of the Domesday Survey', *Archaeologia*, lxvi (1915), 64–6.   [4] Lingard, *Antiquities*, i. 192–6.   [5] Feine, pp. 132–5.

Augustine and ordered that, although all heathen idols must be destroyed, their temples should be preserved and through fitting ceremonies converted into Christian churches. Likewise idolatrous customs were not necessarily to be extirpated, but could when possible be given a Christian form.[1] A transitional stage is reported by Bede. King Redwald of East Anglia had second thoughts after his conversion and maintained a church which offered both cults.[2] Thus it can be assumed that almost from the beginning kings and probably some of the lay nobility possessed private churches on and for their estates.

In Domesday Book can be glimpsed a basic ecclesiastical organization in process of decay. It appears that at one time there had usually been one minster for each hundred or group of hundreds.[3] As the hundred, either individually or grouped, often represented some earlier district originally dependent on a royal *tun*, or vill,[4] it seems that kings had founded in their *tuns* churches to serve the area governed from those centres. These are the 'old minsters' of the tenth and eleventh centuries, churches with large endowments, sometimes still served by a community of priests or canons, and with parochial rights extending over a wide area.[5] Many, of course, by the eleventh century had been alienated by the crown, often to monasteries, and some of them had been much weakened by their new owners. They were also being crowded by newer churches, built by the bishops, abbots, lesser nobility, and sometimes by groups of freemen, to serve smaller private estates and also areas newly colonized. The facility with which ecclesiastical parishes can be explained in terms of secular boundaries is most striking. Within the bishop's parish, normally equivalent to an ancient kingdom or major part of one, the parishes of the old minsters often coincide with the hundreds, and those of the newer churches with the manors or vills. And although the integrity of the parishes of the old minsters was being threatened, it was reaffirmed in a new form by the creation of rural deaneries in the twelfth century.

Churches of all kinds were still being built and rebuilt in the century before the Norman Conquest. The inscription on a sundial now above the south porch of the church at Kirkdale in the North Riding of Yorkshire runs: [6] 'Orm son

---

[1] Bede, *Historia Ecclesiastica*, I, c. 30.   [2] *Ibid.* II, c. 15.   [3] Page, *passim*.

[4] Helen M. Cam, 'Manerium cum Hundredo', 'Early Groups of Hundreds', *Liberties and Communities in Medieval England* (1944).

[5] For the old minsters of the diocese of Canterbury and the other churches within their parishes, see *The Domesday Monachorum of Christ Church Canterbury*, ed. D. C. Douglas (1944), pp. 5 ff., 78–9.

[6] P. H. Blair, *An Introduction to Anglo-Saxon England*, pl. XII. Inscription in Old-English. It should be noticed that all the names except Eadward are Scandinavian.

of Gamal [1] bought St Gregory's minster when it was all ruined and fallen
down, and he caused it to be built afresh from the foundation [in honour of]
Christ and St Gregory in the days of King Eadward and in the days of Earl
Tosti. This is the day's sun-marking at every hour. And Hawarth made me
and Brand [?] the priest.' According to a law of Edmund (I, 5), bishops were
to restore churches on their own property; and from the two extremes of this
period we have examples of the law being observed.[2] We learn as well of
churches built by Benedictine monasteries,[3] priests,[4] kings,[5] earls,[6] and
thegns,[7] even by the people.[8] In size these range from an oratory built by
Edgar's daughter, St Edith, at Wilton [9] to the minsters founded by Cnut and
Harold Godwinesson and Edward's monastic church at Westminster. In
materials they range from a temporary shelter made from the boughs of
trees [10] to elaborate constructions in freestone. According to popular super-
stition the sixth day of the moon was the most propitious for the building of
a church, and the sixteenth for the founding of a minster.[11]

In 1050 Bishop Herman of Wiltshire boasted in Rome not only of the
great number of churches and bells in England but also of the many new

[1] See above, p. 172. He married an earl's daughter, a bishop's great-granddaughter.

[2] St Dunstan had wooden churches built at all the hostels on his estates: Eadmer, *Vita S. Dunstani, Memorials of St Dunstan*, p. 204. St Wulfstan of Worcester acted similarly and urged others to do the same: *Vita Wulfstani*, pp. 21, 52. He also had wooden replaced by stone altars: *ibid.* p. 54.

[3] Abbot Eadnoth of Ramsey built a church on the site of the discovery of the bones of St Yves, *post* 1001: Goscelin, *Vita S. Yvonis, MPL*, clv, coll. 89–90. Bishop Æthelric of Durham retired to Peterborough abbey in 1056 and used his wealth to build roads and churches: Symeon, *HDE*, p. 92.

[4] A rich priest on the island at Abingdon, *c.* 1050: *Chron. Abingdon*, pp. 474, 484, 490. The church is described.

[5] Cnut at Ashingdon: *ASC F* 1020; Florence, i. 183. Edward at Exeter, 1063: K. 814.

[6] Odda at Deerhurst in memory of his brother, *ASC D* 1053; Florence, i. 211; Plummer, p. 238. Harold at Waltham: K. 813.

[7] Copsig at Marsk in Cleveland, nr. Redcar, 1042–56: Symeon, *HDE*, p. 97; a thegn at Leck-hampstead (Berks) on Abingdon loan-land: *Chron. Abingdon*, i. 475; and see Lennard, *Rural England*, pp. 295–6.

[8] According to Symeon (*HDE*, p. 81) all the people helped in building the church of Durham. Cf. II Cnut, 65.1, 'All people should by rights help to repair the church.'

[9] Goscelin, *Vita S. Edithe*: A. Wilmart, 'La Légende de Ste Édith en prose et vers', *Analecta Bollandiana*, lvi (1938), 86–7.

[10] Durham: Symeon, *HDE*, p. 79. When Dunstan went to dedicate the church at Mayfield he found it out of line, and re-orientated it by shoving with his shoulder: *Memorials of St Dunstan*, p. 204.

[11] *Leechdoms*, iii. 178–9, 180–1.

churches being built.[1] There is no reason to suspect Herman of wild exaggeration. The kingdom was wealthy and at peace. A church gave distinction to an estate and its owner, and those lords with wooden edifices could afford to rebuild them in stone.[2] The temporary cooling in religious fervour, which seems to mark the end of this period, may indeed have favoured the building programme. Great piety led usually to the endowment of monasteries.

The history and nature of the privately-owned church (*Eigenkirche*) in the Carolingian Empire and its successor kingdoms has been carefully studied by continental scholars.[3] In England the subject has been relatively neglected,[4] although the evidence, especially for the eleventh century, is more plentiful than for most other countries. A generalized picture of the position of the proprietary church in France and Germany is as follows.[5] The founder of the church established it for the benefit of his family and dependants. He kept a proprietary interest in its endowments and revenue and himself appointed the priest who served it. The lord's church tended to be treated like his mill and oven and other seigneurial monopolies. Lords augmented or diminished the endowments arbitrarily, often took a share of the revenue, and all the revenue when the church was vacant, and could sell, pledge, or bequeath the church, like any other piece of property. At the same time the owner protected the revenues of his church by maintaining its monopoly and by attempting to secure for it all profitable rights of an ecclesiastical nature – for example, burial rights, the right to celebrate marriages, baptismal rights, and the right to take tithe and other church taxes. As the lord appointed the priest, so, although this practice was normally regarded as an abuse,[6] he could dismiss him. In some regions the priest was often of unfree status, and all his possessions fell to the lord at death. In areas where feudal customs developed, there was the tendency to enfeof the priest with his church as a benefice. The priest was invested with the land and revenues and the office. He was an ecclesiastical vassal of his lord. Naturally he often

---

[1] 'de ipsa Anglia ecclesiis ubique repleta, quae quotidie novis locis adderentur novae, de innumera ornamentorum et signorum per oratoria distributione, regumque et divitum in haereditatem Christi amplissima largitate': Goscelin, *Hist. translat. S. Augustini episcopi*, MPL, clv, col. 32.

[2] Cf. Chester-le-Street by Bishop Æthelric of Durham (1042–56): Symeon, *HDE*, p. 92.

[3] Select bibliography in Feine, pp. 139–41.

[4] Cf. bibliography, *ibid.* p. 140. Lingard, *Antiquities*, i. 178 ff., 398–407, is an excellent pioneering study. The other major studies are H. Böhmer, 'Das Eigenkirchentum in England', *Texte und Forschungen zur englischen Kulturgeschichte, Festgabe für Felix Liebermann* (Halle, 1921); W. Page, 'Some remarks on the Churches of the Domesday Survey', *Archaeologia*, lxvi (1915), 61–102, R. Lennard, *Rural England 1086–1135* (1959), pp. 288–338.

[5] Cf. Feine, pp. 131–47, 156–79.   [6] Burchard, *Decretum*, III, cc. 111, 112.

paid the lord for his investiture (a custom which the reformers were to denounce as simony)[1] and the lord usually exacted more than strictly ecclesiastical services from his vassal.

A reading of Domesday Book confirms that most of the basic characteristics, although not all the features, of this Germanic attitude were also present in England before the Conquest. It is quite clear that to commissioners investigating in 1086 tenure, revenues, and other lucrative customs, and to their informers, a church was simply a type of property which differed in no significant way from any other estate or useful building on it and offered no resistance at all to a feudal scheme of classification. This equation is so comprehensive and exact that it need not be unduly laboured. All churches were subject to some lord who expected to make a profit out of them. All churches were *Eigenkirchen*. But in status and value they ranged from those appurtenant to the demesne of a manor, like a mill,[2] wood, salt-pans, or fishing rights, with which the church was often ranged, to those rich estates held in perpetual inheritance under the king. Their economic and tenurial variety is remarkable.

Churches can be classified in several different ways. There is good reason to think that the basic ecclesiastical distinction remained that between the old minsters and the rest. But a more graduated list is given in the late Anglo-Saxon laws – chief minsters, smaller ones, even smaller ones where nevertheless there is a cemetery, and field churches.[3] These are, presumably, episcopal minsters, other old minsters, manorial churches with burial rights, and the rest. Most of the minsters then in existence can be identified from Domesday Book.[4] But there is little evidence for the status and rights of the manorial churches.

Domesday Book, of course, is not concerned with the ecclesiastical status of churches, but with the status of landholders and the values of estates. These classifications, too, are interesting. The record is arranged tenurially, that is to say it is a survey, shire by shire, of the *terrae* held by the king and his immediate vassals. His 'men' are listed according to the order of precedence used in the witness-lists to charters, so that in the sections concerned with clerical vassals we find, each with its index number, the lands of the several bishops, the lands of various saints (abbeys and some collegiate

---

[1] Burchard, *Decretum*, III, cc. 110, 113.

[2] R. Lennard, *Rural England*, pp. 287, 320, notices cases in *DB* where rights in the church are divided into the same fractions as rights over the mill – the result of dividing estates between heirs or heiresses.   [3] VIII Æthelred, 5; I Cnut, 3.2.   [4] Page, *op. cit.*

churches), occasionally the lands of important royal priests or clerks, and, lastly, sometimes a collective heading, 'Clerici tenentes de rege'.[1] This classification throws more light on persons and their status than on the churches themselves.

A more useful distinction for our purpose is that made within the *terrae* between those churches which are listed individually, with the names of the successive holders, a description of the holding, and a statement of its liabilities and value, and those which either appear as appurtenant to a manor (*ibi aecclesia* or *aecclesiolà*) or can be inferred to exist because a priest is mentioned among the manorial tenants (e.g. x *villani et* y *bordarii et presbiter et prepositus inter omnes habent* z *carucas*).[2] The criterion here is usually whether a church is individually responsible for the common burdens – whether it has hidated land and so pays geld. But this feature itself probably serves to distinguish the minsters from most of the newer churches. In general, on the one hand there are honourable tenures and for the most part more valuable churches, and on the other the semi-servile tenures of churches less abundantly endowed.

Individually-listed churches are found in all parts of the country and on most types of estate. But they are more plentiful in the south and on the estates of the larger landholders, especially on royal demesne and on the lands of the bishops and earls. It is easy to believe that most of them once belonged to the king. When observed from the point of view of the Domesday commissioners they are found to vary greatly in tenurial and economic detail, in exactly the same way as secular estates. It is clear that there was no special ecclesiastical tenure. A few very free churches are to be found. In Edward's reign a priest named Eadmer held Hurstmonceaux in Sussex, an estate rated at five hides and valued at £6. He had a church there, seven acres of meadow, and a small wood. He could go with his land where he chose.[3] Here we have a priest in possession of, presumably ancestral, bookland, rated at the thegn's five hides to the common burdens, completely free to choose his lord, and to transfer his commendation at will. No one could be freer in Anglo-Saxon England.

Doubtless there were many hereditary churches under permanent lordship. Any lord could give a church to a priest and allow a son to succeed. In 1086 Bristoard held the church of Bedwyn, on the royal demesne in Wiltshire, which his father had held in Edward's reign.[4] Before the Conquest the

---

[1] See above, p. 131.   [2] For the various formulae, see Page, pp. 63–4, Lennard, pp. 310 ff.
[3] *DB*, i. 18 a i.   [4] *DB*, i. 65 b i.

incumbent of the minster of the king's hundredal vill of Sutton Courtenay in Berkshire was the priest Ælfwine.[1] The neighbouring abbey of Abingdon already had an interest in the church, for it owned, presumably through royal generosity, two parts of the tithe of the vill and also a hide of land, which the priest held of the abbot. So the position remained, until William II, in return for £20, granted the church, with its lands, tithes, and customs, to the abbey. At the same time he protected the life-interest of the priest, who was to change nothing but his lord. Ælfwine, however, was not completely satisfied with the arrangement. He was an expert in English law and had given great help to the abbey in the dangerous years after 1066. So he made a private settlement with the abbot. First he obtained confirmation of his own life-interest. Then it was agreed, in return for £5 and the surrender of the chapel of Milton, that the minster should be granted to Ælfwine's son to hold for his life, but, should the boy die before the father, then the father would recover it for the term of his own life. Here an abbey, influenced by gratitude, deferred breaking hereditary succession, although it wanted to put the church *in commune abbatis et fratrum*. Occasionally hereditary tenure was expressly recognized and safeguarded. A woman, Siflaed, left Marlingford in Norfolk to Bury St Edmunds and stipulated that her church, to which she made gifts, was to be free, and Wulfmaer her priest was to perform the service in it – he and his issue, as long as they were in holy orders. St Edmund was to have no more than the *mund* (protection) of the church.[2]

But it is doubtful whether an hereditary estate in a church was often created by instrument after 1000 for priests who were, after all, officially expected to be celibate. Land was often granted or willed to them. They, like anyone else, could hold private estates under any conditions.[3] The grant of a church to a priest, however, is probably to be regarded as more akin to a loan for one life than to a grant in inheritance. Sometimes this life interest is made clear. About 1040 Stigand, apparently not the future bishop, gave an estate to his priest Ælfgar for life with reversion to Bury St Edmunds.[4] It was often considered safer to make a benefaction to the church rather than to its priest. In 1063 King Edward granted by book an estate as dowry to a church in Exeter at the request of a priest Scepius.[5] The perpetual inheritance was in

---

[1] *Chron. Abingdon*, ii. 26–9; cf. 2.   [2] Whitelock, *Wills*, nos. 37–8.

[3] And so could monks and nuns. Cf. 'Consuetudinis apud Anglos intererat ut monachi qui vellent pecuniarum patrimoniorumque forent susceptibiles, ipsis fruentes quomodo placeret dispensarent': *Chron. Abingdon*, i. 477.

[4] Robertson, *Charters*, no. 92.   [5] K. 813.

favour of the church, not the priest. All the same, ecclesiastical dynasties were founded. And even churches granted by the king to priests who became bishops, or to bishops themselves, tended to become attached to, even if not absorbed in, the bishopric and to be 'inherited' by their successors. In these features clerical were no different from lay estates. Book-land was not without precarious aspects and loan-land could be renewed to an heir when the lease ran out. There was in fact a tendency in the later Old-English kingdom for the two tenures to come together. St Oswald granted some loans of land in perpetual inheritance to thegns by book.[1] It is no doubt because of this convergence, and its completion in Anglo-Norman feudalism, that we cannot discover which priests held their church by book and which as a loan.

The churches listed individually in Domesday Book also vary greatly in their wealth and prestige. The church of Bosham in Sussex, with lands extending to Hampshire, quite separate from the large manor of Bosham which Earl Godwin had held, but having as its parish the hundred of Bosham – presumably the whole district originally dependent on the royal *tun* – will serve as an example of one of the greatest non-episcopal churches.[2] Its lands had been rated at 147 hides and it was valued at £300. Either Cnut or Edward gave sixty-five of these hides, worth £65, to a royal priest named Godwin, and the arrangement recorded in Domesday Book is that he held sixteen of them directly of King Edward (six *in elemosina*) and forty-nine of Earl Godwin. The remainder Edward granted to his Norman clerk Osbern. And this estate, together with the sixteen hides which the priest Godwin had held of the king, Osbern, when he became bishop of Exeter after the Conquest, managed to attach to his bishopric. Much of Osbern's estate was, of course, in the hands of sub-tenants. There was a family of clerks at Bosham, one of whom held lands rated at one hide and four held in common land with the same rating. These clerks had a priest, presumably to serve the church, but themselves

---

[1] E. John, *Land Tenure in Early England*, pp. 129 ff.

[2] *DB*, i. 17 a ii, b i, 27 a i, a ii, 43 a i; J. H. Round, 'Note on the Sussex Domesday', *Sussex Archaeological Collections*, xliv (1901), 140–3. The allocation of the hidage, thanks to Round, is fairly clear. And the value of the priest Godwin's estate, although not necessarily the value to him, is plainly stated. But the value of Osbern's share T.R.E. is by no means clear. He is said to have held Bosham with 65 hides when he received it (the same hidage as Godwin's share). He also held Elsted of 13 hides worth £15 of King Edward. The position of Preston's three hides worth £4 is uncertain. The one hundred-and-forty-seventh hide at Itchenor was held by a tenant of Earl Godwin. Yet Osbern's share of Bosham in 1086 was valued at only £17 10s.; and no addition of given values will come anywhere near £300, the estimated value of the whole church T.R.E. Either there had been severe waste or the statistics are faulty. As Osbern would seem to have held 78 hides, a value of about £80 is indicated.

held the tithes worth £2. There was also at Elsted a priest with one hide and a clerk with half as much. Here we can see how a minster could be broken up to reward royal clerks and provide a picking for an earl. And we can identify four steps in an ecclesiastical 'feudal' ladder: the priest of Bosham held of the clerks, who held of Osbern, who held of the king. A smaller grant of Edward's was the church of Mottisfont, in north Hampshire, with its chapels of Broughton, Pittleworth, East and West Titherley, East Dean, and Lockersley, rated at five hides less one virgate and valued at £4, to Ealdred archbishop of York.[1] But the purpose was different. This estate was obviously to provide the archbishop with a hospice when he visited Winchester, and a house in that city was attached to the church.

A much larger class of churches is formed of those rated at from one to four hides, and of this class the one-hide church is probably the commonest. They are found in fair numbers on royal, comital, and episcopal estates. The churches of the clerks listed as *clerici regis* or *elemosinarii regis* are of from one virgate to about four hides, but are often rated at a half, one, or one-and-a-half hides. Similar churches are found on the estates of the earls. The church of Nether Wallop in Hampshire, on the manor held by Countess Gytha from her husband Earl Godwin, was rated at a hide.[2] In Wiltshire the church on Tostig's manor of Corsham had the same rating.[3] Most bishoprics seem to have had a number of comparable churches on their lands. Buckingham will serve as an example of one of the larger of this class.[4] Rated at five carucates, it had four ploughs, three *villani*, three bordars, ten cottars, a mill worth 10s., a meadow of two carucates, and wood for fencing. Bishop Wulfwig held it from King Edward and it was worth to the bishop £7. Clere in Hampshire, on the estates of the monks of Winchester, was among the smaller of this type.[5] One priest held the church, which with its land was rated at one hide. There was there one plough, one bordar, two slaves, and an acre of meadow, and it was all worth to the bishop £2.

As the values of Domesday Book are almost always the value to the lord whose *terrae* are being considered, the survey provides no evidence for values at tenant level. We do not know what revenues and lucrative rights were enjoyed by the priests who served Buckingham and Clere. We only know that whoever farmed or leased those churches – in the case of Buckingham not necessarily the priest – had contracted to pay £7 and £2 respectively as rent. If they were both fair rents, they can, of course, be used for comparison. It

[1] *DB*, i. 42 a.
[2] *DB*, i. 38 b i.
[3] *DB*, i. 64 a i.
[4] *DB*, i. 143 a i.
[5] *DB*, i. 41 a ii.

is even more risky to compare the values of lay and ecclesiastical estates or to compare their hidages, for churches may have enjoyed beneficial hidage. Nevertheless, for what it is worth, the average larger church was assessed at less than 'the thegn's five hides'.

Besides these important churches, three other types can be distinguished in Domesday Book: churches in boroughs, those in East Anglia owned by partners, and the smaller manorial churches.

The churches in boroughs form an interesting class because they were affected by, if not subject to, burghal customs. There were usually many churches in a borough because most of those who had a substantial holding in it built a church for their tenants. At Nottingham in 1086 the jurors declared that Stori, the *antecessor* of Walter de Aincurt, could make himself a church on his land and in his soke without the need for anyone's licence, and also could send his tithe where he chose.[1] Many of the Norwich churches are mentioned.[2] Archbishop Stigand had the church of St Martin, with 12 acres of land, and the church of St Michael with 112 acres of land, six of meadow, and one plough. His brother, Bishop Æthelmaer, held as part of his patrimony the church of St Simon and St Jude, to which pertained three parts of a mill, a half acre of meadow, and one messuage (*mansura*). The abbot of Bury St Edmunds had half the church of St Laurence and one house. The burgesses themselves held fifteen churches, to which pertained *in elemosina* 181 acres of land and meadow and forty-three chapels. Twelve burgesses held the church of Holy Trinity with 180 acres of land. A 'demesne' burgess of the king, Eadstan, had two churches and the sixth part of a third. In Thetford [3] Archbishop Stigand held the church of St Mary, with its four daughter churches, St Peter, St John, St Martin, and St Margaret, and $5\frac{1}{2}$ carucates of land, five burgesses, 12 acres of meadow, and thirty-five sheep. The abbot of Ely had three churches and the abbot of Bury one.

Some of the special freedoms and restraints characteristic of burgage tenure seem to have applied to these churches. The jurors of Huntingdon deposed [4] that the church of St Mary in the borough, and the land which pertained to it, had belonged to the abbey of Thorney. But the abbot had pledged it to the burgesses (presumably as security for a loan). As a result of an unexplained transaction (possibly the king meeting the debt) King Edward had given it to his priests Vitalis and Bernard, and these had sold it to Hugh, King Edward's chamberlain, who then sold it to two priests of the

[1] *DB*, i. 280 a ii.   [2] *DB*, ii. 116 a i, ff.
[3] *DB*, i. 118 a ii, f.   [4] *DB*, i. 208 a i.

borough. Eustace (the sheriff) had 'invaded' the church. This church had passed in one generation through six owners, and seems to have been the subject of what can only be described as speculation in real estate, mostly by royal courtiers, and with royal approval. The speculators were, of course, buying and selling the church's *valet*. On the other hand true burgesses seem to have been fettered by the burghal tenurial customs. In the city of Lincoln Godric son of Garwine (f.) held the church of All Saints with its appurtenances.[1] He became a monk of Peterborough and gave the church to the abbot. But all the burgesses of Lincoln declared in 1086 that the abbot held it unjustly, for neither Garwine, nor her son, nor anyone else could grant their possessions outside the city or outside the parentage without the king's consent. And a priest, Earnwi, claimed the church as the heir of Godric, his kinsman. In Lincoln churches were hereditary like other property, and, it seems, the church of All Saints had descended through the woman Garwine.

These examples are taken from boroughs in eastern England because it was in this region that fragmentation was carried to extreme lengths. There were some large parishes in East Anglia, but more characteristic are the 'town' churches founded and owned by the freeholders with lands in the township.[2] For example, Wantisden in Suffolk had a church, half of which was attached to a holding of twenty-two freemen, a quarter to that of two other freemen, and a quarter to that of one freeman.[3] At Stonham in Suffolk was a church of 20 acres which nine freemen had given for the salvation of their souls.[4] The shareholders could hold in common or could particularize the individual shares. Moreover, the churches, especially in Norfolk, are often described as being of so many acres – $2\frac{1}{2}$ to 50 acres are mentioned, with the mean lying about 20 acres – and even if these are fiscal and not arable acres, there is still a contrast with most other areas. It is a distinct social and tenurial pattern, connected with the several farming of East Anglia, the rare coincidence between manor and vill, and the partibility of estates.[5] But these churches were no freer from lordship than others elsewhere. Indeed, their division into shares emphasizes the conception of private property. They were in no useful sense people's churches. And there is no good reason for making the Danes responsible for the pattern.

Manorial churches – those established and owned by lords for the benefit

[1] *DB*, i. 336 a ii.   [2] Page, pp. 85 ff.
[3] *DB*, ii. 306 b, 307, 344.   [4] *DB*, ii. 438.
[5] Traces of the system can also be found in Herts, Essex, Lincs, Notts, and Derby: Page pp. 85, 92, 97.

of themselves and the manorial tenants – although sometimes obviously omitted from Domesday Book,[1] must have formed by 1066 the largest class of churches. They are especially associated with the estates of thegns, whether these were book-lands or loan-lands. In the eleventh century a thegn with lands assessed to the common burdens at five hides was expected to have his own church,[2] and the laws of Æthelred, like the Domesday commissioners, assume that each vill can provide a priest and a reeve.[3] It has been suggested,[4] although not altogether convincingly,[5] that the thegn usually built his church only at the head member, the principal estate where he himself lived. It seems likely that custom varied – that where the power of the old minster was still real, a lord might build only for himself and his immediate tenants, but that elsewhere, and especially in East Anglia and Kent, most villages may have acquired a church. We know from ecclesiastical sources that in the eleventh century there were over 400 churches in Kent.[6] Unfortunately, owing to the extreme subjection of manorial churches, we can learn little about them. Except in East Anglia an acreage, rating, or value is rarely assigned to them. In Kent the church is often associated with the slaves,[7] and so with the demesne. In open-field areas the priest is usually associated with the *villani*, and may have held land mixed with their holdings and of a comparable area.[8] But what the measured acreage of a villein's holding was nobody knows, although, as he seems usually to have held a multiple or fraction of a virgate, which was 30 fiscal acres, an equivalent arable holding is often ascribed to him.[9]

On the Continent secular lords gradually filched rights for their own churches from the old baptismal churches. In England disintegration does not seem to have gone so far. Chrism, at least in the diocese of Canterbury, was collected from the bishop mostly by the old minsters (including St Augustine's) for distribution to their daughter churches.[10] This custom proclaimed the minsters' paramount right to baptism and may also have been

---

[1] Lennard, *Rural England*, pp. 14, 288 ff.

[2] *Gethynctho*, c. 2, Liebermann, *Gesetze*, i. 456.

[3] Cf. VII Æthelred, 2.5 (Latin), 2.3 (Old-English); *SSC*, p. 101.

[4] Page, pp. 98 ff.   [5] For Lennard's criticism, see *Rural England*, pp. 290–1.

[6] Gordon Ward, 'The list of Saxon churches in the Textus Roffensis', *Archaeologia Cantiana*, xliv (1932), 'The lists of Saxon churches in the Domesday monachorum, and White Book of St Augustine', *ibid*. xlv (1933).

[7] Cf. *DB*, i. 8 a ii, 'Ibi ecclesia et vi servi et i molendinum de vi solidis et iv acrae prati.'

[8] Lennard, *Rural England*, pp. 310 ff.   [9] *Ibid*. pp. 339 ff.

[10] *The Domesday Monachorum of Christ Church Canterbury*, ed. D. C. Douglas (1944), pp. 5 ff., 77–9.

profitable. There was also the tradition that the five ecclesiastical customs were due to the old minsters. The royal laws expressly safeguarded the minsters' claim to church-scot and tithe. And the lesser nobility may sometimes have built private churches more for their household than for all their estates. Church-scot was by law reserved to the old minsters.[1] Worcester when leasing land often saved its right to the tax,[2] and in 1086 still received it from the whole of Oswaldslow.[3] Pershore was similarly placed within its hundred.[4] Aylesbury (Bucks) took church-scot from eight hundreds,[5] Bensington (Oxon) possibly from its four-and-a-half hundreds,[6] and Headington (Oxon) possibly from its two.[7] No doubt there were some alienations and usurpations, but they can hardly have destroyed the old system.[8] With tithe, the old minsters were forced to make a small surrender. A lord who had a church with a graveyard on his book-land could divert to it one-third of his own tithe (from the inland or demesne). But all the tithe from the geneatland (land held by dependant peasants), and from the whole estate if the lord merely had a church without a graveyard, was to go to the old minster.[9] The privilege is in favour of the thegn's hall, not his estates. Countess Gytha's churches at Wallop in Hampshire illustrate such a partition.[10] Nether Wallop, rated at one hide, had all the church-scot, but only half the tithe of the manor, 46*d.* from the tithe of the villeins, and half (the tithe) of the fields. A chapel (*aecclesiola*) at Over Wallop had 8 acres of tithe. Tithe was a general tax and could properly be diverted to new churches and their minsters. It

[1] II Edgar, 2.2: 'all church-scot is to go to the old minster from every free hearth.'

[2] Cf. Robertson, *Charters*, nos. 34, 35, 112.   [3] *DB*, i. 174 a i.   [4] *DB*, i. 175 b i.

[5] *DB*, i. 143 b ii. The payments ceased with the Norman Conquest.

[6] *DB*, i. 154 b i. Worth 11*s.*

[7] *Ibid.* Worth 10*s.* 6*d.* The priest Vitalis who held the hundredal church of Hurstbourne (Hants) on royal demesne with half a hide, also had church-scot, *DB*, i. 39 a ii.

[8] Archbishop Ealdred when he retained the bishop of Worcester's Warwickshire manor of Alveston, took with it soke and sake, toll and team, church-scot, and all the forfeitures except the four which the king has throughout the kingdom: *DB*, i. 239 b i. See also a grant to Winchcombe in 1059: *A Med. Misc. for D. M. Stenton* (1962), p. 116.

[9] II Edgar, 1. 1–2. Cap. 2.1 runs: 'if anyone has a church without a graveyard he is to pay his priest what he chooses from the ninth part' (i.e. from what remains after he has paid tithe to the old minster).

[10] *DB*, i. 38 b i. Tithe is not often mentioned in *DB* and the entries are not usually very illuminating. A royal almoner, the priest Bristoard, held the churches of Dorchester and Bere Regis, in the hundred of Bere Regis in Dorset, with the tithes: i. 79 a i. The priest on the archbishop of Canterbury's manor of Haddenham (Bucks) had the church with three hides and the tithes: i. 143 b ii. A clerk who held the church of the bishop of Winchester's manor at South Stoneham had one hide of land with all the tithes of the vill and also from the king's land: i. 41 b ii. All these churches look like old minsters.

was sometimes transferred to monasteries. In Edward's reign Abingdon held two parts of the tithe of the hundredal vill of Sutton Courtenay, which was royal demesne.[1] The king had presumably granted it away from the minster. It is possible that in the eastern shires, where there is less evidence of a parish system based on old minsters, and much proof of individual freedom, many freemen could send their tithe where they would.[2] And it may be that when the freemen of a township jointly established a church they assigned all their dues to it. Such an arrangement would give full meaning to the Domesday formula that a church pertained to various named estates.

Less is known about the destination of the other ecclesiastical customs. It may be that plough-alms and light dues were often diverted to a manorial church. Such churches, if they had a cemetery, presumably took the soul-scot of those buried there.[3] But a division of soul-scot could not have greatly damaged the old minsters. Thegns would normally wish to be buried in the mother church and obtain the greater benefits for the dead available from a collegiate establishment.[4] Manorial graveyards were for the poor.

It is in connexion with soul-scot and prayers for the dead that the gilds of laymen are best considered. Men clubbed together in order to get special benefits from the church. The rules of gilds of laymen have survived from Cambridge, Bedwyn (Wilts), a royal manor, Abbotsbury (Dorset), belonging to the monks of that abbey, Exeter, and from Woodbury and several other villages and hamlets near Exeter.[5] It is clear that these gilds differed in social standing and in character and purpose. But all had some religious aspect. The Cambridge fellowship is described as the thegns' gild. That at Abbotsbury clearly had a similar membership, and those at Bedwyn and Exeter were associations of substantial men. The fourteen rural gilds attached to St Peter's, Exeter, seem, however, to have been lower in the social scale, and in some cases the village priest was the leading member.

Most of the gilds were social and mutual-benefit societies, and all were burial societies and possibly confraternities for obits. But the emphasis

---

[1] *Chron. Abingdon*, ii. 27. At Droitwich (Worcs) the king had granted tithe to Westminster Abbey: 'De decima regis de Wich habet S. Petrus £8': *DB*, i. 174 b ii.

[2] Cf. the case of Stori in Nottingham, above, p. 192.

[3] Yet extensive burial rights were often claimed for minsters. For Worcester's claims, see below, p. 204; for Steyning's (Sussex), see Page, p. 79.

[4] Priests were forbidden to sing more than one mass a day. A village priest, therefore, could not properly say many masses for the dead.

[5] Abbotsbury, 'Woodbury', Cambridge, and Exeter, Thorpe, *Diplomatarium*, pp. 605 ff; Cambridge, Exeter, Bedwyn, and Abbotsbury, *EHD*, i. 557 ff. The Bedwyn statutes are incomplete.

varied. One of the main purposes of the Cambridge gild was mutual assurance against legal penalties and other hazards. The Bedwyn and Abbotsbury gilds seem to have been more religious in tone. The Exeter brotherhood appears to have been an association largely concerned with prayers for the dead. The members met thrice a year not to banquet but to allow the priest to sing two masses, one for living friends and one for the dead, and the ordinary brethren each to recite two psalters for the same end. Non-attendance at the meetings was punished by having to provide further masses. This fellowship is like that of the *fratres kalendarii*, found in Exeter in the twelfth century,[1] and may, indeed, be connected. The Devonshire village gilds were again associations for obits.

If we conflate these various aspects, the typical gild had a meeting place with benches – Abbotsbury had a guildhall – an entrance subscription, possibly a probationary period for new members, and rules protected by an oath and fines. Banquets and drinkings were usual. Mutual benefits were arranged to meet calamities, including fire damage to a member's house,[2] and that greatest calamity of all, his death. Provision was sometimes made for the carrying of the corpse to the chosen burial place, especially the church to which the gild was attached,[3] for special services at that church,[4] and for a burial feast.[5] Some gilds made regular provision for religious services [6] or for payments to a priest or church,[7] some distributed alms,[8] and the Exeter gild contributed 5*d.* a head when a member went on a pilgrimage to Rome.

The village gilds attached to the minster at Exeter are the only ones of their kind known.[9] But they cannot have been unique. We have short and

---

[1] Mrs. F. Rose-Troup, 'The Ancient Monastery of St Mary and St Peter at Exeter', *Trans. of the Devonshire Association*, lxiii (1931), 185, 192, believed that the Exeter gild – its regulations are inscribed on an erased folio of an eighth-century lectionary – was founded in Athelstan's reign when the monastery was rebuilt. If so, a direct affiliation with the *fratres kalendarii* is unlikely. For the latter, see *Historical Manuscripts Commission: Report on Manuscripts in Various Collections*, iv (1907), 58.   [2] Exeter, Bedwyn.   [3] Cambridge, Abbotsbury.

[4] Six masses or psalters (Exeter), five masses or psalters (Bedwyn), 1*d.* apiece at the body for the soul (Abbotsbury).   [5] Cambridge, Bedwyn.

[6] Exeter; ½*d.* for their souls at each meeting (Bedwyn).

[7] A young sheep or 2*d.* at Rogation days to the priest (Bedwyn): according to *DB*, i. 65 b i, Bristoard was the priest in 1086, having succeeded his father; 1*d.* or wax to St. Peter's minster (Abbotsbury).

[8] On each death 2*d.* a head for almsgiving, of which a fitting amount went to Ely (Cambridge); food (Abbotsbury).

[9] These associations are post-Conquest, 1072–1103. But Bishop Osbern had been King Edward's priest, almost all the members have English names, and there is no reason to suspect a Norman custom.

similar regulations for two of the Woodbury gilds, and then a list of twelve
other gilds, presumably with similar rules. Eighteen members are listed for
Woodbury I, but only abbreviated lists are given for the others.[1] Twelve of
the gilds are from villages and hamlets to the south-east of Exeter, three from
Woodbury (one called Alwin's guildship), and one from the neighbouring
hamlet of Nutwell, two from Colyton, and one each from Sidmouth, White-
stone, the neighbouring hamlet of Halsford, Exmouth, Clyst St George,[2] and
Broadclyst.[3] There was also a gild in the north-west of the diocese at Bide-
ford and another at 'Lege' (Leigh – unidentifiable).[4] The recorded purpose
of the gilds, and hence the membership lists, is to enter into confraternity
with the canons of the cathedral church of Exeter. The gild members are to
pay the canons 1d. a year from each hearth (at Easter, Woodbury I; at
Martinmas, Woodbury II), and similarly 1d. at the death of each gild-
brother, as soul-scot. In return the canons are 'to perform such service for
them as they ought to perform'.

These gifts are all in favour of minsters and show the hold which the
mother churches had on the religious sentiments of the people. We can also
see from Domesday Book that some of the minsters still preserved all their
rights intact. Mottisfont in Hampshire had six chapels and all the customs of
the quick and the dead.[5] Taunton in Somerset, the minster for a hundred,
had church-scot and soul-scot from almost every landowner within its great
parish.[6] Worcester seems to have collected all the ecclesiastical customs from
all the churches in Oswaldslow.[7] And the Domesday jurors declared that St
Wulfram's in the king's vill of Grantham (Lincs) should receive the tithes
and ecclesiastical customs from all sokes and inlands which the king had in
the wapentakes of Wivebridge and 'Treos'.[8] No litigation over parochial
rights is recorded for the late Anglo-Saxon period. But a case from shortly
after the Conquest illustrates the attitudes.[9] The abbey of Abingdon's vill of
Whistley was within the parish of the hundredal minster at Sonning, which
was held with the manor by the bishop of Ramsbury-Sherborne = Salisbury.
In Abbot Athelm's time there was no church at Whistley, an inconvenience
both to the villagers and to the visiting abbot, especially in winter, for they

---

[1] There is a reference to women beneficiaries in Woodbury I. These may be the wives of members.
But the name Atheleove (Woodbury I) may be feminine and Godgith (Exmouth) was held by
women as well as by men.   [2] 'Cliftwike', Thorpe.   [3] 'Cliftune', Thorpe.
[4] Two priests were members of this gild. East Budleigh lies among the south-eastern group,
and is the most likely candidate.
[5] *DB*, i. 42 a.   [6] *DB*, i. 87 b i.   [7] See below, pp. 252-3.
[8] *DB*, i. 377 a i; cf. 337 b i, 343 b ii.   [9] *Chron. Abingdon*, ii. 18-19.

had to go to Sonning to hear mass. So Athelm, after 1078, built a wooden chapel in his vill which Bishop Osmund dedicated to St Nicholas. In 1087–8, however, the clerk of Sonning complained to the bishop that through the establishment of the chapel he was losing his customs. Osmund suspended the chapel and then in 1089 came to terms with the abbot. In return for the payment of ½M each year to the bishop, the monastery could keep the chapel; and its clerk could perform services and retain for himself all oblations made at the altar. But all the customary rights which the church of Sonning had enjoyed in the vill in King Edward's day were to be maintained intact. Sonning had in fact made only a trivial surrender. Yet it is clear that the minsters as a class were already in decay by 1066 and that the Norman Conquest probably accelerated their transformation.[1]

The smaller churches were founded to serve a lord and his household and to some extent his estates. Eventually the boundaries of manor and parish tended to coincide. But there was still movement in the eleventh century, for Archbishop Wulfstan forbade priests to entice away another priest's parishioner with his tithe and dues.[2] The spiritual rights most coveted for these churches were baptism, confession, and burial, for these were both a convenience to the local inhabitants and a source of revenue for the priest. Archbishop Wulfstan in his 'Ecclesiastical Institutes', a translation of Theodulf's *Capitula*, recognized that the ordinary parish priest heard confessions,[3] received tithe (c. xiv), and had burial (c. ix) and restricted baptismal rights (c. xvii).[4] Burial rights, although they could be lucrative,[5] are those most frequently mentioned and were probably the most widely dispersed. The transportation of corpses over long distances was always resisted by agricultural workers. Babies, however, are easier to carry, and, although many of the smaller churches acquired a font and bought chrism from the old minster,[6] parents may often have chosen to visit the mother church.[7] The attitude of the laity to confessors is more complex.

There remains to be considered the rights of the lords in their churches. In the first place he had the right to appoint the priest. Although the bishop

---

[1] Lennard, 'Some "Minsters" and collegiate churches', *Rural England*, pp. 396–404.
[2] 'Ecclesiastical Institutes' (= Theodulf's *Capitula*), c. xiv, Thorpe, *Ancient Laws*, ii. 410–11.
[3] See below, pp. 269–70.   [4] Thorpe, *Ancient Laws*, ii. 408 ff.
[5] Large soul-scots are specified in wills.   [6] See above, pp. 179–82.
[7] St Wulfstan, when he was prior of Worcester, used to baptise without fee those children brought to him. According to his biographer the action was necessary owing to the avarice of priests, *Vita Wulfstani*, pp. 12–13. Wulfstan may also, of course, have been exercising the traditional rights of the old minster.

had to assure himself of the fitness of a candidate – and sometimes no doubt refused to institute – there are no recorded examples of a refusal in this period. Patronage, apart from the abuse of simony, was a valuable right in itself, and at the higher levels of society it was a necessary part of the machinery of government. The king and the bishops could hardly have done without it. It served both as a ladder of promotion and as a method of paying clerical servants. Stigand climbed from Ashingdon to Canterbury. Bishop Brihtheah of Worcester first gave St Wulfstan the manorial church of Hawkesbury [1] and then proposed to transfer him to a rich suburban church.[2] The corollary, the right to dismiss the priest, which was sometimes attempted when an estate changed hands,[3] was contrary to canon law.

Most lords probably also drew a revenue from their churches. Domesday Book assigns a value to the larger churches, and this we know to be the rent or 'farm' received by the feudal superior. A useful distinction can be drawn here between three types of lord: the king, the bishops and abbots, and the thegns. Royal demesne was a miscellaneous collection of estates and proprietary rights. The bishoprics, most of the abbeys, and many of the minsters [4] were still dominical. And just as there were royal thegns scattered throughout the shires, so in the south of England there were those priests and clerks whom the king had endowed.[5] Characteristic of churches listed individually in Domesday Book – and probably indeed one of the reasons for this treatment – is that they were assessed to the common burdens in hides, carucates, or sulungs. Fiscally they probably ranked as manors. From them the king took his *feorm* (a render of produce, or its commutation), bridge-, borough-, and army-service, and geld, according to the assessment, unless they had been expressly exempted. A church could be fortunate and hold hides which had never gelded, that is to say be exempt from the tax.[6] A

---

[1] *Vita Wulfstani*, p. 47. Hawkesbury, a large manor belonging to the monks, and assessed at 50 hides (*DB*, i. 164 b ii), must have had only a small church, for there is no reference to it or a priest in *DB*.   [2] *Ibid.* p. 8.

[3] Ælfwine, the priest of Sutton Courtenay, obviously felt in danger when the king granted his church to Abingdon Abbey; see above, p. 189.

[4] Edward disposed of minsters. Cf. his writ confirming that the minster of St John of Beverley was under the archbishop of York and subject to him, so that the archbishop was its protector and guardian under the king (Harmer, *Writs*, no. 7), and his grant of the minster of Axminster, with sake and soke, to Eadred, the deacon of Archbishop Ealdred, as a pious benefaction to St Peter's minster at York (*ibid.* no. 120).   [5] See above, p. 131.

[6] Ecclesiastical hides which have never gelded are occasionally found in *DB*. Cf. Wantage and Sparsholt, Berks (57 a i); Blackburn, Lancs, quit of every custom (270 a i); Manchester, Lancs (*ibid.*), quit of every custom except geld; Droitwich, Worcs (174 b ii); Filsham, Sussex (57 a i);

church could be granted land by the king free from all tax and service.[1] A favourite priest could get his assessment reduced.[2] And a priest could hold *in elemosina regis*.[3] Clearly those who held 'in alms' were freed from most, if not all, of the consequences of holding hidated land. And these freedoms prove that from other churches the king exacted the full customs. He could in fact impose any services he chose. He had three churches in Archenfield in southern Herefordshire whose priests had the duties of carrying royal messages into Wales and each singing two masses a week for the king. Each was also responsible for a heriot of 20s.[4]

For the king, then, churches were on the whole like any other dominical estate and produced similar revenues and services. But he was prepared to abate his demands in special cases. Doubtless the king also possessed demesne manors with small churches. The priests of these were less likely to attract special privileges; but royal estates were usually a little freer than others. The king had no interest in grinding the faces of the clergy. And even here some superiority of status is to be expected. On one important matter – the destination of the revenues of a church during a vacancy – no information exists. It may be that the sheriff took over the temporalities for the king. It is difficult to imagine who else enjoyed the revenues. On the other hand vacancies were usually short and the question may not often have arisen.

The position of the clerical estate owner, especially a bishop, abbot, dean, or provost, was rather different from that of a secular lord, for he could enjoy in his private churches not only such royal rights as were transferred to him but ecclesiastical rights as well. Ecclesiastical revenues came lawfully into his hands, and he could quite properly redistribute the resources of his churches. The bishops and most of the abbots had their sees in an old minster with parochial rights extending at least to a hundred, and, through gifts from the king and other laymen, often got possession of other minsters

'canonici de Cicestre tenent communiter xvi hidas quae nunquam geldaverunt, sicut dicunt' (i. 17 a i). But it does not seem that any of the old minsters held land which was not assessed in hides, even when they were on unhidated ancient demesne. Cf. Bedford: 'Terra de hac villa nunquam fuit hidata, nec modo est preter i hida quae jacuit in ecclesia S. Pauli in elemosina T.R.E., et modo jacet recte. Sed Remigius episcopus posuit eam extra elemosinam aecclesiae S. Pauli, ut homines dicunt, et modo tenet et quicquid ad eam pertinet' (*DB*, i. 209 a i; cf. 210 a i).

[1] E.g. Edward's grant of land to St Olave's, Exeter, 1063, 'ut rus praedictae ecclesiae liberum ab omni censu et servitio subiaceat': K. 814.

[2] Some of Archbishop Stigand's estates show beneficial hidage.

[3] Royal almsmen are sometimes grouped near the end of the shire entry in *DB*. Cf. Regenbald who held the two hides of the church of Cirencester, Glos, 'in alms' of King Edward, quit of all service (i. 167 b i). [4] *DB*, i. 179 a ii.

and also estates with smaller churches on them. The attitude of bishops towards their other minsters is various. The archbishops of York fostered Beverley, Ripon, and Southwell as subordinate religious centres. Bishops were always interested in maintaining the rights of those minsters they held in a 'foreign' diocese. But in the smaller dioceses, and often where there was a monastic chapter, the endowments of the minsters were sometimes partly absorbed by the episcopal church. Ramsbury was kept in a sorry state by the bishop of Sherborne, who had apparently also swallowed up the churches at Beaminster, Charminster, and Yetminster.[1] But bishops needed benefices for their kinsmen and servants, and it seems to have been not uncommon for a collegiate church to be reduced to suitable proportions. Hence in most dioceses there remained a number of adequately endowed churches on episcopal demesne.

The English bishoprics and abbeys had been endowed largely by royal generosity, and the effect of booking an estate to the church was to transfer the *feorm* and other customs to the beneficiary while leaving the estate subject to the common burdens.[2] Hence we can assume that a bishop or monastic community normally drew *feorm*, or its commutation, from all the hidated churches it possessed. In Domesday Book we read that one Worcester church in Oswaldslow had to pay all the customs of the *feorm* and one sext of honey.[3] As the *feorm* had been transferred from the king to the church of Worcester as part of the creation of Oswaldslow, it is natural to suppose that all the churches of the bishop and convent within that liberty, which were rated in hides, paid their share of the *feorm* to the ecclesiastical authorities, and that the liability of this church is expressly mentioned not because of the *feorm* – that would normally be taken for granted – but because of the additional payment of honey. The common burdens also had been 'infeudated' to the bishop of Worcester as the holder of this triple hundred; and it was he, as a royal agent, who would exact them from his churches, but in the royal interest. It is likely that much of the *feorm* and possibly some of the common burdens were commuted into money payments. As Domesday values can normally be regarded as the lord's profit, it seems that on Worcester estates *feorm*, together perhaps with other services, was often commuted at £1 the hide, for the *valuit* and hidage are not seldom in agreement. Many Norfolk churches on the demesne of the bishop of Thetford are allotted an acreage

[1] Page, pp. 71–2.   [2] E. John, *Land Tenure in Early England*, ch. II.
[3] Droitwich, 172 b ii.

and a usually corresponding value in pence.[1] This could represent commutation at 10s. the hide.[2]

Just as we cannot learn the value of the benefice to the incumbent, so we do not know who paid this 'value' to the bishop. In a later period it would be the parson, and the payment would be styled a pension. If he himself served the church he would be its rector. But if he were an absentee, or was not in priest's orders, he would have to provide a vicar. Yet even in the thirteenth century there could be confusion between a rector burdened with a pension and a vicar who 'farmed' the church for the proprietor. It is impossible to say whether the eleventh-century 'parson' usually served his church. But as these larger churches were often given to provide a revenue for royal and episcopal clerks, it is likely that the 'parson' himself was more often a sort of owner than a minister.

Monasteries may have been more ruthless exploiters. Since their refoundation in the tenth century they had acquired many estates with their churches and also some minsters as entities, for a church was considered a most suitable gift to a religious house.[3] Although some donors expressly safeguarded the tenure of the priest,[4] relatively few churches are listed on monastic estates in Domesday Book, and sometimes even minsters, which are known to have existed, are omitted.[5] No priest or church is reported from any of the lands of St Albans in Hertfordshire or from those of Coventry in Warwickshire. The holdings of Glastonbury, Muchelney, Athelney, and Bath are almost as deserted. Shaftesbury nunnery had absorbed the minster at Bradford, King Æthelred's benefaction.[6] The great parishes of Worcester and Pershore have already been mentioned. These churches had greatly reduced the minsters at Bredon, Blockley, Fladbury, Hanbury, Kempsey, Kidderminster, and Alderminster.[7] There seems to be clear evidence in the 'manorial' areas for the absorption of individual endowments into monasteries and a repressive policy towards lesser churches. The East-Anglian abbeys,

---

[1] *DB*, ii. 191 a–200 b.

[2] Lennard, pp. 321 ff., regards such payments, admittedly based on the hidage or acreage, as rents for glebe – and so confuses rateable values and 'real' acres and also abandons his general theory that values represent what a farmer pays, or should pay, for the property. It is possible that most values bore some relation to the hidage – for this would determine some of the profits. But in the case of churches the relationship seems especially close.

[3] For example, Bruno of Toul, later pope Leo IX, 'quibus [monasteriis], ad augmentandum in eis sanctae religionis statum, nonnullas tribuit ecclesias', Wibert (= Cardinal Humbert), *Vita S. Leonis*, I, c. xiii, *MPL*, cxliii, col. 480. [4] E.g. Siflaed, above, p. 189.

[5] Page, pp. 61–3 and *passim*. [6] Page, p. 72. [7] Page, p. 94.

however, although they were especially active in acquiring land, and may have wished to exploit their churches as intensively as their agricultural holdings, found local custom resistant. Priests were usually more like freemen or sokemen than villeins.

Cathedral chapters, when monastic, acted like monasteries, although they were often hindered by the bishop's wish to give their churches to his clerks. In 1092, when a dispute between the priests of St Helen's and St Alban's in Worcester over parishes and customs was brought before the bishop's synod, and the prior of Worcester intervened, Bishop Wulfstan appointed recognitors, mostly Englishmen, to report on the status of those churches.[1] They reported that from their own knowledge of Bishop Eald-red's time (1046–62) and from the tradition of their predecessors there was no parish in the whole city of Worcester but that of the mother church (i.e. the cathedral of St Mary), and St Helen's had from the beginning been a vicarage of that mother church. In Bishop Oswald's time (961–92) it had been in the hands of a priest Wynsige (a member of the secular chapter) as vicar and *custos*. When Oswald reformed Worcester in 969, and most of the clerks became monks, and all their churches, with their lands, burial rights, and other customs and dignities, which formerly they had held as private property (*quasi propria*), became the property of the monastic community and were put to common use. Wynsige was among those who became a monk, and he too put St Helen's, its lands, tithes, and all other customs into the common chest. This arrangement had never been disturbed. The recognition of 1092, with its rather faulty history, is contaminated by the struggle of the monks for their freedom from episcopal control and by the rivalry between Worcester and Evesham.[2] But it can probably be trusted on this point and, in any case, reveals the policy of the community.

It was, however, difficult, even for monastic bodies, to exploit churches directly. The simplest way always was to rackrent a church to a farmer; and in practice a farmer was not unlike a parson. Unless the monks or canons themselves served a church, a policy unpopular with reformers, they had to put in a vicar and share the revenues with him. When the income was split it was both convenient and proper for the ecclesiastical owner to take the tithe, or the greater tithes (those from corn), and leave all other payments and

---

[1] *Acta Synodi apud Wigorniam anno MXCII, Anglia Sacra*, i. 542–3.
[2] See below, p. 241. St Alban's belonged to Evesham, Sir Ivor Atkins, 'The Church of Worcester from the eighth to the twelfth century', *The Antiquaries Journal*, xx (1940), 204 ff.

dues as 'altalage' to the priest in charge.[1] In view of the tendency towards hereditary succession, it was probably not unusual to secure an instrument from the vicar confirming the reversion of the church on his death.[2] Vicars, however, often dug themselves in. A late eleventh-century vicar of St Helen's, Worcester, could describe himself as 'the useless slave of God and St Mary',[3] but his humility was spiritual rather than temporal.

Doubtless, besides the larger parish churches, there were also on royal demesne and the estates of the bishops and abbeys many smaller, 'manorial', churches. On the thegn-lands inferior churches were the rule. For a thegn a church was part both of his dignity and his capital equipment. It was sometimes called after him.[4] As he could mortgage, sell, or bequeath his church, and as it was sometimes divided among heirs, a church obviously had some, at least potential, value to the owner. The lord acquitted the priest, as well as the *villani*, of all public burdens placed on land. He had given him a lucrative holding and buildings. And it is unlikely that he was always content with only spiritual services in return, especially when it seems to have been seignorial policy to acquire all possible profitable rights for his church. According to the Council of Winchester of 1076 no clerk, whether in a borough or the countryside (*civilis vel rusticus*), should do more service for his ecclesiastical benefice than was rendered in King Edward's day.[5] But the methods of exploitation cannot be illustrated. The church was appurtenant to the manor and so received little attention from the Domesday commissioners. Nor, surprisingly, does it often appear in ecclesiastical literature, which is at least some indication that, by contemporary standards, there was no great abuse. The royal laws and also the homilies are silent about the taking of ecclesiastical revenues by laymen. Their theme is the withholding, not the misappropriation, of tithe and other customs. It may be allowed that the thegns,

[1] Cf. Worcester's arrangement with Frederic, vicar of St Helen's: 'Hanc [ecclesiam] ipsi fratres . . . commiserunt mihi ad serviendum inde majori ecclesie et ad faciendum proficuum eorum in vita mea. Post autem sine contradictione reciperent sua, et ideo unoquoque anno quicquid lucrari poteram de decimis, conferebam eis ad restaurationem ecclesie sue': *Privilegium Fritherici, Hemingi Chartularium*, ii. 428.

[2] *Ibid.* where the monks granted Frederic confraternity in return for his surrender.

[3] *Ibid.* p. 427.

[4] 'Ordmaeres circe de Hou' (Hoo), 'Deremannes circe de Hou', 'Dodes circe' (Dode in Luddesdown), in the diocese of Rochester: Gordon Ward, 'The List of Saxon churches in the Textus Roffensis', *Archaeologia Cantiana*, xliv (1932), 50; 'Ælsies circe' (Eastbridge), 'Blacemannes circe' (Blackmanstone), in the diocese of Canterbury: *idem*, 'The Lists of Saxon churches in the Domesday Monachorum, and White Book of St Augustine', *ibid.* xlv (1933), 75.

[5] Wilkins, *Concilia*, i. 367.

although they had a proprietary attitude, in general also had a respect for the spiritual office.

When King Æthelred proclaimed that 'All churches are not entitled to the same status in the temporal sense, although they have the same consecration in regard to religion',[1] and declared the classification based on the minster, he was championing an arrangement which, although worldly, had an ecclesiastical justification against an even more worldly pattern created by tenure. There were, indeed, two forces, not necessarily in opposition, which were altering the position of individual churches in the eleventh century. One was the trend towards stronger lordship, the other the effect of ecclesiastical reform. When the two forces were directed by the same person or body, as with a monastery, the changes could be considerable. Endowments could be redistributed and status altered. But hardly anywhere did the two trends come into direct collision, for, in the main, the tenth-century reformers accepted secular lordship. There is nothing subversive and little that is really critical of the existing order in their writings. Their demand was that lordship should be beneficent, that the Christian lord should take his proper place, 'helping the servants of God in their worldly concerns, but leaving them to live according to the direction of their books and the teaching of their spiritual superior'.[2]

Relatively little of the royal ecclesiastical legislation was concerned with the tenure of a priest, mainly, no doubt, because his tenure was basically like that of any other tenant and governed by the same property laws. The selling of God's churches for money was denounced by Ælfric;[3] and he also wrote against lay domination of churches, especially monasteries,[4] in terms which would have satisfied the later 'Gregorian' reformers. But again it was the abuse of lordship rather than lordship itself which was his real target. Æthelred decreed that no man was to bring a church under subjection or traffic illegally in a church, and that no man was to expel a minister from a church without the bishop's consent.[5] These sparse and timid enactments were not really designed to transform the actual scene. There was, however, some concern with the priest's status. It was never enacted that he should be

---

[1] VIII Æthelred, 5.

[2] *Catholic Homilies*, 'On the dedication of a church', ii. 592; *EHD*, i. 852.

[3] 'Likewise some men sell even a church for hire, as if it were worthless mills, the glorious House of God which is dedicated to God for his services', *Lives of Saints*, i. 431; cf. *Catholic Homilies*, ii. 592–3. See also Wulfstan on the buying of another priest's church, *Ecclesiastical Institutes* (= Theodulf's *Capitula*), c. xvi, Thorpe, *Ancient Laws*, ii. 412.

[4] See above, *n.* 2, and cf. *Catholic Homilies*, i. 3, *EHD*, i. 850.

[5] V Æthelred, 10; cf. VI Æthelred, 13, 15.

free. But there are no manumissions of priests in wills, and it can be accepted that any priest, however precarious his economic position, ranked as a ceorl, a freeman. He sometimes received a bequest of land and chattels from his lord.[1] Moreover he was exhorted not to live like a ceorl.[2] The dignity of the priesthood was a favourite theme of the reformers,[3] and Archbishop Wulfstan, in his *Institutes of Polity*, regarded the village priest as the mediator between the lord of the manor and the servile tenants (*nyd-theowan* = *servi testamentales*). He should be the guardian of weights and measures, and should urge both the theows to work for their lords and the lords to protect their theows.[4] When a monk of Ely, in charge of one of the monastery's vills, ordered the rustics to perform labour services on the day on which they always went to St Ives (Hunts.) to make offerings to that saint for their safety and the fertility of their land, it was their priest who spoke up for them and asked that the work should be postponed.[5] And so, although by 1066 tenure could make it possible to classify a priest with the *villani* in manorialized areas, his status was not in the same danger as theirs. By the laws a priest who lived chastely had the status of a thegn.[6] But even a married priest was prevented by his office from sinking into the legal servitude which threatened cultivators of similar economic standing. The warnings of the reformers were addressed more forcibly to the ignorant, lazy, and sinful priest than to the oppressive lord.

Although political realism may have restrained the reformers, they saw that one of the answers to strong secular lordship was the encouragement of education and spirituality among the priests,[7] for then the difference in status would be obvious to all and they would be less vulnerable to economic

---

[1] A widow of an earl to her chaplain for life, ? end of tenth century (K. 968); the aetheling Athelstan to his masspriest, 1015 (Whitelock, *Wills*, no. 20); a woman to her household chaplain, 1035–44 (*ibid*. no. 29); a man to his priest and two chaplains, 1043–4 (*ibid*. no. 31).

[2] Napier, *Wulfstan Sammlung*, no. L, p. 269.

[3] Cf. Wulfstan, *Ecclesiastical Institutes* (= Theodulf's *Capitula*), c. i, Thorpe, *Ancient Laws*, ii. 402; Lingard, *Antiquities*, i. 166–77.

[4] *Episcopus*, Liebermann, *Gesetze*, i. 478; Thorpe, *Ancient Laws*, ii. 314.

[5] Goscelin, *Miracula S. Yvonis, Chron. Ramsey*, pp. lxx–lxxi.   [6] See above, p. 142.

[7] Ælfric emphasizes the necessity of chastity even in his sermons addressed to laymen. Cf. 'We must first overcome . . . lust by chastity, so that the ordained minister of God ever continue in chastity, as the canon plainly tells him' (*Catholic Homilies*, ii. 222–3), and 'To those who serve at God's altar, that is to say priests and deacons, all sexual intercourse is wholly forbidden.' They are not to have unlawful women in their houses; 'and if he secretly or publicly have intercourse with a woman, [know] that he forfeits his order. Let none of them undertake any reeveship or trade': *ibid*. ii. 94–5. The reformers, however, must have expected less success with the village clergy.

pressure. Such an attitude, although not forceful, was justifiable. And bishops were not always timid when action was required against an individual careless lord. Just after the Conquest Ailsi, who had been one of King Edward's thegns, asked Bishop Wulfstan of Worcester to consecrate a church he had built on his manor of five hides at Longney on Severn. Wulfstan came, but objected to a great nut tree in the graveyard which robbed the church of light and under which Ailsi and his friends used to picnic and gamble on summer days. Wulfstan demanded that the tree be cut down, and, when Ailsi refused, cursed it and left the church undedicated.[1] Wulfstan had no great tenderness for the foibles of the lay proprietors of churches. And when private churches were not completely removed from the control of the bishop, the greater abuses of lordship may often have been kept at bay.

4. THE INDIVIDUAL DIOCESES

i. Canterbury	vii. Lichfield	xiii. Wells
ii. Cornwall	viii. London	xiv. Winchester
iii. Devonshire	ix. Ramsbury	xv. Worcester
iv. Dorchester	x. Rochester	xvi. York
v. East Anglia	xi. Selsey	xvii. Durham
vi. Hereford	xii. Sherborne	

i. *Canterbury*

The diocese of Canterbury was restricted to East Kent, but the archbishops also had a superiority over West Kent, the diocese of Rochester. Although easily the smallest diocese in England, it was also the richest, a little wealthier than Winchester. The bulk of the archbishop's lands were in Kent; but he had as well sizeable holdings in Sussex, Surrey, Middlesex, Essex, and Suffolk and smaller ones in Oxfordshire and Buckinghamshire. More than half of the revenues seem to have been allotted to the monks who served the cathedral minster.

The archbishops between Dunstan and Lanfranc were among the least distinguished in the long history of their church. As seven of the nine were raised from the diocesan episcopate, and four of these had also been abbots, their rule was short. Only two of the archbishops had been Christ Church monks. It is likely that the king usually appointed on the advice of his bishops, and that the chapter had little say.

[1] *Vita Wulfstani*, p. 41.

Until 1038 good men were appointed – Sigeric (990–4), successively abbot of St Augustine's, Canterbury, and bishop of Ramsbury; Ælfric (995–1005/6), who had been monk of Abingdon, abbot of St Albans, and bishop of Ramsbury; Ælfheah (1005/6–12), formerly monk of Deerhurst, abbot of a community at Bath, and bishop of Winchester, martyred by the Danes;[1] Lyfing (1013–20), promoted from abbot of Chertsey to bishop of Wells; and Æthelnoth (1020–38), who had been dean of the community. These men, inspired by the reforms of the tenth century and mostly experienced rulers, kept Canterbury at least respectable. But after Cnut's death unsuitable men were raised to the see – Eadsige (1038–44, 1048–50), one of Cnut's priests who became a monk of the house and then bishop of St Martin's, a sickly man; his replacement, Siward (1044–8), sometime abbot of Abingdon; Robert of Jumièges (1051–2), whose translation from London the monks opposed;[2] and, as a final indignity, Stigand, bishop of Winchester which he retained in plurality (1052–70), who was not even a monk. None of these nine archbishops was a real ruler of the English church or even of the province of Canterbury. None, except St Ælfheah,[3] had any lasting reputation.

Stigand's long pontificate is usually dismissed shortly, and little attention has been given to the effects of the eighteen years in which Canterbury was joined to Winchester. As the diocese of Rochester was subject to Canterbury, Stigand created a diocese comprising Kent, Surrey, and Hampshire, and so placed himself on a geographical parity with other bishops. He may well have considered East Kent a derisory parish for an archbishop. This innovation was not to last. But there are two literary displacements better explained by this connexion than by Norman distribution. The 'A' version of the Chronicle was transferred from Winchester to Canterbury some time after 1001.[4] If Stigand removed it no credit falls to him, for the eleventh century is represented in the Chronicle only by jottings. Much more important was the transfer of the Winchester calendar, for this replaced the

---

[1] See also *Vita Wlsini*, c. xii, p. 80; Sir Ivor Atkins, 'The church of Worcester from the eighth to the twelfth century', *The Antiquaries Journal*, xvii (1937), 386.

[2] *Vita Ædwardi*, pp. 18–19. The monks wished to elect one of their number, Ælric, a kinsman of Earl Godwin, described as, 'vir secularis industriae et plurima in mundanis rebus preditus sagacitate, non minus quoque in eadem dilectus congregatione'.

[3] His life was written *c.* 1080 by Osbern, the precentor, at the request of Lanfranc. Osbern quotes Dean Godric as his authority for the account of the translation. *Translatio S. Elphegi*, c. 6, *MPL*, cxlix, col. 390.

[4] A date shortly after the Conquest is usually accepted: see Plummer, pp. xcvi f.

existing Canterbury calendar, which, owing to Dunstan, was derived from Glastonbury. It is possible that Stigand was merely the remover and that it was Lanfranc who then used it as the basis for his reforms. But we cannot be sure.[1]

The metropolitan see was in the minster of Holy Trinity or St Salvator, commonly called Christ Church, at Canterbury. Although the great reformers Oda and Dunstan had been archbishops in the tenth century, Ælfric is said to have found in the minster secular clerks whom he was forced to expel.[2] The house was plundered and burned by the Danes in 1011 when Archbishop Ælfheah was captured,[3] and it is possible that there was never sufficient recovery to carry the standards through a laxer age. After Lanfranc's reforms the monks Osbern and Eadmer wrote with contempt of the old order. Eadmer thought that the decline set in after the martyrdom of St Ælfheah, and, in a famous passage, declared that the brethren lived more like earls than monks, delighting in coloured clothes, fine food, and a variety of musical instruments, and kept horses, hounds, and hawks for hunting.[4] Osbern remembered the scandal caused by the burial of an unbaptized child of Earl Harold close to St Dunstan's tomb.[5] No encouragement can have been given to monastic ideals by Stigand. But Osbern and Eadmer are themselves witness to the scholastic and cultural standards of the monastery when Godric, a disciple of St Ælfheah, was dean.[6] Both mention the strict discipline kept by the schoolmasters,[7] and we can be sure that at least grammar and music were well taught.[8] Also with luxurious tastes there seems to have gone an interest in the arts, to be expected when Stigand was archbishop. Abbot Manni of Evesham, a great artist, made things for Canterbury.[9] A monk

[1] The old Canterbury calendar is in the Bosworth Psalter. See *The Bosworth Psalter*, pp. 15 ff., 126-7. Bishop maintained that Lanfranc abolished the old one and substituted for it 'that of the church of the capital of his master's newly acquired kingdom' (*ibid*. p. 31). It is certain that Lanfranc reformed the Canterbury calendar, but there is no way of knowing which he found in use.

[2] *ASC F* 995, in a later insertion which contains some spurious matter. The clerks had opposed his appointment and had tried to intrude one of themselves. E. Bishop, *The Bosworth Psalter*, p. 129, held, however, that the Benedictine Office was always used at Canterbury.

[3] *ASC* 1011-12; Osbern, *Vita S. Elphegi*, cc. 8-9, *MPL*, cxlix, coll. 381-2; Eadmer, *Epistola ad Glastonienses*, *Memorials of St Dunstan*, p. 418.

[4] Eadmer, *Miracula S. Dunstani*, *Memorials of St Dunstan*, pp. 236-8.

[5] Osbern, *Miracula S. Dunstani*, *ibid*. pp. 141-2; cf. Eadmer, *ibid*. p. 230.

[6] Osbern, *Translatio S. Elphegi*, c. 6, col. 390.

[7] Osbern, *Miracula S. Dunstani*, pp. 137-8, 141; Eadmer, *idem*, p. 229.

[8] Both Osbern and Eadmer had been children in the monastery, Eadmer, probably the younger, entering *c*. 1071. Osbern became precentor. See Stubbs, *ibid*. pp. lxii ff., and M. Rule, *Eadmeri Historia*, RS (1884), pp. cii ff.   [9] *Chron. Evesham*, p. 86.

Æthelwine went with permission to Jerusalem, and, promising St Dunstan a better pall if he returned safely, bought one at Constantinople on the way back.[1] By 1071 there were more than sixty monks.[2] The main fault was 'secular conversation', lack of religious discipline. Lanfranc corrected it.

ii. *Cornwall*

William of Malmesbury knew nothing of the Cornish bishopric except that the see had been in the church of St Petroc the Confessor on the north Cornish coast near the river called. 'Haylemouth' (i.e. Padstow), or, as some said, at St Germans on the River Lynher.[3] But in fact, in the tenth century at least, the see had been at St Germans (the old Lanalet),[4] with perhaps a temporary move at the end of the century, because of the Viking danger, to St Petroc's at Bodmin.[5] We know something about the state of the community of St Petroc's in the second half of the tenth century through the manumissions recorded in the Bodmin Gospels,[6] and the organization is probably typical of the other important Cornish minsters. Although an abbot is named in the early eleventh century [7] and a provost,[8] there seem to have been few monks [9] living beside the priests, deacons, and clerks, some of whom can be traced through the various grades. The expression 'the clerks of St Petroc' recalls 'the clerks of St Cuthbert' at Durham, and it may be that conditions were similar. English and Celtic names are found together, with Biblical and classical names common among the latter. Some forty clerks witness the transactions spread over about half a century; the largest single attestation is eight; [10] and a community of at least ten is likely.

Bishop Conan (appointed by King Athelstan, ? 926) and his successors seem to have been subordinate to the bishops of Crediton, and were

---

[1] Eadmer, *Miracula S. Dunstani*, pp. 245-6; cf. Osbern, *idem*, p. 160, who refuses to tell this story.

[2] Eadmer, *Epistola ad Glastonienses*, *Memorials of St Dunstan*, p. 420.   [3] *GP*, p. 204.

[4] The bishop styled himself, 'Lanaletensis monasterii episcopus': *The Lanalet Pontificial*, ed. G. H. Doble, HBS, lxxiv (1937), 130.

[5] H. P. R. Finberg, 'Sherborne, Glastonbury, and the expansion of Wessex', *Trans. R. Hist. Soc.* 5th ser., iii (1953), 118–22; *idem*, in Hoskins and Finberg, *Devonshire Studies* (1952), pp. 28–9. D. W. Blake, 'The Church of Exeter in the Norman period' (unpubl. Exeter Univ. MA thesis, 1970), pp. 21–2, argues that the see was always at St Germans.   [6] K. 981; *EHD*, i, 561–3.

[7] German, K. iv. 312. An abbot German witnesses after Æthelwold, presumably abbot of Exeter, Cnut's charter of 1019 to Exeter, K. 729.   [8] 'Cufure prauost', K. p. 314.

[9] 'Leucum monachus' witnesses in the middle of the tenth century (p. 315), but he seems also to have been described as a clerk (p. 316).

[10] Seven priests and one deacon (p. 313), two priests, five deacons, one clerk (*ibid.*); early eleventh century: five priests (p. 311).

supported not only by their minster but also by three Cornish manors which had passed from the undivided bishopric of Sherborne to Crediton.[1] In 994, however, King Æthelred freed Bishop Ealdred of St Germans and his diocese from Crediton's jurisdiction and gave him full rights over his bishopric.[2] But Cornwall's freedom was short-lived. In Cnut's reign Lyfing bishop of Crediton added Cornwall on the death of his uncle Brihtwold,[3] and the combination developed into a unity.

iii. *Devonshire*

The bishops of Devon had their see at Crediton from 909 until 1050. Bishop Sideman, who died in 977, had been associated with the reform movement in the church, for Edgar had appointed him tutor to his son and heir, Edward (the Martyr),[4] and the ealdormen of the western provinces from 975 until the second decade of the eleventh century – Æthelweard, his son Æthelmaer, and the latter's son-in-law Æthelweard – were all patrons of monasticism and learning.[5] The will of Bishop Ælfwold (997–1012) [6] illustrates the well-bred culture of the diocese. Ælfwold seemingly belonged to the local nobility, and made bequests of money, horses, and coats of mail to four kinsmen [7] and his brother-in-law, Godric of Crediton, and of tapestries to his sister. He made provision for his heriot and for a gift to the aetheling in the usual currency, horses, war-equipment, a ship, and tents, as well as money; but to Ordulf I, probably the 'founder' of Tavistock Abbey, the uncle of King Æthelred, and the son of Ordgar who had been ealdorman of Devon and Cornwall, he left two books, Hrabanus and a martyrology. He enfranchised all penal and purchased slaves on the episcopal estates. He remembered his priests and his lay servants, Ælfgar the scribe, and Ælfwold the monk; and to his church he gave land for soul-scot, three service books, and a set of mass vestments. The only distant bequest that was not of duty was of a chalice and patten to Wilton. Two relatives, two priests, and the monk witness his will. It is a very

---

[1] Finberg, 'Sherborne, Glastonbury, . . .', pp. 118–19, 121; *EHD*, i. 822.

[2] *Monasticon*, ii. 535; K. 686.

[3] A pontifical which Lyfing owned included a formula of excommunication as used by a bishop of St Germans: *The Lanalet Pontifical*, pp. 130–1, 143.

[4] 'Erat [Eadwardus] doctus divina lege, docente episcopo Sidemanno': *Vita S. Oswaldi, HCY*, i. 449. For his death, see *Chron. Abingdon*, i. 35.

[5] Robertson, *Charters*, pp. 386–7, Whitelock, *Wills*, pp. 144–5, Harmer, *Writs*, pp. 20 ff., 553, 555.

[6] *Crawford Collection of Early Charters*, ed. Napier and Stevenson, no. x; *EHD*, i. 536.

[7] The names Wulfgar, Ælfgar's son, Eadwold, and Æthelnoth link with Ælfwold, which was also the name of a companion monk.

balanced picture. He renders to Caesar and to God, to his kinsmen and to the church, to his lay servants and to his priests, to the secular church and to monasteries. It is a picture of an ecclesiastical nobleman, suitably, but not extravagantly, concerned with the cultural movements of the age.

Little, however, is known of the church and its bishops until Lyfing, abbot of Tavistock, succeeded Eadnoth as bishop in 1027. Lyfing, a politically ambitious man, succeeded to the diocese of Cornwall on the death of his uncle Brihtwold and added the bishopric of Worcester. This pluralism was not unreasonable, for the Cornish and Devonshire churches had suffered from Viking depredations.[1] But Worcester's revenues were no real solution to the problem and his successor had to take new measures. Leofric, a royal priest of Lotharingian education, appointed to Devon and Cornwall in 1046, decided to consolidate the dioceses and change the see. He chose Exeter for its safety and in accordance with the canonical rule that a bishop's see should be in a city,[2] and, no doubt, because it contained a decayed minster which he could appropriate without arousing the sort of opposition which Herman was to meet when he tried to enter Malmesbury. Papal consent for the removal was obtained, probably at the council of Rheims in October 1049.[3] The king agreed to the consolidation of the two dioceses, granted the minster to Leofric, and a few months later, in 1050, possibly on St Peter's day, visited Exeter to put the bishop in possession of his new church.[4]

The monastery of Exeter had been refounded in 968 and in 1019 Abbot Æthelwold and the brethren obtained a charter from Cnut for their burned and dilapidated house. But, although it is possible that there were still later abbots,[5] it is unlikely that even a Lotharingian would have destroyed a truly monastic community.[6] The site of the church is thought to be covered by the

[1] K. 729, 791.

[2] Cf. Burchard, *Decretum*, III, xc. An historical account, based on the papal letter and the 'royal' charter, is in *The Leofric Missal*, ed. F. E. Warren (1883), p. 2.

[3] Letter of Leo IX to King Edward, *ibid*. It contains no mention of the uniting of the dioceses.

[4] For the charters and the circumstances, see above, pp. 116 ff.

[5] An unidentified abbot, Wulfweard, who signs charters, including the Exeter 'foundation charter', from the beginning of the reign until 1050 (*Ord. Survey Facs.*, Exeter xii, K. 769, 778, 792–3, 800) may be of Exeter. Sir Ivor Atkins, 'The church of Worcester from the eighth to the twelfth century', *The Antiquaries Journal*, xx (1940), 16 *n*. and N. R. Ker, 'Hemming's Chartulary', *Studies in Medieval History presented to F. M. Powicke* (1948), p. 75, have suggested that Æva, who signs K. 729, was abbot of Exeter; but, as the grant itself was to Abbot Æthelwold of Exeter (p. 4), who signs above Æva (p. 6), the suggestion cannot stand.

[6] All the clerks of the community (ealra thara hired preosta) witness seven of the manumissions entered in *The Leofric Missal* (pp. 5–6), dated 1030–50 by H. P. R. Finberg, *Devon and Cornwall*

existing Lady Chapel, close to a spring of water,[1] and since there is no tradition of reconstruction by Leofric,[2] we must assume that he found the buildings adequate for his purpose. Leofric gave his canons the rule of St Chrodegang, at the royal behest, so it was believed at Exeter,[3] and introduced a common refectory and dormitory.[4] It is possible that he organized round the nucleus of his foreign household.[5] Later there were twenty-four canons and twenty-four vicars serving the minster.[6] Leofric collected manuscripts assiduously and left a well-furnished church.

The main struggle had been to endow the bishopric adequately. The absorption first of St Germans and the episcopal lands in Cornwall and then of the dilapidated Exeter estates, enabled a start to be made. Leofric busied himself with recovering Exeter claims, possibly withstood Crediton's attempt at independence,[7] added his personal land-holdings, restocked the manors,

Notes and Queries, xxii. 135, and 'The House of Ordgar and the Foundation of Tavistock Abbey', EHR, lviii (1943), 196. It is possible, of course, that Leofric reformed the minster before moving the see. In the 'foundation charter' Edward granted all the possessions of the monastery 'deo sanctoque Petro fratribus canonicis ibi famulantibus' (K. 791). Malmesbury, GP, p. 201, believed, rather credulously, that nuns were ejected, possibly influenced by the double dedication of the church to St Peter and St Mary. In Athelstan's charters, probably reconstructions, it is of St Peter (K. 369), of St Mary (K. 370–1), and of St Mary and St Peter (K. 373). In 1019 it was 'the church of God, his mother Mary, and all saints' (K. 729). In the 'foundation charter' (K. 791) and Leofric's will (Robertson, Charters, p. 227) it is described simply as St Peter's minster. In Leofric's Missal it appears as the minster of St Mary and St Peter (pp. 2b, 3b), and in a common mass for the living and the dead there is mention of 'nos famulos tuos ac locum nostrum et familiam beatissime dei genetricis Marie necnon et sancti Petri apostoli atque sancti Swithuni confessoris Christi' (p. 12a). It is possible that the minster was dedicated originally to St Peter and that St Mary was characteristically added when monks were introduced in 968. The old minster at Worcester was dedicated to St Peter, Oswald's new cathedral to St Mary. In Edgar's reign Abbot Ælfric of Malmesbury changed the dedication of his monastery from the one to the other: Malmesbury, GP, p. 405.

[1] Cyril Fox, The siting of the monastery of St Mary and St Peter in Exeter (Friends of Exeter Cathedral, 1953), p. 8.

[2] The obituary notice in The Leofric Missal (p. 2a) states, 'ecclesias non paucas construxit'. The absence of specific mention of the cathedral church makes it almost certain that Leofric undertook no important rebuilding there. No doubt poverty was the cause.

[3] 'iussuque regis canonicos ibi constituit': The Leofric Missal, p. 2b.

[4] Malmesbury, GP, p. 201, the canons 'contra morem Anglorum ad formam Lotharingorum uno triclinio comederent uno cubiculo cubitarent'. He is, of course, referring to Norman and Anglo-Norman custom.

[5] See above, p. 84, n. 4.

[6] Twelfth- and thirteenth-century documents quoted by G. Oliver, History of Exeter (1821), p. 15.

[7] Bishop Osbern enforced his right: 'de hoc manerio ostendit Osbernus episcopus cartas suas quae testantur ecclesiam S. Petri inde fuisse saisitam antequam rex Edwardus regnaret. Insuper tempore regis Willelmi diratiocinavit coram baronibus regis esse suam': DB, i. 101 b ii.

and raised his bishopric above the poorest.[1] His successor, Osbern, contributed further estates.[2] At Exeter we have an example of Edwardian reform.

iv. *Dorchester*

Dorchester was the largest English diocese, combining, partly as a result of the Viking invasions, the ancient dioceses of Lindsey, Leicester, and Dorchester,[3] and, because of the English retreat, the see-town was badly placed in the extreme south on the Thames. After the Conquest the archbishops of York claimed Lincoln and a large part of Lindsey for St Peter's,[4] but this was based probably as much on historical research as Anglo-Saxon precedent. The bulk of the bishop of Dorchester's lands were in Oxfordshire, with smaller holdings in Buckinghamshire, Huntingdonshire, and perhaps Bedfordshire. He had a moderately rich endowment. Bishop Wulfwig had given a manor worth £10 to his brother Godric,[5] but probably added to the bishopric two valuable churches, Aylesbury and Buckingham, which he had held from King Edward.[6] The cathedral church was a secular minster. Nothing is known about the clerks or their lands.

From 1006 until 1049, although there was no question of the transference of the see, Dorchester was held by monks from Ramsey Abbey, Eadnoth I, the first abbot, Æthelric, and Eadnoth II. These bishops were great benefactors of their monastery, to the resentment of neighbouring Ely.[7] According to the twelfth-century Ramsey chronicle, all three were freely elected by the clergy and people with the consent of the king.[8] But no reliance can be placed on this conventional phrase. Edward broke the tradition in 1049, when he appointed his Norman priest, Ulf, to succeed Eadnoth II; and this change of policy probably helps to explain the vague charges of worthlessness

---

[1] At first he maintained the canons at his own expense: *The Leofric Missal*, p. 2b. For his recoveries and acquisitions, see his will, Robertson, *Charters*, p. 227; *Monasticon*, ii. 528; H. P. R. Finberg, 'Sherborne, Glastonbury, and the expansion of Wessex', *Trans. R. Hist. Soc.* 5th ser. iii (1953), 120–1. For relics, see Exeter MS. 2861 (late twelfth-century list of relics given by Athelstan); *The Leofric Missal*, pp. 3–5; *The Bosworth Psalter*, pp. 48, *n.* 2, 162–3.

[2] See above, pp. 190–1.

[3] Remigius styled himself in his profession to Lanfranc, 'Ego Remigius Dorcacensis et Legoracensis et Lincolniensis provinciae ceterarumque provinciarum quibus antecessores mei praefuerunt . . . antistes': Giraldus Cambrensis, *Opera Omnia*, vii. 151.

[4] Hugh the Chantor, *HCY*, pp. 8–9.

[5] *DB*, i. 144 a i.   [6] *DB*, i. 143 b ii, 143 a i.

[7] Ely snatched the body of Bishop Eadnoth I after the battle of Ashingdon, when it was being taken to Ramsey for burial: *Chron. Ramsey*, p. 119.

[8] See above, pp. 102–3.

brought against Ulf,[1] whom the Ramsey chronicler, hitherto so informative about the doings of the bishops of Dorchester, could not bring himself to mention. Abbot Ælfwine of Ramsey was among the English representatives at Pope Leo IX's council of Rheims on 3 October 1049,[2] where charges of simony were made against some bishops and abbots, bishops who had been invited to attend and had failed to appear or excuse themselves were excommunicated, and canons were issued, including a condemnation of simony. If Ulf's appointment had already taken place, it is likely that Ælfwine complained to the pope about the business. However that may be, Ulf made his way to the papal council held at Vercelli on 1 September 1050, and, according to the 'E' version of the Chronicle, 'they nearly had to break his staff – and would have done so if he had not given more treasure – because he could not perform his duties as he ought'. This, obviously prejudiced, story refers to the threatened deposition of an already consecrated bishop, possibly because of simony. At the Lent synod, held at Sipont, Leo had deposed two archbishops for this sin. Ulf accompanied the papal court on his homeward journey, and was present on 20–22 October at Toul, where Pope Leo translated the new saint, Gerard.[3] Ulf, however, was expelled from his see in the course of the 'English Revolution' of 1052. His successor, Wulfwig, apparently another royal clerk,[4] had to seek consecration abroad, probably in France,[5] owing to Stigand's incapacity, but, unlike Stigand, he seems never to have been regarded by the papal *curia* as an intruder, presumably because of his predecessor's notorious faults. Even if he were an improvement, the first Norman bishop, Remigius, monk of Fécamp, who moved the see to Lincoln, is said to have found his diocese in a bad moral state.[6]

v. *East Anglia*

The bishopric of East Anglia was still regarded as a double diocese in 1086 – the lands were clearly divided between North Elmham in Norfolk and Hoxne in Suffolk [7] – but by then the see had already been moved from Elmham to Thetford, and was to go to Norwich. The bishopric was rather poor,

---

[1] 'which was a bad appointment', *ASC C* 1049; 'but he was expelled from it afterwards because he did nothing like a bishop in it, so much that we are ashamed to say anything more about it', *ASC D* 1050.   [2] *ASC D* 1050, *E* 1046.   [3] Plummer, p. 233.

[4] Harmer, *Writs*, pp. 60–1, produces evidence to connect him with the royal *scriptorium*.

[5] *ASC C* 1053, and see below, p. 303.

[6] Giraldus Cambrensis, *Vita S. Remigii*, c. v, *Opera Omnia*, vii. 20.

[7] Cf. *DB*, ii. 379. Just before 1040 a bishop of Elmham made bequests to bodies of priests at both places: Whitelock, *Wills*, no. 26.

and the last Old-English bishop, Æthelmaer, like his brother Archbishop Stigand, built up a large private estate in the two shires consisting largely in rights over freemen, especially their commendation.[1] The see church, North Elmham, although built in the early eleventh century,[2] was served by clerks, and was completely overshadowed by the flourishing monastic houses of the diocese.

The bishops were in general undistinguished. Ælfgar, the 'alms-giver' (1001–21), who had been Dunstan's private chaplain, gave the church some lustre, but his successor, Ælfwine (1021–23/38), monk of Ely, never lost his interest in the cloister [3] and returned to his convent. Ælfric 'the Black' and Ælfric 'the Small', names given to distinguish them from an earlier bishop, Ælfric 'the Good',[4] made no mark. In 1043 Stigand was appointed, and in 1047, on his transfer to Winchester, left the diocese to Æthelmaer, a local landowner who had been married,[5] and whose main occupation was probably the care of the family estates in the province.[6] Æthelmaer, like Stigand, was deposed in 1070.

vi. *Hereford*

Hereford, the see of the Magonsaetan, the Mercian diocese in the Welsh marches, was a post of danger, and it had only two regularly constituted bishops between 1012 and 1079.[7] Æthelstan's long pontificate (1012–56) spanned five reigns. He built his cathedral church and gained a reputation for holiness. The church was sacked in the year before he died by the Welsh

---

[1] 'Terra ejusdem de feudo', 'feudum episcopi de Tedford': *DB*, ii. 193b, 379. The acquisitions of Stigand and Æthelmaer left many opportunities to the first Norman bishop, Herfast, and in *DB*, after the Norfolk fief, are seven pages 'De invasionibus ejusdem feudi'.

[2] The ruins of the minster can still be seen, the only surviving plan of a cathedral church of this period.

[3] When bishop he gave estates to Ely (*Liber Eliensis*, II, c. 75), and he took part in the founding of Bury St Edmunds (*ibid.* II, c. 86).   [4] Robertson, *Charters*, p. 425.

[5] He held the church of Sts Simon and Jude in Norwich 'de patrimonio' (*DB*, ii. 117b), and before he became bishop he leased lands from Bury St Edmunds, which he later bequeathed to the monastery (Robertson, *Charters*, no. 97). His wife brought him the manor of Blofield, near Norwich: *DB*, ii. 195. His sister had property in Norwich: *DB*, ii. 116. There seems to be no reference in *DB* to his children, but his successor, Herfast, was not without this comfort: 'In Thetford est i ecclesia S. Mariae quam tenebat Stigandus archiepiscopus. Modo tenent filii Arfasti episcopi': *DB*, ii. 118b.

[6] Stigand's private estate in East Anglia was greater than Æthelmaer's, and if we can trust the witness lists to diplomas, the latter was seldom at court.

[7] It was very different after the Conquest: 'vulgatissimo jam per ora hominum infortunio, ut non diu quisquam episcopus apud Hereford superstit': Malmesbury, *GP*, p. 304.

and the outlawed Earl Ælfgar, and in June 1056 Earl Harold's priest, Leofgar, appointed to the see presumably because of his military skill, lost his life in a punitive expedition. Ealdred, bishop of Worcester and Wiltshire, then took over the administration of the diocese and helped to pacify the marches. But in 1058 he departed for Jerusalem and in 1060, on his promotion to York, resigned the see to Walter, a Lotharingian, Queen Edith's priest. Thus, apart from Ealdred's custodianship, Hereford, a secular minster, was ruled by secular bishops.

Walter's acceptance of Hereford proves that it was a desirable diocese. Its estates suffered from the Welsh wars and from the 'invasions' of Earl Harold, perhaps another result of the war. But it was, apart from the exceptional Canterbury and Winchester, one of the better endowed English bishoprics. The lands were divided between the bishop and the priests of St Æthelberht, who had jurisdiction over their own men and estates.[1] Little is known about the cathedral body, except that seven priests were killed during the sack of the church in 1055.[2] The bishop had a moneyer in the cathedral city,[3] and the bishopric was reputed to be rated at 300 hides,[4] a *scipsocn* like Worcester.

vii. *Lichfield*

The history in this period of the large Mercian bishopric of Lichfield, the see of St Chad, is obscure. Lichfield was more remote than Elmham and, unlike the more northerly York, had no connexion with another diocese or with monasteries where annals were kept. The earls of Mercia do not seem to have been benefactors and the bishops were infrequent visitors to the royal court. Perhaps the one gift of the earls was the appointment to the bishopric in 1053 of Leofwine, first abbot of Leofric's monastery at Coventry and possibly a kinsman of the founder.[5] Leofwine married, and he resigned in 1070 to avoid his deposition.[6]

The move of the see to Chester after the Conquest further obscures our

---

[1] *DB*, i. 181 b i; Harmer, *Writs*, no. 49.

[2] *ASC D* 1055; Florence, i. 213. The community at St Æthelberht's minster and the community at St Guthlac (thara twegra hireda) witness a transaction 1043/6: Robertson, *Charters*, no. 99.

[3] *DB*, i. 179 a i, 181 b i.

[4] 'Inter totum sunt in episcopatu 300 hidae quamvis de 33 hidis homines episcopi rationem non dederunt': *DB*, i. 182 b ii.   [5] *FNC*, ii. 360; Harmer, *Writs*, p. 567.

[6] Leofwine refused to attend the legatine council at Winchester in April 1070 to answer the charge that he had a wife and child, was excommunicated, surrendered his bishopric to the king, and returned to Coventry Abbey. Later that year Archbishop Lanfranc consulted the pope while Wulfstan of Worcester was put in temporary charge of the deserted see; and at Christmas 1072 Peter was consecrated to Lichfield. See below, p. 303; Lanfranc, *Ep.* 4 (ed. Giles), i. 21; *Vita*

knowledge of the bishopric. According to Domesday Book the bishop had
held in King Edward's reign lands in Staffordshire, Derbyshire, Chester,
and Shropshire. The Chester lands had been devastated during the Welsh
wars and the bishopric was probably the poorest in England. Nothing is
known about the clerks of this secular minster. Five canons with three
ploughs were still at Lichfield in 1086.[1]

viii. *London*

The diocese of London covered Middlesex, Essex, and Hertfordshire and
represented the old kingdom of the Middle Saxons. The minster of St Paul's,[2]
the see of the great Wulfstan before his translation to Worcester and York in
1002, had mostly monastic bishops until 1051. Ælfhun (1002–12/14) may
have been abbot of Milton Abbas, Dorset.[3] Ælfweard (1035–44), abbot of
Evesham in plurality and originally a monk of Ramsey, was a relative of
Cnut. Robert of Jumièges held the see 1044–51; and it was Edward's intention to replace him by Spearhavoc, monk of Bury St Edmunds and abbot of
Abingdon; but in the end a Norman priest of the king, William (1051–75),
was consecrated bishop. As usual these monkish bishops of a secular church
seem to have cared more for their old homes. Ælfhun, it is true, tried to get
possession of the relics of St Edmund which, for fear of the Danes, were de-
posited in St Gregory's, London (1010–13).[4] But Ælfweard before his resig-
nation because of leprosy had transferred from London to Evesham many
religious and secular books, and he also bought in Holland for Evesham the
relics of St Odulph.[5] Robert sent a splendid Missal to Jumièges.[6] And

Wulfstani, pp. xxviii–xxxi, 24–7; *EHD*, ii. 632; James Tait, 'An alleged charter of William the
Conqueror', *Essays in History presented to R. Lane Poole* (1927), pp. 155–8.

[1] *DB*, i. 247 a i.

[2] 'ecclesia apostoli Pauli, quae usitate Paules-Berig appellatur': Goscelin, *Historia translat. S.
Augustini*, *MPL*, clv. col. 43. For the history of St Paul's in this period, see C. N. L. Brooke in
A History of St Paul's Cathedral, ed. W. R. Matthews and W. M. Atkins (1957), pp. 12 ff., biblio-
graphical note, pp. 361 ff; D. Whitelock, *Some Anglo-Saxon bishops of London* (Chambers Mem.
Lect., 1974).

[3] Robertson, *Charters*, no. 69. He may have been tutor to the aethelings Edward and Alfred
(Florence, i. 167). They were sent to Normandy under his charge (*ASC*).

[4] Liebermann, *Ungedruckte*, p. 205.

[5] *Chron. Evesham*, p. 83; *Translat. et mirac. S. Odulphi*, *ibid.* pp. 313–14. As Evesham refused
to receive a leper, Ælfweard transferred the books to Ramsey (Florence, i. 198–9; *Chron. Ramsey*,
pp. 157–8).

[6] *The Missal of Robert of Jumièges*, ed. H. A. Wilson, HBS (1896); cf. *The Benedictional of
Archbishop Robert*, ed. *idem*, HBS (1903).

Spearhavoc, the goldsmith, is said to have robbed not only the king but also his bishopric when he was pushed out of his see and fled abroad in 1051.[1] It was possibly because of such depredations that London was by no means a rich church in 1066. The Norman bishop William took advantage of the Conquest greatly to increase his estates.

The bishops were also hampered by the unusual freedom of the chapter.[2] In Domesday Book the church of St Paul's is treated as a tenant-in-chief, the canons holding their estates – of about the same value as the bishop's – independently of their ecclesiastical superior; and it seems that some individual prebends existed before 1066. Whether these peculiarities were due to urban conditions or Norman influence since 1044 is uncertain. But the canons lived under a rule, and it is agreed that the chapter was not greatly affected by the Conquest and that the continuity is responsible for the abnormality of its post-Conquest constitution. An archdeacon of London, Edward, became a monk at Canterbury in Archbishop Lanfranc's time. But the earlier history of the office is unknown.

ix. *Ramsbury*

The diocese of Wiltshire and Berkshire, created in 909 out of the diocese of Winchester, had provided three archbishops of Canterbury in the tenth century, and for most of the eleventh was ruled by two men – Brihtwold from Glastonbury (995/1005–45) and Herman, a royal priest from Lotharingia (1045–78). The diocese had been spoiled by the removal of the see from the obvious centre, Wilton, to the isolated episcopal manor of Ramsbury, inexplicable except as a retreat from a royal vill and a fashionable nunnery. Hence both Brihtwold and Herman were dissatisfied and restless. Brihtwold, cut off from the monastic life, was a benefactor and probably a frequent visitor to his old monastery. Herman, detached from the royal court, tried to remedy the situation in which he found himself. First he attempted to move his see into Malmesbury Abbey. Then he retired to St Bertin's at St Omer where he became a monk, and Ealdred took over (1055–8). He returned when he was offered the diocese of Sherborne as well, and probably had his see in that

---

[1] *Chron. Abingdon*, i. 463. He also lost a most precious ring of Queen Edith (*ante* 1046) and recovered it after invoking St Letard at St Augustine's, Canterbury: Goscelin, *Historia translat. S. Augustini*, col. 46.

[2] See below, pp. 240–1.

monastery. But he is often found at Wilton, and in the end, possibly imitating Leofric, planned the move to (Old) Salisbury.[1]

Herman is said to have complained that Ramsbury had neither a convent of clerks nor revenues suitable for his maintenance: his predecessors had been natives, but he was a foreigner without the support of kinsmen.[2] Goscelin of St Bertin found the conditions primitive when he joined the bishop after 1058.[3] It is possible that Brihtwold had dilapidated the church, for the bishop's four great manors in Wiltshire and large estate in Sonning in Berkshire endowed him more than adequately by contemporary English standards. Nothing is known about the secular chapter. There were a few priests at Ramsbury in 1086.[4]

x. *Rochester*

St Andrew's, Rochester, the second bishop's see in Kent, is entirely obscure in this period. William of Malmesbury knew nothing but the names of the bishops. One or more with the name of Godwin ruled from 995 to 1046 and Siward, abbot of Chertsey, whom Stigand consecrated, was bishop from 1058 to 1075. Post-Conquest tradition is strong that the bishops of Rochester were under the patronage, if not the lordship, of the archbishops;[5] and the gap of 1046–58 may in fact be a vacancy due to the unsettled condition of the arch-see. The inferiority of Rochester will also account for its lack of distinction.

Rochester was a secular minster,[6] and it was left by Siward in a sad state, served by four or five canons living in squalor and poverty. Lanfranc

---

[1] For Herman generally, see *Vita Ædwardi*, pp. xlvii f., 91 ff.

[2] Malmesbury, *GP*, p. 182.

[3] Goscelin, *Liber Confortatorius*, ed. C. H. Talbot, *Studia Anselmiana*, fasc. xxxvii = *Analecta Monastica*, 3rd ser. (Rome, 1955), p. 102.   [4] *DB*, i. 66 a i.

[5] At Rochester Dunstan 'sedit plane potestate, etsi non corporali sessione. Sedit inquam potestate; imperio sedit; defensione sedit; beneficiis sedit': Osbern, *Vita S. Dunstani*, *Memorials of St Dunstan*, p. 108. 'Nam qui ecclesiae Cantuariensi per pontificatum praesidet, Rofensi ecclesiae, quae sub patrocinio beati Andreae subsistit, per episcopi institutionem, per horum et intus et extra, cum res exigit, dispositionem, utpote suo dominio praesidet': Eadmer, *idem*, *ibid*. p. 200. 'Qui enim Cantuariensis archiepiscopus est in Rofensi ecclesia proprius vel dominus si saevus, vel patronus si bonus': Malmesbury, *ibid*. p. 293. In 1077 Archbishop Lanfranc 'elected' Gundulf, sent him to the king for the royal assent, and then consecrated him at Canterbury: *Vita Gundulfi*, *Anglia Sacra*, ii. 279–80. Gundulf acted as Lanfranc's vicar-general and administered Canterbury after his death: *ibid*. ii. 284–5. Archbishop Anselm 'elected' his successor: *ibid*. ii. 291–2.

[6] R. A. L. Smith, 'The early community of St Andrew at Rochester, 604–*c*. 1080', *EHR*, lx (1945), 289 ff.

reformed the church by restoring some of its possessions and introducing monks. Gundulf, whom Lanfranc brought from Bec, rebuilt the church.[1] According to Domesday Book it was a very poor daughter of a rich mother. The lands of the canons are not distinguished.

xi. *Selsey*

Little is known about the diocese of the South Saxons in the late Anglo-Saxon period. Three of the bishops may have been monks of Christ Church, Canterbury – Æthelric I (c. 1032–8), who was probably from Dunstan's circle and certainly was greatly attached to Archbishop Æthelnoth,[2] Grimketel (1039–47), who, although not behaving like a monk was buried at Christ Church,[3] and Ælthelric II (1058–70), an indubitable Canterbury monk [4] who was deposed during the purge of the English episcopate. The one royal priest to hold the see was Heca (1047–57).

The see was moved inland to Chichester after the Conquest. According to Domesday Book the bishopric in Edward's reign was one of the poorest in England. One manor, suitably named Preston, always belonged to the minster, and the canons of Chichester held in common 16 hides which had never gelded.[5] It is possible that in both cases we are concerned with the clerks of Selsey minster.

xii. *Sherborne*

Sherborne, the original diocese for the western parts of Wessex, was reduced to the single shire of Dorset in the tenth century, and in 1058 it was joined to Ramsbury, once part of the diocese of Winchester. Throughout our period Sherborne, although without the renown of Worcester, was clearly a thoroughly respectable monastic see. It owed its condition to Wulfsige III, appointed abbot of Westminster by Edgar and bishop of Sherborne in plurality by Æthelred.[6] It is Wulfsige who is said to have introduced monks into both

---

[1] *GP*, pp. 135–6; *Anglia Sacra*, i. 336–7. One of the canons, Æthelric, became priest of Chatham, and made a gift to the monks for the soul and burial of his wife, Godgifu: *ibid.* i. 340. Others took the vow: *Vita Gundulfi, ibid.* ii. 280. Gundulf divided the estates between the bishop and the monks: *ibid.* ii. 283, 288.   [2] See above, p. 74.

[3] He is said to have bought Selsey from Harold Harefoot and Elmham (1043–4) from Edward: Malmesbury, *GP*, p. 205, Florence, i. 193. For his burial, *ASC C* 1047.

[4] *ASC E* 1058. He was consecrated by Archbishop Stigand.   [5] *DB*, i. 16 b ii.

[6] Before the publication of Goscelin of St Bertin's *Vita Wlsini* the accepted dates for the bishops were: Wulfsige 992–1001/2, Æthelric 1001/2–1009/12, Æthelsige 1009/12–1014/17, Brihtwine

places.[1] He created a library at Sherborne.[2] And his cult, which started twelve years after his death, kept his spirit alive in that monastery. There still survived in 1040 one monk who had known him,[3] and there is no doubt that a regular monastic life was maintained without interruption.[4]

Wulfsige was recognized as a saint by Archbishop Ælfheah and the *witan* about 1012, and the body was translated from the porch into the church by Wulfsige's successor, Æthelric. When Cnut and Emma once visited Sherborne they expressed indignation at the dilapidated state of the roof above the shrine, and ordered its restoration, Emma giving £20 and promising more.[5] But it was Bishop Ælfwold (1045/6–58), a monk of Winchester and a great ascetic, who thoroughly restored the monastery. He made a more imposing shrine for St Wulfsige.[6] He then rebuilt the church and translated the saint again.[7] He transferred the relics of St Juderwara from nearby Halstock.[8] He introduced an image of St Swithun. He was devoted to St Cuthbert and visited Durham.[9] And he adorned his church with many gold and silver crosses and shrines.[10] Miracles seem to have been frequent at the

1014/17–?1023, *ante* 1027–1045/6, Ælfmaer, abbot of St Augustine's, ?1023– *ante* 1027, Ælfwold 1045/6–1058, Herman 1058–1078. But the *Vita Wlsini*, written *c.* 1080 by Goscelin on the authority of the monks of Sherborne and *libelli* of miracles, is based on a slightly different chronological framework. Goscelin maintains that Wulfsige was a pontiff for twenty-five years (pp. 77, 79) and that miracles began twelve years after his death (pp. 78–9). Wulfsige was appointed to Westminster by Edgar (959–75) (pp. 75–6) and his body was translated on the authority of Archbishop Ælfheah (1005–12) by Bishop Æthelric. As Wulfsige cannot have been appointed after 975, or translated after 1012, the terminal date for his death is 1000, with the likelihood of its being earlier. Goscelin also writes (p. 82) that Wulfsige's successor, Æthelric, died in the reign of King Eadwi, by whom he means Edmund Ironside (cf. p. 81). Æthelric must be a slip for his successor, Æthelsige, and we may, therefore, have a firm date, 1016, for the latter's death.

[1] 'Testantur sane quod utrumque locum contubernio monachorum primus instituerit et utrique familie primus abbas et in pontificali culmine prefulserit': *Vita Wlsini*, p. 76.

[2] Paris B.N. MS. Lat. 943 (early eleventh century) includes a list of books 'quos custodit Dodo': Stubbs, *Memorials of St Dunstan*, p. cxiii.

[3] *Vita Wlsini*, p. 73.

[4] Some of the monastic provosts (priors) are mentioned in the *Vita Wlsini*: Æthelweard under Ælfwold (p. 82), Wulfric under Herman (p. 73), and Ælfric under Osmund (p. 84).

[5] *Ibid.* p. 81. The name of the bishop is not given. Cnut intruded into Sherborne Ælfmaer abbot of St Augustine's, who, on going blind, retired to his old monastery and allowed Brihtwine to return (*ibid.* p. 82; Goscelin, *Historia translat. S. Augustini*, MPL, clv, col. 30). Although it has often been denied that Ælfmaer was the traitor who let the Danes into Canterbury, and so caused the martyrdom of Ælfheah, he received this reward from Cnut. The king, however, made amends to Sherborne by allowing Brihtwine to be succeeded by his brother Ælfwold.

[6] *Vita Wlsini*, pp. 82–3.

[7] 'ubi novum monasterium veteri adiunxit': *ibid.* p. 83.

[8] *Ibid.* p. 84.

[9] Malmesbury, *GP*, pp. 179–80.

[10] *Vita Wlsini*, p. 83.

shrines of both St Wulfsige and St Juderwara.[1] Bishop Herman (1058–78), who combined Sherborne with Wiltshire, and had his see in the monastery,[2] won a lawsuit with the aid of the relics of St Wulfsige,[3] and asked Goscelin of St Bertin to write the saint's life.[4] All the same, Herman decided to move his see to (old) Salisbury.

Although William of Malmesbury considered Sherborne a rich see,[5] Bishop Æthelric at the beginning of the century was complaining bitterly about its losses,[6] and, on Domesday evidence, it seems in 1066 to have been poorer than Ramsbury and about the same as Wells. Nine manors in Berkshire are described as 'de victu monachorum'.[7]

xiii. *Wells*

The bishopric of Somerset,[8] founded in 909, with the see in St Andrew's, Wells, was in the beginning at the heart of the kingdom of Wessex, and the first two bishops were translated to Canterbury. Although the cathedral church was not reformed as a monastery, it was ruled by promoted abbots from 974 until 1033, and in that period probably declined in importance, since it lay outside the main stream of reform and also became geographically more remote from the new centres of royal power. Lyfing-Æthelstan (999–1013), who had been abbot of Chertsey, and who was translated to Canterbury after the disasters which followed Ælfheah's martyrdom, was in the old tradition. But in 1033 Cnut appointed his Saxon or Lotharingian priest Duduc, and in 1060 Edward his priest from the diocese of Liége, Giso, to the bishopric, and a new era began. The rule of monastic bishops was often disastrous for non-monastic sees, and these foreign bishops found their estates badly encumbered. Duduc was unable to make much change. But Giso was a successful reformer, recovering estates and establishing a regular life for his canons.

Wells, probably because of the depredations, was one of the poorer bishoprics in Edward's reign, and the canons' share was small.[9]

---

[1] *Vita Wlsini, passim.* The cures were mostly of local people. A Londoner, however, is mentioned (p. 79). It may be presumed that a *libellus* of Wulfsige's miracles was kept at Sherborne, and used by Goscelin, like the *libellus* of St Juderwara, to which he refers (p. 85).

[2] Florence, i. 236.   [3] *Vita Wlsini*, pp. 83–4.   [4] *Ibid.* p. 73.
[5] *GP*, pp. 176–7.   [6] Harmer, *Writs*, no. 63.   [7] *DB*, i. 77 a ii.
[8] J. Armitage Robinson, *The Saxon Bishops of Wells*, Brit. Acad. supplemental papers iv (1918). Giso, *Historiola, Ecclesiastical Documents*, pp. 9–21.
[9] Robinson, pp. 52 ff. Harmer, *Writs*, nos. 64–72.

xiv. *Winchester*

The 'capital' see of Wessex, the see of St Æthelwold and St Ælfheah, the nursery of Ælfric the Homilist, the true centre of the tenth-century reformation, Winchester was completely without distinction between 1005 and 1070. Ælfheah's successor, Cenwulf, who had been abbot of Peterborough, received the dedication of Ælfric's Life of St Æthelwold.[1] And it was probably Cnut's appointment of his priest Ælfwine (1032–47) [2] and the succession of another royal priest, Stigand (1047–70), which damped down the religious life. Nor can Winchester's combination with Canterbury (1052–70) have been advantageous to the western diocese. It is in this period that the 'A' version of the Chronicle, which had been written at Winchester, peters out.[3] Yet it is possible that conditions were not so bad as the obscurity would suggest. Ælfwine certainly was given a foul reputation by the malicious monks [4] and Stigand was not remembered with gratitude.[5] But there are signs that Stigand encouraged the Old Minster's artistic tradition,[6] and the church must have been connected with the royal treasury. Moreover, the monastery, describing itself as 'the humble congregation of brethren in the church of Sts Birinus, Swithun, and Æthelwold', protested vigorously to the pope when it was threatened with suppression in 1071. It wrote with pride of its monastic tradition. Alexander II both confirmed its customs and advised the monks carefully to observe the Rule.[7] It may be that Winchester was like Canterbury, rich and worldly, but cultured and not ruined beyond repair.

The diocese covered Hampshire and Surrey and the bishopric was after Canterbury the richest in England. More than half the estates were in Hampshire, but there was a good holding in Wiltshire and smaller holdings in Somerset, Berkshire, Surrey, Oxfordshire, Cambridgeshire, and Buckinghamshire. There is no reason to suppose that Stigand had neglected Winchester's interests. About half the estates seem to have been allocated to the monks, which made them a little richer than those at Christ Church, Canterbury.

[1] *Chron. Abingdon*, ii. 255.

[2] Thomas Rudborne, *Historia Major Wintoniensis*, *Anglia Sacra*, i. 233, asserts however that Ælfwine became a monk at Winchester.   [3] Plummer, p. xcvii.

[4] Thomas Rudborne, *op. cit.* i. 233–4, 237–8; *Annales Ecclesiae Wintoniensis, ibid.* i. 291–3.

[5] *Anglia Sacra*, i. 239, 249–51. In 1122–3 Winchester asked for reciprocal prayers from Savigny for Bishops Ælfwine and Walkelin, Stigand's predecessor and successor: *Rouleau Mortuaire du B. Vital, abbé de Savigni*, ed. Léopold Delisle (Paris 1909), p. xliii, tit. 182.

[6] See above, p. 79.   [7] *Anglia Sacra*, i. 320–2.

xv. *Worcester*

The see of the Hwicce, which St Dunstan and St Oswald had held in turn, was ruled throughout the period by monks, mostly from West-country abbeys, of whom all were able and some were good. Oswald had held Worcester with York for twenty years (972–92), and the practice was sometimes revived. Wulfstan I (*Lupus*) joined the two 1003–16; Ælfric Puttoc obtained Worcester 1040–1; but Ealdred, who intended to hold both, was forced by the pope in 1062 to provide a substitute in the south. All the same, he retained paramount control over Worcester [1] and treated it in rather the same way as the archbishops of Canterbury treated Rochester. Worcester was also combined with Devon and Cornwall (1038–40, 1041–6) under Lyfing, and with Wiltshire (1055–8) and Hereford (1056–60) while Ealdred built up his ecclesiastical empire in the West. A sentimental tie at least was kept with Ramsey Abbey which Oswald had founded.[2] Worcester also wielded an important influence over the Norse-Irish see of Dublin.[3]

Despite these irregularities and a tradition of episcopal nepotism, Worcester was the one see which kept the reform movement alive throughout the eleventh century.[4] Wulfstan I dominated the English church at the beginning of the period and Wulfstan II (1062–95) provided the last Old-English saint. It was from the diocese of Worcester that, immediately after the Conquest, monasticism was revived in the province of York. There was a fine theological library at Worcester, and somewhere in the diocese the 'D' version of the

---

[1] Malmesbury, *GP*, p. 253, calls him 'tutor episcopatus'. After the Conquest Thomas I of York claimed Worcester for his archbishopric, and some modern observers have held that in the century before 1070 Worcester was, *de facto* at least, often within the northern province. Certainly there was confusion; and it may be that York was creating a prescriptive title. But it does not seem that there was any formal change of the historic boundary.

[2] Eadmer, *Mirac. S. Oswaldi*, *HCY*, ii. 53. Cf. also Eric John, *Land tenure in Early England* (1960), pp. 111–12; Francis Wormald, *English Kalendars before A.D. 1100*, HBS (1934), p. vii.

[3] *Vita Wulfstani*, p. 59. The second bishop of Dublin, Patrick, was a Worcester monk: Aubrey Gwynn, *The Writings of Bishop Patrick, 1074–84* (Scriptores Latini Hiberniae, i, Dublin, 1955). It was possibly because of this Irish connexion that the Chronicle of Marianus Scotus was chosen as a basis for 'Florence's' work.

[4] Sir Ivor Atkins, 'The church of Worcester from the eighth to the twelfth century', *The Antiquaries Journal*, xvii (1937), 371–91, xx (1940), 1–38, 203–29; Eric John, 'An alleged Worcester charter of the reign of Edgar', *BJRL*, xli (1958), 54 ff., 'The King and the Monks in the Tenth-Century Reformation', *ibid.* xlii (1959), 61 ff., 'Some Latin Charters of the Tenth Century Reformation in England', *Revue Bénédictine*, lxx (1960), 333 ff., *Land tenure in Early England*, pp. 80 ff.

Chronicle was written.[1] The cathedral chapter was clearly a school of sound learning. In the middle of the eleventh century it produced scholars as diverse in their talents as Hemming the sub-prior and archivist,[2] Patrick bishop of Dublin, poet and theologian,[3] and Florence, perhaps the annalist.[4] The reason for Worcester's distinction is clearly the persistence of the monastic ideal. It was the one cathedral monastery which did not suffer from episcopal government.

The church (Oswald built the new cathedral dedicated to St Mary) had been endowed by the creation in 964 by King Edgar of the triple hundred (300 hides) of Oswaldslow, a *scipsocn* in which the bishop had extensive political and jurisdictional rights.[5] In Edward's day, according to Domesday Book, the bishopric was the wealthiest after Canterbury and Winchester, although falling far behind those two giants. The bulk of its endowments still lay within Oswaldslow, but there were also large estates in Gloucestershire and a smaller holding in Warwickshire. The estates, like Oswaldslow itself, seem to have been divided between bishop and monks in the proportion of two to one. But St Wulfstan's attempt to act as a true abbot in the monastery caused constitutional strains.[6]

xvi. *York*

York, the metropolitan see of Northumbria, was by English standards a great city.[7] It had been the capital of a Norwegian kingdom in the tenth century, and later some of its earls, as Eric, Siward, and Tostig, were Scandinavian in whole or in part. Even Morcar, the last earl of Northumbria, had

---

[1] Plummer, pp. lxxiv ff.; Sir Ivor Atkins, 'The origin of the Later part of the Saxon chronicle known as D', *EHR*, lv (1940), 8–26. On the other hand, D. Whitelock, *EHD*, i. 111, and *The Peterborough Chronicle, The Bodleian Manuscript Laud Misc. 636* (Copenhagen, 1954), 27–32, favours York.

[2] Cf. N. R. Ker, 'Hemming's Cartulary', *Studies in Medieval History presented to F. M. Powicke* (1948), pp. 49–75.   [3] See above, p. 226, *n*. 3.

[4] See Wolfgang Keller, *Die literarischen Bestrebungen von Worcester, Quellen und Forschungen zur Sprach- und Kulturgeschichte*, lxxxiv (1900), 70 ff; R. R. Darlington, *Vita Wulfstani*, pp. xi–xviii, *Anglo-Norman Historians* (1947); *EHD*, ii. 204.   [5] See above, pp. 169 ff.

[6] For Worcester administration, see below, pp. 241–3, 246–8, 252–4.

[7] A description, written *c*. 1000, is in the *Vita Oswaldi*, 'Est civitas Eboraca metropolis totius gentis Northanimbrorum, quae quondam erat nobiliter aedificata, et firmiter muris constructa; quae nunc est dimissa vetustati; quae tamen gaudet de multitudine populorum, non minus virorum ac mulierum, exceptis parvulis et pubetinis, quam xxx millia eadem civitate numerati sunt; quae inedicibiliter est repleta, et mercatorum gazis locupletata, qui undique adveniunt, maxime ex Danorum gente': *HCY*, i. 454.

a Scandinavian name. But the Northumbrian church had always looked, if not to Canterbury, at least south. No archbishop of York seems ever to have dreamed of establishing a province embracing the Scandinavian world. The sea-route to Denmark lay across the English Channel not the North Sea. York was in direct contact only with Ireland and the Norwegian lands. Hence Northumbrian 'separatism' had no message for the archbishops. Moreover, since all monasteries north of the Humber had disappeared, southerners were appointed by the king to the metropolitan see. They remained quite detached from local politics and ambitions.

It is, indeed, possible that the kings regarded the archbishops as their agent within an area of doubtful loyalty. Some of the ablest men in the English church were appointed to York and all fostered Christianity in these semi-heathen parts. Three were monks – Wulfstan the Homilist, Ælfric Puttoc (1023–51), formerly prior of Winchester, and Ealdred (1060–9), the most experienced of Edward's bishops. Only once was a royal priest, Cynsige (1051–60), appointed. The tie with Worcester, which began with St Oswald, was not completely broken. Some of these archbishops held the other diocese in plurality, or, in Ealdred's case, through a *chorepiscopus*. But, most remarkable for the time, they seem to have used Worcester revenues for the advancement of the northern minsters. The archbishops were also in close touch with Peterborough, the nearest monastery. Wulfstan planned to be buried there, but went to Ely instead. Ælfric Puttoc and Cynsige left their bodies and fine mortuaries to Peterborough, and the latter may have become a monk before he died. Thus, although the Peterborough chronicler, in connexion with a story that the monk Æthelric was consecrated archbishop but was expelled and had to be satisfied with Durham, claimed that the canons and clerks of York were hostile to monks, it is clear that York had a monastic tone and that the canons had a Rule.[1] The great reform drive in Northumbria started by Wulfstan was still alive under Ealdred. Men turning to Christianity from heathenism offered perhaps a more fruitful field for a ministry than was to be found elsewhere in England: the challenge may have brought out the best in the archbishops. There is a parallel with the seventh century. And the work of these men was crowned, but after their time, with a great renascence of monasticism in their province.

The diocese covered Yorkshire and part of Nottinghamshire, including Southwell. After the Conquest Lindsey and Lincoln were claimed. Partly

[1] See above, pp. 71, 73, 81, 88–90.

because of its great size and partly because Wulfstan turned his legal experience to its problems, the bishopric had a model administration unmatched elsewhere in the kingdom. The four minsters – York, Ripon, Beverley, and Southwell – with their colleges of canons, served as local centres. Parish priests were organized in gilds; archdeacons existed; and diocesan synods were held.[1] Folcard wrote of York's provincialism.[2] But in some directions it showed the way. Nevertheless, the first Norman archbishop of York, Thomas I, doubtless because of the rebellions and invasions which had devastated his diocese and city between 1065 and 1070, found his see in a poor condition. Only three of the seven canons of York were in residence at his accession.[3] Also the bishopric was relatively poor. By Canterbury standards there was not an archbishop's endowment. The acquisitiveness of the archbishops of York is easily explained.

xvii. *Durham*

At Durham an attenuation of the original monastic establishment had produced a curious hybrid arrangement. When the church of Lindisfarne was abandoned in 875 owing to the Danish invasion, the surviving monks dispersed, and custody of the body of St Cuthbert and of the other treasures of the church was assumed by some clerks who had been educated from infancy by the monks.[4] These men accompanied Bishop Eardwulf and Abbot Ealdred of Luel on the celebrated wandering through Northumbria, and, after the church had been re-founded at Chester-le-Street, established themselves as an hereditary corporation – the clerks of St Cuthbert – with the descendants of the seven porters of the body assuming a place of special honour. A grandson of an original porter served again when the final move was made to Durham in 995, and the genealogies of two are known to seven generations.[5]

These clerks of St Cuthbert were under a head who, after the Conquest at least, was called a dean,[6] and have been described as canons. They were usually married men, living in their own houses,[7] and enjoying an hereditary

---

[1] See below, pp. 245–6.   [2] *Vita S. Johannis, HCY*, i. 241.
[3] Hugh the Chantor, *HCY*, p. 11.   [4] Symeon, *HDE*, i. 57–8.
[5] Symeon names four of the porters of 875 (i. 65), gives the genealogies of two (i. 79–80), and mentions three descendants living at the time of writing. It is possible, therefore, that some of the original families had died out. They had, of course, been dispossessed by Bishop William of St Calais.   [6] *Ibid*. i. 122.
[7] When the church was moved to Durham houses were assigned by lot: *ibid*. i. 81.

estate. But, owing to the education of the founder clerks, they maintained a monastic type of service in the church.[1] It was an article of faith at Durham that monasticism had never completely died out in the community. All the bishops, except one, we are assured, had been monks,[2] and these had always had two or three companions.[3] Apparently it was not unusual for clerks of St Cuthbert to renounce the world and assume the monastic habit,[4] and it was a necessary step when one of them was elected bishop.[5] They must, however, have been monks without a cloister.[6] The monastic tradition was also maintained by the regulation that no woman could enter any church in which the body of St Cuthbert had rested, nor even the cemetery except in case of war or fire. The scandals at the double monastery of Coldingham in St Cuthbert's lifetime were supposed to be the origin of this rule;[7] and it was preserved into the fourteenth century with the aid of a collection of monitory stories.[8]

It is clear, however, that by the time of Bishop Aldhun's death (1018) monasticism had collapsed. A three-years' vacancy occurred because none of the clerks would abandon the world, and when a priest, Edmund, who is described as one of their number, but was clearly outside the circle of electors,[9] agreed to accept the conditions, he was elected with alacrity. He made his profession as monk before his consecration, but none of the clerks followed his example, and he had to apply to Peterborough Abbey for a monk to instruct him in the rule and serve as a companion.[10] The intrusion of foreign monks into the church led to trouble. Two of them, the brothers Æthelric and Æthelwine, succeeded Edmund in turn, apparently through the influence of the earls of Northumbria and certainly against the wish of the clerks,[11] and both were regarded as aliens who despoiled Durham for the sake

---

[1] Symeon, *HDE*, i. 57–8, 106.   [2] *Ibid*. i. 58, 106.   [3] *Ibid*. i. 58.
[4] Cf. Riggulf, *ibid*. i. 80.   [5] *Ibid*. i. 86.
[6] Solitary monks and nuns, more properly styled anchorites, were always common enough. A monk Eadmer suggested Durham as a resting place for the saint in 995 (*ibid*. i. 79). Bishop Aldhun's daughter after her repudiation by two husbands returned to Durham and took the veil, remaining a nun until her death ('De obsessione Dunelmi', *ibid*. i. 217). A later example, famous in Durham history, is St Godric.   [7] Symeon, *HDE*, i. 58–9.
[8] Cf. *ibid*. i. 60–1, 94; *Historiae Dunelmensis scriptores tres*, ed. James Raine, Surtees Soc. ix (1839), 117.
[9] Malmesbury, *GP*, p. 270, says that no one had thought of inviting him.
[10] Symeon, *HDE*, i. 85–6.
[11] After Bishop Edmund's death, Eadred, one of the clerks 'qui post episcopum secundus erat' (presumably the dean), bought the bishopric with the church's money from King Harthacnut, but died before assuming office. The monk Æthelric succeeded, possibly by King Edward's and

of Peterborough.[1] After these unhappy experiences the clerks accepted William's nomination of Walcher, a secular clerk, without demur and tolerated his abolition of the Benedictine office, the monastic form of service.[2]

The value of the church's estates in King Edward's reign is unknown, for the lands north of the Tees are omitted from Domesday Book, and the bishop's holding in Yorkshire was small before the Conquest.[3] The internal arrangements are obscure and became controversial in the Norman period.[4] It seems that the clerks had prebends, and, as the bishop had to become a monk, it may be that his share was small.

Earl Siward's help, and after three years was expelled by the clerks because he was a foreigner and elected against their will. We can imagine that the priest Alfred, guardian of the relics and schoolmaster, was one of the ring-leaders (*ibid.* i. 87, 89). Earl Siward forced them to take him back (*ibid.* i. 91). Æthelwine succeeded, after his brother had resigned, owing to Earl Tostig's favour (*ibid.* i. 92). For the Peterborough side of the story, see *Chron. Peterborough*, pp. 73–4.

[1] Symeon, *HDE*, i. 87, 89, 91–2, 94.   [2] *Ibid.* i. 105–6.

[3] For Durham's estates *ante* 1066, see Sir Edmund Craster, 'The Patrimony of St Cuthbert', *EHR*, lxix (1954), 177 ff.

[4] F. Barlow, *Durham Jurisdictional Peculiars* (1950), pp. 5 ff.

CHAPTER IV

Ecclesiastical Government

Pope Gregory I had instructed Augustine to divide England into two provinces, with sees in London (for which Canterbury was substituted) and York. Each province was to contain twelve dioceses. Based on a memory of Roman geography, this scheme was unsatisfactory, for the province of York could never equal that of Canterbury. But a sensible attempt of the Mercian kings to create a third province, based on Lichfield, carved out of the southern province, failed. The English church was to remain unequally and disadvantageously divided. Canterbury, with in the eleventh century twelve or thirteen suffragans,[1] was one of the largest provinces in Christendom. York, with one or two,[2] was among the smaller. The bishops of Ireland, Wales, and Scotland were not organized in provinces, and remained a field for English metropolitan expansion. It was sometimes convenient, and entailed little danger of dependence, for bishops from those parts to go to England for consecration. About 1028 the first bishop of the Norse-Irish city of Dublin, Donatus or Dunan, was consecrated probably by Æthelnoth of Canterbury, just as his successor, Patrick, monk of Worcester, was by Lanfranc.[3] It is also likely that a few Welsh bishops were consecrated by English metropolitans. According to English tradition Ælfric of Canterbury (995–1005) consecrated a bishop of Llandaff and two bishops of St Davids, Æthelnoth of Canterbury (1020–38) one bishop to each see, and Cynsige of York a bishop of 'Llandaff' in 1056.[4] Bishop Æthelstan of Hereford, when

---

[1] St Germans-Crediton = Exeter, Sherborne-Ramsbury, Winchester, Wells, Selsey, London, Rochester, Dorchester, Elmham, Lichfield, Hereford, and Worcester. There were also those outside England.

[2] Durham and perhaps at times Worcester.

[3] Aubrey Gwynn, *The Writings of Bishop Patrick* (Scriptores Latini Hiberniae, vol. i, Dublin 1955), pp. 1–2.

[4] Haddan and Stubbs, *Councils*, i. 287–93; J. Conway Davies, *Episcopal Acts relating to Welsh Dioceses 1066–1272* (Hist. Soc. of the Church in Wales, no. 1), i (1946), 54–66, where there is unnecessary nationalist bias. The evidence may be 'dubious, false, or negative', but bishops had to be consecrated, and English bishops sometimes sought consecration abroad. A tradition which included the notice, most inconvenient for Canterbury, that Herewald was consecrated by an archbishop of York, cannot be dismissed lightly.

blind, employed the Welsh bishop Tramerin who died in 1055.[1] As for Scotland it was remembered at York that Cynsige had consecrated two bishops of Glasgow.[2] York, it seems, despite its geographical advantage, had less power of attraction; and it was probably kept in mind, at least at Canterbury, that Pope Gregory had subjected the British bishops to Augustine. But it is unlikely that true metropolitan rights, as were claimed on such evidence after the Conquest, were involved before 1066. English archbishops gave their services when approached and probably without conditions.

England also exercised some influence over the Scandinavian churches, and Adam of Bremen gives a prejudiced account of activities which threatened the rights of his own church, for Hamburg-Bremen claimed to be the metropolitan of the North. Those Scandinavian kings who feared German domination naturally looked to England for bishops and to Canterbury for their consecration. Cnut appointed his own bishops throughout his empire, and one of these, Gerbrand, appointed to Zealand, after his consecration by Archbishop Æthelnoth of Canterbury was captured by Archbishop Unwan and forced to promise obedience. Cnut is said to have agreed not to act in future without Bremen's advice.[3] Olaf of Norway recruited bishops and priests in England,[4] and Harold Hardrada was accused by Archbishop Adalbert of having his bishops ordained in England and Gaul.[5] The Orkneys occasionally had English bishops.[6] Englishmen even found their way to Sweden.[7] Some northern bishops retired to England.[8] It is doubtful, however, whether Canterbury, even in Cnut's time, exercised true metropolitan powers in Scandinavia. By Edward's reign Archbishop Adalbert (1043-72) seems to have made his claims good. He even received legates from the churches of Iceland, Greenland, and the Orkneys.[9]

A sharply defined hierarchical construction had never been characteristic of the English church, and the reforms of the tenth century, based as they were on Carolingian attitudes,[10] had not been directed towards that end.

---

[1] *ASC CD* 1055; Florence, i. 214.

[2] And also, it was claimed, received charters of profession from them, documents which had perished in the fire at York: Hugh the Chantor, *HCY*, p. 32. Cf. Malmesbury *GR*, p. 353.

[3] Adam of Bremen, *Gesta pontificum Hammaburgensis ecclesiae*, II, c. 53, *MPL*, cxlvi, col. 539.

[4] *Ibid.* II, c. 55, col. 540.

[5] *Ibid.* III, c. 16, col. 571. Pope Alexander II (? 1061) wrote to Harold complaining of this practice: *MPL*, cxlvi, col. 128.

[6] Adam of Bremen, *op. cit.* IV, c. 8, col. 426, c. 34, coll. 652-3.

[7] *Ibid.* II, c. 60, col. 543.   [8] See above, p.15, *n.* 4.

[9] Adam of Bremen, *op. cit.* III, c. 23, col. 576, c. 42, coll. 615-7, IV, cc. 35-6, col. 655.

[10] For which cf. Fournier and Le Bras, i. 130 ff.

Indeed, the rapid and unbalanced changes then introduced intensified the incoherence, while the exaltation of the king as the patron of the church made its remedy both unnecessary and undesirable. Moreover, owing to the smallness of the kingdom and the centralizing policy of the kings, there were no provincial capitals, no episcopal cities with a real life of their own where the bishop could normally be found ruling as a local prince, attracting his own clientèle. York was no Hamburg. As a result, the *ecclesia Anglorum* takes on its firmest shape only in relation to the king and the kingdom. From the standpoint of the royal court the bishop was the king's ecclesiastical servant; he could be employed as best suited the temporal and ecclesiastical affairs of the kingdom; and his diocese was the district which the king had entrusted to him. This 'national' organization blurred the truly ecclesiastical structure of the church.

The two English metropolitans, however, were always given precedence over the bishops. They normally attested diplomas as *archiepiscopus*, although Archbishop Ælfric Puttoc of York (1023–51) preferred the variant *archipraesul*, which was also occasionally used by others. *Archipontifex* seems to have been less common.[1] Few of their own documents have survived. Oswald (972–92) may have styled himself, 'dei gratia Eboracensis archiepiscopus',[2] Wulfstan of York (1008), 'ego N. [Wulfstanus] gratia domini dispensante Eboracensium archiepiscopus',[3] and (1017), 'dei omnipotentis providentia archipontifex',[4] and Eadsige of Canterbury (1044), 'gratia dei archiepiscopus'.[5] In literary compositions of the late tenth century archbishops were awarded some astonishing styles;[6] but afterwards, it seems, the trend was towards simplicity, possibly through the influence of the writ. On two occasions in charters archbishops were described as primate – in 1019, 'Ego Lyuing Dorovernensis basilicae primas'[7] and in 1031 'Ego Æthelnoth Eboracensis (*recte* Dorovernensis) basilicae primas'.[8] But this style is probably to be regarded as a variant of 'Metropolitanus archipraesul', used by Lyfing in 1018,[9] and expressing archiepiscopal rather than true primatial dignity.

---

[1] Wulfstan of York, 1019, K. 729, 1313.   [2] K. 1286*.
[3] c. 40.2, of the Latin version of V and VI Æthelred.
[4] K. 1313.   [5] K. 1333*.
[6] 'perprudenti domino archonti Albrico' (Archbishop Ælfric addressed by the Saxon priest, B.): *Memorials of St Dunstan*, p. 3; 'consentaneo typici nominis praesagio Sigerico, apostolico summi praesulatus ciriceo largiflua dei gratia decorato [*decorated by the pallium*]'; 'dilectissimo in Christo patri Sigerico misteriarchae' (Archbishop Sigeric): *ibid.* pp. 399–400.
[7] K. 729.   [8] K. 744.   [9] K. 727.

Pope Gregory I had ruled that, after Augustine, seniority should belong to the archbishop with the earlier consecration.[1] It is uncertain whether this rule was regularly observed. In the late Old-English period Canterbury normally signed before York in the witness lists to charters, although there is one significant exception.[2] And the 'ancient custom' asserted in the twelfth century that when one metropolitan died the other exercised archiepiscopal functions in the vacant province,[3] does not bear directly on the problem. Gregory's decision implied, of course, legal parity between the metropolitans. It could not be used, without misrepresentation, by either see to support a claim to primacy. Nor is there evidence that Canterbury ever made such a claim before 1070. Theodore was probably fortified by special privileges, but these may be assumed to have been personal. Certainly when Lanfranc put forward in 1070–2 Canterbury's claim to a primacy over York he could produce no historical or documentary evidence of any real legal value. He carried the day because his own importance and royal support were too much for the isolated and ill-prepared archbishop of York. His stated case was both historically and juridically weak, and after 1072 it gradually collapsed.[4]

Nevertheless, although Lanfranc badly strained his evidence to support the claim to a legal primacy, his confidence, and to some extent his success, were due to an historical background which made his assertions plausible, without, however, furnishing much proof suitable for use in a court. The desirable evidence was a papal privilege, expressly granting the right, which the reigning pope could be induced to confirm. Such a document Canterbury did not possess. Inferences from history were a very inferior kind of evidence. But it is possible that Lanfranc, as a stranger to the English past, did not make the most of the historical evidence. On a broad view of the Anglo-Saxon period it appears that Canterbury had enjoyed a natural primacy which had required no assertion. Canterbury was the mother church and was seated in Kent which for long had formed part of Wessex. York was remote and poor and had had a chequered history. In these circumstances the archbishops of Canterbury had acquired a prescriptive right to crown the English (Wessex) kings and had usually acted as their chief ecclesiastical adviser.

---

[1] *Historia Ecclesiastica*, I, c. xxix.

[2] In 1015 the old Wulfstan of York signed before his junior, Archbishop Lyfing (K. 1310), and between 1020 and his death in 1023 he usually signed before the newly appointed Æthelnoth (K. 734–5, 740, with 736 as an exception).   [3] Hugh the Chantor, *HCY*, p. 7.

[4] For the latest views on Canterbury's case, see Margaret Gibson, *Lanfranc of Bec* (1978), pp. 116 ff., 231 ff.

Consequently, when the king held 'national' ecclesiastical councils, the archbishop of Canterbury normally acted as head of the church. In this period
these rights were as much as a primate could expect to enjoy. Indeed, active
primacies had more of a secular than an ecclesiastical colouring. There was
never much ecclesiastical interest in primacies.[1] Both the subject archbishops
and the pope regarded the intermediate step as a nuisance. Only strong kings,
anxious to centralize the church under their power, to control an administrative hierarchy, and to eliminate or canalize outside interference, encouraged
the position. But these considerations had only a limited validity in the late
Old-English kingdom. The kingdom was small; only one of the two church
provinces was of real importance; and the effective head of the church was
the king. There was no administrative need to stress Canterbury's primatial
rights over York. And, as papal interference did not begin until the very last
years of the kingdom's history, there was no need to assert Canterbury's
primacy against the pope. Hence the position was that Canterbury had a
natural primacy, which seems never to have been challenged by York – even
Ealdred seems to have yielded precedence to Stigand [2] – and rarely to have
been disregarded by the kings. Also British and Scandinavian bishops had
visited Canterbury for consecration, so that Lanfranc could easily infer that
his predecessors had been at least primates of all Britain. But in fact the
Anglo-Saxon archbishop of Canterbury exercised no legal rights as primate:
he merely enjoyed some privileges in the kingdom, and without, deriving
from the history of his see.

An archbishop was archbishop in his diocese and metropolitan in his
province, although the distinction was often ignored even in more legalistic
ages.[3] Metropolitan rights were no more popular than primatial in western
Christendom after the collapse of the Roman system of church government.[4]
Bishops valued their independence;[5] the popes, except for a short time

[1] Cf. Feine, *Kirchliche Rechtsgeschichte*, i. 196. The Isidorian reformers of the ninth century
were studiously vague about the role of primates and patriarchs: Fournier and Le Bras, i. 133.
[2] Cf. K. 808, 810, 813, 817, 819; and cf. his precedence at the Worcester council, above, p. 106.
[3] For metropolitan rights, see Robert Brentano, *York Metropolitan Jurisdiction and Papal
Judges Delegate, 1279–1296* (Univ. of Calif. publicns. in History, lviii, 1959), pp. 1–22.
[4] Feine, *op. cit.* i. 193–5; Fournier and Le Bras, i. 132–3.
[5] Cf. Bruno of Toul's objection to the nature of the profession required of him by Poppo
archbishop of Trier in 1026. It contained a *lex* which was *superflua atque impossibilis a nemine
servanda*. Conrad II made Poppo moderate it. Wibert (= Cardinal Humbert), *Vita S. Leonis*, I,
c. xii, *MPL*, cxliii, coll. 479–80. Hugh the Chantor, in connexion with the 'fraudulent' charter
recording that in 1070 Thomas of York made his profession by oath to Lanfranc of Canterbury,

during the reform period of the eleventh century, regarded archbishops as rivals; and kings often found their pretensions inconvenient and unnecessary. The metropolitan rights of Rouen were useful to the dukes of Normandy for they served to create a ducal church; but for that very reason they were without interest to the kings of France. In Germany and England extensive metropolitan rights were inconvenient to the kings, for the rulers dealt directly with the bishops and treated them as immediate servants. Under such conditions metropolitan rights were few. Archbishops retained their traditional power of supervising their bishops – even if they did not visit, an interest in their appointment (reduced usually to advice, confirmation, and consecration), the right to call provincial synods, and a theoretical right to hear appeals from the legal judgments of the bishops.

None of these metropolitan rights, except for participation in the appointment of bishops,[1] can be illustrated from the later years of the Anglo-Saxon kingdom. Archbishop Wulfstan of York included a chapter on Synods in his *Institutes of Polity* [2] and clearly was thinking of a provincial or national meeting of bishops. Each bishop was to attend with his *witan* and have with him a book of canons. The purpose of the synod was to achieve concord among themselves, promote Christianity, and suppress heathenism. Disputes among the bishops should be settled without recourse to laymen. They were to take common action against powerful sinners and wrongdoers, but, if the task was beyond them, they should refer the matter to the king. Bishops should avoid worldly pomp, hunting and hawking, and avarice and simony.

This account, so general and vague, inspires no confidence that such synods actually met. There was, indeed, no need for them in the southern province when royal ecclesiastical councils were the rule and legislation was usually issued by the king. And, although there is evidence for the meeting of synods in the northern province,[3] doubtless under Wulfstan's inspiration, these are more likely to have been diocesan than truly provincial. No example can be given in either province of a judicial appeal from a bishop to an archbishop. Indeed, owing to Stigand's irregular position, few metropolitan rights were exercised between 1052 and 1066. Several English bishops were

wrote, 'nec abbas episcopo suo, nec episcopus metropolitano subieccionem iureiurando promittit, soli summo pontifici, ex consuetudine Romane ecclesie metropolite': *HCY*, p. 5.

[1] See above, pp. 109–11.

[2] *Polity*, pp. 210 ff. The Isidorian reformers favoured provincial councils rather than metropolitan monarchy: cf. Fournier and Le Bras, i. 132–3.   [3] See below, p. 246.

consecrated by foreign metropolitans or by the pope.[1] So careless were the archbishops of Canterbury of their rights that the register of professions of faith made by the bishops to the archbishop before consecration runs only from the end of the eighth century to 870 and, apart from an isolated entry from the mid-tenth century, does not start again until after the Conquest.[2] From York no such register has survived.

Equally revealing is the apparent absence of rules of precedence for the bishops. The order in which the bishops are given in the witness lists to diplomas makes little ecclesiastical sense.[3] In Germany in 1063 the men of the abbot of Fulda and of the bishop of Hildesheim fought a bloody battle in the abbey of Goslar over which of the two prelates should sit next to the archbishop of Mainz.[4] No such procedural disputes are recorded for England. Moreover, even the geographical boundary between the provinces was obscured in the last century of the Old-English kingdom, primarily by the custom, which started with St Oswald, of the northern metropolitan holding Worcester with York, and secondarily by the confusion flowing from Stigand's incapacity. As a result, the first Norman archbishop of York was able to claim Worcester, Lichfield, and Lindsey for his province. It seems that the ecclesiastical provinces counted for little in the strong kingdoms of Cnut and Edward.

In vernacular documents and the chronicles the bishop, like the king or an earl, is simply given his rank without adornment. Few episcopal documents in Latin have survived and these provide a miscellany of styles. 'Ego Oswaldus Wigornensis aecclesiae episcopus' (961–72),[5] 'Ego Lyfing superni rectoris fultus iuvamine praesul' (1042),[6] 'Ego Ealdredus Wigornensis aecclesiae episcopus' (1053–7),[7] and 'Ego Wlstanus, licet indignus servus servorum dei, Wigornensis ecclesie antistes' (1089)[8] – all from Worcester –

---

[1] 'Abroad', Wulfwig of Dorchester (*ASC C* 1053) and Leofwine of Lichfield (Florence, i. 211); at Rome, Giso of Wells and Walter of Hereford (*Vita Ædwardi*, p. 35).

[2] *Anglia Sacra*, i. 78–82.

[3] Many of the lists may be dislocated through copying. But no sign of an order based on episcopal seniority can be detected, nor, except for the possible case of Winchester, which usually has the place of honour after the archbishoprics, of a precedence according to the dignity of the see. In Edward's reign, at least, there was a tendency to group curial bishops at the head of the list; and in 1050 Robert bishop of London (consecrated in 1044, and previously an abbot) was placed at the bottom in the Abingdon charters (K. 792, 793, 800). Such indications as there are point to the dominance of secular values. The order of seating at 'general councils' was determined at London in 1075: Malmesbury *GP*, p. 67; *GR*, p. 353; Florence i. 280.

[4] Lambert of Hersfeld, *Annales*, *MPL*, cxlvi, coll. 1072–4.   [5] K. 1287.

[6] K. 765.   [7] K. 805.   [8] *Hemingi Chartularium*, ii. 424.

exemplify the diploma style. From letters come, 'Divinitatis suffragio Lana-latensis monasterii episcopus' (tenth century, St Germans),[1] 'W. humilis minister S. parrochiae' (c. 1000),[2] 'Lupus Lundoniensis episcopus' (996–1002),[3] and 'Wulstanus servorum dei minimus Wigornensis ecclesiae episcopus rito indignus' (1094).[4]

Each cathedral minster had a body of clergy to serve it. But this *hired*, family, household, or community, does not seem to have been called a *capitulum*, chapter, and was often rather different from the later cathedral chapters. The cathedral clergy were either monks, as at Canterbury, Winchester, Worcester, and Sherborne, or clerks.[5] But although secular bodies were the more numerous, the dominant tone was monastic, for the aim of most bishops was that the clerks of their minsters should form true communities and enjoy their endowments in common.[6] Certainly at London, York, Exeter, and Wells the clerks were given a quasi-monastic rule, based on the *Institutio canonicorum* of the Council of Aachen (817); and the clerks of St Cuthbert had preserved a monastic tradition. This was a custom which did not survive the Conquest. Norman bishops preferred to create individual prebends for the cathedral canons.[7] The tendency to regard chapters as monasteries, due largely to the history of the Old-English church, had important effects. The bishop had no powerful subordinates. He was both free from ecclesiastical restraint and also without officials who could act for him.

The economic relationship between bishop and chapter varied from diocese to diocese. In some secular minsters, like Rochester, Selsey, Ramsbury, Dorchester, North Elmham, and Lichfield, the clerks may have held no more, and sometimes less, than the lands belonging to the cathedral

---

[1] *The Lanalet Pontifical*, ed. G. H. Doble, HBS, lxxiv (1937), 130.

[2] *Memorials of St Dunstan*, p. 408, where attributed to St Wulfsige of Sherborne. K. Jost, *Wulfstanstudien*, p. 21, thinks that it is Wulfstan of London.

[3] D. Bethurum, *The Homilies of Wulfstan*, pp. 374–5. Cf. 'Siwardus episcopus' (coadjutor at Canterbury, 1045–8), *Chron. Abingdon*, i. 458.

[4] Eadmer, *Historia Novorum*, p. 46.

[5] *Canonicus* is a rare term in England before 1066. *Preost/clericus* is usual.

[6] Cf. V Æthelred, 7 (VI Æthelred, 4), 'And canons, where there is property such that they can have a refectory and dormitory, are to hold their minster with right observance and with chastity, as their rule directs.' The view probably was that canons were those who observed one of the Carolingian rules for such; the others were clerks.

[7] For York, see Hugh the Chantor, *HCY*, p. 11. Non-episcopal churches were similarly treated. In St Martin's Dover, 'T.R.E. erant praebendae communes, et reddebant lxi libras inter totum. Modo sunt divisae per singulos per episcopum Baioc.': *DB*, i. 1 b i. In St Mary's Bromfield, 'In hoc manerio erant xx hidae et totum habebant xii canonici ipsius aecclesiae. Unus eorum, Spirtes nomine, tenebat solus x hidas': *DB*, i. 252 b ii.

church itself – that is to say, they were like any other community of priests serving a minster. The bishops, however, had acquired, and depended on, estates which pertained not to the minster but to the bishopric. Thus there was a long-standing distinction between the two *mensae*, and the chapter, or the hereditary cathedral priests, had lands which they regarded very much as their own. Where there had been reform, the bishop had usually increased the endowments so that a larger number of canons or a house of monks could be maintained; and, since the tenth century, cathedral communities, especially the monastic, had received benefactions from outside sources. But whenever extensive estates passed into the hands of cathedral bodies bishops tended to interfere. Provision had been made for communities and not for individuals. Where there were monks, the bishop was abbot; and he varied the allotment as he thought fit. Domesday Book seems to recognize this attitude. Except in the case of London, all the lands are the lands of the bishop. Estates allocated to cathedral bodies are noted and are described in different ways. Sometimes they are treated as sub-fiefs; sometimes merely the destination of the revenue is indicated; and sometimes we are told that a holding had always belonged to the church or is and always was for the food or clothing of the monks.[1] Thus the jurors were trying to describe an internal arrangement. London was exceptional. The lands of St Paul's minster are collected separately from the bishop's and are given individual headings and index numbers. The church is treated as a tenant-in-chief on the same footing as the bishop. It is possible that the canons even had prebends.[2]

---

[1] In the monastic bishoprics the lands of the monks are clearly indicated, and in the case of Canterbury, Winchester, and Worcester phrases are occasionally used which show that it is an old division, e.g. 'de vestitu monachorum fuit semper', 'semper fuit in monasterio', 'S. Trinitas tenuit T.R.E.' (Canterbury, *DB*, i. 16 b i, b ii; ii. 373); 'semper fuit in ecclesia', 'T.R.E. de victu monachorum' (Winchester, 41 a i); 'S. Maria de W. tenuit et tenet' (Worcester, 164 b ii). As some of the secular sees were abandoned for monasteries after the Conquest, the land for three ploughs held by 5 canons of Lichfield (247 a i) and the six hides held by priests of Ramsbury (66 a i) are probably ancient possessions. The four vills 'de victu canonicorum' of Exeter and the sixteen hides which never gelded held communally by the canons of Chichester = Selsey (16 b i) are probably no novelty. Among the lands held by the canons of Hereford, one was held by two canons T.R.E. (181 b ii). And for Wells we have the explicit, 'canonici S. Andreae de episcopo. Ipsi tenebant T.R.E.' (89 b i). At York a new arrangement was made by Archbishop Thomas; but 'habuit et habet S. Petrus' (303 a ii, b i) is suggestive; and we know that the seven canons of York had held lands in common before 1070. The clerks of St Cuthbert also had held lands before the Conquest (F. Barlow, *Durham Jurisdictional Peculiars*, pp. 1 ff.). The canons of Rochester, Dorchester, and North Elmham seem to have left no trace in *DB*.

[2] 'Terra S. Pauli Lundoniensis' or 'Terra canonicorum S. Pauli' in Surrey (34 a i), Herts (136 a ii), Beds (211 a i), Essex (12 a ii); in Middlesex, index, 'Episcopus Lundon. et canonici

Perhaps we may see here innovations which the Norman bishops Robert and William had introduced.

The monastic chapters were organized like any other monastery of the time, except that, as the bishop was the abbot, the resident superior was a dean or prior. The arrangement did not work easily. Cathedral convents rarely welcomed the bishop's interference. And when St Wulfstan, who was imbued with the ideals of the tenth century, attempted to repair the remissness of his busy and often absent predecessor, there occurred at Worcester one of the earliest conscious reactions against the scheme. Although there is nothing in the *Vita Wulfstani* to suggest that the monks resisted Wulfstan's assertion, or re-assertion, of the principle that the bishop was abbot in the monastery and had direct rule over the monks, there is so much about Wulfstan's interference and stern discipline that it is not surprising to find the evidence elsewhere. After 1062 the priory asserted its rights against the bishop, claimed a distinct share in the privileges of the whole church, and prepared forgeries which supported its case – essentially the case that Oswald when he introduced monks into Worcester appointed a prior to rule them and gave him and them various privileges.[1] The ideal of the bishop-abbot, with all things in common, had ceased to work under the most favourable circumstances. At Sherborne, when it was joined to Ramsbury, doubtless the monks enjoyed much independence. And the problem was solved at Winchester and Canterbury by the appointment of secular priests as bishop.

The organization of the secular chapters is obscure. These bodies seem to have been small. Seven priests were killed at Hereford in 1055.[2] There were only seven canons at York,[3] a church which was considered a reformed and flourishing minster, and fewer at Wells,[4] Rochester,[5] and Lichfield.[6] It would not be rash to think that a community of five clerks formed a typical

ejus' (126 b ii). See also Marion Gibbs, *Early Charters of the Cathedral Church of St Paul, London*, Camden 3rd ser., lviii (1939), pp. xvi ff; C. N. L. Brooke, 'The Composition of the Chapter of St Paul's 1086–1163', *Camb. HJ*, x (1951), 111–32; *idem* in *A history of St Paul's Cathedral*, ed. W. R. Matthews and W. M. Atkins (1957), pp. 12–14.

[1] Cf. Eric John, 'An alleged Worcester charter of the reign of Edgar', *BJRL*, xli (1958), 54–80. Wulfstan's attitude is probably revealed by his appointment of his brother, Ælfstan, to replace him as prior in 1062: *Hemingi Chartularium*, ii. 407.

[2] *ASC D* 1055; seven canons, Florence, i. 213.

[3] Cf whom only three survived in 1070: Hugh the Chantor, *HCY*, p. 11.

[4] Four or five clerks: *Ecclesiastical Documents*, pp. 16–17.

[5] Malmesbury, *GP*, pp. 135–6; *Anglia Sacra*, i. 336–7, cf. 340; *Vita Gundulfi, ibid.* ii. 280.

[6] 'ibi (Lichfield) v. canonici habent iii car.': *DB*, i. 247 a i.

secular chapter. Few documents have survived from the secular minsters and we do not know how the communities were organized. It may be thought that those churches which had a *regula* based on the collection issued by the Council of Aachen (817) would have had some capitular officials – a senior or head, a schoolmaster,[1] and a steward for the common chest – but we do not know how they were named or how far they corresponded to later dignitaries in function. Archbishop Thomas found no acceptable arrangement at York in 1070; and it was he who appointed a dean, treasurer, precentor, and chancellor (master of the schools),[2] the 'four-square' constitution which was generally adopted in the Norman period.

In all the western kingdoms of Christendom the most vital unit in the church was the bishop's parish or diocese.[3] The bishop had the strongest tradition of rights, and the diocese was often of a size that could be governed by the resources of the age. Even so, the bishop's parish did not escape from the disruptive forces of the early Middle Ages. He ruled over no centralized, uniform entity. Proprietary rights limited him severely, and he was largely reduced to his own proprietary rights and such powers of his order as he could exercise over a largely independent clergy. Hence it was often administratively advantageous, and not necessarily harmful to the church, for a good and energetic bishop to accumulate a group of small or poor dioceses.[4] But the rather haphazard attempts to reorganize diocesan geography which took place in Edward's reign were to come to little.

The English bishop, like his continental brethren,[5] was closely circumscribed in his own diocese. As we see from the Life of St Wulfstan, he normally lived on his own estates, occupied with the problems of those directly subject to him – the cathedral chapter and his private churches – and turning aside mostly when invited or compelled to do so. Wulfstan attended the shire and royal courts when summoned,[6] and visited the private churches of others when invited.[7] As his estates were scattered, and

---

[1] Earl Harold appointed a distinguished schoolmaster to his minster at Waltham: *Vita Haroldi*, p. 23; cf. 17–19.   [2] Hugh the Chantor, *HCY*, p. 11

[3] 'diocesis vel parochia = bisceoprice': Ælfric, *Glossary*, p. 299.

[4] Later hagiographers were, of course, troubled. See Goscelin's excuses for St Wulfsige of Sherborne: *Vita S. Wlsini*, p. 76; Eadmer's explanation of St Oswald's pluralism: *Vita S. Oswaldi*, *HCY*, ii. 28; and of that of his successor, Ealdwulf: *ibid*. ii. 46; and Osbern's justification of Dunstan's pluralism, *Memorials of St Dunstan*, pp. 105–6.

[5] Cf. Feine, *op. cit.* i. 156 ff., 180. For the duties of English bishops, see Lingard, *Antiquities*, i. 96 ff.   [6] *Vita Wulfstani*, pp. 21, 31, 34, 48; Malmesbury, *GP*, p. 282.

[7] *Vita Wulfstani*, pp. 38, 40, 45, 55.

invitations to travel outside fairly frequent, he could exercise a pastoral ministry in a simple fashion. Those who required his services could approach him as he travelled around, all the more easily since he planned his circuits carefully in advance.[1]

The bishop inherited from the church of the classical world considerable powers.[2] He had the *potestas ordinis*: he was the primary dispenser of the sacraments, especially baptism at Easter and Whitsun (but without the exclusive right), confirmation, ordination of priests, and dedication of ecclesiastical buildings, altars, vessels, and chrism. He had the *potestas magisterii*: the office of instructing the clergy and laity. And he had the *potestas jurisdictionis*, the power to govern, legislate, and administer justice for his diocese. His duties were many, and, as Ælfric the homilist wrote, 'it is very hurtful that a bishop be careless'.[3]

The dispensing of the sacraments and the instruction of the flock were duties which all bishops performed at all times, although with differing standards of competence and zeal. Ælfric wrote in his sermon on the Greater Litany, 'A bishop should constantly instruct his people with book-learning and set them a good example, reprove the perverse, and love the virtuous, be to them a faithful shepherd under Christ, overseeing all, as his name indicates; and not conceal evil nor consent to injustice. Bishops and priests are set as cryers, to announce the faith to lay people, and also to intercede for them to Almighty God. It therefore befits them to have goodness and to be adorned with fair morals.' [4] This theme was repeated in I Cnut, c. 26, 'The bishops are God's heralds and teachers, and they shall proclaim and zealously give example of our duty towards God – let him who will take heed.' They and their priests were shepherds of their flocks and were to cry out continually against the ravening wolves. St Wulfstan of Worcester exemplifies the conscientious shepherd. No doubt others were more remiss. Clearly it was easier to administer the sacraments in a small south-western diocese than in one of the large eastern and northern ones. There were obvious difficulties when the archbishop of York spent much of his time in Worcestershire or at court, or when one bishop administered several sees. But the population was small, the ceremonies were often cursory – Wulfstan is credited with confirming more than 3,000 in a day [5] – and the ordinary person had need of a bishop only once in his lifetime.

[1] *Vita Wulfstani*, p. 51.
[2] Cf. Feine, *op. cit.* i. 179 ff.
[3] *Lives of the Saints*, i. 292–3.
[4] *Catholic Homilies*, ii. 320–1.
[5] *Vita Wulfstani*, p. 36.

Less immutable was the *potestas jurisdictionis*, which tended to be strongly affected, in its nature, procedure, and extent, by the contemporary secular scene. Most noticeable, perhaps, in the early eleventh century, are the restrictions on a bishop's powers. Many of the churches and monasteries in his diocese were outside his direct control, and there is no evidence that English bishops normally interfered.[1] They visited to perform episcopal functions when invited. The position of the monasteries is particularly interesting. The tenth-century reformation, by putting the greater monasteries directly under the king, had re-established the abbots as a class similar, although a degree less in dignity, to the bishops. They had direct access to the king and were often to be found among his *witan*. Episcopal rights over monasteries had not been – could not have been – legally restricted, but their exercise had not been encouraged. It seems to have been tacitly accepted that jurisdiction over the greater abbeys belonged to the king and his *witan*. Rules for the monasteries were enacted by king and council,[2] and the king took action against unsatisfactory convents.[3] Indeed there is no recorded case in this period of a bishop taking disciplinary action against an abbot.[4] Monasteries seem to have welcomed retired bishops into the community, and such domestic bishops may have exercised, with or without permission, *episcopalia* inside the walls. The absence of recorded conflict does not signify. It is not impossible that one or two monasteries possessed papal privileges according them immunity from the diocesan, although all extant privileges are of doubtful authenticity.[5] Yet, in the absence of the need, there can have been little desire for the right. Some bishops, of course, ruled their own monasteries[6]

---

[1] We have no evidence about the institution of priests to private churches. But bishops would at least be aware of their rights: cf. *Institutio Canonicorum* of the Council of Aachen, 817, c. lxxvi, *Enlarged Rule of Chrodegang*, ed. A. S. Napier, EETS, 150 (1916), p. 83.

[2] E.g. *Regularis Concordia;* V Æthelred, 4.1, 6.1; VI Æthelred, 2–3; VII Æthelred, 6.3; VIII Æthelred, 25, 31.1.   [3] See above, p. 103, *n.* 1.

[4] Bishop Æthelric of Dorchester, a former monk of Ramsey, *c.* 1020/34 rebuked the abbot and monks of that house for slackness (*Chron. Ramsey*, pp. 139–40); but he was in a sense still a member of the community.

[5] Harmer, *Writs*, pp. 140–5; W. H. Stevenson, *Cartulary of Muchelney and Athelney*, Somerset Rec. Soc. xiv (1899), 41, *n*, lists charters purporting to grant this privilege and condemns them all. The Isidorian reformers were hostile to monastic exemptions: cf. Fournier and Le Bras, i. 132. Burchard of Worms ignored them in his *Decretum: ibid.* i. 390–1.

[6] When they were abbots *ex officio* (as at Canterbury, Winchester, Sherborne, and Worcester) or when they had proprietary rights. Bishop Oswald of Worcester-York was co-founder of Ramsey with Earl Æthelwin, and acted as abbot until his death. In 991, after the dedication of the new church of Ramsey, the bishop and earl presided, and Oswald addressed the monks, 'ecce pater vester dominus aldermannus et ego . . . patronali vobis vice praesidentes' (*Chron. Ramsey*, pp. 98-9;

and some had influence in individual houses.[1] There was also a tendency in Edward's reign, noticeable too in Germany about the same time, for bishops to impropriate monasteries – collect abbacies.[2] But all these relationships were based on proprietary rather than canonical rights.

The bishops were not only hindered by a proprietary pattern, they were also handicapped by the scarcity of institutions or agents of government. In England there was a dangerously wide gap between the bishops and the parish priest. There was a kind of institutional hierarchy in the dioceses, the legacy of the history of the English church, in that the 'old minsters', the ancient and large foundations served by a body of priests, had rights which transcended the newer parish boundaries; and these could, in a way, serve as secondary cathedrals. Certainly in East Anglia, besides the see at Elmham, Hoxne was maintained as a centre for Suffolk,[3] and in the diocese of York the great minsters at Beverley and Southwell functioned as the religious capitals of the East Riding and the district of Nottingham respectively. It is probable that they were centres for the distribution of chrism,[4] but of other administrative functions we know nothing.

There would seem always to be a need for occasional diocesan synods to deal with local church problems. Archbishop Wulfstan in his writings takes them for granted.[5] And some were certainly held in the dioceses of Worcester

cf. pp. 100, 104–6). But after Oswald's death in 992 the first abbot was ordained, who is said to have reserved his obedience to the bishop of Dorchester (*ibid.* p. 110).

[1] Most monastic bishops kept closely in touch with their old houses. Nunneries as a class were possibly under the closer supervision of the diocesan. Certainly Herman of Ramsbury took a great interest in Wilton (*Vita Ædwardi*, pp. 94 ff.); but Herman was a protégé of Queen Edith, who, as queen, was the patron of nunneries and, because of her education at Wilton, specially concerned with that community.

[2] A Hauck, *Kirchengeschichte Deutschlands*, iii. 728–9. In England Archbishop Stigand was the most notorious collector of monasteries (above, p. 78); but Archbishop Ealdred had Winchcombe and St Peter's Gloucester (above, p. 88, *n.* 5). Bishop Herman of Ramsbury, however, was successfully resisted when he attempted to annex Malmesbury (above, p. 82). Secular minsters were in every bishop's hands.

[3] Whitelock, *Wills*, nos. 1, 26; *DB*, ii. 379a, *VCH Suffolk*, i. 515: 'In hoc manerio est ecclesia sedes episcopatus de Sudfolc T.R.E.'

[4] Cf. F. Barlow, *Durham Jurisdictional Peculiars*, p. xiv, *n.* 2. It may be significant that Bishop Wulfstan of Worcester, on his way to bless chrism for Archbishop Thomas at York and perform other *episcopalia*, is found at Nottingham, *Vita Wulfstani*, p. 44.

[5] 'Canons enacted under King Edgar', cc. 3–6: Thorpe, *Ancient Laws*, ii. 245–6. They were expected to issue decrees and last for three days. Cf. also 'Ecclesiastical Institutes' (= Theodulf', *capitula*), *ibid.* ii. 404. In Wulfstan's chapter on Priests in his 'Institutes of Polity': *Polity*, p. 176 the archbishop writes that the priests will assemble at some time every year for their common need; cf. also 'Ecclesiastical Institutes', c. xxviii: Thorpe, ii. 424. See Lingard, *Antiquities*, i. 106–9.

and York in the eleventh century. Ealdwulf, bishop of both sees, held a synod in Worcestershire to discuss the matter of St Oswald's translation.[1] The *Law of the Northumbrian Priests* supposes regular meetings at York.[2] Ealdred of York held a synod and issued decrees shortly before the Conquest,[3] and St Wulfstan of Worcester, although the evidence is for after the Conquest, did likewise.[4] After the year 1002 a monk of Ramsey had a vision of St Ives presiding at a synod and, in the fashion of synods, the seats rose in tiers, divided into their ranks and benches.[5] This ideal pattern of the hierarchical order can hardly have been seen in England; and it is doubtful whether diocesan synods were a regular feature in the English church in the half-century before the Conquest.[6] But, as there are few records from the secular sees, it would be unwise to hold that such meetings were quite unusual. All the same, it is likely that the bishop met his parish clergy most often at the shire court, and that, just as some of the meetings of the king's court could be regarded as 'national' church synods, so the shire court, under the earl and bishop, or bishop and sheriff, could take on some of the characteristics of a diocesan synod. Certainly it was there that the bishop proclaimed and enforced the royal ecclesiastical laws.[7] In England mixed forms seem general from top to bottom.

Little progress, therefore, was being made in organizing episcopal administration. The monastic or quasi monastic constitutions of some of the sees and the appointment of monks to bishoprics may have had a retarding influence. Monastic bishops were more likely to rely on the spiritual help of some of the brethren than to organize a diocesan administration. Characteristic of a rather primitive attitude to government is the employment of *chorepiscopi*, usual at Canterbury and occasional elsewhere.[8] These domestic

---

[1] *c.* 1000, 'Deinde Wigornenses conveniens quos summa causa, quos tenor negotii praecipue respiciebat, sua et illorum voluntas atque consilium an in eodem esset, diligenter perscrutatus est': Eadmer, *Mirac. S. Oswaldi, HCY*, ii. 47.

[2] Cf. cc. 4, 6, 44, Liebermann, *Gesetze*, i. 380, 382, *EHD*, i. 435, 437.

[3] Fulcard, *Vita S. Johannis, HCY*, i. 241, cf. *Vita Ædwardi*, pp. liii ff.

[4] *Vita Wulfstani*, p. 53; *Anglia Sacra*, i. 542.

[5] Goscelin, *Mirac. S. Ivonis, Chron. Ramsey*, p. lxv.

[6] Cf. Council of London (1075), 'Et quia multis retro annis in Anglico regno usus conciliorum obsoleverat, renovata sunt nonnulla quae antiquis etiam canonibus noscuntur definita': Wilkins, *Concilia*, i. 363-5.

[7] See above, pp. 146 ff. and Lingard, *Antiquities*, i. 101-3.

[8] There was usually a bishop of St Martin's, Canterbury; and, according to Canterbury tradition he was between the pontificates of Theodore and Lanfranc a substitute for an archdeacon, *Fragmentum de institutione Archidiaconatus Cantuariensis, Anglia Sacra*, i. 150. The bishop of

bishops had been discarded in most provinces of the western church,[1] and their retention in England reveals the old-fashioned view that there were no ranks between the bishop and the priest.

The real key to pure ecclesiastical government, the use of archdeacons,[2] was rather neglected in England, possibly because the tenth-century reformers had encouraged the bishops themselves to minister to their flocks. There is no reference to archdeacons in the royal laws; but the development of the office may have come after Cnut's codes, for there is good evidence for the existence of an archhdeacon, even if he was only the bishop's personal assistant, in several sees. As the rule of St Chrodegang required the appointment of an archdeacon, it may be presumed that they existed at London, Wells, Hereford, and Exeter. In fact Edward, archdeacon of London, became a monk at Canterbury after the Conquest.[3] There were also archdeacons at Winchester before 1066.[4]

The best evidence for the active employment of archdeacons comes from the dioceses of Worcester and York, which were held together by St Oswald (972–92) and by some of his able successors. Worcester tradition, as stated by a commission appointed in 1092 by Bishop Wulfstan,[5] but tainted by the priory's claim to a peculiar,[6] was that archdeacons and rural deans had existed in the diocese at least from Oswald's day, for the saint had freed the monastic churches from their interference. Wulfstan's recognitors, mostly Englishmen, including his archdeacon Ailric and the archdeacon's brother, Edwin, both possibly monks, claimed to have first-hand knowledge of conditions under Bishop Ealdred (1046–62). Wulfstan, who confirmed their findings, had lived all his life in the diocese and had started his ecclesiastical career

St Germans seems to have been subordinate to the bishop of Crediton in the tenth century, H. P. R. Finberg, 'Sherborne, Glastonbury, and the expansion of Wessex', *Trans. R. Hist. Soc.*, 5th ser., iii (1953), 118–22. Ealdred abbot of Tavistock may have been Lyfing's deputy in Worcester before 1046 when, on Lyfing's death, he became full bishop: Finberg, *Tavistock Abbey* (1951), p. 4. And Ealdred, when archbishop of York, treated St Wulfstan of Worcester as a 'chorepiscopus': *Vita Wulfstani*, pp. 19–20, *HCY*, ii. 348. When blind, Bishop Æthelstan of Hereford employed a Welsh bishop, Tramerin: *ASC CD* 1055. For Bishop 'Begard', see F. E. Harmer, 'A Bromfield and a Coventry Writ of King Edward the Confessor', *The Anglo-Saxons*, ed. Peter Clemoes (1959), p. 94.

[1] Cf. Feine, *op. cit.* i. 166, 170. The Isidorian reformers were hostile to them: cf. Fournier and Le Bras, i. 132.   [2] Feine, i. 170–2, 182–5.

[3] See above, p. 220.

[4] Barlow, Biddle, von Feilitzen and Keene, *Winchester in the Early Middle Ages* (1976), p. 58 (no. 176); cf. p. 64 (no. 242).

[5] *Acta Synodi apud Wigorniam anno MXCII*, *Anglia Sacra*, i. 542–3. See also above, p. 204.

[6] See above, p. 241, and below, pp. 252–3.

under Bishop Brihtheah (1033–8). Evidence for York comes from the *Law of the Northumbrian Priests*, a code attributed to the senior Bishop Wulfstan (Worcester, 1002–16; York, 1002–23), Brihtheah's uncle. According to this source an archdeacon was working as the agent of the bishop, holding synods and having disciplinary powers over the lower clergy which included suspension from office.[1] It should also be noticed that Archbishop Ealdred's deacon, a namesake, and so possibly a kinsman, was important enough to be granted the church of Axminster with sake and soke by King Edward as a benefaction to St Peter's, York.[2]

In view of these facts the Worcester tradition cannot be entirely devoid of truth. Either Oswald or Wulfstan I could easily have established archdeacons. The former had been educated at Fleury and was open to continental influence, the latter was familiar with continental canonical literature.[3] Both were reformers, and both were faced with the need to provide subordinates to act during their absences from one or the other of their dioceses. And it may well be that the reform was of necessity developed farther at York.[4] We do not have to believe that rural deans had the same history. In 1092 men might be excused for thinking that if there were archdeacons there must have been deans. But nothing can be produced in support of the idea.

When the governmental activity of the bishops was small, the operations of their subordinates must have been even smaller. It is significant that in the biography of St Wulfstan very little is heard of his archdeacon. We know only that he was sent ahead to announce the bishop's arrival in the parishes.[5] It is unlikely that the archdeacon normally had jurisdictional powers. He may well have administered the ordeal in the public courts.[6] Worcester tradition seems to associate him with the collection of the episcopal customs from churches.[7] If he was, in fact, except in the remote and enormous diocese of York, little more than the bishop's chief deacon, a personal servant who performed such occasional services as the bishop

[1] cc. 6–7, Liebermann, *Gesetze*, i. 380; *EHD*, i. 435.   [2] Harmer, *Writs*, no. 120.
[3] E.g. with the *Institutio Canonicorum* of the council of Aachen, 817, c. viii, which deals with the disciplinary powers of the archdeacon: *Enlarged Rule of Chrodegang*, ed. A. S. Napier, EETS, 150 (1916), pp. 16–17.
[4] At York the memory of the activities of the deacon James may have been helpful.
[5] *Vita Wulfstani*, p. 51. He built a church on one of his estates: *ibid.* pp. xxxv–xxxvi. Sir Ivor Atkins, 'The Church of Worcester from the eighth to the twelfth century', *The Antiquaries Journal*, xx (1940), 37–8, maintains that Ailric was a Worcester monk.
[6] Cf. William I's writ of *c.* 1072, c. 2: Liebermann, *Gesetze*, i. 485.
[7] 'Omnes ecclesiasticas consuetudines prior sicut summus decanus episcopi pro suis ecclesiis episcopo persolvat': *Acta Synodi MXCII*, p. 543.

required, it would not be rash to think that most bishops had such an official.[1] But it would be going against the evidence to hold that the archdeacon was generally of constitutional importance in this period. He had not acquired a separate competence or ordinary powers. After 1070 his office would develop for a time with the widening authority of his master, and then each would go his own way.

If there were few well-developed institutions of government in the English church there were some surprisingly vital voluntary organizations. Anglo-Saxon society was rich in gilds of various kinds,[2] and among them we find gilds of priests. These were organized for mutual benefit and protection, and were governed by rules which set professional standards. They may be regarded as an ecclesiastical variety of the tithings and hundreds, and it is possible that orders in the royal laws for the expulsion of criminous clerks from 'the fellowship of those in holy orders', and for their providing surety for their good behaviour in the future, refer to such gilds.[3] The statutes of the gild of priests at York have been preserved.[4] All members are to co-operate, with the help of the bishop, to obtain compensation due to any member who has been injured.[5] Each is to provide himself with twelve sureties that he will observe the rules.[6] And the rules are protected by fines payable to the bishop or, occasionally, the archdeacon, who can be regarded as an ecclesiastical reeve. If such gilds existed in every diocese the need for more official organization would have been reduced. But we have evidence for their existence only at Canterbury,[7] Winchester,[8] and York.

By the twelfth century there were all kinds of 'peculiars' in the English church, that is to say, disturbances in the diocesan organization due to the

---

[1] Makower, para. 38, p. 307, hazarded, 'Towards the end of the Anglo-Saxon period there was, as a rule, one archdeacon appointed in every diocese'; see also para. 42, pp. 316–17. Ælfric in his *Glossary*, p. 299, lists 'archidiaconus = ercediacon'. For Leofsige, deacon in Lindsey, who had been a married nobleman and who eventually with his wife and son took monastic vows, see *Chron. Ramsey*, pp. 153–4. It is not impossible that Leofsige was Bishop Eadnoth II's deacon in Lindsey.   [2] Thorpe, *Diplomatarium*, pt. III; *EHD*, i. 557 ff.

[3] VIII Æthelred, 27; I Cnut, 5.3; cf. *Law of the Northumbrian priests*, c. 45. Wulfstan's 'Canons enacted under King Edgar', Thorpe, *Ancient Laws*, ii. 244 ff., seem to assume that priests were organized in gilds: cf. cc. 7, 9.

[4] *Law of the Northumbrian Priests*, Liebermann, *Gesetze*, i. 380–5; *EHD*, i. 434–9. Chapters 1–45 (less, perhaps, 19–24) are properly the priest's laws.   [5] c. 1.   [6] c. 2.3.

[7] In Canterbury '32 mansuras quas tenent clerici de villa in gildam suam': *DB*, i. 3 a i. But W. Urry, *Canterbury under the Angevin Kings*, p. 125, suggests that these are the canons of St Gregory.

[8] The ealdorman Æthelmaer left money to the gild of the priests and the gild of the deacons at Winchester, 971–83: Whitelock, *Wills*, no. 10.

importance of the patrons (formerly proprietors) of some of the individual churches.[1] A bishop's churches within the diocese of another were usually privileged. Within his own diocese his own churches and those of the cathedral chapter were specially administered. Some monasteries enjoyed exemptions of varying degree. In the twelfth and thirteenth centuries these franchises were still in a relatively plastic state. There was much dispute and litigation over area and the privileges enjoyed, and the many compromises led to the constitutional stability of the later Middle Ages.

The fundamental strand in most of these franchises was a proprietary attitude towards ecclesiastical property: the rights of landlords were opposed to those of office-holders. In a way, therefore, their history goes back far beyond the Norman Conquest. But recognizable franchises are the answer to government, and their changing form in the twelfth century was due to changes in diocesan administration. As the bishop's government developed so did the counter-claims of the immunist. Hence, if peculiars as such existed before the Conquest, something more rudimentary must be looked for. It can be assumed that they would be more general in scope, more expressive of landlordship, more financial than jurisdictional in nature. It can also be accepted that if there was a need for franchises in the Anglo-Saxon period they would have existed. There was nothing in the polity which hindered irregularity. Indeed, there were many factors which encouraged it. Anglo-Saxon conditions were suitable for the development of any kind of franchise. The only question is whether there was sufficient irritant in an organization completely informed by privilege – a church which was the sum of a number of relatively passive immunities – to produce a contrast between areas of ordinary and peculiar government.

The privileged position of a bishop's churches within the diocese of another expresses a simple principle which is valid at all times, and in some instances can certainly be traced back to the Anglo-Saxon kingdom. It is known that the archbishop of Canterbury enjoyed this right in several dioceses, and the bishop of Durham probably in the diocese of York.[2] It may well have been a general rule, and Edward's grant of the rank of a diocesan bishop to that great pluralist, his servant Regenbald,[3] may have conferred a useful ecclesiastical franchise.

As a bishop could satisfy all the requirements of his churches, those lying outside his own diocese often became recognized as detached parts of

[1] F. Barlow, *Durham Jurisdictional Peculiars.*   [2] *Ibid.* pp. 53 ff.
[3] Harmer, *Writs,* no. 44.

it. So it was at Canterbury.[1] The Anglo-Saxon position, which may not
have been so legally precise, is illustrated well by the correspondence between
Archbishop Anselm and Bishop Wulfstan of Worcester in 1094. The bishop
of London had objected to Anselm's dedication of the archbishop's church
at Harrow.[2] Anselm claimed, on general testimony, that archbishops of
Canterbury had always had the dignity, right, and custom, and had long
possessed it without challenge, to exercise all episcopal rights, namely dedication and everything else, within any vill or church belonging to the archbishop as archbishop of Canterbury, in whosesoever diocese it lay. And he
quoted Lanfranc's and Dunstan's peaceful possession of the right.[3] Wulfstan
confirmed Canterbury's claims. He believed that no one had ever before
questioned the exercise of this right in the archbishop's private churches
(*propriae ecclesiae*). Anselm's predecessor Stigand had obtained churches in
the diocese of Worcester by secular grant, and had dedicated these in
Wulfstan's time and before without reference to the diocesan bishop. There
had been no opposition since it was recognized as a special power of the
metropolitan bishop. Wulfstan knew of no litigation on this point of law, and
he thought that the archbishop had the right in any diocese.[4] Anselm apparently received similar testimony from other bishops and maintained his
peculiars intact. It may be inferred that before the Conquest a bishop, if he
wished, could exercise *episcopalia* within his proprietary churches wherever
situated. But the imprecision of Wulfstan's statement of the law should be
noticed. He implies that Canterbury's was a metropolitan privilege, although
in fact Stigand's metropolitan status was doubtful. He was giving a faulty
and specious ecclesiastical justification for what in his heart he recognized
had been the right of an episcopal proprietor.

The privileged position of a bishop's churches within his own diocese – a
domestic arrangement by which the bishop kept the ordinary diocesan
officials out of his own property – does not make sense until the diocese had

---

[1] Irene Churchill, *Canterbury Administration*, i. 62 ff.

[2] Eadmer, *Historia Novorum*, pp. 45–7.

[3] 'semper archiepiscopus Cantuariae hanc habuit potestatem et consuetudinem, ut intra
cuiuscumque episcopi diocesim haberet ecclesia Cantuariae villam aut ecclesiam, eiusdem archiepiscopi proprii iuris esset quidquid de eadem villa vel ecclesia pertineret ad episcopale officium,
sive dedicatio sive aliquid aliud': *S. Anselmi Opera Omnia*, ed. F. S. Schmitt, ep. 170, iv (1949),
51–2.

[4] 'nullus aliquando exstitit, qui . . . ne dedicationem propriarum dumtaxat ecclesiarum publice
faceret defenderet. . . . utpote hanc specialem potestatem eiusdem metropolitani episcopi esse':
ibid. ep. 171, iv. 52–3.

a fixed administration from which the bishop wanted to be free. Although we may be certain that the churches of an Old-English bishop were separately administered, it may be that the position was the reverse of that which obtained in the twelfth century: that instead of the archdeacons and rural deans being excluded from the bishop's estates in favour of peculiar officials, those estates were the one area to which his subordinates had free access. In other words, the episcopal estates were the only area of ordinary administration.

The peculiars possessed by most cathedral chapters and some monasteries were often regarded by the thirteenth century as forming private archdeaconries. That is to say, while rarely hindering the bishop as ordinary, they excluded the archdeacon and rural deans. Ecclesiastically they were similar to the bishop's peculiar jurisdictions, and, in the case of the chapters, had the equitable justification that they were enjoyed by an associate in the government of the diocese. In some ways they were the ecclesiastical counterpart to the private hundred; and, since the parish of the old minsters was usually coterminous with a hundred or group of hundreds, franchises may sometimes represent the persistence of old parish rights despite episcopal centralization. Old parishes, or hundreds, were often reorganized as rural deaneries, and the ecclesiastical owners of such ancient jurisdictions may have felt that they should accordingly enjoy private deaneries. As secular immunities, including the private hundred, were common in the Anglo-Saxon period, the existence of ecclesiastical liberties is to be expected. But since the archdeacon had not then those powers which he acquired after the Conquest, and the presence of rural deans is doubtful, they cannot have been directed quite so purposefully as later against those officials. The most explicit, but unfortunately unreliable, evidence for a capitular franchise comes, as might be expected, from one of the most actively administered dioceses – Worcester. In 1092 the commission of inquiry set up by Bishop Wulfstan, some of whose findings have already been discussed, reported that Bishop Oswald granted to Wynsige, whom he made prior of the community *c.* 972, and to all Wynsige's successors, that the priors of Worcester were to be deans over all the monastery's churches and priests, so that no dean or archdeacon should take action concerning the churches or clerks of the monks except through the prior. And the prior, acting as the bishop's chief dean (or, in the same way as the bishop's chief dean),[1] was to pay the ecclesiastical customs due from his churches directly to the bishop.

---

[1] See above, p. 248, *n.* 7. The title 'prior' is anachronistic: 'provost' is more likely than 'dean'.

The story cannot be believed in detail. It was part of a case which the monastery was assembling in order to secure, or regain, an independent share in all the franchises enjoyed by the church of Worcester – one of the three hundreds of Oswaldslow and similarly part of the church's estates with the privileges which pertained to them. To strengthen the case against the bishop the date of Wynsige's appointment as prior was falsified and some documents were tampered with.[1] It is likely that Wynsige was made prior when Oswald became archbishop of York and felt the need to provide for the subordinate government of the monastery; and although it may well be that Oswald gave him some other rights at the same time, these can hardly have been those specified in the story. Nor need the grant have been in full legal form. It is possible that the separation of powers between bishop and prior developed gradually or spasmodically according to the habits of the several bishops of Worcester – pluralist and absentee bishops giving the prior a relatively free hand – and that it was St Wulfstan's attempt to put back the clock, to achieve the ideal of a true bishop-abbot, which caused the monastery to try to give legal form to privileges which had been informal and had existed on the weak basis of tolerance and prescription.

The negative franchise claimed by the monks in 1092 – freedom for their churches from the interference of archdeacons and (rural) deans – is almost certainly anachronistic for 972. The positive franchise – that just as the archdeacon collected the bishop's financial customs from the episcopal churches, so the prior collected them (but not for retention) from the monastery's churches – is, even if it does not owe its origin to Oswald, less objectionable. It is a small privilege. The key to the whole situation, its origin and fluctuations, is probably to be found in the term *decanus*. The multiplicity of meanings of this word – dean of a chapter (prior of a monastery), deacon, archdeacon, and rural dean, to mention those relevant – not only can cause difficulty of interpretation now, but could lead to the perversion of a tradition. It may well be that Wynsige was given a 'deanery' both over the monastery and over the monastery's churches. But exactly what such a deanery implied at the time and subsequently cannot be told. In some ways the story is reminiscent of what happened at Durham *c.* 1093, when Bishop William of St Calais, who had replaced the clerks of St Cuthbert by monks, proclaimed the new prior, Turgot, archdeacon or dean in the diocese.[2] This

[1] Eric John, 'An alleged Worcester charter of the reign of Edgar', *BJRL*, xli (1958), 54–80.
[2] F. Barlow, *Durham Jurisdictional Peculiars*, p. 3 and *n.*

event became later part of the monastic case for an archdeaconry covering the monks' churches within the diocese. In both the Worcester and Durham instances, although separated by a century, the bishop's intention may have been basically the same – to give the prior a share in the government of the diocese. As time passed that share had often to be defined anew owing to the changing pattern of the diocesan government.

It would not be surprising if the greater monasteries enjoyed franchises covering their parishes similar to those possessed by the bishops' chapters. Abbots were important and their possession of hundreds accustomed them to regional government. But their ecclesiastical franchises were more vulnerable than the capitular, for they conflicted with the ancient view of the bishop's ordinary powers, and they were liable to summary suppression in any period when the bishop strove to reform diocesan administration.

In general, therefore, the disorders in the Anglo-Saxon church were not of serious consequence. There was a relaxation of government typical of the age rather than a formal dispersal of legal rights. The malady could be cured whenever the bishops, conscious of their powers and inspired by new ideals, exerted themselves to create a purer ecclesiastical administration and to apply more stringently the principles of canon law. English conditions were remarkable only in detail.

CHAPTER V

Ecclesiastical Jurisdiction

The reforming bishops of the middle of the tenth century had influenced the English kings to support their crusade. Royal laws and secular penalties had furthered their programme; and, since the bishops were important among the king's *witan* and presided with the earl or sheriff in the shire courts, the contemporary view of the world, in which the king, as the servant of Christ, sat enthroned in majesty above the twin hierarchies, was realized more completely perhaps than anywhere else in western Christendom. Yet there was always the temptation to conflate. As Æthelred's charter of 984 proclaimed,[1] 'The hierarch of the heavenly kingdom has widely divided the copious gifts of his bounty among divers ranks, among kings, bishops, princes, abbots, and reeves, so that each, in his turn and with no holding back, should on the day of reckoning make a two-fold render for the talent delivered to him for trading on the earth.'

The distinction between Church and State, the clergy and the laity, was not at its starkest in the Anglo-Saxon period, for it was but one among many social divisions. An elaborate caste system, with appropriate laws and values attached to the different ranks of men, could easily comprehend the various classes of the clergy. Clerical privilege was unremarkable in a society ruled by privilege.[2] And even though church leaders were professionally aware that the church was separate from the world, in practice they were unwilling to push the theory too hard. One of the questions put to Archbishop Egbert [3] – 'If a layman kills a clerk or a monk, should the blood price reckoned according to the law of his natural parents be paid to his kinsmen, or should a larger sum be paid to his ecclesiastical superiors?' – reveals the conflict of laws. And the archbishop's answer, which is not entirely to the point, embodies a compromise in favour of the church: 'A layman who kills a bishop,

---

[1] K. 1281.

[2] Cf. 'And we enjoin that no high-born priest despise the lower-born, because, if it be rightly considered, then are all men of one birth': Wulfstan's 'Canons enacted under King Edgar', 13, Thorpe, *Ancient Laws*, ii. 247.

[3] The dialogue of Egbert (732/66), qu. xii, Haddan and Stubbs, *Councils*, iii. 408–9.

priest, deacon, or monk should perform the appropriate penance and pay the proper ecclesiastical blood price to his church . . . unless the dignity of the slain man's birth or the nobility of his stock should require a higher price. For it is not just that holy service in a higher Order should be penalized by the loss of what would have been due according to kinship law for a secular life in the lay habit.' In other words, the church would take the compensation (*had–bot*) calculated according to his clerical or secular rank, whichever was the greater.

When justice was very much the application of the appropriate tariff of compensation, the church's interest lay more in the maintenance of the correct scale for its members and in the proper destination of the penalties than in private courts of law. Yet the desire to secure the monetary compensation, the necessity to traverse or supplement the rights of a clerk's kinsmen, did push the church in the direction of claiming its own justice. Another question put to Egbert illustrates this point. He was asked,[1] if, when monks were guilty of sexual vice, the penalty for the crime should go to the secular kinsmen, and answered, going beyond the question:

No part of the penalty due from those within the church who commit either grave or light offences pertains to those outside the church, especially since the Apostle says all ecclesiastical cases ought to be settled by the priests. If indeed ecclesiastical persons commit any crime among laymen, such as homicide, fornication, or theft, then they are completely at the mercy of the secular persons against whom they have sinned, unless they shall have a mind to make satisfaction to the church for these matters. But laymen who fornicate with nuns shall not atone in the way that the public law ordains for the punishment of fornicators, but pay double, that is, the adulterers shall pay 60 silver coins to the church, for graver cases need graver and harsher cures.

Thus Egbert lays down three principles: when a cleric offends/sins against a cleric, the penalty goes to the church; when a clerk offends/sins against a layman, the penalty normally goes to the layman; and when a layman offends/sins against a clerical person, a special heavy penalty goes to the church. Also he claims ecclesiastical jurisdiction over the first type of case.[2]

The intervention of the state in church affairs and the participation of the bishops in secular business should not obscure the purely ecclesiastical

---

[1] Qu. viii, *ibid.* pp. 406–7.

[2] Cf. also *Confessionale Ps.–Egberti*, c. xxiii (Wasserschleben, p. 310): 'Si quis episcopum vel presbyterum occiderit, id ad regis judicium pertinet vel episcopi. Quicunque sacerdotem vel monachum occiderit, id est juris episcopi utrum arma deponat et in monasterium eat an VII annos jejunet'; c. xxiv: 'Si quis patrem suum vel matrem suam, sororem vel fratrem, filium vel filiam occiderit, id est juris episcopi; nonnulli volunt ut X annos in terra peregrina poeniteat.'

activity of the prelates. The jurisdiction of the church was not regarded as residuary. The law of Christ was pre-eminent. And the helping hand which the king held forth was not intended to restrict the moral responsibility of prelates.[1] What is more, although church and state spoke formally with the same voice about sin and crime, and a homilist like Ælfric had no doubt that most robbers would rightly both be led to death in chains and also go to the torments of Hell, and recognized that temporal death was the robber's due even if he repented and cried to God for mercy 'before the sharp sword swayed to his neck',[2] the church's concern with penitence and absolution introduced complications which hindered the administration of justice.[3] The confessional took more account of circumstances than did a court of law. Penitent criminals could be an embarrassment to confessors. And the church sometimes hesitated before the inflexible brutality of secular penalties.[4] This difference in outlook is illustrated well by an incident at Durham about 1060.[5]

Tostig, earl of Northumbria, was working hard to reduce that anarchical province to order, and his ferocious, if impartial, justice was renowned.[6] On this occasion he had succeeded in arresting a man named Aldan-hamal, a malefactor notorious for theft, robbery, murder, and arson. The criminal was condemned to death, despite attempts by kinsmen and friends to bribe the earl; and while in fetters at Durham awaiting execution, when all efforts at rescue had failed, his conscience was smitten, he repented of his crimes, and he promised St Cuthbert that if he could go free he would make full atonement. St Cuthbert heard his prayer, struck off his fetters, and allowed him to make a lucky escape into the church. The guards, under Tostig's thegn Barcwith, went in pursuit and considered breaking open the doors of the cathedral, for freedom of sanctuary, they thought, would allow all thieves, robbers, and murderers to laugh in their faces. But Barcwith was immediately struck down by heaven for his impiety and within an hour or two died

---

[1] Cf. Wulfstan's 'Edward and Guthrum', 3, 4. Liebermann, *Gesetze*, i. 130–1.

[2] *Lives of the Saints*, i. 424–7.

[3] Cf. 'Cum omne crimen atque peccatum oblatis Deo sacrificiis deleatur . . .': Burchard, *Decretum*, V, i; cf. v.

[4] Wulfstan of York limited the scope of the death penalty in the royal codes for which he was responsible. See K. Jost, *Wulfstanstudien*, pp. 25–6, 38–41.

[5] *Historia translationum S. Cuthberti*, c. v, ed. Hodgson Hindle, Surtees Soc., li (1868), 168–70. Cf. also Symeon, *HDE*, p. 95. Ælfric, however, who tells similar stories (from Lantfred) about a bondwoman condemned to be flogged and a fettered serf, both freed by St Swithun, is careful to make the point that the one was guilty of a very slight fault and the other only of carelessness (*Lives of the Saints*, i. 452–3, 466–7). Cf. the miraculous healing of the innocent man unjustly mutilated for theft (*ibid.* pp. 458–9). [6] *Vita Ædwardi*, p. 51.

raving mad; and Earl Tostig, terrified by his fate, pardoned the criminal and, later, held him in esteem. The other guards made rich expiatory offerings on the tomb of St Cuthbert which were used to adorn a cross and a New Testament with gold and silver and jewels, and so produce memorials of the event which were carefully preserved in the monastery as a warning to others. There are hints in the story that Aldan-hamal was reformed. For the church saving a soul was more important than doing justice on a criminal, and sanctuary involved such fundamental ecclesiastical rights [1] and aroused such deep feelings that no man could violate it with impunity.

In theory [2] the bishop punished his clergy for breaches of discipline and the laity for infractions of the moral code. He had also acquired jurisdiction over marriages and some interest in wills. But the tendency was for the bishop to abandon jurisdiction over the non-noble classes of laity to the priests and, where they existed, the archdeacons, except for certain grave offences. The ultimate weapon of his jurisdiction was the anathema,[3] which corresponded to the lay outlawry, except that excommunication did not entail complete expulsion from the church, owing to the belief in the indelible nature of baptism. It entailed temporary or permanent loss of church rights and, by the eleventh century, could take various forms, usually expressed in the form of an interdict. For a priest the chief punishment was always loss of office, ranging in severity from degradation to temporary suspension. For a repentant layman there were the penances of differing severity and duration, calculated according to a tariff.

The influence of Germanic custom on ecclesiastical penalties was considerable. It was no less influential on the legal procedure of the church. The church administered the various ordeals in all types of court, including its own, for the laity. But probably more characteristic of the church courts was the Germanic clearing oath, the solemn oath taken by the accused, with or without helpers, according to a tariff of compurgation.

Little illustration can be given of the activities of the ecclesiastical courts in this period. We know from the penitentials, the canonical decrees and pastoral letters of bishops, the homilies, and the royal ecclesiastical laws

---

[1] Lingard, *Antiquities*, i. 273-7. For sanctuary at Wilton nunnery, see *Vita Edithe*, pp. 272-3, 293. [2] Feine, *Kirchliche Rechtsgeschichte*, i. 179 ff.

[3] Formulae are in Liebermann, *Gesetze*, i. 432 ff. A form used by the bishop of St Germans, Cornwall, is in *The Lanalet Pontifical*, ed. G. H. Doble, HBS, lxxiv (1937), 130-1. See also T. P. Oakley, *English penitential discipline and Anglo-Saxon law in their joint influence* (New York, 1923), pp. 86 ff.

what sins and derelictions of duty among the clergy and laity caused the authorities most concern, and we can reconstruct the probable course of events. But concrete examples are hard to find.

Most cases must have been dealt with through the *forum internum*, the confessional. The penitent sinner confessed and performed his penance. Public and unrepentant sinners, however, were presumably first admonished from the pulpit or, occasionally, by the bishop in synod.[1] If they refused to submit, then excommunication would follow. Defiant excommunicates would be constrained by the lay power to stand trial at the shire court, and there, if found guilty, they would receive an ecclesiastical penalty, and sometimes a secular penalty as well, at the discretion of the episcopal judge. The greatest gap in our knowledge is with contentious jurisdiction. One cause of our ignorance must be its relatively small amount. There had not yet started that lively litigation between ecclesiastical persons and corporations which was later to be the mainstay of the ecclesiastical courts. There can have been few if any disputes over jurisdiction, exemption, and status. The monastic chronicles are not yet chronicles of lawsuits. Disputes over land and revenues were probably heard in the ordinary way in the shire courts, although, in Wulfstan's canons, it was enacted that no dispute between priests was to be referred to the judgment of secular men, but was to be settled among themselves or, if necessary, by the bishop.[2] Probably the only contentious cases involving laymen which concerned the bishop were matrimonial and testamentary, and even these could hardly have required a formal ecclesiastical court. When land could be left by will, nullity and bastardy suits must have been infrequent; and it is likely that most matrimonial disputes were more matters for the confessional than cases requiring a definitive judgment. Testamentary cases, on the other hand, are likely to have been heard by the bishop in the shire court. Witnesses were necessary and a public judgment was desirable.

The sins to which the laws drew special attention were heathenism and the various forms of witchcraft, sexual offences, murder, and the breaking of oaths.[3] The legislation concerning heathenism begins with V Æthelred (1008)

---

[1] 'And we enjoin that every priest declare in the synod if, in his confessional district, he know any man contumacious to God, or miserably sunk in deadly sins, whom he cannot incline to *bot*, or dare not for wordly opinion': Wulfstan's 'Canons enacted under King Edgar', c. 6, cf. 5, Thorpe, *Ancient Laws*, ii. 245–6.   [2] c. 7, *ibid*. ii. 247.

[3] Cf. Cnut's proclamation of 1020, cc. 14–15: bishops abhor the violation of oaths and pledges, parricide, murder, perjury, witchcraft, sorcery, adultery, and incest.

c. 1, and it is likely that the Scandinavian invasions had led to a dilution of Christian belief and practice which became even more alarming when new Viking settlers had to be accommodated. Certainly the legislation reached its climax in II Cnut (1020–3), where detailed information is given about heathen customs.[1] Not unexpectedly, the *Law of the Northumbrian Priests*, cc. 48–54, and 'Edward and Guthrum', c. 2.2, also pay attention to the subject. A recrudescence of witchcraft may have been due to the same causes. The special concern of the reformers was black magic and murder.[2] In primitive societies no death is natural, and the partial barbarization of society due to the Viking wars and conquest seems to have led to increased belief in the dark forces. It is, perhaps, significant that a *cause célèbre* of the period concerns Danes charged with witchcraft and secret killing.[3] But characteristic of England, there was no need to legislate against heresy.

The campaign against unlawful marriages was an original part of the reformers' programme, and the most famous case occurred before the renewal of the Viking attacks.[4] But it is possible that the looseness of the marriage tie among the Danes[5] explains the spate of legislation about marriage and incest. Dunstan had attacked irregular marriages,[6] but the first detailed decrees are in VI Æthelred (for the province of York, 1008), repeated in I Cnut.[7] Monogamy is enjoined, marriage within six degrees prohibited, and marriage with spiritual relations, nuns, or divorced women proscribed. Adultery and unchastity are forbidden for men as for women. Whores are to be banished.[8] Priests are to be celibate.[9] Other sins mentioned by name in the laws are covetousness and greed, gluttony and intemperance,[10] frauds and deceits such as false weights and measures,[11] perjuries such as lying evidence and breaches of oaths and pledges,[12] and those crimes the church abhorred, murder, homicide, theft and robbery, and sacrilege.[13]

---

[1] c. 5. Cf. also Wulfstan's 'Canons enacted under King Edgar', cc. 16–18, Thorpe, *Ancient Laws*, ii. 249.

[2] *Law of the Northumbrian Priests*, c. 48; I Edmund, 6, VI Æthelred, 7, II Cnut, 4a–5.

[3] Below, p. 273.   [4] Dunstan and the illegal marriage of a thegn; see below, p. 300.

[5] Cf. above, pp. 172–3.

[6] Auct. B, *Memorials of St Dunstan*, p. 49; Adelard, *ibid.* p. 67; Osbern, *ibid.* p. 106.

[7] VI Æthelred, 11–12, I Cnut, 7; cf. also I Edmund, 4, V Æthelred, 10, Cnut, 1020, cc. 16–17.

[8] VI Æthelred, 7, II Cnut, 4a.

[9] I Edmund, 1, IV Edgar, 1, 7, V Æthelred, 9, VI Æthelred, 3–5, VIII Æthelred, 28–30, I Cnut, 6a.   [10] V Æthelred, 25, VI Æthelred, 28.

[11] V Æthelred, 24, VI Æthelred, 28; Wulfstan, *Episcopus*, Liebermann, *Gesetze*, i. 477.

[12] V Æthelred, 24–5, VI Æthelred, 28, 'Ecclesiastical Institutes' (= Theodulf's *Capitula*), cc. xxi, xxvii, Thorpe, *Ancient Laws*, ii. 422.   [13] V Æthelred, 25, VI Æthelred, 28.

The church was also concerned with its discipline. All men were to go to church, confess often, and prepare themselves for communion at least three times a year.[1] They were to learn and understand the Pater Noster and Creed.[2] They were to keep all festivals and fasts, and, especially, were to avoid unsuitable behaviour, such as marketing, legal business, and hunting on Sundays.[3] They were to pay their dues to the church [4] and respect the clergy and all ecclesiastical rights.[5]

Priests were, of course, under more detailed control. Dunstan is said to have had royal decrees issued against priests who gave themselves to hunting, business, or immorality,[6] and in a 'general council' to have ordered all canons, priests, deacons, and sub-deacons either to live chastely or lose their churches.[7] Synodal decrees on the subject of the dress of the clergy and their behaviour were issued by Archbishop Ealdred of York.[8] The *Law of the Northumbrian Priests* shows that the conduct of the clergy was closely regulated. There are listed the sins of disobedience: neglect of a superior's summons (cc. 4, 6), disregard of his command (cc. 3, 7, 45), absence from synod (c. 44), obtaining ordination outside the diocese without permission (c. 12), and desertion of an office (c. 28); the sins of uncanonical behaviour: bigamy (c. 35), brawling, and unfriendly actions between clerks (cc. 29–33), drunkenness and singing in taverns (c. 41), neglect of the tonsure (c. 34), embezzlement of a church's possessions (c. 27), and buying or accepting a church which was not vacant (c. 2); and the sins of ignorance and inefficiency: careless or criminal neglect of baptism and confession (cc. 8, 10), misdirection about festivals and fasts (c. 11), failure to fetch chrism at the proper time (c. 9), irregularities in the celebration of mass (cc. 13–18), placing unsuitable ornaments in a church (c. 26), improper conduct of duties (cc. 36–8), including the ordeal (c. 39), concealment of sins in the parish (cc. 40, 42), and remissness over the collection of church dues (c. 43).

[1] V Æthelred, 22, VI Æthelred, 27, I Cnut, 18–19, Cnut, 1020, c. 19.

[2] I Cnut, 22; cf. also Wulfstan's 'Canons enacted under King Edgar', cc. 17, 22, 'Ecclesiastical Institutes' (= Theodulf's *Capitula*), c. xxii, Thorpe, *Ancient Laws*, ii. 418.

[3] II Edgar, 5, V Æthelred, 12–14, 17–20, 22, VI Æthelred, 22–5, 27, VIII Æthelred, 16–17, I Cnut, 14–17, Cnut 1020, 18-19; Wulfstan's 'Canons enacted under King Edgar', cc. 19, 23–5; 'Ecclesiastical Institutes' (= Theodulf's *Capitula*), c. xxiv, Thorpe, *Ancient Laws*, ii. 420.

[4] I Edmund, 2, II Edgar, 2–5, IV Edgar, 1, 4–6, V Æthelred, 11–12, VI Æthelred, 16–21, 42, VIII Æthelred, 7–9, 11–13, 34, I Cnut, 8–14, Cnut, 1027, 16–17.   [5] Cf. I Cnut, 21.

[6] *Memorials of St Dunstan*, p. 110. It is also reported that he forbade King Edgar to hunt on Sundays, Eadmer, *ibid.* p. 207. See Wulfstan's 'Canons enacted under King Edgar', Thorpe, *Ancient Laws*, ii. 244 ff.   [7] Eadmer, *Vita S. Oswaldi, HCY*, ii. 20.

[8] Folcard, *Vita S. Johannis, HCY*, i. 241; cf. *Vita Ædwardi*, pp. liii ff.

The comprehensiveness of these rules for the Northumbrian clergy is most impressive. The synodal decrees of the thirteenth century do not start at a point much in advance. And although this reform drive in the province of York and, presumably, in the diocese of Worcester, was the personal contribution of Wulfstan (*Lupus*), it is unlikely that he aimed at a standard much higher than that which obtained in the southern province.

The basic disciplinary institution was the *forum internum*.[1] According to eleventh-century theologians contrition was one of the three principal sacrifices which had to be rendered to God, and perfect contrition was in two parts, anguish of soul and penance.[2] Archbishop Wulfstan taught that sins ought to be confessed to God in prayer at least once or twice a day and that there should be confession to the parish priest in the week immediately before Lent.[3] The duty of regular confession was enjoined by the royal laws [4] as well as by the homiletic literature, and the late Old-English church was much concerned about the proper enforcement of ecclesiastical punishments.

The Celtic and English churches had created between the sixth and eighth centuries a penitential system which was a remarkable aberration from the main tradition of ecclesiastical law. It consisted not only in the regulation of private penance (whereby the confessor without ceremonial prescribed to the sinner not the ancient status of a penitent, but the performance of certain penitential works) but also in the virtual replacement of the canonical system of public penance by this new development. Thus the old distinction between public and secret sins and between the associated public and private penance was disregarded.[5] Great importance was given to the priest's office as judge and much reliance placed on his *discretio*. The system

---

[1] For penitential literature, see especially Wasserschleben; Lingard, *Antiquities*, i. 329 ff.; O. D. Watkins, *A History of Penance* (1920); T. Pollock Oakley, *English penitential discipline and Anglo-Saxon law in their joint influence* (New York, 1923); G. Le Bras, *Pénitentiels (Dict. Théol. Cathol.)*; P. Fournier, 'Études sur les pénitentiels', *Revue d'histoire et de littérature religieuse*, vi–ix (1901–4); Fournier and Le Bras, i. 50 ff., 71 ff., 108 ff.

[2] Cf. St Peter Damiani, *Sermo (lxx) ii in dedicatione ecclesiae*, *MPL*, cxliv, coll. 904–5.

[3] 'Ecclesiastical Institutes' (= Theodulf's *Capitula*), cc. xxx, xxxvi, Thorpe, *Ancient Laws*, ii. 426 ff. H. Logeman has printed some late tenth- and eleventh-century prayers and general confessions, one in Latin the rest in English, *Anglia*, xi. 97 and xii. 497.

[4] V Æthelred, 22, VI Æthelred, 27, I Cnut, 18b.

[5] The principle, however, is recognized in some Anglo-Saxon MSS. See B. Fehr, 'Über einige Quellen zu Ælfrics "Homiliae Catholicae" ', *Archiv für das Studium der neueren Sprachen und Literaturen*, cxxx (1913), 381. And Oakley, pp. 78 ff., would allow the existence of some public penance in England from Theodore's time.

was private in root and branch, and the attempt to father it on Theodore shows how lacking it was in *auctoritas*. In England almost all penances were private, and penance was generally interpreted as fasting.[1] The circumscription of penance was due in part to Celtic tradition, the preoccupation with morals and asceticism, and in part to the difficulty which a missionary church had found in enforcing public shame on free and proud Germanic warriors. And it became lasting when the royal governments began to enforce ecclesiastical discipline. The penalties of the secular courts imposed on public sinners became a substitute for public penance. This insular creation was carried to the Continent by Celtic and English missionaries and had there an enormous success. Although it served an obvious need at a time when formal ecclesiastical discipline was in ruins, its influence is usually deplored by the historians of canon law.[2]

The ceremonies connected with public penance were reserved primarily to the bishop.[3] Private penance, however, was of its nature less centralized, and, although there are signs that serious matters remained the bishop's concern,[4] the parish priest became the ordinary confessor.[5] It was generally understood that in case of necessity confession could be profitably made to a clerk, a layman, or even to God himself. But penitential lore was to be kept secret within the circle of the competent.[6]

For imposing private penance the bishop and priest needed a handbook of the various sins with appropriate penalties. The secular laws, with their tariffs of compensation calculated according to the rank of the persons involved, served as a pattern, and the ecclesiastical penalty was likewise called a *bot*.[7] The origins of, and relationship between, the early penitentials is an obscure and controversial subject. Celtic collections, e.g. the *Vinnianus* (*c*. 550), *Excerpta quedam de libro Davidis* (550–600), and *Cummeanus* (*c*. 650), led the way,[8] and then at the end of the seventh and the beginning of the eighth century many hundreds of judgments attributed to Archbishop Theodore of Canterbury (*ob*. 766) were collected in several recensions,

[1] Cf. Oakley, pp. 50 ff.   [2] Cf. Fournier and Le Bras, i. 57–61, 64–5.   [3] Oakley, pp. 43 ff,
[4] Cf. 'Quod de criminibus soli episcopi poenitentiam tribuant': Council of Winchester, 1076. Wilkins, *Concilia*, i. 365.
[5] Cf. Wulfstan, 'Canons enacted under King Edgar', c. 65, Thorpe, *Ancient Laws*, ii. 259.
[6] Cf. *P. Ps.-Bede* (Wasserschleben, p. 251), *P. Ps.-Theodore*, xlviii. 25 (*ibid.* pp. 619–20).
[7] Wulfstan, 'Of penitents', c. 3, Thorpe, *Ancient Laws*, ii. 278; *Polity*, p. 214; 'Ecclesiastical Institutes' (= Theodulf's *Capitula*), c. xxxi, Thorpe, ii. 428; *Law of the Northumbrian Priests*, c. 1; cf. 'Of ecclesiastical penalties or bots', Thorpe, ii. 240 ff.
[8] Fournier and Le Bras, i. 53–4; Oakley, pp. 27 ff.

probably in England.[1] The sources of the *Poenitentiale Theodori* are various. Doubtless some of the *judicia* attributed to Theodore are indeed his, and a Greek tradition is clearly to be seen. But there is also a strong Celtic admixture. Nor are these collections purely penitentials: they include much customary insular church law. It was their comprehensiveness, as well as their attribution to Theodore, which made the work so influential in the eighth and early ninth century.

The attempt in the later eighth century to end the period of anarchy in the church within the Carolingian empire and reform ecclesiastical law, the reception of the great collections of ancient law, the *Dionysiana = Dionysio Hadriana* and the *Hispana*, and the marriage of these in the *Dacheriana*, led immediately to the questioning of the authority of the insular penitentials.[2] An attempt was made to reform the penitential system by a return to more acceptable authorities, such as the Fathers, oriental and African councils, and papal decretals, and also to restore more regular practices, including public confession and penance. Hence in the middle of the ninth century new penitential manuals, less dependent on Theodore, were made in the Frankish empire. Some signs of this reform are to be found in England in the tenth and eleventh centuries. But since the reformers had little success on the Continent there is no reason to think that they did better in England.

The last great English penitential was Egbert's (archbishop of York, 732/4–66),[3] a fairly comprehensive, but not particularly well-arranged production, drawn from a wide selection of sources: Gildas, Theodore and Bede, and Frankish compilations based on *Columbanus* and *Cummeanus*. It was still being used in the eleventh century.[4] But perhaps in commoner use were the *Confessionale Ps.–Egberti*,[5] the *Poenitentiale Ps.–Egberti*,[6] and the *Poenitentiale Ps.–Theodori*,[7] all produced in, or deriving from, the Frankish

---

[1] Haddan and Stubbs, iii. 173; Wasserschleben, pp. 182–219; Fournier and Le Bras, i. 54–6; Oakley, pp. 105 ff.   [2] Fournier and Le Bras, i. 91 ff.

[3] Haddan and Stubbs, iii. 413; Wasserschleben, pp. 231–47; Fournier and Le Bras, i. 88; Oakley, pp. 121 ff. It was known to Archbishop Wulfstan: D. Bethurum, 'Archbishop Wulfstan's commonplace Book', *PMLA*, lvii (1942), 916.   [4] See below, p. 285.

[5] Thorpe, *Ancient Laws*, ii. 128 ff. (in O.E. and Latin); Wasserschleben, pp. 300 ff.; Fournier and Le Bras, i. 88; Oakley, pp. 131 ff. It is still disputed whether it is Egbert's, whether English or Frankish in origin, whether written originally in English or Latin.

[6] Thorpe, *Ancient Laws*, ii. 170 ff. (in O.E. and Latin); Wasserschleben, pp. 318 ff.; Fournier and Le Bras, i. 353; Oakley, pp. 133 ff.

[7] Thorpe, *Ancient Laws*, ii. 1 ff; Wasserschleben, pp. 566 ff.; Fournier and Le Bras, i. 111. It was written between 830 and 847, and was an important authority for Ælfric and Wulfstan: D. Bethurum, 'Archbishop Wulfstan's Commonplace Book', pp. 916, 927.

kingdom in the ninth or tenth century. When Archbishop Wulfstan issued a penitential,[1] he abbreviated the *Poenitentiale Ps.–Egberti*.[2] The first work (the *Confessionale*), in forty-one chapters, is still largely based on Theodore. The second, however, in four books, is an adaptation of books iii–v of Halitgar of Cambrai's penitential in six books,[3] with, as an Appendix, a miscellany of pieces not found in Halitgar. It is, therefore, rather different in tone from the *Confessionale*, for Halitgar was one of the reformers who based his practice not on earlier penitentials but on more ancient canonical literature. The third work, the false penitential of Theodore, is the most comprehensive and eclectic of them all, drawing on a wide variety of sources, including Halitgar's collection of canons. Consequently it is repetitive and contradictory and would seem to be unsuitable for general use. Also to hand in England were legal compilations such as the *Institutio Canonicorum* of the council of Aachen, 817, which dealt, among other things, with private and public penance.[4] Thus the eleventh-century English church had available not only the penitential customs deriving from English and Celtic sources but also the more strictly canonical law which the Carolingian reformers were trying to re-establish. None of the surviving penitentials, however, is in the form of questions to be put by the priest to the penitent, a form which, because of its utility, became popular in the eleventh century. And it is possible that the village priest used a simpler, more practical handbook, written, we may be sure, in English.

The essential features of private confession were the private award by the priest or bishop of penances expressed in fasts for terms of years or months and a tariff of commutation. The penitentials are lists of sins, each with its traditional *bot*. They were concerned with all aspects of human behaviour recognized as sinful by the Christian church; but, although there were some fluctuations in emphasis, the subjects which generally received the most detailed attention were sexual sins and violence. A typical chapter in a penitential is:[5]

---

[1] 'Modus imponendi poenitentiam', Thorpe, ii. 266–77 (in O.E. and Latin). See Karl Jost, 'Einige Wulfstantexte und ihre Quellen', *Anglia*, lvi (1932), 288 ff. D. Bethurum, *op. cit.* p. 927.

[2] It contains sixteen chapters of Book II and eighteen chapters of Book IV, all in order, and adds little original material. Wulfstan also used this penitential for his Homily X b.

[3] Fournier and Le Bras, i. 108–10. Books III and IV are largely based on the *Dacheriana*, Book V is derived from the *Excerpta* (an epitome) of the *Hispana*.

[4] See cc. xxvii, xxx, l, lxiii; in English translations of the first half of the eleventh century, *Enlarged Rule of Chrodegang*, ed. A. S. Napier, EETS, 150 (1960).

[5] *Confess. Ps.–Egberti*, c. xxii.

If anyone kills another as murder, that is to say in anger and secretly, let him fast four years; some require seven years. If anyone consents to a homicide which is later committed, let him fast five years – some require seven – and for forty days not enter the church. If anyone kills his own man, let him fast one year. If anyone injures a man in his genitals or wounds him in the face, let him make amends to the victim for the wound and do his work for him until the wound is healed, and also let him fast two or three legitimate fasts. If he does not know how the money can be paid, let him fast twelve months. If anyone kills a man [? to avenge his brother], let him fast three years. If later he is willing to pay compensation to a man's kinsman, then let him fast a year-and-a-half. If anyone [? strikes and] wounds another man, let him fast forty days for the spilling of blood.

Several points of interest are exemplified by this piece. In the first place the text is uncertain, and one of the doubtful passages is of some importance. It is also possible that, although alternative penalties are given, the approved scale is imperfect, for murder would seem to be more heinous than consenting to a homicide. More generally the passage is interesting for its illustration of how penitential regulations accepted, and took into account, the secular law. In the case of less serious crimes the criminal who honoured his obligations under the secular law was awarded a shorter penance by the church. The two systems were not in rivalry but were regarded as complementary.[1]

All penitentials took into account the gravity of the sin,[2] some of the circumstances, and the rank or order of the offender, with the rule that the higher the status the heavier the penalty. But there was also left to the confessor some discretionary power. Sometimes an *Ordo poenitentialis* or *Ordo ad dandam poenitentiam*, advice on how the manual was to be used, is given as a preface;[3] occasionally they are found unattached.[4] The introduction to Egbert's true penitential explains the system in a piece which comes from Bede and which was often quoted:[5]

The holy custom made in the days of our fathers never departed from the true road, and established for penitents and those mourning their diseases and sins the remedies of eternal salvation,[6] for diversity of sin produces diversity of remedies for the penitent. Physicians of the body make various remedies and potions for various sicknesses, and good

[1] Oakley, pp. 166 ff. stresses this point.

[2] The distinction between *criminalis culpa* (*crimen*) and *peccatum* was recognized: K. Jost, *Wulfstanstudien*, p. 54.

[3] E.g. Preface to *Confess. Ps.–Egberti*; Book i of *Poenit. Ps.–Egberti*; c. i of *Poenit. Ps.–Theodori*; cc. i–iii of Wulfstan's 'Modus imponendi poenitentiam'.

[4] Cf. Wulfstan's 'De confessione' (Latin and O.E.), Thorpe, ii. 260–5, 'Of penitents' (O.E.), *ibid.* ii. 278–87.

[5] Wasserschleben, pp. 231–3. There is a version in *The Lanalet Pontifical*, ed. G. H. Doble (HBS, lxxiv, 1937), pp. 125–7.

[6] This passage is very corrupt in the manuscripts.

and just judges of secular cases weigh and handle the various judgments so that they may judge rightly between the poor and the rich and between case and case. How much more, then, you priests of God, should the remedies for the souls of living men be weighed and handled, lest through a foolish remedy the wounds of the soul are made worse. . . . There are some who are raised to the priesthood who are like blind dogs running to the corpses of the dead or like the crows of the air, men whose zeal is less for God than for earthly honour, men blind to divine wisdom. . . . Therefore, my brothers, let him who wishes to accept priestly authority first think of God, and, before the hand of the bishop touches his head, gather together his weapons, that is to say, a psalter, a lectionary, an antiphonary, a missal, a book on baptism, a book of saints arranged chronologically for preaching, a *computus* with its tables of cycles, for this is the law of priests, and his penitential – the book which you have here, set out according to the authority of the canons, so that you may perceive the distinguishing features of all cases, without which there can be no true judgments. For it is written: In nothing should you appear indiscriminate; but you should distinguish why, where, how long, when, and how you should act. For all should not be weighed in the same balance although they are all fettered by the same vice, but there should be a distinction between each of them.[1] There should be a distinction between the rich and the poor, the freeman and the slave, the child, boy, youth, and the man, the layman and the clerk, the monk, bishop, priest, deacon, subdeacon, and lector; whether in Orders or not, married or single, virgin or woman, canoness or nun; between the weak and infirm and the healthy; concerning the nature of the beasts and the men; between the chaste and the unchaste, intentionally or by chance, whether in public or in private, with what compunction he makes amends, by necessity or voluntarily, between places and times. . . . And so do not overlook those who persevere in evil doing, but make a severe judgment according to the canons, so that others shall be afraid.

Archbishop Wulfstan stated more simply [2]

When anyone comes to his confessor for the sake of telling him his needs and confessing his sins then ought the confessor earnestly to ask him about those things which he confesses to him, how they were done, whether intentionally or unintentionally, and whether suddenly or in a premeditated way; and let him then for every misdeed prescribe the *bot* according as the deed has been done. Very unlike is the man who defending himself slays another to him who seeks out another to slay him; so it is, both in adulteries and in every misdeed.

The *Ordo poenitentialis* also usually gave advice on how penances could be commuted. Fasting was always supposed to be accompanied by gifts of alms – money saved by the austerities. But it was recognized that there were circumstances, such as sickness, which made fasting impossible, and so alternative penances were allowed.[3] The *Confessionale Ps.–Egberti* specified

[1] Cf. II Cnut, 68 (Archbishop Wulfstan): 'religious penance and secular judgments must take into account weak/strong, sick/sound, age/youth, wealth/poverty, freedom/slavery, compulsion/necessity, and intention.'
[2] 'Ecclesiastical Institutes' (= Theodulf's *Capitula*), c. xxxi, Thorpe, ii. 428.
[3] Cf. Oakley, pp. 52 ff.

psalm-singing and genuflections, or, as the ultimate relaxation, the simple distribution of alms.[1] A three-year penance could in fact be performed by distributing 26s. in the first year, 20s. in the next, and 18s. in the third, or, possibly, by laying out 64s. at once. Among pieces associated with Wulfstan is a tract explaining how 'a powerful man, rich in friends, may with the support of these, greatly lighten his penance'.[2] Such a man could, using the principle of oath-helpers,[3] accomplish a seven-year penance in three days with the aid of twelve and then seven times twelve men, all fasting together for that short period. In an entirely different spirit, by means of psalm-singing and scourging, the ascetic eremitical monks of Italy could perform centuries of penance in the space of days.[4]

By the eleventh century the penitential system suffered from both rigidity and flexibility. The list of sins had remained largely unaltered since the seventh century. But great cultural changes had taken place. Burchard of Worms introduced many new categories into his *Corrector*,[5] a work which does not seem to have found its way into England, and it is hard to believe that such a revision was not generally required. The antiquity of the tariff must have given additional discretionary powers to the priest; and since it is clear that commutation of penance was usual,[6] the system must have been in a state of collapse. What appears rigid, must in practice have been utterly formless. When we also take into account that many confessors would have possessed garbled texts of penitentials which at their best were confused and

[1] c. ii, Wasserschleben, p. 303.

[2] 'Of powerful men', Thorpe, ii. 286 ff.; cf. also 'Of penitents', cc. xviii, xix, *ibid*. ii. 284–7, (Ps.) Wulfstan, Homily XLVI and K. Jost's commentary on it, *Wulfstanstudien*, pp. 236 ff.

[3] The thegn, of course, was a twelf-hynde man, i.e. his wergild was 1,200 shillings.

[4] At St Peter Damiani's monastery of Fonte Avellana the tariff was 20 psalters (3,000 psalms) = 300,000 scourgings = 100 years' penance. Peter's disciple, St Dominicus Loricatus (*ob.* 1062) could chant three psalters a day (occasionally he could do nine, but never ten), while birching himself with each hand. Hence he could regularly perform a hundred years' penance in six days and a thousand years' within Lent. See P. Damiani, *Vita SS. Rodulphi et Dominici Loricati*, *MPL* cxliv, coll. 1015–17. St Rodulf (monastic-bishop of Gubbio, *ob.* 1063) used to perform, in a similar way, a hundred years' penance in twenty days, *ibid.* col. 1011.

[5] Wasserschleben, pp. 624 ff.; *MPL*, cxl, coll. 949 ff.

[6] The only problem is how often penance was commuted into a money payment. The eleventh-century use of *bot* for penance suggests that it usually was. Commutation into money is generally understood as alms to the poor. The rich woman who tempted St Wulfstan suggested that they could easily redeem their sin by alms: *Vita Wulfstani*, p. 12. But the *bot* may, of course, have been taken by the confessor. St Peter Damiani relates of St Rodulf bishop of Gubbio that at his annual synod, 'ne a lapsis quidem commodum aliquod, praeter solam penitentiam, requirebat': *Vita S. Rodulphi*, *MPL*, cxliv, col. 1012, and Archbishop Wulfstan urged bishops 'not to be too eager for money . . . at penance': *Polity*, p. 213.

often contradictory as well, the church's long tolerance of the disorder is remarkable. One man, however, attacked it passionately. St Peter Damiani, deeply stirred by the indulgence of confessors to those guilty of sodomy and other unnatural sins, quoted in his *Liber Gomorrhianus*, dedicated to Pope Leo IX, chapter V of the *Poenitentiale Egberti*,[1] and then covered it with scorn and denounced all similarly unauthentic works. Who, he asked, were the authors of these false canons with such uncertain attributions? – these 'incantations in which lost men confide with vain presumption', 'lying and sacrilegious deceptions of the devil', 'ravings in which men trust as though in the portents of dreams', 'a snare for the lost and a net for errant souls', 'a monster created by man, with the head of a horse and the hooves of a goat', 'diabolical figments instituted to deceive the souls of the simple with cunning devices', 'Siren's songs', 'theatrical ravings'.[2]

It was a system coming to a dishonoured end. But, as with all systems, everything depended on the operator. St Wulfstan bishop of Worcester was a famous confessor. According to William of Malmesbury's version of Coleman's Life, Wulfstan received those coming to confess their sins with good cheer and put them in good heart. He heard their confessions with gracious humanity and never showed any aversion – stooping with tears to their sins and not recoiling as from things unheard of. As a result men came to him from all over England, unashamed to confess to him things that they were ashamed of having done and dare not confide to anyone else. In return Wulfstan imparted grace, warned them against despair, and instructed them how to avoid sin in the future and atone for those they had committed. Confession and penance created a bond, and the bishop took an increased interest in those whom he had shrived.[3] Here is the good confessor. And we know that Earl Harold went out of his way to confess to Wulfstan.[4] But what repentance Harold showed for his manifest sins will never be known.

The attempt to introduce ninth-century Frankish reforms into the tenth-century English church meant the introduction of a more authoritative tariff of penances – with the exclusion of some English peculiarities, such as Theodore's laxity in matrimonial cases – and of public penance centralized in the hands of the bishop. There is no evidence that public penance during Lent and the public reconciliation of penitents by the bishop on Maundy Thursday was widely practised in England before the tenth century,[5]

---

[1] V. 3, 4, 17–19, 20, 22, Wasserschleben, pp. 236–7.
[2] Caps. X–XII, *MPL*, cxlv, coll. 169–72. [3] *Vita Wulfstani*, pp. 49–50.
[4] *Ibid.* p. 13. [5] Cf. *P. Ps.-Egberti*, i. 12 ,*P Ps.-Theodori*, c. 41.

although the liturgical forms were available from the eighth. There is an *Ordo ad dandam poenitentiam* and *Reconciliatio poenitentium in Cena Domini* in Archbishop Egbert's Pontifical, and for the eleventh century in the Benedictional of Archbishop Robert, the Lanalet and Salisbury Pontificals, and in the Canterbury and Magdalen College Benedictionals, all really pontificals.[1] And it seems that at least some bishops introduced the ceremony into their already heavy programme on Maundy Thursday [2] without, however, attempting a general reform in the diocese. Wulfstan of York, because of his study of canon law, advocated public penance and apparently tried to enforce it.[3] His own penitential, being an abbreviation of the *Poenitentiale Ps.-Egberti*, opens with an *ordo* based on public confession: 'These are the customs which are observed across the sea'.[4] In his homiletic writings for priests he always assumes that these will act as private confessors,[5] but he also indicates that, according to the gravity of the sin, absolution may be reserved to the diocesan bishop, the archbishop, the pope, or even to God himself.[6] This is characteristic of Wulfstan's high conception of a bishop's duties and also of his hierarchical view of the church. The role he gives to the pope is not supported by any English penitential. Clearly he was attempting to introduce more authentic canonical procedures; and he admitted that there was opposition to his policy.[7] Later, St Wulfstan of Worcester, al-

---

[1] (*a*) ed. W. Greenwell (Surtees Soc. xxvii, 1854), p. 120; (*b*) ed. G. H. Doble (HBS, lxxiv, 1937), pp. 72–80, 140–3, prefaced, pp. 68–72, by instructions for private confession and penance; (*c*) N. R. Ker, 'Three Old English Texts in a Salisbury Pontifical', *The Anglo-Saxons*, ed. Peter Clemoes (1959), p. 263; (*d*) ed. H. A. Wilson (HBS, xxiv, 1903), pp. 57–60; (*e*) ed. R. M. Woolley (HBS, li, 1917), pp. 13 ff., 29–35; (*f*) ed. H. A. Wilson (HBS, xxxix, 1910), pp. 155–6, 284–6. And see B. Fehr, *Über einige Quellen zu Ælfrics 'Homiliae Catholicae'*, p. 381.

[2] Cf. Napier: *Wulfstan Sammlung* (Berlin 1883), no. XXXII, *Sermo de cena domini*, 'And I tell you all . . . that bishops exclude from church at the beginning of Lent those men who are guilty of manifest deadly sins, and then, after they have earnestly repented, lead them back into church on the day of *cena domini*, which is today.' The bishop had also to bless chrism and perform his Maundy duties to the poor.

[3] D. Bethurum, *The Homilies of Wulfstan*, pp. 345 ff., 'Archbishop Wulfstan's Commonplace Book', *PMLA*, lvii (1942), 925–7. Wulfstan collected liturgical directions for Ash Wednesday, including a sermon by Abbo of St Germain, which he rewrote as Homily XXXII (Napier).

[4] Thorpe, *Ancient Laws*, ii. 266–7.

[5] Cf. 'Ecclesiastical Institutes' (= Theodulf's *Capitula*), cc. xxx, xxxi, xxxvi, *ibid.* ii. 426 ff. And, although public penitents had to present themselves to the bishop on Ash Wednesday (*caput ieiunii*), Ælfric, in his sermon for that day, *Lives of Saints*, pp. 261 ff., although he deals with fasting, the ashes, penitence, and confession, makes no clear reference to public penance, and, indeed, seems concerned throughout with private penance. His last words are, 'and it behoveth you that you be shriven in this week, or at least in the second': pp. 282–3.

[6] Homily LI (Napier). See K. Jost, *Wulfstanstudien*, pp. 54, 107, 198.

[7] Homily XIV (Bethurum).

though he heard private confessions,[1] also reconciled penitents on Maundy Thursday. The full account of the service which Coleman gave in his Life of the saint was omitted by William of Malmesbury with the explanation that his aim was to describe the bishop's life not his office and that it was otiose to describe what all bishops did and what they could not do otherwise than as prescribed in the books. William contents himself with saying that Wulfstan showed a gracious, angelic countenance to the penitents, who, as was human nature, expected to gain remission of their sins through a saint, and that Wulfstan, as was customary, dined with them.[2]

It is possible that Coleman's prolixity is a sign that he regarded the ceremony as a little unusual in his time. Certainly few accounts of public penance are to be found. But Bishop Æthelric of Dorchester, c. 1020, imposed a public penance on a witch, who had confessed to making a love-potion and being involved in the murder of a child. This he did on account of the people, whose feelings had already been wounded by her doubtful reputation.[3] And it would seem that, at least from the tenth century, and possibly from the beginning, the two methods existed side by side in England until in the twelfth the whole system was transformed.

Although the penitentials do not enjoin secrecy on the confessor,[4] the working of the penitential system cannot be properly illustrated. Earl Æthelwine, the pious co-founder of Ramsey Abbey, confessed that he had indulged in the sins of the flesh, had taken too much pleasure in the pomp and delights of earthly power, and had given unjust judgments in the law courts.[5] But this record stands alone. As for penance, the only references are to parricides. For this sin the penalty was, according to the *Confessionale Ps. -Egberti* (c. xxiv) ten years' pilgrimage (and a case reserved for the bishop), or, according to the *P. Ps.–Theodori* (III, 1–4), seven to fourteen years' exile according to the circumstances. The continental custom seems to have been to bind the sinner in chains and require him to travel abroad as a pilgrim at least until the irons fell off. Hence the presence of such men is noticed at

[1] See above, p. 269.
[2] *Vita Wulfstani*, p. 58. A German monk at Worcester had objected to Wulfstan, when prior, c. 1050, preaching to the people, on the grounds that 'solius pontificis esse populo praedicare, qui solus tradita sibi et indulta potestate peccata posset absolvere': *ibid.* p. 14.
[3] *Chron. Ramsey*, p. 132. For the case, see below, p. 273.
[4] Here we have the sharpest distinction between the Penitentials and the thirteenth-century Manuals for Confessors. The reason, presumably, is that in the earlier period private confession was merely a relaxation of public confession.
[5] *Chron. Ramsey*, p. 104.

English shrines when the chains miraculously broke.[1] And there exist from England models for letters dimissory to be given to such sinners, from which we learn that Wulfstan I usually imposed pilgrimage for life in exile, especially to Rome.[2] In one case the pope had awarded a life penance of fasting, wearing a woollen garment, and going bare-foot on Mondays, Wednesdays, and Saturdays, a haircut only thrice a year, and deprivation of communion until the moment of death. The sinner could, however, attend church at Christmas and Easter and eat meat on Sundays and the principal feasts. The bishop could moderate this sentence if he thought fit.[3] The Ely chronicler records another papal judgment from Wulfstan's time.[4] After Leofwine, the son of Æthelwulf, had fatally wounded his mother during a quarrel, he was advised by the priests and other prudent men to go to Rome and consult the pope. The penance imposed by the Roman pontiff was that he should give his eldest son, Æthelmaer, to a poor monastery, enrich that church with lands, and bestow alms generally. Leofwine chose Ely. On an earlier occasion, however, a penitent was actually dissuaded from going to Rome; and these two cases may well illustrate a change in attitude. According to Peterborough tradition,[5] Ealdwulf, King Edgar's 'chancellor', so loved his only son that he had him sleep between him and his wife. One night, when the parents were drunk, the boy was suffocated. Ealdwulf went to Bishop Æthelwold of Winchester for confession and announced his intention of going to Rome. But the bishop persuaded him instead to restore a church. And so he contributed to the refoundation of Medeshamstead (Peterborough), became its abbot, and was (in 992) promoted bishop of Worcester and archbishop of York. Cain's offence was the oldest and deadliest; and its punishment is the most fully recorded. Pilgrimage to shrines in England, barefoot and clad in wool, is met with in another connexion,[6] and may have been a penance awarded for sins less serious than parricide.

[1] Venetian consul and a man from Cologne at Ramsey (Goscelin, *Miracula S. Yvonis, Chron. Ramsey*, pp. lxvii–lxviii), three Saxon brothers at Ely and Ramsey (*ibid.*), Saxons at Worcester (Eadmer, *Miracula S. Oswaldi, HCY*, ii. 44–5), and a foreigner at Winchester ('Goscelin', *Miracula S. Swithuni, MPL*, clv, col. 76). Cf. a German doing seven years' penance 'pro culpa voluptatis et contumaciae' freed from the devil at Canterbury (Osbern, *Miracula S. Dunstani, Memorials of St Dunstan*, p. 135), and Thierry, one of the mad dancers of Kölbigk, and English criminals and penitents released at Wilton (*Vita Edithe*, pp. 285–93, 305).

[2] Letters printed D. Bethurum, *The Homilies of Wulfstan*, appendix II; *Memorials of St Dunstan*, p. 409 (attributed by Stubbs to Wulfsige III of Sherborne, by K. Jost, *Wulfstanstudien*, pp. 16–21, to Wulfstan).

[3] Bethurum, *op. cit.* pp. 375–6.

[4] *Liber Eliensis*, II, c. 60.

[5] *Chron. Peterborough*, pp. 29–31.

[6] *Vita Ædwardi*, p. 65.

In general it appears that in England the confessional, except *in articulo mortis*, was for the pious.[1] The public or hardened sinner was normally punished by the bishop in the public courts. The conjunction of these two disciplines produced a satisfactory working system, which hardly needed supplementation. But there remains to be considered the *forum externum*, the public jurisdiction of the church exercised in a synod or ecclesiastical court, a jurisdiction which, in theory at least, is to be distinguished, on the one side, from the public penitential ceremonies and, on the other, from the ecclesiastical business of the shire court. We know that Archbishop Wulfstan envisaged a system of synods under which the priests would report recalcitrant sinners to the bishop's synod, and the bishops to the provincial or national synod, with final recourse to the king.[2] But of the operation of a diocesan synod as a court of law only one example can be given; and this, it must be admitted at once, could possibly be a case heard by the bishop according to ecclesiastical law in the shire court.

About 1020 Bishop Æthelric of Dorchester brought a case against Thorkell the Tall, the famous Jómsviking, earl of East Anglia, and his (second) wife, Edith, after a witch had confessed that she had been an accessory to the murder of Thorkell's son by the step-mother.[3] The bishop's act was courageous, for Thorkell, Æthelred's old captain, was powerful with King Cnut, and his regent in 1020. It was also at first ineffective, for the earl disregarded the three summonses to attend the bishop's synod. Æthelric thought it prudent to take no further action until Cnut became available.[4] He then reported Thorkell's contumacy. The earl did

---

[1] Wulfstan, in his *Sermo ad Anglos*, laments that sinners 'because of idle calumny are ashamed to atone for their misdeeds as the books teach': *EHD*, i. 858.

[2] 'Ecclesiastical Institutes' (= Theodulf's *Capitula*), c. xxviii, Thorpe, *Ancient Laws*, ii. 424; Wulfstan, *Polity*, pp. 214–16; 'Canons enacted under King Edgar', cc. 5–6, Thorpe, ii. 244.

[3] *Chron. Ramsey*, pp. 129–34. The date must lie between 1016 and Martinmas 1021, when Thorkell was banished. If the banishment was connected with the trial, a late date is required. As there is a hint that Cnut was not available at the time when Thorkell was first accused, the date 1019–20, when Cnut was in Denmark and Thorkell was regent, is indicated. The case was regarded as one of the English against the Danes; and it was possibly an attempt to damage the government of the conquerors in the absence of the king. For the procedure, see M. M. Bigelow, *History of procedure in England from the Norman Conquest* (1880), chs. VI–X. For another case of swearing on, and losing, a beard, see *Chron. Evesham*, p. 42.

[4] Cf. 'Laici vero, si de crimine suo accusati fuerint et episcopo suo obedire noluerint, vocentur semel, et iterum, et tertio. Si post tertiam vocationem emendare noluerint, excommunicentur. Si autem post excommunicationem ad satisfactionem venerint, forisfacturam suam, quae Anglice vocatur oferhyrnesse seu lahslite, pro unaque vocatione episcopo suo reddant': Council of Winchester, 1076, Wilkins, *Concilia*, i. 367.

not fail to obey the summons to the king's court, and, when charged by the bishop in the presence of the king, replied that he and his wife were innocent. As the defendant had traversed the charge, the medial, or proof, judgment was that he, with eleven compurgators, and his wife, with as many female compurgators, should clear themselves by oath when and where the bishop appointed. Æthelric chose the meadow where it was said that the murdered child was buried as the place of the trial, and ordered the abbot of Ramsey to produce the monastery's best relics for the ceremony of the oaths. At the trial, which was held in the presence of a great crowd of laymen and clerks, Thorkell first swore his own innocence, and then, to spare his wife, swore on his beard that she too was innocent. But, although his beard came away in his hand, Edith still denied the charge, and was only brought to confession when the bishop ordered the secret tomb to be opened. Final judgment was that Thorkell was guilty of perjury and the countess of homicide, and for these sins penances were awarded. The earl had also incurred the penalty of *oferhyrnes* for having flouted the bishop's jurisdiction, and he gave the bishop a piece of land, which Æthelric transferred to Ramsey.[1] In 1021 Thorkell was outlawed;[2] but the events may be unconnected.

Although the king's intervention was necessary to bring the earl to trial and the medial judgment was declared in the king's court, and although thereafter we may be reading an ecclesiastical description of a shire court, the process exemplifies the purest kind of ecclesiastical justice to be expected at the time. This one illustration of a humble monk-bishop bringing the greatest of the earls, and one of the most illustrious of the Jómsvikings, to justice is sufficient to prove that the laws were enforced in Cnut's reign. If one earl was tried in an ecclesiastical court, some thegns and many ceorls must have been brought to justice too.

Shortly after the Conquest, William I and his *witan* decided that episcopal jurisdiction had hitherto not been properly exercised according to canon law; and in a writ of *c.* 1072, addressed to the secular magnates of the shires of Essex, Hertfordshire, and Middlesex (i.e. the bishopric of London) and those of the diocese of Dorchester-Lincoln,[3] ordered certain reforms. No bishop or archdeacon was to hold the bishop's ecclesiastical pleas in the hundred courts, or bring any case concerning the rule of souls to the

---

[1] This fact explains why we have a record of the case.

[2] *ASC CDE;* Florence, i. 183. He was present at the dedication of the church of Ashingdon in 1020 between Cnut's return and the banishment.

[3] Liebermann, *Gesetze*, i. 485; *SSC*, pp. 99-100.

judgment of secular men. In future such cases were to be heard in a place appointed by the bishop, according to canon and episcopal law and not according to the law of the hundred. Recalcitrant offenders were to be excommunicated, and their attendance would be secured by the king's justiciar or sheriff. No sheriff, reeve, or royal servant was to interfere with the bishop's ecclesiastical jurisdiction, nor any layman bring another to the ordeal except in the presence of the bishop's justiciar. The ordeal was to be held only in the episcopal see or in some other place appointed by the bishop.

This writ has usually been understood as effecting, or starting, the separation of ecclesiastical and secular courts. Certainly it is concerned with separation. But the scope of the order is difficult to determine. Only the hundred court is named – and even the general prohibition against the hearing of ecclesiastical cases by laymen is qualified by a reference to the law of the hundred – and, if the king was concerned only with that court, then the reform was indeed limited.[1] To overthrow the Anglo-Saxon system the shire court had to be remodelled. But not only is that court ignored – an almost incredible drafting error if it were in question – but also is missed by the terms, for, as we have seen, the hearing of ecclesiastical cases in the shire court did not necessarily lead to a lay trial. The early-eleventh-century reformers both condemned the taking of episcopal cases to laymen [2] and also accepted the dual competence of the shire court. And so it is hard to believe that the purpose of the writ of c. 1072 was to effect a drastic reform. If it was concerned with the shire court at all, it must have been aimed at aspects of its procedure which had fallen out of favour or at abuses which had crept in. It is possible, for instance, that the supplementary secular punishments for ecclesiastical offences [3] had become general and had fallen to the sheriff. The writ's prohibition could easily cover such a practice. It is even possible that some bishops had become lax in their attendance at the shire and had allowed ecclesiastical cases to be heard in their absence.

The writ cannot be used to prove that there was little true ecclesiastical jurisdiction in the Anglo-Saxon period. Clearly there was a great deal of a kind – perhaps too much. And it is just possible that one of the purposes of William's ordinance was to protect the secular courts from undue clerical interference. However that may be, there had been sufficient confusion in the

---

[1] See above, pp. 146 ff.

[2] Cf. Wulfstan, *Polity*, pp. 214–16; 'Canons enacted under King Edgar', c. vii, Thorpe, *Ancient Laws*, ii. 246; *Law of the Northumbrian Priests*, c. v, Liebermann, *Gesetze*, i. 380.

[3] See above, pp. 141 ff., 149–50.

old system to prejudice a reformer influenced by stricter canonical attitudes and all too willing to believe that things had been wrong, and no doubt there had been many abuses and slacknesses which a study based on the laws cannot reveal. The writ drew attention to the canonical rules, warned lay justiciars to keep to their proper sphere, and gave authority to those bishops who so wished to hold their spiritual courts separately. It would, perhaps, allow for radical reform. But there is no clear sign that this was its prime purpose or even its immediate effect. The extreme 'Hildebrandine' reformers of the period had the disengagement and separation of the church from the world as one of their ends. But William and his bishops gave this aim only lukewarm support, and modest success came long after the advocacy.

CHAPTER VI

The Education and Heritage of the Clergy

The clergy was a professional body and needed professional training.[1] To carry out its duties properly it required, in the eleventh century, a good knowledge of Latin, some acquaintance with music and arithmetic, and a grasp of theology and ecclesiastical law. The essential library of a parish priest was considered to be the service books (psalter, lectionary, gospel-book, antiphonary, and missal) and a handbook on baptism, a martyrology, or book of saints, to provide sermons, a *computus*, the guide to the ecclesiastical calendar, and a penitential.[2] The desirable standard of education was in fact too high ever to be generally attained. Although a parish priest was technically handicapped if he knew no more Latin than was necessary to stumble through the services, for Latin was the language of the church, his ministry was conducted in the vernacular, and there was a recognized distinction between the pursuits of the scholars (*bōceras*) and those of the parish priests. The law of the priest was the *computus*, not a Latin grammar.[3] The scholars accepted the distinction by writing their books for the education of the parish clergy in English. The monks and the higher clergy, however, were for the most part literate in both English and Latin. Bishops who were monks had been properly trained. Most of the foreign clerks appointed by Edward to bishoprics were Latinists. But it cannot be assumed that all the English clerks who were raised to the bench shared their attainments. It was believed in the twelfth century that Archbishop Stigand, 'like most of his fellow bishops', had been illiterate;[4] and it may well be that his knowledge of Latin was slender or had slipped away.

The most systematic education was provided in the monasteries,[5] and that is one reason why monks were so often promoted to bishoprics. Some

---

[1] See Lingard, *Antiquities*, i. 161–5.

[2] *Poenitentiale Egberti:* see above, p. 267; Ælfric's Pastoral Letters: see Bernhard Fehr, *Die Hirtenbriefe Ælfrics* (Bibl. der Angelsächsischen Prosa, ix, Hamburg, 1914), pp. lxxxvi f. Cf. the *Institutio Canonicorum* of the council of Aachen, 817, c. lxxvii, Old-English translation, *Enlarged Rule of Chrodegang*, ed. A. S. Napier, EETS, 150 (1916), p. 84.

[3] Heinrich Henel, Ælfric's *De Temporibus Anni* (EETS, 1942), p. 96.

[4] Malmesbury, *GP*, p. 36.   [5] See G. N. Garmonsway, Ælfric's *Colloquy*, pp. 11 ff.

monasteries offered instruction to a few who were not oblates; [1] but they were in no sense public schools. In contrast the recruitment and education of the secular clergy was haphazard and largely informal. Instruction could be obtained at some of the minsters and, doubtless in a more casual way, from any of the educated clergy. Some men entered the household of a bishop and others rose more humbly through helping a parish priest. [2] Archbishop Wulfstan, following Theodulf, ordered every priest to have a school in his house. [3] Yet there must have been many up-country priests serving proprietary churches whose technical equipment was unsatisfactory. They had learned little from teachers who themselves were ignorant. [4] Such men Ælfric chided: 'What secular art can be learned without study and labour? And do you not see that the secular arts are flourishing everywhere? No one ploughs who has not learned the art of agriculture. . . . How can you acquire or use your spiritual art without hard work? Spiritual artificers should not be inferior to secular ones.' [5]

The great need in such a church was for centres of scholarship which could supply the bishops with learned treatises written in Latin and the lower clergy with simple textbooks written in the vernacular. The tenth-century revival in the English church took a form which met these requirements perfectly. The foundation or restoration of monasteries entailed their equipment with a theological, legal, and liturgical library and with the standard educational manuals. Search had to be made for books to be copied and thought had to be given to the compilation of suitable collections of canon law. The leaders imported books and teachers from the best houses in Europe, from Fleury on the Loire with its fine library and from several Lotharingian monasteries, and made certain that the English establishments

---

[1] St Wulfstan was educated first at Evesham and then at Peterborough in the third decade of the century without apparently having a monastic career in mind: *Vita Wulfstani*, pp. 4–6.

[2] Cf. Ælfric, ed. Fehr, *Die Hirtenbriefe Ælfrics*, Ep. 3, cc. 38–41, 90, and Wulfstan's 'Canons enacted under King Edgar', c. 10, 'And we enjoin that no priest receive another's scholar without leave of him whom he had previously followed': Thorpe, *Ancient Laws*, ii. 247; cf. also c. 51.

[3] 'Ecclesiastical Institutes' (= Theodulf's *Capitula*), c. xx, *ibid*. ii. 414. In the previous chapter he invites priests, wishing to put their relations to learning, to send them to one of his own churches.

[4] Ælfric, in his preface to *Genesis*, writes of the ignorant priest who was his teacher: *The Heptateuch*, ed. S. J. Crawford (EETS, 160, 1922), pp. 76 ff.

[5] *Die Hirtenbriefe Ælfrics*, Ep. 2, cc. 145–55. Cap. 11 of Wulfstan's 'Canons enacted under King Edgar', *ut supra*, orders that every priest should in addition to lore, diligently learn a handicraft. See also 'Ecclesiastical Institutes' (= Theodulf's *Capitula*), Thorpe, *Ancient Laws*, ii. 404.

would be centres of learning and art.[1] Thus England drew deeply on the Carolingian renaissance, which in its turn had been stimulated by English scholars.

There was, therefore, a strong insular tradition deriving both directly from the Roman missionaries to Britain and indirectly by way of the Frankish Empire. This heritage appeared strange to the Normans and aroused their disapproval, sometimes even hostility. The English church was old-fashioned. There were the customs introduced by St Gregory and St Augustine, the use of the Roman psalter, never abandoned for the Gallican or vulgate version, and the use of a Bible similar to the *versio antiqua*, again preserved against the competition of the vulgate text.[2] The Normans also preferred William of Dijon's new-fangled version of Gregorian plainsong.[3] The church of St Salvator (Christ Church) Canterbury was suposed to be modelled on St Peter's Rome.[4] But, even if it had not been burned, Lanfranc would probably have pulled it down in favour of a more modern building in the fashionable style. There was the monastic constitution of the church and the use of the Benedictine Office in many cathedrals.[5] There were the primitive penitential and dietary laws stemming from the Roman missionaries, the Celtic church, and Theodore.[6] Then there were the insular accretions: the vernacular literature and the insular script, the church calendars, peculiar to each church, but as a family distinctly English and in some respects repugnant to outsiders.[7] The English church was not remarkable in being individual.

[1] Cf. Mary Bateson, 'Rules for monks and secular canons after the revival under King Edgar', *EHR*, ix (1894), 690–1. H. W. Keim, 'Æthelwold und die Mönchreform in England', *Anglia*, xli (1917), 405–43, stresses the importance of Æthelwold and Winchester. Sir Frank Stenton, *Early History of Abingdon* (1913), p. 7, and Eric John, 'The King and the Monks in the tenth-century Reformation', *BJRL*, xlii (1959), p. 69, emphasize the influence of Æthelwold and Abingdon.

[2] *The Bosworth Psalter*, pp. 6–14.

[3] Abbot Thurstin, 'Gregorianum cantum aspernatus', wanted the monks to learn 'cujusdam Willelmi Fiscanensis cantum'. They refused, 'quippe qui jam tam in hoc quam in alio ecclesiastico officio secundum Romanae morem ecclesiae insenuerant'. The bloody result is well known. See Malmesbury, *De Antiqu. Glaston. ecclesie*, i. 113–16.

[4] Eadmer, *De reliquiis S. Audoeni et quorundam aliorum sanctorum quae Cantuariae in ecclesia domini salvatoris habentur*, *HCY*, i. pp. xlv–xlvi.

[5] *The Bosworth Psalter*, p. 129. In 1071, when the monks of Winchester were threatened with ejection, Pope Alexander II wrote, 'Sunt etiam nonnulli qui asserunt fere omnes majores ecclesias ejus terrae consuetudinem monastici ordinis ex eo cepisse et tenuisse quod S. Augustinus . . . in hac forma religionis et cultu praecipue constituit et ordinavit. . . . statuta mutare vel infringere indignum esse ducimus, praesertim cum ea catholicae fidei eruditionibus obesse non invenimus': *Anglia Sacra*, i. 321.   [6] See above, pp. 262 ff.

[7] Gasquet and Bishop believed that the large 'martyrological' element in the English calendars was derived from the Breviate of the *Martyrologium Hieronymianum*, going under the name of the

But individuality and deep-seated traditions were no longer in favour. Custom was no defence against customs familiar to a new master or against what a revolutionary Roman church believed to be the law.[1]

The English church was, however, unaware of this danger. From the new monastic centres English learning was diffused; and it spread even more purposefully through the efforts of Ælfric and Wulfstan, reformers of the second generation, Ælfric the pupil of St Æthelwold of Winchester, Wulfstan, possibly from the same school, but as bishop and archbishop able to tap many sources.[2] There was, however, one serious weakness in the situation. Few of the scholars could write plain and simple Latin. Mostly they wrote in a 'babu' style, usually opaque through the use of clichés, often turbid owing to the desire to impress, and almost always, except in the simplest narrative, a barrier between the writer and his readers. In short, linguistic skill in Latin was generally insufficient. And although Ælfric could produce in his *Colloquy* easy conversational pieces for monastic oblates, fashion still favoured, for communication between adults, a pompous and rhetorical style and a difficult vocabulary, as Greek as possible.[3] The Anglo-Saxons loved their riddles; and such 'Hisperic' Latin was unsuitable for educational purposes. Information could not be disseminated among the mass of the clergy in this medium. And instead of developing a 'basic' Latin which might have been within the reach of the lower clergy, it was decided, probably quite realistically, to use English. As a result there was in the last century of the Old-English kingdom a great reflorescence of English literature. The vocabulary was enriched through loan words and borrowed technical expressions, the grammar was reformed by Latinists, and in the end there was no branch of

Martyrologium Gellonense, introduced into England soon after its making, probably in Offa's reign (*The Bosworth Psalter*, pp. 145–57). The 'sacramentary' element was, of course, variously derived. There was always a large English admixture. The Normans were suspicious of the English saints – Lanfranc even dropped St Dunstan from the Canterbury Calendar (*ibid.* pp. 32, 63–4) – and they disliked and suppressed such peculiarities as the feast of St Benedict in March, commemorating his death and burial at Monte Cassino, instead of in July, commemorating the translation of his relics to Fleury (*ibid.* p. 23), and the feasts of the Conception of the B.V.M. (8 December) and her Oblation in the Temple (21 Nov.), introduced into England possibly from Greek monasteries in Southern Italy in the eleventh century (*ibid.* pp. 43–52).

[1] It is, of course, disputed whether the Gregorian age should be considered a period of revolution or of reform. For a view of this and a discussion of the 'antipathetical concepts' of *veritas/lex* and *consuetudo*, see G. B. Ladner, 'Two Gregorian letters', *Studi Gregoriani*, v (1956), 221 ff.

[2] For Wulfstan and Ælfric, see also above, pp. 68 ff.

[3] Cf. Lantfred of St Swithun, *Anglia Sacra*, i. 322. See further Michael Lapidge, 'Three Latin poems from Æthelwold's school at Winchester', *Anglo-Saxon England*, ed. Peter Clemoes, i (1972), 85; 'The hermeneutic [*sic*] style in tenth-century Anglo-Latin literature', *ibid.* iv (1975), 67.

learning which could not be satisfactorily expressed in the vernacular. Latin could be translated with ease into idiomatic English.[1] It was a great achievement, and, despite, the Norman Conquest and the introduction of French, of more than ephemeral importance. But the writers were always a little ashamed of their work [2] and this vernacular achievement made no impression on the Latin world. Sigebert of Gembloux, in his catalogue of ecclesiastical authors which he finished in 1111, included only Bede (c. 68), Alcuin (c. 83), Boniface (c. 121), and Aldhelm (c. 132) of the English pre-Conquest writers,[3] and Bede is the only one of these to get a substantial notice.

Ælfric worked out a comprehensive educational programme and forged for himself a distinctive and excellent vernacular style. His main output was while he was at Cerne Abbas (Dorset) as monk, parish priest, and teacher (987–1005).[4] First came his two volumes of *Catholic Homilies* (989; 992),[5] which he had probably preached himself and which would serve any priest, together with an Appendix, *De temporibus anni*,[6] a manual on ecclesiastical astronomy and the reckoning of time. He produced next his *Grammar*, the first Latin grammar in any vernacular and also remarkable for its grammatical treatment of English, his *Glossary*,[7] and his delightful *Colloquy*,[8] to give monastic oblates practice in speaking Latin. At the same time (992–1002) he was working on his *Lives of Saints*, with, as an Appendix, a version of Alcuin's *Interrogationes Sigewulfi*.[9] He had also started to translate parts of the Old Testament, and continued with this work, reaching Judges,[10] until he became abbot of Eynsham in 1005.

This library for priests was a great bequest from the tenth to the eleventh century. Homiliaries and martyrologies were, of course, common books. But

---

[1] Cf. Peter Goolden's Introduction to his *The Old English Apollonius of Tyre* (1958). For recent studies of the vernacular literature, see the bibliographies and various articles in *Anglo-Saxon England* (1972 →). [2] Cf. Ælfric, *Grammar*, p. 1. [3] *Liber de Script. Eccles, MPL*, clx, coll. 547 ff.

[4] P. A. M. Clemoes, 'The Chronology of Ælfric's Works', *The Anglo-Saxons* (1959), pp. 212–47.

[5] For the date, see Kenneth Sisam, 'Ælfric's *Catholic Homilies*', *Studies in the History of Old English Literature* (1953), pp. 157–60.

[6] Ed. Heinrich Henel (EETS, 1942).

[7] *Ælfrics Grammatik und Glossar*, ed. Julius Zupitza (Berlin 1880).

[8] Ed. G. N. Garmonsway (Methuen's Old English Library, 2nd edn., 1947); and see *idem*, 'The Development of the Colloquy', *The Anglo-Saxons*, ed. Peter Clemoes, pp. 248–61.

[9] G. E. MacLean, 'Ælfric's version of Alcuini Interrogationes Sigewulfi in Genesin', *Anglia*, vi (1883), 425 ff., vii (1884), 1 ff.

[10] *The Old English version of the Heptateuch, Ælfric's Treatise on the Old and New Testament, and his preface to Genesis*, ed. S. J. Crawford, EETS, 160 (1922).

Ælfric reworked the material and went behind the current editions.[1] For his legends of the apostles and saints he used one or more collections of these, and his exegetical homilies were based primarily on those of Gregory the Great, on the commentaries and mathematical-scientific treatises of Bede, and on St Augustine's sermons and commentaries. But he reveals acquaintance with many other theologians, including the English Alcuin, Alcuin's pupils, Haymo monk of Fulda and bishop of Halberstadt (*ob.* 853) and Amalarius of Metz archbishop of Trier (809–14), Theodulf bishop of Orleans (*ob.* 821), Smaragdus abbot of Aniane (*ob.* 843), and Ratramnus monk of Corbie (*ob.* after 868).[2] Ælfric's *De temporibus anni* relies almost entirely on Bede's *De temporum ratione*, *De temporibus*, and *De natura rerum*. Every parish priest was supposed to have his *computus* (OE gerim) – a textbook on ecclesiastical arithmetic, especially for the reckoning of Easter – and he needed clear instruction on how to use it. Although Ælfric's treatise is severely practical and eschews all Bede's scientific curiosity, it could not have been entirely satisfactory, for in 1011 Byhrtferth attempted an improvement with his *Handbóc*.[3] Ælfric's *Grammar*, on the other hand, was a very popular text.

Ecclesiastical law was a branch of theology, and Ælfric's work in this field was of the greatest importance, although overshadowed a little by the greater influence of Wulfstan's studies. Ælfric's main contribution was to compose what are usually called his pastoral letters for the use of bishops.[4] He wrote three of these in Latin, which he also translated into English, the first (*c.* 992–3) [5] for his diocesan bishop, St Wulfsige III of Sherborne, the other two, after he had been consulted by Wulfstan on various points of law,[6] and after he had become abbot of Eynsham, for the archbishop (after 1005).[7] Letters I and II open with a homily on chastity, then give instruction on the clerical grades, and finally lay down the duties of priests and the faults they

---

[1] Max Förster, 'Über die Quellen von Ælfrics Homiliae Catholicae', *Berlin Philos. Dissert.* 1892, 'Ueber die Quellen von Ælfrics exegetischen Homiliae Catholicae', *Anglia*, xvi (1894), 1–61; B. Fehr, *op. cit.* pp. lxxxiv f., 'Über einige Quellen zu Ælfrics "Homiliae Catholicae" ', *Archiv für das Studium der neureren Sprachen u. Literaturen*, n.s. xxx (1913), 378–81; J. H. Ott, *Über die Quellen der Heiligenleben in Ælfrics Lives of the Saints*, Halle-Wittenberg Philos. Dissert. 1892.

[2] His teaching on the Eucharist was sometimes suspected of heresy.

[3] Heinrich Henel, *Studien zum altenglischen Computus* (Beiträge zur englischen Philologie, xxvi, Leipzig, 1934). Dr Henel suggests, p. 22, that the prototype of the *computus* used in the eleventh century was composed *c.* 970.   [4] Ed. Bernhard Fehr, *op. cit.*

[5] For the date, see K. Sisam, *op. cit.* pp. 169–71.

[6] Ælfric's reply, printed Fehr, pp. 222 ff.

[7] Wulfstan seems also to have made his own English version of Ep. 2. See Fehr, pp. lxv ff. and K. Jost, *Englische Studien*, lii (1918), 105–12.

should avoid. 'The canons are those rules which the Holy Fathers established, in which are written how canons, that is regular clerks, should live. In these we read, and you too can read if you choose, the following:'.[1] These letters are in fact *Epistolae de canonibus*, or episcopal capitularies such as the Frankish bishops had issued at the end of the eighth and in the ninth century.[2] They enact, in the form of episcopal injunctions, the Rule for priests. Letter III is concerned for the most part with the liturgy, with the proper handling of the sacraments; but the last ten chapters repeat what Ælfric had written earlier to Wulfstan on the wrongfulness of the clergy judging robbers and thieves. Ælfric also re-edited the tenth-century Rule for English monks, the *Regularis Concordia*, for his monastery and issued a special version suitable for secular clergy.[3]

Ælfric was the scholar; Wulfstan was as well the high prelate. He reestablished ecclesiastical discipline in his wild and semi-pagan province,[4] issuing laws for the clergy and laity, providing a Rule for his minsters, composing treatises on legal themes important at the time, and, like Ælfric, preaching sermons which became popular. His *Institutes of Polity*, in the tradition of the Carolingian 'Königsspiegel' literature, is an interesting essay on the duties of the English governing classes. Moreover, by writing the reform programme into the royal laws, he gave it the widest circulation and an added authority. This Worcester-York stream of reform is one which can be traced right through our period. Wulfstan's nephew, Brihtheah, succeeded to Worcester in 1033, and was a patron of Wulfstan II of Worcester, the saint and reformer (1062–95).[5] Ealdred, bishop of Worcester (1046–62) and archbishop of York (1061–9), enacted canons for his province on the eve of the Norman Conquest.[6] And it was from the diocese of Worcester that the impetus came which re-established monasticism in the North of England after the Conquest.

The sources used by Ælfric and Wulfstan have received some attention.[7] They are essentially the books collected during the monastic reform of the

---

[1] Ep. 2 (Latin), cc. 84–5.   [2] Fournier and Le Bras, i. 112–4.
[3] Fehr, pp. cxxiv ff; printed in part, *ibid*. pp. 234 ff.   [4] See above, pp. 70–1.
[5] Wulfstan II of Worcester incorporated his namesake's sermons into his own homiliary: D. Bethurum, *The Homilies of Wulfstan*, p. 56.
[6] Folcard, *Vita S. Johannis*, HCY, i. 241–2. See *Vita Ædwardi*, pp. liii ff.
[7] For Ælfric, see Max Förster, *op. cit.* pp. 1–61, and B. Fehr, *op. cit.* For Wulfstan, see especially K. Jost, 'Einige Wulfstantexte und ihre Quellen', *Anglia*, lvi (1932), 265–315, *Wulfstanstudien* (Bern, 1050), and D. Bethurum, *op. cit.* where there is a list on pp. 109–10. See also above, p. 282, *n*. 1.

tenth century, and so go back to the compilations made in the Frankish empire in the century before – products of the Carolingian renaissance. Ælfric probably relied mainly on the collections made by Æthelwold at Winchester, Abingdon, and other monasteries. Wulfstan, who plundered Ælfric, was at least as widely read, for he found a fine library at Worcester, rich especially in legal manuscripts, and perhaps some relics of Alcuin's library at York. It was his habit to make scrapbooks of useful extracts, and some of his own working collections have survived.[1]

The most important sources used by Ælfric and Wulfstan were the compilations which the Carolingian reformers fathered on Charlemagne and Lewis the Pious, the *Capitula a sacerdotibus proposita*, approved by Charlemagne at Aachen in 802, and the enactments of the council of Aachen in 817,[2] the *Memoriale* and the *Capitulare monasticum* inspired by Benedict of Aniane,[3] and the *Institutio canonicorum*,[4] drawn up by either Amalarius of Metz, Alcuin's pupil, or Ansegisius abbot of St Wandrille. Ælfric probably knew the *Capitula a sacerdotibus proposita*, a piece attached in several English manuscripts to the false penitential of Egbert, as *Jura sacerdotum* or *Jus sacerdotale*.[5] Wulfstan translated a chapter of the *Institutio canonicorum*.[6] Ælfric also used the *Excerptiones Ps.–Egberti*, a collection of canons probably made in the second half of the ninth century either in England or western Francia.[7] The sources of this work are the fourth book of the Frankish collection of canons, the *Collectio Vaticana* or *Quadripartitus*, thought to be the 'lost' *De Vita sacerdotum* of Halitgar bishop of Cambrai (816–31),[8] the

---

[1] Mary Bateson, 'A Worcester Cathedral Book of Ecclesiastical Collections, made c. 1000 A.D.', *EHR*, x (1895), 712 ff.; D. Bethurum, 'Archbishop Wulfstan's Commonplace Book', *PMLA*, lvii (1942), 916–29, *Homilies*, pp. 98–101. Miss Bethurum suggests that Ælfric furnished Wulfstan with many of the texts.

[2] Hefele-Leclercq, *Histoire des conciles*, iv. 9 ff.; Hauck, *Kirchengeschichte Deutschlands*, ii. 595 ff.; Fournier and Le Bras, i. 93.

[3] Cf. Mary Bateson, 'Rules for monks and secular canons after the revival under King Edgar', *EHR*, ix (1894), 693 ff.

[4] *Ibid.* pp. 691 ff.; B. Fehr, *Die Hirtenbriefe Ælfrics*, p. cxvii; J. C. Dickinson, *The Origins of the Austin Canons and their introduction into England* (1950), pp. 18 ff.; *Enlarged Rule of Chrodegang*, ed. A. S. Napier (EETS, 150, 1916).

[5] Fehr, *op. cit.* pp. xciv ff.; Bethurum, *Archbishop Wulfstan's Commonplace Book*, p. 919. It was a source for Wulfstan's 'Canons enacted under King Edgar'.

[6] Wulfstan, *Polity*, pp. 248 ff.

[7] Thorpe, *Ancient Laws*, ii. 97; Wasserschleben, *Die Bussordnungen*, pp. 45 ff.; Fehr, *op. cit.* pp. xcvii ff.; Fournier and Le Bras, i. 316 ff.

[8] Mary Bateson, 'The supposed Latin penitential of Egbert and the missing work of Halitgar of Cambrai', *EHR*, ix (1894), 320–6.

Capitula a sacerdotibus proposita, mentioned above, Frankish capitularies collected by Ansegisius, a collection of councils known as *Statuta ecclesiae antiqua*, and the Irish collection of canons, the *Hibernensis*.[1] Ælfric and Wulfstan were also acquainted with Amalarius's *De ecclesiasticis officiis libri quattuor* [2] and with various episcopal capitularies, such as those of Theodulf bishop of Orleans (*ob.* 821), Alcuin's companion at Charlemagne's court, and Gerebald bishop of Liége (787–809).[3] Wulfstan used as well the much more recent Atto of Vercelli's (*ob.* 961) *De pressuris ecclesiasticis*.[4] Ælfric and Wulfstan were probably familiar with several penitentials, the manuals for confessors. Ælfric certainly made use of the *P. Ps.–Theodori*,[5] a Frankish work of the ninth century, and the true and false penitentials of Egbert.[6] They naturally had access to various pontificals, the service books for bishops; and it goes without saying that the Bible and the Rule of St Benedict were always in their mind.

This corpus of canonical writings, although traditional and sound, is to be regarded as a little old-fashioned for the eleventh century. It is noteworthy that no direct use seems to have been made either of the great ancient collections received by the Carolingian church – the *Hadriana* and the *Hispana* – or of the Isidorian forgeries of the mid-ninth century. The avoidance of the apocrypha was doubtless due to the reserved attitude of Fleury and Lorraine in the tenth century to these productions.[7] The English contribution to canon law is sometimes despised and often depreciated. The insular tradition, with its penitentials, can be viewed as perverted. The writing of legal works in the vernacular carries no prestige. And the failure to produce an outstanding or influential collection in the tenth and eleventh centuries makes England of little importance in general histories. But penitentials,

---

[1] For which see Fournier and Le Bras, i. 62–4. Ælfric may have used the *Hibernensis* directly, Fehr, *op. cit.* p. cxix.   [2] Bateson, *Rules*, pp. 702 ff.; Fehr, *op. cit.* p. cxvii.

[3] These were based mainly on the *Hadriana* and *Hispana*. A. Werminghoff, 'Capitula episcoporum saec. VIII et IX', *Neues Archiv*, xxvi (1901), xxvii (1902); Fournier and Le Bras, i. 112–14. Theodulf's *Capitula* was a text widespread in England. It was in the Wulfstan collection: D. Bethurum, 'Archbishop Wulfstan's Commonplace Book', *PMLA*, lvii (1942), 916. An Old-English version, under the title 'Ecclesiastical Institutes', is in Thorpe, *Ancient Laws*, ii. 400–42, and an incomplete version in *Capitula of Theodulf*, ed. A. S. Napier, EETS, 150 (1916).

[4] *MPL*, cxxxiv.

[5] For which see Fournier and Le Bras, i. 111, and above, p. 264. For Ælfric's and Wulfstan's collection of penitentials, see D. Bethurum, *Archbishop Wulfstan's Commonplace Book*, p. 927.

[6] Haddan and Stubbs, *Councils*, iii. 413; Thorpe, *Ancient Laws*, ii. 170. For *P. Ps.–Egberti* see Fournier and Le Bras, i. 108–10, and above, pp. 264–5.

[7] B. Fehr, *op. cit.* pp. cxvi ff.; Fournier and Le Bras, i. 328–9.

although always despised by purists, were indispensable.[1] The vernacular renderings secured for Christian rules an unparalleled influence in the secular kingdom. And the unhappy conditions which stimulated the assembly, or fabrication, of new collections of canons elsewhere in Christendom – despair at the humiliation of the church, domestic controversy, and the absence of legislation – simply did not exist in England. Mediocrity of achievement can indeed be allowed. But it was due less to mental torpor than to a tolerable situation and respect for the accustomed authorities.

Ælfric and Wulfstan were also widely read in the Carolingian theologians and liturgiologists, such as Pirmin (*ob.* 753/4), Alcuin and Ps.–Alcuin (Wulfstan especially being attracted to Alcuin's letters), and Alcuin's pupil, Rabanus Maurus, abbot of Fulda and archbishop of Mainz (*ob.* 856),[2] an encyclopaedic writer. Wulfstan made a special study of baptism, and had read Theodulf and Jesse bishop of Amiens (799–836) on the subject.[3] They knew a few later writers, such as Abbo Cernuus, monk of St Germain-des-Prés, Paris (*ob.* after 921) [4] and the 'Anonymous of Boulogne',[5] and some earlier authorities, such as Rufinus of Aquileia (*ob. c.* 410), Caesarius of Arles (*ob.* 543), Isidore of Seville (*ob.* 636), and St Eligius of Noyon (*ob.* 660). No doubt they were also directly acquainted with some of the Early Fathers. But neither was a pure scholar. They usually took what they wanted from the most convenient sources of information.

For his liturgical knowledge Ælfric drew mostly, of course, on the English revision of the Rule of St Benedict, the *Regularis Concordia*, for which his teacher, St Æthelwold, was largely responsible. Its liturgy is based ultimately on the *Ordines Romani*. Ghent and Fleury, monasteries represented at the council which drew up the English rule, may have exerted some influence; but English practice seems in the main to have been derived from Corbie. It was from that Frankish house that Æthelwold drew monks to teach Gregorian plainsong to his monasteries,[6] and it has been noticed that

---

[1] It is interesting to note that Burchard of Worms in 1008-12, although he doubted the authority of Theodore, nevertheless included pieces from Theodore in his *Decretum* and simply suppressed the *inscriptio* : Fournier and Le Bras, i. 379-80.

[2] 'De clericorum institutione', *MPL*, cvii; 'De ecclesiastica disciplina', *MPL*, cxii.

[3] 'De ordine baptismi', 'Epistola de baptismo', *MPL*, cv.

[4] 'De cena domini', *MPL*, cxxxii. An Old-English translation is in Corpus Christi College Cambridge, MS. 190, ff. 353-9.

[5] For this MS. see B. Fehr, *op. cit.* pp. x ff. It had belonged to St Bertin and may be of English origin. Certainly it contains Ælfric's letter (2a) to Wulfstan.

[6] *Chron. Abingdon*, i. 129.

some of the peculiarities of the *Regularis Concordia* are similar to those in the *Codex Ratoldi*, a sacramentary apparently copied for an abbot of Corbie who died in 986. Thus an *Ordo Romanus* supplied by Corbie may have served as the basic text.[1] Wulfstan, as we have seen,[2] went to Metz for his *Regula canonicorum*.

It is clear that the ecclesiastical revival in England was firmly based on traditional theological and legal literature. Ælfric and Wulfstan were not original thinkers. They were less creative than Bede. But they found in the writings left by the ninth-century Frankish church material which was applicable to English conditions two centuries later. The tone was exactly right. Carolingian reform had been effected by the king working through and in co-operation with his bishops. Hence it is not surprising that themes which were soon to become important among the canonists, such as the powers of the papacy, the rights of appeal from one level to another, the technicalities of ecclesiastical jurisprudence, and the independence of the church from royal control, find little or no place in the English productions.

Ælfric and Wulfstan were interested only in current problems; and the greatest of these was the instruction of the clergy and laity in Christian practices and discipline. Their natural inclinations were, however, dissimilar.[3] Ælfric was essentially the moralist, who taught by historical example and allegory, whose aim was to please as well as improve. At the centre of his religious thought was the antithesis between good and evil. Wulfstan was without Ælfric's tenderness and charm and purely literary interests. He was the instructor, the disciplinarian, the judge. For him things were right or wrong. By establishing the duties of all ranks and orders he gave to the English people a Christian rule to follow. Thus these two great teachers, complementary in their attitude and method, provided a body of instructional literature of the greatest importance. And their works were still being copied in the twelfth century and read, if with difficulty, in the thirteenth.[4] How far the law was observed is another matter. As Ælfric and Wulfstan knew, the besetting sin of the clergy was indifference to their vocation; and, when the temptations of the world were so great, satisfactory standards in both clergy and laity could be achieved only through constant goading. We

---

[1] B. Fehr, *op. cit.* pp. cxxiii f. Cf. also Thomas Symons, *Regularis Concordia* (Nelson's Medieval Classics, 1953), pp. xlv ff., *The Missal of the New Minister, Winchester*, ed. D. H. Turner (HBS, xciii, 1962).   [2] See above, p. 284.

[3] K. Jost makes an interesting comparison in *Wulfstanstudien*, pp. 168 ff.

[4] Cf. B. Fehr, *op. cit.* pp. xx f.; D. Bethurum, *Homilies*, pp. 24–5, 104.

may be sure that when there was a good bishop, as often at Worcester and York, some attempt was made to enforce the Rule. But where the bishop was worldly and indifferent the laws with their guardians slept.

At its worst the ecclesiastical culture of the eleventh century was a swamp formed by brackish trickles from ancient civilizations. There was variety enough. A priest could even read much of the pleasant romance *Apollonius of Tyre* in an excellent translation. But only fragments of learning were to hand, and usually in such debased forms that only the most outstanding scholars could make anything of them. Science was at its lowest ebb. Some priests no doubt dabbled in astrology, a forbidden subject, and were acquainted with 'the last fading traces' of Greek medicine,[1] a decomposed and revolting study. And it was only the superhuman efforts of a few men which kept the air fresh above the nastiness of the sub-antique, the stagnant end of an old world.

[1] Charles Singer, Introduction to *Leechdoms* (1961), p. xlvii.

CHAPTER VII

England and the Papacy

Anglo-papal relations rightly come last in a constitutional study of the English church in the first half of the eleventh century because they were of relatively small importance at the time and also because the subject forms a bridge to a new age. The divine institution of the papacy, the pope's primacy in the church, and his power to legislate, govern, and judge were recognized in all the great collections of canon law current in western Christendom. It was both a tradition and a theory. In fact the bishops were, ecclesiastically, almost autonomous. The ninth-century Isidorian collectors and forgers stressed papal supremacy, but only in the interest of the bishops. Burchard bishop of Worms, in his great and influential *Decretum* (1008–12), naturally regarded the bishop as the ordinary and normal organ of spiritual government. The bishop had occasionally to co-operate with his fellows in provincial councils; and above them all was the pope. But the pope was distant and his intervention unexpected.[1] The pope was the necessary apex of the hierarchy – for a system which could not be expressed in monarchical terms was almost inconceivable – the keystone of the arch. And he was not expected, despite his theoretical powers, to get out of place.

Reverence for the papacy is quite another matter. Italy was too close to be impressed. The other fragments of the Carolingian church had independent traditions. Respect was greatest in England. Rome was the mother church. Bede's Ecclesiastical History kept alive the story of the special relationship between the two churches. No other daughter could show a greater tradition of love and untroubled obedience than the Anglo-Saxon community, and there were even elements in England's willing subjection to Rome which could lead the more ambitious and legally-minded popes of the later eleventh century to believe that the kingdom of England itself was subordinate to the papacy.[2] The frequent dedication of sacred buildings in

---

[1] Fournier and Le Bras, i. 133, 387–90.

[2] Cf. Alexander II to William I, *ep.* cxxxiv, *MPL*, cxlvi, col. 1413, Jaffé-Wattenbach, *Regesta Pontificum Romanorum* (1885), no. 4757, 'Novit prudentia tua Anglorum regnum, ex quo nomen Christi ibi clarificatum est, sub apostolorum principis manu et tutela extitisse, donec quidam . . . pactum dei abjecerunt et Anglorum populum a via veritatis averterunt.'

England to St Peter and St Paul was a memorial to the bond;[1] Rome-scot was perhaps a less welcome reminder; and the custom of pilgrimage to the threshold of the apostles made manifest and nourished the devotion of the people. Many Englishmen, no doubt, were content with humbler shrines; but few aspired higher than Rome.[2]

In Rome was a permanent settlement of Englishmen, known as the *Schola Saxonum*,[3] one of the four *scholae* of foreigners situated in Trastevere in the 'vicus Saxonum' on the Vatican hill in the Leonine city.[4] The English called it their 'burh' or borough,[5] a name which still survives as *il Borgo*. In the borough was the church of St Mary in Saxia; and on this site Innocent III founded in 1204 the church and hospital of Santo Spirito in Sassia. The borough was twice destroyed by fire in the ninth century, and had most recently been restored by Pope Leo IV (847-55), who built the church.[6] The exact nature of the corporation is uncertain. A *schola* was a guild or association, which could exist for various purposes. The Roman militia was organized on the basis of regional *scholae*; but, although the foreign schools helped on occasion to defend the city, it seems unlikely that the *Schola Saxonum* was an expatriate military unit[7] like the Varangian regiment of the imperial guard at Byzantium. Nor could it have been an educational establishment or seminary. Most probably it was an organization founded by English *peregrini*, pilgrims and merchants, who decided to settle in the city and who drew some of their livelihood from their more transient successors.[8] It was a privileged body. King Alfred had obtained for it freedom from all taxation,[9] and Pope Leo IX in 1053 respected its right to the burial of all

---

[1] W. Levison, *England and the Continent in the Eighth Century*, pp. 33 ff.

[2] See above, pp. 20 ff.

[3] *Liber pontificalis*, ed. L. Duchesne (1955), ii. 53, and Pope Alexander II, *ep.* cxxxiv, refer to it as the *Schola Anglorum*.

[4] See O. Jensen, 'The "Denarius sancti Petri" in England', *Trans. R. Hist. Soc.*, n.s., xv (1901), 174-7.

[5] 'gentis Anglorum . . . habitatio, quae in eorum lingua burgus dicitur': *Liber pontificalis*, ii. 53. It was built of wood: hence the fires.   [6] *Liber pontificalis*, ii. 128.

[7] As W. H. Stevenson believed, *Asser's Life of King Alfred* (1904), p. 243; and cf. Levison, p. 40. For William Lunt's criticism, see *Financial relations of the papacy with England to 1327* (1939), pp. 12-13.

[8] As Lunt argues, p. 13. Cf. *Asser's Life of King Alfred*, p. 53, 'scholam Saxonum in Roma morantium'. *Liber pontificalis*, ii. 128, refers especially to *peregrini*. St Albans's tradition attributed its foundation to King Offa of Mercia: see Malmesbury, *GR.* i. 85, 109; *Gesta abbatum monasterii S. Albani*, i. 5.

[9] From Pope Marinus (882-4), *ASC* 885; *Asser's Life of King Alfred*, p. 53. According to Florence, i. 185, Cnut obtained a similar privilege in 1027 from Pope John XIX.

Englishmen who died within.[1] It was supposed to be the burial place of English kings,[2] and had a romantic appeal to Englishmen at home. The *schola* was also maintained partly at their charge, for Peter's Pence seems connected with it, and in the eleventh century part of that tribute went to its church.[3] Its existence is proof of the age-long interest that Englishmen showed in Rome; and its presence no doubt made things easier for the pilgrim.

In the eleventh century King Cnut's splendid pilgrimage of 1027 set the example.[4] 'I learned from wise men', he wrote, 'that the holy Apostle Peter had received from the Lord great power to bind and to loose, and was the keeper of the keys of the kingdom of heaven; and I considered it very profitable diligently to seek his special favour before God.' [5] His jarl Harold followed him in 1042.[6] About 1056 Earl Harold, Godwin's son, made the journey,[7] and in 1061 his younger brothers, Tostig and Gyrth.[8] As the earls, so the thegns,[9] and a number of lesser people too.[10] Men made their wills before the 'south-fare'.[11] The journey was hazardous even for the great. Cnut took advantage of the concourse for the coronation of the Emperor Conrad II to complain about the lack of security and the unreasonable barriers and tolls on the routes to Rome, and persuaded the emperor, King

[1] Jaffé-Wattenbach, *Regesta Pontificum Romanorum*, no. 4292, *MPL*, cxliii, col. 704: 'praeter Anglos venientes de Anglia, qui, si in scola Saxiae infirmantur et ibi moriuntur, ibi sepeliantur.'

[2] Stevenson, *Asser's Life of King Alfred*, p. 244.

[3] Pope Alexander II, *ep.* cxxxiv, and see below, p. 295. Stevenson, *Asser's Life*, pp. 211, *n.* 2, 244, will not accept that Peter's Pence was established for the maintenance of the school. Lunt, pp. 13–16, is more cautious. St Albans believed that Offa started the tribute to maintain the school: see Jensen, pp. 178 ff., and cf. Henry of Huntingdon, *Historia Anglorum*, ed. T. Arnold (RS 1879), p. 124.

[4] *ASC D* 1031; Florence, i. 185; *Enc. Emmae*, pp. lxii–lxiii, 34–8; Plummer, pp. 206–7. F. Barlow, 'Two Notes: Cnut's Second Pilgrimage and Queen Emma's disgrace in 1043', *EHR*, lxxiii (1958), 649.

[5] Liebermann, *Gesetze*, i. 276; *EHD*, i. 417.

[6] Adam of Bremen, *Gesta pontificum Hammaburgensis ecclesiae*, II, c. 75, *MPL*, cxlvi, col. 554.

[7] See above, p. 59.

[8] *Vita Ædwardi*, pp. 34 ff.; *Vita Wulfstani*, pp. 16–17; Malmesbury, *GP*, p. 252.

[9] E.g. Archbishop Stigand's thegn, Ketel, apparently with his stepdaughter, between 1052 and 1066: Whitelock, *Wills*, no. 34; a Lincolnshire thegn, Askell, same period, K. 806. Both have Scandinavian names.

[10] A dumb man of Canterbury: 'Mirac. of St Egwin', *Chron. Evesham*, p. 47; a woman cured by St Cuthbert: Symeon, *HDE*, p. 82. Cf. also Goscelin, *Vita S. Yvonis*, *MPL*, clv, col. 89, and 'Goscelin', *Miracula S. Swithuni*, *ibid.* col. 72. The Exeter guild statutes make provision for visits to Rome – 'aet suthfore [Thorpe translates "funeral"] aelc mon v. pening': Thorpe, *Diplomatarium*, p. 614, and the concessions which Cnut obtained at Rome in 1027 imply that the number of English travellers was considerable.

[11] The expression occurs Robertson, *Charters*, p. 4, and in the Exeter Guild Statutes (see previous note). For a will, see Whitelock, *Wills*, no. 34.

Rudolf of Burgundy, and some other princes to issue solemn decrees, supported by an oath, that the passage of both merchants and pilgrims should be eased and protected.[1] But the jarl Harold was killed on his way back to Denmark,[2] and Earl Tostig and his party were ambushed and robbed close to Rome.[3]

It was a long journey even by the shortest route. In 990 Archbishop Sigeric of Canterbury returned from Rome with the pallium by eighty stages to the English Channel.[4] His party passed through Sutri, Viterbo, Siena, and Lucca, and reached the River Po at Piacenza in thirty-eight stages. Ten halts later, having gone through Pavia, Vercelli, and Ivrea, and entered the kingdom of Burgundy below Aosta, they were at St Remy, under the Great St Bernard. Six further stages took them to Lausanne on Lake Geneva, another five to Besançon, and then they crossed the Saône out of the kingdom into the duchy of Burgundy. The party travelled through Champagne in eight stages by way of Brienne and Châlons-sur-Marne, made stops at Rheims and Laon, and with the seventy-fifth halt reached Arras in Flanders. The road through Thérouanne and Guines brought them finally to the Channel port of Wissant.[5] This was the direct route, the obvious choice for a prelate hurrying home. But it was not the only road. Tostig and his party went by 'Saxony and the upper Rhine'.[6] Princely travellers often had diplomatic duties on the way.

Journey's end was Rome, the holy city. Important men had business to do at the papal court; but for all there were the pilgrim's tasks, the visits to the most famous churches,[7] the gifts at the shrines, and the purchase of

---

[1] Liebermann, *Gesetze*, i. 276; *EHD*, i. 417. It is, of course, possible that Cnut went to Rome primarily for political reasons. He had possibly been specially invited to Conrad's coronation.

[2] His murderer was Duke Ordulf of Saxony, who had just married the sister of King Magnus of Norway, and the motive was political: Adam of Bremen, *ut supra.*   [3] *Vita Ædwardi*, pp. 35–6.

[4] *Memorials of St Dunstan*, pp. 92–5. For the route from Rome to Lucca, see Julius Jung, 'Das Itinerar des Erzbishofs Sigeric von Canterbury und die Strasse von Rom über Siena nach Luca', *Mittheilungen des Instituts für österreichische Geschichtsforschung*, xxv (1904), 31 ff; and see the map in J. N. L. Baker, 'Medieval Trade Routes', *Social Life in Early England* (ed. G. Barraclough, 1960), pp. 232–3. For Sigeric's route, see map above, pp. 12–13.

[5] He had been invited by Abbot Otbert of St Bertin, at St Omer, to visit the house so as to fulfil the promise made by his predecessor Æthelgar on his pallium journey (*Memorials of St Dunstan*, pp. 338–9). The visit may have been paid, of course, on the way out.

[6] *Vita Ædwardi*, p. 34. Presumably Tostig and Judith visited Count Baldwin V of Flanders, Judith's half-brother. Even if they then travelled by way of Basle, they probably crossed the Alps by the Great St Bernard pass. Harold's route (*ibid.* p. 33) is not stated.

[7] Cf. Cnut's letter of 1027, 'But now I give thanks to Almighty God, who has granted me in my lifetime to visit his holy Apostles, Peter and Paul, and every sacred place which I could learn of

relics and keepsakes.[1] In 990 Archbishop Sigeric stayed two or three days in the city.[2] On the first he toured the great basilicas outside the gates. Leaving St Peter's,[3] he visited St Mary's in the English school, crossed the Tiber by the Ponte S. Pietro, and, after calling at one of the churches of St Laurence,[4] passed through the Porta Flamina to visit St Valentine's by the Ponte Milvio. Then, moving in a clockwise direction, he made other sorties from the city, visiting the churches of St Agnes, one-and-a-half miles up the Via Nomentana from the Porta Pia, St Laurence, a little more than half a mile up the Via Tiburtina, St Sebastian, about two miles up the Appian way, and St Anastasius (now St Vincent and St Anastasius at the Three Fountains) and St Paul's at the second milestone, both on the Ostian way. He then traversed the Aventine, visiting the churches of St Boniface (now St Alexis), St Sabina, and St Mary in Cosmedin,[5] crossed the river probably by the Ponte S. Maria into Trastevere, where he viewed the churches of St Cecilia, St Chrysogonus, and St Mary, went through the Porta Aurelia to visit the church of St Pancras, and returned home, presumably to the *Schola Saxonum*, about a mile away.

The following morning Sigeric visited the churches of St Mary ad Martyres (the Pantheon)[6] and of the Holy Apostles on his way to take lunch with the pope at St John Lateran. Afterwards he visited S. Croce in Gerusalemme, and returned home by way of St Mary Major and St Peter ad Vincula, both on the Esquiline, and St Laurence in Panisperna,[7] on the highest point of the Viminal, the site of the martyrdom. In two days he had visited the 'Seven churches of Rome' – St John Lateran, St Peter, St Paul, St Laurence, St Mary Major, S. Croce, and St Sebastian – and sixteen other ancient buildings.

within the city of Rome and outside it, and in person to worship and adore there according to my desire': *EHD*, i. 417.

[1] Pavia, a staging point on the journey, was also a great market for relics; see Plummer, p. 204; Stevenson, *Asser's Life of King Alfred*, p. 209. Cf. Malmesbury. *GP*, p. 311.

[2] Two or possibly three days' itineraries are described: *Memorials of St Dunstan*, pp. 391-2.

[3] Where possibly he had received the pallium; cf. Æthelnoth's official visits, below, p. 298.

[4] The entry is 'S. Laurentium in craticula' (gridiron), a church which is listed again at the end of the itinerary as 'S. Laurentium ubi corpus ejus assatus est', i.e. the church built on the site of the martyrdom, St Laurence in Panisperna. Cf. the descriptions, 'S. Laurentii in Panisperna ubi; positus fuit in craticula' (*Codex urbis Romae topographicus*, ed. C. L. Urlichs, 1871, p. 175) and 'In thermis Olympiadis, ubi assatus fuit S. Laurentius, et vocatur ibi Panisperna' (*Ye solace of Pilgrimes*, ed. C. A. Mills, 1911, p. 101, *n.* 2). The duplication is probably a mistake; and the itinerary is simplified if we understand here St Laurence in Lucina or possibly St Laurence in Damaso. See also G. G. Willis, *Further Essays in Early Roman Liturgy* (1968), pp. 1 ff.   [5] 'S. Maria schola Graeca.'   [6] 'S. Maria rotunda.'   [7] See above, *n.* 4.

The visit to Rome was always costly and could be unreasonably expensive. Cnut complained about simony in so far as it affected the English church. Tostig made a fuss about the insecurity of the roads. But papal politics and morals and civic shortcomings were irrelevant to the purpose. It is possible, indeed, that the rapacious marketing of spiritual benefits enhanced their value to the ordinary purchaser. And Rome was worth any price. The magnitude of its ancient buildings, the splendour of its basilicas, and the profusion of the relics and associations still impress. In the eleventh century, when men built so small, acquired so little, they were astounding.

Yet the tarnished magnificence of Rome was not without danger for unsophisticated Christians. Corrupt religious practices in such a setting were most infectious. There was in all things an emphasis on outward show, beauty without piety, authority without ethical purpose; and the papal court, by selling privileges, set a bad example to prelates. Although not all the popes appointed by the Roman house of Tusculum – Benedict VIII (1012–24), his brother, John XIX (1024–32), and their nephew, Benedict IX (1032–46) – were worthless,[1] they were essentially prince-bishops with limited interests and influence. In 1046 the Emperor Henry III started the reform of the papacy by appointing Suidgar bishop of Bamberg (Clement II) to the office, and completed it by naming in 1048 his cousin, Bruno bishop of Toul. With Leo IX the popes began to rule again, and by 1057, when the last of Henry's nominees, Victor II, died, the papacy was established as a power with its own policy and ambitions. The relaxation of imperial control which followed Henry III's death gave the cardinals of the reform party their chance, and, triumphing over the renewed interference of local interests, which led to the 'intrusion' of Benedict X in 1058, they launched the papacy on its independent career. Nicholas II (1058–61) and Alexander II (1061–73) not only continued the moral drive which had started under imperial direction but also escaped from the tutelage of secular powers.

Even for the remote English church these events were momentous. Until 1048 every overture came from the English side. After that date papal policy became a factor that had to be taken into account. It was a disturbing influence in English ecclesiastical affairs.

England had two permanent business connections with the papacy. It owed tribute and its archbishops required the pallium.

[1] The first two have found defenders: cf. É. Amann and A. Dumas, *L'Église au pouvoir des laïques* (Paris, 1948), pp. 80–9.

Thietmar, bishop of Merseburg (1009-18), knew little English history; but he recorded in his Chronicle how shameful it was that the English, who took their name either from their angelic (that is, beautiful) appearance or from living in an angle of the land, and who were *tributarii* of Peter the prince of the apostles and spiritual sons of their holy father, St Gregory, should now have been forced to pay tribute to the Danish pirates.[1] The payment from England of an annual tribute to the pope was already an ancient custom in the eleventh century, and, like most ancient customs, its origin, history, and nature are obscure.[2] No other kingdom paid such a tax. According to a letter of Pope Alexander II, written between 1067 and 1073, the money was divided between the churches of St Peter and St Mary *in Schola Saxonum*, but in what proportion is unknown.[3] Originally it must have been a free-will gift from pious English kings. By the tenth century, however, it was a duty which had been transferred to the people,[4] presumably by means of an assessment laid on the king's *tuns*, which led to its association with the hundred, and, sometimes perhaps, to units of 100*d*. Liability spread from the kingdom of the original imposer of the tax to other regions in England as unification took place. But it was never paid from Wales or England north and west of the Tees,[5] and there were franchises.[6] There may, of course, have been regional differences in the method of assessment. The tax was called Rome-scot, *Romefeoh*, Rome-penny, and hearth-penny, and payment was due on 1 August, St Peter's day. It was levied by collecting 1*d*. from some householders. But by the eleventh century it was a customary payment and had often become entangled with other customs.[7] In some areas payment was

---

[1] *Chronicon*, VII, c. 26, *MPL*, cxxxix, col. 1381.

[2] The most thorough and recent investigation is Wm E. Lunt, *Financial relations of the papacy with England to 1327* (1939), ch. i. See also O. Jensen, 'The "Denarius sancti Petri" in England' *Trans. R. Hist. Soc.*, n.s., xv (1901), 171 ff.

[3] *MPL*, cxlvi, col. 1413, Jaffé-Wattenbach, no. 4757.

[4] It is first mentioned in the laws in I Edmund, c. 2 (942-6).   [5] Lunt, pp. 17-22.

[6] The monks of St Albans claimed in the thirteenth century that their exemption was based on a charter of King Offa, their traditional founder, whom they credited with the institution of Peter's Pence for the maintenance of the *schola* which he had established during a visit to Rome: 'Offa . . . denarium qui dicitur 'Sancti Petri' de maxima parte regni sui concessit, sane retento censu de tota terra S. Albani, ecclesiae S. Albani futuris temporibus die S. Petri ad Vincula persolvendo': *Gesta abbatum monasterii S. Albani*, p. 5. It will be noticed that St Albans collected the tax from its estates but retained it.

[7] The laws prescribe payment on 1 August: cf. II Edgar, c. 4, VIII Æthelred, c. 10. So does 'Romescot', Liebermann, *Gesetze*, i. 474, and *Law of the Northumbrian Priests*, c. 57.1. Likewise the homilies: cf. Napier, *Wulfstan Sammlung*, nos. XXIII, LXI. But the *Rectitúdines singularum personarum* (attributed to Archbishop Wulfstan) states that the thegn (c. 1) and the geneat (c. 2)

made by the hundreds – which also represented the parishes of the old minsters – to the bishops,[1] and by them to the archbishop.[2] But in the diocese of Canterbury, East Kent, in Lanfranc's time (and it must be remembered that he was an administrative reformer), the forty-five paying units were estates, once an estate-holder, and payment was direct to the archbishop.[3] Yet even here there are traces of arbitrary arithmetic which point to the fragmentation of a regional scheme;[4] and what had happened to geld must be kept in mind. When there were intermediaries between the contributors to Rome-scot and the archbishop, it is likely that each collector raised what he could and passed on only the traditional sum to the higher authority. In the eleventh century the archbishop of Canterbury collected £16 6s. 1d. from his diocese, while his contribution to the total, in the later Middle Ages at least, was £8. Certainly in later times far more was collected than was sent to the pope.[5] If English prelates had a private interest in the tax, and even

paid alms-money, and that the cottar, like every other freeman (c. 3.4), and the gebur (c. 4.2a) paid hearth-penny, due on Maundy Thursday. Although Easter hearth-penny was a different tax (for its payment to the archbishop in the diocese of Canterbury, see above, pp. 180–2), Rome-penny also was a hearth-tax, and the liability of St Augustine's Canterbury to each was 600d. It is therefore possible that either some free hearths paid twice a year or that the destination of these compulsory alms was various. In a document stating the services due to Taunton in 1066 (Thorpe, Diplomatarium, pp. 432–3) hearth-penny appears, characteristically for the period, among a miscellany of customary payments and services. See also N. Neilson, Customary Rents (Oxford Studies in Social and Legal History, ii, 1910), pp. 197–201.

[1] In Northumbria in each wapentake two thegns and a priest were sworn as collectors, to deliver the money to the bishop's see: Law of the Northumbrian Priests, c. 57.2. In the Taunton document (see previous note) hearth-pennies are associated with hundred-pennies.

[2] 'and wite aelc b. be tham, the he wille beon with god geborgen, and with Sce. Peter, thaet aelc penig cume forth of tham romfeo on his b. scire and siththan tham aerceb. to handa on Cristes cyrcean; and, locahwa hit gewanje, thaet hit forth na cume tham arceb. to handa, si he Judas gerefa, the Crist belaewde': Napier, Wulfstan Sammlung, no. XXXIII, p. 118 n.

[3] 'Romscot in Eastekent', The Domesday Monachorum of Christ Church Canterbury, ed. D. C. Douglas (1944), p. 80. Hugh de Montfort, who held a divisio based on the castle of Saltwood (VCH Kent, iii. 190), is the tenant. Although most of the old minsters are listed their payments are not outstandingly heavy.

[4] The total is 3,913d., that is to say almost four-thousand, or 25 marks of silver. There were four lests in East Kent, based on royal tuns, containing in all some 40 hundreds (VCH Kent, iii. 179–81). St Augustine's paid 600d.; the next four items add up to 500d., the next four to 600d., and the next five to 200d. After that the neatness disappears, although it is not difficult, by shuffling, to make other groups of 200d.

[5] Lunt, pp. 39, 78–9. The standard payment from the twelfth century was 299 silver marks annually. The reason for this sum is unknown and the system of repartition between the dioceses is not arithmetically obvious. There is a rough relationship between the number of shires or archdeaconries in a diocese and the sum for which it was responsible, and the unit of £5½ seems to lie behind some of the assessments. The Mercian bishoprics (London £16½, Lincoln + Ely =

retained it when remittances to Rome were suspended, it would help to explain why it was usually associated with tithe and church-scot in the royal laws, and its payment enforced by secular penalties.[1]

The pope regarded Peter's Pence as an annual tribute to which he had a right.[2] But we know little about the method used to convey the tax to Rome or about the regularity with which it was paid. It is, perhaps, significant that Cnut on his way back from Rome in 1027 should have ordered his English officials to secure the collection of Rome-scot.[3] And since Earl Tostig, after his misadventure in Rome in 1061, threatened the *curia* with suspension of payment, it is possible that he had been entrusted with its conveyance.[4] It is not unreasonable to suppose that the tribute was rendered sporadically, sometimes with arrears, when a suitable opportunity presented itself. The visit of an archbishop for his pallium would be an obvious occasion. Doubtless there were interruptions. According to Pope Alexander II, in a letter written after 1066 to King William,[5] payment had been stopped by members of Satan who had turned England from the way of truth. And for this stoppage not only Tostig's threats but also Stigand's suspension and Ealdred's punishment may have been responsible. Although the tribute was not immense, it was always welcome, and it could be treated as a diplomatic asset by English kings and their ecclesiastical advisers.

Dorchester £47, Lichfield £10¼, Worcester £10¼, Hereford £6) contributed £90, a nice round sum; but the Kent and Wessex figures are ragged, both singly and in combination. There is no obvious clue to the date of this scheme.

[1] See above, p. 145. The penalties became extremely severe, a sign, perhaps, of reluctance to pay. Lunt, pp. 4–5, suggests that the king enforced payment because the tribute represented royal alms.

[2] According to Otto of Freising, *Chronicon*, VI, c. 32, ed. G. H. Pertz (Hanover, 1867), i. 287, Benedict IX, when he surrendered the papacy in 1045, reserved for himself the revenues from England, 'quia maioris videbatur auctoritatis esse'. Pope Alexander II, *MPL*, cxlvi, col. 1413, called it an annual pension.   [3] Liebermann, *Gesetze*, i. 277; *EHD*, i. 417.

[4] *Vita Wulfstani*, p. 16; Malmesbury, *GP*, p. 252. L. Thomassin quotes from a letter of King Edward to Pope Nicholas II (1059–61), 'Ego augeo et confirmo donationes et consuetudines pecuniarum, quas habet S. Petrus in Anglia, et ipsas pecunias collectas cum regalibus donis mitto vobis, ut oretis pro me et pro pace regni mei coram corporibus SS. apostolorum': *Vetus et nova ecclesiae disciplina*, III, i. c. xxxii, *n*. 4; vii (1787), 240. According to Osbert of Clare, *Vita Eadwardi*, *Analecta Bollandiana*, xli (1923), 87–8, Edward sent the archbishop and the bishops to Rome in 1061: 'Voluit enim per eum etiam renovare et confirmare consuetudines et donationes pecuniarum quas antecessores sui reges beato Petro instituerant propter summam devocionem et fidem quam erga eum et eius vicarios semper habebant.' Both are referring to K. 825, pp. 182–3, a document probably forged by Osbert. After the fire of 1843 a hoard of about 1,000 coins was found under the campanile of St Paul's without the Walls, including about 100 English – 33 of Edward the Confessor, and the rest Cnut's and Æthelred's, Jensen, p. 192.   [5] *Ep.* cxxxiv, *MPL*, cxlvi, col. 1413.

The general custom that a metropolitan archbishop should receive a pallium from the pope had developed out of English practice. After the Conversion the English archbishops had been the pope's vicars, and had sought his confirmation and the token of this special relationship.[1] The pallium or pall was a variety of stole worn round the shoulders over the alb. It was in the form of a circular band of white woollen cloth, with a pendant before and behind, embroidered with crosses, such as appears on the seal of the archbishops of Canterbury. It was part of the pope's insignia, and he granted it to others as a sign of favour and as a symbol of delegated authority. The presentation ceremony is described by the Anglo-Saxon chronicle 'D', on the occasion of Æthelnoth's visit in 1022. On Sunday, 7 October, the pope placed a pallium, presumably his own, on the archbishop's shoulders; the archbishop then celebrated mass and afterwards lunched with the pope. Later he took a second pall from St Peter's altar and returned home.[2] He had probably submitted in advance the written profession of faith required from those seeking this honour.[3] The theory was accepted in England that the pallium conferred metropolitan authority on a bishop, empowering him to govern a province and consecrate and rule over diocesan bishops. Without it no bishop could exercise that authority.[4]

But, according to English thinking, it was an honour which was due. An archbishop-elect should be consecrated at home by the other archbishop and his helpers and there was no obligation on the new metropolitan to fetch the pallium in person. In a period of easier communications and renewed zeal, however, Canterbury from at least 927 and York from 1026 [5] began to make 'these long journeys which the highest priests have to make'.[6] Almost from the start the expedition was found dangerous,[7] and almost from the begin-

---

[1] W. Levison, *England and the Continent in the Eighth Century*, pp. 20 ff.

[2] Plummer, p. 204; cf. Archbishop Sigeric's engagements in 990, above, p. 293. In 1071 Lanfranc went to Rome for his pallium: 'et duo pallia ob signum praecipue amoris tribueret. Quorum unum Romano more ab altare accepit; alterum vero ipse papa, unde missas celebrare consueverat, sua manu porrexit': *Acta Lanfranci*, J. Earle, *Two of the Saxon Chronicles parallel*, p. 271.

[3] For such professions, see Levison, Appendix ii. Hugh the Chantor, *HCY*, p. 5, cf. 6, declares that postulants for the pallium swore obedience and fealty to the pope.

[4] As we can see from Stigand's case, below, pp. 303 ff.

[5] Levison, pp. 21–2, 242.   [6] Auct. B., *Memorials of St Dunstan*, p. 38.

[7] For the danger from Saracens in the Alps in the first half of the tenth century, see Flodoard, *Chronicon*, s.a. 921, 923; J. Armitage Robinson, *The Saxon Bishops of Wells*, Brit. Acad. supplemental papers, iv (1918), 59–60. In 959 Ælfsige of Canterbury was frozen to death in the Alps although his feet were plunged into the belly of a disembowelled horse: Auct. B., Osbern, Eadmer, *Memorials of St Dunstan*, pp. 38, 107, 198; Malmesbury, *GP*, p. 26; Eadmer, *Vita S. Odonis*,

ning it was believed in England that the pallium could be bought.[1] And so extortionate had the papal *curia* become by the eleventh century that 'the bishops and priests of the whole island of Britain' sent a letter of protest, composed by Archbishop Wulfstan of York, to one of the popes.[2] It is possible that Wulfstan himself had withstood a request for a personal visit to Rome and that he was ready with a brief when the demand was renewed for Canterbury. Basing his case on Bede's Ecclesiastical History and a letter of Alcuin, Wulfstan made the points that it had not been the custom in the past for English archbishops to go to Rome for the pallium, that English archbishops after Augustine had normally been consecrated in England by the surviving archbishop, and that the pall used to be given gratis without the taint of simony. The second point suggests that a suspicion was forming in the English church that the new custom of personal visits might easily lead to the archbishop-elect seeking, or being required to seek, consecration at Rome.[3] The English church can have obtained no satisfaction from the *curia*, for later it incited the king to protest. In 1027 John XIX agreed to abate the demands for money.[4] But even if he and his successors observed the promise there were still the customary gifts to be made. The corruption of the papacy, however, led to the postulant, provided he was furnished with official documents to prove his election,[5] receiving the pallium without further ado. No other concession was made to the English church. The movement towards centralization had begun. However, after the Conquest, when Alexander II sent the pallium to Thomas of York, the expression *ex more* was included in the grant.[6]

The reform of the papacy after 1049 actually created new difficulties for the English church. Robert of Jumièges obtained the pallium from Leo IX

Anglia Sacra, ii. 86. In 1007 Archbishop Ælfheah was robbed on his way to Rome: Osbern, *Vita S. Elphegi*, c. 5, *MPL*, cxlix, col. 379; *ASC D* 1007.

[1] For the attitude of the chapter of Canterbury in 995, or at the time of the insertion of the account, see above, p. 103.

[2] Printed Wilkins, *Concilia*, i. 166, Haddan and Stubbs, *Councils*, iii. 559. For the date, Levison, Appendix iii, pp. 241–8. For the authorship, D. Bethurum, 'A letter of protest from the English bishops to the Pope', *Philologica: The Malone Anniversary Studies*, ed. T. A. Kirby and H. B. Woolf (1949), pp. 97–104.

[3] The two Canterbury clerks who, according to a 'spurious' passage in *ASC F*, tried to forestall Ælfric in 995 by 'buying' a pallium at Rome, presumably also sought from the pope the consecration of one of them as archbishop.

[4] Cnut's Letter of 1027, Liebermann, *Gesetze*, i. 276, *EHD*, i. 417, makes it clear that he had protested before: 'conquestus sum iterum coram domino papa.'

[5] As the Canterbury case of 995 proves, above, p. 103.   [6] *Ep.* lxxxii, *MPL*, cxlvi, col. 1364.

in 1051, although he was translated from London probably without refer-ence to the pope.[1] Stigand, who replaced him at Canterbury, acquired nothing better than a pallium from an 'intrusive' pope, Benedict X, in 1058.[2] Even Cynsige of York delayed his visit until 1055 when Victor II succeeded.[3] Hence for three years England was without a metropolitan. In 1061 Ealdred of York was at first refused the pallium by Nicholas II – even perhaps tem-porarily broken – for having dared to move from Worcester to York and to hold the two sees in plurality without papal consent.[4] Times had changed. The next to go to Rome for his pall was Lanfranc in 1071.

Before 1049 the periodic visits of the English archbishops to Rome were probably the main occasions on which business was done.[5] Few memorials of this intercourse have survived; and, even though papal letters and privi-leges have probably been lost, it is likely that transactions were few. There is no trace of legal consultation. Archbishop Dunstan was enraged and defiant when a nobleman, whom he had excommunicated for an unlawful marriage, obtained papal letters of absolution.[6] Other bishops shared his attitude.[7] But Archbishop Wulfstan, under the influence of his legal studies, allowed only limited powers of absolution to the various ranks in the church

[1] See above, pp. 47–8.

[2] Benedict sent the pallium, *ASC DE* 1058. There is no mention of a special embassy; and it is possible that Stigand's agents in Rome seized the opportunity of the election of a pope of the old type. We know that Stigand's thegn, Ketel, visited Rome in this period: Whitelock, *Wills*, no. 34. According to Malmesbury, *GR*, i. 244, Stigand bought the pallium.

[3] *ASC D* 1055. The delay may have been protracted owing to Leo IX's military campaign in 1053, his capture by the Normans, and the one year's vacancy at Rome.

[4] *Vita Ædwardi*, pp. 34–5.

[5] Whether or no Lyfing-Ælfstan took the letter of protest from the English church about papal exactions for the pallium (see above, p. 299), he certainly brought back papal complaints about English conditions: see Cnut's letter of 1020, Liebermann *Gesetze*, i. 273, *EHD*, i. 415.

[6] 'Sed ipso apostolico mente altior in se solidus perstitit, "scias", inquiens legato, "nec capitis plexione me a domini mei auctoritate movendum".' He would stand firm like John before Herodias, etc. Adelard in *Memorials of St Dunstan*, p. 67; Eadmer, *ibid.* pp. 200–2.

[7] Aribo, archbishop of Mainz, attacked Count Otto of Hammerstein for his uncanonical marriage between 1018 and 1023, when the wife appealed to the pope. Aribo replied by calling a synod and decreeing *inter alia* that penance must be performed before an appeal could be made to the pope, and that the appeal could be made only with the bishop's permission. Pope Benedict VIII, however, accepted the appeal and punished Aribo by taking away his pallium. The archbishop continued to fight until the Emperor Conrad stopped further proceedings against the count. See Hauck, *Kirchengeschichte Deutschlands*, iii. 431, 434, 533–6, 538, 552. Bishops who took this attitude could find support in the canons, and their attitude reflected both their impatience at papal interference and also their distrust of the papal administration. Burchard of Worms in his *Decretum* (1008–12), II, c. 80 (cf. Fournier and Le Bras, i. 392) supported the episcopal attitude.

according to the gravity of the sin, and reserved certain cases to the pope.[1] Hence it was written into English law that papal absolution was needed by certain sinners, including those who withheld Peter's Pence.[2] Wulfstan's attitude, however, can be regarded as negative. He was not requiring the help of the pope. There is no reason to think that he would have welcomed papal interference. He was merely trying to make life harder for the worst kind of sinner. Another type of business which was to be so important later – the seeking of papal privileges – was also sparse. Monasteries reformed under royal patronage in the tenth century had little reason to go to Rome. Nor was the pope a force in European diplomacy. Æthelred and Richard of Normandy apparently made a treaty of amity in 991 under papal supervision,[3] but papal interests were still limited and local.

In 1049, however, the papacy ceased to be an institution which provided a few services to a distant church at a price. It suddenly became a political power whose diplomacy reached even to England. For the first time we can with reason speak of Anglo-papal relations. In 1049 Pope Leo IX launched an attack on current ecclesiastical abuses and pressed it with spectacular effect in a series of councils held in the next three years.[4] Bishops and abbots were interrogated and put on trial. Consciences were troubled, confessions made, and disciplinary action was taken. At the Rome synod of 1050 Hugh of Breteuil, bishop of Langres, made his sensational surrender to the pope following his condemnation for various sins at the council of Rheims in the previous year. At Rome and Vercelli (September 1050) Lanfranc of Pavia, the future archbishop of Canterbury, developed his charges against the teaching of Berengar of Tours on the dogma of the Eucharist. At all these stirring councils English bishops were present. Edward answered Leo's invitation to send representatives to Rheims by dispatching a bishop and two abbots. The delegation was sent 'so that they might inform the king of whatever was there decided in the interests of Christendom',[5] and, according to the Ramsey chronicle, the king ordered that whatever was done or said there should be written in English and a copy kept in the king's treasury under the

---

[1] See above, p. 270.   [2] See above, p. 145.

[3] *Memorials of St Dunstan*, p. 397; *EHD*, i. 823-4.

[4] Hefele-Leclercq, *Histoire des conciles*, iv. 1002 ff.; N. N. Huyghebaert, 'Saint Léon IX et la lutte contre la simonie dans le diocèse de Verdun', *Studi Gregoriani*, i (1947), 417 ff.

[5] *ASC* E 1046, *D* 1050; Florence, i. 204. Goscelin of St Bertin, *Historia de translat. S. Augustini episcopi*, *MPL*, clv, coll. 31-2, states that Wulfric of St Augustine's was sent by Edward 'pro ecclesiasticis magistratibus et gente sua responsurus', and that when the orders of the English delegation were investigated they were found more innocent than most.

care of Hugh the chamberlain.[1] What is more, in that year, possibly after the council, Leo announced in a letter to Edward that he was going to send a legate to England to investigate among other things the unsatisfactory location of the episcopal sees.[2]

The visit to Rheims was the prelude to exceptionally close Anglo-papal relations. In 1050 bishops Herman and Ealdred were at the Easter council of Rome 'on the king's business'.[3] In September Bishop Ulf was at the Council of Vercelli.[4] In the spring of 1051 Archbishop Robert went to Rome for the pallium. Among the ecclesiastical business transacted with the pope in these three years was the removal of the see of Crediton to Exeter and possibly the consolidation of the dioceses of Devon and Cornwall, the disputes over the elections to Dorchester and London, and probably the king's plan to rebuild Westminster Abbey. The abbot of Ramsey obtained at Rheims a papal privilege for his abbey,[5] and the abbot of St Augustine's papal permission to rebuild his monastery.[6] There may also have been diplomatic exchanges about Flanders and the succession to the English throne, both matters of concern to the Emperor Henry III, the pope's patron.

Although nothing was decreed at these councils which had not appeared in English ecclesiastical and royal legislation of the tenth and early eleventh centuries, the new attack must have jolted severely a church in which zeal was declining. The old ideals were presented again in a challenging form. A new wind was beginning to blow through the English church. But it was stopped within three years by the appointment of Stigand to Canterbury.

The attitude of the English church towards the new reform movement and the view taken by the papacy of Stigand and the English church form one of the greatest mysteries of Edward's reign. Stigand was deposed by papal legates in the Council of Winchester at Easter 1070.[7] No record of the disciplinary actions was kept. Canterbury's view of the proceedings, however, is stated in the professions made by three bishops to Archbishop Lanfranc

---

[1] *Chron. Ramsey*, p. 170.

[2] *The Leofric Missal* (ed. F. E. Warren, HBS), p. 2b; *MPL*, cxliii, col. 639.

[3] *ASC C* 1049, 1050; *D* 1050; *E* 1047; Florence, i. 204; Goscelin, *op. cit.* col. 32; list of bishops and abbots present, *MPL*, cxliii, col. 617.

[4] *ASC E* 1047; and see above, p. 216.

[5] *Chron. Ramsey*, p. 171.   [6] Goscelin, *op. cit.* col. 33.

[7] Summons of the Cardinal-priests John and Peter and Ermenfrid bishop of Sion to Wulfstan of Worcester to be at Winchester with all the abbots of his diocese on the third day after Easter (7 April) in *Vita Wulfstani*, pp. 189-90. The headings to 16 canons issued at Winchester which may be attributed to this council are printed in Wilkins, i, 365; Mansi, xx. 400-2, 460.

after his appointment later in that year.[1] According to these, Stigand had expelled Robert from Canterbury by force and guile, had invaded his see, and had worn Robert's pallium. 'Florence of Worcester' makes this the second of three charges, the others being Stigand's holding Winchester and Canterbury in plurality,[2] and his acceptance of the pallium from Benedict X. It is easy to believe that all three charges were brought against Stigand in 1070 and possible to suggest reasons why the English church preferred to remember only one. The professions of Wulfstan and Remigius then add, almost word for word, that, because of the 'invasion', Stigand was summoned, excommunicated, and condemned by Popes Leo (IX), Victor (II), Stephen (IX), and Nicholas (II). He, however, remained obdurate; and each of these popes sent legates, or letters, into England prohibiting anyone to go to him for ordination and, according to Wulfstan's profession, to show him episcopal reverence. This statement, too, must have come from the official process against Stigand.[3] Two bishops then make a personal statement. Wulfstan's is that because of the papal prohibition some bishops went to Rome, some to France, and some to neighbouring bishops for consecration.[4] He went to Ealdred of York, but made no profession of canonical obedience to him. Remigius's statement is that he was not fully aware of the situation and so went to Stigand for consecration, made his profession to him, and received his episcopal office from him. Shortly afterwards Pope Alexander II sent legates to England with orders to depose Stigand and either to degrade or to suspend from their offices all those who had

[1] 'Non post multos dies Lanfrancus ab universis regni Anglici episcopis, qui diversis temporibus, diversis in locis, ab aliis archiepiscopis vel a papa tempore Stigandi sacrati sunt, professionem petiit et accepit': Miles Crispin, *Vita B. Lanfranci*, c. x, *MPL*, cl, col. 48. Wulfstan's profession, *Vita Wulfstani*, p. 190; Remigius's, *Giraldi Cambrensis Opera* (RS, ed. J. F. Dimmock), vii. 151–2; Herfast's, *Anglia Sacra*, i. 80. For the relevant part of the texts, see below, p. 309.

[2] There is a hint of this in Remigius's profession. Cf. Malmesbury, *GP*, p. 35, 'quondam dimisso Anglorum Orientalium episcopatu, sullimiorem gradum meditatus, Wintoniensem invaserat'. An alternative charge, reflected here, would be that Stigand had changed bishoprics without papal consent. It was this crime rather than pluralism which confounded Ealdred in 1061 (*Vita Ædwardi*, pp. 34–5). Hugh the Chantor, *HCY*, p. 2, wrote that Stigand was degraded because he was archbishop, bishop of Winchester, and abbot of several monasteries at the same time, and for other reasons as well.

[3] Its absence from Herfast's profession does not count. Herfast was appointed in the interregnum after Sigand's deposition. He was entirely in the clear, and it was really unnecessary to bring the charges against Stigand into his profession. They are in fact only briefly resumed.

[4] Wulfwig of Dorchester and Leofwine of Lichfield went 'abroad' in 1053, and Giso of Wells and Walter of Hereford went to Rome in 1061. That is to say, with Wulfstan, five out of seven bishops avoided Stigand. But Wulfstan was alone in seeking a consecrator in England. The reason he gave in 1070–1 was no doubt a simplification suitable for the time.

been ordained by him. Remigius was presumably suspended, for he goes on to say that he went with Lanfranc to Rome (in 1071) to ask for pardon, which he received. And, as he has learned from Alexander that Stigand was not Lanfranc's *antecessor* nor Lanfranc his successor, he makes his profession to Lanfranc. The third bishop, Herfast, had nothing to explain away.

The charges preferred against Stigand in 1070 were inevitable and are unremarkable. It had been decided to depose him and a case could easily be framed. The one charge that Lanfranc chose to record for posterity was presumably the one which he considered most cogent and also most relevant to the matter at hand. Yet even this charge – Stigand's expulsion of the lawful archbishop and his 'invasion' of the see during Robert's lifetime – is not unanswerable. It is doubtful whether Stigand was in any way personally responsible for Robert's expulsion. And obviously the one unexpected part of the charge, that Stigand wore Robert's pallium (for the celebration of mass), was inserted to show that Stigand had been a true usurper – that he took complete seisin – that he had in fact 'invaded' the see and not merely taken over the administration of a vacant diocese. Whether the story is true is another matter. Certainly Stigand exercised no metropolitan rights until he received the pallium from Benedict.

Lanfranc gave no publicity to the 'crimes' of pluralism and accepting the pallium from a pope who turned out to be an intruder. The one was embarrassing. One of the greatest English saints of the tenth century, St Oswald, had added York to Worcester. Some recent popes had retained their bishopric on promotion to the papacy.[1] At home Leofric still held Devon and Cornwall and Herman Wiltshire and Sherborne. It was a charge to use and forget. The other was a moot point which could have troubled a dialectician.

It is, however, the papal reaction to Stigand's crimes, as stated in the professions of Wulfstan and Remigius, which needs careful consideration. Was Stigand cited, excommunicated, and condemned by every pope between 1052 and 1070? Did all these popes denounce in England Stigand's incapacity as a metropolitan and even his suspension from the episcopal office? 'Florence of Worcester' does not record this charge. Remigius of Dorchester pleaded that he was not fully aware of the state of affairs.[2] William of Malmesbury, who was not a fool, found it difficult to reconcile the story of unremitting papal action with the historical facts, and had to explain that

---

[1] Clement II, the first of the reforming popes, never surrendered his bishopric of Bamberg. Leo IX kept Toul for a time (1049–51), and Victor II (1055–7) Eichstädt.

[2] 'Ego vero hujus negotii nec ex toto ignarus, nec usquequaque gnarus.'

Stigand owed his immunity before 1070 to his use of delays and bribes to avoid his frequent citations to the papal court.[1] But William does not tell us whom he bribed.

Three aspects of the story need investigation. Was England aware of Stigand's incapacity as archbishop, of his suspension from his episcopal office, and of his excommunication? There is no doubt that during Edward's reign Stigand was not recognized as an archbishop except in 1058 after the receipt of his pallium.[2] Until that year he consecrated no bishop. By 1061, when two bishops went to Rome for consecration,[3] his incapacity was again notorious. The Normans, too, were either aware of the position or learned it in England.[4] William, who needed a traditional and legitimate coronation, must have disregarded Stigand with the greatest reluctance. But from 1067 until 1070 Stigand seems to have been accorded full metropolitan respect by the Normans.[5] Expediency or William's arbitrariness may have been the cause.

On the other hand there is no evidence that anyone regarded Stigand as suspended from his episcopal office. He appears in all the witness-lists to 'royal' diplomas. He is known to have blessed abbots in 1061, 1065, and 1066.[6] In 1094, when Anselm inquired from Bishop Wulfstan about some archiepiscopal privileges, Wulfstan had the effrontery not only to match Anselm's citation of their peaceful exercise by Archbishop Lanfranc and Dunstan by referring to their equally peaceful exercise by 'your excellency's predecessor' Stigand, but also to describe them as 'the special power of that metropolitan bishop'.[7] Nothing at all can be put against the case that Stigand always acted as a bishop and was regarded as one.

[1] GP, p. 252.   [2] Stigand consecrated the bishops of Selsey and Rochester: ASC DE 1058.
[3] Giso of Wells and Walter of Hereford.
[4] Cf. William of Poitiers, II, c. 1, ' . . . Stigandi, justo zelo apostolici et anathemate ministerio sacerdotum privati'. But he was writing after 1070.
[5] Malmesbury, GP, pp. 36–7. Malmesbury states that Stigand recognized William as son and king on condition that William recognized him as archbishop and father, and that he appealed to this agreement in 1070. William of Poitiers, II, cc. 28, 35, 40, emphasizes Stigand's power and importance and gives an explanation of King William's motives. See also above, pp. 77 ff.
[6] The abbot of St Augustine's in 1061, ASC E 1061. Goscelin, Historia de translat. S. Augustini episcopi, MPL, clv, col. 33, states that Æthelsige 'in palatio regis consecratur', and then went to the pope for his mitre and sandals. The abbot of St Edmunds in 1065, according to 'Heremanni archidiaconi miracula S. Eadmundi', Ungedruckte Anglo-Normannische Geschichtsquellen, ed. F. Liebermann, p. 256, cf. p. 245, where it appears that Baldwin was consecrated by the archbishop in a royal court at Windsor on 15 April. The abbot of Ely in 1066, Liber Eliensis, II, cc. 98, 118.
[7] Eadmer, Historia Novorum, pp. 45–7. S. Anselmi Opera Omnia, ed. F. S. Schmitt, epp. 170–1, iv (1949), 51–3.

The third question is already answered. Clearly Stigand was never re-garded in England as an outcast from the faithful. There is no strictly con-temporary evidence that he was at any time shunned by the English kings, prelates, or laity.

What then is to be made of the story accepted in 1070? It may well be thought that this account of the papal actions was brought in by the legates. It was from them that Remigius heard it. Accordingly there are two possi-bilities. Either the popes took these drastic actions and the English and then Anglo-Norman government and episcopate simply disregarded them. (And in this lies another of William of Malmesbury's difficulties: how could the saintly Edward have been so contumacious?) Or the legates' story was wish-ful thinking. Although it needs courage to reject official versions, in this case there appears to be no alternative. Undoubtedly some of the popes must have censured Stigand's behaviour. Certainly he was forbidden to use Benedict's pallium and exercise metropolitan rights. But obviously this is the limit to the steps taken by these popes. According to the *Vita Ædwardi*,[1] in a section denouncing the state of the English church written probably in 1067, the queen and some other pious folk knew in 1066 'that the Christian religion was chiefly dishonoured by men in Holy Orders, and that the pope of Rome, by means of legates and letters, and the king and queen, by frequent admoni-tion, had often proclaimed this fact'. Archbishop Stigand (and the author does not anywhere avoid the title) 'will repent too late or not at all'. Here we seem closer to the truth. We can understand that there had been general denunciations, no doubt pointed complaints, but that decisive measures had never been taken.

We are very ill-informed about Anglo-papal relations between 1052 and 1066. In 1061 an important English legation went to Rome and returned with papal legates (including one of Stigand's deposers in 1070).[2] It is hard to believe that these Roman *missi*, although they were sent for disciplinary reasons, published a sentence of excommunication against Stigand, for it is related in the *Vita Wulfstani*[3] that Stigand sat in the Worcester council of 1062 with the king and the earls, the papal legates, Ealdred of York and the bishops, and took his appropriate place – after the legates and before York –

---

[1] p. 77.

[2] Ermenfrid bishop of Sion. R. R. Darlington, *Vita Wulfstani*, p. xv *n.*, is inclined to suspect confusion. But Ermenfrid was an expert on depositions. He was Leo IX's legate to the council of Lisieux (?1054) at which Duke William secured the removal of Mauger archbishop of Rouen: 'Historia archiepisc. Rothomagensium', Bouquet, *Recueil*, xi. 70.   [3] p. 18.

in the election of Wulfstan to the see. A little laterAbbot Ælfwine of Ramsey was sent by Edward to Rome 'on some royal business' – and obtained a privilege from Alexander II for his own monastery.[1] Unfortunately no genuine papal latters addressed to Edward or his bishops have survived. But Pope Nicholas II sent out the decrees of the council of Rome (1059) to all cathedral bishops, clergy, and people,[2] and Alexander II similarly notified all catholic bishops of the decrees of the council held at Rome in 1063.[3] Presumably copies of these letters reached England, and in both of them pluralism was condemned.

The truth of the matter cannot be exactly as stated in 1070. Stigand's position had been irregular and had probably been condemned by some of the popes. But there was much irregularity in Christendom and the papal reform drive was a novelty. Realists in the *curia*, although lavish with manifestos, did not tilt at windmills. The English church was remote and had never completely lost its mission status. No pope in his senses would have attempted the impossible because of irregularities in that province. Even Gregory VII was to hold back his hand. It seems then that the legates in 1070 stated as a fact what the popes should have done. Possibly instructed by Cardinal Hildebrand, they announced the law rather than a true history of the case.

All the same, Stigand, and in some degree the English church, was in disgrace between 1052 and 1070; and England was indifferent to it. No English bishop was a papalist, none was directly inspired by Roman reform. The circumscribed cult of St Leo IX found an adherent in Leofric of Exeter,[4] but his gratitude was particular. It is indeed possible that the reformed papacy inspired less respect in England than had the old, remote, corrupt and passive, but potent symbol of Christian unity. A dominant theme in the story of Tostig and Ealdred's adventures at Rome in 1061 is how they turned the tables on the Romans and their pope. But the bishop triumphed through humility and suffering. Elsewhere in the Ealdred cycle of legends, where he came up against the secular power, he was victorious through religious confidence and strength. The English church probably thought itself misunderstood.

The situation was not peculiar to England. Large areas of Christendom remained sheltered from the storm or were resisting its onslaught, and

---

[1] *Chron. Ramsey*, pp. 176–7. Ælfwine's health collapsed as a result of this mission.
[2] *MPL*, cxliii, coll. 1314–5.
[3] *MPL*, cxlvi, coll. 1289–90.
[4] *The Bosworth Psalter*, p. 162.

everywhere were to be found men of the past, bishops, some of them good bishops, completely old-fashioned in outlook. Even pious kings acted according to political expediency. Neither Edward nor William ever aligned himself seriously with papal policy and ambitions. No one could have expected that the papal crusade for reform and the drive to create a papal monarchy could be so well sustained or so successful. But the substitution of Stigand for Robert of Jumièges at Canterbury, even if not a deliberate affront to the reformers, or directly occasioned by the application and rejection of papal policies, was a real turning-point in English history. The English church lost, perhaps refused, the opportunity to put its own house in order, but possibly because the reformers were too uncompromising in tone. The support given by the papacy to William's invasion in 1066 reveals the dominance in the Roman *curia* of a party too anxious for quick results and, in its impatience with fourteen years of discord, too forgetful of the four-and-a-half centuries of English tolerance which had gone before.

Stigand's Deposition

Florence[1]	Wulfstan's Profession	Remigius's Profession	Herfast's Profession
In quo concilio[a] Stig-andus Doruberniae[b] archiepiscopus degradatur tribus ex causis, scilicet:[c] [1] quia episcopatum Wintoniae cum archiepiscopatu injuste possidebat [2b] et quia, vivente archiepiscopo Roberto, non solum archiepiscopatum sumpsit, [c] sed etiam ejus pallio, quod Cant-wariae remansit, [a] dum	[2b] Sanctam Dorobernensem ecclesiam ... Stigandus iam-pridem invaserat, [a] metropolit-anum eiusdem sedis vi et dolo	Cum enim, contempta Helmeanensis ecclesiae mediocritate, translatus esset ad Wentanae civi-tatis episcop[at]um, stim-ulante adhuc majoris honoris ambitu, post paucos annos [2a] Robertum archiepiscopum partim vi partim insidiis expulit, [b] metropolem invasit,	Deposito enim Stigando, [2a] qui praefatam ecclesiam, expulso archiepiscopo Roberto, [b] invaserat

[1] ii. 5; collated with the, presumably derivative, passage in *Radulfi de Diceto Opera Historica*, ed. W. Stubbs, RS, i (1876), 201 (D).

a Ubi D   b Dorobernensis D   c om. scilicet D

[c] usumque sibi pallii sine sedis apostolicae auctoritate usurpare praesumpserat.

———

[c] pallium quod a sede apostolica ipse detulerat cum ceteris ablatum usurpare non metuit.

[4] Qua temeritate Romae audita, a Romanis pontificibus saepe vocatus, tandem damnatus et excommunicatus est. Ipse tamen in sui cordis obstinatione novem annis in sui cordis obstinatione permansit. Quo tanti temporis intervallo, praefatae Romanae ecclesiae pontifices, Leo, Victor, Stephanus, Nicholaus, Alexander, legatos suos suis quisque temporibus in Anglicam terram transmiserunt; et ne aliquis ad eum ordinandus accederet, apostolica authoritate prohibuerunt.

om. aliquandiu D   g *om. sancta* D   h suscepit D

---

expulerat,

[c] usumque palii quod ei abstulit contempta sedis apostolice auctoritate temerare presumpserat.

vi d injuste ab Anglia pulsus est,e

[3] et post a Benedicto, quem sancta g Romana ecclesia excommunicavit, eo quod pecuniis sedem apostolicam invasit, pallium accepit.h

[4] Unde a Romanis pontificibus Leone, Victore, Stephano, Nicholao, Alexandro vocatus, excommunicatus, damnatus est. Ipse tamen ut cepit in sui cordis obstinatione permansit. Per idem tempus iussa eorum pontificum in Anglicam terram delata sunt prohibentium ne quis ei episcopalem reverentiam exhiberet, aut ad eum ordinandus accederet.

d *om.* vi D   e pulsus est ab Anglia D

APPENDIX II

The Monasteries

In the year 1000 there were more than forty Benedictine monasteries in England, of which at least thirty were for men.[1] All, except St Augustine's, Canterbury, and the nunnery of Shaftesbury, which seem to have had an unbroken history from earlier times, were products of the tenth-century reformation, half refoundations of previous communities, half new creations.[2] Mostly set up in the 960s and 970s by Dunstan, Æthelwold, and Oswald, they were less than forty years old at the turn of the century. Two monasteries and one nunnery were founded in Æthelred's reign and four more for men under Cnut and Edward the Confessor. Some smaller houses, dependent on existing monasteries, may also have been established after 1000. But no community of any importance was founded between 1043 and 1067 (Battle). On the other hand, few well-known monasteries disappeared. Exeter was suppressed in 1050 and several nunneries fell out of record; but there were probably as many active monastic communities in 1066 as in 1000. Nevertheless, the monastic movement which had begun under King Edmund (939–46) lost momentum under Æthelred and came virtually to a halt with the accession of Edward the Confessor. It had lasted almost exactly a century.

It is disputed whether the sad state of the monasteries at the beginning of the tenth century was due primarily to the Viking raids.[3] But there is little reason to think that the renewed warfare which began in 980 was

[1] For the general background see Friedrich Kempf, 'The renewal of Monastic and Canonical Life', *The Church in the Age of Feudalism* (Handbook of Church History, ed. Hubert Jedin and John Dolan, iii, trans. Anselm Biggs, 1969), ch. 39. Cf. *Tenth-Century Studies*, ed. David Parsons (1975). The statistics in this Appendix are derived from David Knowles and R. Neville Hadcock, *Medieval Religious Houses in England and Wales* (1953) and *The Heads of Religious Houses in England and Wales, 940–1216*, ed. Knowles, C. N. L. Brooke, and Vera London (1972).

[2] For the reforms see David Knowles, *The Monastic Order in England, 943–1216* (1940, 1949), pp. 31 ff.; D. H. Farmer, 'The progress of the Monastic Revival', in *Tenth-Century Studies*; D. A. Bullough, 'The Continental Background of the Reform', *ibid.* See further several articles by E. John, especially 'The King and the Monks in the tenth-century Reformation', reprinted in *Orbis Britanniae and Other Studies* (1966).

[3] E. John argues that true monasticism had already disappeared before the start of the raids.

directly harmful to monasticism. No important abbey was sacked or dispersed; the Danish conquerors were not in general hostile to Christianity; and even the burden of taxation and confiscations of land does not seem to have been crippling. The insecurity of the times and the need for intensified intercession with God, both to spare the unhappy kingdom from its enemies and to have mercy on the departed, could have worked to foster the monastic order. The introduction of new royal dynasties and the rise of new aristocracies led to some new foundations. Cnut founded Bury St Edmunds and St Benet of Hulme and Earl Leofric of Mercia founded Coventry. But Edward the Confessor only refurbished an existing house (Westminster), while the new earls of Northumbria did not found monasteries and the new comital dynasty in Wessex was if anything unfriendly to the movement.

The expansion slowed down for more basic reasons. Medieval monastic revivals were always relatively short-lived. Monasticism flourished from the time that the enthusiasm of the laity was aroused until that encouragement either subsided or destroyed the ascetic way of life. In England both factors operated, but in different ways according to the time and place. North of the Humber, probably because society was too lawless, monasticism did not catch on again before 1070. In the South there were by 970 sufficient establishments to meet society's need. Under Cnut and Edward the Confessor peace brought prosperity. Wealthy monasteries lost their zeal and wealthy landowners showed little interest in mortification of the flesh. Rich widows seem to have been able to live safely on their own estates. These developments were not fatal. Monasteries could survive periods of prosperity. But riches and torpor made them vulnerable not only to predators but also to reformers.

Geographically the monasteries were most unequally spaced. In Greater Wessex were some of the oldest and most famous houses. In the diocese of Crediton/Exeter were Tavistock and Exeter. In Wells were Bath, Glastonbury, Athelney, and Muchelney. In Sherborne were the cathedral community, Abbotsbury, Milton Abbas, Cerne, two nunneries, Shaftesbury and Wareham, and one or two obscure houses. In Ramsbury were Malmesbury, Abingdon, and Cholsey, and the nunnery of Wilton. In Winchester were the three convents in the city, the cathedral community, New Minster, and Nunnaminster (f.), Chertsey, and two other famous nunneries, Romsey and Wherwell. In the diocese of Canterbury were the two great houses in the city, the cathedral community and St

Augustine's, and possibly some small monastic remnants in Sheppey and Thanet.

Greater Mercia, even when deprived of the diocese of Wells, was well endowed. In the diocese of Worcester were the cathedral community, Evesham, Pershore, Gloucester, Tewkesbury, Winchcombe, and the mysterious nunnery at Berkeley.[1] There were no Benedictine houses in Wales. In Dorchester were Eynsham, St Ives, Ely, Thorney, Ramsey, Peterborough, and Crowland. In the diocese of London were Westminster, St Albans, and the nunnery of Barking. In East Anglia were Cnut's two foundations, Bury St Edmunds and St Benet of Hulme.

The attenuation already noticeable in East Anglia is even more pronounced to the north. The only abbeys in the large diocese of Lichfield were Burton-on-Trent founded in 1004 and Coventry founded in 1043. In the dioceses of York and Durham and in Scotland were no Benedictine monasteries. A line drawn westwards from the Wash to Burton, then south to Coventry, and continuing south-westerly to Worcester contains to its south all the Benedictine communities.

With the great foci of tenth-century reform located at Glastonbury, Abingdon, Winchester, and Worcester, and the leading reformers occupying the sees of Canterbury, Winchester, and Worcester, such a geographical distribution of the abbeys was almost inevitable. The pattern, however, was most irregular: the three saints not only reformed and founded communities in their own dioceses but also operated outside. Æthelwold and Oswald had a special interest in the Danelaw. As a result there were by 970 three main groups of monasteries, each looking to one of the leaders.[2] These leagues criss-crossed each other and had little respect for either diocesan or regional boundaries. It was because of this situation that a common customary for all the monasteries, the *Regularis Concordia*, was devised by a council which met at Winchester between 965 and 975.[3]

The history of English monasticism from the death of the three great reformers (984–92) until the Norman Conquest is extremely obscure. The obscurity is not due to a lack of literature but to its subject matter. The several versions of the Anglo-Saxon Chronicle, and the annals which

[1] Freeman, *NC*, ii. 544 ff.

[2] Diagram in Knowles, *The Monastic Order*, p. 721; cf. pp. 48 ff.

[3] Ed. T. Symons (1953). See also Symons, '*Regularis Concordia*: History and Derivation', in *Tenth-Century Studies*.

underlie it, were written in monasteries; but they are outward rather than inward looking. Although Ælfric the Homilist, Wulfstan (*Lupus*), Byrhtferth of Ramsey, and Folcard and Goscelin of St Bertin, to mention some of the best known authors of the period, were all monks, little of their writing throws much direct light on the monasticism of their own times.[1] Important abbots found no biographers, probably because their lives were judged inferior to those of the heroes of the golden age. There are no collections of letters. The monastic buildings have not survived, even in fragments, and there have been few archaeological reports.[2] There are, however, some collections of charters and other legal documents which illustrate the monasteries' behaviour as landowners.[3]

To the carelessness of record was added destruction after the Norman Conquest. Foreign abbots were at first little interested in their 'ignorant' and 'unworthy' predecessors. English monks, like Eadmer, hastened to conform. And when William of Malmesbury in 1118 started to write the history of the Anglo-Saxon church, it was too late to recover much of the story of the recent past.[4] The regnal lists of monasteries between 1000 and 1066 are pitifully thin. For many monasteries no names at all have survived. The lists of abbots for even famous houses are most insecure.

Because of the lack of material the history of no individual house in this period can be written in detail. The life of no monk, bar a few monk-bishops, can be told even in outline. The pattern of affiliations within the monastic order cannot be traced because few books of confraternity have survived[5] and the provenance of most abbots is unknown. All the same the historian is not faced with a blank sheet. Sometimes he at least starts from

[1] The main exception is Goscelin's *Liber Confortatorius*, which reveals much about Wilton nunnery in the 1060s. See F. Barlow, *Vita Ædwardi*, pp. 94 ff.

[2] Although little work has been done on the domestic buildings, the churches have attracted considerable interest: see H. M. and Joan Taylor, *Anglo-Saxon Architecture* (2 vols, 1965); H. M. Taylor, 'Tenth-century Church Building in England and on the Continent', in *Tenth-Century Studies*.

[3] Several of these are incorporated in twelfth-century charter-chronicles, e.g. *Chron. Abingdon*, *Chron. Ramsey*, *Liber Eliensis*.

[4] He tried to give for each diocese, after a history of the bishopric and its bishops, an account of all the monasteries, their site, foundation, succession of abbots, buildings, and cults. He was, however, often defeated by the lack of records, especially Lives of their saints and abbatial lists. Cf. *GP*, p. 202 on Tavistock.

[5] The most important Benedictine survival is *Liber Vitae: Register and martyrology of New minster and Hyde abbey, Winchester*, ed. W. de Gray Birch (Hants Record Soc., 1892). Cf. also *Liber Vitae ecclesiae Dunelmensis*, ed. J. Stevenson (Surtees Soc., 13, 1841); facsimile, ed. A. Hamilton Thompson (*ibid.* 136, 1923).

the known and only gradually loses touch; and there are many scraps of information which indicate what changes took place.

The almost unanimous contemporary opinion, both native and foreign, was that there had been deterioration in the state of English monasteries since 980;[1] yet, although this must be accepted as largely true, some caveats must be entered. To be taken into account are the ingrained pessimism of Christian observers and their preoccupation with the enormity of present ills. It must also be allowed that the 'Norman' abbots were prejudiced and ignorant observers of the English past and that the Conquest itself may well in the beginning have disorganized monastic life. It is clear that shortly after the Conquest, sometimes after a painful period, most English convents recovered quickly. The great abbeys of the Anglo-Danish kingdom remained the great abbeys under the Normans and Angevins. Obviously they had had no failings which could not be rectified fairly easily: they did not have to be refounded. Moreover, there were individual houses in 1066 which were maintaining high standards. Worcester and Evesham are famous examples. And some monasteries of which we know little, like Westminster, can hardly have been completely degenerate. Nor should it be overlooked that the period produced two popular monastic saints, Ælfheah (Alphege), abbot of Bath and archbishop of Canterbury, martyred by the Danes at Greenwich on 19 April 1012, and Wulfstan, monk and bishop of Worcester, who lived until 19 January 1095. It is probably an unremarkable scene, a mixture of good, bad, and indifferent convents without inspired leadership at provincial or national level and no shared urgent purpose. It is the monastic world at its most ordinary.[2]

In eleventh-century England, as elsewhere in Europe, monasteries, like other churches, had an owner: they were *Eigenklöster*. On the Continent the kings had lost possession of many monasteries both to those servants to whose protection they and the bishops had entrusted them, the advocates (*advocati*),[3] and to local counts, like the dukes of Normandy, and other feudal lords. There were also monasteries, like Cluny and St Victor, Marseilles, which had been put into the ownership of St Peter at Rome.[4] The position in England was rather different. It

[1] Cf. *Vita Ædwardi*, pp. 40–1.

[2] Knowles, *The Monastic Order*, pp. 73 ff. paints an even rosier picture. See also D. F. Farmer, *op. cit.* pp. 15 ff.

[3] Kempf, *loc. cit.* pp. 271–3.

[4] H. E. J. Cowdrey, *The Cluniacs and the Gregorian Reform* (1970), pp. 172–4.

had been the common aim of the tenth-century episcopal reformers to destroy the hold of local landowners on monasteries, and to achieve this by putting them under the ultimate control of the monarchy. The *Regularis Concordia* is hostile to the authority of the ordinary laity (*secularium prioratus*) and stresses the authority of the king and queen, the consort taking a special place in the government of the nunneries. Royal guidance of abbatial elections is specially mentioned.[1]

In practice the king and queen shared their authority with other interested parties. Although advocates in the technical Continental sense seem never to have existed in England – or in Normandy – monasteries did not always lack a local protector who would speak for them. For example, Wulfric Spot, the Mercian nobleman who founded Burton, probably because he had no son made careful arrangements for the protection of the abbey after his death. In his will he expressed the hope that King Æthelred would be its lord and that Archbishop Ælfric and his brother Ælfhelm would act as its protectors, friends, and advocates against all living men – not as though they owned it but as something belonging to St Benedict's order.[2] The first abbot, Wulfgeat, to judge by his name, was a relation of the founder; the next was a monk of Winchester: local control had been broken, apparently through dynastic failure and possibly through the ineffectiveness of the lay advocate. Whether earls in their official capacity had any authority over abbeys is uncertain; but it is clear that Leofric of Mercia had a large say in the ordering of his foundation at Coventry and that his family retained its influence for some time. There is little evidence after 1000 of conflict between the king and other landowners over the control of monasteries;[3] and the general position may have been that the royal family was not much interested in the smaller houses, particularly those which were not on royal demesne, an attitude which would allow founders some rights and the earls some interest under the overriding authority of the king. If so, the position was little changed by the Conquest.

This general proposition would also cover the place of the founder-bishops. Most of the great monasteries of the period had been refounded or created by Dunstan, Æthelwold, and Oswald; and the power of these

---

[1] *Regularis Concordia*, chs. 3, 9, 10.

[2] Whitelock, *Wills*, no. XVII; *Chron. Abingdon*, p. 411. The grantor's brother and the archbishop were to be 'mund & freond & forespreocan'.

[3] But Edward the Confessor may have tried to increase the influence of the court at the expense of local interests. See F. Barlow, *Edward the Confessor* (1970), p. 78–9, 104–6.

over their establishments seems to have been as much proprietorial as
episcopal. Only ownership will explain the authority they wielded within
the diocese of another bishop. Occasionally, in order to intensify their
ownership, they also assumed the office of abbot: for example, Oswald
bishop-abbot of Worcester, was as well abbot of his monastery at Ramsey
in Huntingdonshire in the diocese of Dorchester. Such pluralism was not
unusual in the monastic order. It was common for leading reformers, like
William of Dijon, to act as abbot of several abbeys, their moral purpose
and sheer necessity rebutting the traditional prejudice in the church
against pluralism. In England the bishop-proprietors operated subject to
royal authority; but in routine matters their power would seem to have
been the more effective.

The changing pattern of lordship within the monastic order cannot be
traced in detail. It seems that there was an ever-shifting scene, similar to
the mobility in secular society. It is unlikely that the three great leagues
long survived their founders and in Edward the Confessor's reign some
new monastic lordships appeared.[1] Ealdred held Winchcombe with
Worcester as well as other important benefices.[2] Earl Leofric's nephew of
the same name is said to have been abbot of Peterborough, Burton,
Coventry, Crowland, and Thorney,[3] although in most of those places he
may have appointed a surrogate abbot. Archbishop Stigand, who was not
a monk, was credited by the twelfth-century Ely chronicler with holding
the abbacies of Ely, Winchester, Glastonbury, St Albans, and St Augustine's Canterbury towards the end of Edward's reign. The inclusion of
Glastonbury seems to be a mistake, and, like Leofric, he appointed
deputies.[4]

All these, it should be noticed, were, even if irregular, ecclesiastical
'empires'. For the tenth-century reformers freedom meant freedom for
the monasteries to pursue their ends unhampered by local tyrants. They
accepted that freedom was attainable only when guaranteed by a strong
king, and, since they were bishops, they never contemplated allowing

[1] Cf. Knowles, *The Monastic Order*, pp. 72 ff.

[2] *ASC D* 1053; Florence, i. 211–12.

[3] *ASC E* 1066, where it is said that the king gave him those abbeys. Cf. *Chron. Peterborough*, pp.
66–7.

[4] *Liber Eliensis*, p. 168. Winchester he held as bishop. He may have appointed abbots to St
Albans, *ibid.* pp. 176–7, St Augustine's in 1061 (Æthelsige was a Winchester monk), and Ely in 1066
(Thurstan). The abbey of Gloucester with which he is sometimes credited was the secular minster of
St Oswald: see above p. 75, *n.* 5 and 'Vita S. Oswaldi', in Symeon, *Opera Omnia*, i. 370.

their monasteries much freedom from their control. Benevolent government by the episcopal proprietors, backed by the royal power would, they
thought, produce ideal conditions for the monks. They would not have
cared for Stigand's lordship, but they could not have objected to the
others on principle.

In apparent conflict with that attitude are the papal privileges which
some of the reformers are said to have obtained for their monasteries.
Glastonbury had a probably genuine privilege of Pope John XIII dated
971 which was issued at the request of King Edgar and Archbishop
Dunstan, its founders. This allows the monks free election of their abbot,
the abbot and convent choice of any bishop for the ordination of their
clerks and monks, and the Isle of Glastonbury freedom from all outside
jurisdiction.[1] Ramsey too claimed that it had a privilege from a Pope John
granted at the request of its founder, Bishop Oswald, which confirmed its
right of free election of its abbot.[2] If these instruments are indeed authentic, they must have been obtained by the great reformers in pursuit of
their dominant aim to safeguard the future of the monasteries they had
reformed. It is possible that Dunstan and Oswald were prepared in antici-
pation of their death to relinquish proprietorial rights over houses outside
their own diocese. But it is by no means impossible that papal privileges
were solicited and accepted without much concern with the exact implication of the formulae such documents contained.

Some changes were bound to occur once the strong hands of the
founder bishops were removed. English abbots must have been aware of
monastic ambitions on the Continent. Cluny had a conception of freedom
which, although not unchanging, was consistently defended against not
only the secular powers but also the local bishops and archbishops;[3] and
the English monastic order had been deeply influenced by Cluny through
her daughter, Fleury (St Benoît-sur-Loire, Loiret). Abbo, monk of
Fleury, may have helped to draft the *Regularis Concordia*, and he lived
and taught at Oswald's abbey of Ramsey for two or three years before he
became abbot of Fleury in 988. In 1004 he was murdered while trying to
reform a monastery in Gascony at the request of the duke of Aquitaine.
He was a great champion of monastic rights and papal authority against

---

[1] *Regesta Pontificum Romanorum*, ed. P. Jaffé and G. Wattenbach (2 vols, Leipzig 1885–8), i, no.
3734.
[2] *Chron. Ramsey*, p. 99.
[3] Cowdrey, *op. cit.* pp. 3 ff.

bishops. He made a collection of canon law which clearly reflected his views, and in 997 got a papal privilege for Fleury which gave his monastery some freedom from the bishop of Orleans.[1]

In the next fifty years the relations between English monasteries and the Continent were as close as before.[2] At the imperial coronation of Conrad in Rome in 1027 was present, besides Cnut and Abbot Lyfing of Tavistock, Abbot Odilo of Cluny, who took the opportunity to acquire from John XIX four bulls of exemption.[3] Edward the Confessor brought Robert abbot of Jumièges to England, and that house had been reformed by disciples of William of Dijon, a Cluniac monastic reformer who had no great respect for bishops.[4] Throughout the period abbots were much used in diplomacy; and just as foreign abbots were frequently at the English royal court, so English prelates travelled abroad. According to the Ramsey chronicle Abbot Ælfwine (1043–1079/80) in 1049, when he attended Leo IX's Council of Rheims, and towards the end of Edward's reign, when he went on a royal legation to Alexander II, obtained papal privileges granting apostolic protection to his monastery and confirmation of its rights and possessions.[5] It is therefore by no means unlikely that views on what constituted freedom far more radical than those held by bishops were current in some English monastic circles.

Monasteries ambitious for freedom had to fight on several fronts, against the various secular powers and against episcopal authority, and often as not in England they found the king and his bishops in league against the rest. Their one recourse was to the pope, who for a consideration would take them into the protection (*tuito, defensio, protectio* etc.) of the holy see;[6] but popes were in no position to enforce the terms in England, and English abbots seem to have been extremely cautious in their use of bulls. Few genuine privileges dating from this period exist, and it is impossible to compare the terms of any individual grant with the grantee's actual performance. Limited privileges, such as the right of an

---

[1] *Ibid.* pp. 29–32. Abbo's *Collectio canonum* is printed *MPL*, cxxxix. 473.

[2] Cf. Bullough, 'The Continental Background of the Reform', *loc. cit.*

[3] Cowdrey, *op. cit.* p. 35.

[4] *Ibid.* p. 33.

[5] *Chron. Ramsey*, pp. 170–1, 176. The documents are not reproduced. The second was, 'in perpetuum ecclesiae patrocinium contra suspectam futurorum nequitiam'.

[6] Willy Szaivert, 'Die Entstehung und Entwicklung der Klosterexemtion bis zum Ausgang des 11. Jahrhunderts', *Mitteilungen des Instituts für österreichische Geschichtsforschung*, lix (Innsbruck, 1951), 286; summary, p. 296. For papal privileges obtained by English monasteries, see also above, pp. 302, 305, *n.* 6.

abbot to wear the mitre and sandals of a bishop, which St Augustine's obtained in 1063,[1] were probably exceptional and also honoured; but more comprehensive privileges had only a marginal usefulness within powerful monarchies before the twelfth century. The two most important freedoms to which some monasteries aspired were freedom of election to the abbacy and freedom from the jurisdiction of the diocesan bishop. Even if these were granted or confirmed by a papal privilege they could not be asserted against a hostile king or a hostile bishop if supported by the monarch. In England monastic liberties depended on the indulgence of the king and his *witan*.

The king controlled the election of bishops and was only slightly less interested in the appointment of abbots. The *Regularis Concordia* required that abbots should be elected according to the provisions of the Rule of St Benedict and with the consent and advice of the king. Since the Rule, although it expected the election of the best candidate in the community or, as second best, a good monk from another house, also allowed, if there were difficulties, the intervention of the diocesan bishop and other local well-wishers,[2] extreme views of freedom of election were entirely out of place. The English Rule clearly envisaged a petition to the king for his *congé d'élire* and then royal confirmation of the election.[3] Such a procedure allowed the king, with the advice of his counsellors, to appoint to bishoprics; and examples of arbitrary royal appointments to abbeys are easy to find. Æthelred nominated Ælfsige to Ely about 996 and Ælfweard to Evesham about 1014.[4] Edward was particularly imperious. About 1044 he appointed his goldsmith Spearhavoc to Abingdon and at Winchester his kinsman Wulfric to Ely. In 1051, when he was at his most wilful, he replaced Spearhavoc with an aged Scandinavian bishop, his 'kinsman' Rothulf.[5] On the other hand it was quite common for a member of the community, often its provost, to be elected abbot, and in

[1] *Regesta Pontificum Romanorum*, i, no. 4541.

[2] *Regularis Concordia*, ch. 9. See also above, pp. 101 ff.

[3] A clear account of a possible procedure is given in *Chron. Evesham*, pp. 87–8, in connexion with the substitution of Æthelwig for the paralysed Manni in 1058. Bishop Ealdred of Worcester sent Æthelwig with a company of monks and honourable laymen to King Edward with the request that he would grant the abbacy to Æthelwig and make him abbot. The king, who was holding his court at Gloucester, agreed and had Ealdred consecrate him on the festival of St George (23 April) in Easter week. As Easter Sunday was on 19 April in 1058 and 4 April in 1059, it is clear that Æthelwig was made abbot in the former year.

[4] *Liber Eliensis*, p. 129; *Chron. Evesham*, p. 81.

[5] *Liber Eliensis*, p. 164; *Chron. Abingdon*, pp. 462–4.

many such cases the king must have paid attention to the wishes of the convent. Edward, when he forced Rothulf on Abingdon, promised the monks free election next time; and when the bishop died in the following year they successfully elected Ordric, a monk of the house. Ramsey was ruled by one of its own monks from 993 until 1079 except for the brief interlude of 1016–20, when a German, Wythman, appointed presumably by Cnut, held the post. Needless to say the outsider was not only critical of the conditions but also a most unpopular ruler.[1]

Other authorities also could influence abbatial elections. The first three abbots of Earl Leofric's abbey at Coventry were Leofwine I, Leofric, and Leofwine II, all doubtless close relatives of the founder; and to the second, his nephew, he also granted other monasteries. But in 1066 the Peterborough monks elected their provost, Brand. Abbot Leofric and Archbishop Stigand, as has already been noticed, appointed to monasteries; and it is only to be expected that the wishes of the diocesan bishop[2] or of a local landowner could often have had effect in the case of one of the smaller convents.

If we had more biographical details it would be easier to determine how the abbots obtained their office. The fragmentary evidence available supports no simple generalization. The two extremes, free election by the community and an arbitrary appointment by the king or other external authority, are well attested; and no doubt there were many intermediate situations. It is likely that much depended on the attitude of the king. Æthelred and Edward, both autocrats, are known to have nominated. Cnut may have been more indulgent. All kings seem to have required the abbey to petition for the *congé d'élire* and for confirmation of the election. They then granted the abbey to the elect, probably in the same way as a bishop received his office; but again it is uncertain whether the prelate was invested through a ring or other spiritual symbols.[3] The abbot also needed to be blessed (consecrated) by a bishop, and an unworthy candidate could be refused. There seem to be cases of abbots-elect having difficulty in obtaining a blessing;[4] but there is nothing remarkable in this.

[1] *Chron. Ramsey*, pp. 120 ff.

[2] Cf. above, p. 317 and p. 320, *n*. 3.

[3] See above, pp. 99 ff. The king's permission had also to be obtained for other important changes. When Abbot Siward of Abingdon (1030–44) proposed to rebuilt Æthelwold's monastery he approached the king, apparently Cnut: *Chron. Abingdon*, p. 444.

[4] Leofsige of Ely had long been without the benediction when Cnut succeeded and ordered Æthelnoth archbishop of Canterbury to consecrate him: *Liber Eliensis*, p. 152.

The second ambition, freedom from diocesan control, had little support in traditional canon law. The councils and synods of the early middle ages had subjected monasteries to the diocesan bishop, and although the reforming popes of the eleventh century were sympathetic to monastic liberty, which they regarded as a model for the freedom of the whole church, few monasteries were strong enough to take advantage of this trend. In England there were only a handful of convents which could have nourished so great an ambition.

Monasteries required the services of a bishop for the blessing of their abbot, for the profession of their monks and the conferment of orders on them, and for the performance of other *episcopalia*, such as the dedication of an altar, when the need arose. Any bishop would do, and at least one monastery is known to have enjoyed *de facto* freedom from its diocesan. In the twelfth century Ely claimed that it had always been free from the bishop of Dorchester/Lincoln and had enjoyed the liberty without question. The abbots had usually been blessed by the archbishop of Canterbury,[1] and recourse had been to any bishop of their choice for the performance of *episcopalia*. The first two abbots had used bishops of Elmham and two bishops of that see retired to the monastery. Later the abbey lodged the Swedish bishop Osmund.[2] No papal privilege is cited, and Ely's immunity clearly depended on Cnut's indulgence to his favourite house. On the other hand neighbouring Ramsey, although also in royal favour and originally tied to Worcester, seems to have been on the closest terms with its diocesan bishop, partly no doubt because from 1006 until 1049 the bishops of Dorchester were Ramsey monks.

The tenth-century reformers created an anarchical situation and also established a relationship with their monasteries which was more pastoral than legal in tone. Episcopal visitation is a touchstone. There are no accounts in this period of disputes between bishops and abbots on this sensitive matter; on the contrary, there are many stories which show how amicable relations often were. Ramsey seems always to have welcomed visits from those bishops of Dorchester who had been monks of the house. The unpopular outsider, Abbot Wythman (1016–20) complained to Bishop Æthelric of the monks' inobedience and relaxed discipline,

<hr/>

[1] Ælfsige (*c.* 996) was blessed by the bishop of Winchester; Leofsige (1029), Wulfric (*c.* 1044), and Thurstan (?1066) were blessed by archbishops of Canterbury: *Liber Eilensis*, pp. 129, 152, 164, 168.

[2] *Ibid.* pp. 137 ff., 168–9. But cf. Blake, *ibid.* p. 403.

particularly of their lack of stability. The bishop decided to make a secret inspection. He arrived early one morning disguised as an ordinary traveller wishing to say his prayers, and before he was recognized had a good look round. He saw some of the monks celebrating private Masses, others praying at the principal altar, many more sitting in the cloister industriously reading, writing, or practising some other honest craft, and all behaving in a proper manner. Whereupon he gave the abbot a severe dressing down for making false charges; but he also warned the brethren that they were to obey their abbot.[1] Æthelric again visited the abbey for disciplinary reasons probably when Æthelstan was abbot: he had heard that the abbot was ruling laxly and that the monks had become remiss, and with Cnut's permission went to restore discipline. He called them all together in the chapter-house and gave then a great scolding; but when the whole community submitted without a murmur and humbly promised to amend its ways, the bishop consoled the monks with a gift of land.[2]

Evidence from the diocese of Worcester in the later part of the period is not dissimilar. Wulfstan's relations with Abbot Æthelwig of Evesham were uneasy, and in the one account we have of the bishop visiting the abbey there is no mention of the abbot being in residence. Wulfstan called in on the way to a meeting of the shire court at the pressing invitation of the monks, made his devotions to St Egwin, and cured a monk named Æthelric.[3] Once when he was at Gloucester Abbot Serlo and the monks begged him to dine with them.[4] Likewise when he chanced to visit Wilton in the diocese of Ramsbury he received a warm welcome from the nuns and cured Gunnhildr, King Harold's daughter, of a tumour on the eye.[5] Coleman implies that Wulfstan received many such invitations.[6] There is no suggestion that he ever forced his attentions on a monastery: he visited them as a welcome guest and to perform the services asked of him. His attitude was social and pastoral.

Some monasteries were targets for episcopal schemes. Malmesbury abbey can hardly have welcomed reconnoitring visits from Bishop Herman of Ramsbury, who wanted to move his see into that house.[7] But in general bishops do not seem to have meddled unnecessarily in monastic affairs nor to have been particularly sensitive over their diocesan rights,

---

[1] *Chron. Ramsey*, pp. 121–2.

[2] *Ibid.* pp. 139–40.

[3] *Vita Wulfstani*, pp. 21–2. R. R. Darlington's side note, 'Visitation of the diocese', conveys a too formal and legal sense.

[4] *Ibid.* p. 37.　　　[5] *Ibid. p. 34.*　　　[6] *Ibid.* p. 54.　　　[7] Above, p. 82.

while monasteries welcomed congenial (that is to say, monastic) bishops into their company. As almost all the chronicles are monastic, this may be a rosy picture; it is also one of lax, or at best relaxed, government. The irregularities caused by the tenth-century reformation became a source of weakness after the great reformers had died.

Monasteries were maintained by landed estates, which were the gift of the faithful. According to Domesday Book (1086) seven houses had gross incomes of between £500 and £900 (in descending order of wealth: Glastonbury, Ely, Christ Church Canterbury, Bury St Edmunds, St Augustine's Canterbury, St Swithun's Winchester, and Westminster), seven between £200 and £500 (Abingdon, New Minster at Winchester, Ramsey, Peterborough, St Albans, and two nunneries, Wilton and Shaftesbury), six between £100 and £200, and twenty-five less than £100.[1] By that time there was a relatively small aristocracy of wealth; and, although there must have been changes since 1000, the general pattern is probably that of the pre-Conquest period. As a result of Edgar's patronage of monastic reform the larger convents were established as great powers in their neighbourhood. They had been granted important secular immunities by the king, either whole hundreds or immunity from hundredal jurisdiction; they possessed the usual seigneurial jurisdiction of sac and soke; and as owners of hidated bookland they had public military and financial duties. They were surrounded by vassals and servants whom they had enfeoffed with land.[2]

The methods of estate management employed by Athelney with estates worth £20 and Glastonbury with over £800 are unlikely to have been the same; but all convents had some problems in common. Monasteries were a little different from other estate holders in that they were stationary and relatively enclosed. Food and drink and other necessities had to be transported to the house on a regular basis, either from home farms, central stores, or markets in which they were bought with money received in part from agricultural rents. Monks, with the help of lay servants, managed the estates, but were not, of course, working farmers or labourers. Such manual work as they did was within the monastery.[3] The

[1] Table in Knowles, *The Monastic Order*, p. 702.
[2] See above, p. 98.
[3] Symons, *Regularis Concordia*, pp. xxxiii–xxxv.

best documented scheme of estate management is Ely's, instituted under Cnut. The monastery was concerned directly with land situated in 116 villages in six shires. This it had divided into two parts. It had organized a little over half into units which provided quotas of food ('food farms'), each sufficient to meet the abbey's needs for a week; and the rest was used to grow crops and breed stock for sale in the market.[1] This was estate management as efficient as could be achieved in the circumstances. Smaller monasteries could probably manage with something simpler and, perforce, more flexible.

One aim of the tenth-century reformers was to abolish the partition of a minster's estates between the individual 'monks' and put all back into a common fund. In the twelfth century, with the evolution of the obedientiary system, there developed not only a division between the lands pertaining to the abbot and those of the community, but also an allotment of particular estates to the several great spending officials and also to particular funds. In the eleventh century something intermediate may have existed. Some relaxation of the strictest conception of a common purse may have crept in. We are specifically informed that Wulfstan, when bishop-abbot of Worcester, dined either with the monks in the refectory or in the hall with his knights, as he believed that it was wrong to dine in private.[2] Others must have behaved differently. The Ely system entailed divisions and different funds. The Abingdon chronicle mentions the English custom by which monks could administer their inherited lands and rents, and gives two examples of monks holding private manors.[3] A Ramsey example exemplifies several matters. In a bargain made before Bishop Eadnoth of Dorchester (1034–49) a rich deacon named Leofsige gave his son, Morcar, whom he had had when in minor orders, to the monastery as an oblate together with various estates. The convent in return promised Leofsige that he could become a monk at Ramsey and the mother that she could take the veil there whenever they wished. When Leofsige died and Morcar inherited his remaining estates, the monk granted them in the shire court of Lincoln to the abbey; but the abbot allowed him to retain them as a 'farmer' or life tenant at an agreed annual rent.[4] Domesday Book occasionally lists monks and nuns as landholders: in

---

[1] *Liber Eliensis*, pp. 152–3; Reginald Lennard, *Rural England 1086–1135* (1959), pp. 104 ff. for the system, see especially 130 ff. and 131, *n.* 1 for Ely; Edward Miller, *The Abbey and Bishopric of Ely* (1951), pp. 36 ff.

[2] *Vita Wulfstani*, p. 46, cf. 54.

[3] *Chron. Abingdon*, p. 477.

[4] *Chron. Ramsey*, pp. 153–4.

two cases monks held of the abbot.[1] But it is unlikely that the old system had completely disintegrated. The Normans found commonalty of possession even in some secular minsters – and promptly abolished it in favour of individual prebends.

Even more distinct from secular social habits was the way of life within the monastic communities. They were one-sex societies of all ages. Besides the monks (or nuns) were the children offered to God (oblates) who would make their profession at puberty, and the old and dying laity who had taken the cowl in preparation for death.[2] There were also the servants, usually ordinary laymen. The basic accommodation required by each community was a church, a dormitory for sleeping, a refectory for eating, a cloister for their non-liturgical activities, a chapter house for meetings, latrines, an infirmary, a guest house, a kitchen, a cellar, and a larder. Some small houses could have managed with less; some rich convents would have added even more specialized rooms: the *Regularis Concordia*, for example, regulates the use of the room where a fire was lit in cold weather.[3] Whether there was a typical or common plan for a monastic complex at this time is, however, unknown.

Monks and nuns took the triple vow of poverty (no private possessions), chastity, and obedience. All these obligations were difficult to observe; and monasteries were run on quasi-military lines. At the head of each was an abbot (or abbess) with dictatorial powers; and he had a number of officers whom he appointed and could dismiss.[4] The internal arrangements are not clearly revealed for this period by either the *Regularis Concordia* or the records of individual monasteries. The English Rule, which is concerned almost entirely with the ritual, vouches for the existence of the sacrist (*aedituus*),[5] who was in general charge of the

---

[1] List in Knowles, *The Monastic Order*, p. 81. Abbot Æthelstan of Ramsey (1020–43) rented one estate to a monk who was a relative and put out another to provide beans, salt, and honey for the brethren: *Chron. Ramsey*, pp. 144–5.

[2] Both oblates and the old were sources of income. For grants of land with oblates, cf. *Liber Eliensis*, pp. 131, 139–40, 143–4. At least two abbots, Leofsige and Thurstan, had been oblates. For grants *ad succurrendum*, pp. 140, 157–8. Early in the eleventh century Æthelstan, a vassal of the bishop of Worcester, and his wife Wulfgifu took religious vows when they became old and less prosperous; the man entered the cathedral priory, the woman possibly became a recluse in the city: *Vita Wulfstani*, p. 7.   [3] *Regularis Concordia*, ch. 29.

[4] Kassius Hallinger, *Gorze-Kluny* (1950, reprinted Graz, 1971), pp. 781 ff.; Knowles, *The Monastic Order*, pp. 427 ff.   [5] Ch. 20 and *passim*.

church and services, of the cantor (precentor),[1] who was in charge of the choir and the singing, and of the master of the school,[2] that is to say, the teacher of the oblates. Those three were the key men in producing the unceasing curriculum of church services.

The *Regularis Concordia* is far less informative about the disciplinary and administrative officers. For these it commonly uses the word *prior*, a general term which could cover any superior and frequently meant the abbot.[3] (It should never be understood in the sense of the claustral prior of the post-Conquest period.) A provost and a dean are mentioned;[4] and it would seem that the Rule took for granted that the abbot appointed a provost as his deputy, and that beneath the provost were one or more deans, the immediate superiors of the ordinary monks. This was the four-storey constitution which was probably to be found in most continental monasteries in the tenth century, including primitive Cluny and Fleury.[5] The provost was concerned mostly with economic and external matters (the estates), the deans with internal discipline. The one disciplinary official to which the *Regularis Concordia* pays special attention is the *circa*, or inspector, an officer who was peculiar to Lotharingian monasteries.[6] Under the direction of the dean he patrolled the cloister and choir, looking for infractions of the rules, which he denounced at the next meeting of Chapter.

It is quite clear from the evidence of monastic chronicles that in all houses where there was a choir were also to be found a sacristan, cantor, and master or keeper of the boys. At Worcester Wulfstan held in turn the offices of master (*custos*) of the children, cantor, sacristan (*secretarius*), provost, and bishop.[7] Provosts are noticed at, besides Worcester, Christ Church Canterbury, Winchester (? New Minster), Abingdon, Peterborough, Ramsey, and Ely, and were not infrequently elected

---

[1] Ch. 25 and *passim*.

[2] Ch. 19 and *passim*. There were also at least two keepers (*custodes*) of the boys: p. 61. There seems to have been confusion between the terms *magister* and *custos*. Eadmer (see below, p. 333, *n.* 2) refers to four (or four sets of) *magistri* in control of the boys at Canterbury.

[3] Ch. 21 and *passim*. Whether the head is called *abbas* or *prior* presumably depends on the source for the Rule at that point. Once, p. 41, the two terms occur together. For *prior* in this sense, see Hallinger, pp. 854, 860.

[4] Provost, p. 39; dean, pp. 39, 56. Cf. Hallinger, p. 866.

[5] Hallinger, pp. 759 ff.

[6] Ch. 57. Hallinger, pp. 897–8, 959 ff.

[7] *Vita Wulfstani*, pp. 9, 11.

abbot.[1] Once Abingdon promoted its sacristan.[2] In the customary which Lanfranc composed after 1079 for Christ Church it is stated that the officer called 'provost' in the Rule of St Benedict had become known as the prior;[3] and there can be little doubt that the second-in-command in pre-Conquest abbeys was usually termed the provost (*praepositus*).

Monastic deans, however, are far more elusive. The best attested deans are at Christ Church Canterbury, where they seem to have had a prominent position. Dean Æthelnoth was elected archbishop in 1020, and Dean Godric, a pupil of St Ælfheah (1005/6–12), was involved in the translation of the saint in Cnut's reign, and lived to describe the event to Osbern; he also saved Osbern and other children in the monastery from a whipping as St Dunstan had just worked a miraculous cure, and not surprisingly earned the epithet of 'good'.[4] An Evesham claim to have had a 'dean of Christianity' in the Vale may also be a confused memory of the other office.[5] It will have been noticed that Wulfstan, although a famous disciplinarian, is not credited with having been a dean at Worcester,[6] and the paucity of evidence suggests that in general the office was relatively junior.

The internal economic arrangement of the monasteries is even more obscure.[7] The cellarer was the most important traditional officer; and in every

[1] For Canterbury, Osbern, 'Miracula S. Dunstani', *Memorials of St Dunstan*, pp. 141–2. For Winchester, Florence, i. 184 (Symeon *HR*, ii. 156, *Chron. pont. eccles. Ebor.* in *HCY*, ii. 342), *Liber Vitae . . . of New Minster and Hyde Abbey, Winchester*, p. 32: Ælfric Puttoc was elected archbishop of York in 1023. For Abingdon, *Chron. Abingdon*, i. 482: Ealdred was elected abbot in 1066. For Peterborough, *ASC E*, p. 142: Brand was elected abbot in the same year. For Ramsey, *Chron. Ramsey*, pp. 127, 156: Ælfwine was elected abbot in 1043. Ely has recorded the names of Leofric (*Liber Eliensis*, p. 150), Leofwine (pp. 84, 92, 368–9) who may be the same as Leo (pp. 123, 290), Sihtric (pp. 291, 293), Thurstan (pp. 219, 293–4, 338–9), and Wulfwine (p. 291). Leofwine, Leofric, and Thurstan became abbots. The provost was like Martha and was placed *extrinsecus*: p. 123.

[2] Æthelstan the *aedituus* (*c.* 1044), *Chron. Abingdon*, i. 452.

[3] *Decreta Lanfranci* (*The monastic constitutions of Lanfranc*), ed. David Knowles (Nelson's Medieval Classics, 1951), p. 75, revised and improved edition in *Corpus Consuetudinum Monasticarum*, ed. K. Hallinger (Sieburg, 1947), iii. 36. For the date, see Margaret Gibson, *Lanfranc of Bec* (1978), pp. 240–1. Eadmer, 'Miracula S. Dunstani', *Memorials of St Dunstan*, p. 164, probably using post-Conquest terminology, claims that an Æthelred had held the offices of sub-prior and cantor at Canterbury before becoming a *praelatus* under Wulfstan at Worcester.

[4] *ASC* 1020: 'decanus'. Osbern, 'Translat. S. Elphegi', *MPL*, cxlix, col. 390; 'Miracula S. Dunstani', *Memorials of St Dunstan*, pp. 137–8.

[5] *Chron. Evesham*, p. 83, cf. 48.

[6] The only evidence for a dean at Worcester is the witness of Æthelwig 'decanus' to a doubtful charter of King Edward (1044–51) granting an estate in that shire: K 797 = P. H. Sawyer, *Anglo-Saxon Charters* (1968), no. 1058.

[7] For the monastic officials, see Knowles, *The Monastic Order*, pp. 427 ff.

house there must have been monks deputed to oversee the kitchens, the guest house, the infirmary, and other domestic activities. None of these officials, however, is mentioned in the *Regularis Concordia*; and they are not featured in the monastic annals of the time. It is possible that these domestic duties were undertaken by a wide circle of brethren on a rota basis.

The daily chapter, held in the morning after the Morrow Mass, was the monks' court.[1] There sins and transgressions were confessed and denounced and punishment was awarded by the abbot. In strict houses discipline was severe. Punishment was often a scourging (*disciplina*) carried out publicly on the spot. On the other hand, provided the sinner showed due contrition, there was no lasting shame or obloquy. It was recognized that the ordinary Christian was capable of committing every imaginable enormity, in thought if not in deed, and that the monastic way of life made man specially prone to some kinds of sin. Monks were expected to confess their secret sins once a week to the abbot, or someone appointed by him.[2]

The main purpose of the monastic community was to perform a prescribed series of communal religious exercises (the *opus dei*). It was a work of intercession with God of benefit to all mankind and more particularly to named persons, founders, benefactors, deceased brethren, those in confraternity, and, of course, the community itself. The daily time-table (*horarium*) was quite unlike the pattern followed by ordinary men and women in the world. It was closer to the watches kept on ships at sea or guard duty in the army: recurrent spells of arduous work divided by periods of rest. Services in the choir alternated with times for sleep, food, and other necessities, work (usually domestic), reading, meditation, and private prayer. Chanting was arduous in itself. There were as well the liturgical movements and the walking from place to place, often up stairs. In summer the working day, spent mostly in the choir, ran from about 1.30 a.m. until about 8.15 p.m.; in winter the monks had a little longer in bed at night.[3] As St Hugh of Cluny pointed out to the doubting Peter Damiani, it was a régime which made great physical demands on its

---

[1] *Regularis Concordia*, ch. 21.   [2] *Ibid*. ch. 22.

[3] For the liturgical time-table as reconstructed from *Regularis Concordia*, see Symons, *ibid*. pp. xliii–xliv; Knowles, *The Monastic Order*, p. 714.

practitioners and fully justified one or two (according to season) heavy, if simple, meals a day.[1]

The aim was always to do more than duty required: hence the increasing burden of services. At Worcester St Wulfstan increased the severity of the days by fasting and of the nights by vigils. He had no mattress on his bed, indeed no bed at all, for he snatched winks of sleep in the church or where he was reading. Every day he went down on his knees at every verse of the seven penitential psalms, and he did likewise at nocturns with Psalm 119. Seven times a day he prostrated himself before each of the eighteen altars which were in the old minster (Oswald's church). He performed private devotions in the chapel of All Saints in the western porticus, and began to visit at night other churches in the city in order to pray in each. Unafraid of ghosts, he walked serenely through the cemeteries; but once, when he entered the minster of St Peter, he was attacked by a 'devil', a peasant whose sleep he had disturbed, and was roughly handled before he managed to put the 'stinking demon' to flight.[2]

The *horarium* was not only arduous but also extremely complicated, with variations according to the season (winter or summer) and the day (festival or fast, etc.). By the mid-tenth century it had become so elaborate and intricate that only monks who had been educated in the monastery since childhood could properly carry it out. The *schola*, divided like the rest of the choir monks into the left choir and the right, had an important part to play in the services.

The liturgy for all English monasteries was laid down by the *Regularis Concordia*.[3] It is a confused document which can scarcely be understood even by modern Benedictine monks of great experience. One reason for the confusion is that it is an imperfectly digested and harmonized collection from a number of other customaries. It was the aim of the reformers to produce a consuetudinary which exhibited the best practices of Western monachism. Essentially, they tried to conflate the observances of St Peter's, Ghent, and its family with those of Fleury and its parent, the primitive Cluny, and graft those on to traditional English custom. Since

---

[1] Anonymous II, in *Bibliotheca Cluniacensis*, ed. Martin Marrier and André Du Chesne (Paris, 1614, reprinted Mâcon, 1915), coll. 460–2.

[2] *Vita Wulfstani*, pp. 9–11.

[3] Hallinger, pp. 897 ff.; Knowles, *The Monastic Order*, pp. 40 ff. Cf. also Milton McC. Gatch, 'Old English literature and the liturgy: problems and potential', *Anglo-Saxon England*, vi (1977), 237.

Ghent had a mixed observance derived from both Gorze (near Metz) and Brogne (near Namur), and Cluny had not yet diverged greatly from the early ninth-century practices of the Carolingian monasteries as established by Benedict of Aniane, the differences between the main traditions were still mostly in detail. What seems to have happened is that Dunstan and Æthelwold took the chronological framework from (old) Cluny, but a good number of special observances and customs from Gorze-Brogne. At one point the compiler declared, 'For we have ordained that the goodly religious customs of this land, which we have learnt from our forefathers, shall in no way be abandoned but . . . be observed everywhere.'[1] The most striking English liturgical peculiarity was the recital at most services of special prayers for King Edgar and his queen.

The council of Winchester required all the English houses to observe the new Rule in all its detail and avoid novelties in the future.[2] When it is considered how unsettling and unpopular innovations always are, how difficult it must have been to change from one complicated *horarium* to another, and how unclear the new Rule was, it can hardly be doubted that variety of observance not only remained but also developed. Ælfric 'the Homilist's' directions for Eynsham early in the eleventh century have been described as a distinct customary.[3] Despite diversity, however, it is likely, especially since some special English customs were retained and Cluny was drawn on before it made its idiosyncratic changes, that the English customaries on the eve of the Conquest formed a distinct, rather old-fashioned, family. It was a tradition which the newcomers found strange and did not much like.

From a reading of the Rule it could be imagined that almost all the monks were almost all the time engaged in the communal activities described. That was the ideal. In practice some monks had to be excused choir service. There were the sick, those on journeys, those engaged in administration, and perhaps those allotted special tasks, such as the craftsmen, the scribes, illuminators, goldsmiths, and so on. There were also the lazy. St Wulfstan, we are told, behaved humanely towards those negligently absent from matins. He did not shout at the sleeping monks or kick

---

[1] *Regularis Concordia*, p. 30, cf. 33.

[2] *Ibid.* chs. 6–7.

[3] Gatch, *op. cit.* pp. 241–2. The document was edited by Mary Bateson in *Compotus Rolls of the obedientiaries of St Swithun's Priory, Winchester*, ed. G. W. Kitchin (Hants Record Soc., 1892), pp. 171–98.

them awake; he merely made them recite the office afterwards when the others retired to rest.[1]

Monasteries were regarded as asylums, refuges from the world. Essentially they cared for their own wounded; but they also received the victims of the world at their gate and sometimes let them in. The *Regularis Concordia* pays special attention to charitable activities.[2] Monasteries looked after the traveller in their guest house and the sick in the infirmary; and they distributed alms to the poor, for in them, it was taught, Jesus Christ was received and adored.[3] The English Rule assumed that a monastery would have a regular clientèle of paupers, and made provision for daily Maundies to a selection of these. A ration of food was also to be given to poor travellers when they left. Charity was dispensed at most medieval courts; but the monastic gate was probably the most reliable source of relief for the poor.[4] It was also among the least dangerous dispensaries of medical care. Cultivation of a herb garden and study of medicine were traditional monastic activities.[5] Most of these charitable services were probably maintained by all convents according to their means. Visitors were always welcome except at the very poorest and most austere houses. But there was probably no exact connexion between strictness of discipline and the provision of social services. The reception of visitors and the care of the old, sick, and dying could be profitable; and it was the richest and most extravagant communities which had most to distribute in alms.

All monasteries had to maintain a school of some sort for their children. Ælfric's *Colloquy* gives a genial view of the oblates' life,[6] and Abbot Eadnoth (993–1006) of Ramsey behaved mercifully when four of

---

[1] *Vita Wulfstani*, p. 51.   [2] Chs. 62–3.

[3] *Regularis Concordia*, p. 61. Cf. Rule of St Benedict, ch. 53. For St Wulfstan's maundies in Lent, see *Vita Wulfstani*, p. 17; for his great gifts to the poor on Maundy Thursday, *ibid*. pp. 58–9.

[4] Characteristically Abbot Leofric of St Albans in the early eleventh century when there was a severe famine in England sold all the building materials which his predecessors had excavated in Verulamium with a view to rebuilding their church, and gold and silver vases for the relief of the poor. He retained only some precious gems, for which he could find no buyer, and the famous cameos (see above, p. 20), which were reserved for decorating the shrine. His action caused some controversy, but the chronicler defends it: *Gesta monasterii S. Albani*, pp. 29–30, and also below, p. 335, *n.* 4. Abbot Æthelstan of Ramsey was murdered in 1043 by an Irish almoner whom he had first befriended and then disgraced: *Chron. Ramsey*, pp. 155–6.

[5] Cf. *Cassiodori Senatoris Institutiones*, ed. R. A. B. Mynors (1937), I, xxxi, 'De medicis', p. 78.

[6] See above, p. 281. Cf. also, Earl R. Anderson, 'Social idealism in Ælfric's *Colloquy*', *Anglo-Saxon England*, iii (1974), 153.

the boys (including the nephew of the founder and a future bishop of Dorchester) on a walk outside the cloister pealed the bells in the west tower of the church so carelessly that they cracked one of them.[1] But at Christ Church, Canterbury, Osbern and Eadmer remembered a most brutal regime just about the time of the Conquest, with masters armed with whips of cowhide and knotted thongs. According to Eadmer it was the custom to whip the boys on the fifth day before Christmas not for any specific faults but as a general corrective. Only miracles worked by St Dunstan could save them from such floggings.[2] The main purpose of the school was to train the children to carry out their choral duties, and the cantor must have had a part in its management and in the teaching. But as the boys also needed to read, write, and converse in Latin, they were probably taught all the arts subjects, grammar,[3] logic, and rhetoric (the *trivium*), and arithmetic, geometry, astronomy, and music (the *quadrivium*), at an elementary level. The more talented children could, of course, take their studies further.

The monastic *schola* was not a public school in any sense; but some monasteries allowed outsiders to attend. Daughters of the nobility were sometimes educated in nunneries and often left in order to marry.[4] Boys, however, were almost without exception (and, as scholars, by definition) clerks, although not all in later life proceeded to major orders, and so remained free to marry, bear arms, and follow most secular careers. In the early eleventh century Wulfstan, a son of a vassal of the bishop of Worcester and clearly intended for a clerical career through the episcopal household, was sent to Evesham abbey for his elementary education and to Peterborough for more advanced schooling. At the latter Earnwig, a skilled scribe and book illustrator who became abbot in 1041, was his master. Wulfstan's conversion to the monastic life occurred much later when he was a parish priest and was not connected directly with his education.[5]

The services for the laity and secular clergy already described were traditional. Monasteries also at times engaged in activities for which there was less authority. It was never intended that monks should exercise an

---

[1] *Chron. Ramsey*, pp. 112–14, 120, 128, 146.

[2] 'Miracula S. Dunstani', *Memorials of St Dunstan*, pp. 137–8, 140–2 (Osbern), 229–30 (Eadmer).

[3] An important identification of three St Augustine Canterbury's school reading books is in A. G. Rigg and G. R. Wieland, 'A Canterbury classbook of the mid-eleventh century', *Anglo-Saxon England*, iv (1975), 113.

[4] For example, Edith, Earl Godwin's daughter, the future wife of King Edward. was at Wilton: *Vita Ædwardi*, pp. 46 ff.   [5] *Vita Wulfstani*, pp. 4 ff., 47, 94.

active ministry in the world: that was the very opposite of their purpose. Not all monks, and originally and at some times and places very few of them, were in major orders. But it must have seemed natural for boys who had been taught in the school and possessed all the necessary skills to proceed to the priesthood. The *Regularis Concordia* assumes that among the monks were priests, deacons, and subdeacons,[1] and the eighteen altars in St Oswald's church at Worcester suggest that a good proportion of the monastic community were priests.[2] Monks are found at Ramsey celebrating private Masses.[3] In these circumstances the only obstacle to an outside ministry was ecclesiastical law and discipline, and it became not unusual for monasteries to supplement the parochial work of a sparse and sometimes remiss priesthood. These intra- and extramural activities do not seem to have caused much offence in the eleventh century. In the twelfth, however, a bitter controversy arose between monks and clerks on this matter.

Most English monasteries, since they were attached to an ancient church, had extensive parochial rights; and although their duties could have been deputed, in whole or in part, to secular priests, it was often attractive to the convent for a variety of reasons to perform some of them. The *Regularis Concordia* takes for granted that the laity will attend the chief Mass in the monastic church on Sundays and festivals. Bells were rung to summon the faithful, and a sermon would usually be preached.[4] It was an occasion for worship at the shrines and for miraculous healings to occur.[5] It seems too that monasteries offered some of the sacraments to the people, most commonly perhaps baptism and confession, with the Eucharist at Easter.[6] It is also likely that some monasteries served a few of the

[1] Cf. pp. 66–7. Orderic (Vitalis), born in 1075 and given as an oblate to St Evroul in Normandy at the age of ten, was ordained subdeacon at sixteen, deacon at eighteen, and priest at thirty-three: *The Ecclesiastical History of Orderic Vitalis*, ed. and trans. Marjorie Chibnall (Oxford Medieval Texts), vi (1978), 554.

[2] *Vita Wulfstani*, p. 9.   [3] See above, p. 323.

[4] *Regularis Concordia*, ch. 23. For Wulfstan building a bell tower at Worcester, see *Vita Wulfstani*, p. 15.

[5] Evesham recorded miracles which occurred at St Egwin's altar and shrine. Twice there is a reference to these happening on the Sabboth, which may in this context mean Sunday: *Chron. Evesham*, pp. 47, 48, 50. Also mentioned is the presence of a multitude of people on the festival of St Egwin: *ibid.* p. 51. Cf. the similar situation at the Lotharingian monastery of Lobbes (nr Charleroi): 'Miracula SS. Ursmari et Ermini', ed. O. Holder Egger, *Monumenta Germaniae Historica, SS*, xv (2), 833 (cap. 16).

[6] In connexion with the principal Mass on Sundays, *Regularis Concordia*, ch. 23, refers to the Eucharist partaken by monks, but not by the laity. But at the abbey of Lobbes a crowd of people took communion on Easter Sunday: 'Miracula SS. Ursmari et Ermini', p. 833 (cap. 17).

parochial churches they owned.[1] This proved to be the least defensible of their encroachments, although in the turmoil of the Gregorian reform monks were often the only unspoilt priests available to the reformers.[2]

St Wulfstan when provost of Worcester exercised an active external ministry. 'Every day' between the day offices and sext, or even vespers, he stood before the door of the church offering help to victims of oppression and free baptism to the children of the poor. Soon the wealthy imitated, and it became the general custom to ask Wulfstan to baptize. He was also prepared to confess the laity. A rich and beautiful woman, who only went to church to show herself off, once approached the provost, who, thinking she wanted to make her confession, took her aside. Instead she made the startling proposal that he might care to undertake the administration of her property and also share her bed. Wulfstan smacked her face in the full sight and hearing of the people. Every Sunday and festival the provost preached to the congregation, and 'like the prophets of old he hurled his thunderbolts at the sinners and rained sweet showers on the elect'. A foreign monk in the community who objected to Wulfstan's ministry was shown the error of his ways in a vision;[3] but William of Malmesbury's obvious interest in this clash of views probably reflects the twelfth rather than the eleventh-century attitude.

The tenth-century reformation had led to a great reflorescence of art: monasteries had to be built and furnished. The furnishings suffered severely during Æthelred's reign when danegelds and other ransoms had to be paid, for works of art in precious metals had to be melted down. When peace was restored and agriculture and trade flourished again, although there was some rebuilding activity, it was more usual to spend on restoring and improving the furnishings.[4] Relics and statues and all kinds of objets d'art were purchased abroad,[5] and English workshops seem

---

[1] *Regularis Concordia* makes no mention of this, but does regulate the procession of the monks on the Purification of the B. M. V. (Candlemas) to one of the town churches: p. 33.

[2] See F. Barlow, *The English Church 1066–1154* (1979), p. 52.

[3] *Vita Wulfstani*, pp. 11–15; for his preaching see also pp. 36, 39–40, 95. Cf. William of Malmesbury, *GP*, pp. 281, 286.

[4] For example, Abbot Ealdred of St Albans destroyed many of the buildings of the Roman Verulamium because they were the haunts of robbers and harlots, and put aside usable material for the rebuilding of his church. Although great foundation trenches were dug, he died before the rebuilding was carried out: *Gesta Abbatum Monasterii S. Albani*, pp. 24–8. Abbot Leofric sold most of the collection, including stone columns, for the relief of the poor: see above, p. 332, *n*. 4.

[5] Cf. above, pp. 20–1.

once more to have been in active production. Stone sculpture is difficult to date and all large castings in metal have disappeared. But there is literary evidence for the commissioning of major statues in bronze and other metals.[1] Among the artistic centres was Evesham, where the master of the workshop was a monk Manni who was elected abbot in 1044 and became paralysed in 1058. Like Dunstan he was not only well read in the classical and sacred authors, but also a master of all the other arts, singing, calligraphy, painting, and smithery. His work was to be found at Canterbury, Coventry, and many other places. At Evesham he rebuilt the church and furnished it splendidly. He provided a shrine for St Egwin made out of gold, silver, and precious stones (in it were three 'stones' which illuminated most of the church at night), and shrines for St Odulf and St Credan, and with his own hand wrote and illuminated a Missal and a Psalter. His main assistant was a goldsmith named Godric, who, when fitting the small figures on to St Egwin's shrine, pierced his left hand with a sharp tool, but the saint cured the wound. Godric's son, Clement, later became prior of Evesham, and Godric himself took the cowl under Abbot Walter (after 1077).[2]

Literary work was not a great feature of the reformation; but the first generation of monks educated in the reformed monasteries produced a spate of writing in both Latin and English. The works were almost all technical and utilitarian: grammars, homilies, lawbooks, bibles, service books, theology, calendars, lives of saints, mathematical treatises, and such like.[3] They met the educational needs of the monks and also, when written in English, of the parish priests. There was little literary self-indulgence. Not even much history was written. The various annals which make up the Anglo-Saxon Chronicle dried up after describing the military campaigns in Æthelred's reign, and only came briefly to life

[1] *Ibid.* pp. 79, 89–90. For Abbot Leofric's commissions for Peterborough, see *Chron. Peterborough*, p. 66; for Earl Leofric's commissions of statues, see *Chron. Evesham*, p. 82. For metal work, see D. M. Wilson, 'Tenth-century Metalwork', *Tenth-Century Studies*, p. 200; David A. Hinton, 'Late Anglo-Saxon metal-work: an assessment', *Anglo-Saxon England*, iv (1975), 171. For stone carving, see Rosemary Cramp, 'Anglo-Saxon Sculpture of the Reform period', *ibid*. p. 184.

[2] *Chron. Evesham*, pp. 44, 86–7, 99; cf. 317–18.

[3] Cr. above, ch. VI. See further, Peter Clemoes, 'Late Old English Literature', *Tenth-Century Studies*, p. 103; C. E. Hohler, 'Some Service Books of the Later Saxon Church', *ibid*. p. 60; M. R. Godden, 'Old English composite homilies from Winchester', *Anglo-Saxon England*, iv (1975), 57; K. D. Hartzell, 'An unknown English Benedictine gradual of the eleventh century', *ibid*. p. 131; Michael Lapidge, 'The hermeneutic [sic] style in tenth-century Anglo-Latin literature', *ibid*. p. 67; Milton McC. Gatch, 'Beginnings continued: a decade of studies of Old English prose', *ibid*. v (1976), 225.

again for the stirring events of 1049–56.[1] Such works as *Encomium Emmae* and *Vita Ædwardi Regis*, written by foreign monks, although interesting, are propaganda rather than true history.[2] The literary output, after the first explosion, was respectable rather than outstanding in its amount and quality. Its vernacular component was, however, unique; and the heavy losses which this branch of literature suffered, not only after the Norman Conquest but also when Old English ceased to be comprehensible even to English readers, may conceal the magnitude and variety of the achievement.[3]

Never in doubt at the time, after the Conquest, or subsequently was the high quality of English book production. The beauty of the script, the liveliness of the illustration, and the general technical mastery shown in all the processes made them prized possessions. By the middle of the eleventh century there was a variety of decorative styles, all derived from older, often classical, exemplars, but also executed in a recognizable English idiom.[4] The pictures saved many otherwise obsolete books from destruction.

The Normans after the Conquest were greatly impressed by the wealth of the monasteries and the profusion of their ornaments. They were great treasure houses which could be looted for the highest motives. The splendour was proof of the enthusiasm which the monastic ideal had aroused at times in the people, and it also displayed popular religion at its best. Monastic churches with their stained glass windows, shrines, pulpits, and roods provided a rich setting for an impressive ritual, and were prob-

---

[1] Cf. Cecily Clark, 'The narrative mode of *The Anglo-Saxon Chronicle* before the Conquest', *England before the Conquest* (Dorothy Whitelock *Festschrift*, 1971), ed. Peter Clemoes and Kathleen Hughes, p. 215.

[2] For *Vita Ædwardi*, see also Barlow, 'The purpose of the *Vita Ædwardi Regis*', in *Edward the Confessor*, pp. 291 ff.

[3] The attribution in recent years of MSS to English monasteries in the mid-eleventh century is making the Edwardian monastic scene (and Stigand's Winchester and Canterbury) even more respectable: cf. above, pp. 333, *n*. 3, 336, *n*. 3 and Barbara Raw, 'The probable derivation of most of the illustrations of Junius II from an illustrated Old Saxon *Genesis*', *Anglo-Saxon England*, v (1976, 133.

[4] J. J. G. Alexander, 'Some aesthetic principles in the use of colour in Anglo-Saxon art', *Anglo-Saxon England*, iv (1975), 145, is not only itself interesting, but also has references to many other works on Anglo-Saxon illuminated MSS. Among the standard works are D. Talbot Rice, *English Art 871–1100* (1952), pp. 173 ff. and Francis Wormald, *English Drawings of the Tenth and Eleventh Centuries* (1952).

ably unrivalled by any secular church in England, except the northern minsters. Moreover so important was their work of intercession with God held to be that there was a great eagerness to 'buy' their services. The repentant, the sick, and the dying contributed their riches or their mites. Moreover, to people anxious for fame and immortality monasteries offered the nearest thing to be found on earth, constant commemoration. On the high altar of the church was kept the *Necrologium*, which besides being a roll-call of the dead was also a *Liber Vitae*, a Book of Life, for men passed from death unto life (1 John 3:14). Edward the Confessor cannot have been disappoined by the services he got from Westminster Abbey in return for his donations. Thanks to them his memory has been kept green for over 900 years.

Index

339

DATE DUE